Jane Austen
made a patchwork coverlet.

She painstakingly folded scraps of fabric
over tiny diamonds of paper and meticulously
stitched the fragments together to
make a bigger picture.

Who was
Jane Austen?

The historical record is threadbare.

The following narrative has been patchworked
together from Austen's own words, gleaned
from her novels, her poems, and from
what remains of her letters.

AUTHOR'S NOTE:

The following is a fictional account of factual events. The quotes from which the text has been constructed are reproduced in the notes at the back of the book, where I have also highlighted any aspect of the story which, for dramatic purposes, departs from the historical record.

Austen is a novelist, and the summaries of her work contained here include some spoilers. Her books are so good that I hope the reader will derive pleasure from them whether or not they know what is coming next.

The currency of Regency England is the pre-decimal system of "£" pounds, "s" shillings and "d" pence, where there are 12 pence to the shilling, 20 shillings to the pound, and 21 shillings to the guinea. Very approximately, Regency prices correspond to today's prices with the addition of two zeros to each pound, so £1 in Jane Austen's time is about £100 today and a shilling about £5. Wages for the poor were very different than today's rates. A farm labourer in Regency England earned only about £20 a year, (£2000 nowadays).

Irregularities in Capitalisation & Spelling in this book are inspired by Austen's idiosyncratic prose.

First published by Verso 2025
© Kate Evans 2025

All rights reserved
The moral rights of the author and artist have been asserted

1 3 5 7 9 10 8 6 4 2

Images of the Austen quilt on the title page, endpapers and page 179 appear courtesy of Jane Austen's House. Photography by Richard Warburton.
The wallpaper design on page 152 is *Chawton Leaf* © Hamilton Weston Wallpapers Ltd. Reproduction quilt fabrics appear courtesy of Riley Blake Designs.

Verso
UK: 6 Meard Street, London W1F 0EG
US: 207 East 32nd Street, New York, NY 10016
versobooks.com

Verso is the imprint of New Left Books

ISBN-13: 978-1-80429-622-6
ISBN-13: 978-1-80429-623-3 (UK EBK)
ISBN-13: 978-1-80429-627-1 (US EBK)

British Library Cataloguing in Publication Data
A catalogue record for this book is available from the British Library

Library of Congress Cataloging-in-Publication Data
A catalog record for this book is available from the Library of Congress

Printed and bound by CPI Group (UK) Ltd, Croydon CR0 4YY

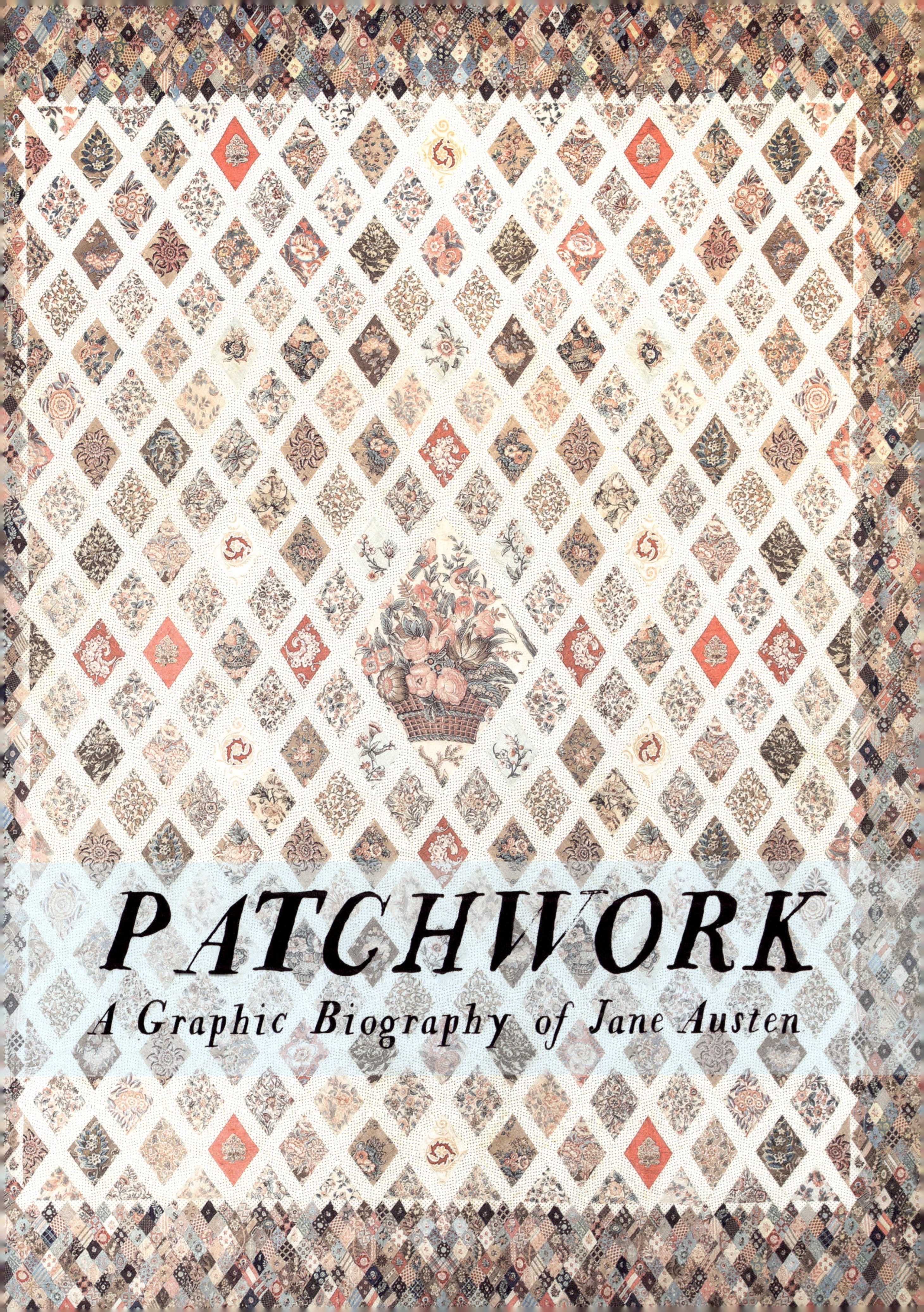

PATCHWORK

A Graphic Biography of Jane Austen

TABLE OF

THE FABRICS

BIRTH 1

CONGREGATION 5

LITTLE WORTH 11

SCHOOL HOUSE 17

EFFUSIONS OF FANCY BY A VERY YOUNG LADY
IN A STYLE ENTIRELY NEW 31

COMING OUT 51

I WRITE ONLY FOR FAME 59

Mrs LEIGH-PERROT BUYS SOME LACE 79

EXILE 83

THE WAVES 93

INTERLUDE

THE MUSLIN 100
THE CHINTZ 104
THE LINEN 108
THE COTTON 112

CONTENTS

THE PAPERS

CHAWTON! A HOME!..128

TO BUSINESS!..133

CATHARSIS..139

YOUNG LADIES OF AN INTERESTING AGE........143

THE PIG OF PALL MALL......................150

PLAN OF A NOVEL ACCORDING TO HINTS
FROM VARIOUS QUARTERS...................160

WRITS & STITCHES.........................166

PASSION.................................170

SICK...................................173

ST SWITHIN'S DAY........................177

BEHOLD ME IMMORTAL....................183

notes 186
bibliography 225
what did Jane Austen look like? 228
acknowledgements 229

THE

FABRICS

BIRTH

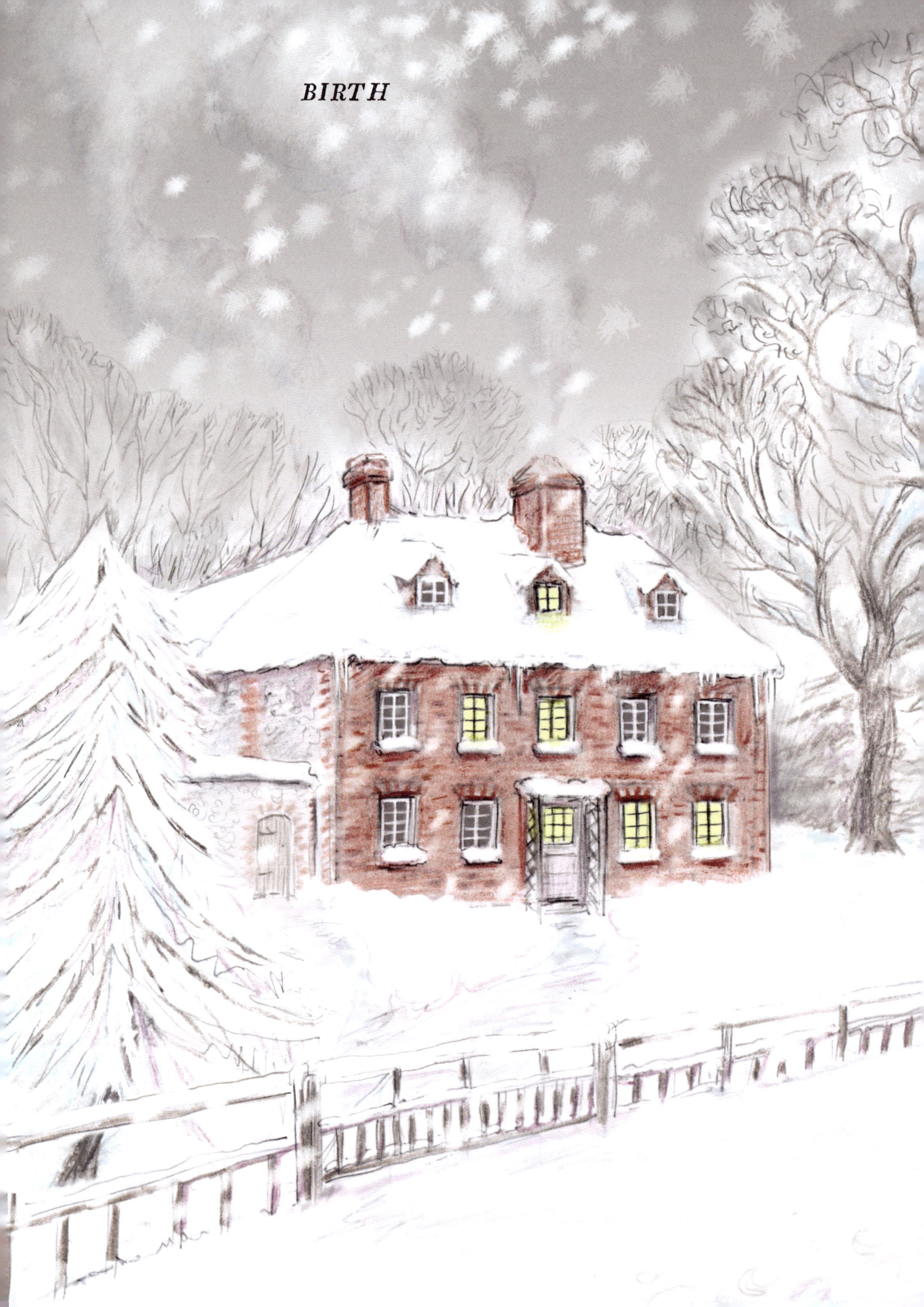

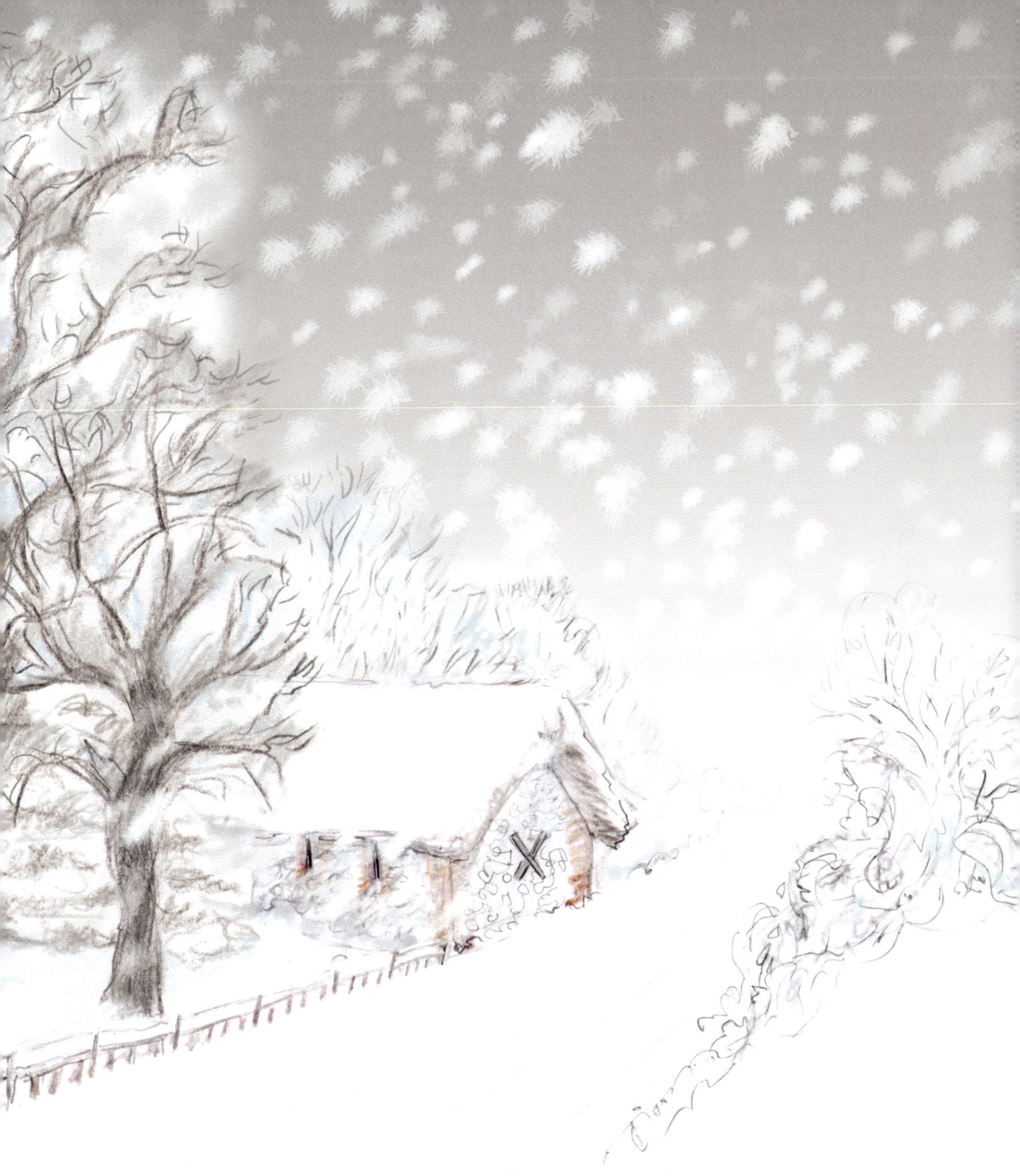

17th December 1775.

Snow blankets Steventon Rectory.

Frost traces patterns on the window panes.

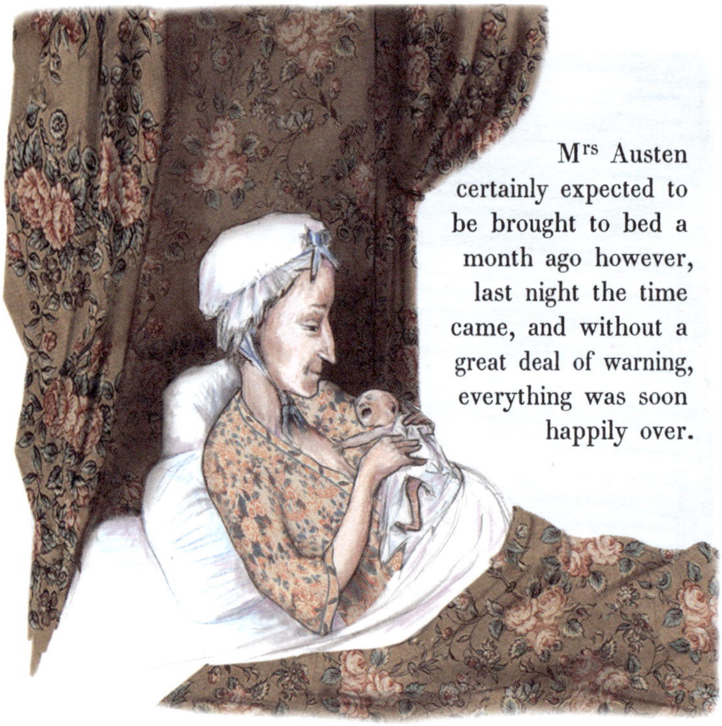

Mrs Austen certainly expected to be brought to bed a month ago however, last night the time came, and without a great deal of warning, everything was soon happily over.

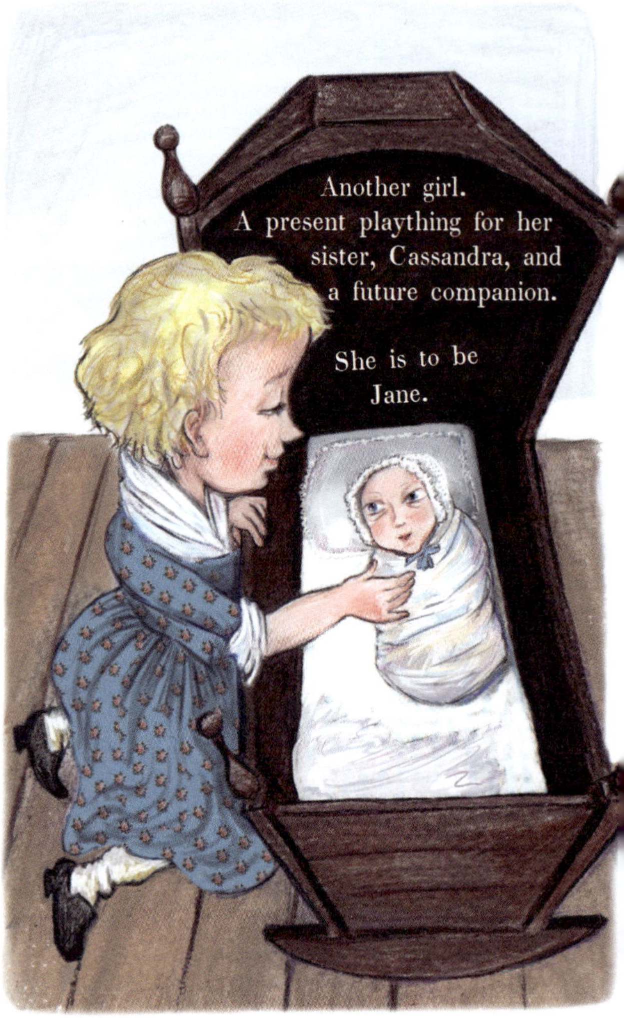

Another girl. A present plaything for her sister, Cassandra, and a future companion.

She is to be Jane.

Mrs Austen is, thank God, pure well after it, but she is weary. Jane is her seventh child and won't be the last. She has on her short robe of Indian chintz, the better to feed the baby. For the next six weeks of her confinement she will have no occasion to put on her stays.

Mrs Hilliard tucks in the baby, draws the bed curtains tight against drafts, shutters the windows, banks up the fire, picks up a pail of unmentionable linens and ushers young Cassandra from the room.

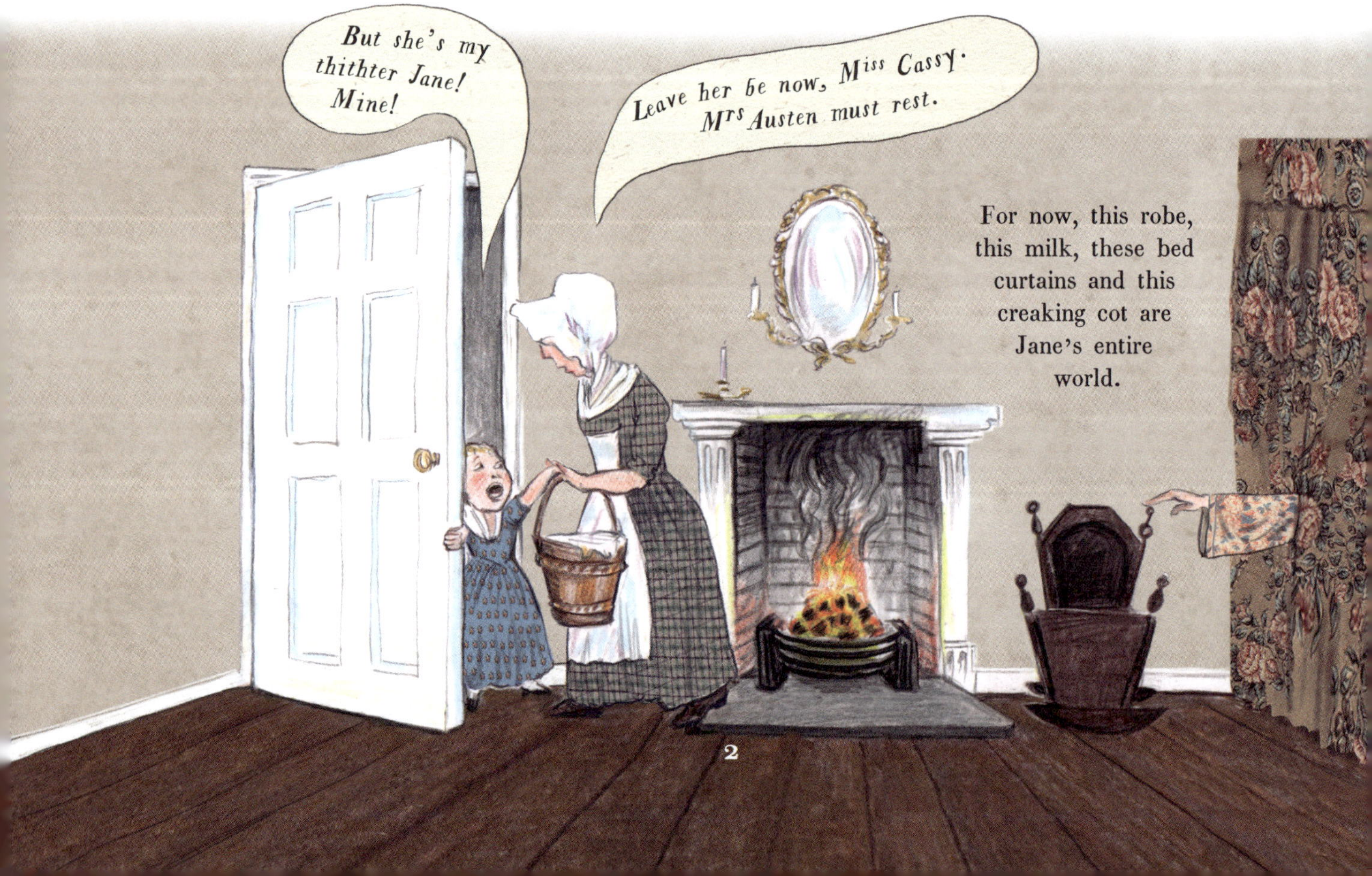
But she's my thithter Jane! Mine!
Leave her be now, Miss Cassy. Mrs Austen must rest.

For now, this robe, this milk, these bed curtains and this creaking cot are Jane's entire world.

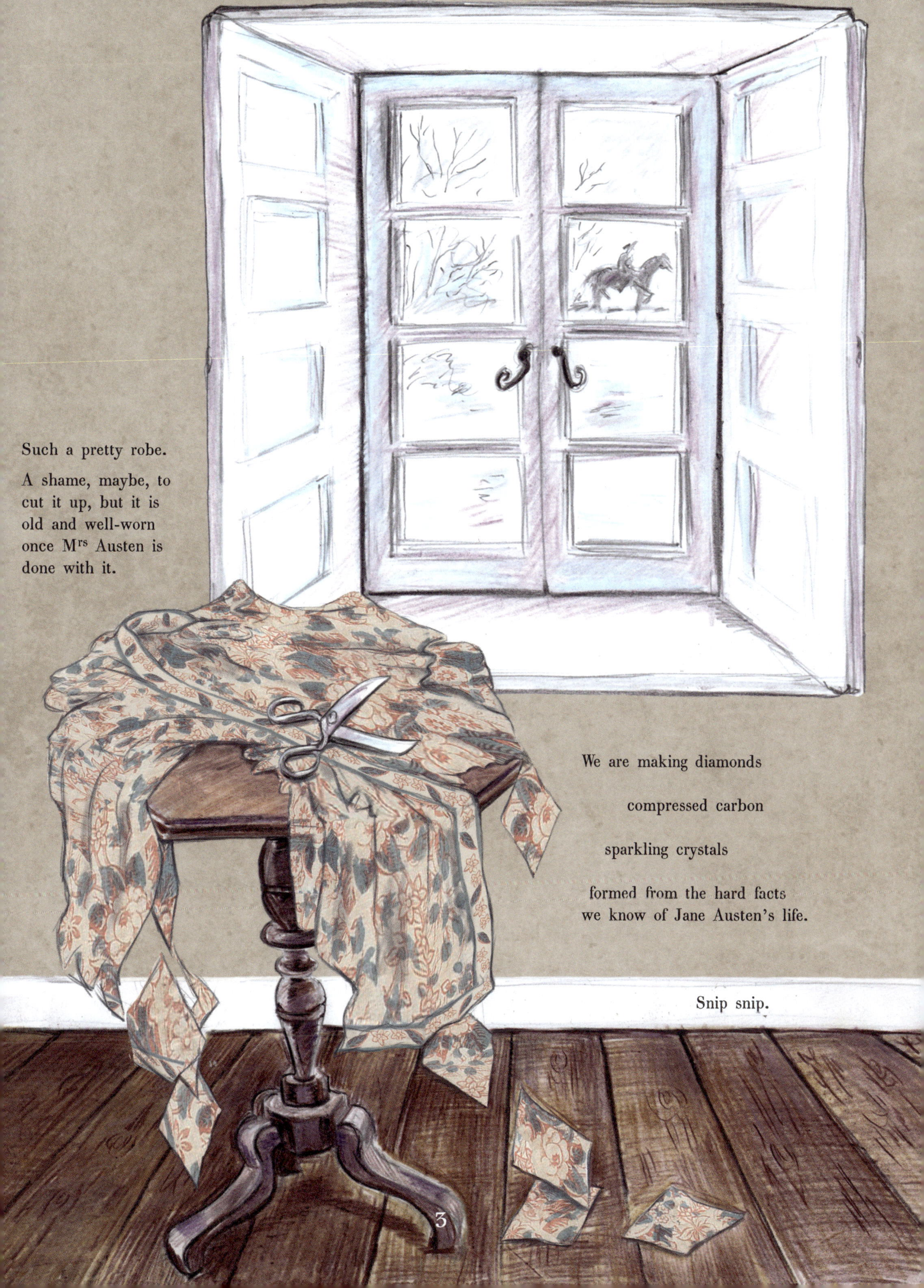

Such a pretty robe.

A shame, maybe, to cut it up, but it is old and well-worn once Mrs Austen is done with it.

We are making diamonds

compressed carbon

sparkling crystals

formed from the hard facts
we know of Jane Austen's life.

Snip snip.

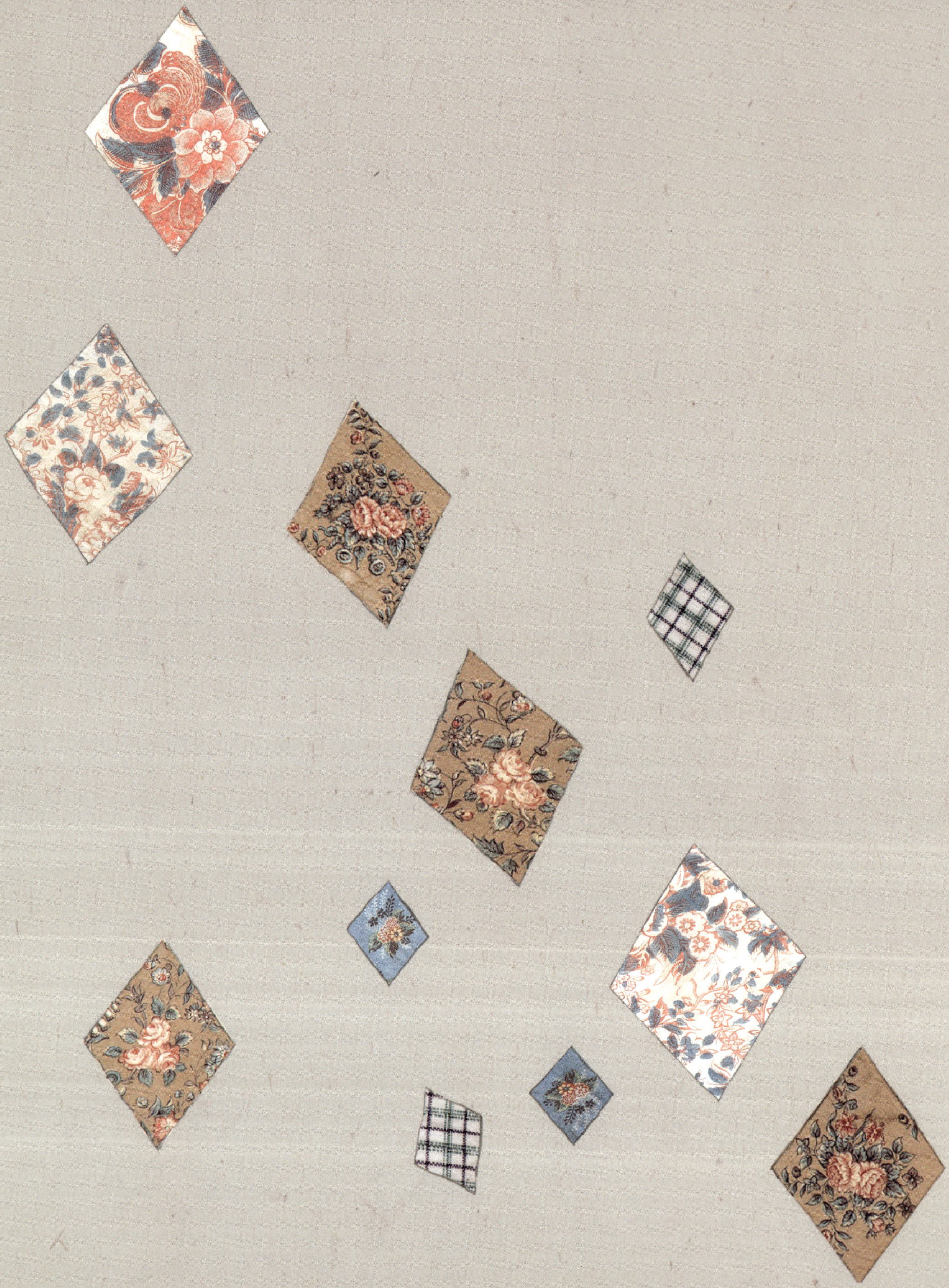

THE CONGREGATION

Good Friday, 5th April 1776,
Steventon church.

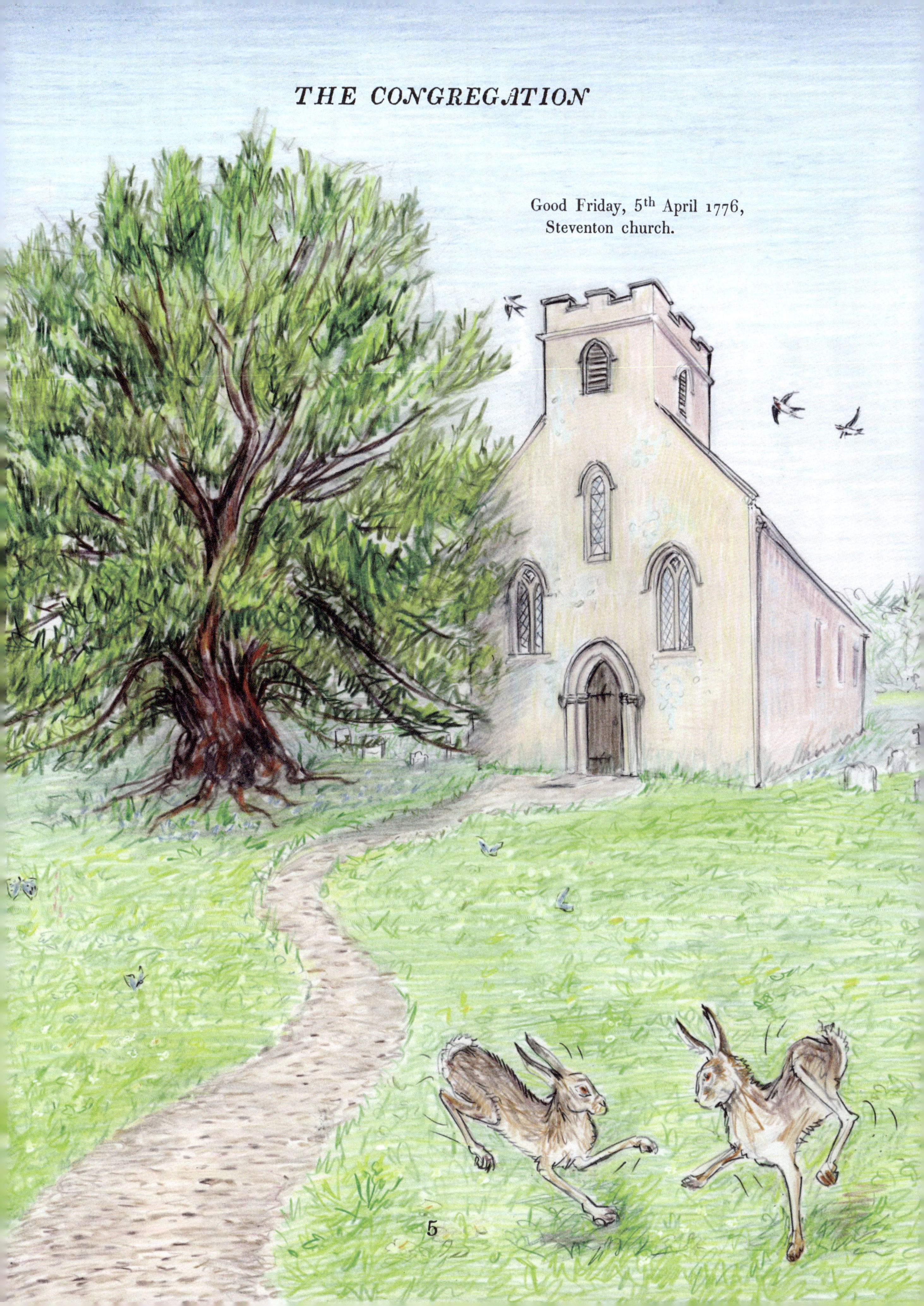

THE GOOD PEOPLE OF STEVENTON are assembled for the morning service. The gentry, snug in their box pews, charcoal braziers at their feet. The common folk clustered at the back.

The Reverend George Austen ascends his pulpit, opens the Book of Common Prayer and reads, with great propriety:

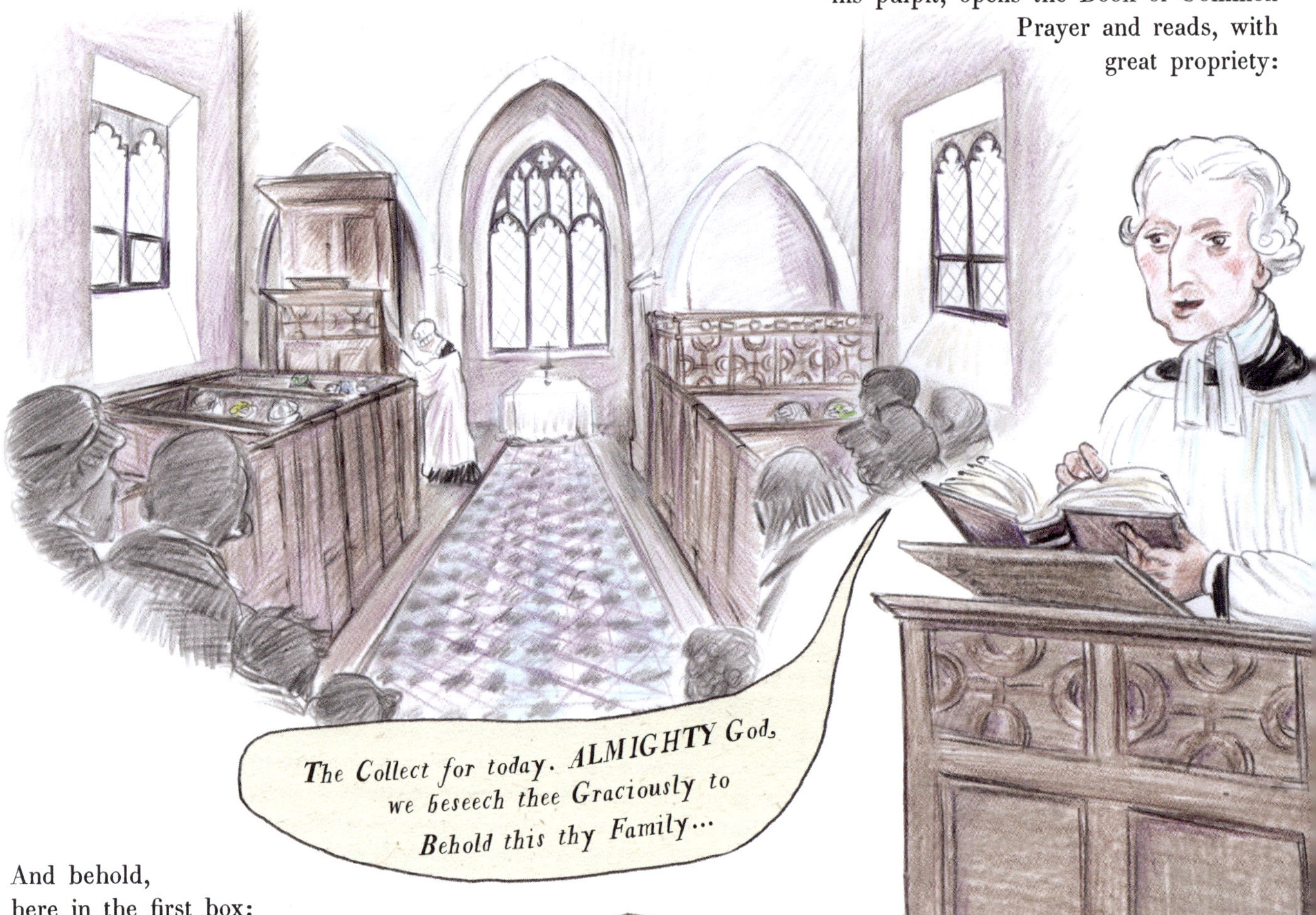

The Collect for today. ALMIGHTY God, we beseech thee Graciously to Behold this thy Family...

And behold, here in the first box: Mrs Austen, sitting very straight, keeping a wary eye on her brood.

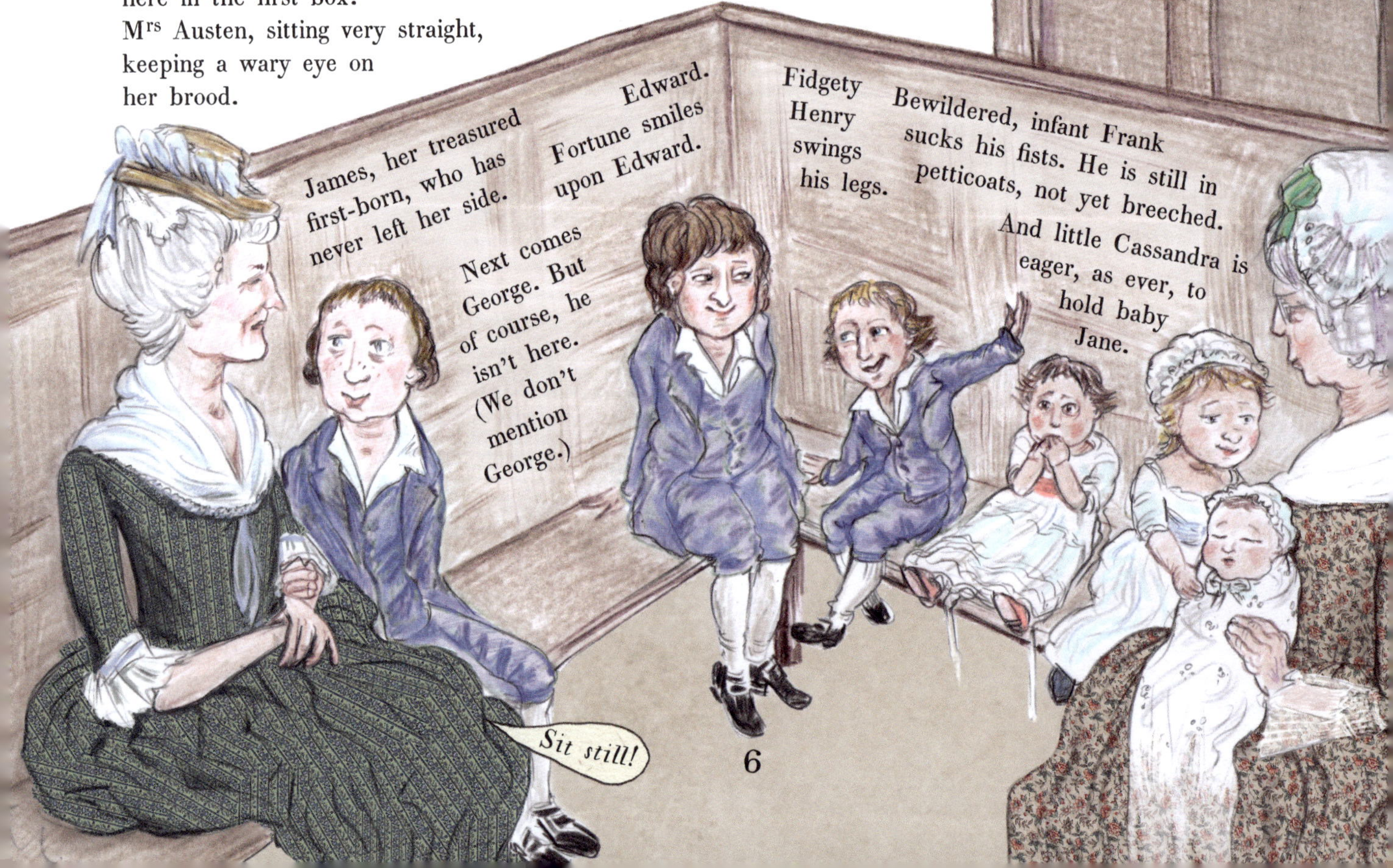

James, her treasured first-born, who has never left her side.
Next comes George. But of course, he isn't here. (We don't mention George.)
Edward. Fortune smiles upon Edward.
Fidgety Henry swings his legs.
Bewildered, infant Frank sucks his fists. He is still in petticoats, not yet breeched.
And little Cassandra is eager, as ever, to hold baby Jane.
Sit still!

Once the sermon is done, three other family members rise slowly to their feet and proceed to the font with the baby. Three aged, distant great-aunts and second cousins, strategically selected to be godparents with an eye to their riches and advancing years. An inheritance would be useful for this baby, for the Austens, it could be said, enjoy a superfluity of children, and a want of almost everything else.

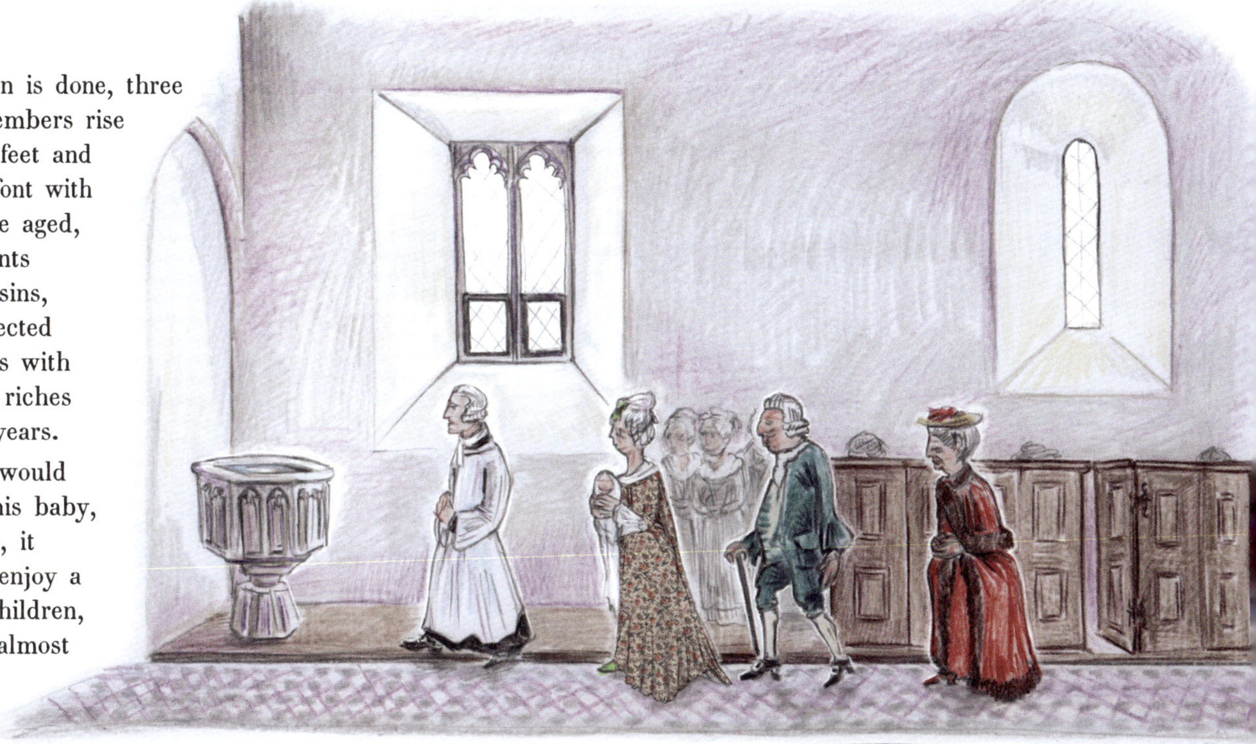

George Austen cradles his daughter tenderly as he unties her bonnet strings and intones the phrase:

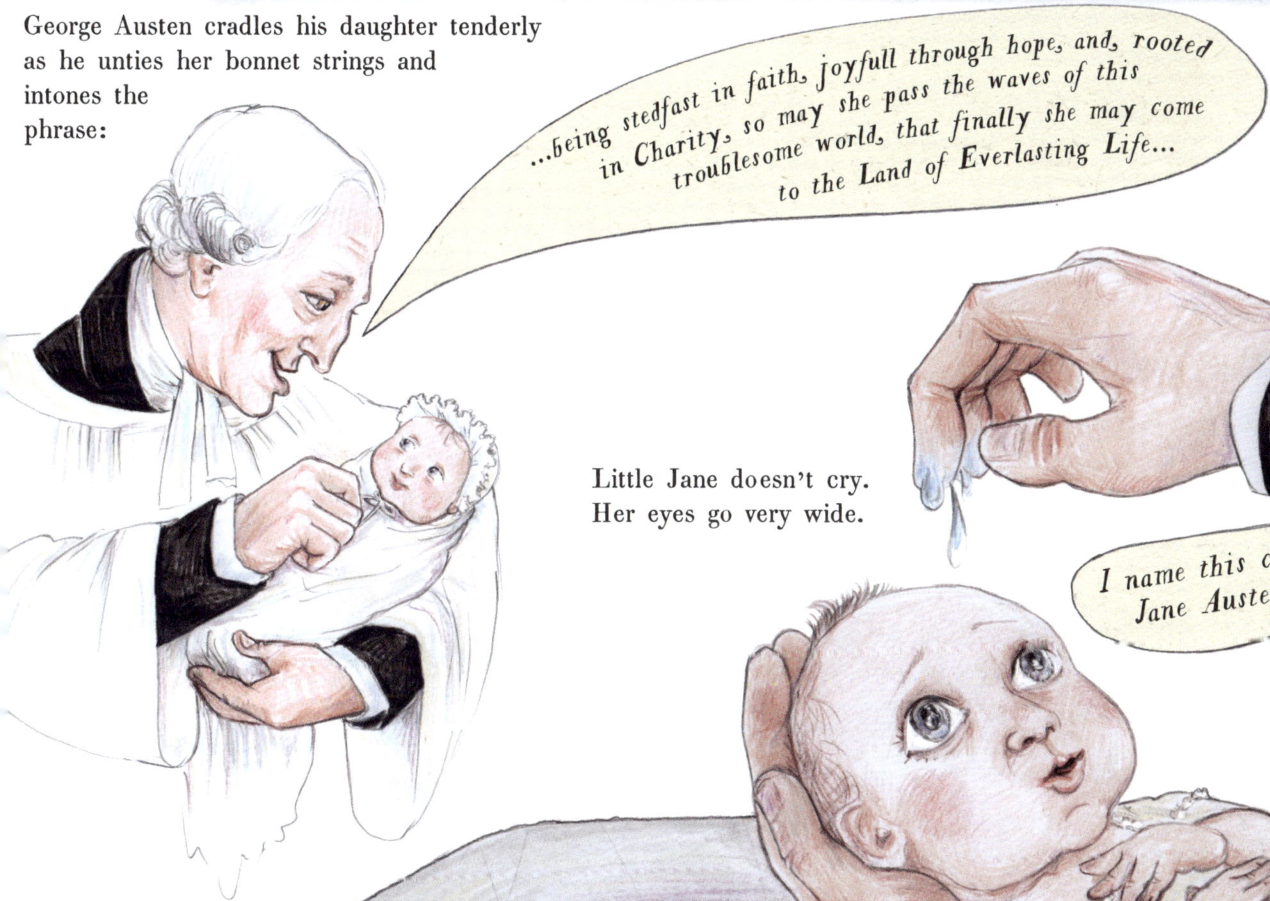
...being stedfast in faith, joyfull through hope, and, rooted in Charity, so may she pass the waves of this troublesome world, that finally she may come to the Land of Everlasting Life...

Little Jane doesn't cry.
Her eyes go very wide.

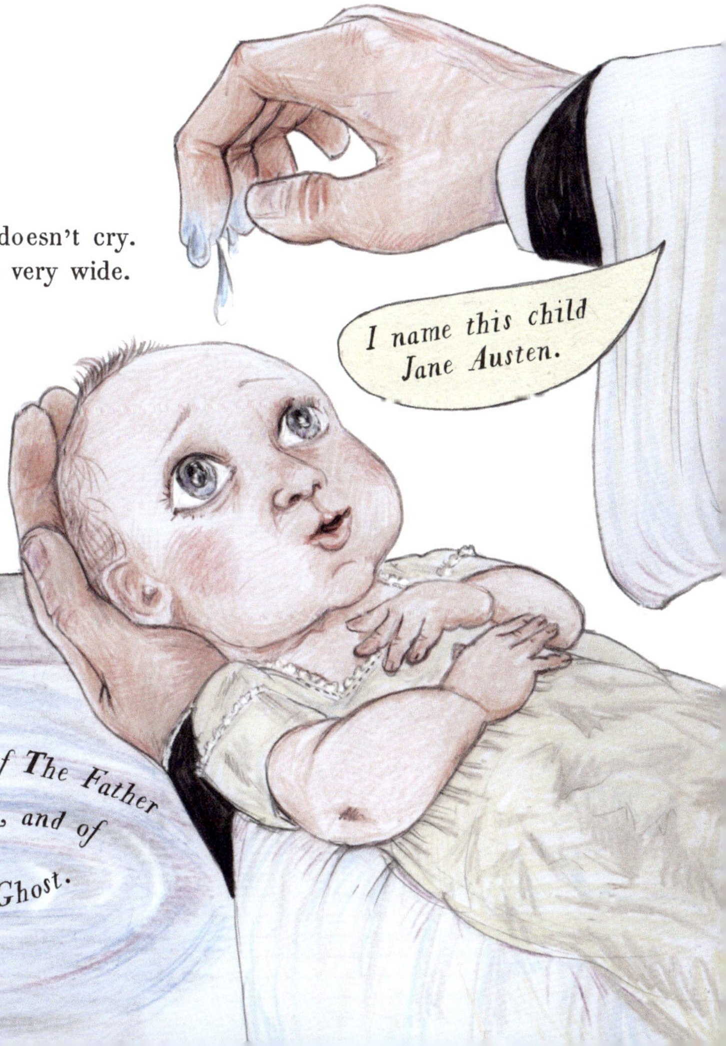
I name this child Jane Austen.
I baptise thee in the name of The Father and of the Son, and of the Holy Ghost.

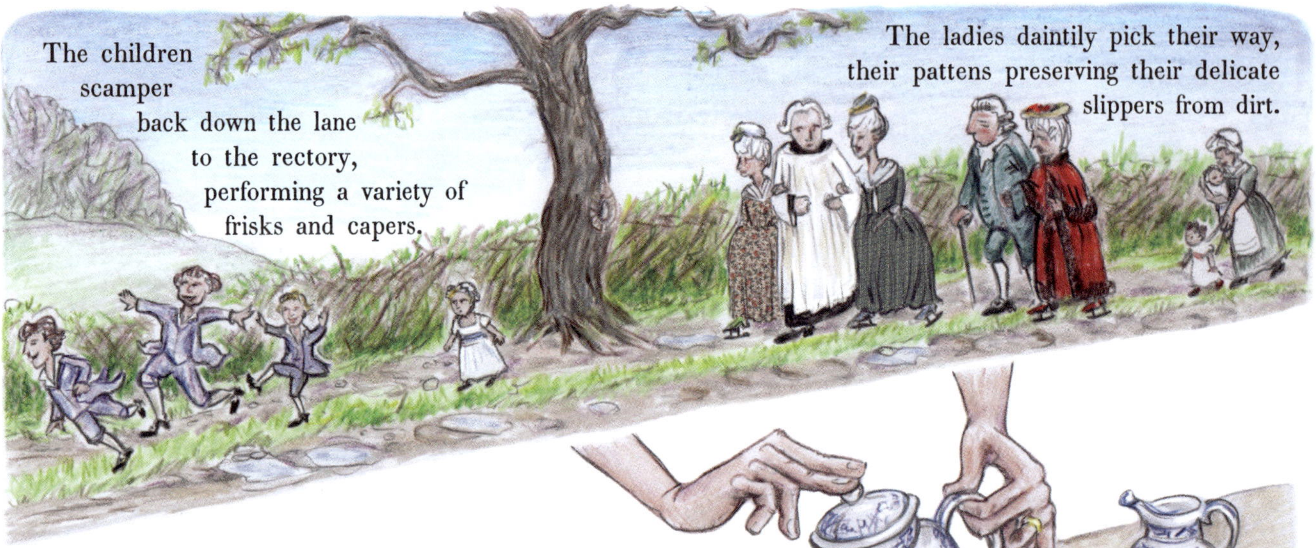

The children scamper back down the lane to the rectory, performing a variety of frisks and capers.

The ladies daintily pick their way, their pattens preserving their delicate slippers from dirt.

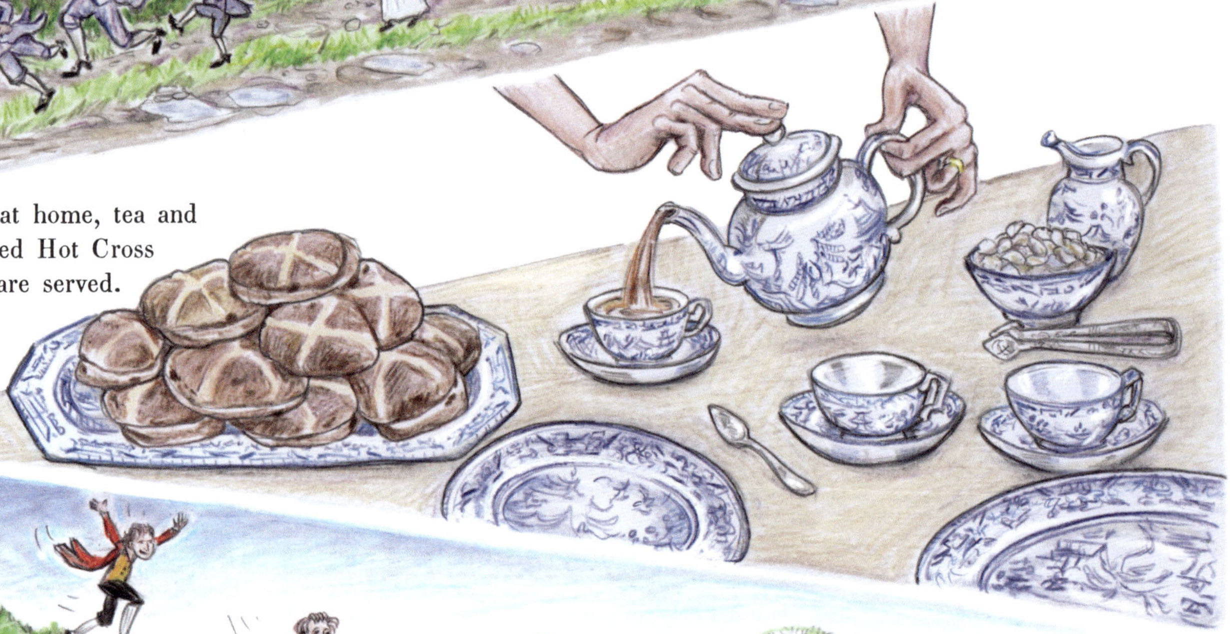

Back at home, tea and buttered Hot Cross buns are served.

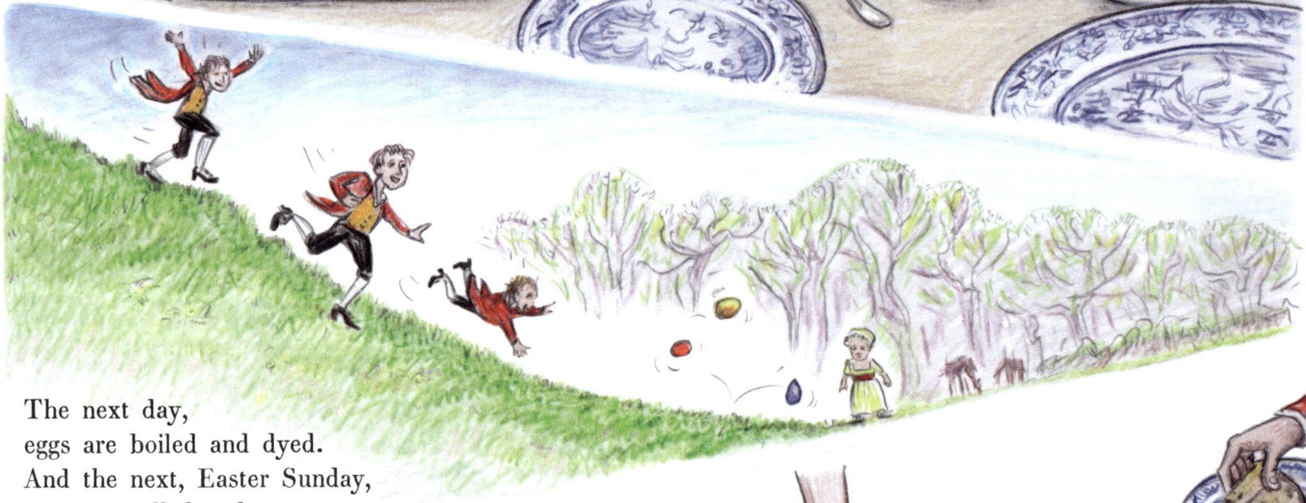

The next day, eggs are boiled and dyed. And the next, Easter Sunday, eggs are rolled and cracked.

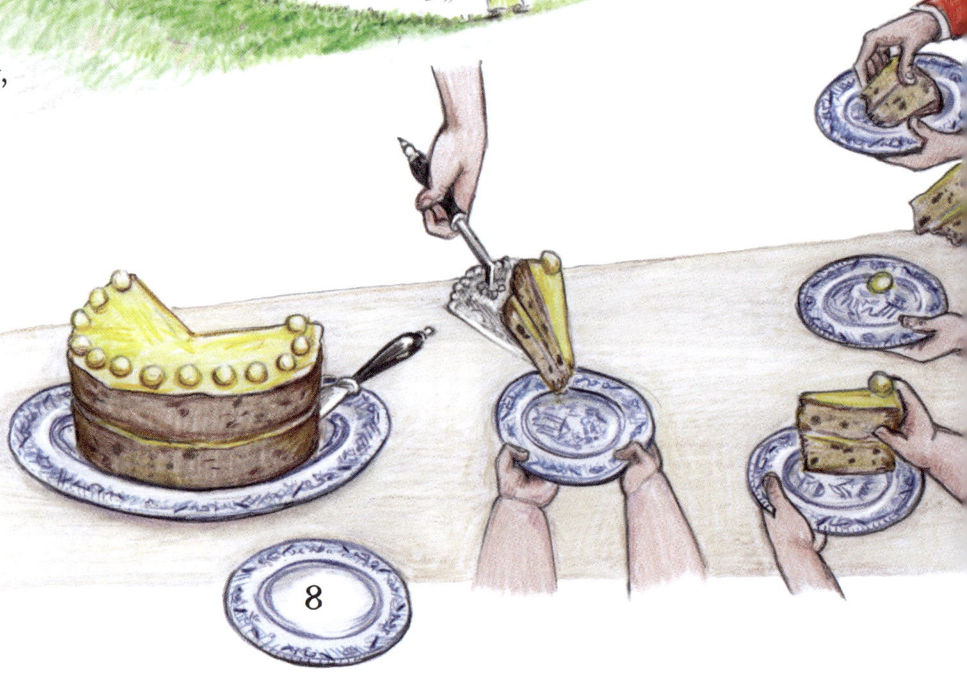

And in the evening, when the last crumbs of simnel cake have been licked from sticky fingers and the children bundled off to bed...

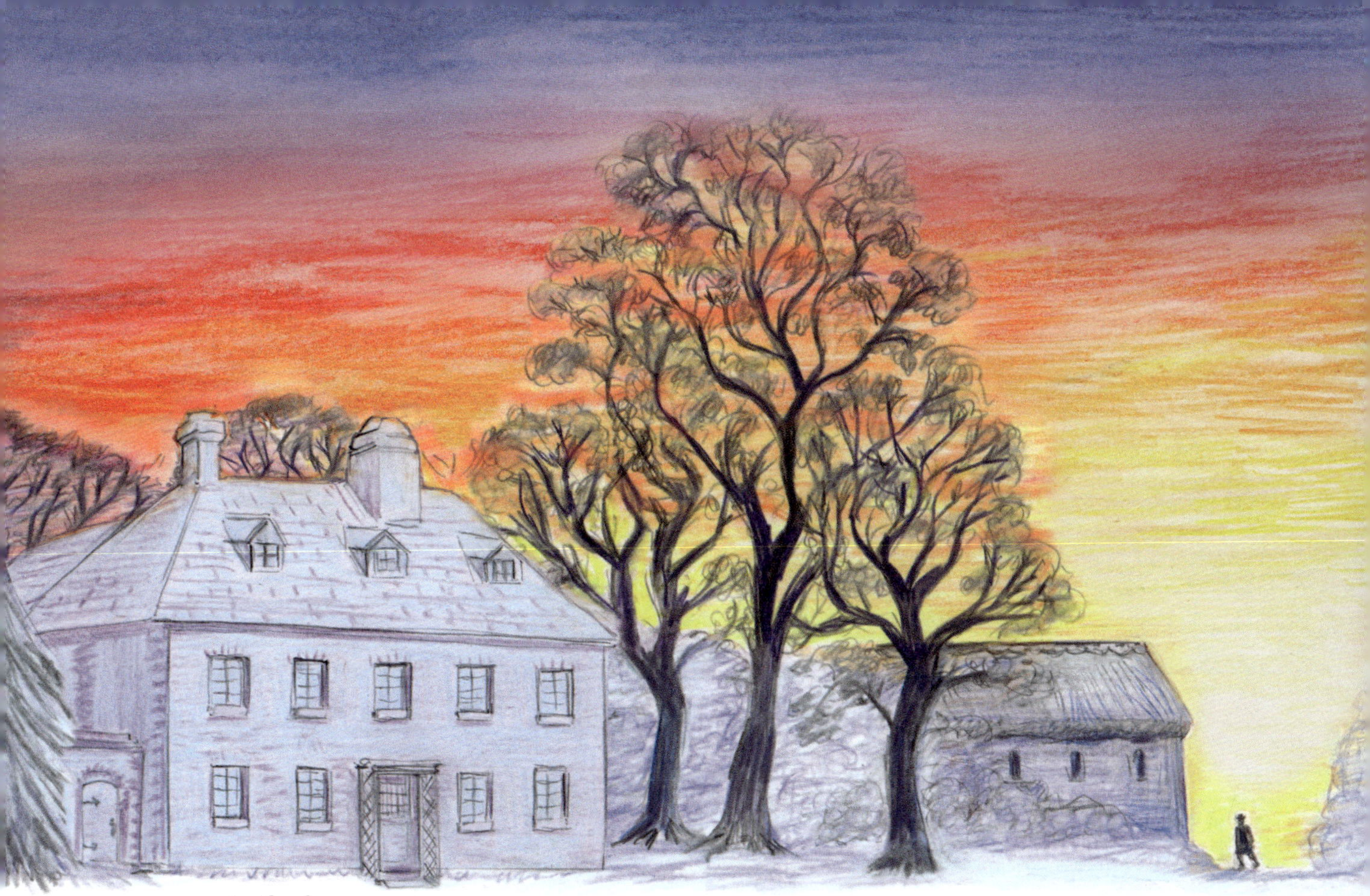

...a man comes to the house.
He doesn't approach the main entrance. He knows his place.
He skirts around through the side gate and knocks at the back door.

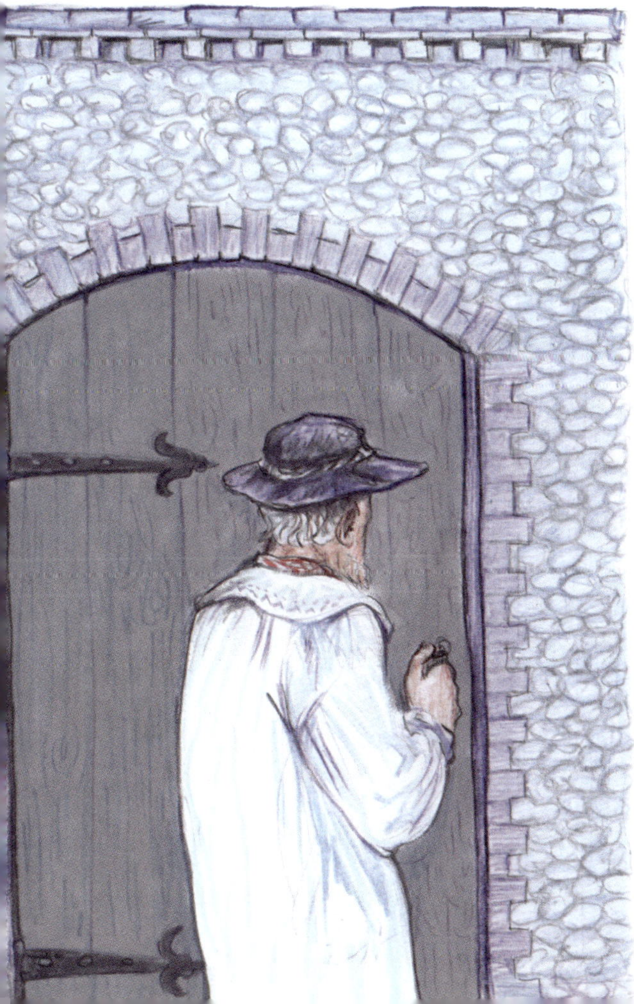

And there he takes delivery of a bundle containing a small loaf of the best Barbadoes sugar, and a baby.

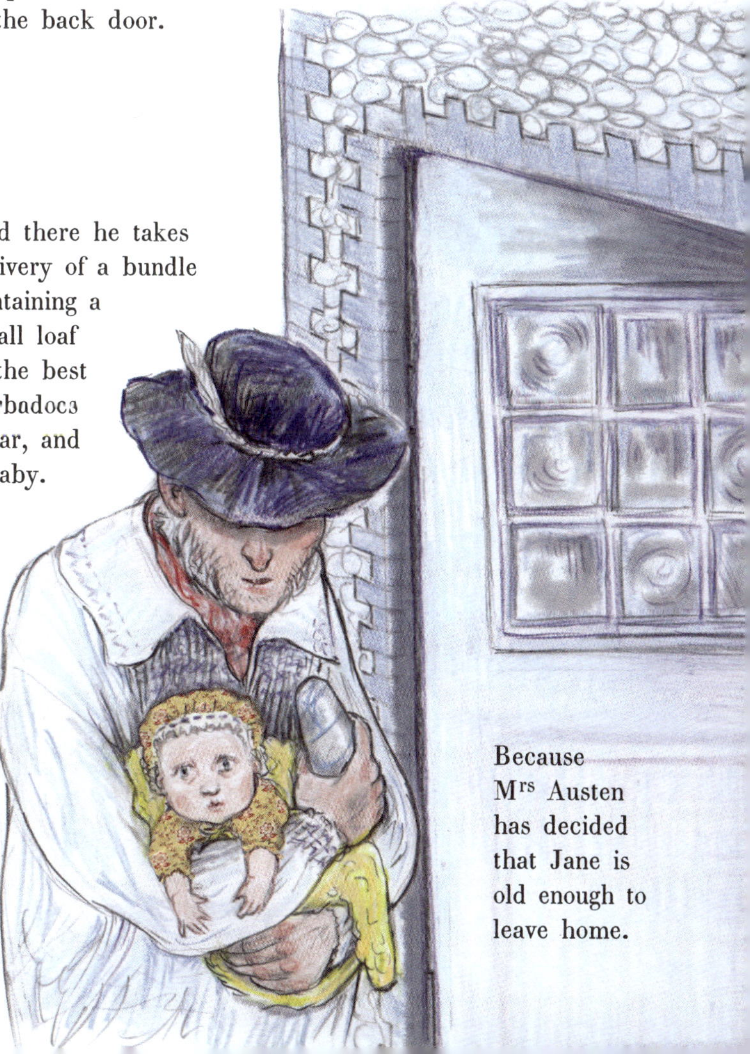

Because Mrs Austen has decided that Jane is old enough to leave home.

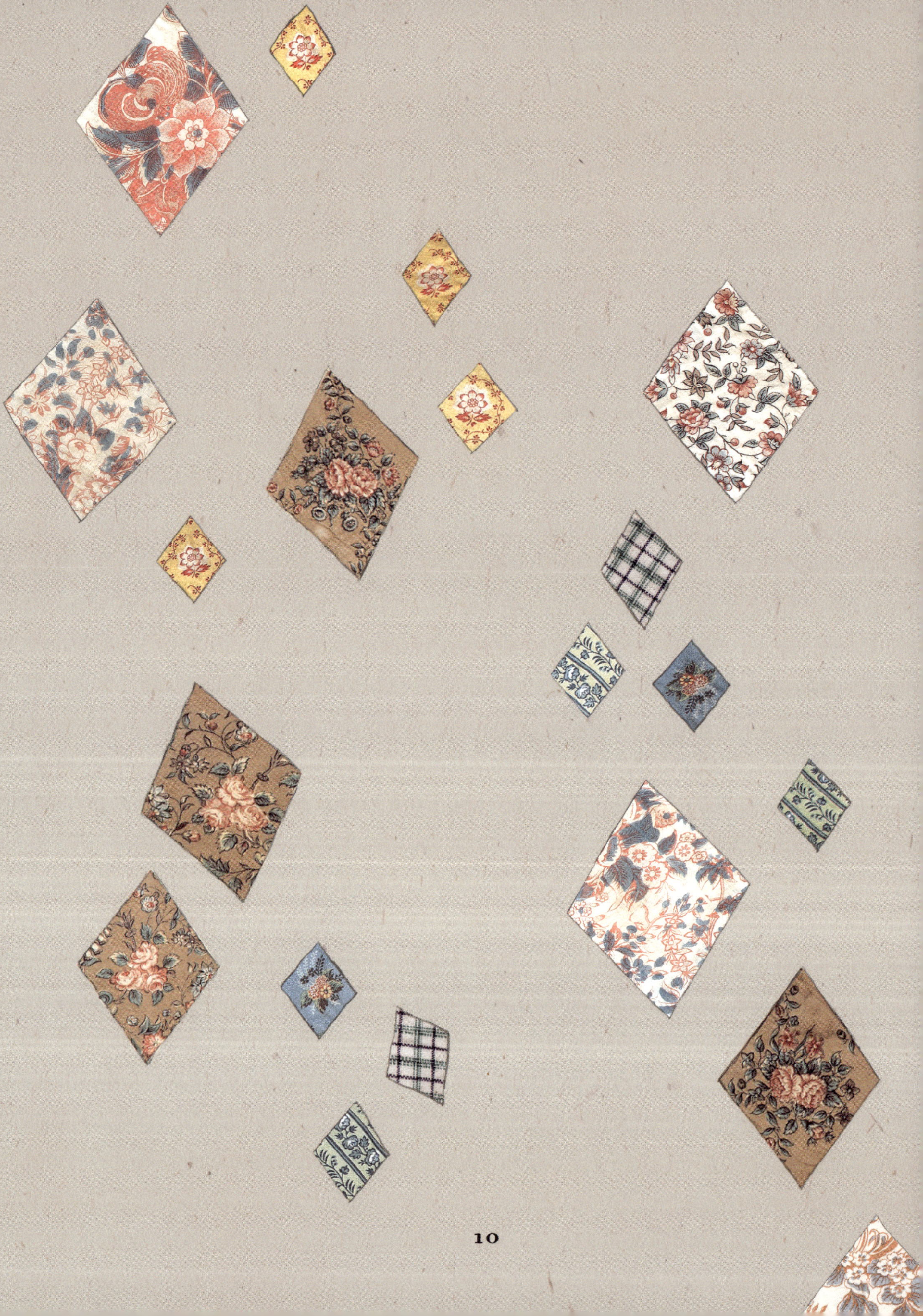

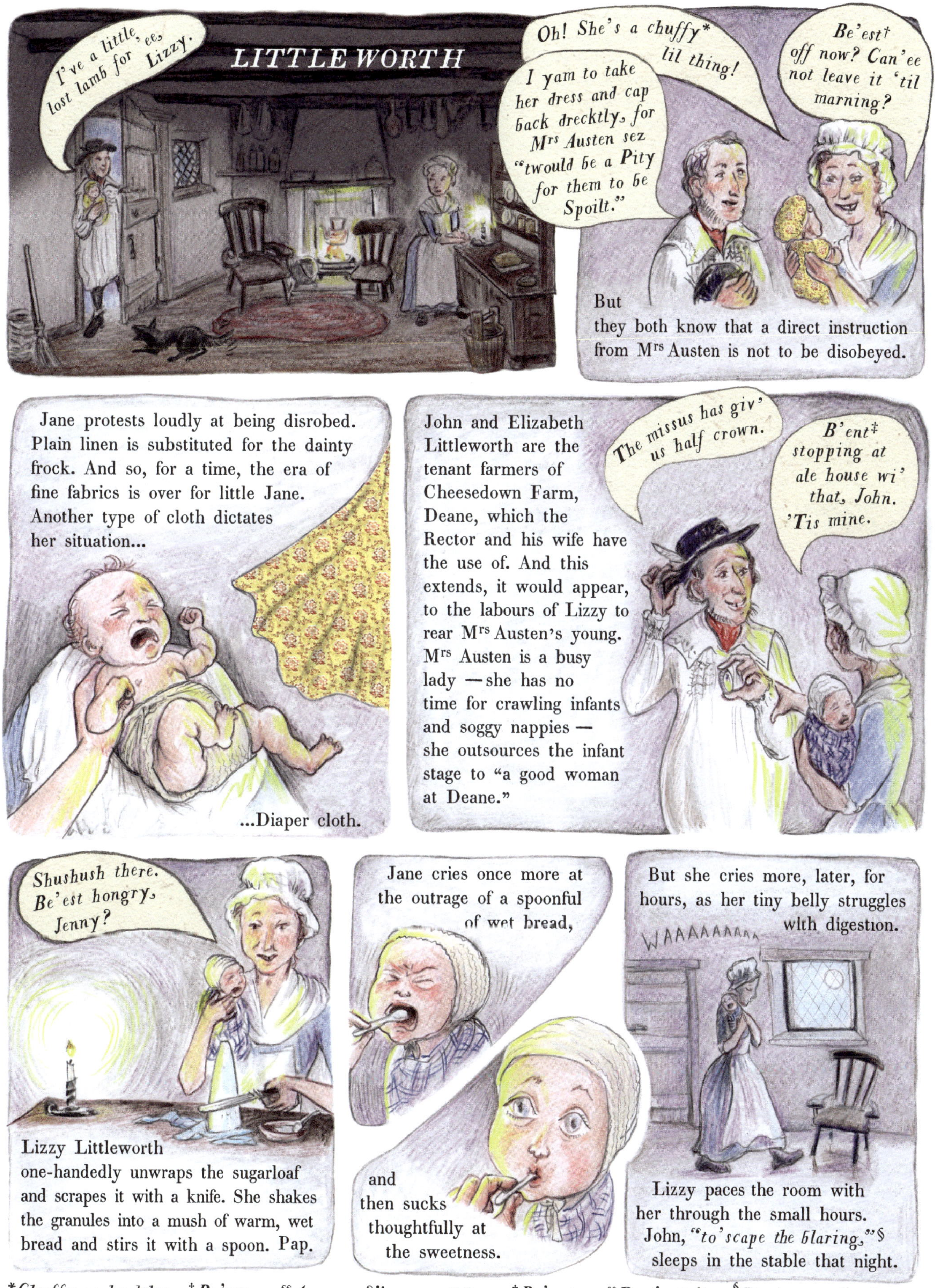
LITTLEWORTH
I've a little, lost lamb for ee, Lizzy.
Oh! She's a chuffy* lil thing!
I yam to take her dress and cap back drecktly, for Mrs Austen sez "twould be a Pity for them to be Spoilt."
Be'est† off now? Can'ee not leave it 'til marning?
But they both know that a direct instruction from Mrs Austen is not to be disobeyed.
Jane protests loudly at being disrobed. Plain linen is substituted for the dainty frock. And so, for a time, the era of fine fabrics is over for little Jane. Another type of cloth dictates her situation...
...Diaper cloth.
John and Elizabeth Littleworth are the tenant farmers of Cheesedown Farm, Deane, which the Rector and his wife have the use of. And this extends, it would appear, to the labours of Lizzy to rear Mrs Austen's young. Mrs Austen is a busy lady — she has no time for crawling infants and soggy nappies — she outsources the infant stage to "a good woman at Deane."
The missus has giv' us half crown.
B'ent‡ stopping at ale house wi' that, John. 'Tis mine.
Shushush there. Be'est hongry, Jenny?
Lizzy Littleworth one-handedly unwraps the sugarloaf and scrapes it with a knife. She shakes the granules into a mush of warm, wet bread and stirs it with a spoon. Pap.
Jane cries once more at the outrage of a spoonful of wet bread,
and then sucks thoughtfully at the sweetness.
But she cries more, later, for hours, as her tiny belly struggles with digestion.
WAAAAAAAAA
Lizzy paces the room with her through the small hours. John, "to'scape the blaring,"§ sleeps in the stable that night.

*Chuffy = healthy †Be'est = "Are you?" ‡Be'ent = "Don't be" §Blaring = Crying

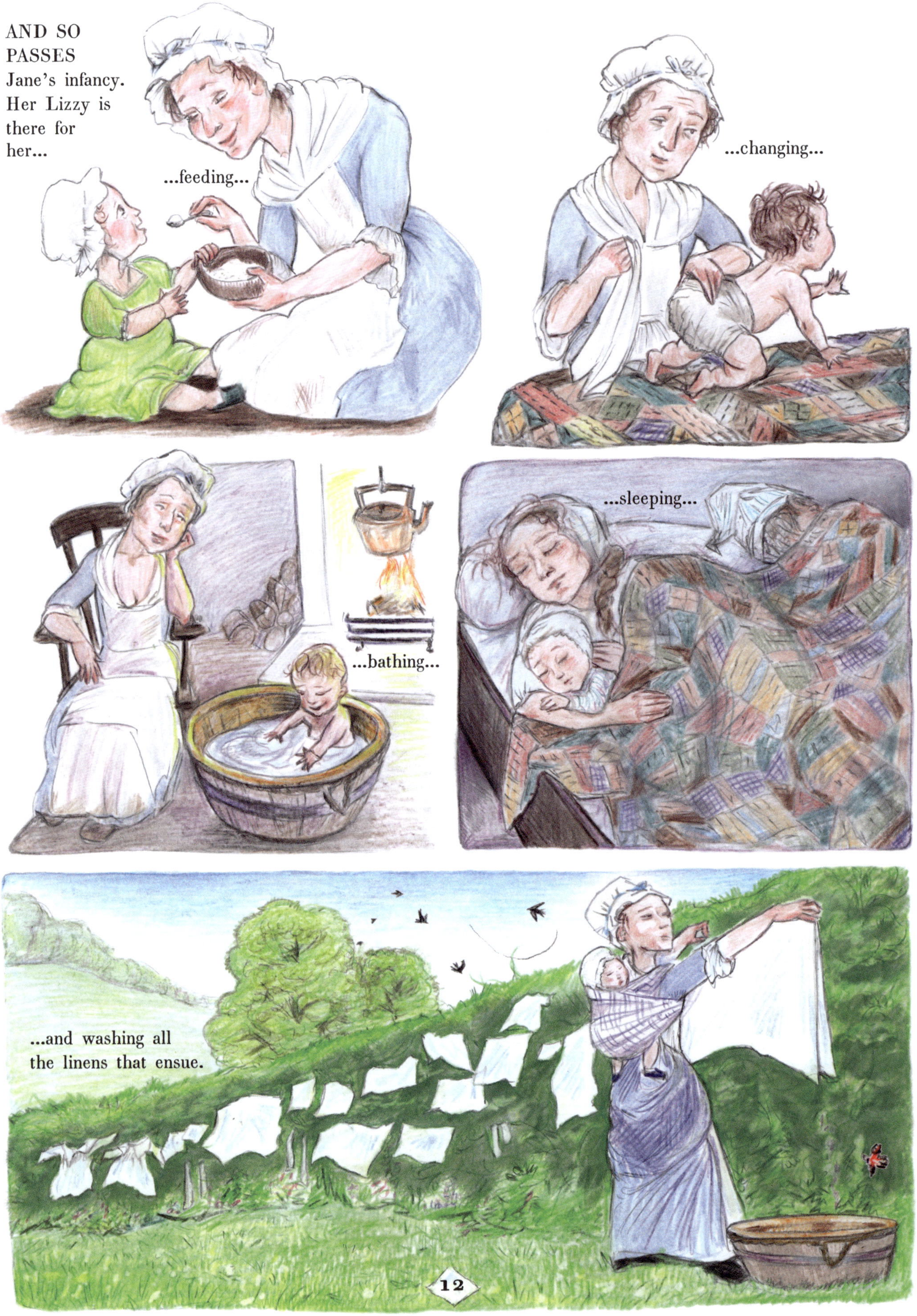
AND SO PASSES Jane's infancy. Her Lizzy is there for her...
...feeding...
...changing...
...bathing...
...sleeping...
...and washing all the linens that ensue.

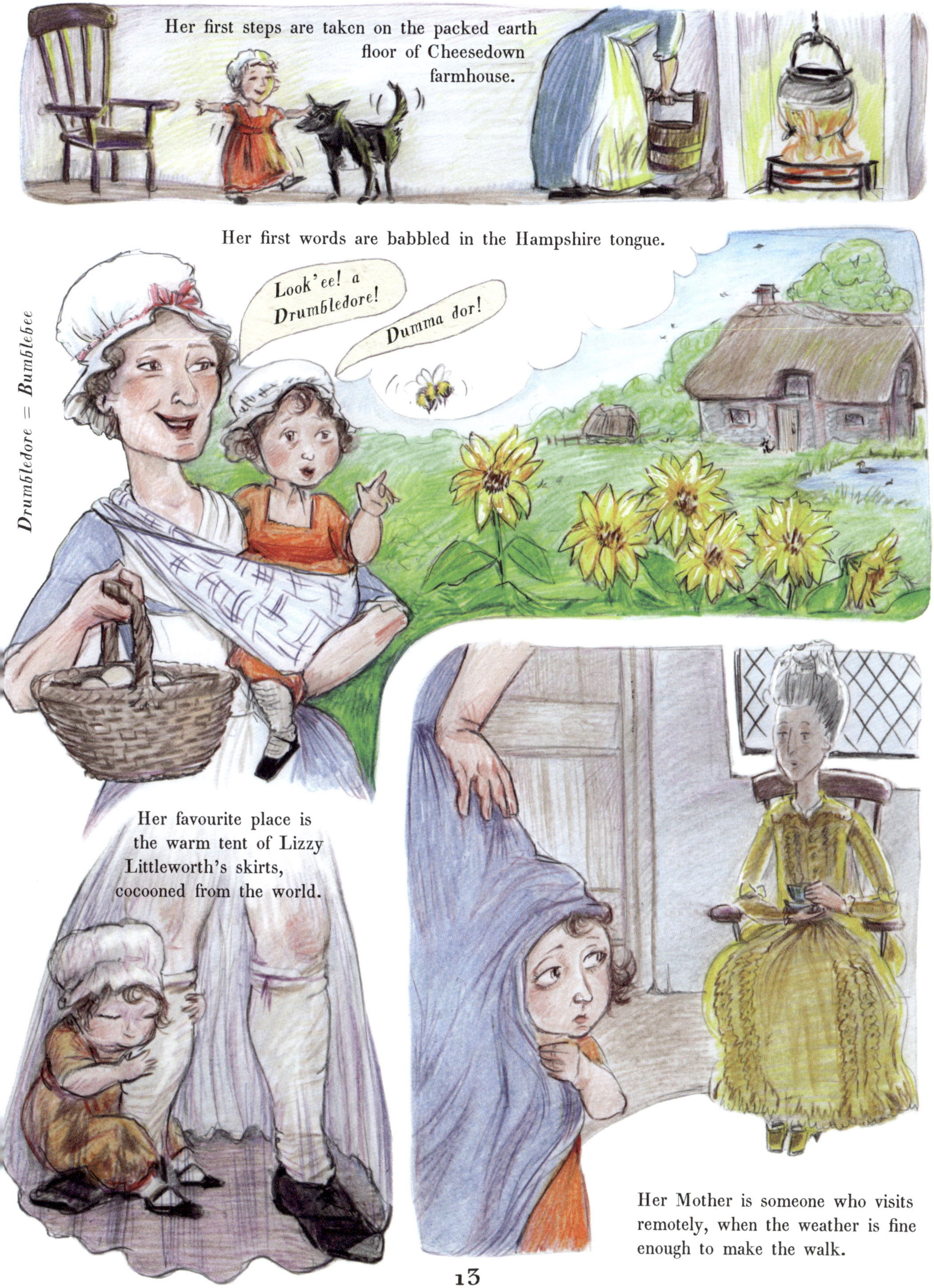
Her first steps are taken on the packed earth floor of Cheesedown farmhouse.
Her first words are babbled in the Hampshire tongue.
Look'ee! a Drumbledore!
Dumma dor!
Drumbledore = Bumblebee
Her favourite place is the warm tent of Lizzy Littleworth's skirts, cocooned from the world.
Her Mother is someone who visits remotely, when the weather is fine enough to make the walk.

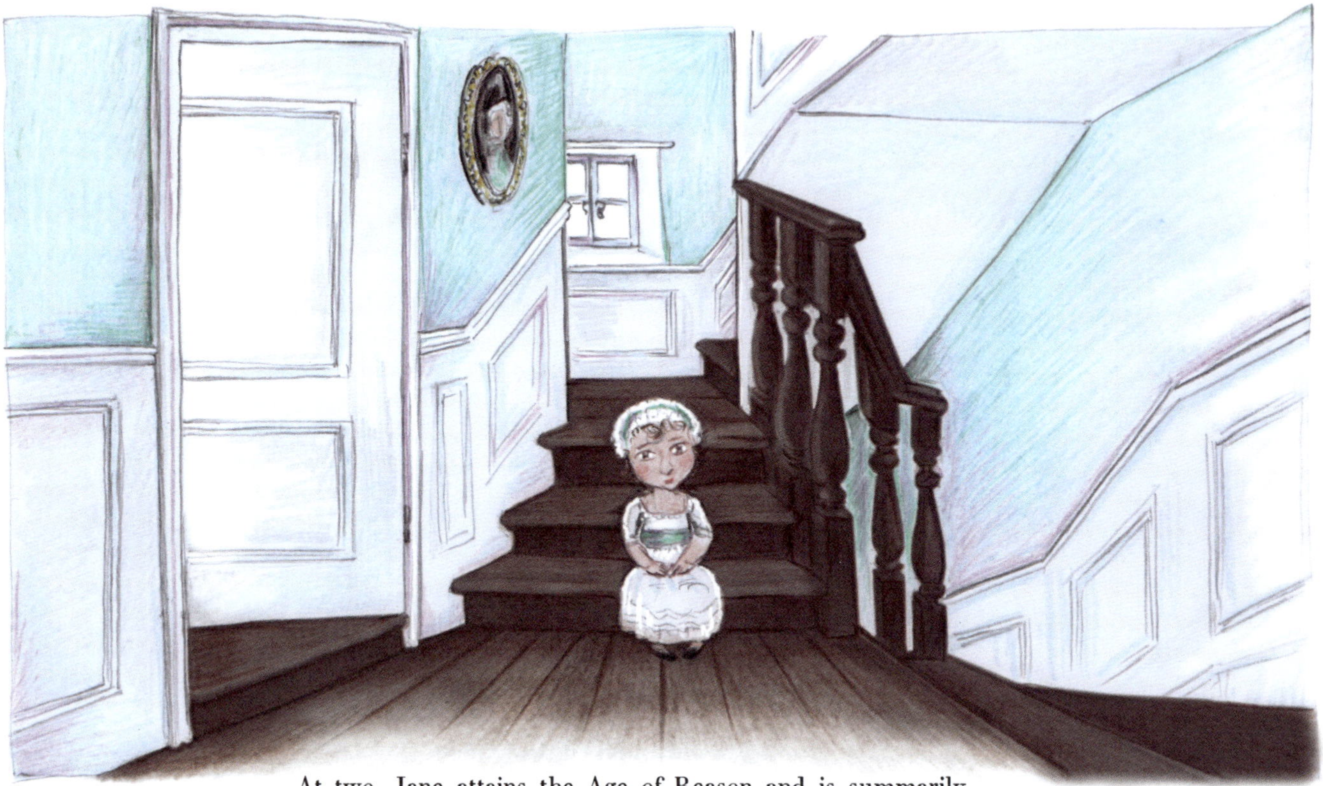

At two, Jane attains the Age of Reason and is summarily transplanted from her cosy cottage back to the many-roomed parsonage.

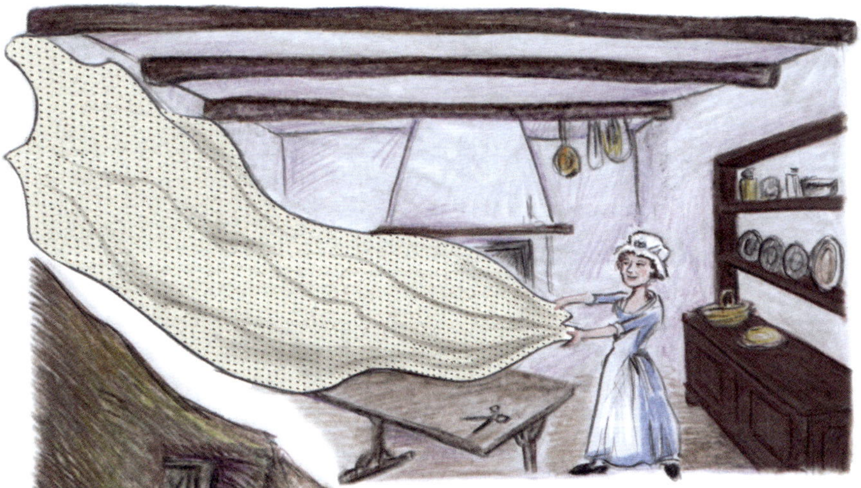

Elizabeth Littleworth buys seven yards of spotted calico with her hard-gotten gains. By sputtering tallow candle-light, she stitches herself a bright, white gown for Sunday best.

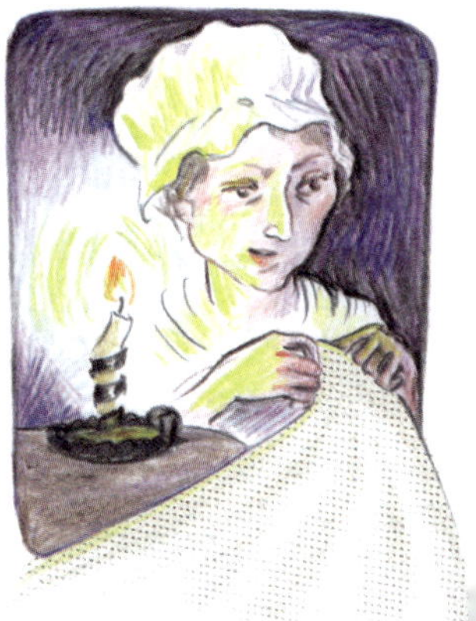

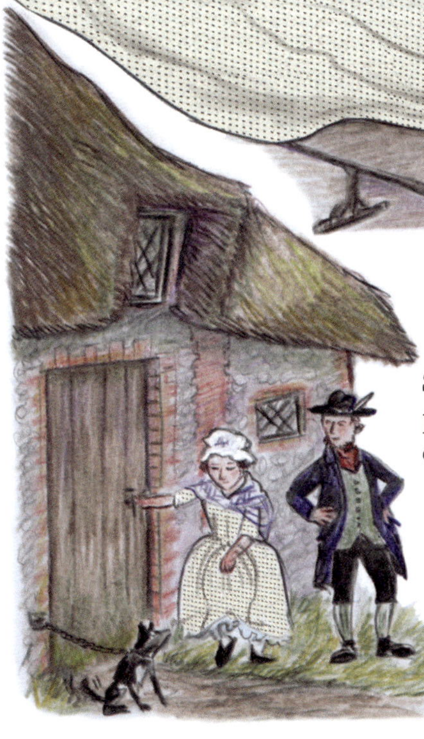

She is inordinately proud that it has no dirt upon the hem, and sallies forth to church.

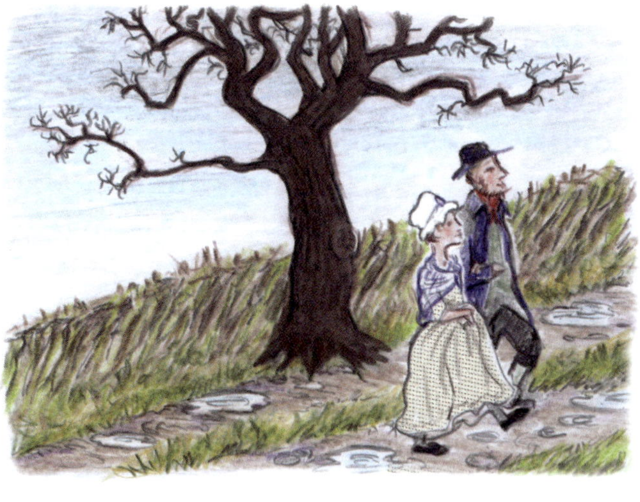

Jane spots her and races eagerly to her, burrowing into her skirts.

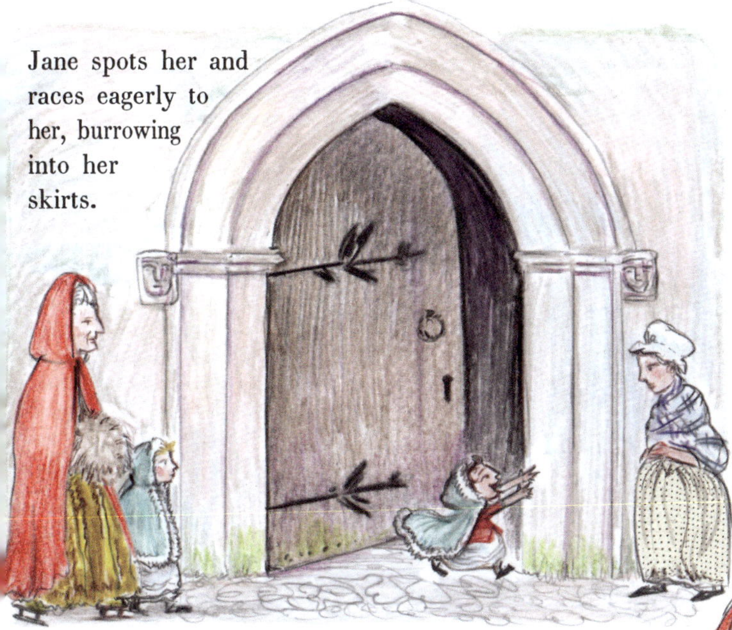

But strong hands pull her away, and Lizzy unclasps her fingers, concerned that the cheap cotton will tear.

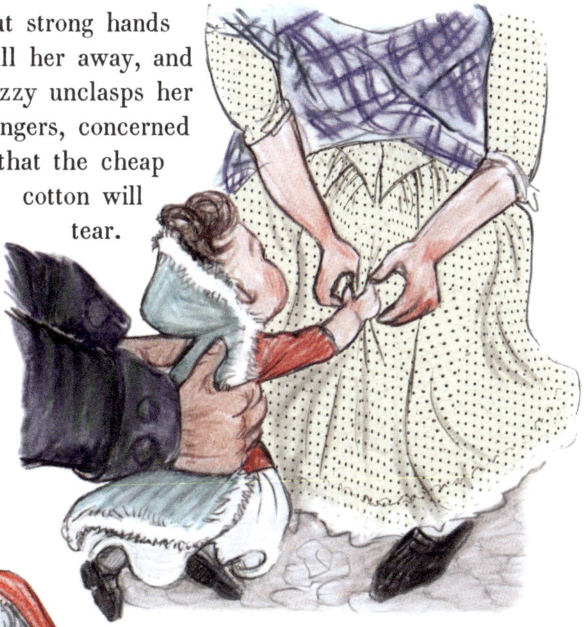

Jane screams.

Lizzy blushes.

Mrs Austen tuts.

Cassie understands.

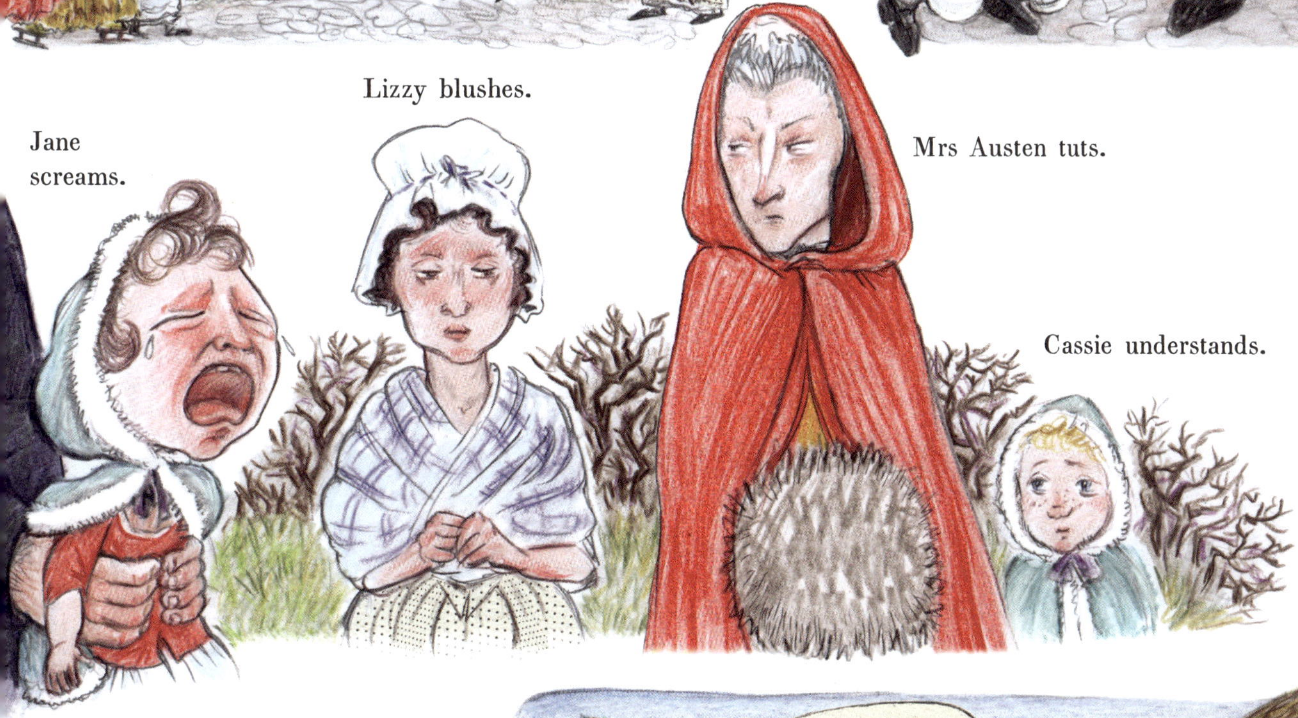

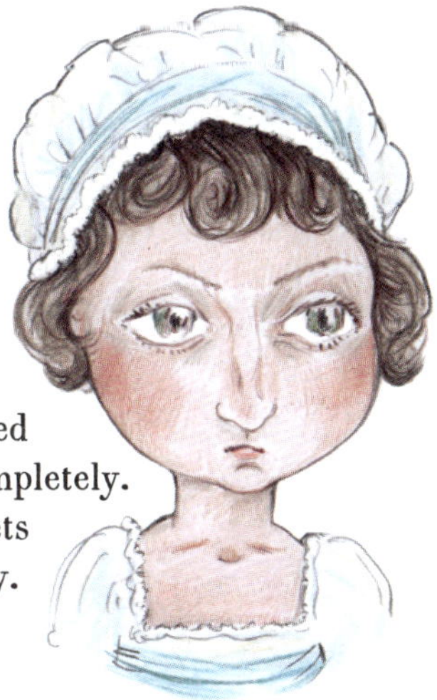

Jane forgets the spotted dress completely. She forgets her Lizzy.

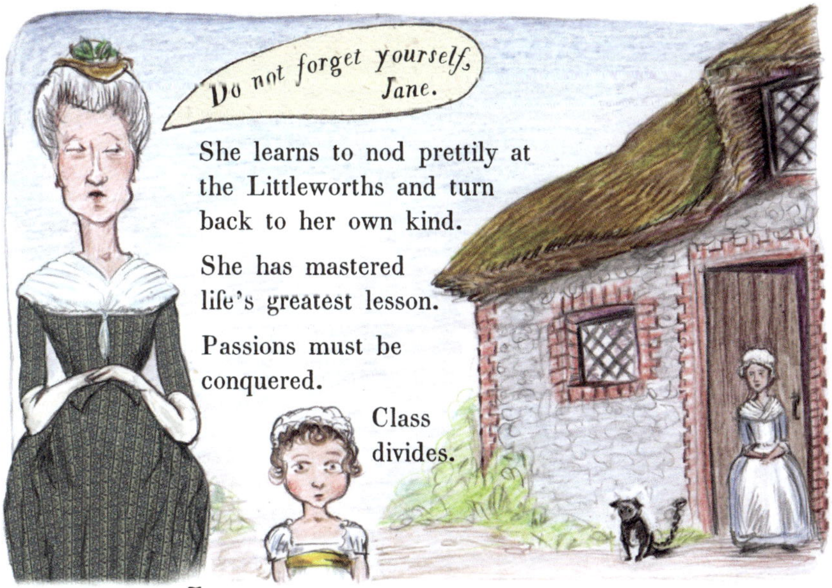
Do not forget yourself, Jane.

She learns to nod prettily at the Littleworths and turn back to her own kind.

She has mastered life's greatest lesson.

Passions must be conquered.

Class divides.

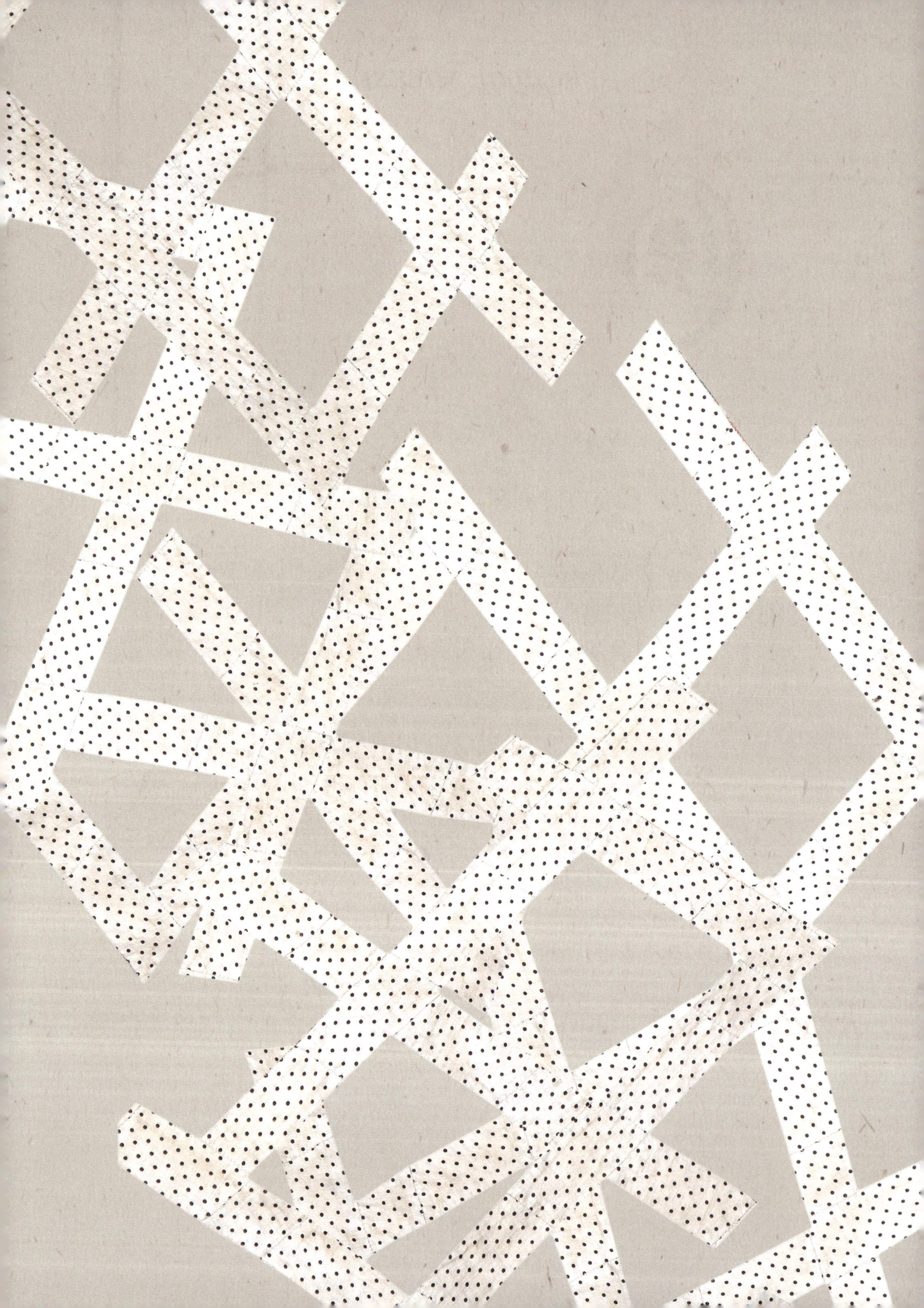

SCHOOL HOUSE

GEORGE AUSTEN SITS in his study, his face reflected thoughtfully in the bow window.

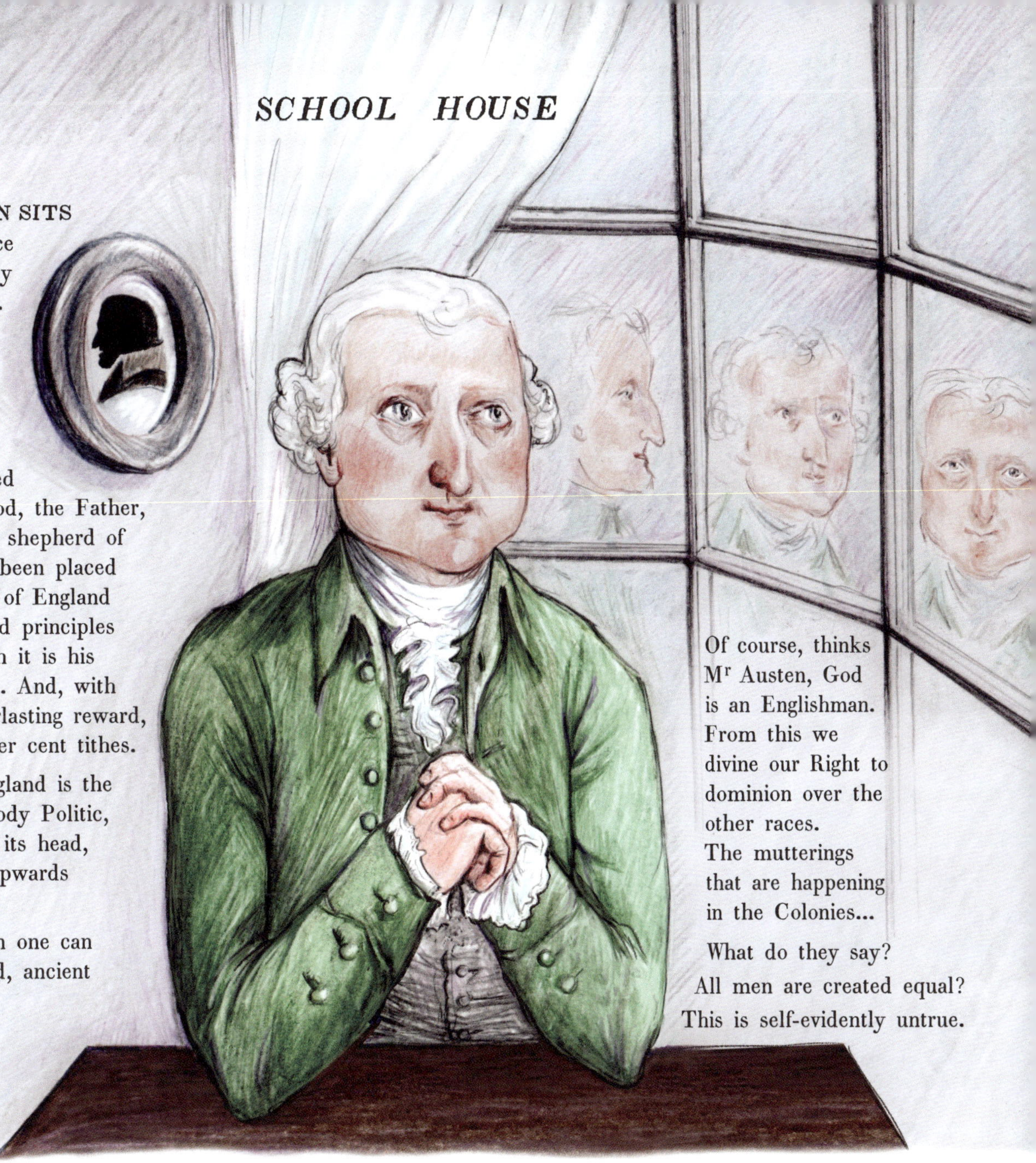

His head.

He is the head.

Head of his family, and as the appointed representative of God, the Father, head of his Parish, shepherd of his Flock. He has been placed here in this corner of England to imbue those good principles in the people which it is his duty to recommend. And, with the promise of everlasting reward, to collect the 10 per cent tithes.

The Church of England is the right arm of the Body Politic, the King stands at its head, and wealth flows upwards through its veins.

Whatever connection one can claim to established, ancient wealth determines one's standing.

Family, ties.

Of course, thinks Mr Austen, God is an Englishman. From this we divine our Right to dominion over the other races. The mutterings that are happening in the Colonies...

What do they say? All men are created equal? This is self-evidently untrue.

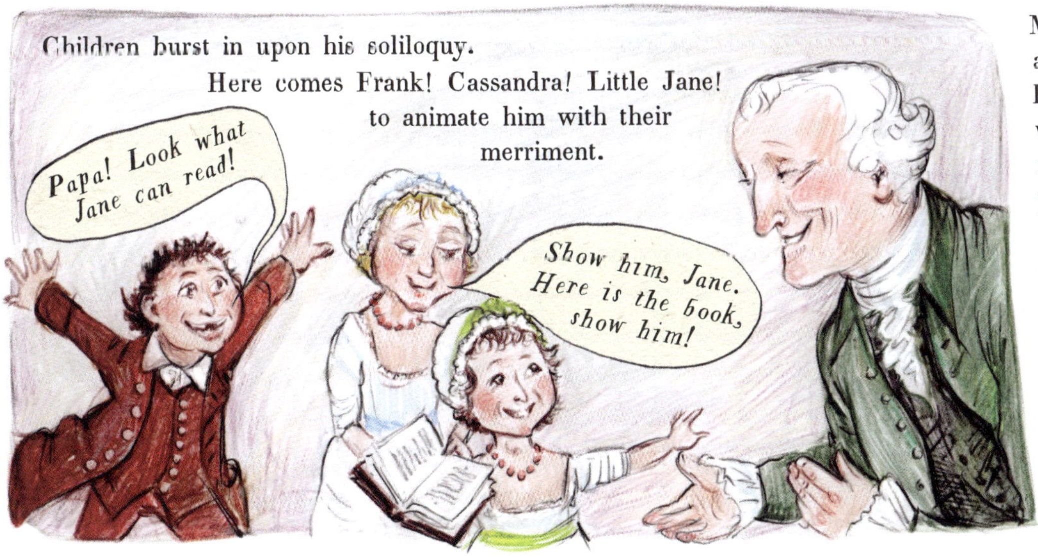
Children burst in upon his soliloquy.
Here comes Frank! Cassandra! Little Jane! to animate him with their merriment.
Papa! Look what Jane can read!
Show him, Jane. Here is the book, show him!

Mr Austen's duties are not onerous. Regular meetings with the curate, the magistrate and the parish overseer have it all in hand. But raising eight children (or is it seven?) to the standards of the Gentry requires a considerable outlay, more than his poor parishioners can supply.

What more can be done?

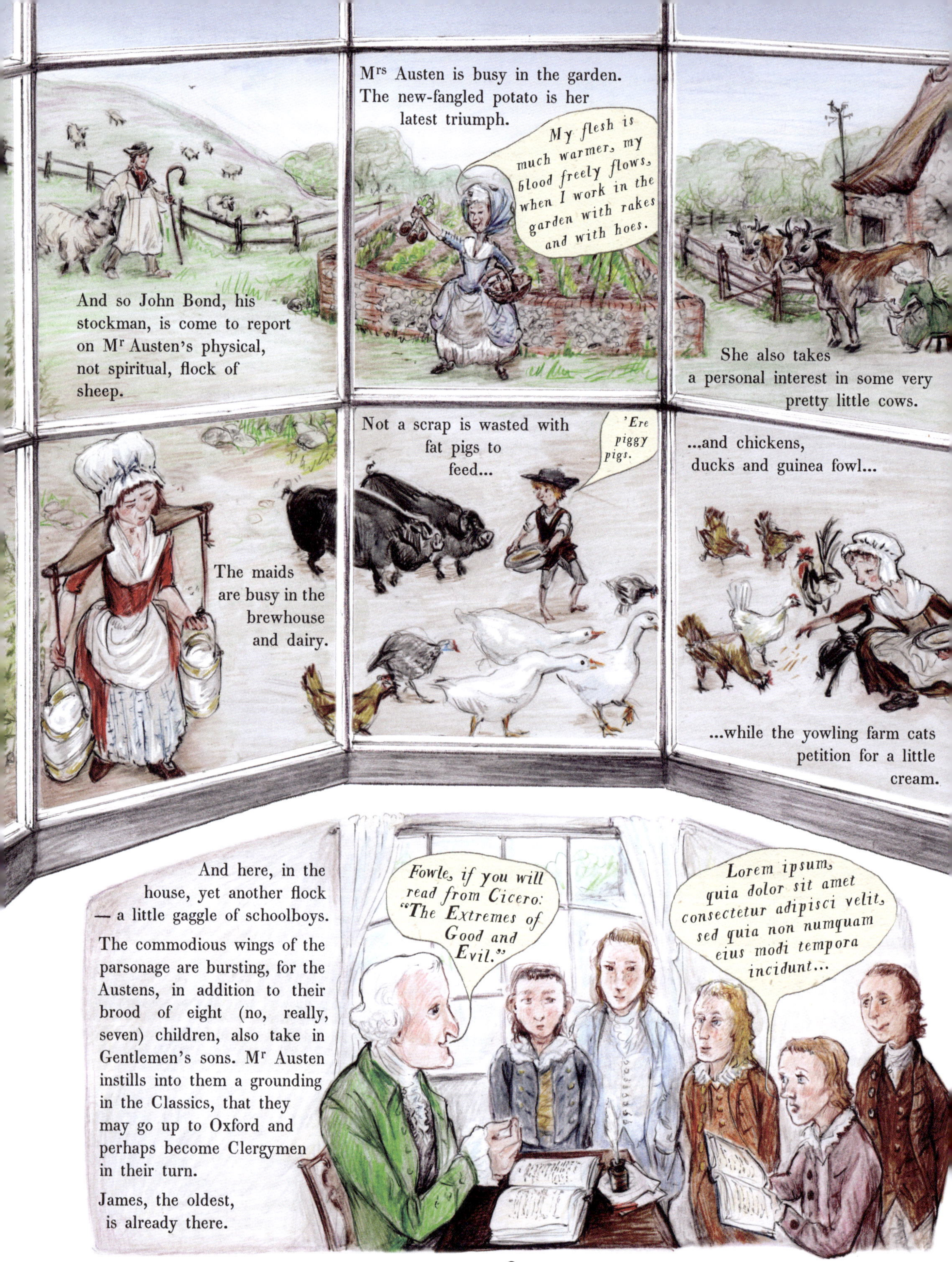
And so John Bond, his stockman, is come to report on Mr Austen's physical, not spiritual, flock of sheep.
Mrs Austen is busy in the garden. The new-fangled potato is her latest triumph.
My flesh is much warmer, my blood freely flows, when I work in the garden with rakes and with hoes.
She also takes a personal interest in some very pretty little cows.
The maids are busy in the brewhouse and dairy.
Not a scrap is wasted with fat pigs to feed...
'Ere piggy pigs.
...and chickens, ducks and guinea fowl...
...while the yowling farm cats petition for a little cream.
And here, in the house, yet another flock — a little gaggle of schoolboys.
The commodious wings of the parsonage are bursting, for the Austens, in addition to their brood of eight (no, really, seven) children, also take in Gentlemen's sons. Mr Austen instills into them a grounding in the Classics, that they may go up to Oxford and perhaps become Clergymen in their turn.
James, the oldest, is already there.
Fowle, if you will read from Cicero: "The Extremes of Good and Evil."
Lorem ipsum, quia dolor sit amet consectetur adipisci velit, sed quia non numquam eius modi tempora incidunt...

Schoolboys, but they have all the grandeur of men, to little Jane. Full of life and spirits, they seem born only for expense and enjoyment.

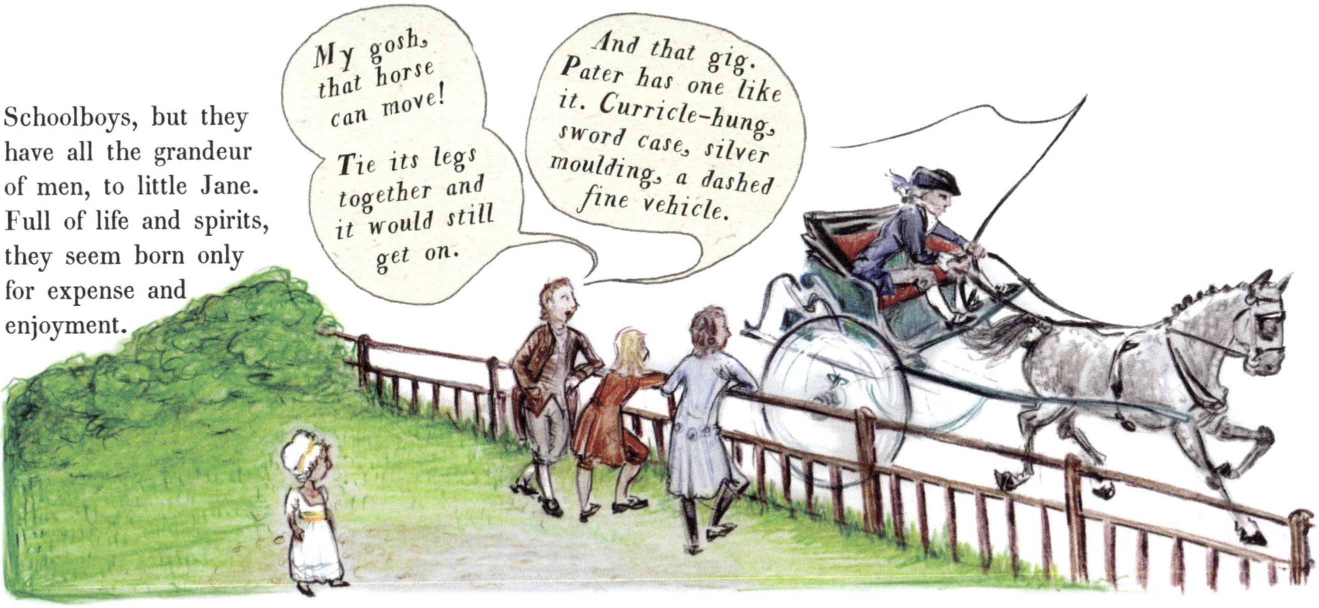
My gosh, that horse can move!
Tie its legs together and it would still get on.
And that gig. Pater has one like it. Curricle-hung, sword case, silver moulding, a dashed fine vehicle.

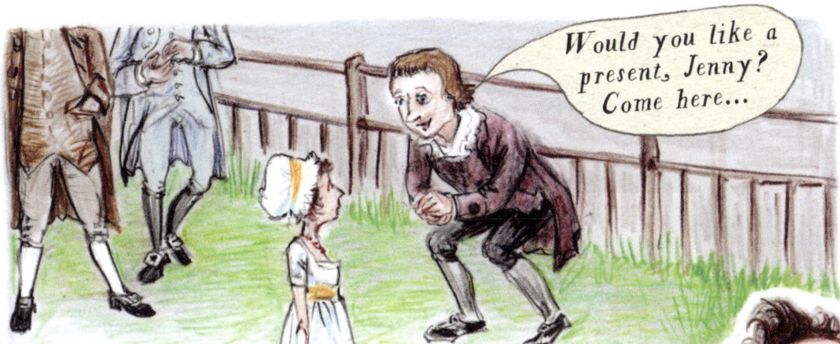
Would you like a present, Jenny? Come here...

And they think the little ones are fair sport.

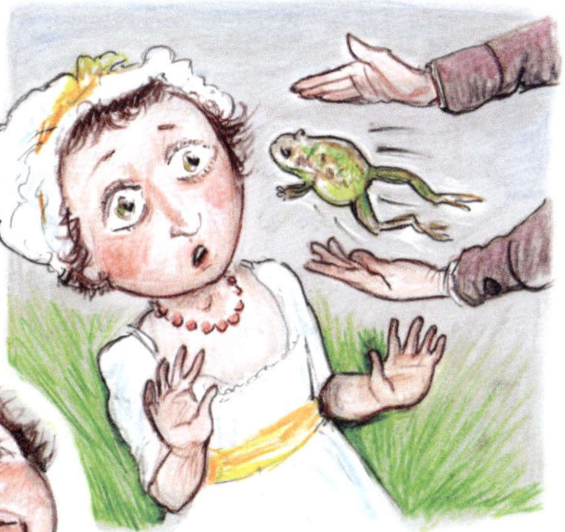

In this mælstrom, it is inevitable that Cassy, Frank, Jane and the latest and last baby, Charles, are left to shift for themselves.

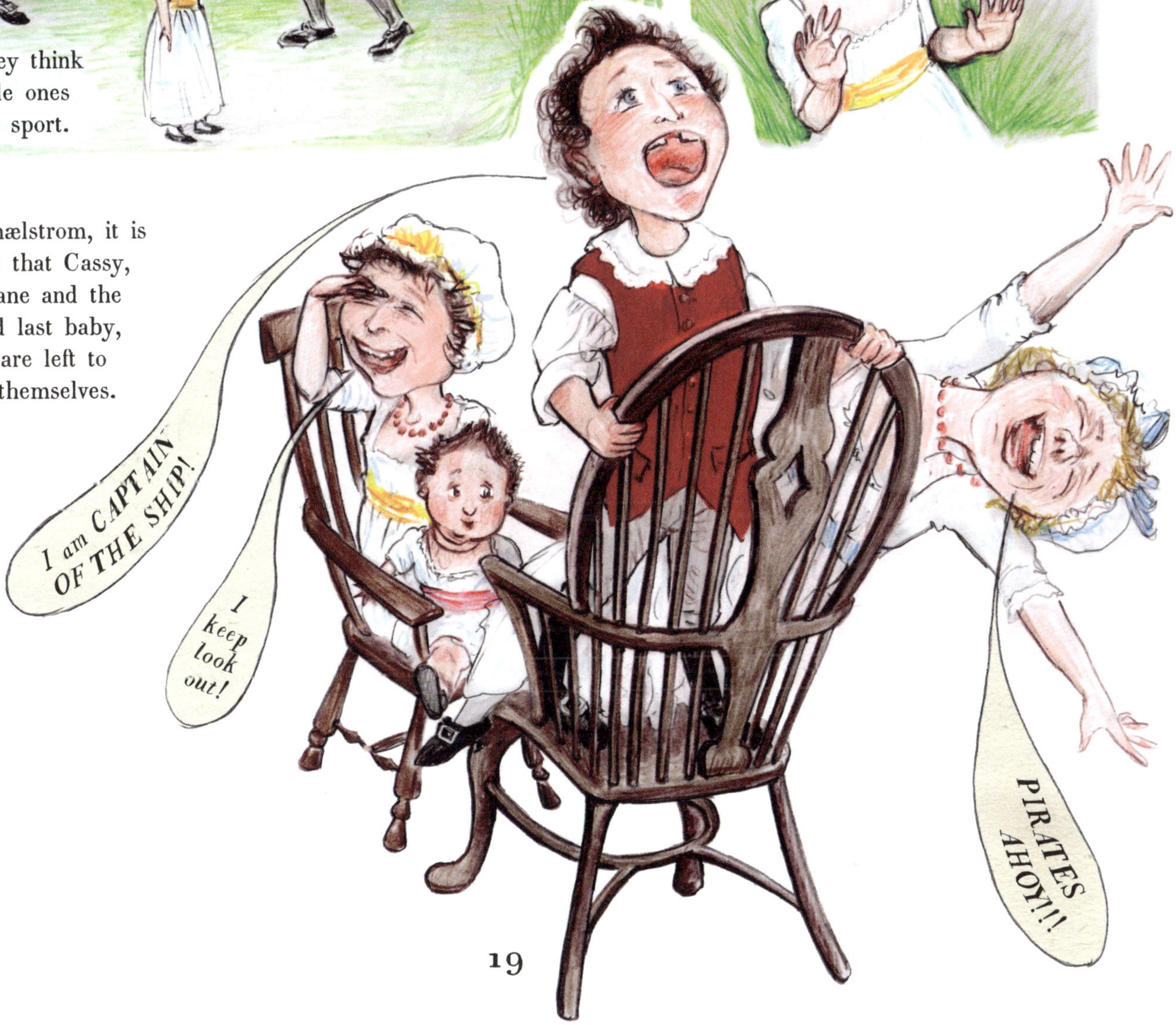
I am CAPTAIN OF THE SHIP!
I keep look out!
PIRATES AHOY!!!

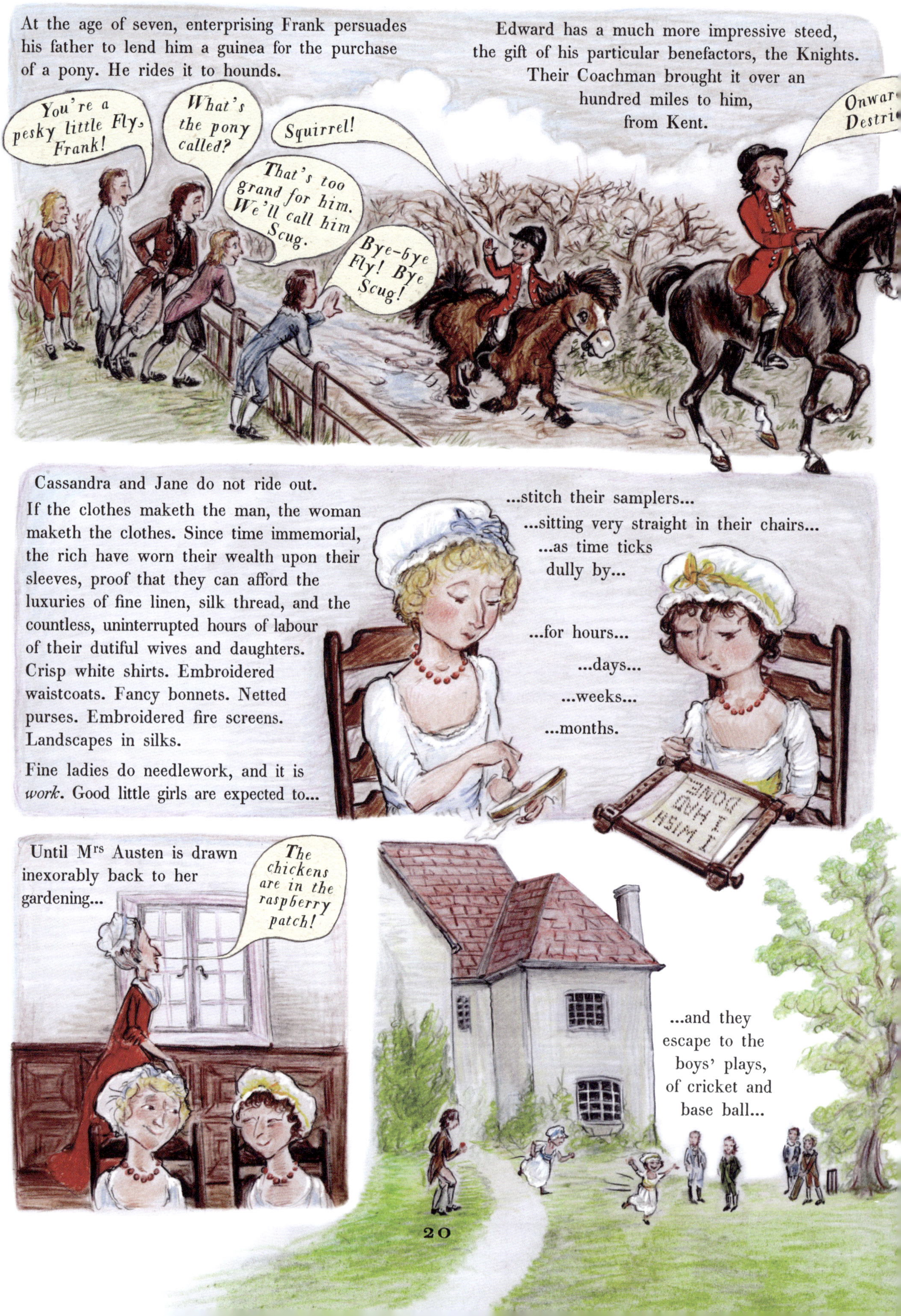
At the age of seven, enterprising Frank persuades his father to lend him a guinea for the purchase of a pony. He rides it to hounds.
You're a pesky little Fly, Frank!
What's the pony called?
Squirrel!
That's too grand for him. We'll call him Scug.
Bye-bye Fly! Bye Scug!
Edward has a much more impressive steed, the gift of his particular benefactors, the Knights. Their Coachman brought it over an hundred miles to him, from Kent.
Cassandra and Jane do not ride out.
If the clothes maketh the man, the woman maketh the clothes. Since time immemorial, the rich have worn their wealth upon their sleeves, proof that they can afford the luxuries of fine linen, silk thread, and the countless, uninterrupted hours of labour of their dutiful wives and daughters. Crisp white shirts. Embroidered waistcoats. Fancy bonnets. Netted purses. Embroidered fire screens. Landscapes in silks.
Fine ladies do needlework, and it is *work*. Good little girls are expected to...
...stitch their samplers...
...sitting very straight in their chairs...
...as time ticks dully by...
...for hours...
...days...
...weeks...
...months.
Until Mrs Austen is drawn inexorably back to her gardening...
The chickens are in the raspberry patch!
...and they escape to the boys' plays, of cricket and base ball...

...leaping from the hayloft in the barn...

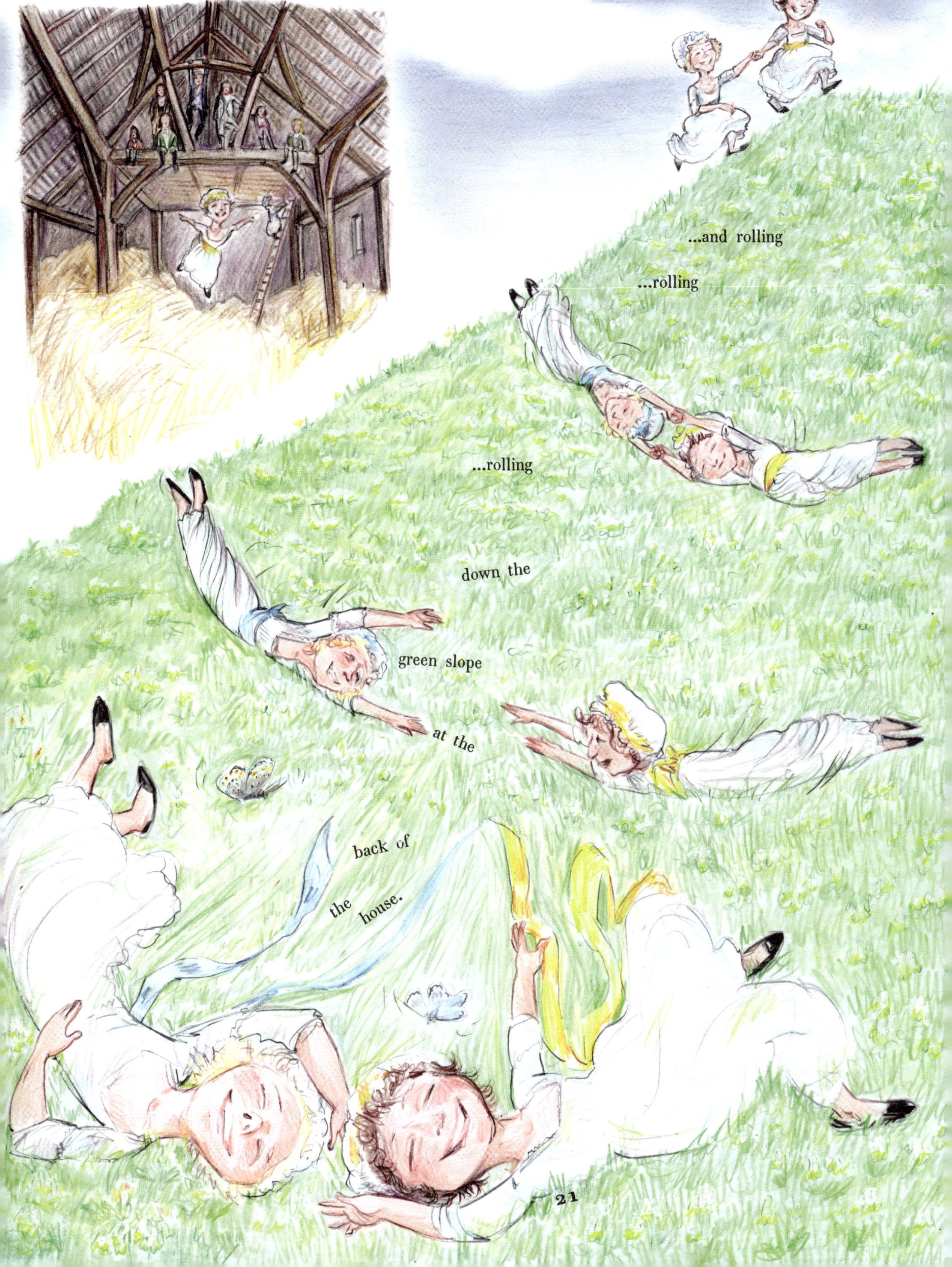

...and rolling

...rolling

...rolling

down the

green slope

at the

back of

the house.

It is a fine summer's afternoon, and Jane is six and a half. It is a wash day, and Dame Bushell is scrubbing grass stains from small white dresses.

Jane is bored.

Cassandra is away, staying with their cousins, the Coopers, but today is the day she is due back, and Papa has taken a hired chaise to Andover to fetch her home.

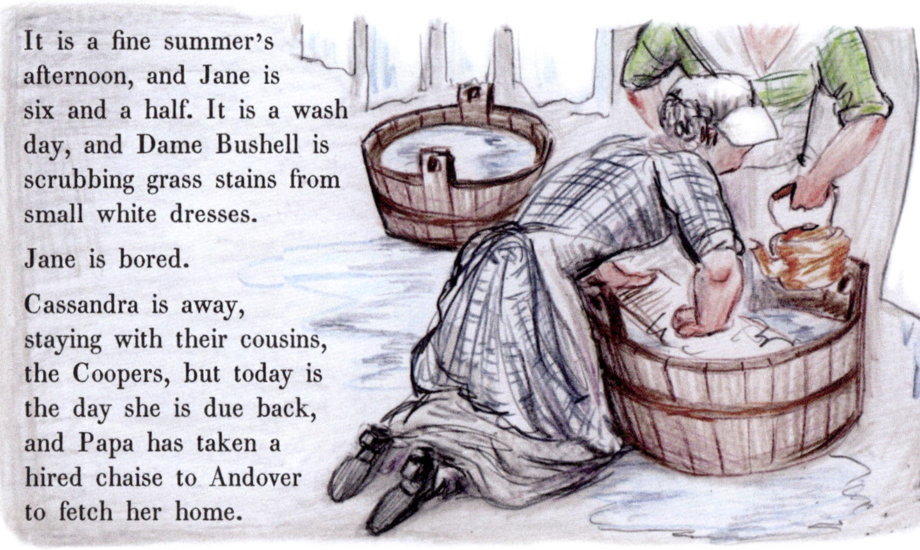

She grasps little Charles by his fat little hand and pulls him along on his sturdy little legs.

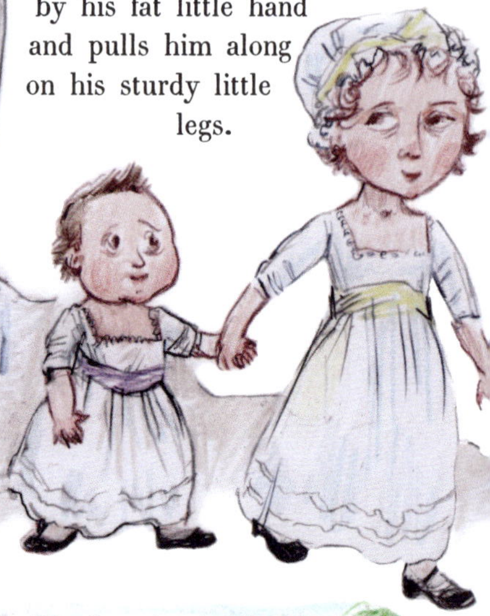

They slip out of the house, crunch down the gravel drive and go out of the gate.

Maybe nobody even notices that they are gone.

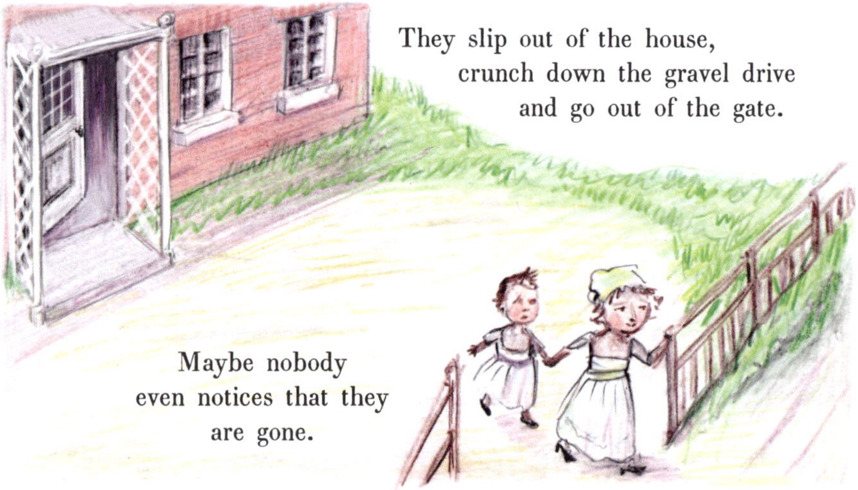

The lane is pitted with cart grooves, but dusty and dry.

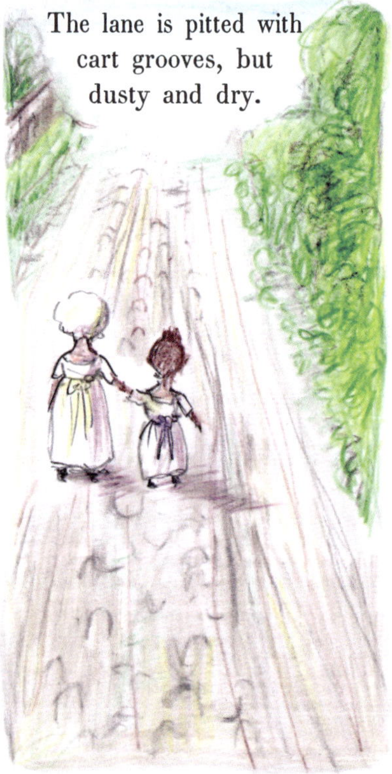

They march past the tithe barn,

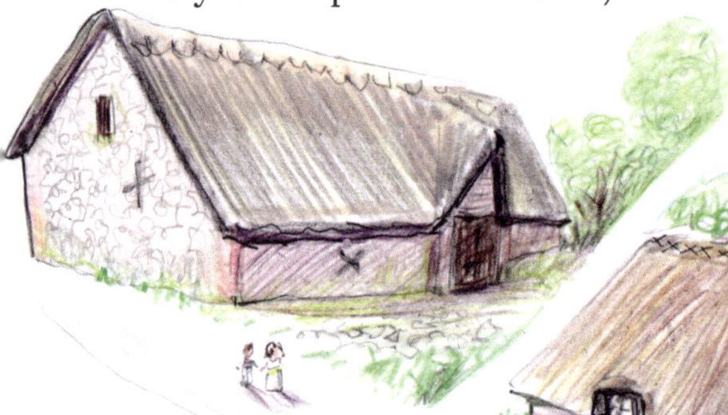

past the cottages,

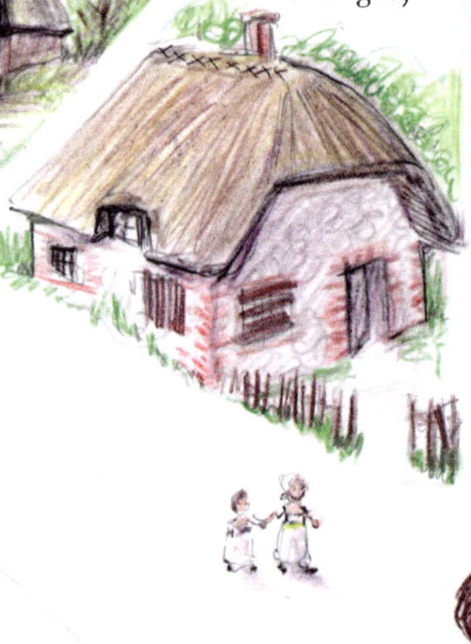

past the unblinking stares of the ragged children,

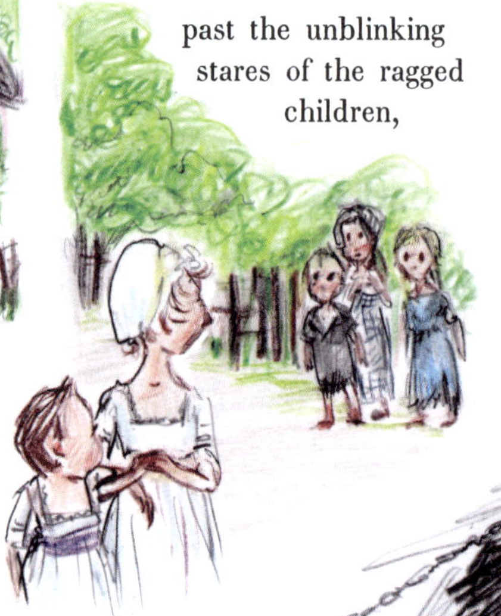

past the barking village dogs.

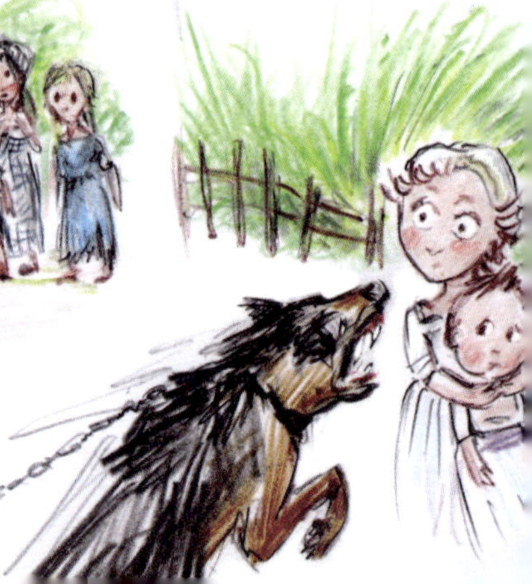

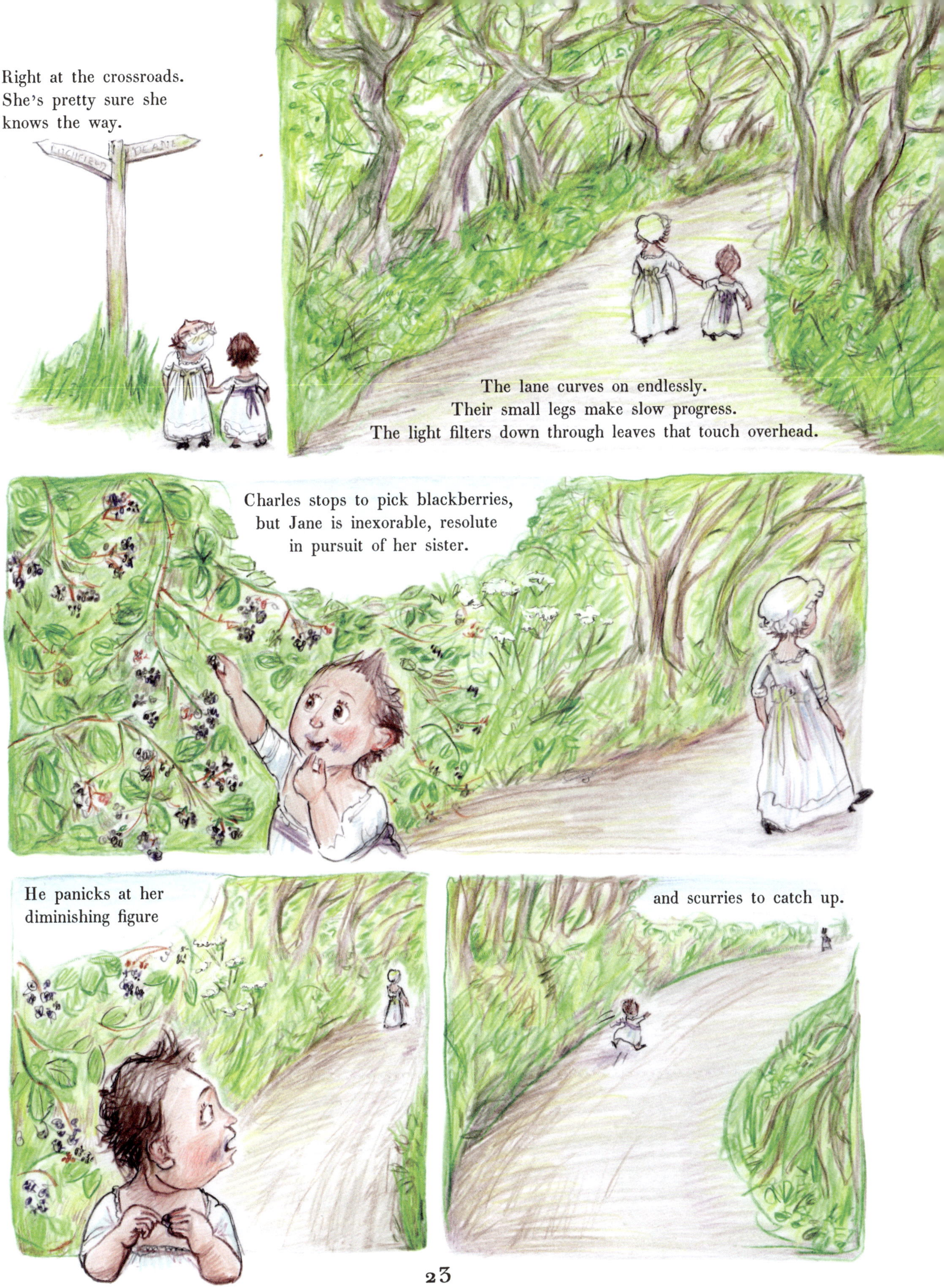
Right at the crossroads.
She's pretty sure she
knows the way.
DEANE
The lane curves on endlessly.
Their small legs make slow progress.
The light filters down through leaves that touch overhead.
Charles stops to pick blackberries,
but Jane is inexorable, resolute
in pursuit of her sister.
He panicks at her
diminishing figure
and scurries to catch up.

The children gain the Deane Gate Inn. This is as far as Jane has ever been before, when they go to collect the letters.

The inn sign creaks in the summer breeze. A man is wrestling a stone from a horse's hoof.

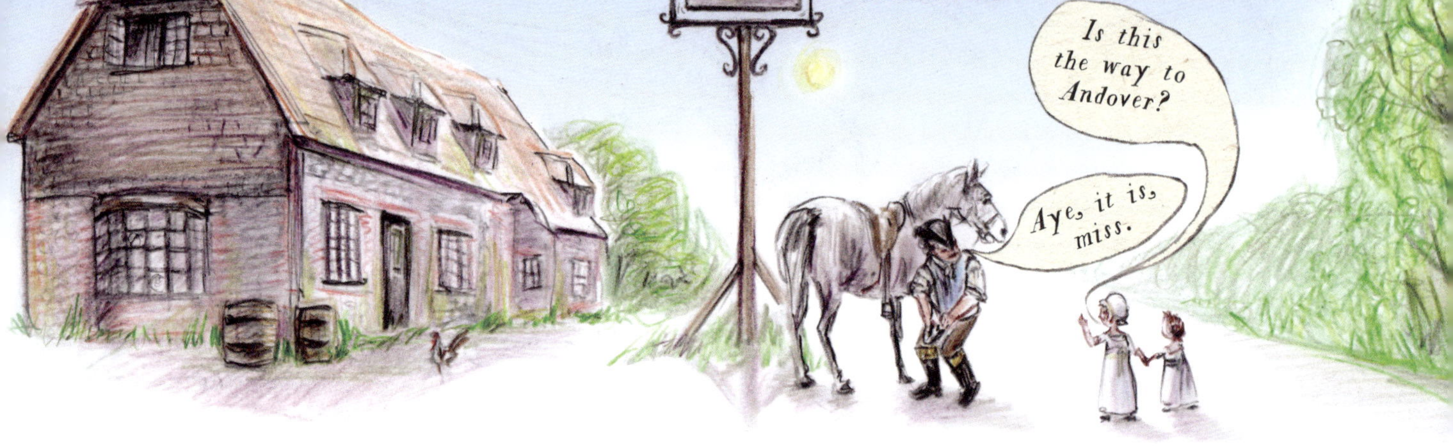
Is this the way to Andover?
Aye, it is, miss.

So the children turn westward, towards the sun that keeps slipping closer to the horizon.

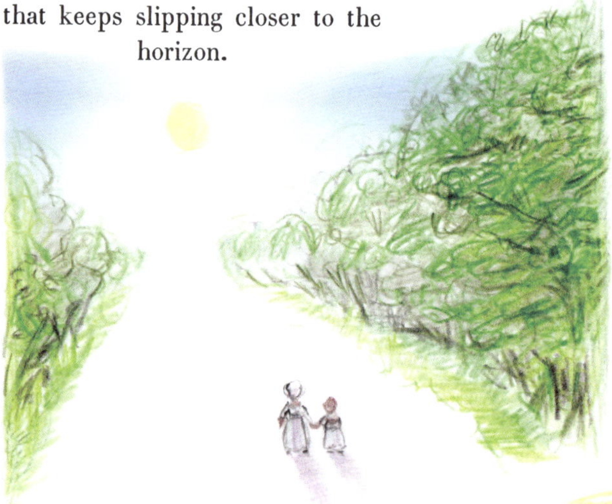

They meet a man on a mule with a chicken under his arm. He drops the reins to tip his hat, graciously.

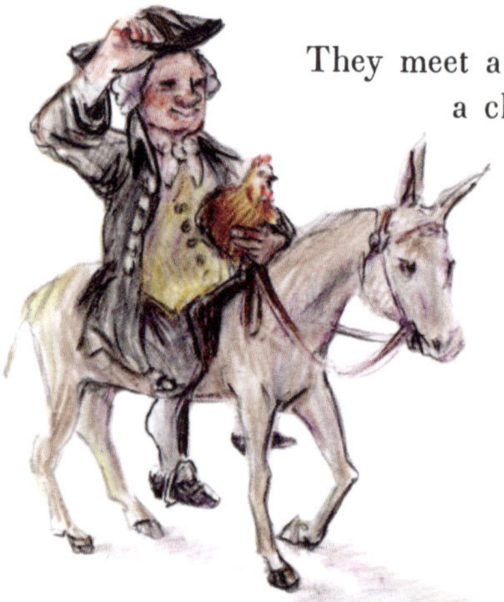

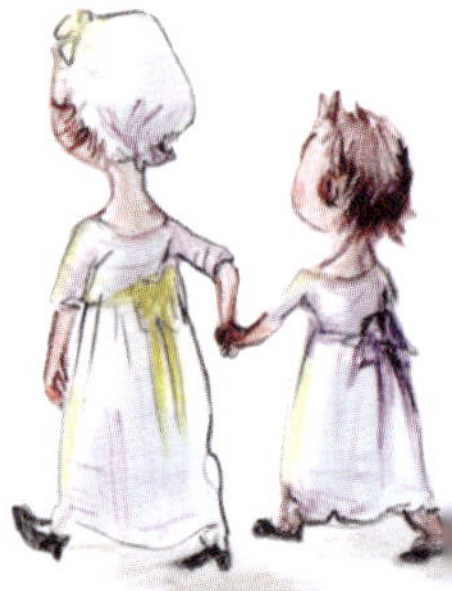

They are passed by a farm cart so laden with hay that the driver cannot even offer them a ride.

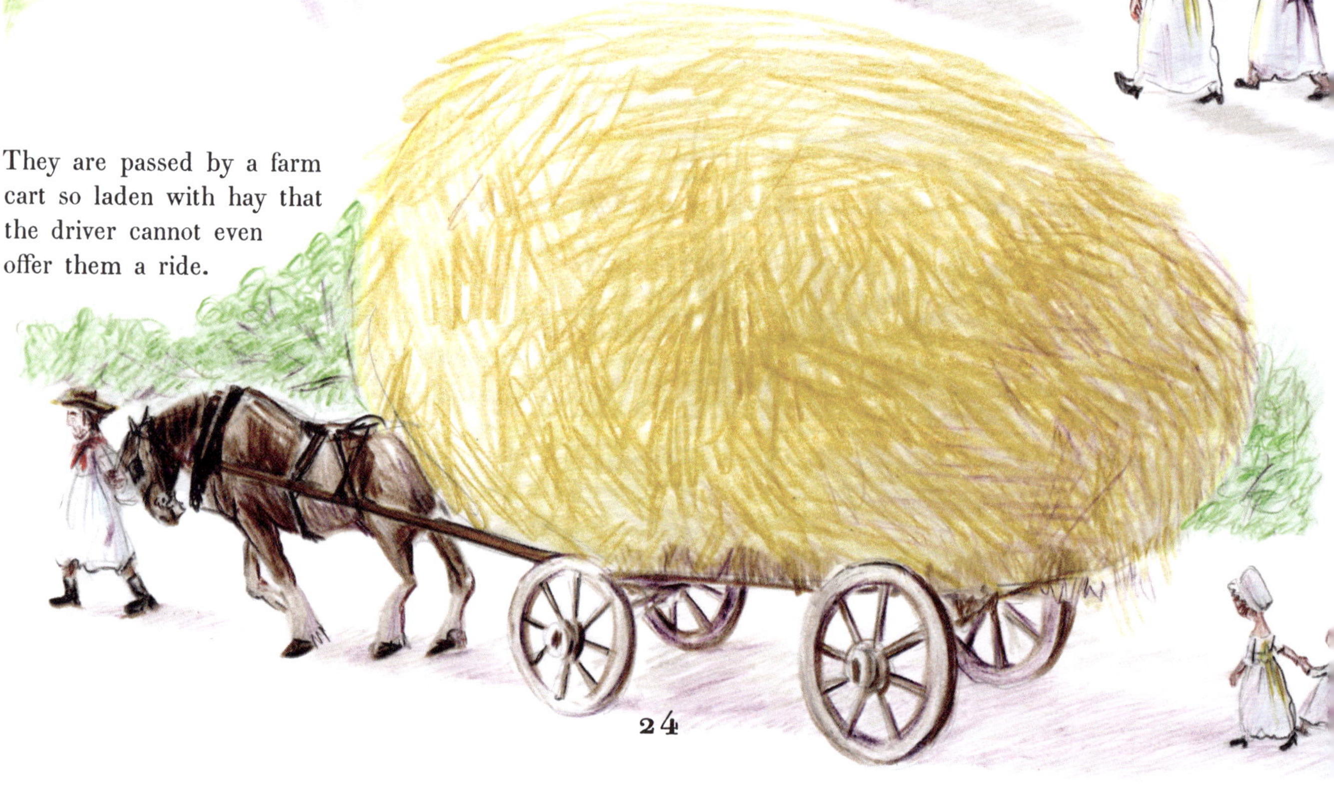

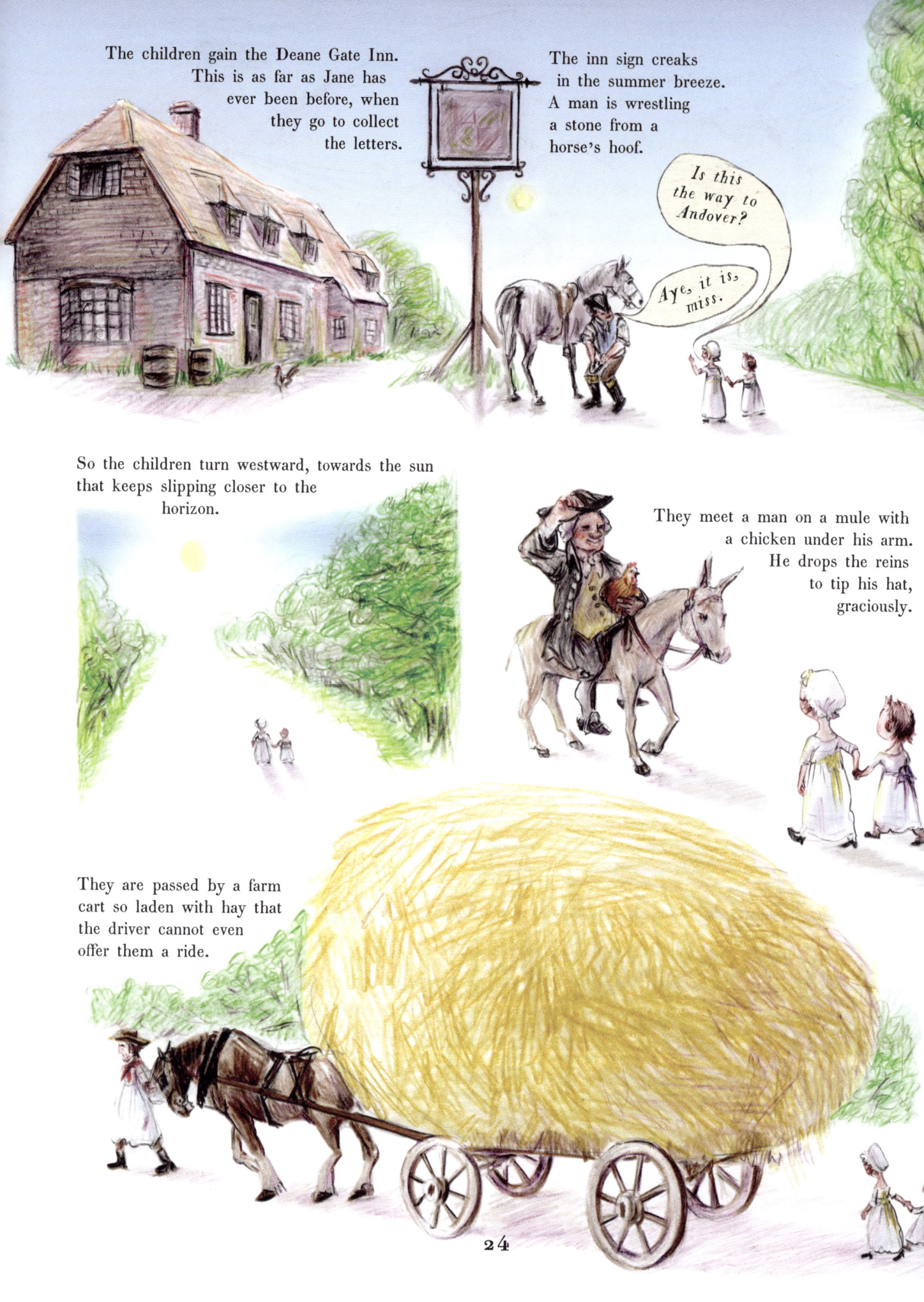

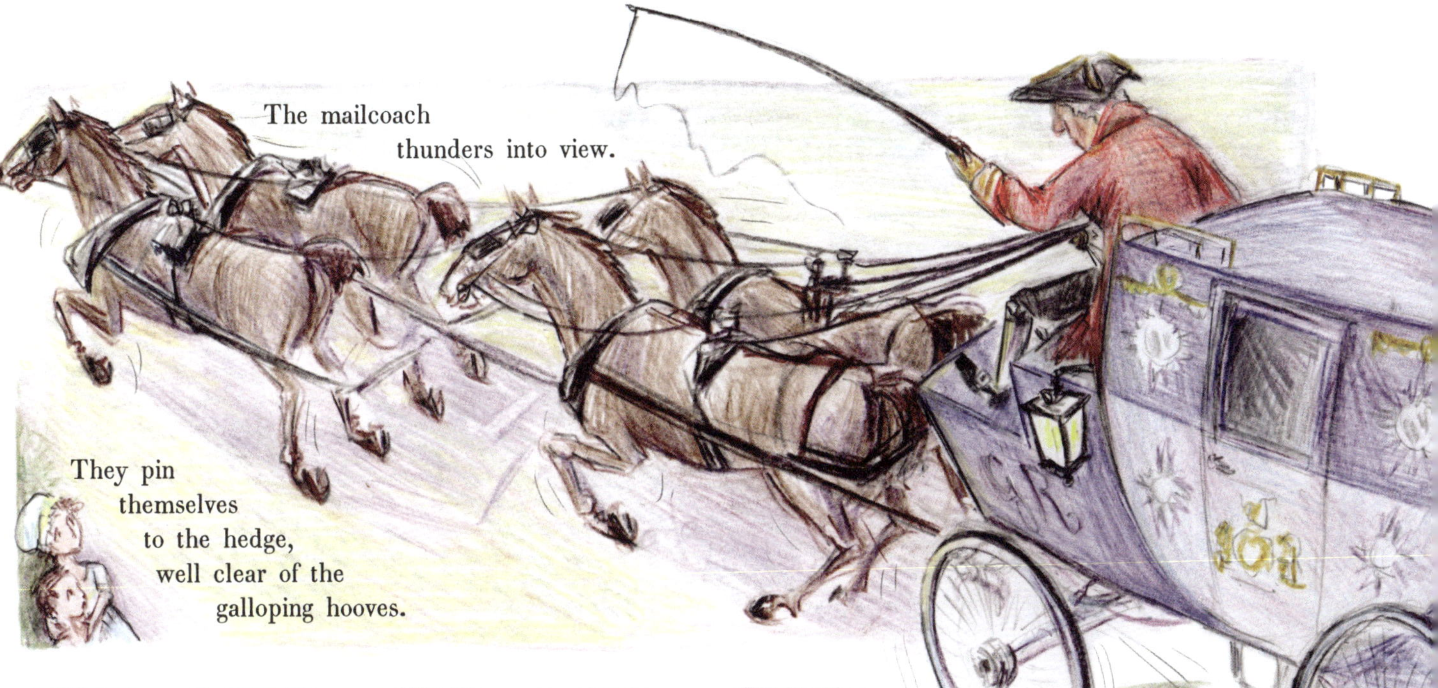
The mailcoach
thunders into view.
They pin
themselves
to the hedge,
well clear of the
galloping hooves.

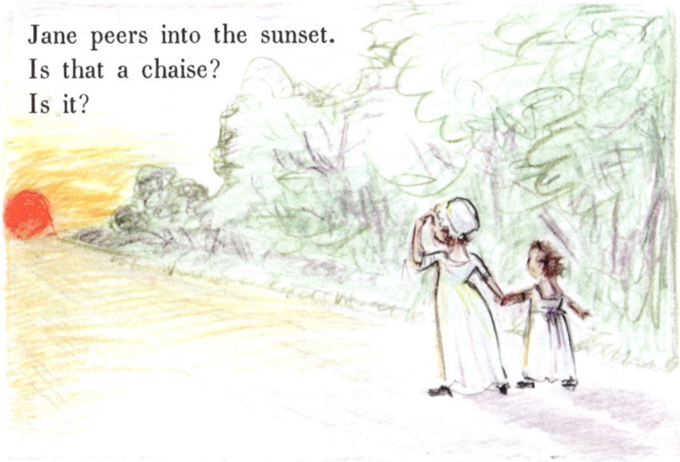
Jane peers into the sunset.
Is that a chaise?
Is it?

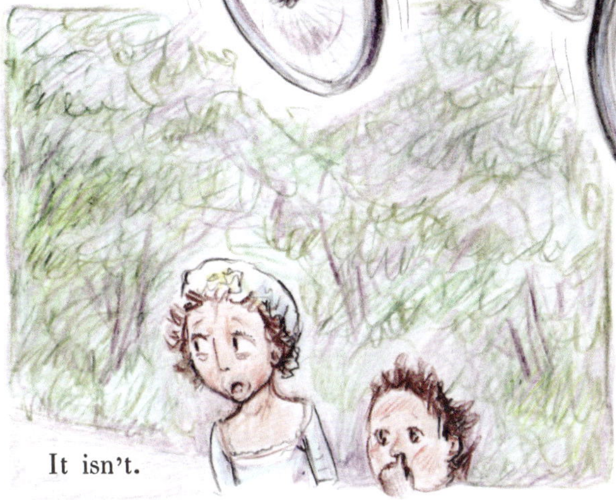
It isn't.

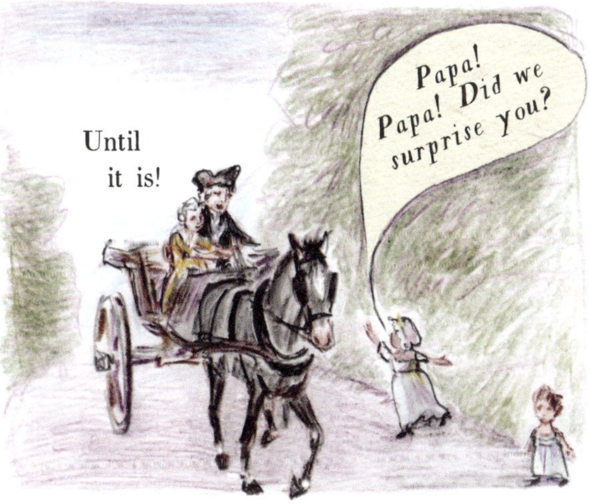
Until
it is!
Papa!
Papa! Did we
surprise you?

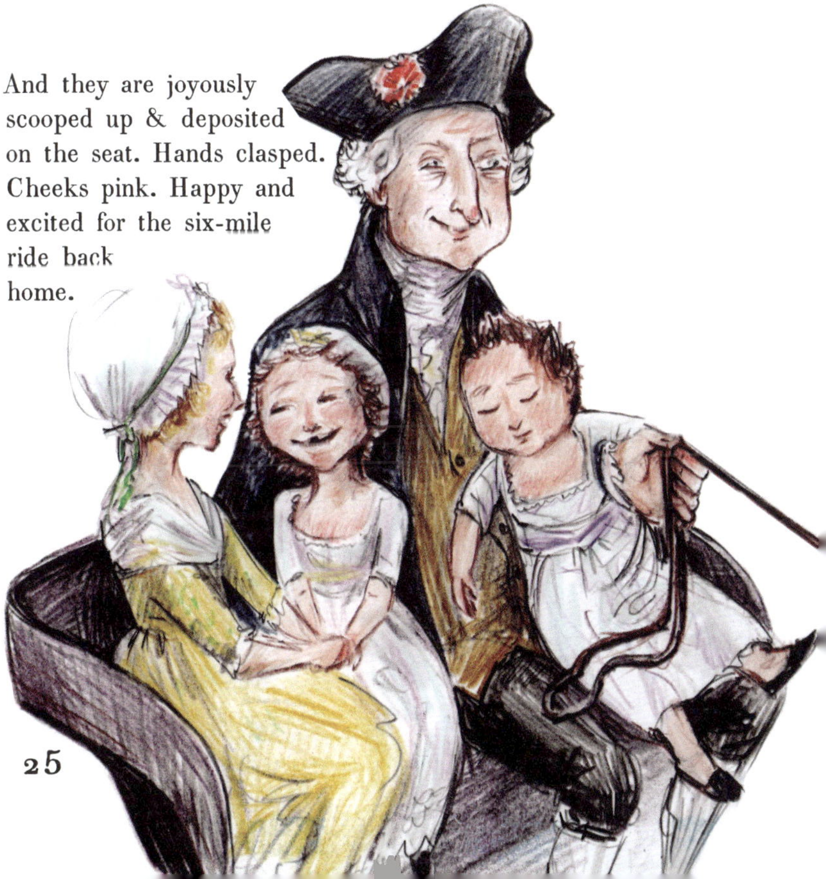
And they are joyously
scooped up & deposited
on the seat. Hands clasped.
Cheeks pink. Happy and
excited for the six-mile
ride back
home.

1783. Jane is seven.

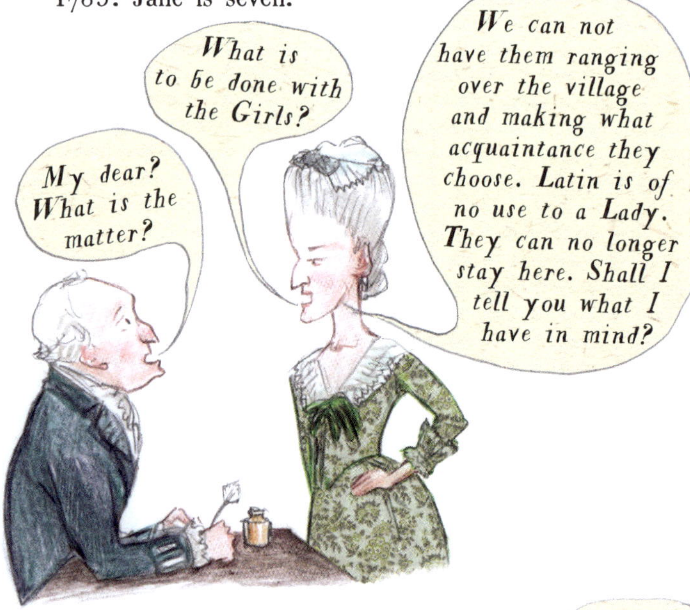
My dear? What is the matter?
What is to be done with the Girls?
We can not have them ranging over the village and making what acquaintance they choose. Latin is of no use to a Lady. They can no longer stay here. Shall I tell you what I have in mind?

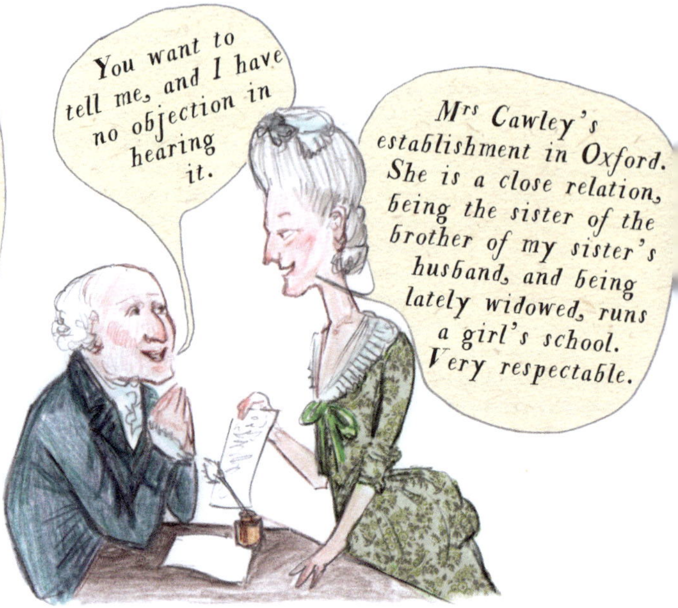
You want to tell me, and I have no objection in hearing it.
Mrs Cawley's establishment in Oxford. She is a close relation, being the sister of the brother of my sister's husband, and being lately widowed, runs a girl's school. Very respectable.

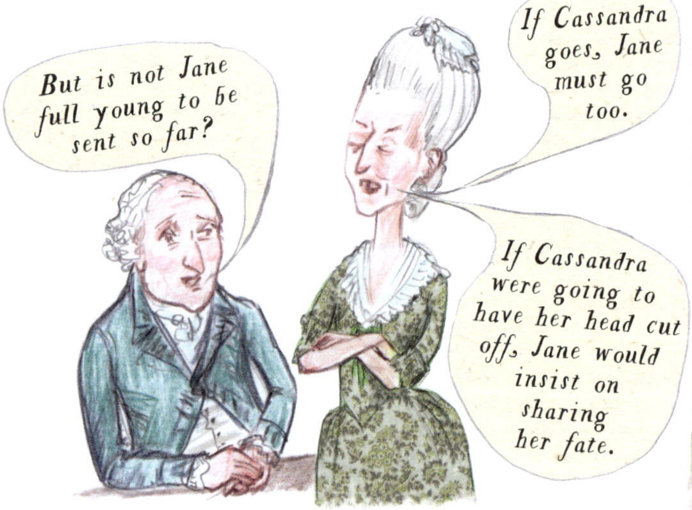
But is not Jane full young to be sent so far?
If Cassandra goes, Jane must go too.
If Cassandra were going to have her head cut off, Jane would insist on sharing her fate.

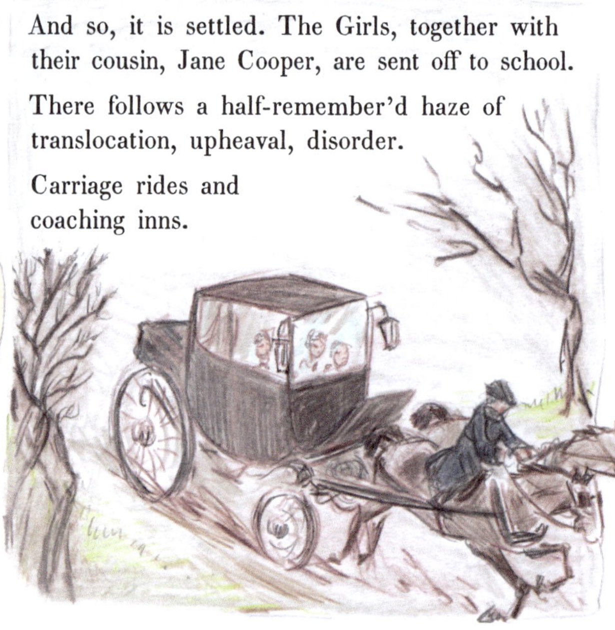
And so, it is settled. The Girls, together with their cousin, Jane Cooper, are sent off to school.
There follows a half-remember'd haze of translocation, upheaval, disorder.
Carriage rides and coaching inns.

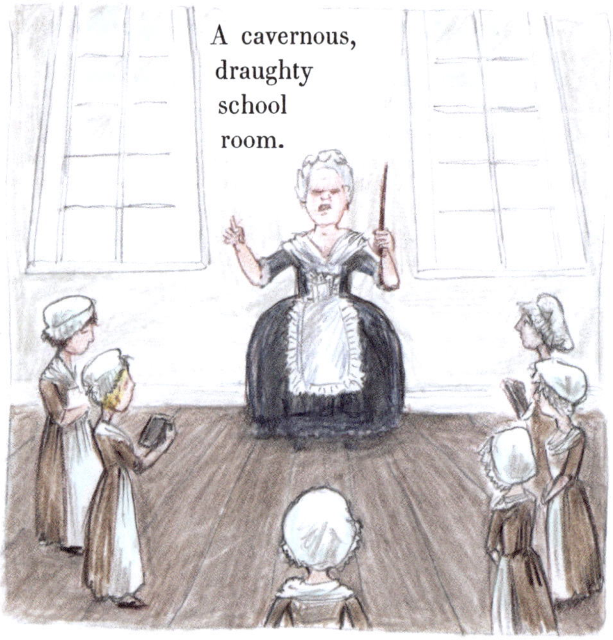
A cavernous, draughty school room.

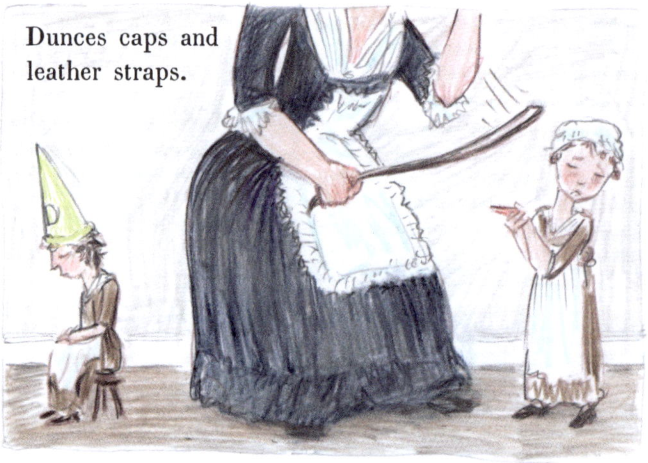
Dunces caps and leather straps.

And then danger! Contagion! MEASLES in Oxford!

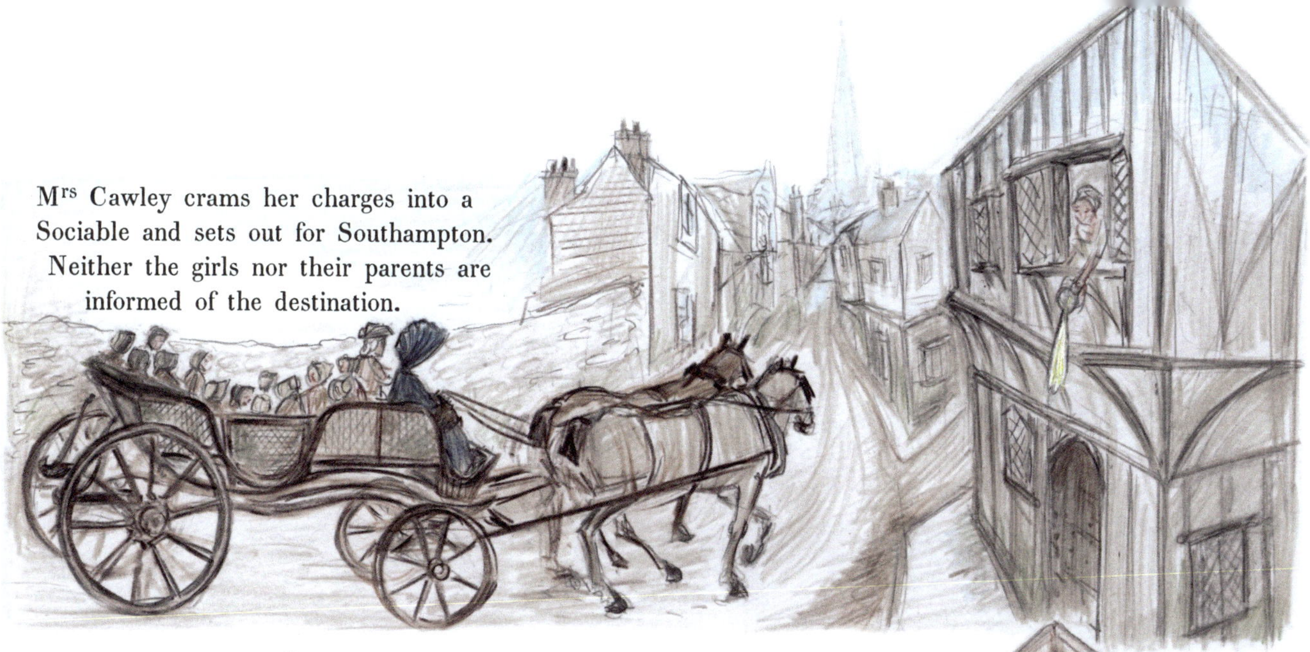
Mrs Cawley crams her charges into a Sociable and sets out for Southampton. Neither the girls nor their parents are informed of the destination.

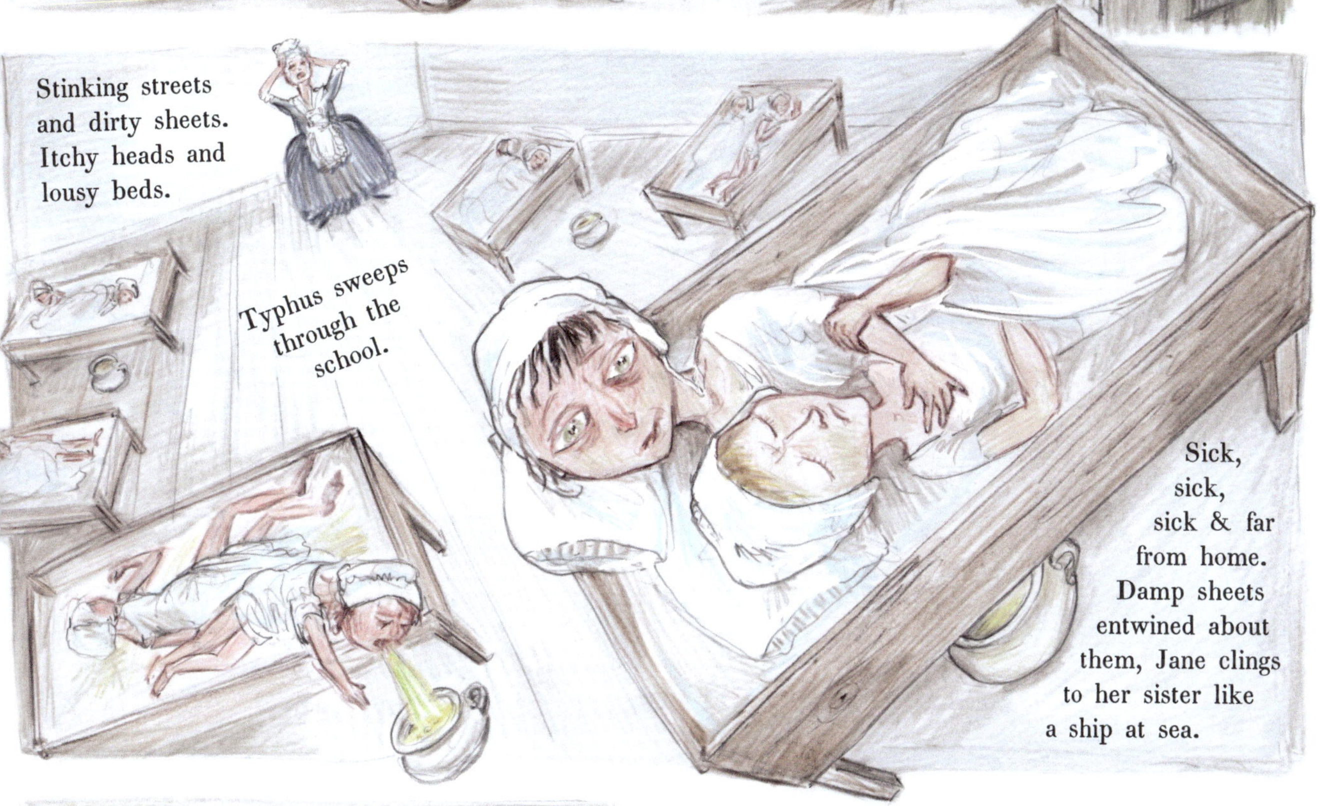
Stinking streets and dirty sheets. Itchy heads and lousy beds.
Typhus sweeps through the school.
Sick, sick, sick & far from home. Damp sheets entwined about them, Jane clings to her sister like a ship at sea.

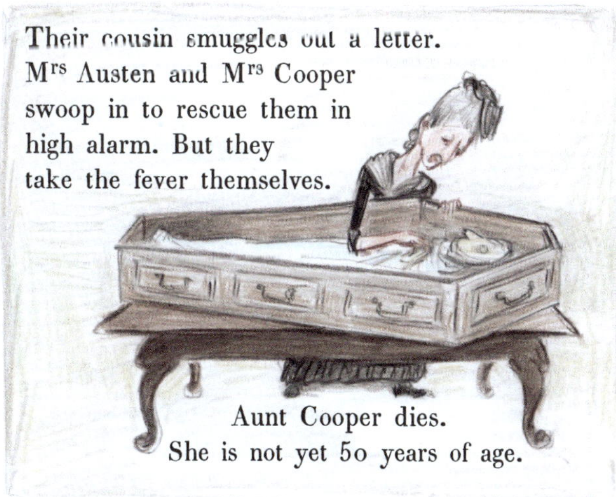
Their cousin smuggles out a letter. Mrs Austen and Mrs Cooper swoop in to rescue them in high alarm. But they take the fever themselves.
Aunt Cooper dies. She is not yet 50 years of age.

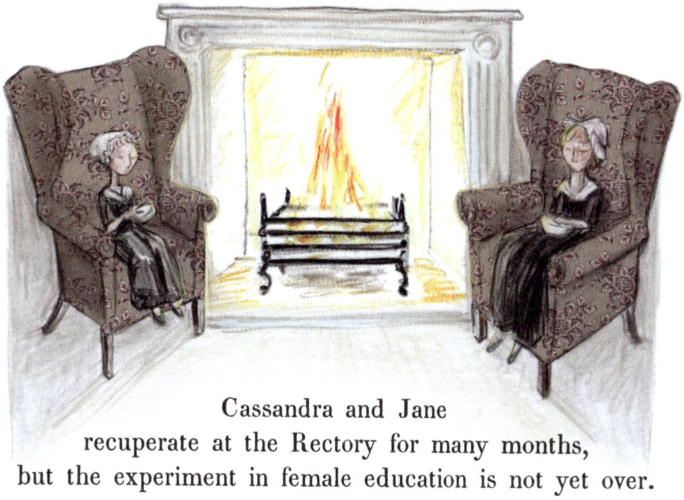
Cassandra and Jane recuperate at the Rectory for many months, but the experiment in female education is not yet over.

1785. Jane is nine.

Mrs Latournelle runs an old-fashioned Boarding-school where a reasonable quantity of accomplishments are sold at a reasonable price. Girls may be sent there to scramble themselves into a little education, without any danger of coming back prodigies.

It is reckoned to be a very healthy spot.

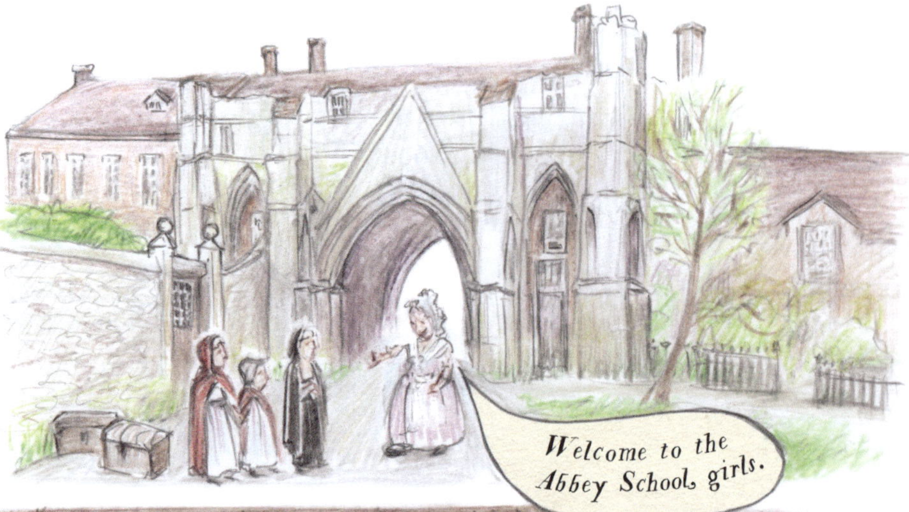
Welcome to the Abbey School girls.

Jane Cooper makes a sombre companion, grieving for the loss of a mother whom she had dearly loved & suffering as a girl of 14, of strong sensibility, must suffer at such a time.

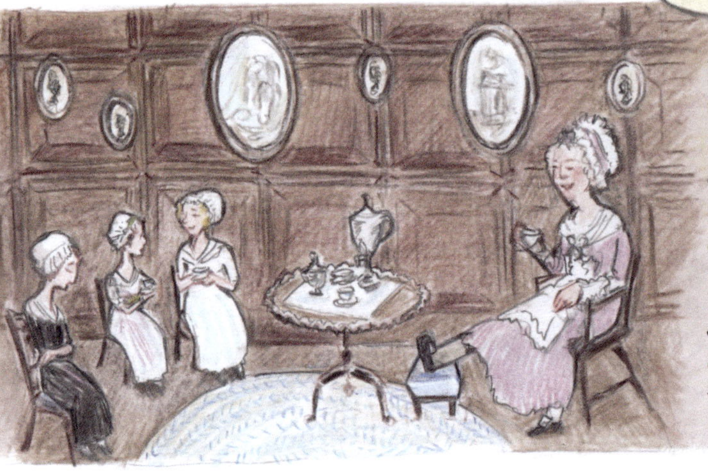

But Mrs Latournelle is honest, and kind, and feeds them plenty of wholesome food. She lets them run about in summer, and in the winter, she dresses their chilblains with her own hands.

Jane, Jane and Cassandra drink tea in her parlour and wordlessly speculate about her cork leg.

Little Jane is aukward, and foolishly shy. Fearful of not doing exactly what is right, she can not endure the incessant noise and demands of sixty girls together. Her nerves are under continual irritation, in an agitation of mind.

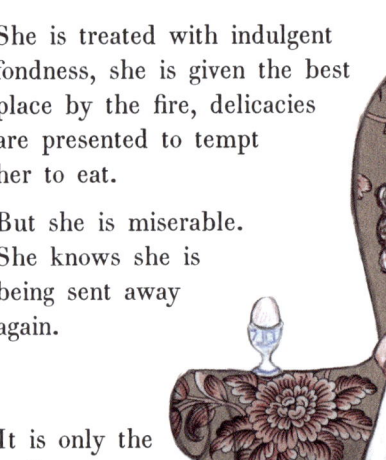

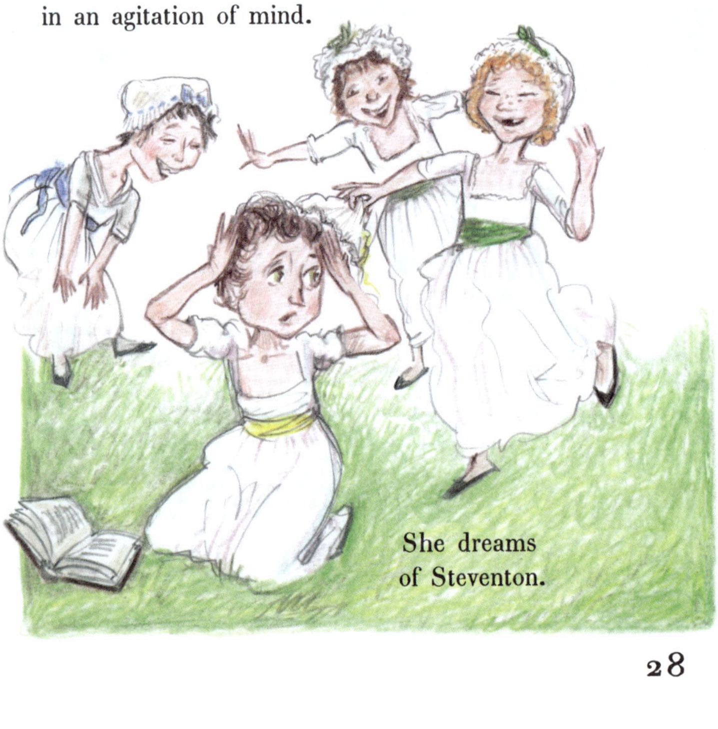
She dreams of Steventon.

Here she is, at home for Easter in 1786. She must leave for school in the morning.

She is treated with indulgent fondness, she is given the best place by the fire, delicacies are presented to tempt her to eat.

But she is miserable. She knows she is being sent away again.

It is only the ordinary trauma of the English upper class.

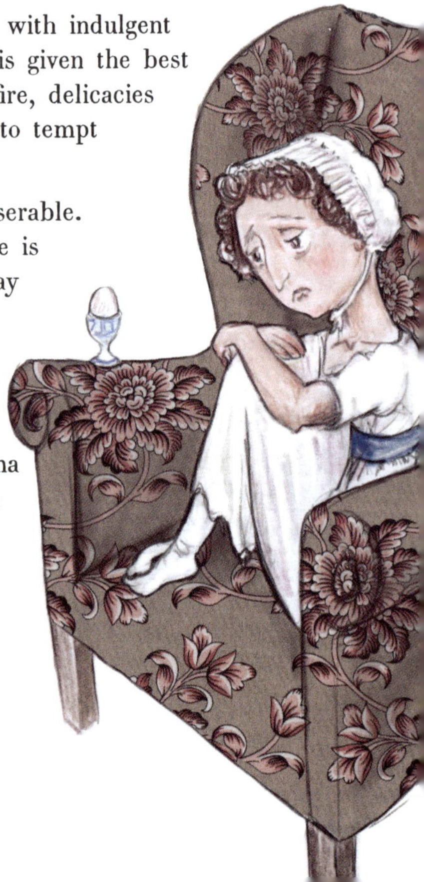

There is someone
missing from the picture.

Somebody cut from
the frame.

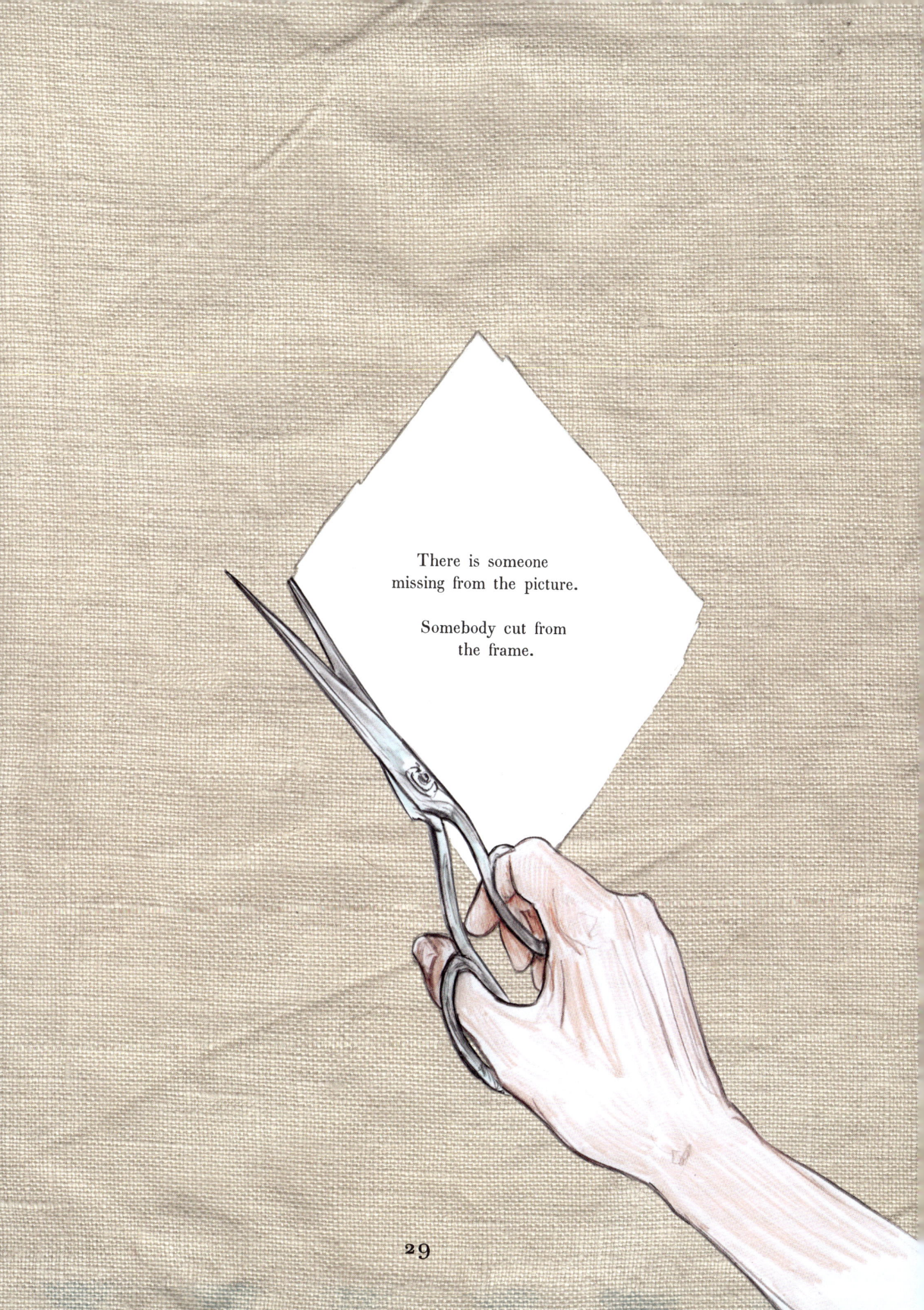

A little boy, George, 9 years Jane's senior.

He has fits.
He starts. He stumbles.
He blushes easily. His ears are a little too large and his face is a little too long. Long after it is expected, his speech fails to come.

Mrs Austen recognises the signs. Her baby brother was the same.

*December 9, 1770.
My poor little George is come to see me to-day. He had a fit lately; it was near a twelve-month since he had one before, so was in hopes they had left him, but must not flatter myself so now.*

Mr Austen philosophises:
We have this comfort, he cannot be a bad or a wicked child.

Snippets.
What is George's disability? What is his crime?

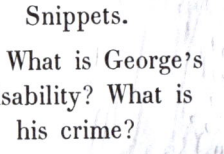

He is sent away to a farm ten miles off.
A whole life sentence.

Is he ever allowed home? Does Jane ever see him? Jane can talk with her fingers. Was this with her brother?

George's story remains untold.
He cannot speak.
He has no voice.

EFFUSIONS OF FANCY BY A VERY YOUNG LADY

IN A STYLE ENTIRELY NEW

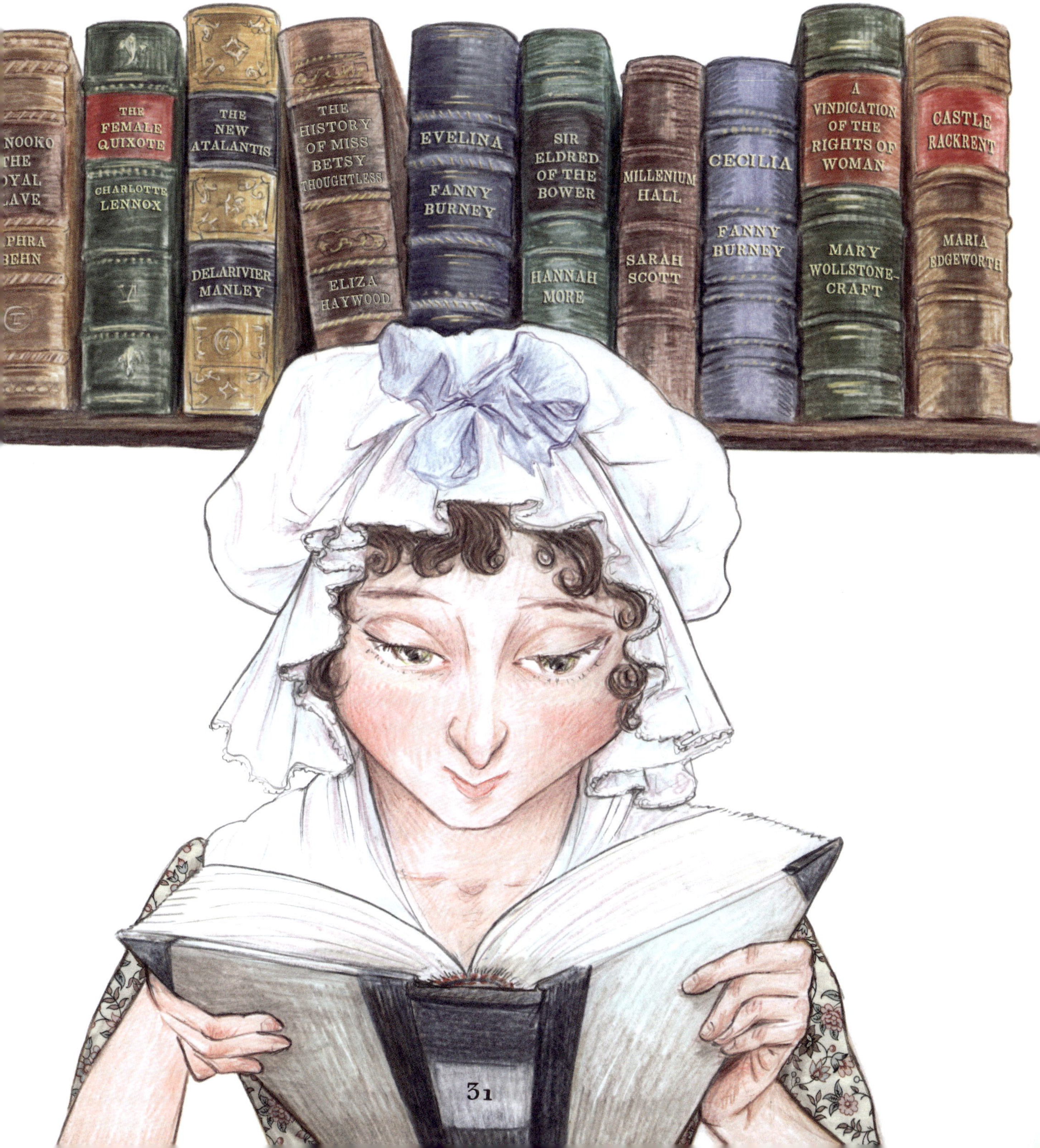

NOOKO THE YAL AVE
PHRA BEHN
THE FEMALE QUIXOTE
CHARLOTTE LENNOX
THE NEW ATALANTIS
DELARIVIER MANLEY
THE HISTORY OF MISS BETSY THOUGHTLESS
ELIZA HAYWOOD
EVELINA
FANNY BURNEY
SIR ELDRED OF THE BOWER
HANNAH MORE
MILLENIUM HALL
SARAH SCOTT
CECILIA
FANNY BURNEY
A VINDICATION OF THE RIGHTS OF WOMAN
MARY WOLLSTONE-CRAFT
CASTLE RACKRENT
MARIA EDGEWORTH

JANE IS TWELVE, Cassandra fifteen, and their official education is over. They are abandoned to the free exploration of Mr Austen's bookcases. If they wish to learn, they do not want the means. If they choose to be idle, they certainly might.

Give Jane a book, and she will read all day long. She does not know when anyone speaks to her. She is regardless of time.

And what edifying volume thus engrosses our heroine? Has she chosen a work by one of our best moralists? A collection of the finest letters? A memoir of a character of worth and suffering, calculated to rouse and fortify the mind by the highest precepts?

No! What is this trash! A duodecimo volume? An illustrated frontispiece? Everything announces this to be...

a **NOVEL!!!**

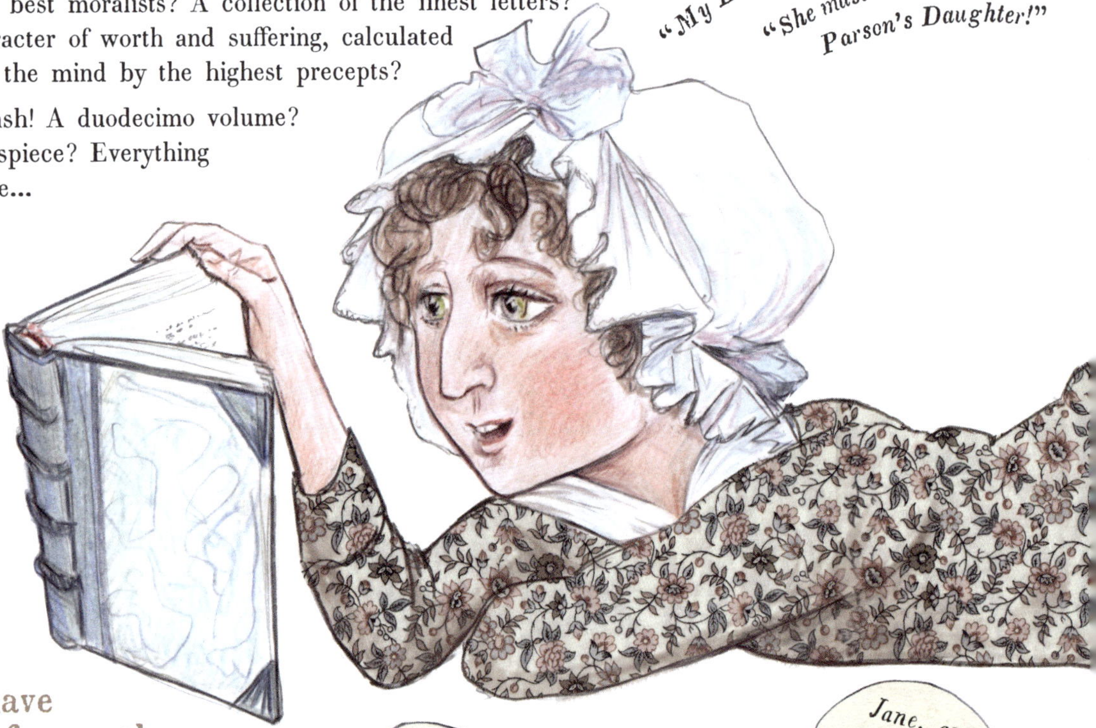

"My Lord, I cannot learn who she is."
"She must be a Country Parson's Daughter!"

NOVELS have been long and frequently regarded not as being merely USELESS to society, but even as *PERNICIOUS*.

Women, of every age, of every condition, contract a taste for novels. The **DEPRAVITY IS UNIVERSAL**. One's sight is everywhere offended by these *FOOLISH*, yet DANGEROUS, books.

Exhibiting scenes and ideas which **SOFTEN THE MIND**; they nourish a VAIN INDOLENCE, which lays the mind open to ERROR and the heart to *SEDUCTION*.

NOVELS inculcate a **RIDICULOUS** WAY OF THINKING...

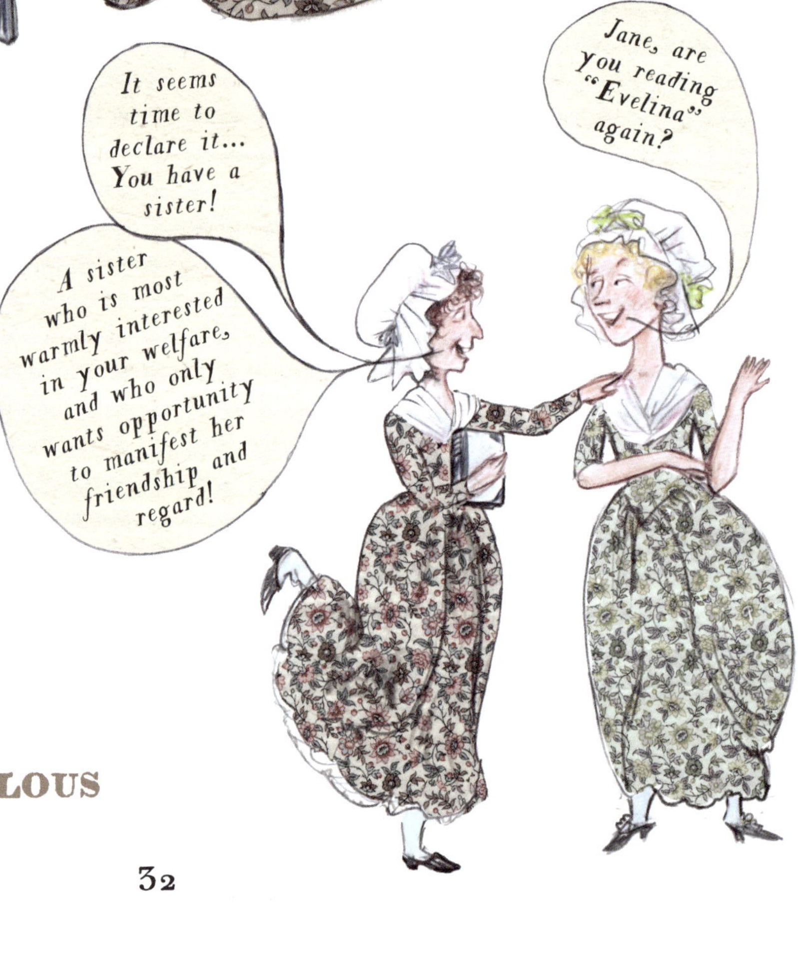

It seems time to declare it... You have a sister!
A sister who is most warmly interested in your welfare, and who only wants opportunity to manifest her friendship and regard!
Jane, are you reading "Evelina" again?

If Jane is looking for dramatic stories, she can find them in the lives of her nearest and dearest.

Her Father was orphaned at the tender age of eight and expelled from his home by his evil stepmother.

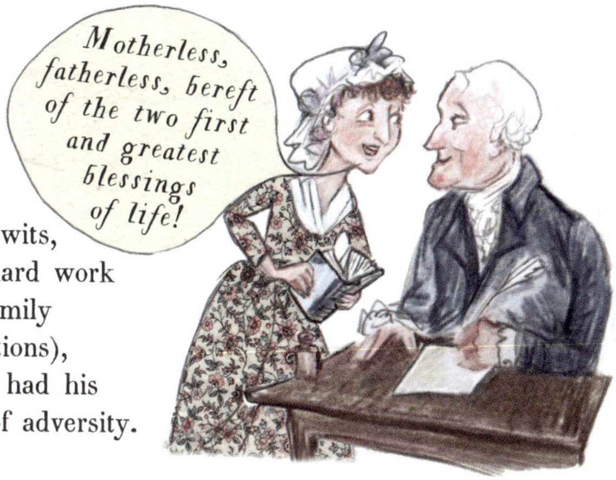
Motherless, fatherless, bereft of the two first and greatest blessings of life!

Reliant on his wits, luck, hard work (and family connections), he has had his share of adversity.

Her Mother is, as she will remind one, of noble birth. She is mighty proud of her aristocratic Nose.

She married in a Red Riding Habit, but is she more adoring Grand mama? Or wolf?

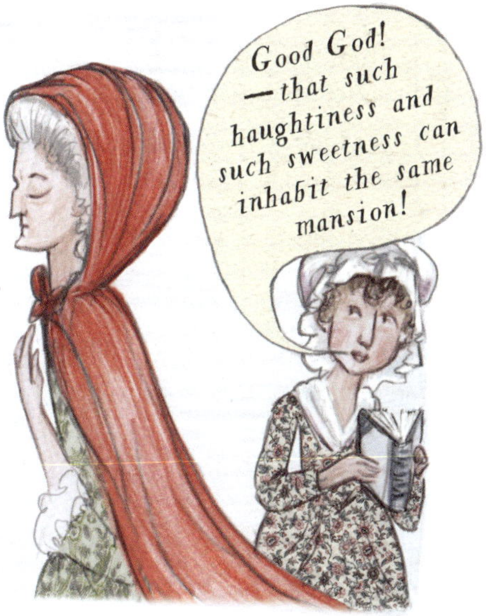
Good God! —that such haughtiness and such sweetness can inhabit the same mansion!

Brother Edward has the most extraordinary turn of luck. At the age of twelve, he so enchanted the Knights, — childless, wealthy, Third Cousins — that he has been adopted as the Heir to their Country Estates. His story wants only a glass slipper to render it a true life Fairy Tale.

He has embarked upon a Grand Tour of the Continent in fine style.

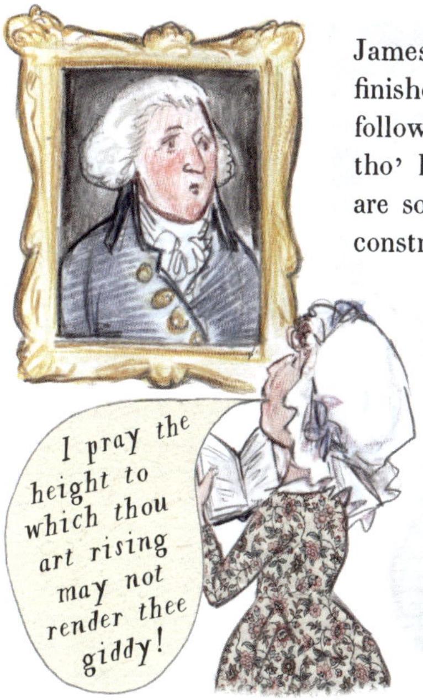
I pray the height to which thou art rising may not render thee giddy!

James, the eldest, has finished his studies and followed him abroad, tho' his finances are somewhat more constrained.

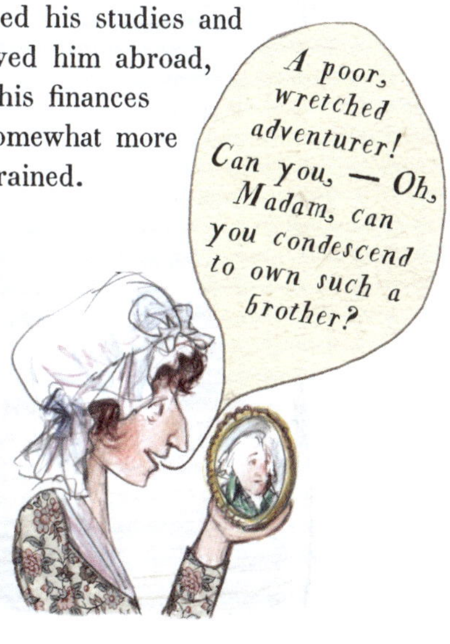
A poor, wretched adventurer! Can you, — Oh, Madam, can you condescend to own such a brother?

Frank has left for the Royal Naval Academy.

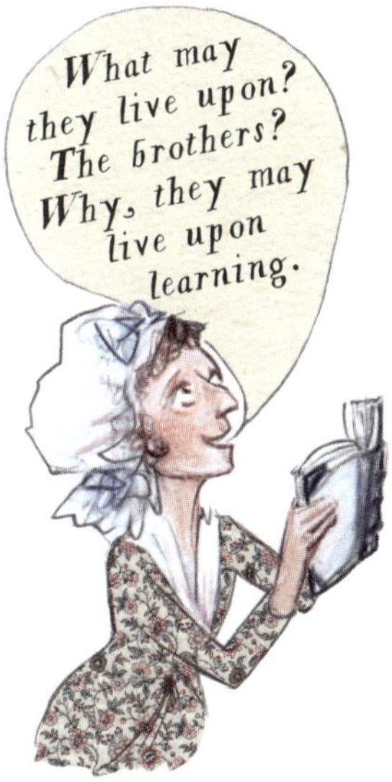
What may they live upon? The brothers? Why, they may live upon learning.

Henry is tall and dashing, quite the young Gentleman. He is mastering his Latin and Greek...

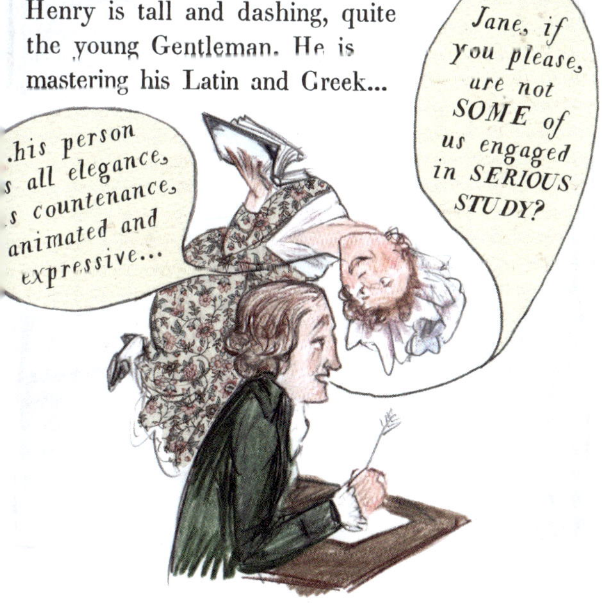
..his person is all elegance, his countenance, animated and expressive...
Jane, if you please, are not SOME of us engaged in SERIOUS STUDY?

...while little Charles is struggling with the basics.

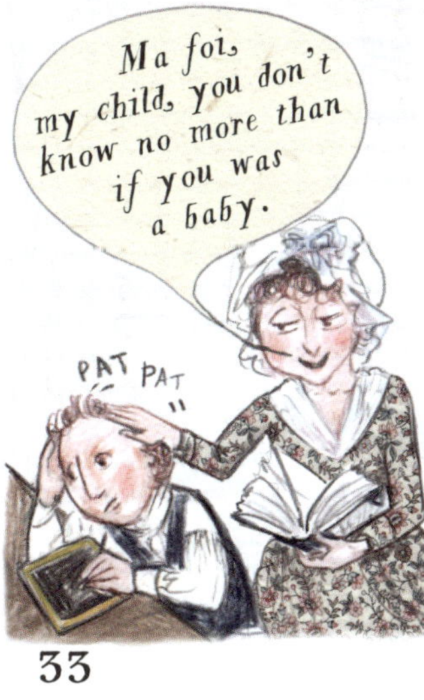
Ma foi, my child, you don't know no more than if you was a baby.
PAT PAT

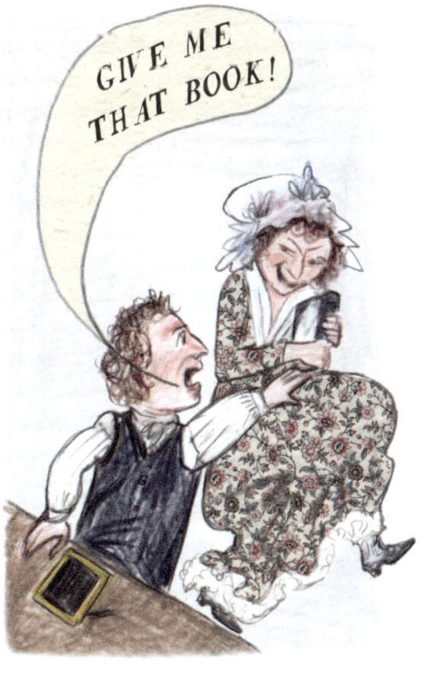
GIVE ME THAT BOOK!

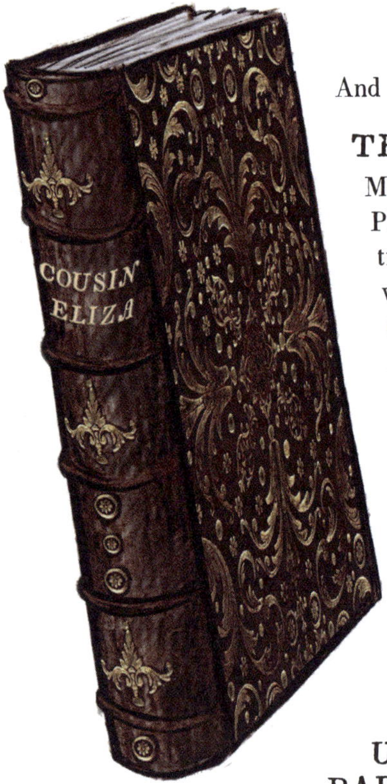
COUSIN ELIZA

And then Jane's wider family supplies her with the most spectacular romantic heroine...

THE HEART RENDING BACK STORY...

Mr Austen's sister, Philadelphia, likewise tragically orphaned, was forced to (gasp!) **WORK** for **A LIVING** as a **MILLINER** as a girl of 15.

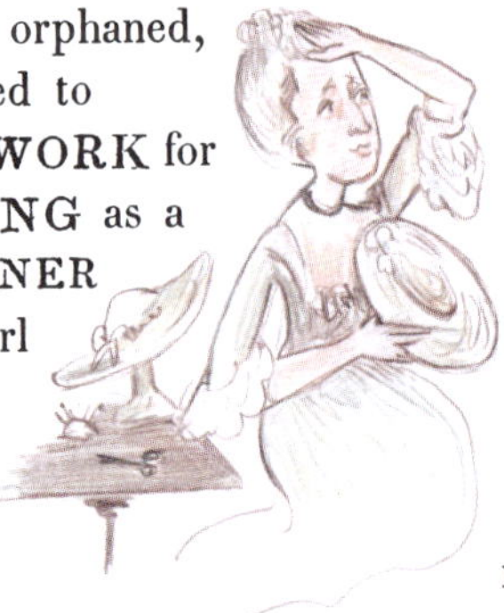

To escape such **DESPERATE CIRCUMSTANCES**, her passage was paid to India, in return for marriage to a man she had never met.

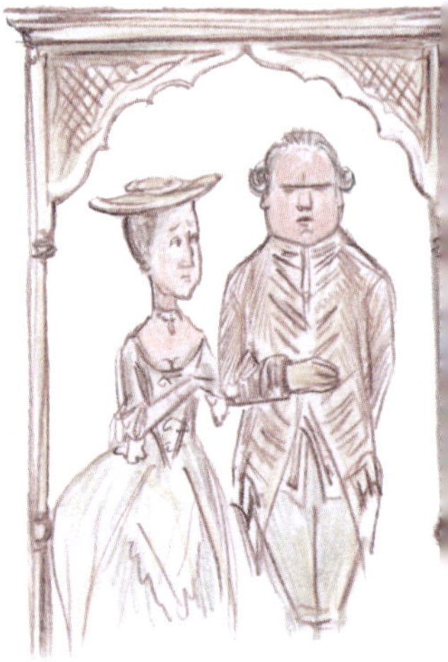

THE UNCERTAIN PARENTAGE...

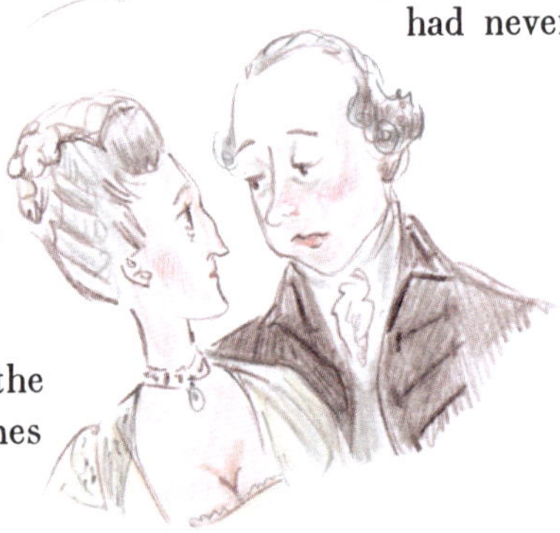

Philadelphia catches the notice of the Great Warren Hastings, who becomes "godfather" to her child.

THE BEAUTY... THE GRACE... THE INNOCENCE...

Enter... **COUSIN ELIZA!**

Eliza smells of attar of roses.
Born in exotic Calcutta, she eats pickled mangoes and cassoondy sauce.
She plays the harpsichord.
She rides a horse.
She wears Indian chintzes, seersuckers, dimities, muslins lighter than air, silks from Malda, Pullicat and Cossimbazar.

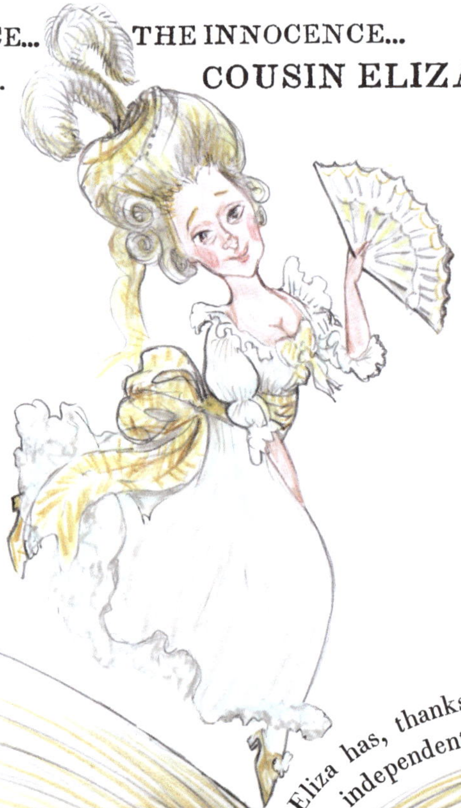

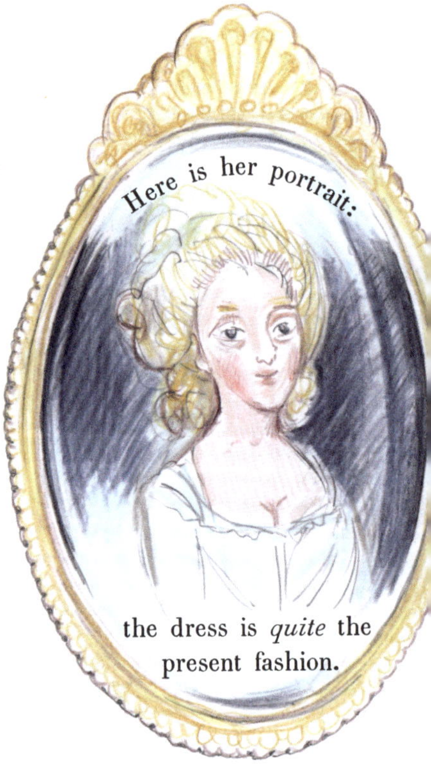

Here is her portrait:

the dress is *quite* the present fashion.

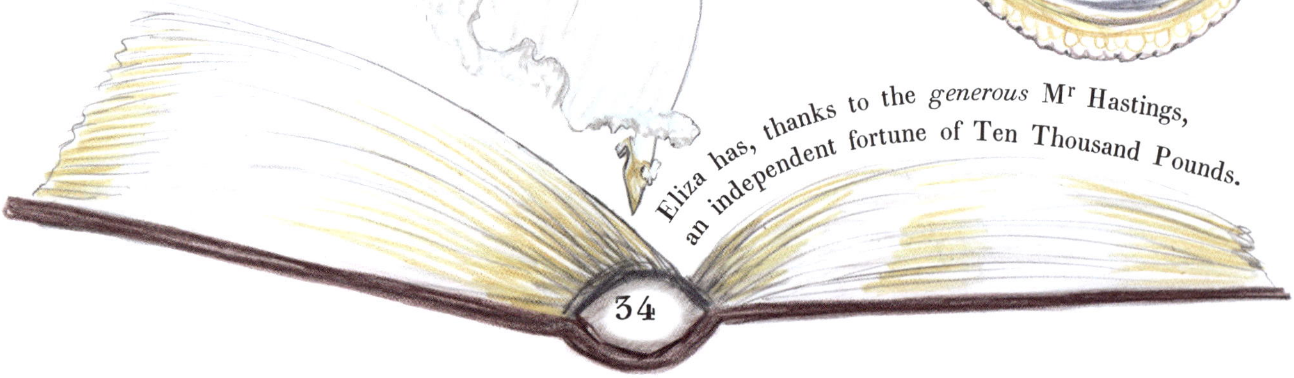

Eliza has, thanks to the *generous* Mr Hastings, an independent fortune of Ten Thousand Pounds.

Eliza settles in Paris with her mother.

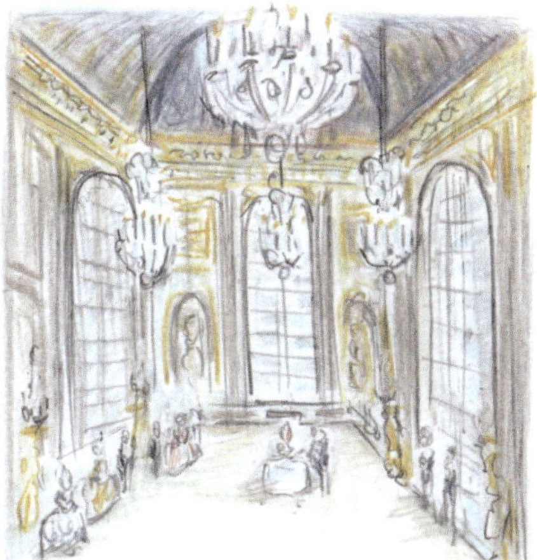

She is at Versailles with Marie Antoinette.

She parades at Longchamp in a fine carriage.

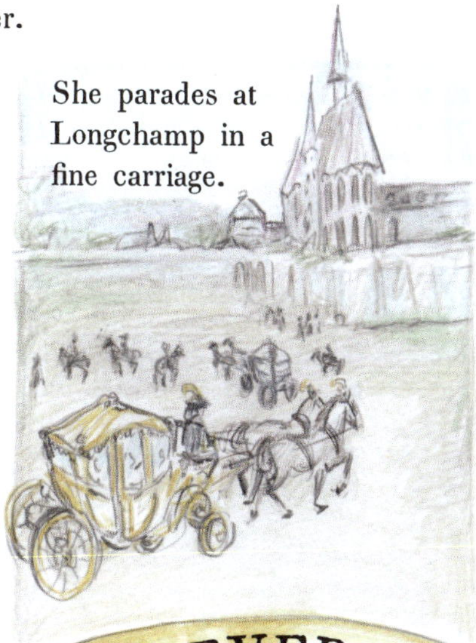

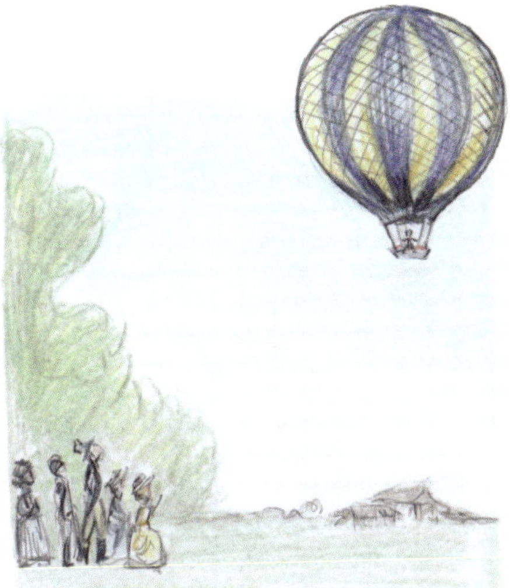

She sees Blanchard take to the skies in a Hot Air Ballon.

She marries a Comte (at least, *he says* he is) with enormous Tracts of Land. He adores her (at least, *she says* he does). She is now the Comtesse de Feuillide.

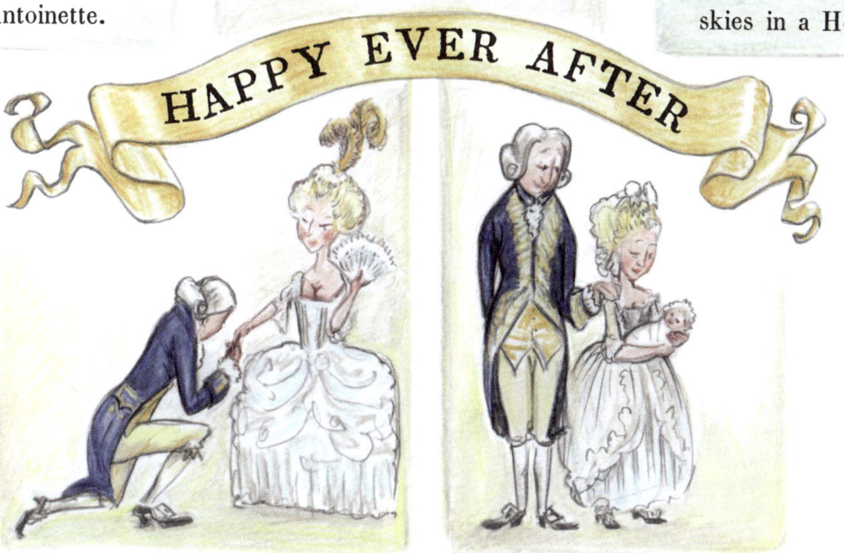
HAPPY EVER AFTER

A child soon follows — a son and heir, of course. A charmed life.

Eliza calls flirting "trade."

Christmas, 1787. Eliza, Aunt Phila and baby Hastings grace Steventon with a visit.

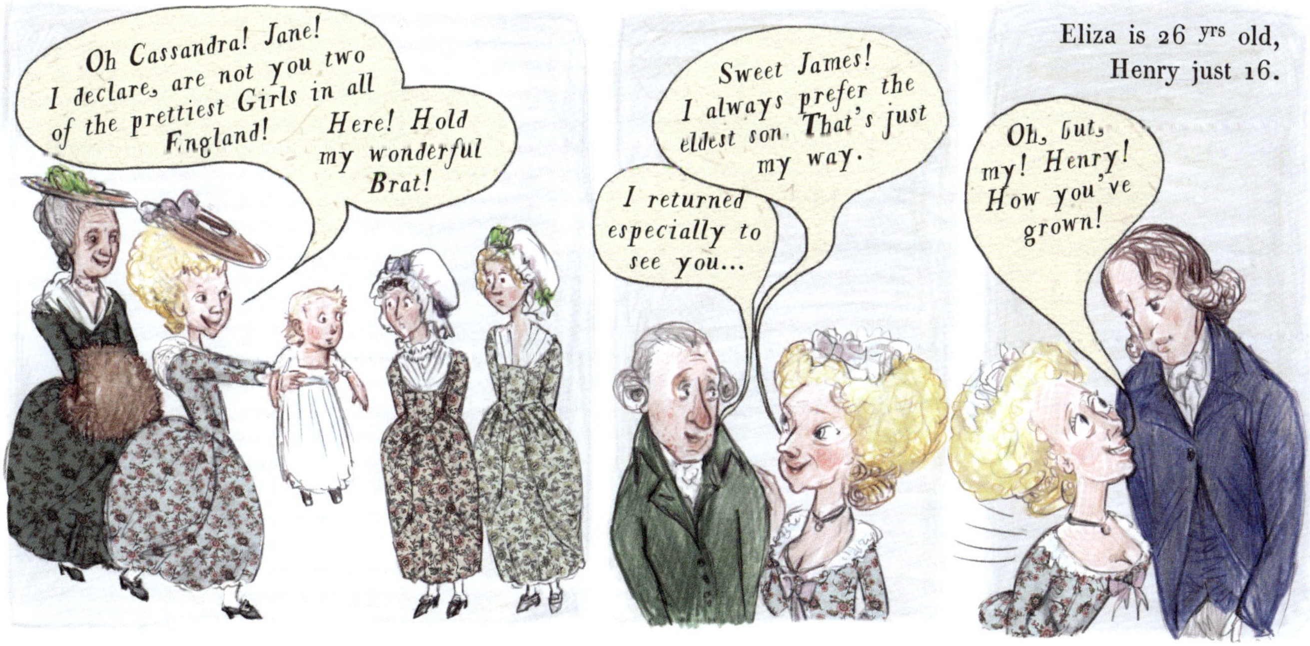
Oh Cassandra! Jane! I declare, are not you two of the prettiest Girls in all England!
Here! Hold my wonderful Brat!
Sweet James! I always prefer the eldest son. That's just my way.
I returned especially to see you...
Oh, but, my! Henry! How you've grown!

Eliza is 26 yrs old, Henry just 16.

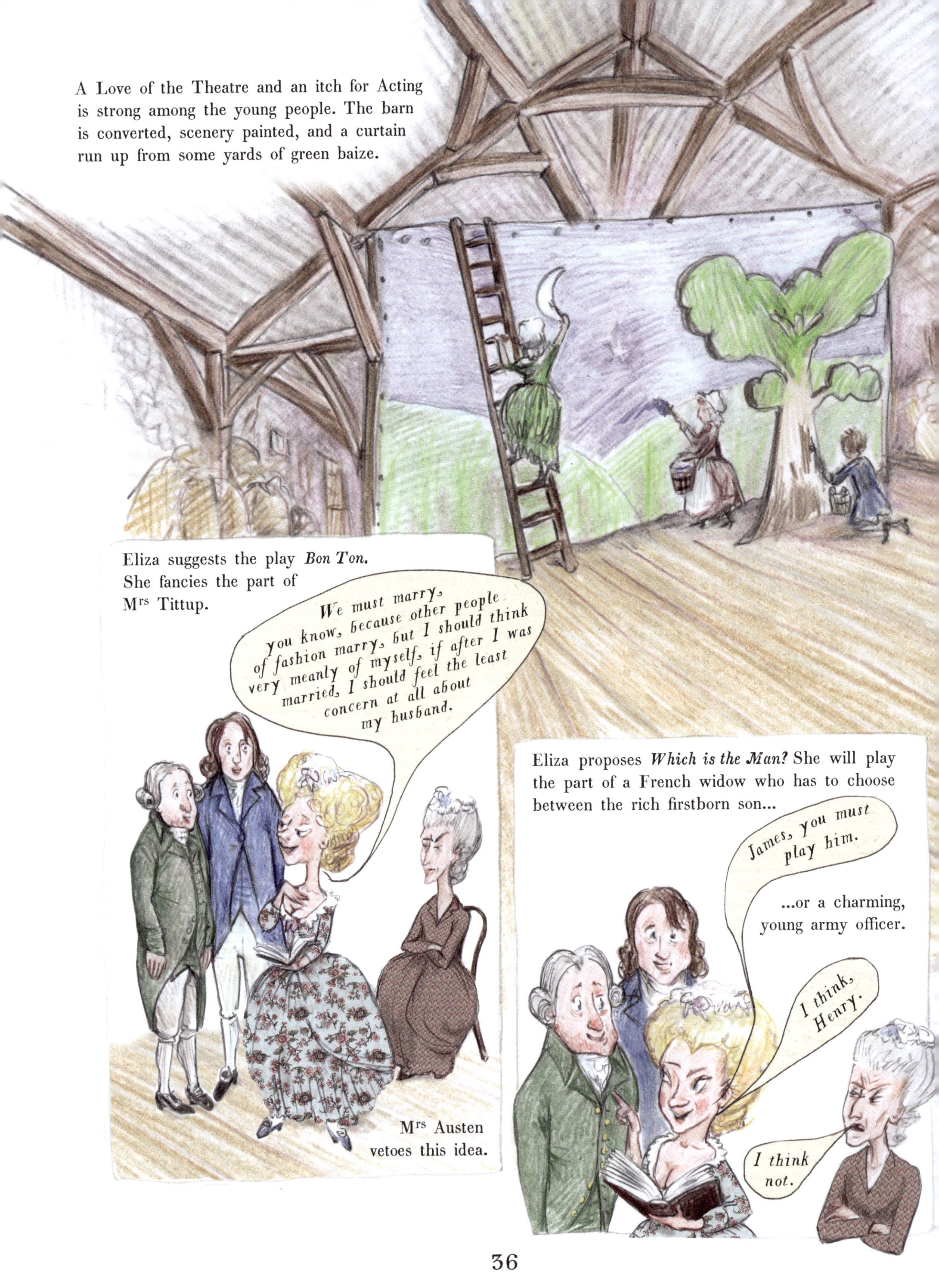
A Love of the Theatre and an itch for Acting is strong among the young people. The barn is converted, scenery painted, and a curtain run up from some yards of green baize.
Eliza suggests the play *Bon Ton.* She fancies the part of Mrs Tittup.
We must marry, you know, because other people of fashion marry, but I should think very meanly of myself, if after I was married, I should feel the least concern at all about my husband.
Mrs Austen vetoes this idea.
Eliza proposes ***Which is the Man?*** She will play the part of a French widow who has to choose between the rich firstborn son...
James, you must play him.
...or a charming, young army officer.
I think, Henry.
I think not.

The company settles upon *The Wonder! A Woman Keeps a Secret!*

There is fighting!

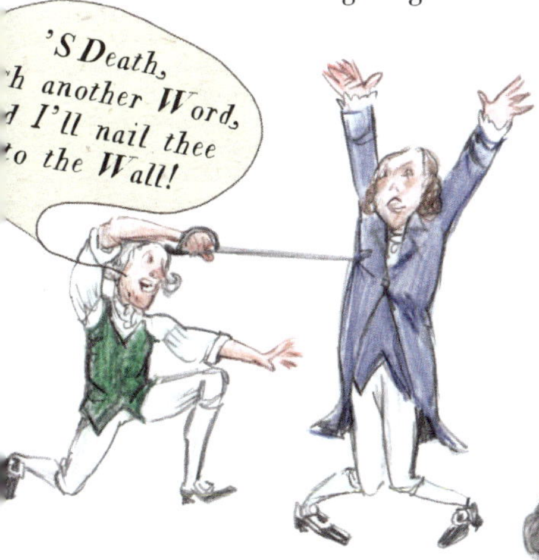
'S Death,
h another Word,
d I'll nail thee
o the Wall!

Passion!

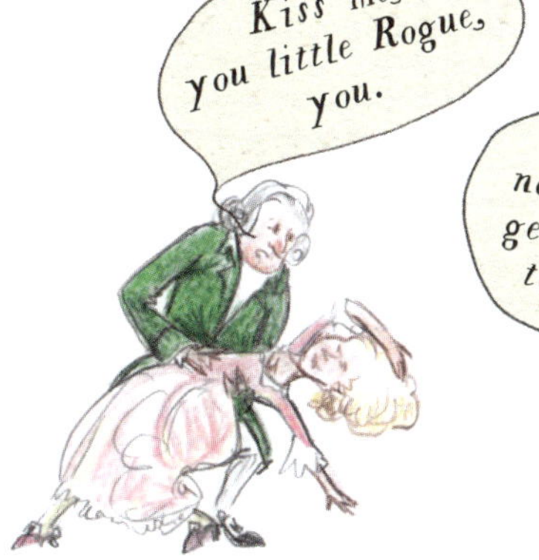
Kiss me, you little Rogue, you.

And appalling Scottish accents.

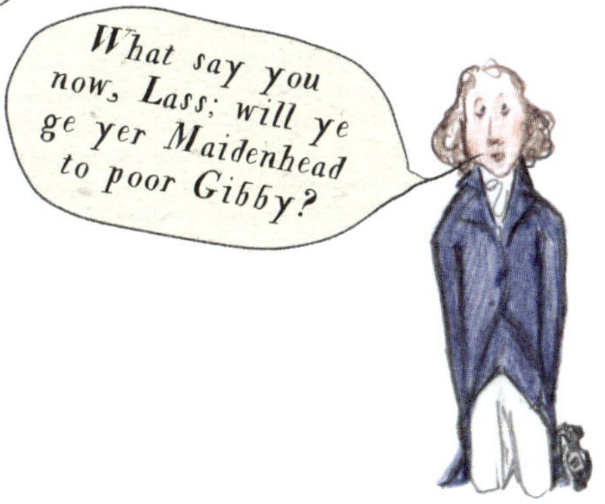
What say you now, Lass; will ye ge yer Maidenhead to poor Gibby?

Each has their part, their dress, their favourite scene. Everybody is gay and busy. The local gentry come to watch. A triumph!

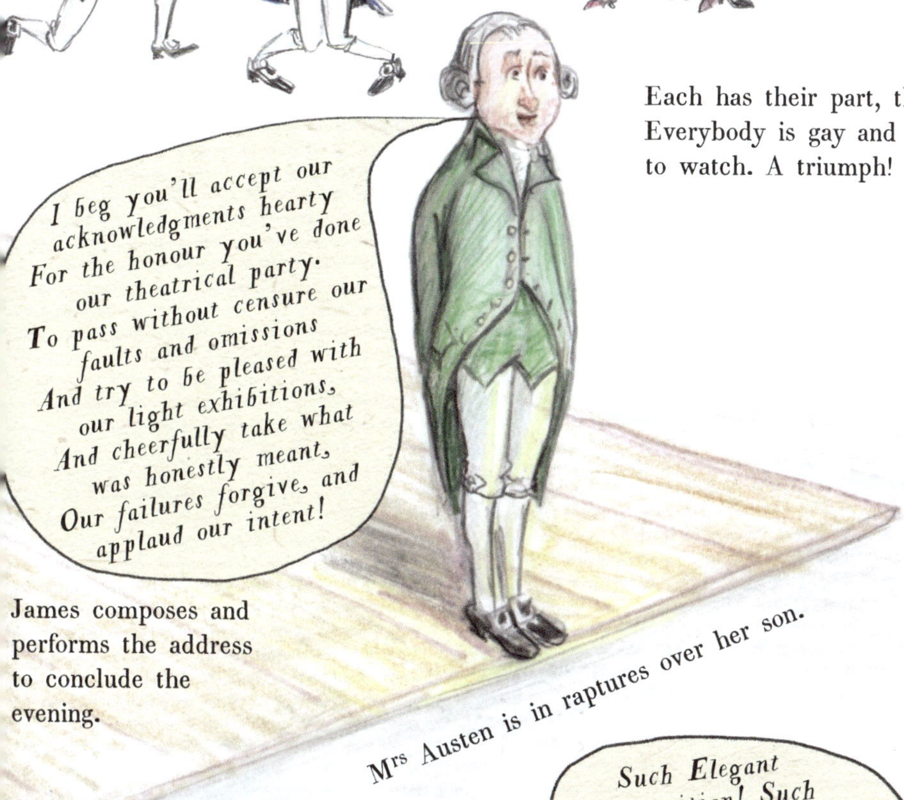
I beg you'll accept our acknowledgments hearty
For the honour you've done our theatrical party.
To pass without censure our faults and omissions
And try to be pleased with our light exhibitions,
And cheerfully take what was honestly meant,
Our failures forgive, and applaud our intent!

James composes and performs the address to conclude the evening.

Mrs Austen is in raptures over her son.

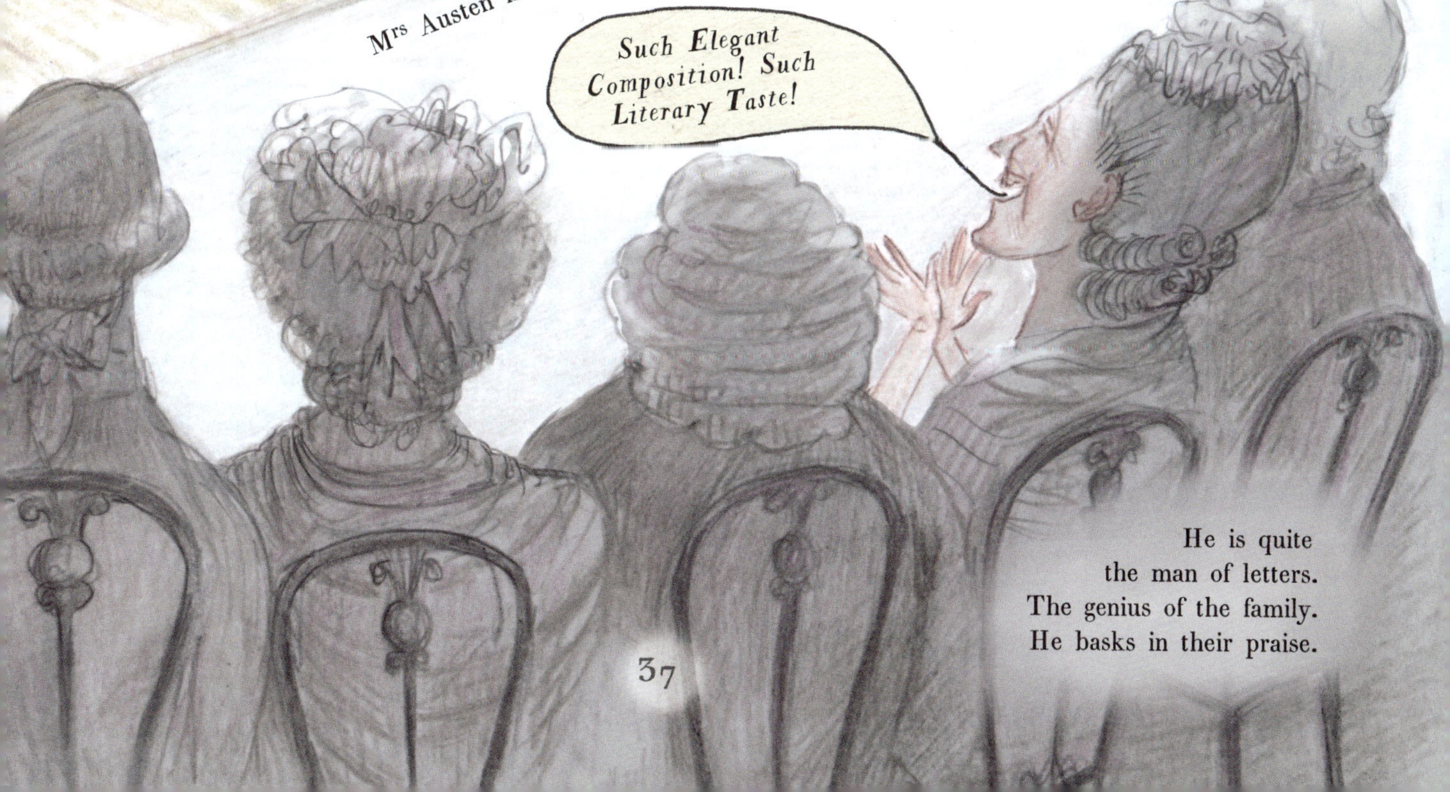
Such Elegant Composition! Such Literary Taste!

He is quite the man of letters. The genius of the family. He basks in their praise.

NOVELS inculcate a **RIDICULOUS WAY OF THINKING** whereby every **RAW GIRL** while she reads, is tempted to think that she can also **WRITE**

But! what is Jane subversively scribbling?

A NOVEL!

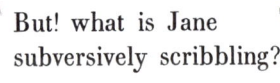

Henry & Eliza...

When the Ladies returned, their amazement was great at finding the following note: "Madam, We are married & gone."

Her Grace flew into the most violent passion, & sent out after them 300 armed men, intending to have them put to Death in some torturelike manner.

Henry & Eliza continued their flight to the Continent. There they remained three years, became the parents of two Boys, & at the end of it Eliza became a widow without any thing to support her.

Immediately on her Husband's death, Eliza set sail for England in a man of War of 55 Guns, which they had built in their more prosperous days.

But as she stepped on Shore at Dover, with a Child in each hand, she was seized by the officers of the Dutchess.

No sooner had Eliza entered her Dungeon than the first thought which occurred to her, was how to get out of it again.

She went to the Door; but it was locked. She looked at the Window; but it was barred with iron. She dispaired of effecting her Escape, when she fortunately perceived in a Corner of her Cell, a small saw & Ladder of ropes.

In a few weeks she had displaced every Bar but one to which she fastened the Ladder. A difficulty then occurred. Her Children were too small to get down the Ladder by themselves, nor would it be possible for her to take them in her arms when she did.

At last she determined to fling down all her Cloathes, of which she had a large Quantity, & then having given them strict Charge not to hurt themselves, threw her Children after them. She herself with ease discended by the Ladder, at the bottom of which she had the pleasure of finding her little boys in perfect Health & fast asleep.

Her wardrobe she now saw a necessity of selling, for the preservation of her Children. With the money she got for them, bought others more usefull, some playthings for Her Boys, & a gold Watch for herself...

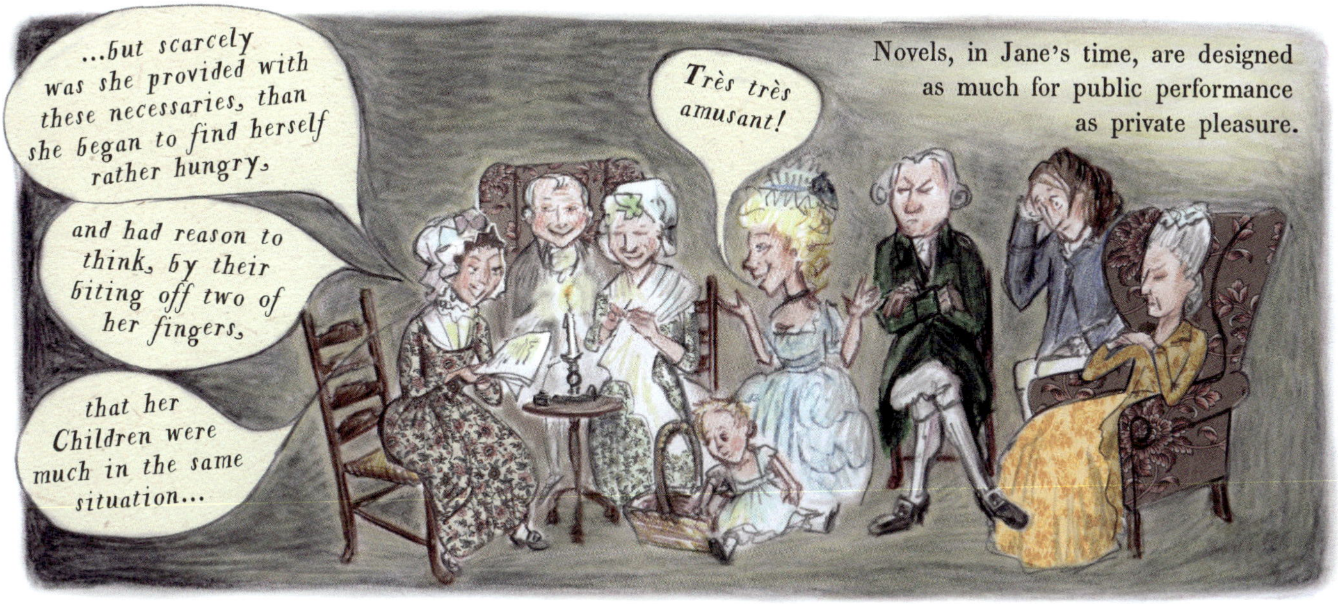
...but scarcely was she provided with these necessaries, than she began to find herself rather hungry,
and had reason to think, by their biting off two of her fingers,
that her Children were much in the same situation...
Très très amusant!
Novels, in Jane's time, are designed as much for public performance as private pleasure.

The evening conversation, when the family is all assembled, is often enlivened by reading aloud. The skill is practised and prized — attention must be paid to modulation, emphasis, foresight, a clear manner, good delivery.

Jane's performances of her compositions are superlative. Laughter resounds around Steventon rectory as an unstoppable fountain of silliness flows from Jane's quill.

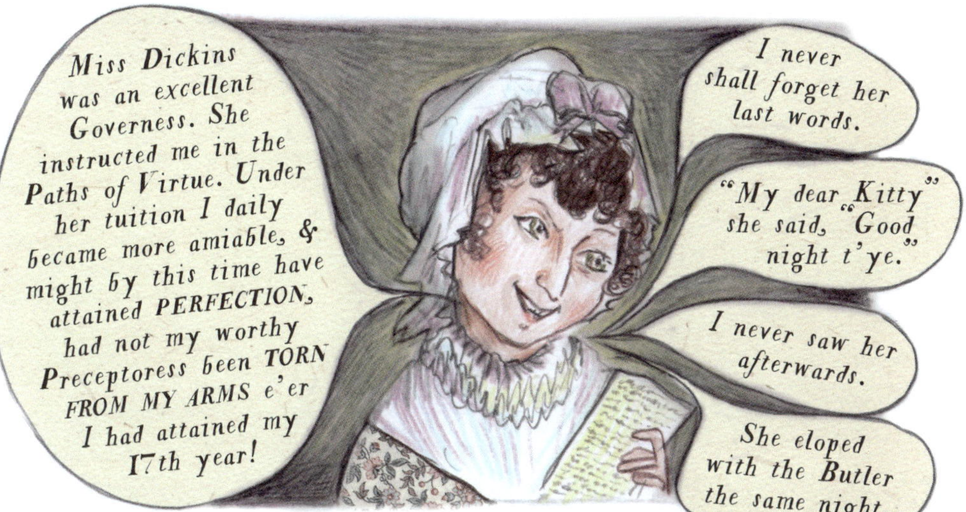
Miss Dickins was an excellent Governess. She instructed me in the Paths of Virtue. Under her tuition I daily became more amiable, & might by this time have attained PERFECTION, had not my worthy Preceptoress been TORN FROM MY ARMS e'er I had attained my 17th year!
I never shall forget her last words.
"My dear Kitty" she said, "Good night t'ye."
I never saw her afterwards.
She eloped with the Butler the same night.

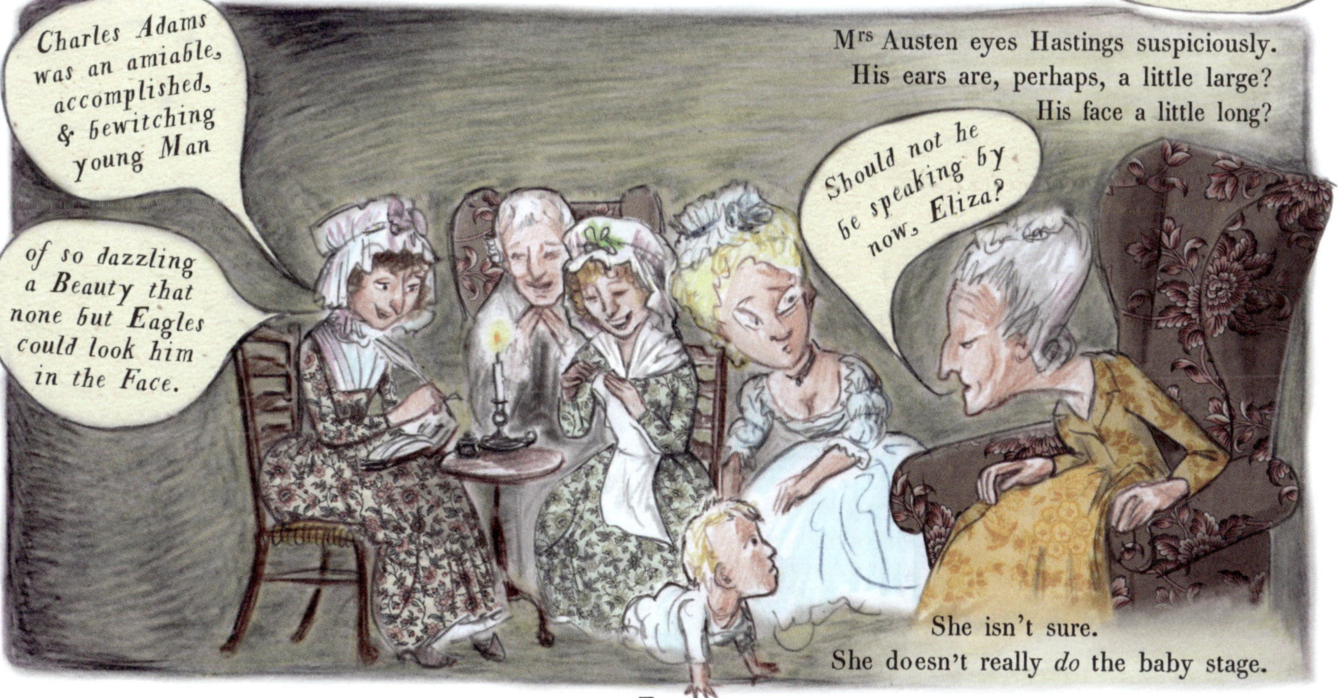
Charles Adams was an amiable, accomplished, & bewitching young Man
of so dazzling a Beauty that none but Eagles could look him in the Face.
Mrs Austen eyes Hastings suspiciously. His ears are, perhaps, a little large? His face a little long?
Should not he be speaking by now, Eliza?
She isn't sure. She doesn't really *do* the baby stage.

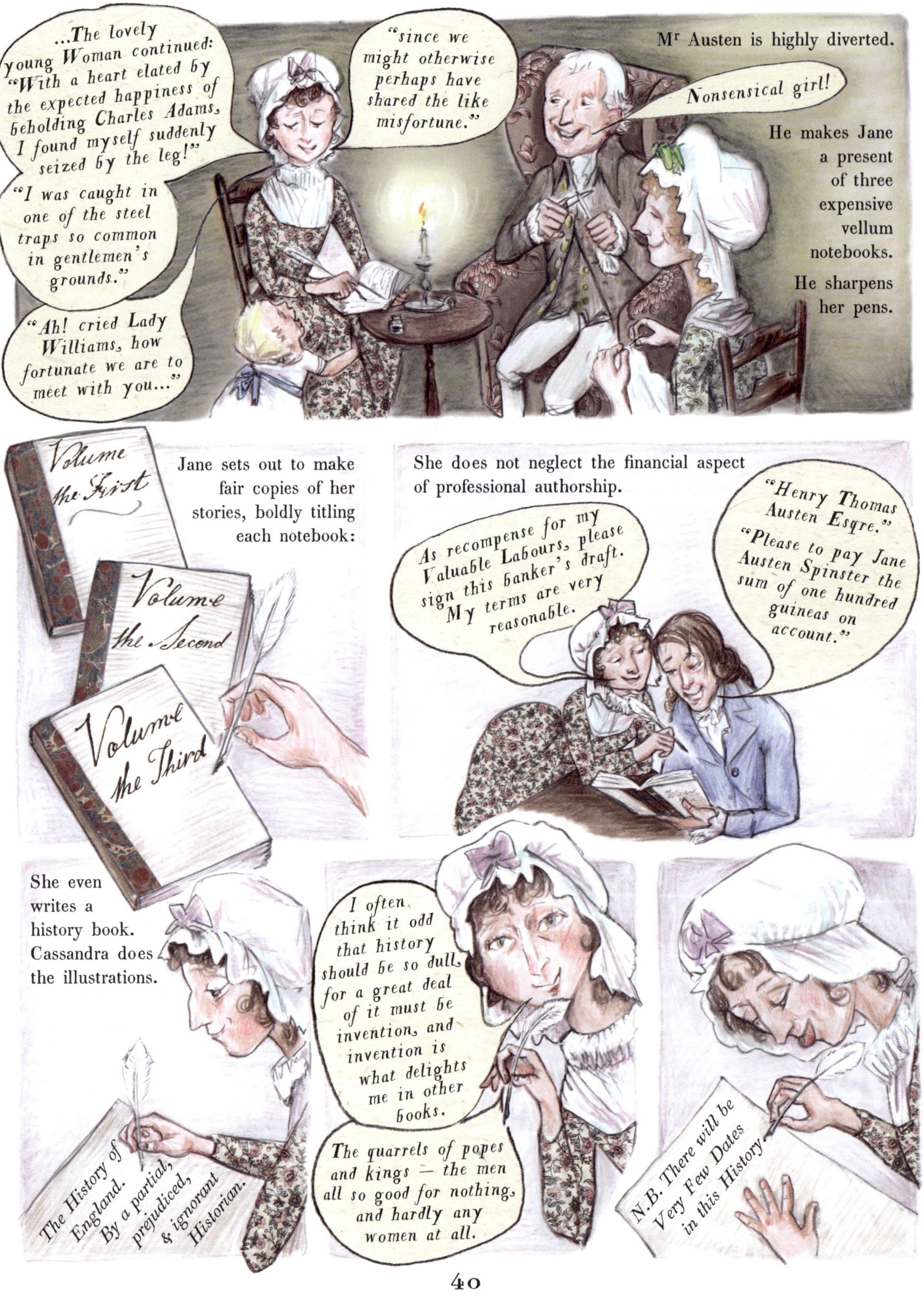
…The lovely young Woman continued: "With a heart elated by the expected happiness of beholding Charles Adams, I found myself suddenly seized by the leg!"
"I was caught in one of the steel traps so common in gentlemen's grounds."
"Ah! cried Lady Williams, how fortunate we are to meet with you…
"since we might otherwise perhaps have shared the like misfortune."
Mr Austen is highly diverted.
Nonsensical girl!
He makes Jane a present of three expensive vellum notebooks.
He sharpens her pens.
Jane sets out to make fair copies of her stories, boldly titling each notebook:
Volume the First
Volume the Second
Volume the Third
She does not neglect the financial aspect of professional authorship.
As recompense for my Valuable Labours, please sign this banker's draft. My terms are very reasonable.
"Henry Thomas Austen Esqre."
"Please to pay Jane Austen Spinster the sum of one hundred guineas on account."
She even writes a history book. Cassandra does the illustrations.
The History of England. By a partial, prejudiced, & ignorant Historian.
I often think it odd that history should be so dull, for a great deal of it must be invention, and invention is what delights me in other books.
The quarrels of popes and kings — the men all so good for nothing, and hardly any women at all.
N.B. There will be Very Few Dates in this History

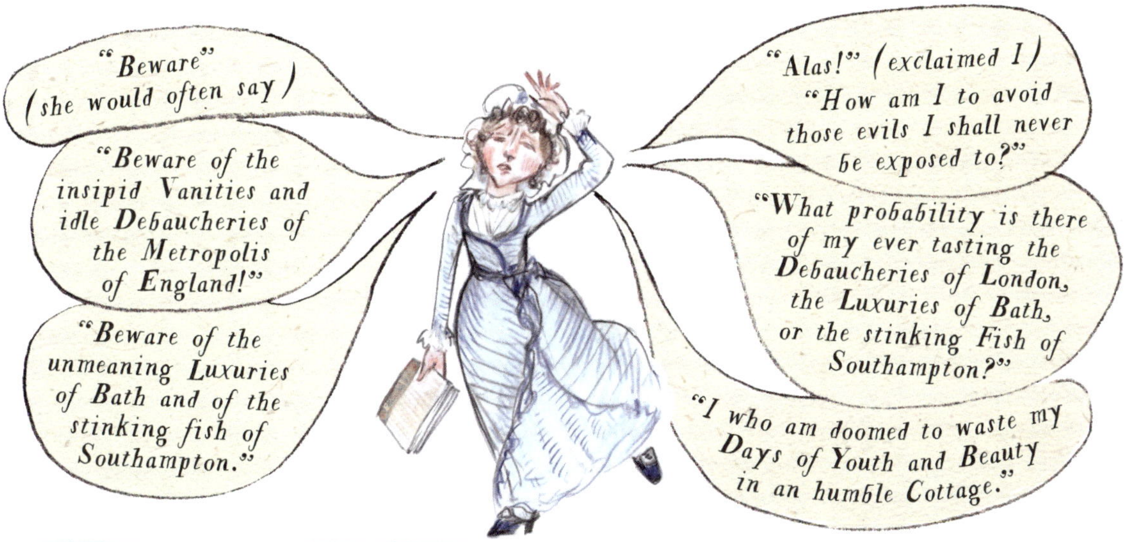
"Beware" (she would often say)
"Beware of the insipid Vanities and idle Debaucheries of the Metropolis of England!"
"Beware of the unmeaning Luxuries of Bath and of the stinking fish of Southampton."
"Alas!" (exclaimed I) "How am I to avoid those evils I shall never be exposed to?"
"What probability is there of my ever tasting the Debaucheries of London, the Luxuries of Bath, or the stinking Fish of Southampton?"
"I who am doomed to waste my Days of Youth and Beauty in an humble Cottage."

Mr Austen takes his Girls on a trip to Sevenoaks to visit his Uncle Francis (who just happens to be very elderly, and very rich).

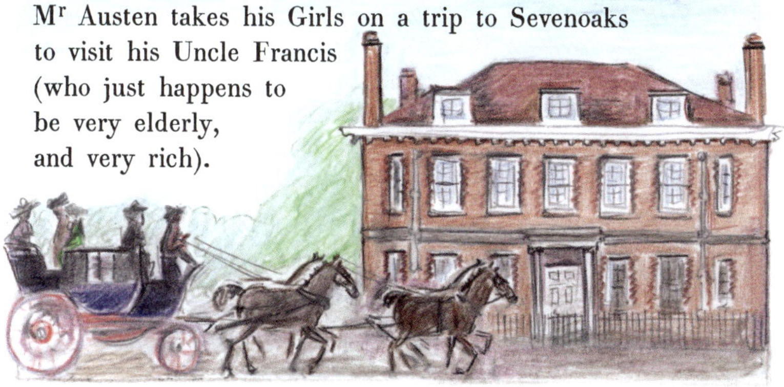

Jane is judged to be "very prim" by her cousins, but she is only exceedingly shy.

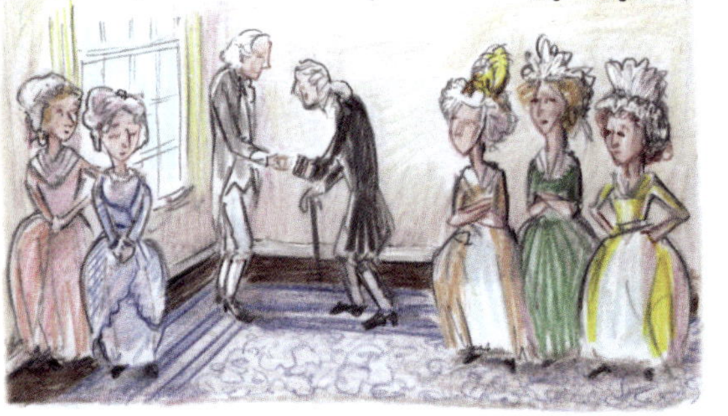

The Girls are taken to London, to visit Eliza.

With familiar people, Jane regains her sparkle.

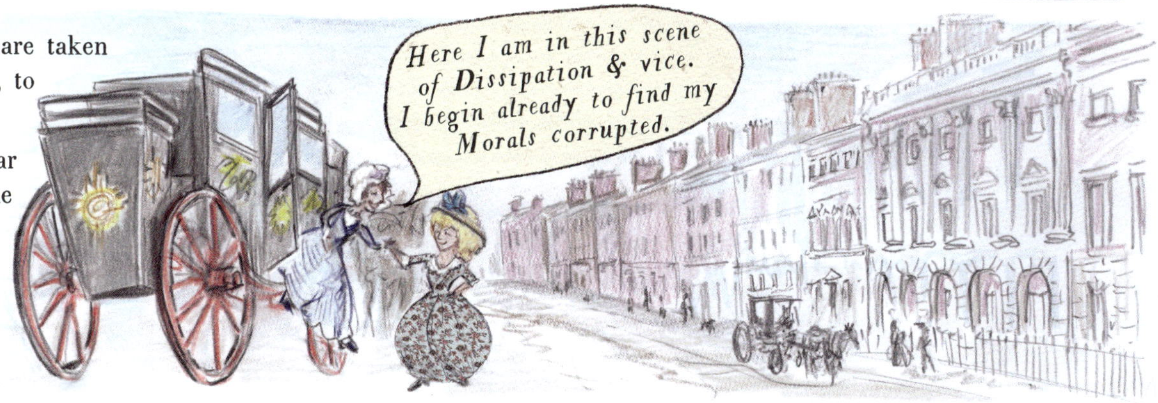
Here I am in this scene of Dissipation & vice. I begin already to find my Morals corrupted.

On her return to the Rectory, Jane immortalises Cassandra's adventures in Town with a dedicated literary work.

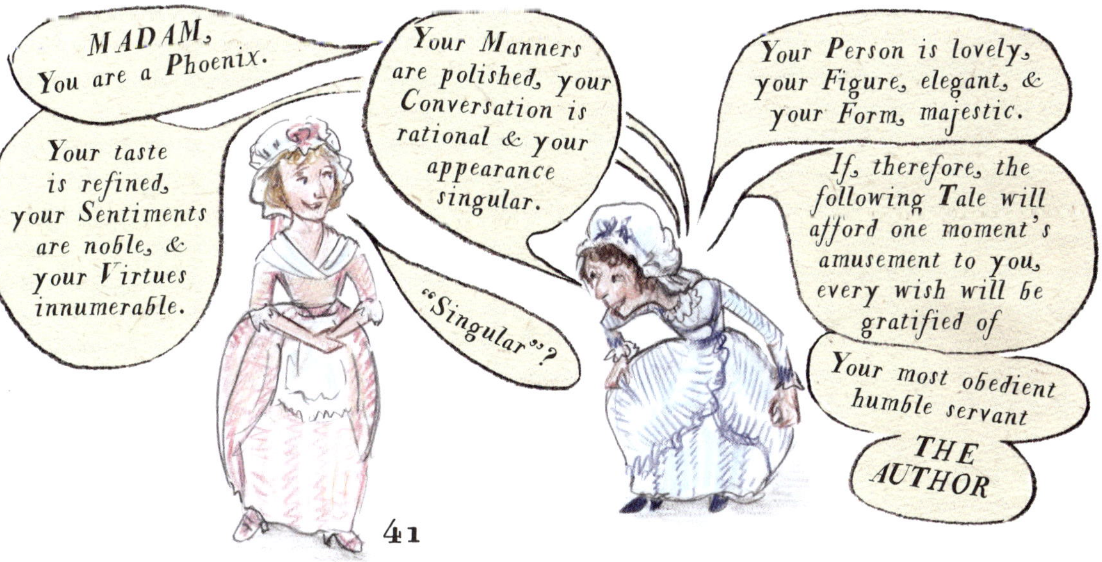
MADAM, You are a Phoenix.
Your taste is refined, your Sentiments are noble, & your Virtues innumerable.
Your Manners are polished, your Conversation is rational & your appearance singular.
"Singular"?
Your Person is lovely, your Figure, elegant, & your Form, majestic.
If, therefore, the following Tale will afford one moment's amusement to you, every wish will be gratified of
Your most obedient humble servant
THE AUTHOR

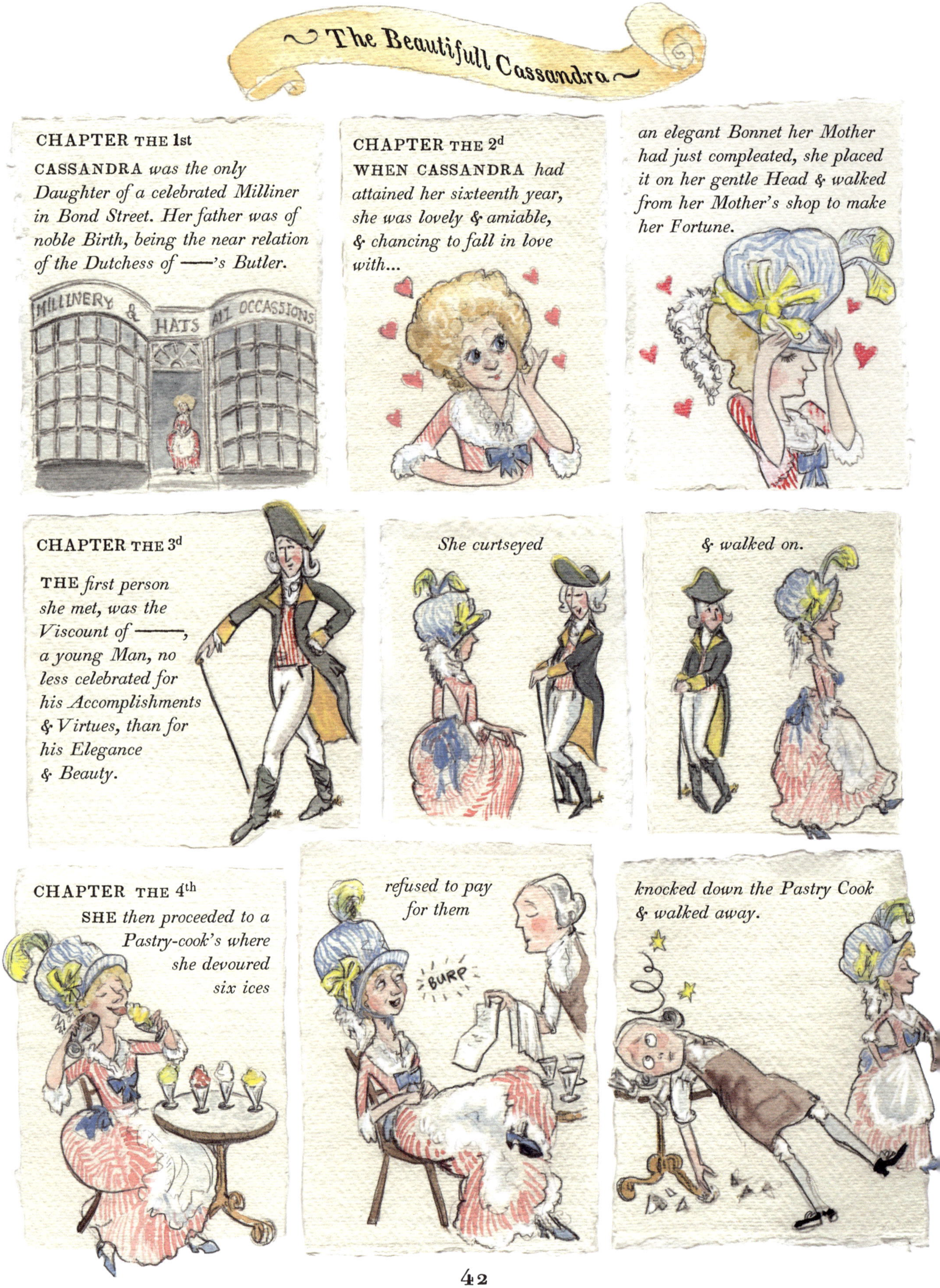
~ The Beautifull Cassandra ~
CHAPTER THE 1st
CASSANDRA *was the only Daughter of a celebrated Milliner in Bond Street. Her father was of noble Birth, being the near relation of the Dutchess of ——'s Butler.*
MILLINERY & HATS ALL OCCASSIONS
CHAPTER THE 2d
WHEN CASSANDRA *had attained her sixteenth year, she was lovely & amiable, & chancing to fall in love with...*
an elegant Bonnet her Mother had just compleated, she placed it on her gentle Head & walked from her Mother's shop to make her Fortune.
CHAPTER THE 3d
THE *first person she met, was the Viscount of ——, a young Man, no less celebrated for his Accomplishments & Virtues, than for his Elegance & Beauty.*
She curtseyed
& walked on.
CHAPTER THE 4th
SHE *then proceeded to a Pastry-cook's where she devoured six ices*
refused to pay for them
BURP
knocked down the Pastry Cook & walked away.

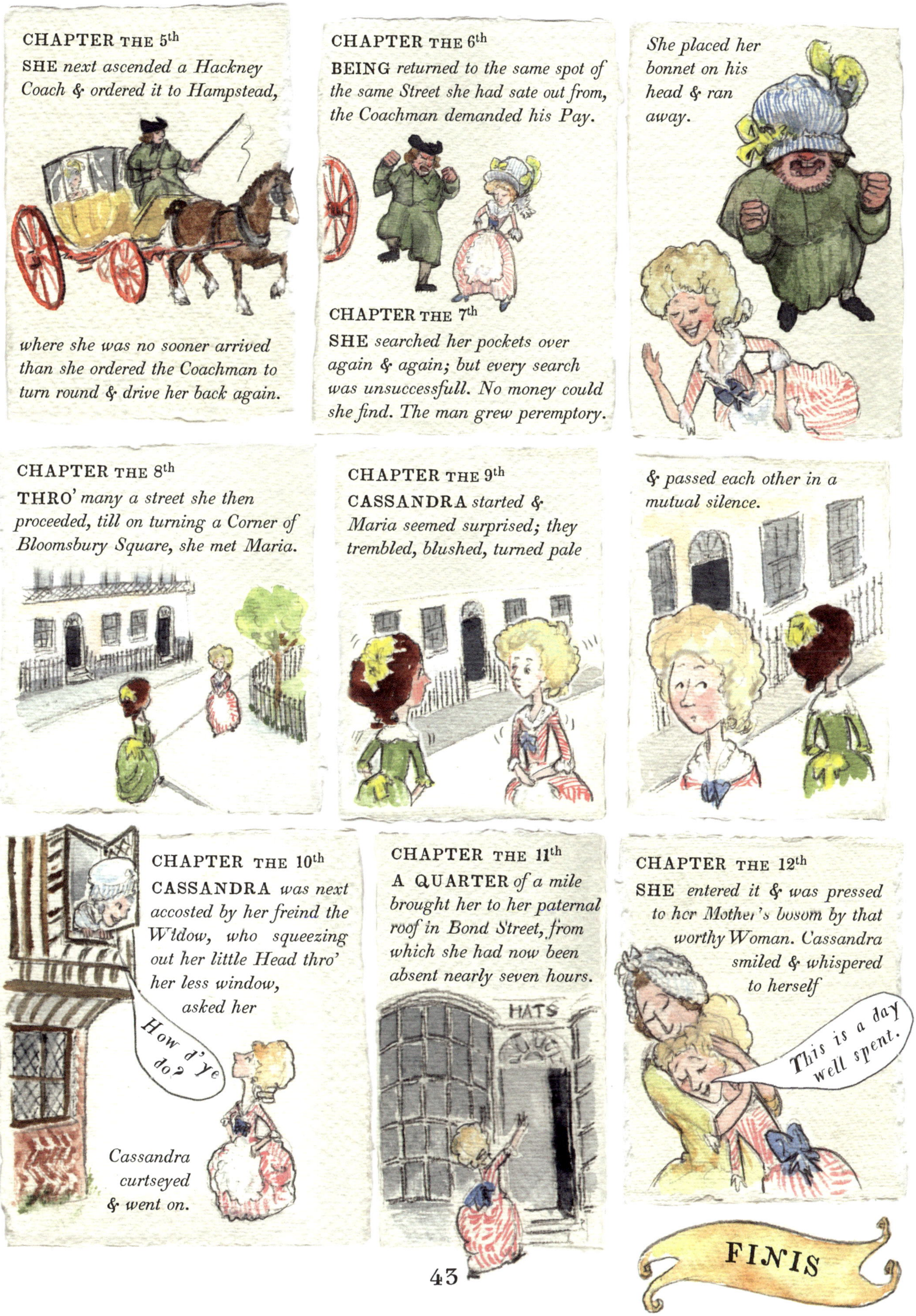
CHAPTER THE 5th
SHE next ascended a Hackney Coach & ordered it to Hampstead,
where she was no sooner arrived than she ordered the Coachman to turn round & drive her back again.
CHAPTER THE 6th
BEING returned to the same spot of the same Street she had sate out from, the Coachman demanded his Pay.
CHAPTER THE 7th
SHE searched her pockets over again & again; but every search was unsuccessfull. No money could she find. The man grew peremptory.
She placed her bonnet on his head & ran away.
CHAPTER THE 8th
THRO' many a street she then proceeded, till on turning a Corner of Bloomsbury Square, she met Maria.
CHAPTER THE 9th
CASSANDRA started & Maria seemed surprised; they trembled, blushed, turned pale
& passed each other in a mutual silence.
CHAPTER THE 10th
CASSANDRA was next accosted by her freind the Widow, who squeezing out her little Head thro' her less window, asked her
How d'ye do?
Cassandra curtseyed & went on.
CHAPTER THE 11th
A QUARTER of a mile brought her to her paternal roof in Bond Street, from which she had now been absent nearly seven hours.
HATS
CHAPTER THE 12th
SHE entered it & was pressed to her Mother's bosom by that worthy Woman. Cassandra smiled & whispered to herself
This is a day well spent.
FINIS

Jane's life touches very little on politics or international events, but even somnolent Steventon is disturbed by the news from France in 1789.

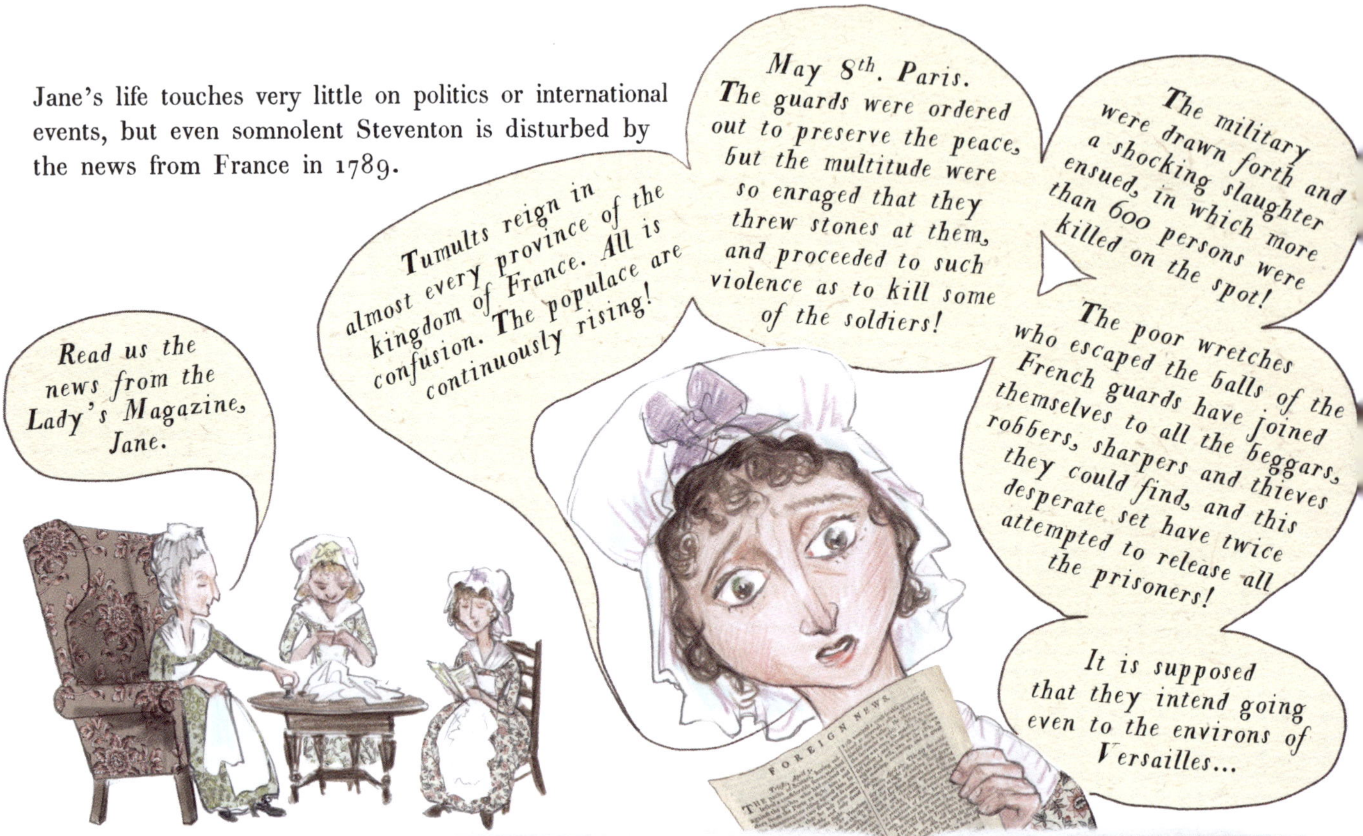

Read us the news from the Lady's Magazine, Jane.
Tumults reign in almost every province of the kingdom of France. All is confusion. The populace are continuously rising!
May 8th. Paris. The guards were ordered out to preserve the peace, but the multitude were so enraged that they threw stones at them, and proceeded to such violence as to kill some of the soldiers!
The military were drawn forth and a shocking slaughter ensued, in which more than 600 persons were killed on the spot!
The poor wretches who escaped the balls of the French guards have joined themselves to all the beggars, robbers, sharpers and thieves they could find, and this desperate set have twice attempted to release all the prisoners!
It is supposed that they intend going even to the environs of Versailles...
FOREIGN NEWS

The Bastille stormed, the Treasury empty, the King's authority challenged, their cousin quite a refugee...

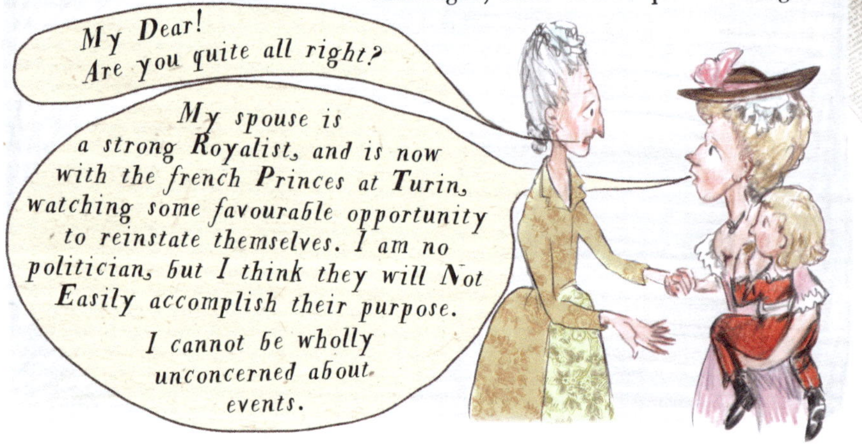

My Dear! Are you quite all right?
My spouse is a strong Royalist, and is now with the french Princes at Turin, watching some favourable opportunity to reinstate themselves. I am no politician, but I think they will Not Easily accomplish their purpose.
I cannot be wholly unconcerned about events.

And Little Hastings is afflicted with convulsions. He neither walks nor talks.

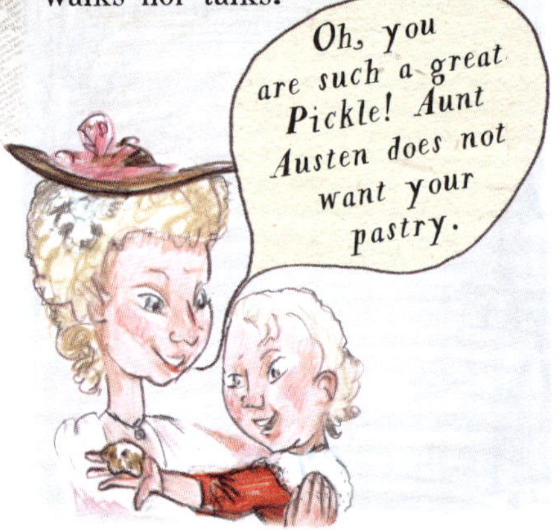

Oh, you are such a great Pickle! Aunt Austen does not want your pastry.

Mrs Austen is at last convinced.

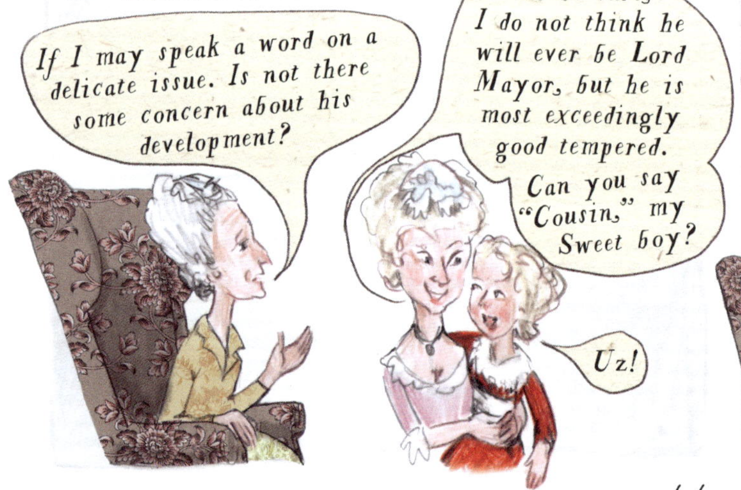

If I may speak a word on a delicate issue. Is not there some concern about his development?
To be sure, I do not think he will ever be Lord Mayor, but he is most exceedingly good tempered.
Can you say "Cousin," my Sweet boy?
Uz!

And when Mrs Austen presses the point and suggests the only sensible recourse...

Eliza is outraged. She swiftly leaves for Margate.

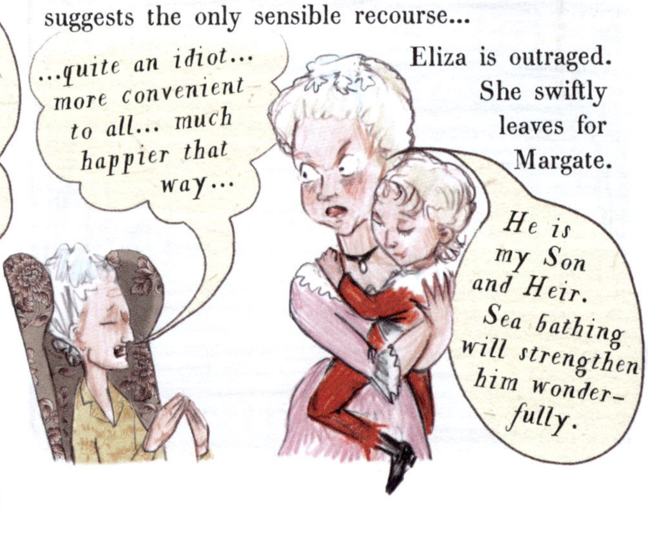

...quite an idiot... more convenient to all... much happier that way...
He is my Son and Heir. Sea bathing will strengthen him wonderfully.

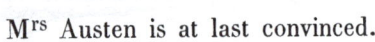

THE PUBLIC IS APPRAISED OF A PERFORMANCE, FOR ONE NIGHT ONLY

BY "THE STEVENTON PLAYERS" OF a DRAMATICK WORK

by a Playwrightess of newly discovr'd Talent

MISS JANE AUSTEN

THE MYSTERY

Dramatis Personae:

MEN

Colonel Elliott – MR HENRY AUSTEN
Sir Edward Spangle – MR EDWARD AUSTEN
Old Humbug – REV. GEORGE AUSTEN
Young Humbug – MASTER CHARLES AUSTEN
and Corydon – MR JAMES AUSTEN

WOMEN

Fanny Elliott – MISS CASSANDRA AUSTEN
Mrs Humbug – MRS AUSTEN
and Daphne – MISS JANE AUSTEN, HERSELF

Act the First. Scene the 1st: A Garden.

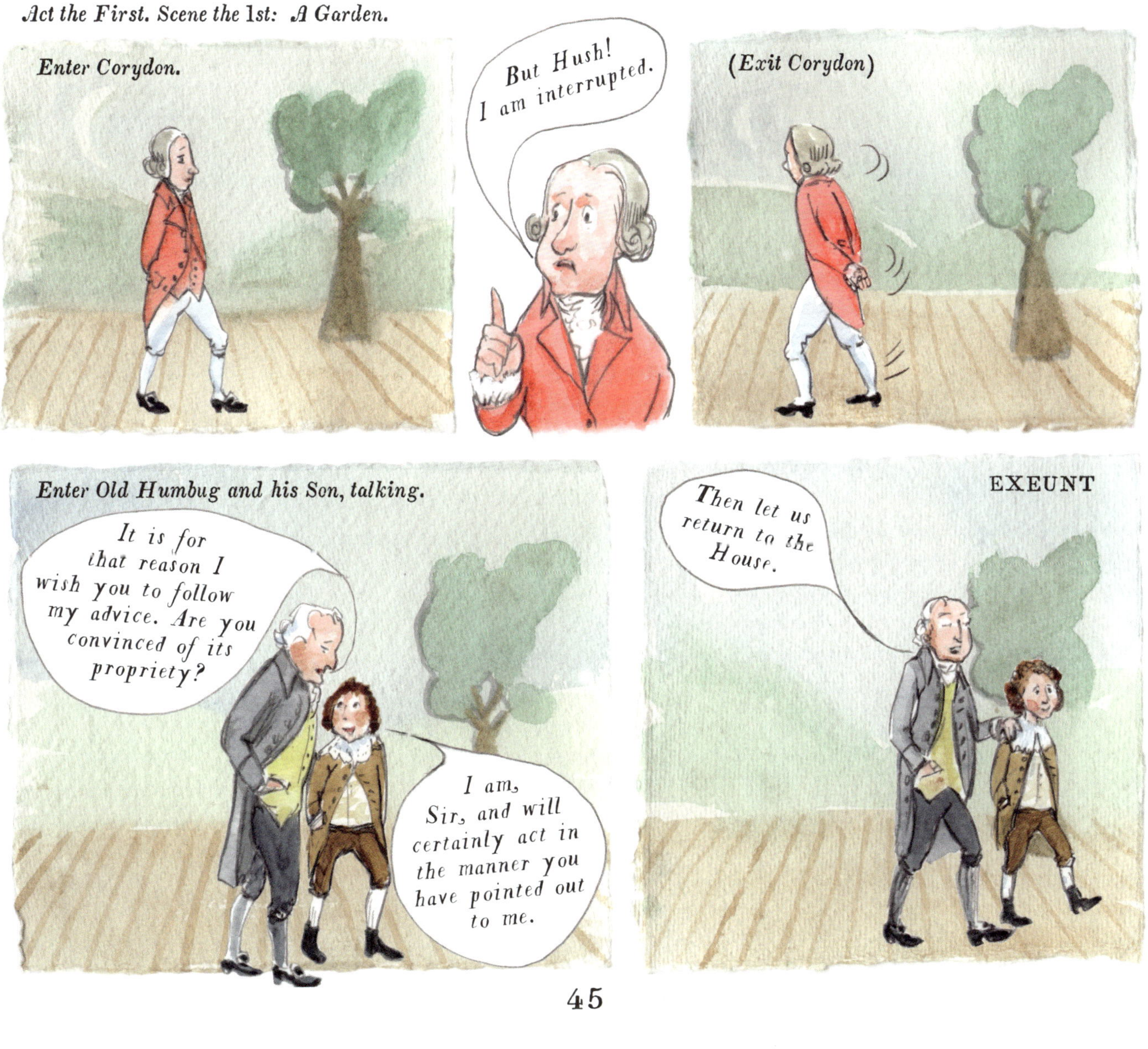
Enter Corydon.
But Hush! I am interrupted.
(Exit Corydon)
Enter Old Humbug and his Son, talking.
It is for that reason I wish you to follow my advice. Are you convinced of its propriety?
I am, Sir, and will certainly act in the manner you have pointed out to me.
EXEUNT
Then let us return to the House.

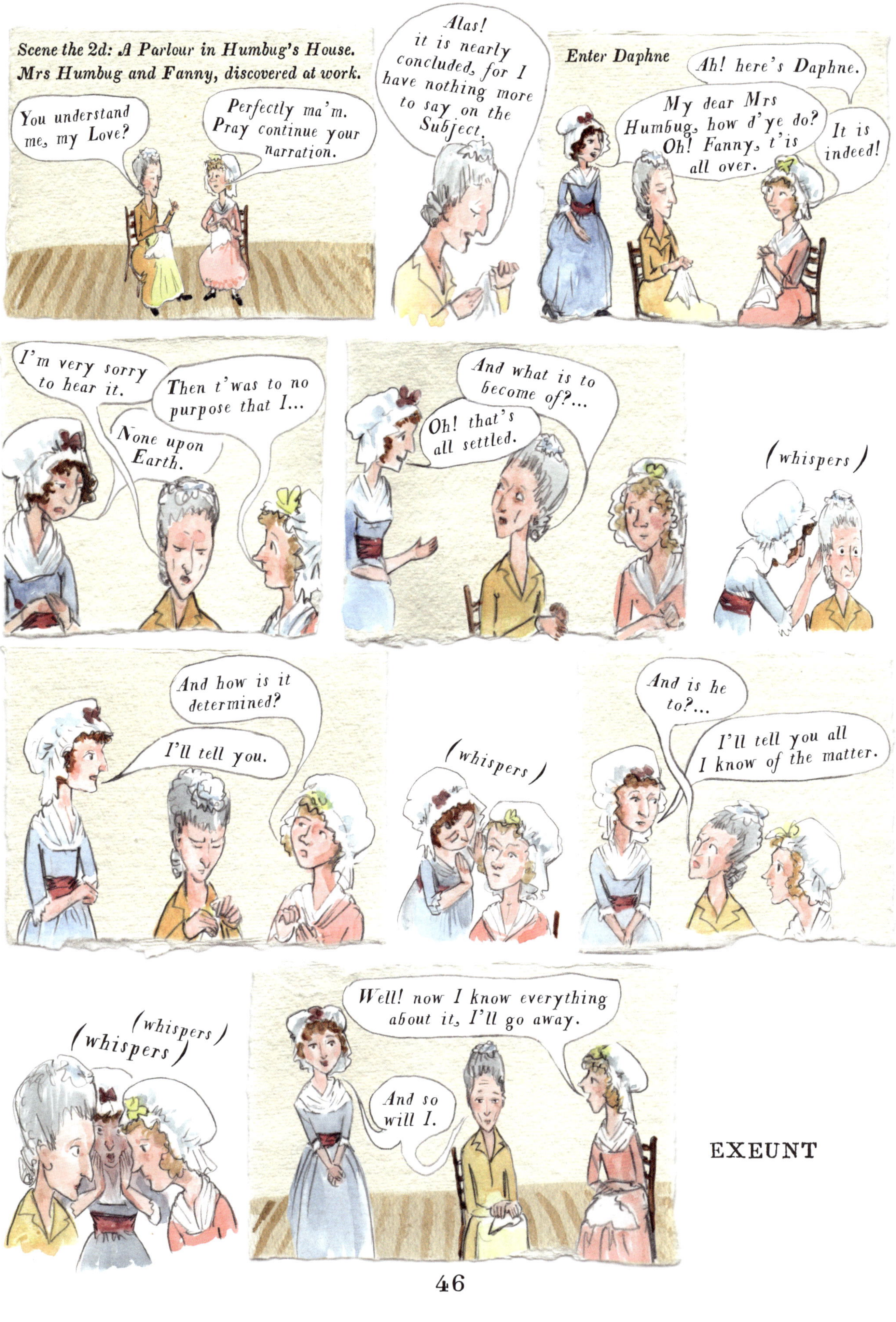
Scene the 2d: A Parlour in Humbug's House.
Mrs Humbug and Fanny, discovered at work.
You understand me, my Love?
Perfectly ma'm. Pray continue your narration.
Alas! it is nearly concluded, for I have nothing more to say on the Subject.
Enter Daphne
Ah! here's Daphne.
My dear Mrs Humbug, how d'ye do? Oh! Fanny, t'is all over.
It is indeed!
I'm very sorry to hear it.
Then t'was to no purpose that I...
None upon Earth.
And what is to become of?...
Oh! that's all settled.
(whispers)
And how is it determined?
I'll tell you.
(whispers)
And is he to?...
I'll tell you all I know of the matter.
(whispers)
(whispers)
Well! now I know everything about it, I'll go away.
And so will I.
EXEUNT

Scene the 3d: the Curtain rises and discovers Sir Edward Spangle reclined in an elegant Attitude on a sofa, fast asleep.

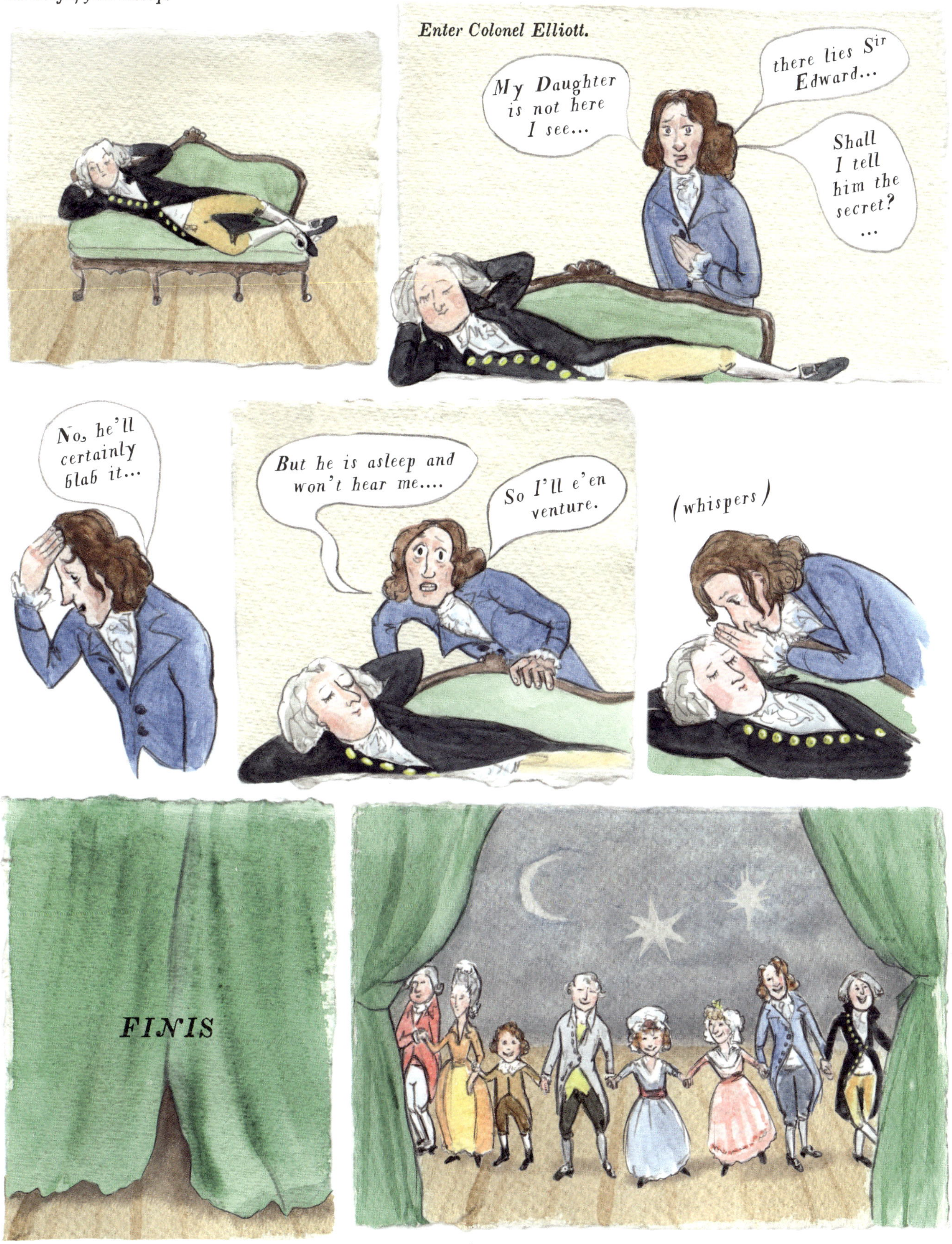
Enter Colonel Elliott.
My Daughter is not here I see...
there lies Sir Edward...
Shall I tell him the secret? ...
No, he'll certainly blab it...
But he is asleep and won't hear me....
So I'll e'en venture.
(whispers)
FINIS

The tides of fate start to sweep away members of the Austen clan.

July 1791, Charles follows his brother's footsteps to the Royal Naval Academy.

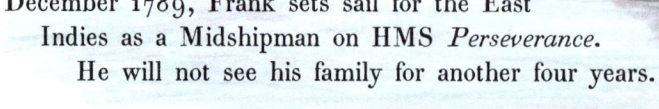

December 1789, Frank sets sail for the East Indies as a Midshipman on HMS *Perseverance*. He will not see his family for another four years.

A Breast Cancer claims Aunt Phila a few months later. Eliza nursed her through her painful, hideous illness.

Edward marries eighteen-year-old Elizabeth Bridges on the day after Boxing Day, 1791.

"The daughter of a Baronet, you know."

James takes Orders, and gains the curacy of the neighbouring parish of Deane. He marries Anne Mathew, the grand-daughter of a Duke.

However much he loves God, or his Wife, he loves Fox Hunting more.

Henry is also intended for the Church. Eliza has opinions about this matter.

"Men love to *Distinguish* themselves by *Action*. You really are fit for something better, something smarter."

"Come, do change your mind. It is not too late."

But here's the Mystery. How will Jane distinguish herself? What is her Fate?

Jane can write a copperplate hand (tho' not as neat as Cassandra's) and is sometimes called upon by her Father to fill out parish paperwork.

It is a summer's morning. Steventon church is empty. She takes the printed specimen page at the front of the marriage register and doodles her dreams of her future.

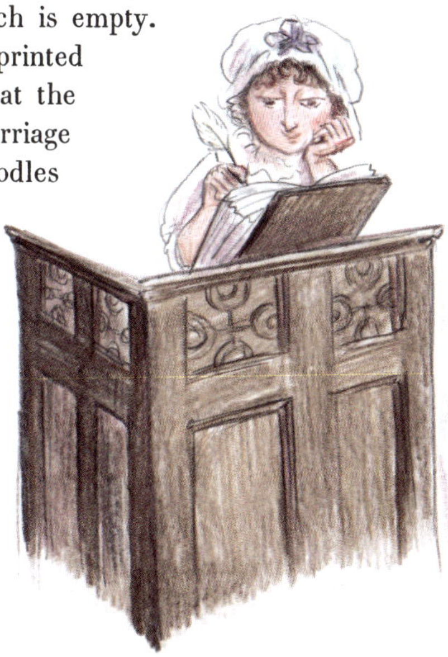

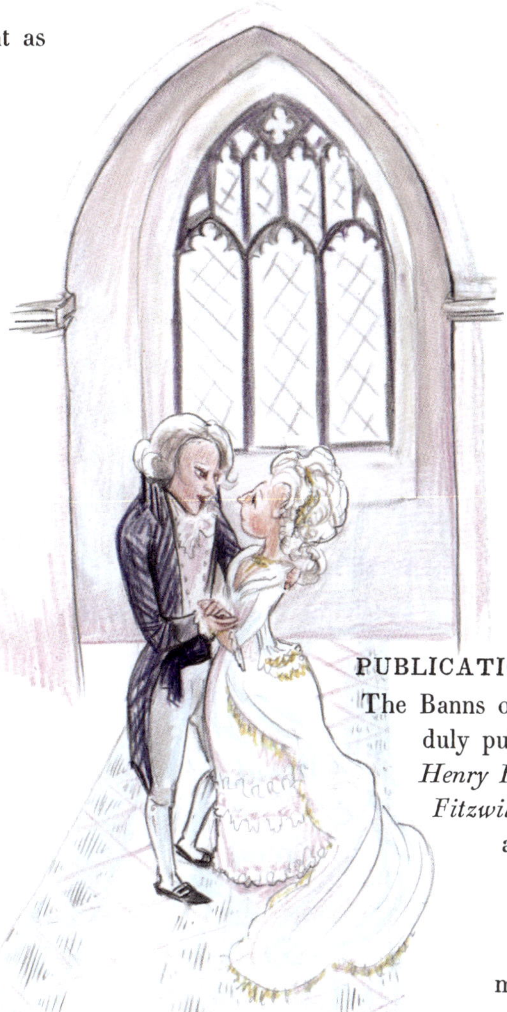

PUBLICATION OF BANNS

The Banns of Marriage were duly published between *Henry Frederic Howard Fitzwilliam* of *London* and *Jane Austen* of *Steventon*

The dashing man about Town. What a catch! The fictional Fitzwilliams are a Family of note.

AN ENTRY OF A MARRIAGE

Edmund Arthur William Mortimer, of Liverpool, and *Jane Austen, Steventon* were married in this church.

Liverpool? A fortune acquired by trade, more's the pity, but a fortune, still.

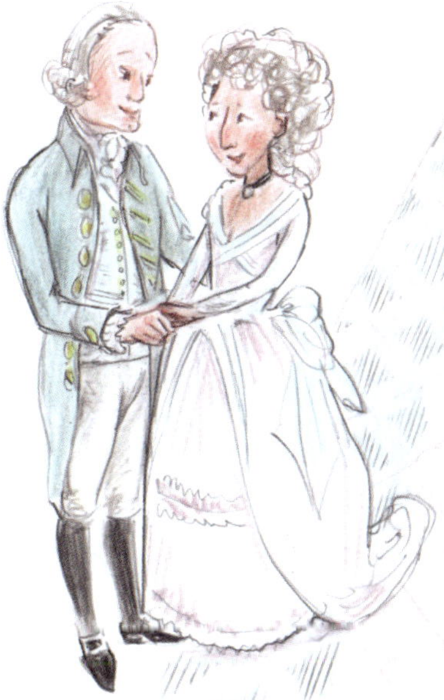

Or then again...

This Marriage was Solemnized between *Jack Smith* and *Jane Smith, late Austen.*

Plain Jack Smith?

Plain Jane?

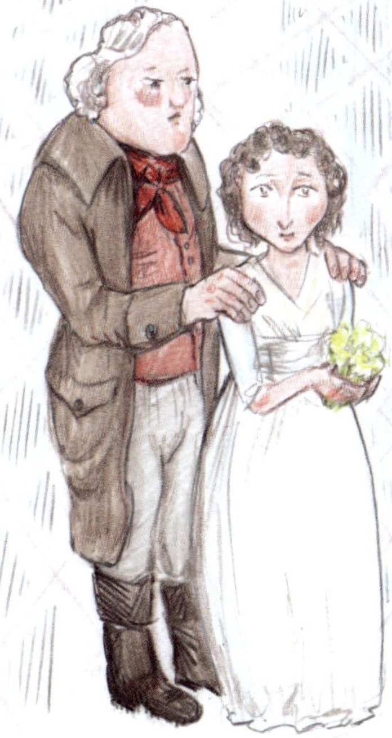

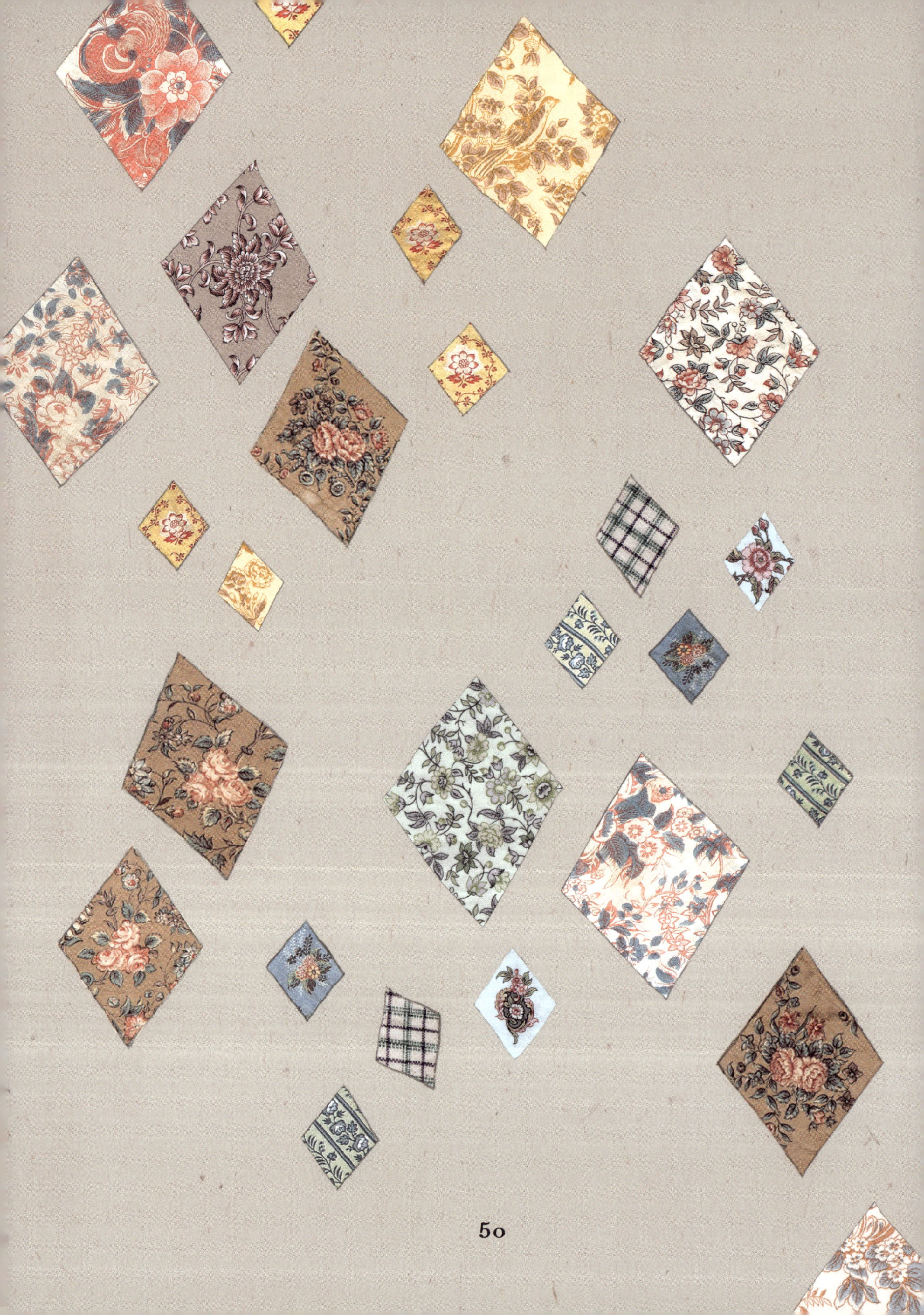

COMING OUT

Autumn 1792. At the tender age of sixteen, we find Jane in preparation for her Appearance. Henceforth, she has been invisible to Society: absent from engagements, head close-covered in a cap, demure, never saying a word. All that is about to change.

But first, there are agonies of decisions to be made. Trimmings for her robe? Feathers for her hair? The yellow shoe roses or the blue? Yards of the finest Irish are stitched into petticoats. Silk stockings? Satin gloves? She lies awake debating between the spotted and the tamboured muslin.

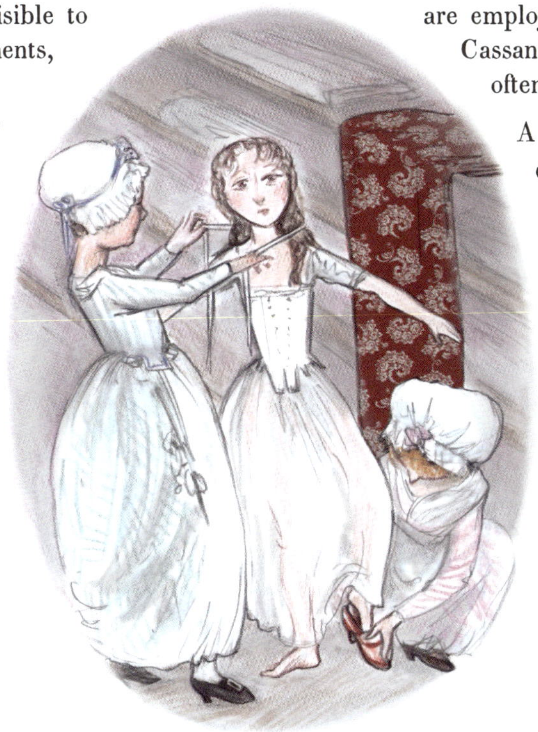

For this Occasion the services of a mantua-maker are employed, but the drama of Jane and Cassandra's costumes lies in the fact that, often, they make them themselves.

A "gown" means a length of uncut cloth, as well as a finished garment. A gown enables one to pass in high society. A gown must reflect the latest fashion. A gown is a puzzle. A challenge. An obsession.

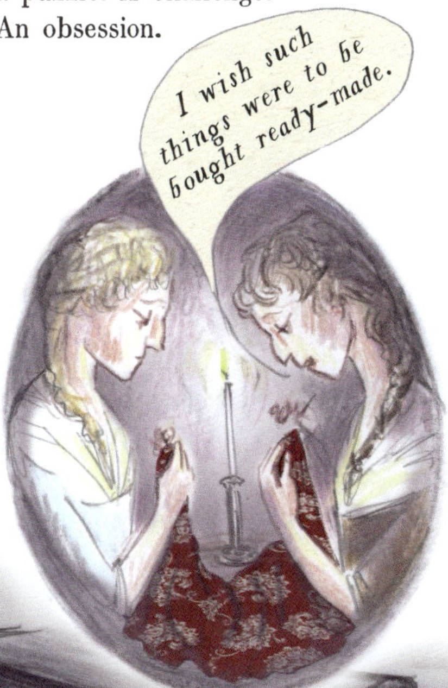
I wish such things were to be bought ready-made.

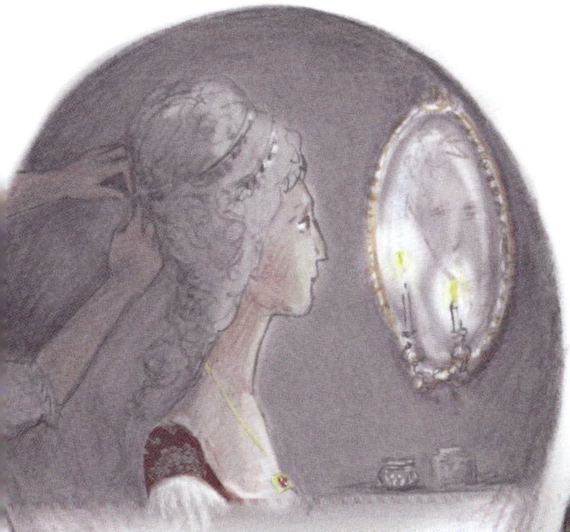

The evening arrives. Jane's hair is pomaded and papered and powdered. It feels stiff & strange.

She is handed into her father's Carriage. (A recent acquisition. They have never been able to afford such a thing before.)

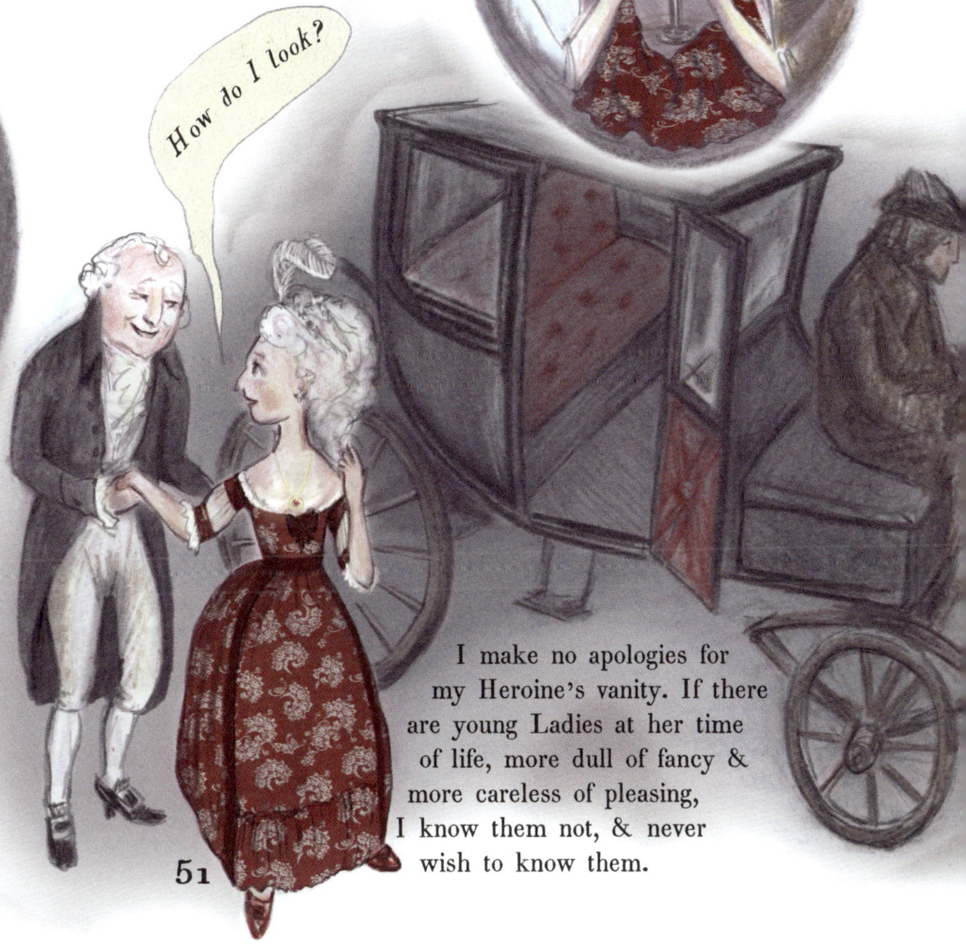
How do I look?

I make no apologies for my Heroine's vanity. If there are young Ladies at her time of life, more dull of fancy & more careless of pleasing, I know them not, & never wish to know them.

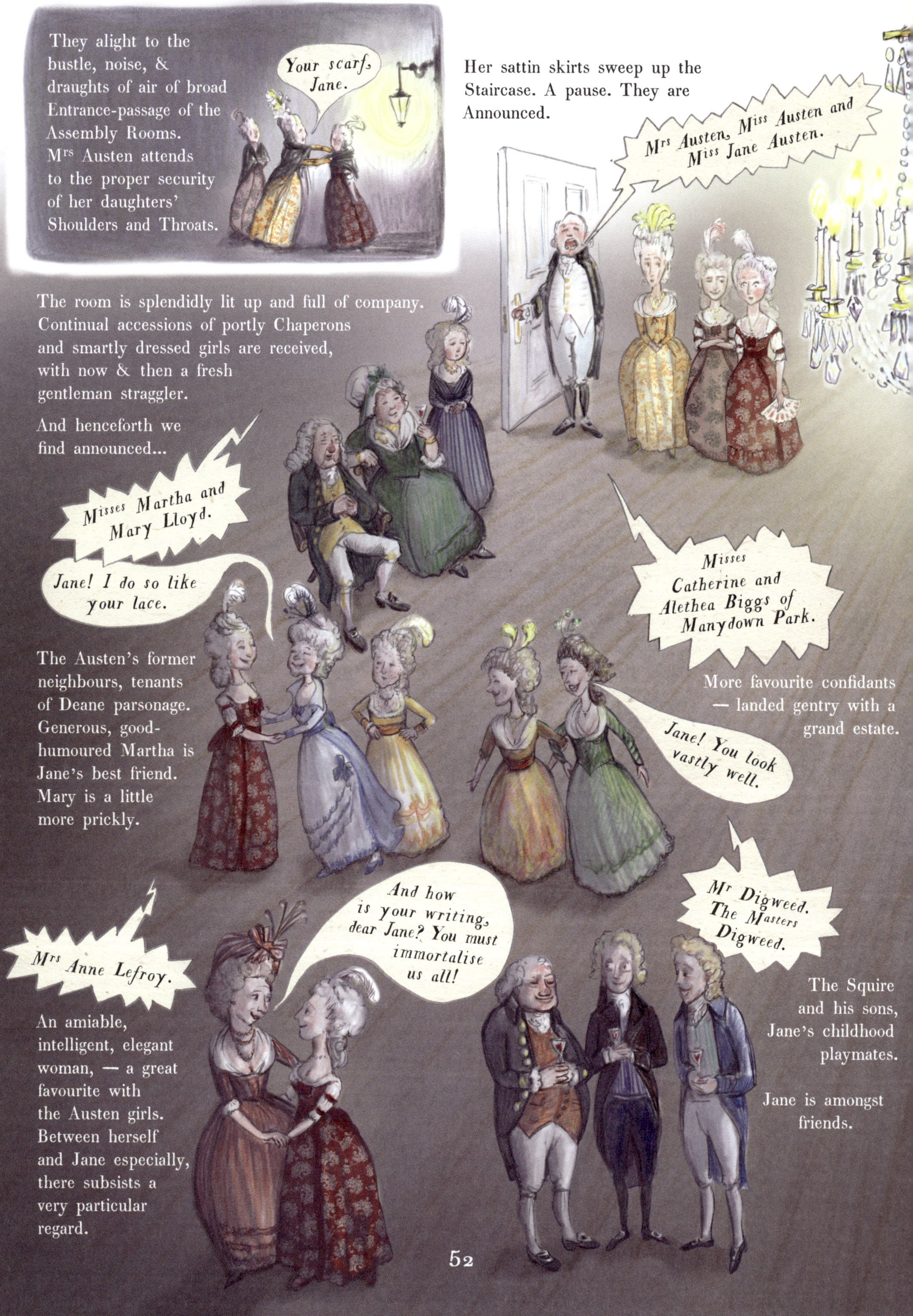
They alight to the bustle, noise, & draughts of air of broad Entrance-passage of the Assembly Rooms. Mrs Austen attends to the proper security of her daughters' Shoulders and Throats.
Your scarf, Jane.
Her sattin skirts sweep up the Staircase. A pause. They are Announced.
Mrs Austen, Miss Austen and Miss Jane Austen.
The room is splendidly lit up and full of company. Continual accessions of portly Chaperons and smartly dressed girls are received, with now & then a fresh gentleman straggler.
And henceforth we find announced...
Misses Martha and Mary Lloyd.
Jane! I do so like your lace.
The Austen's former neighbours, tenants of Deane parsonage. Generous, good-humoured Martha is Jane's best friend. Mary is a little more prickly.
Misses Catherine and Alethea Biggs of Manydown Park.
More favourite confidants — landed gentry with a grand estate.
Jane! You look vastly well.
Mrs Anne Lefroy.
And how is your writing, dear Jane? You must immortalise us all!
An amiable, intelligent, elegant woman, — a great favourite with the Austen girls. Between herself and Jane especially, there subsists a very particular regard.
Mr Digweed. The Masters Digweed.
The Squire and his sons, Jane's childhood playmates.
Jane is amongst friends.

Some cousin or brother or other invites Jane to dance.
It does not much signify who.

Jane abandons herself to the experience,
finds her feet in the rhythm
of the country dance

the whirl of the couples pass about her,
she bounds down the set, flies down the middle,
she is in a continuous course of smiles.

They break
for refreshment.
A general spirit
of ease and enjoyment
is diffused upon the company.
They all stand about and talk
and laugh. Every moment has its
pleasure.

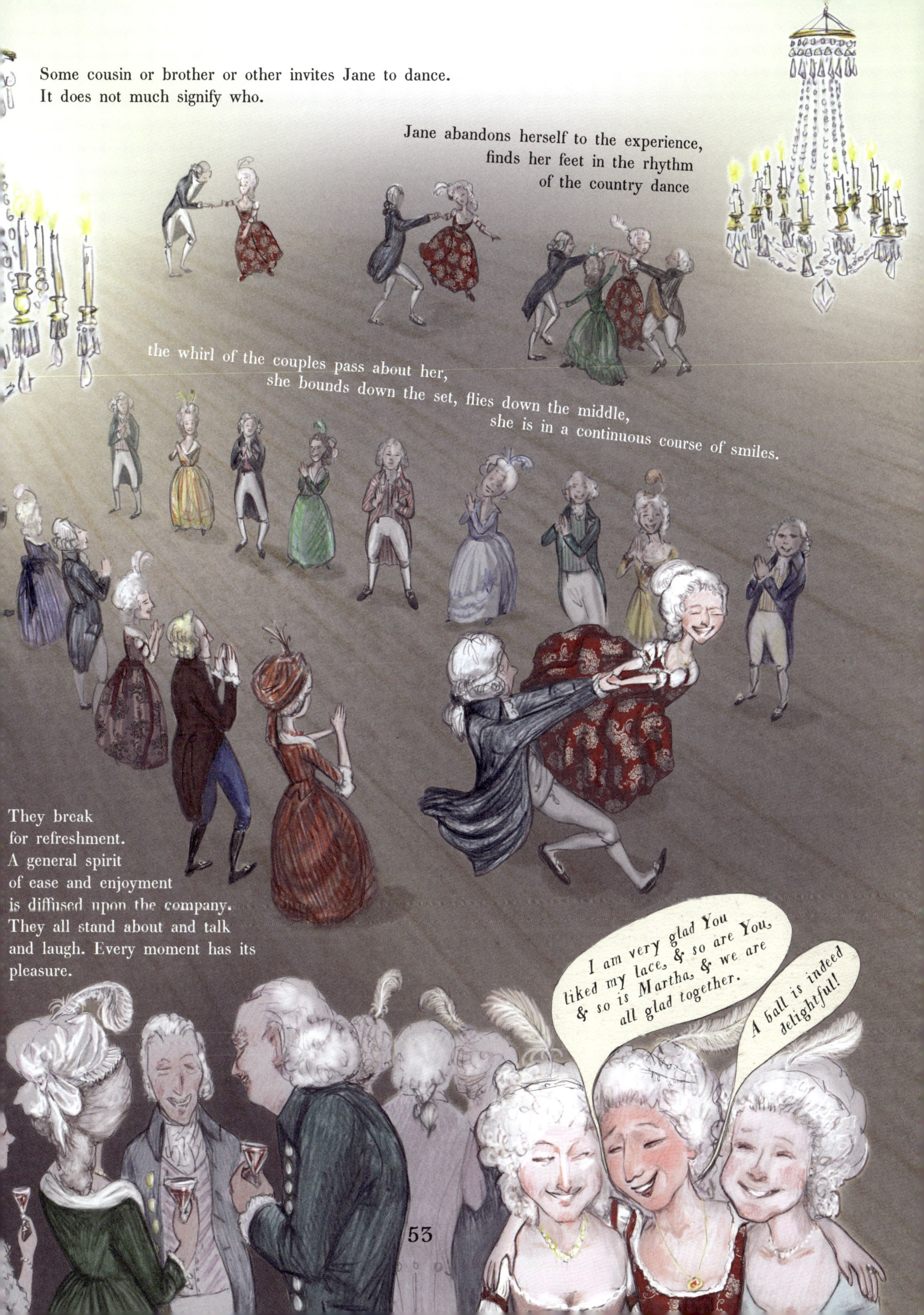
I am very glad You liked my lace, & so are You, & so is Martha, & we are all glad together.
A ball is indeed delightful!

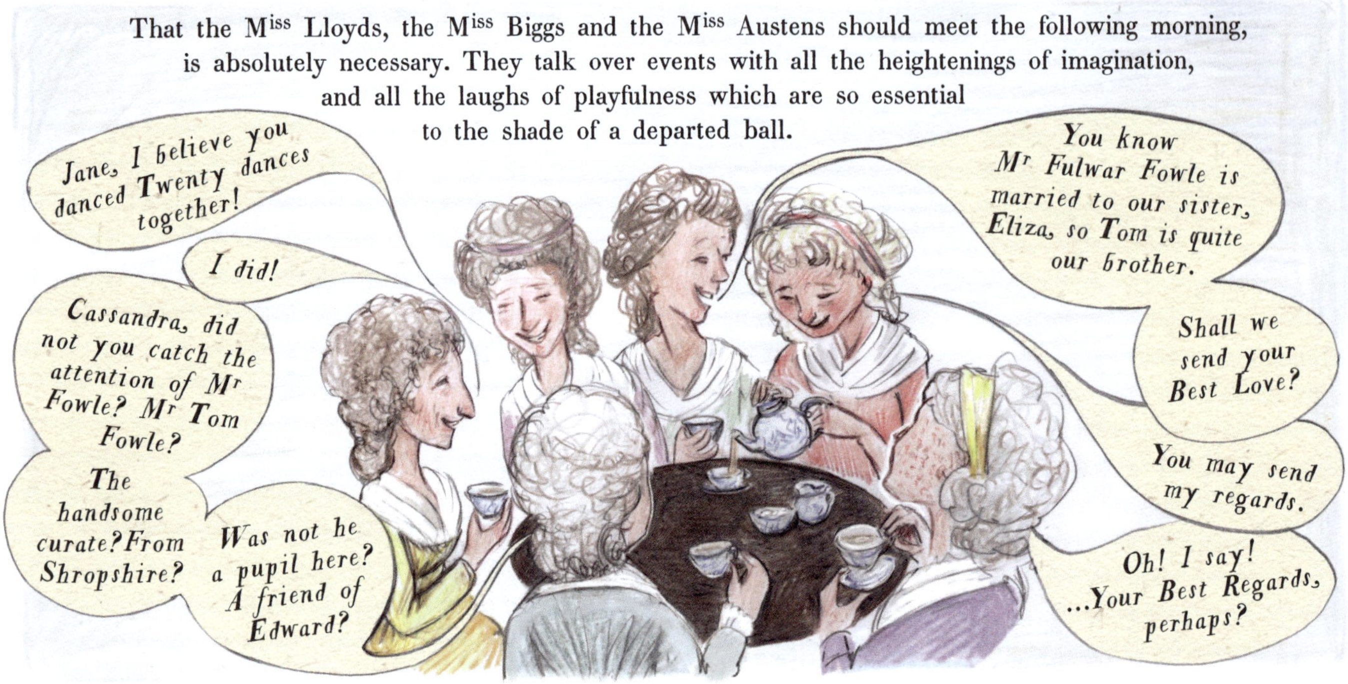
That the Miss Lloyds, the Miss Biggs and the Miss Austens should meet the following morning, is absolutely necessary. They talk over events with all the heightenings of imagination, and all the laughs of playfulness which are so essential to the shade of a departed ball.
Jane, I believe you danced Twenty dances together!
I did!
Cassandra, did not you catch the attention of Mr Fowle? Mr Tom Fowle?
The handsome curate? From Shropshire?
Was not he a pupil here? A friend of Edward?
You know Mr Fulwar Fowle is married to our sister, Eliza, so Tom is quite our brother.
Shall we send your Best Love?
You may send my regards.
Oh! I say! ...Your Best Regards, perhaps?

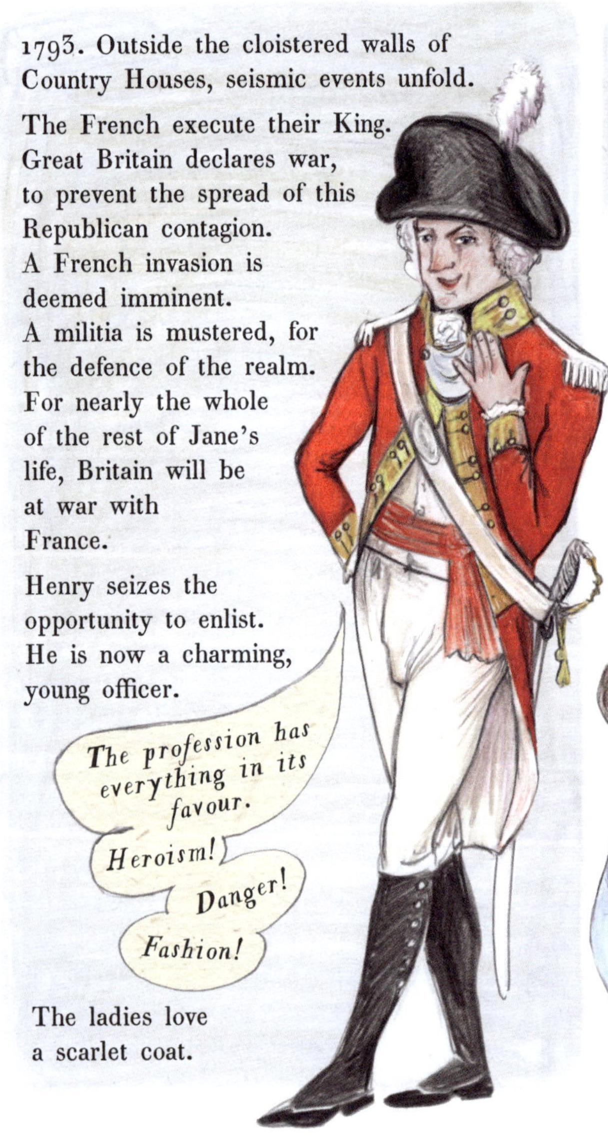
1793. Outside the cloistered walls of Country Houses, seismic events unfold.
The French execute their King. Great Britain declares war, to prevent the spread of this Republican contagion. A French invasion is deemed imminent. A militia is mustered, for the defence of the realm. For nearly the whole of the rest of Jane's life, Britain will be at war with France.
Henry seizes the opportunity to enlist. He is now a charming, young officer.
The profession has everything in its favour.
Heroism!
Danger!
Fashion!
The ladies love a scarlet coat.

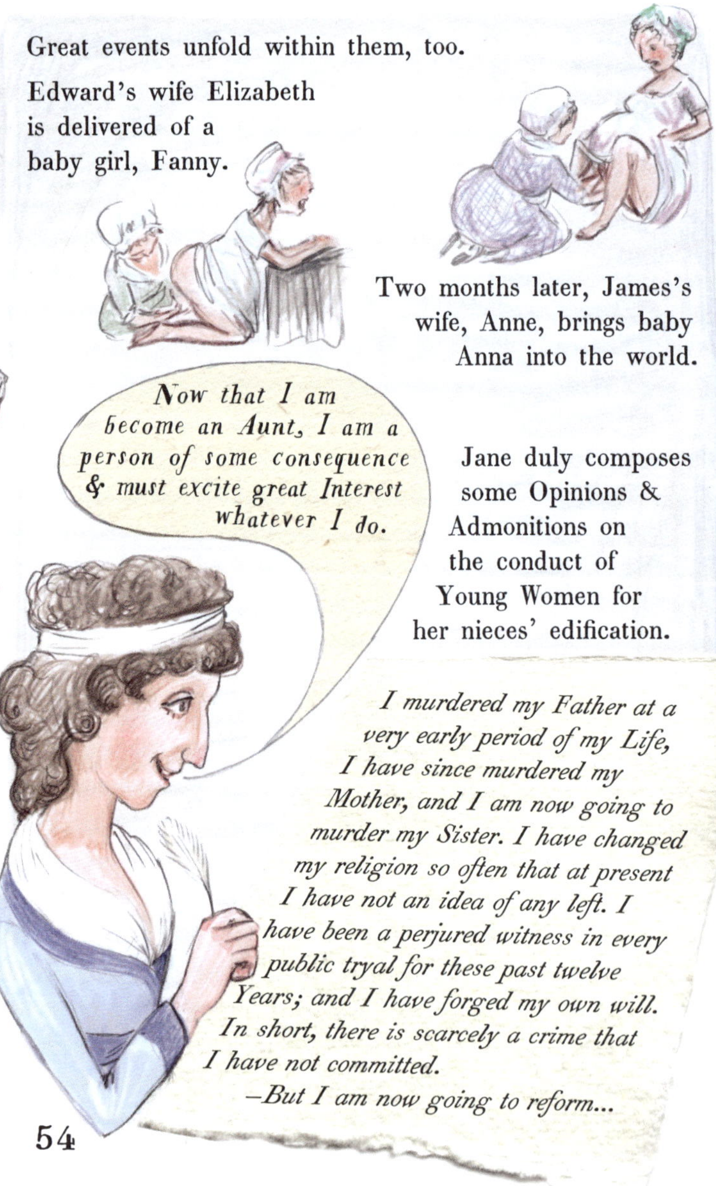
Great events unfold within them, too.
Edward's wife Elizabeth is delivered of a baby girl, Fanny.
Two months later, James's wife, Anne, brings baby Anna into the world.
Now that I am become an Aunt, I am a person of some consequence & must excite great Interest whatever I do.
Jane duly composes some Opinions & Admonitions on the conduct of Young Women for her nieces' edification.
I murdered my Father at a very early period of my Life, I have since murdered my Mother, and I am now going to murder my Sister. I have changed my religion so often that at present I have not an idea of any left. I have been a perjured witness in every public tryal for these past twelve Years; and I have forged my own will. In short, there is scarcely a crime that I have not committed.
–But I am now going to reform...

Autumn. At the grand age of 14, little Charles is off to sea on HMS *Daedelus*.

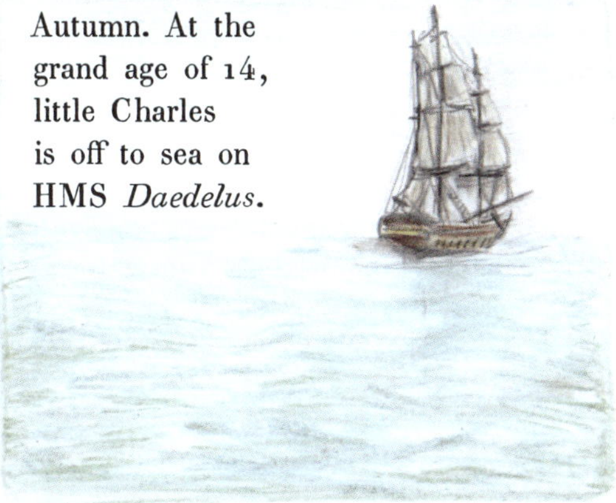

Winter. Frank returns! A very different person. No longer a boy — he is taller, stronger, more graceful in his lieutenant's uniform. Sunburnt and gregarious, he tells of storms, shipwrecks, deprivations, privateers.

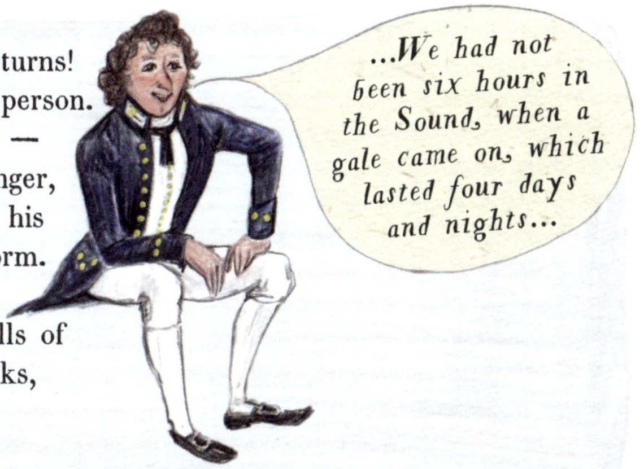
...We had not been six hours in the Sound, when a gale came on, which lasted four days and nights...

Eliza, in London, is greatly distressed to hear that Marie Antoinette is beheaded.

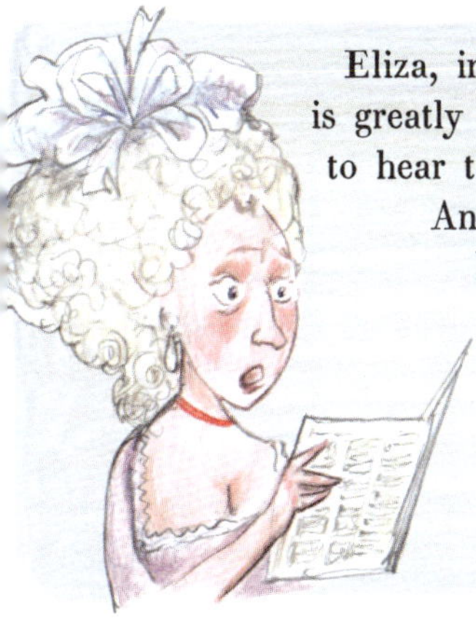

And far less perturbed to learn, in her morning paper the following March, that the Comte de Feuillide has been sent to the guillotine.

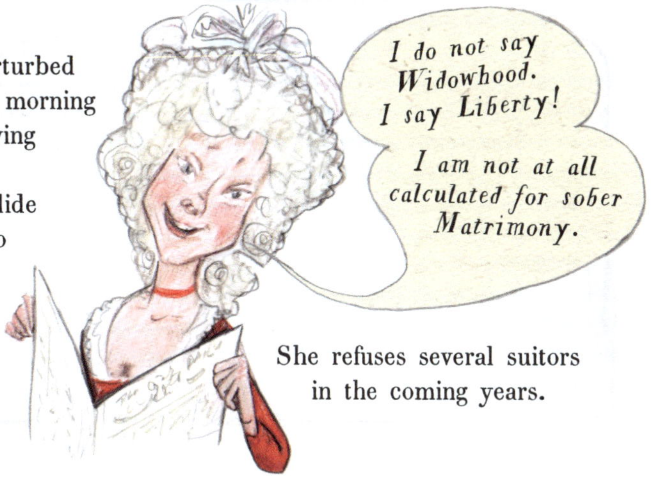
I do not say Widowhood. I say Liberty!
I am not at all calculated for sober Matrimony.

She refuses several suitors in the coming years.

Just as Eliza celebrates her disengagement, Cassandra has an announcement:

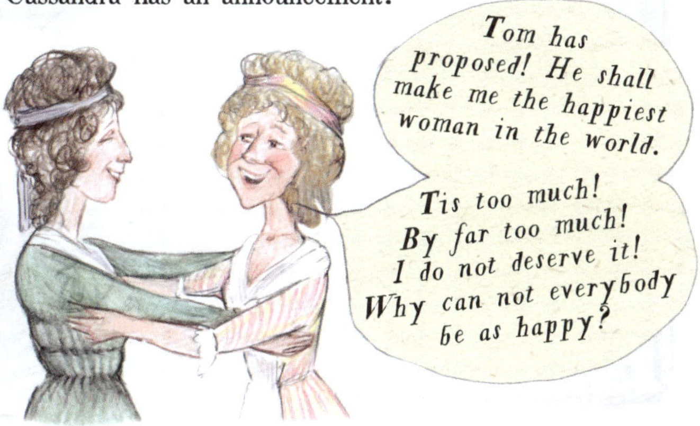
Tom has proposed! He shall make me the happiest woman in the world.
Tis too much! By far too much! I do not deserve it! Why can not everybody be as happy?

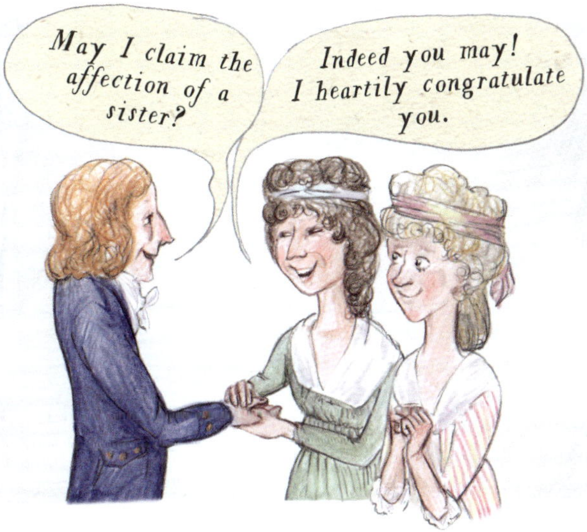
May I claim the affection of a sister?
Indeed you may! I heartily congratulate you.

There are practical considerations.

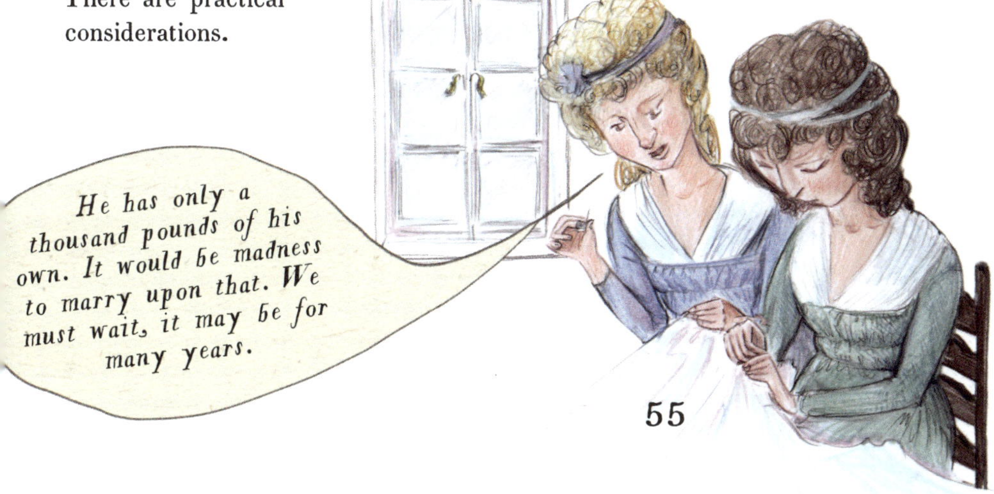
He has only a thousand pounds of his own. It would be madness to marry upon that. We must wait, it may be for many years.

Cassandra and Jane embark upon the enormous task of sewing her bridal wardrobe — linens, petticoats, pockets, tiny baby clothes for her life to come.

Why cannot everybody be as happy? The year is 1795. Jane is twenty.

It is Christmas, that festival which requires more than an ordinary share of private balls to proclaim its importance. Jane's fancy is caught by a most interesting young man. He has a pleasing countenance, and if not quite handsome, he is very near it.

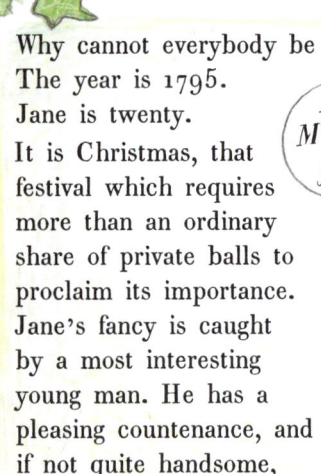

My nephew, Mr *Tom Lefroy, from Ireland.*

May I have the pleasure of this dance?

A pleasing flutter of the heart! With what sparkling eyes and ready motion she grants his request. She feels herself in high luck.

Imagine to yourself everything most profligate and shocking in the way of dancing and sitting down together! Jane listens to Mr Lefroy, and finding him irresistible, becomes so herself.

But alas! Tom has one, two, three, four, five older sisters.

...then Phoebe, Lucy, Catherine, Elizabeth and Sarah are all back home in Longford. My family have great ambitions for me...

A handsome young fellow like him may go paying compliments, but he knows he must marry for Money.

Jane laughs herself out of the situation.

Jane, I would have you be on your guard. Do not involve yourself, or endeavour to involve him, in an affection which the want of fortune would make so very imprudent.

If he had the fortune he ought to have, I should think you could not do better. But as it is, you must not let your fancy run away with you.

Dear Mrs *Lefroy, do not be uneasy. I do not care sixpence for him.*

Besides, he has a serious fault. His morning coat is a great deal too light.

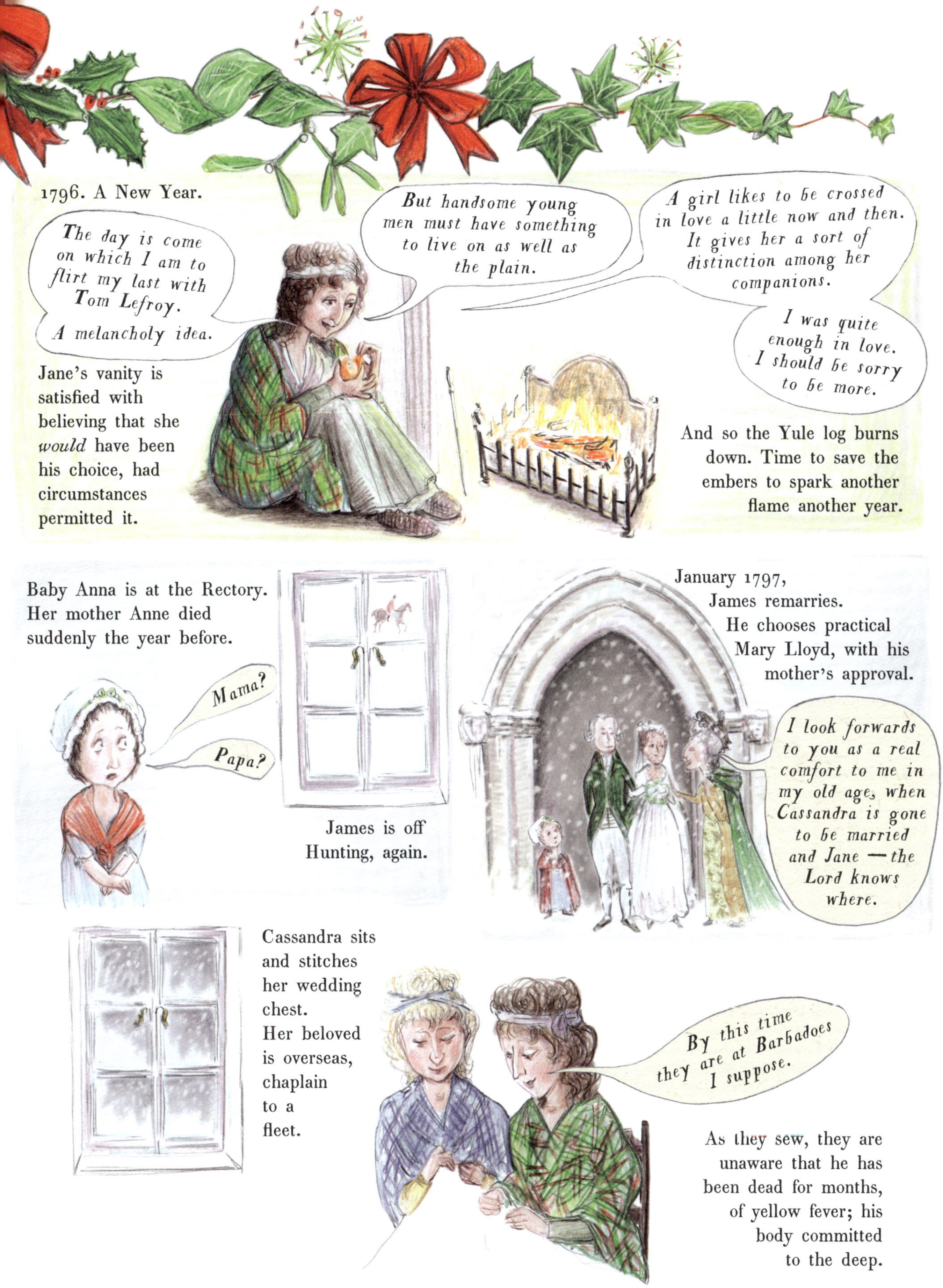
1796. A New Year.
The day is come on which I am to flirt my last with Tom Lefroy. A melancholy idea.
But handsome young men must have something to live on as well as the plain.
A girl likes to be crossed in love a little now and then. It gives her a sort of distinction among her companions.
I was quite enough in love. I should be sorry to be more.
Jane's vanity is satisfied with believing that she *would* have been his choice, had circumstances permitted it.
And so the Yule log burns down. Time to save the embers to spark another flame another year.
Baby Anna is at the Rectory. Her mother Anne died suddenly the year before.
Mama?
Papa?
James is off Hunting, again.
January 1797, James remarries. He chooses practical Mary Lloyd, with his mother's approval.
I look forwards to you as a real comfort to me in my old age, when Cassandra is gone to be married and Jane — the Lord knows where.
Cassandra sits and stitches her wedding chest. Her beloved is overseas, chaplain to a fleet.
By this time they are at Barbadoes I suppose.
As they sew, they are unaware that he has been dead for months, of yellow fever; his body committed to the deep.

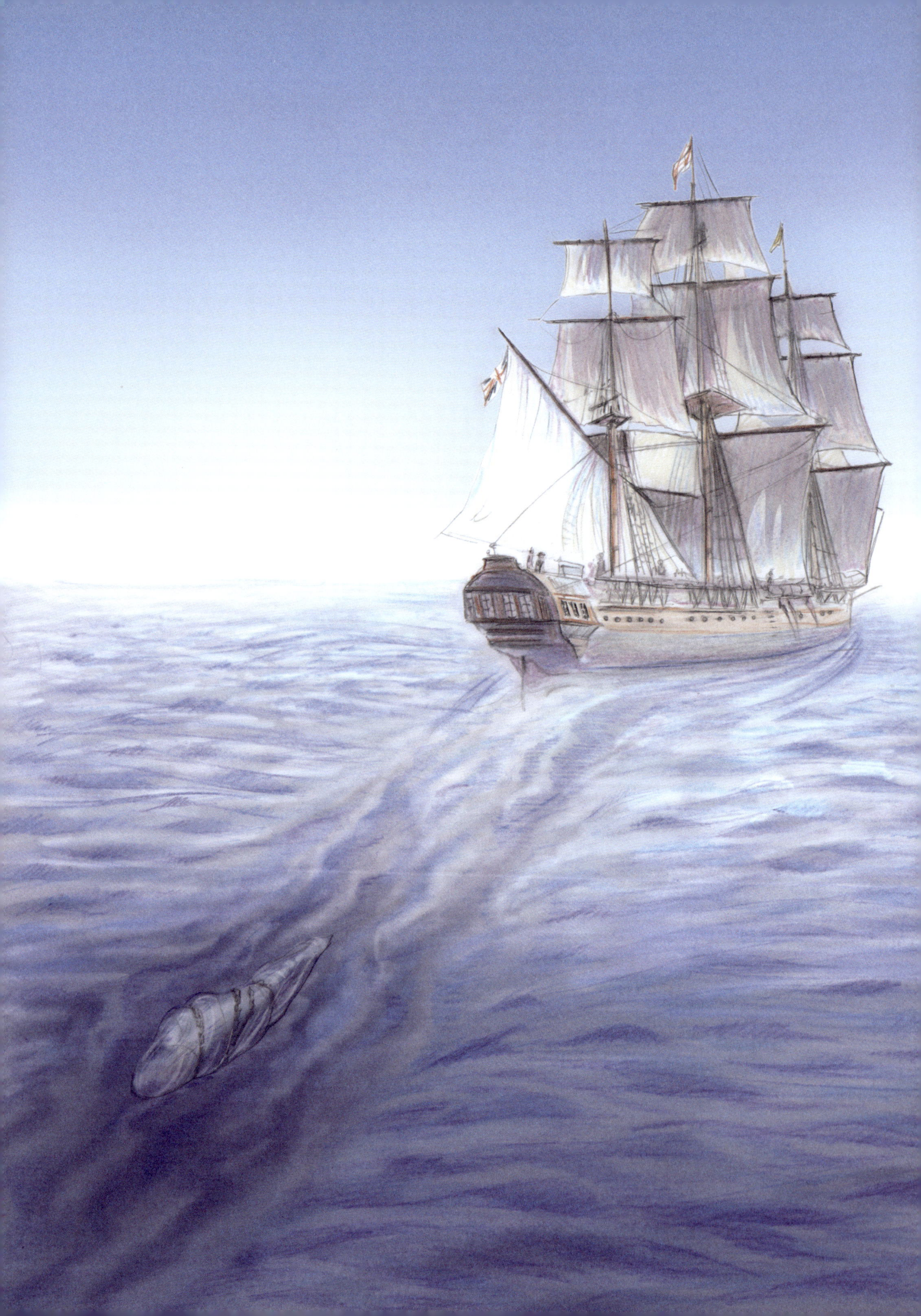

I WRITE ONLY FOR FAME

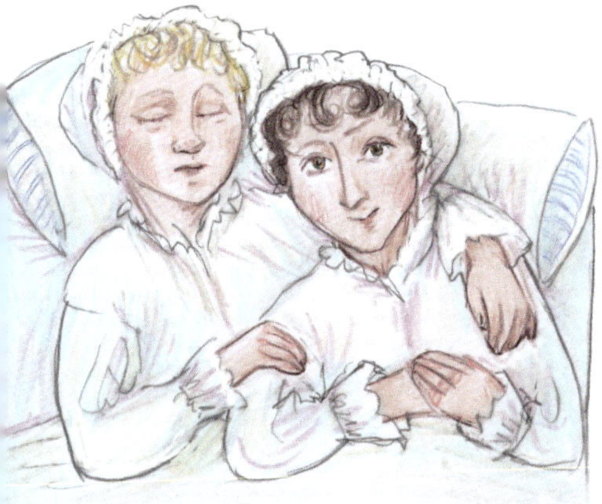

Let us rewind a little.
Because Jane has been busy.

She slips out from her sister's sleeping embrace and rises early. The household is still quiet. The fire is not yet made. She shrugs her feet into stout slippers and gathers a shawl around her.

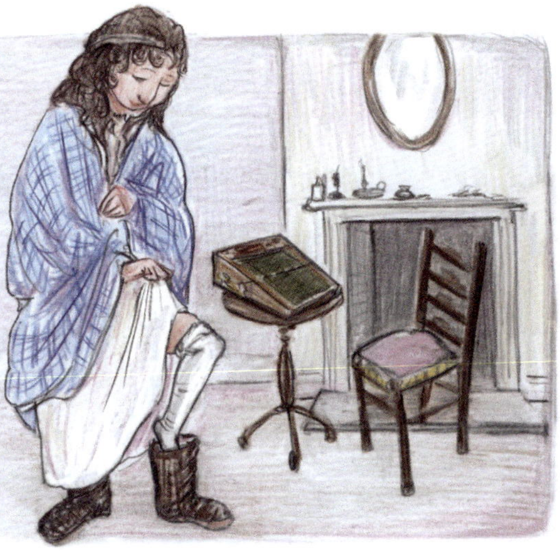

Before her is her laptop, a mahogany writing box with a smooth sloping surface.
She slides her quill out of its long sleek drawer, and tops up the inkwell with oak gall ink.

What is Jane writing?

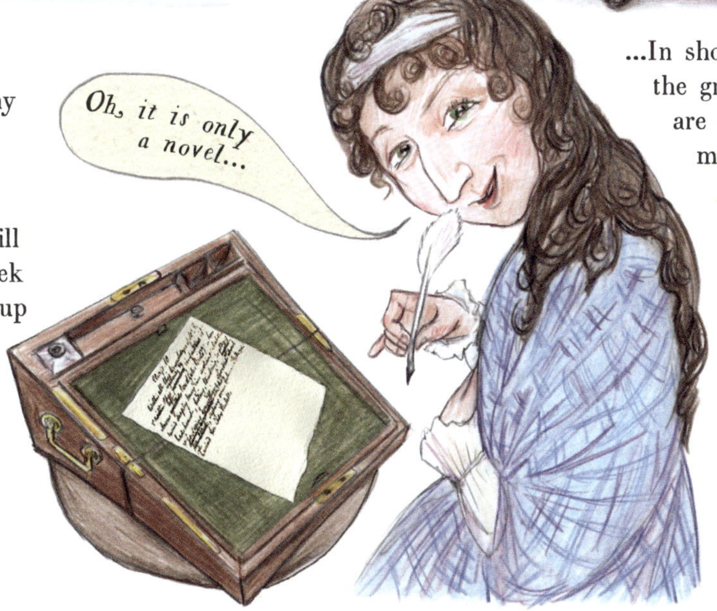
Oh, it is only a novel...

...In short, only some work in which the greatest powers of the mind are displayed, in which the most thorough knowledge of human nature, the happiest delineation of its varieties, the liveliest effusions of wit and humour, are conveyed to the world in the best-chosen language.

Jane's work has altered, extended, achieved more focus, more scope, more range. She has moved from the ridiculous to the sublime.

Her first creation is *Lady Susan*. She uses a series of letters to sketch a scheming, duplicitous anti-heroine — an extended meditation on the power of the Coquette.

The work is flawed. Lady Susan is too forthright in her machinations.
Jane is undeterred. She throws together a hasty Conclusion and moves on.

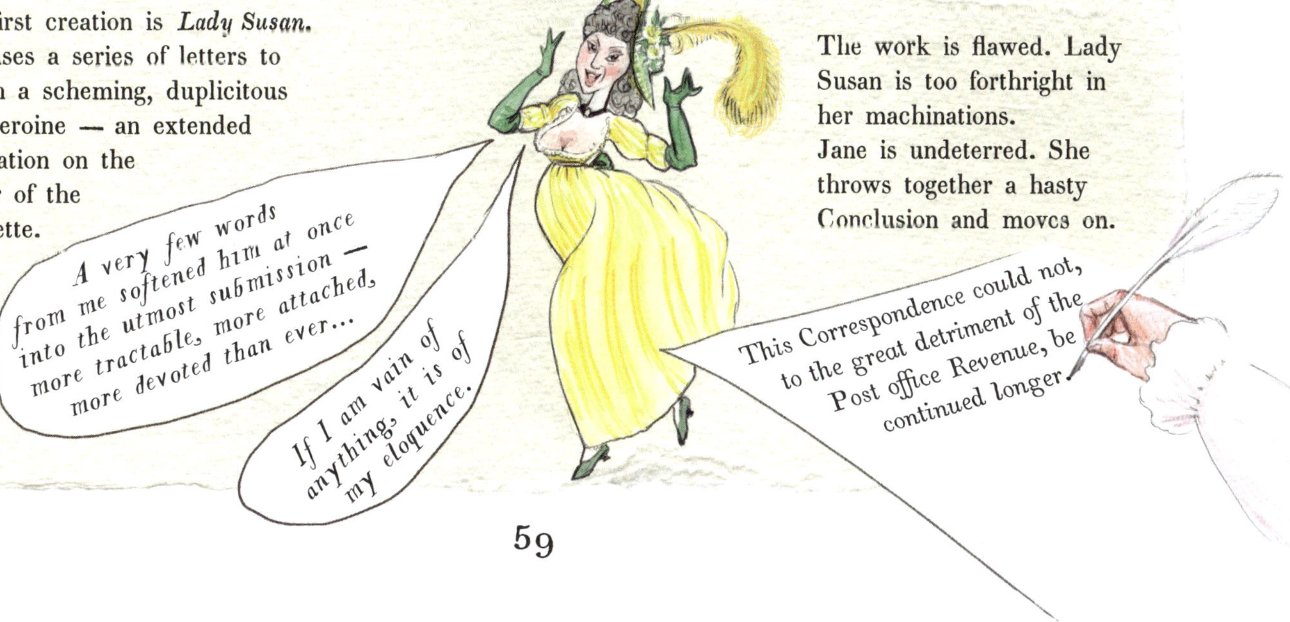
A very few words from me softened him at once into the utmost submission — more tractable, more attached, more devoted than ever...
If I am vain of anything, it is of my eloquence.
This Correspondence could not, to the great detriment of the Post office Revenue, be continued longer.

With her next work, ***Elinor and Marianne***, Jane hits upon the format that she will revisit and refine throughout her work.

She collects her People:
There shall be

Some sisters...

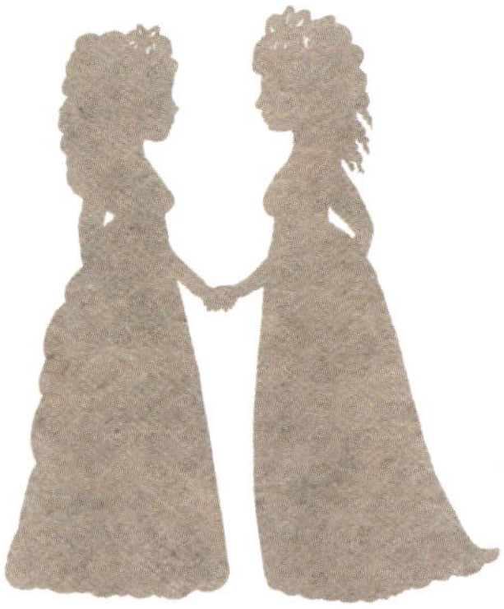

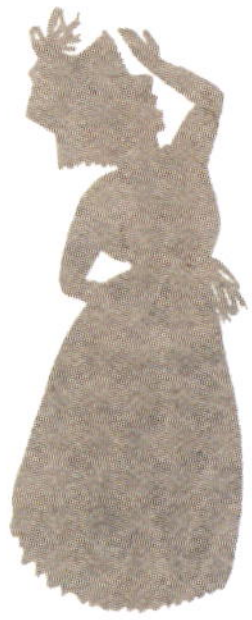

An absent or ineffectual mother...

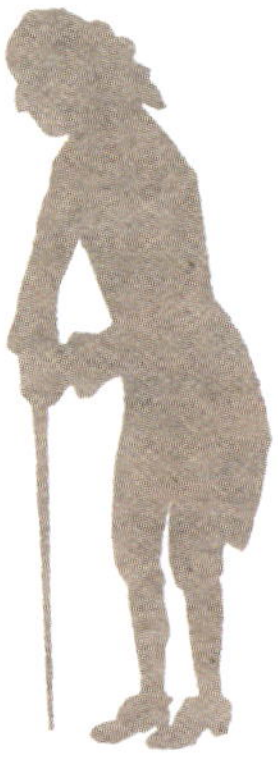

A well-meaning but misguided father...

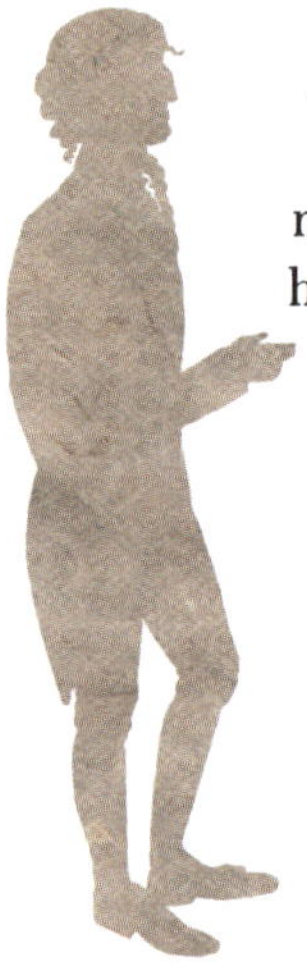

A hero, who is not what he seems at first sight...

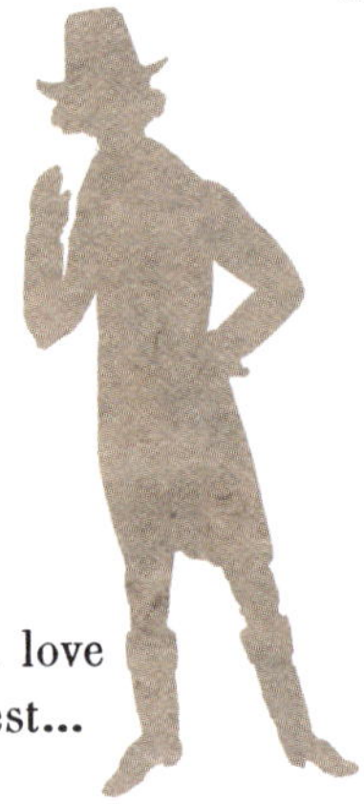

A rival love interest...

And three or four other families besides.

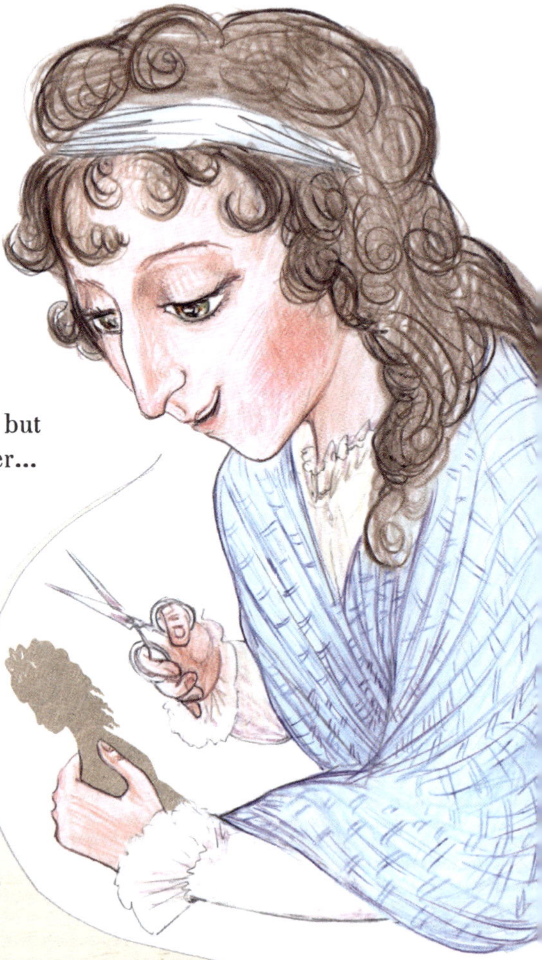

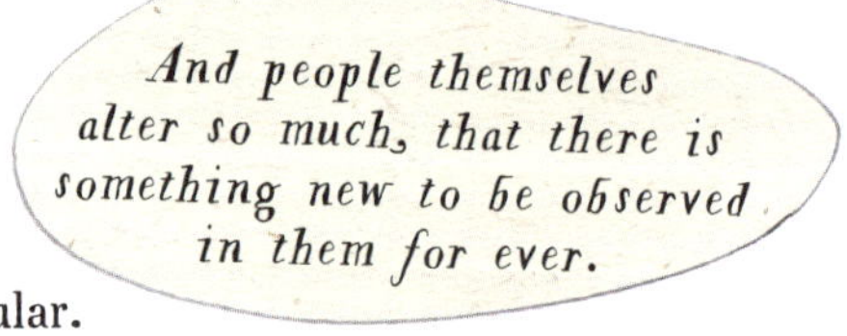
And people themselves alter so much, that there is something new to be observed in them for ever.

She then arranges them in a Country Village. An unusual choice, perhaps, for a dramatist, as a country neighbourhood consists in a very confined and unvarying society. But Jane's genius lies in the Particular.

At first, this novel too is written as letters between the two sisters.

But Jane hits a hurdle. Her characters *speak* to her. She hears their conversation and her hand rushes to trap the words upon the page. Credulity is strained when the letter writer minutely recounts speeches which passed some time before.

Inspired by Fanny Burney's latest, ***Camilla***, Jane entirely rewrites the story from a third person perspective.

And a delightful ironic dissonance emerges in that narrative voice. It is something quite new.

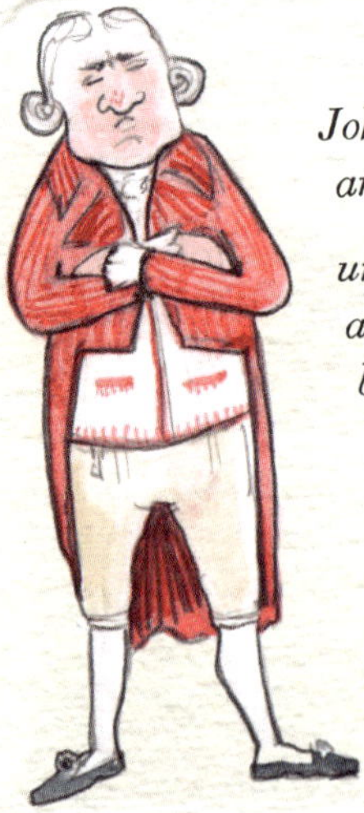

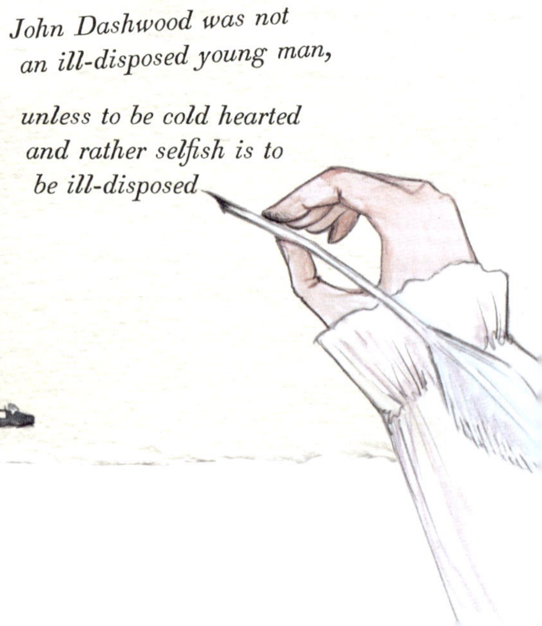
John Dashwood was not an ill-disposed young man,
unless to be cold hearted and rather selfish is to be ill-disposed

Elinor and Marianne (not its final title) is an imperfect novel. Jane has a clunky tendency to tell rather than show who her characters are. She is writing in reaction to the craze of the "novel of sentiment," so it carries a didactic moral on the importance of suppression of emotion: Elinor Dashwood's self-governance is contrasted with the pathos of her sister Marianne.

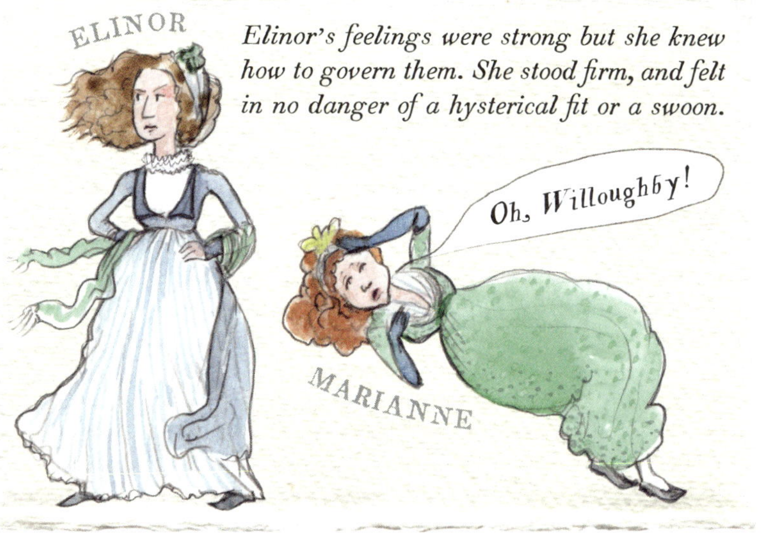
ELINOR
Elinor's feelings were strong but she knew how to govern them. She stood firm, and felt in no danger of a hysterical fit or a swoon.
Oh, Willoughby!
MARIANNE

But it shows enough of Jane's genius to set it apart from anything that has been written before. The perils that her heroines endure are ordinary, and believable, and all the more affecting for that.

At the outset of the novel, the Dashwood sisters' father dies, his estate is entailed, and they are left reliant on the generosity of John, their rich, older half-brother, and his wife...

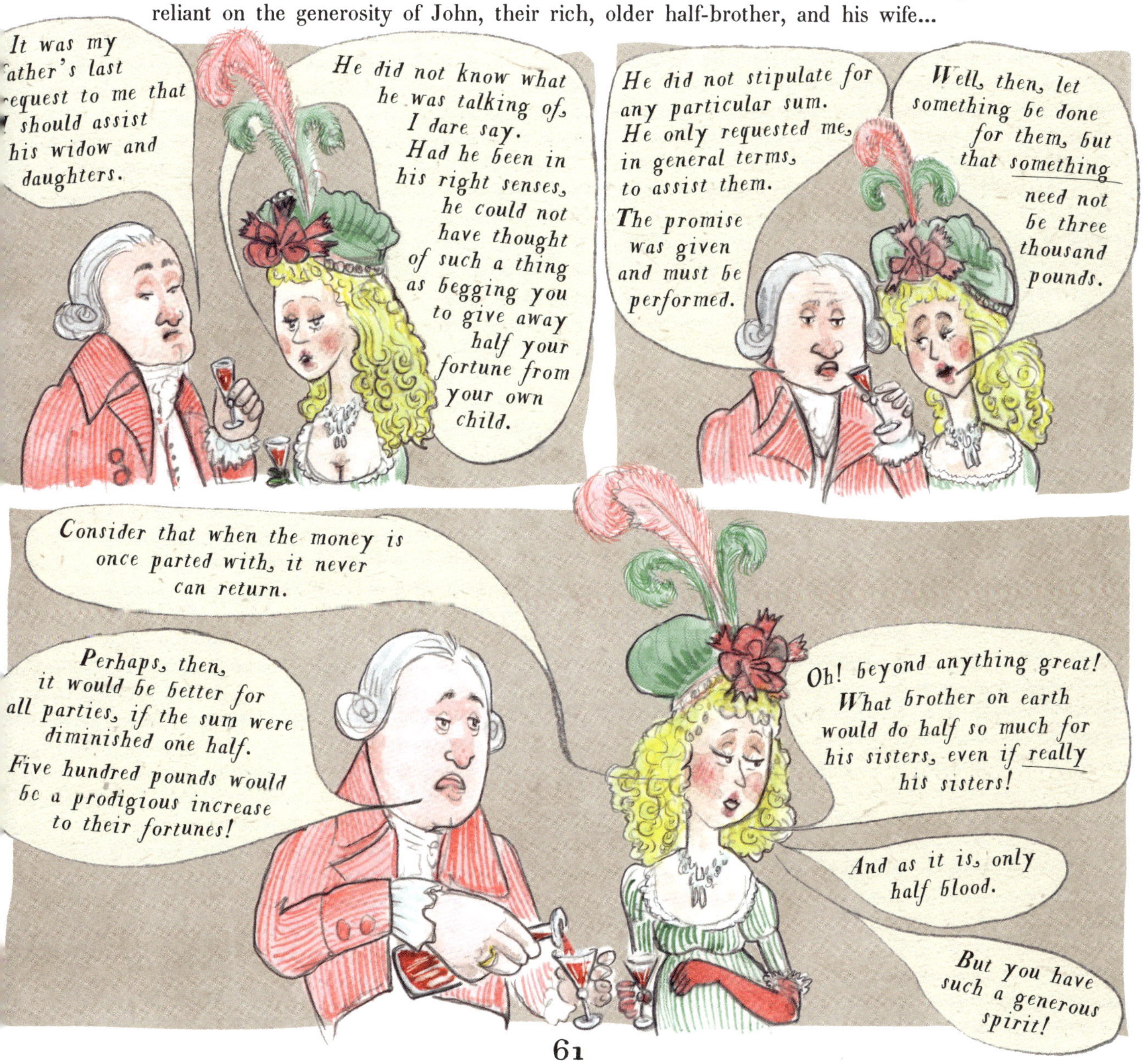
It was my ather's last equest to me that should assist his widow and daughters.
He did not know what he was talking of, I dare say. Had he been in his right senses, he could not have thought of such a thing as begging you to give away half your fortune from your own child.
He did not stipulate for any particular sum. He only requested me, in general terms, to assist them.
The promise was given and must be performed.
Well, then, let something be done for them, but that something need not be three thousand pounds.
Consider that when the money is once parted with, it never can return.
Perhaps, then, it would be better for all parties, if the sum were diminished one half. Five hundred pounds would be a prodigious increase to their fortunes!
Oh! beyond anything great! What brother on earth would do half so much for his sisters, even if really his sisters!
And as it is, only half blood.
But you have such a generous spirit!

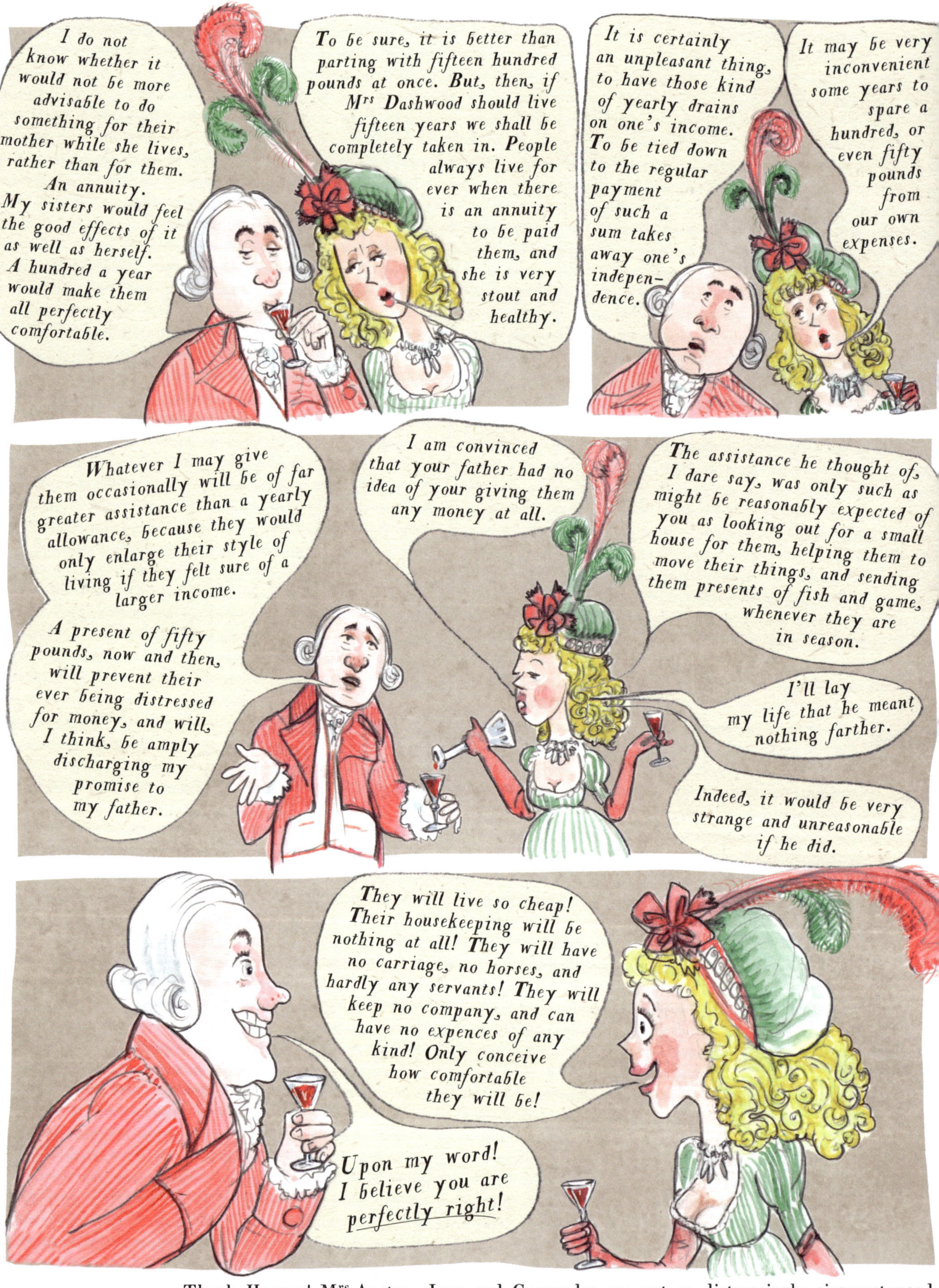
I do not know whether it would not be more advisable to do something for their mother while she lives, rather than for them. An annuity. My sisters would feel the good effects of it as well as herself. A hundred a year would make them all perfectly comfortable.
To be sure, it is better than parting with fifteen hundred pounds at once. But, then, if Mrs Dashwood should live fifteen years we shall be completely taken in. People always live for ever when there is an annuity to be paid them, and she is very stout and healthy.
It is certainly an unpleasant thing, to have those kind of yearly drains on one's income. To be tied down to the regular payment of such a sum takes away one's indepen-dence.
It may be very inconvenient some years to spare a hundred, or even fifty pounds from our own expenses.
Whatever I may give them occasionally will be of far greater assistance than a yearly allowance, because they would only enlarge their style of living if they felt sure of a larger income.
A present of fifty pounds, now and then, will prevent their ever being distressed for money, and will, I think, be amply discharging my promise to my father.
I am convinced that your father had no idea of your giving them any money at all.
The assistance he thought of, I dare say, was only such as might be reasonably expected of you as looking out for a small house for them, helping them to move their things, and sending them presents of fish and game, whenever they are in season.
I'll lay my life that he meant nothing farther.
Indeed, it would be very strange and unreasonable if he did.
They will live so cheap! Their housekeeping will be nothing at all! They will have no carriage, no horses, and hardly any servants! They will keep no company, and can have no expences of any kind! Only conceive how comfortable they will be!
Upon my word! I believe you are perfectly right!

Thank Heaven! Mrs Austen, Jane and Cassandra are not so distressingly circumstanced.

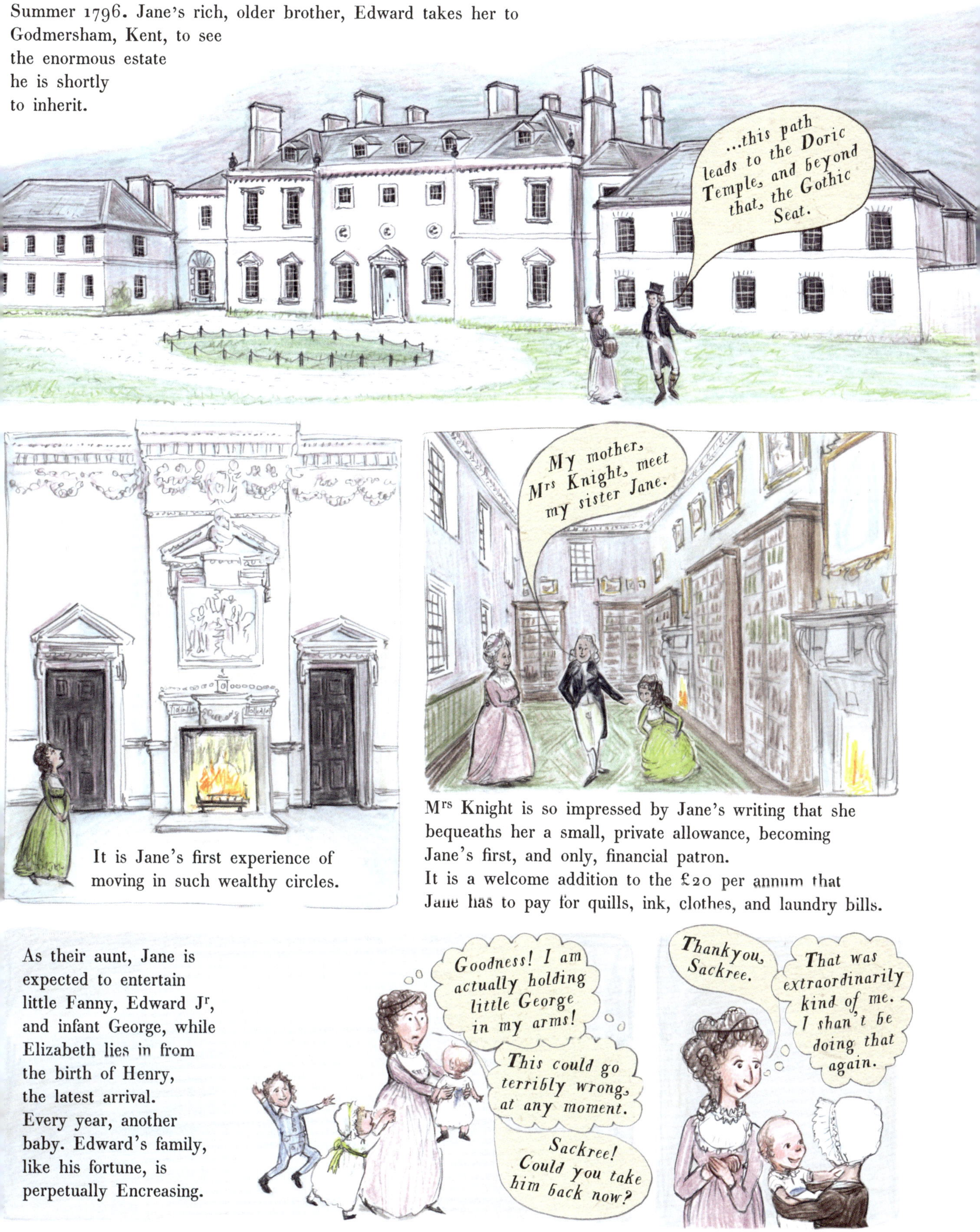
Summer 1796. Jane's rich, older brother, Edward takes her to Godmersham, Kent, to see the enormous estate he is shortly to inherit.
...this path leads to the Doric Temple, and beyond that, the Gothic Seat.
It is Jane's first experience of moving in such wealthy circles.
My mother, Mrs Knight, meet my sister Jane.
Mrs Knight is so impressed by Jane's writing that she bequeaths her a small, private allowance, becoming Jane's first, and only, financial patron.
It is a welcome addition to the £20 per annum that Jane has to pay for quills, ink, clothes, and laundry bills.
As their aunt, Jane is expected to entertain little Fanny, Edward Jr, and infant George, while Elizabeth lies in from the birth of Henry, the latest arrival.
Every year, another baby. Edward's family, like his fortune, is perpetually Encreasing.
Goodness! I am actually holding little George in my arms!
This could go terribly wrong, at any moment.
Sackree! Could you take him back now?
Thankyou, Sackree.
That was extraordinarily kind of me. I shan't be doing that again.

Jane's next novel is about class. She takes a girl of moderate means, invents for her an enormously wealthy hero, and declares them to be equal. In its startlingly original opening lines, Austen makes a playful poke at the financial ramifications of love and romance.

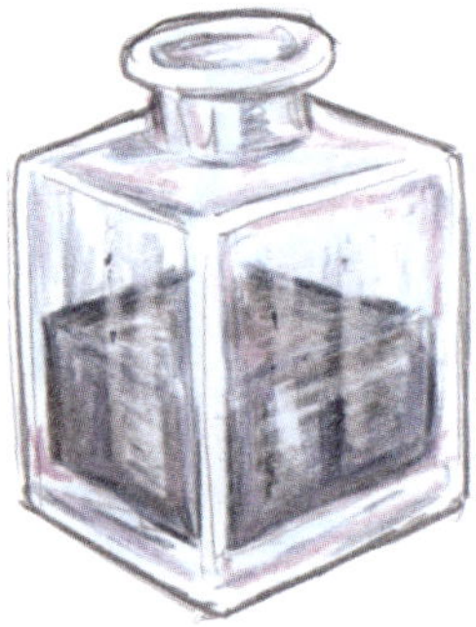

It is a truth universally acknowledged, that a single man in possession of a good fortune must be in want of a wife.

However little known the feelings or views of such a man may be on his first entering a neighbourhood, this truth is so well fixed in the minds of the surrounding families, that he is considered as the rightful property of some one or other of their daughters.

And immediately, the reader is transported to the Bennet family's breakfast table, with conversation in full flow...

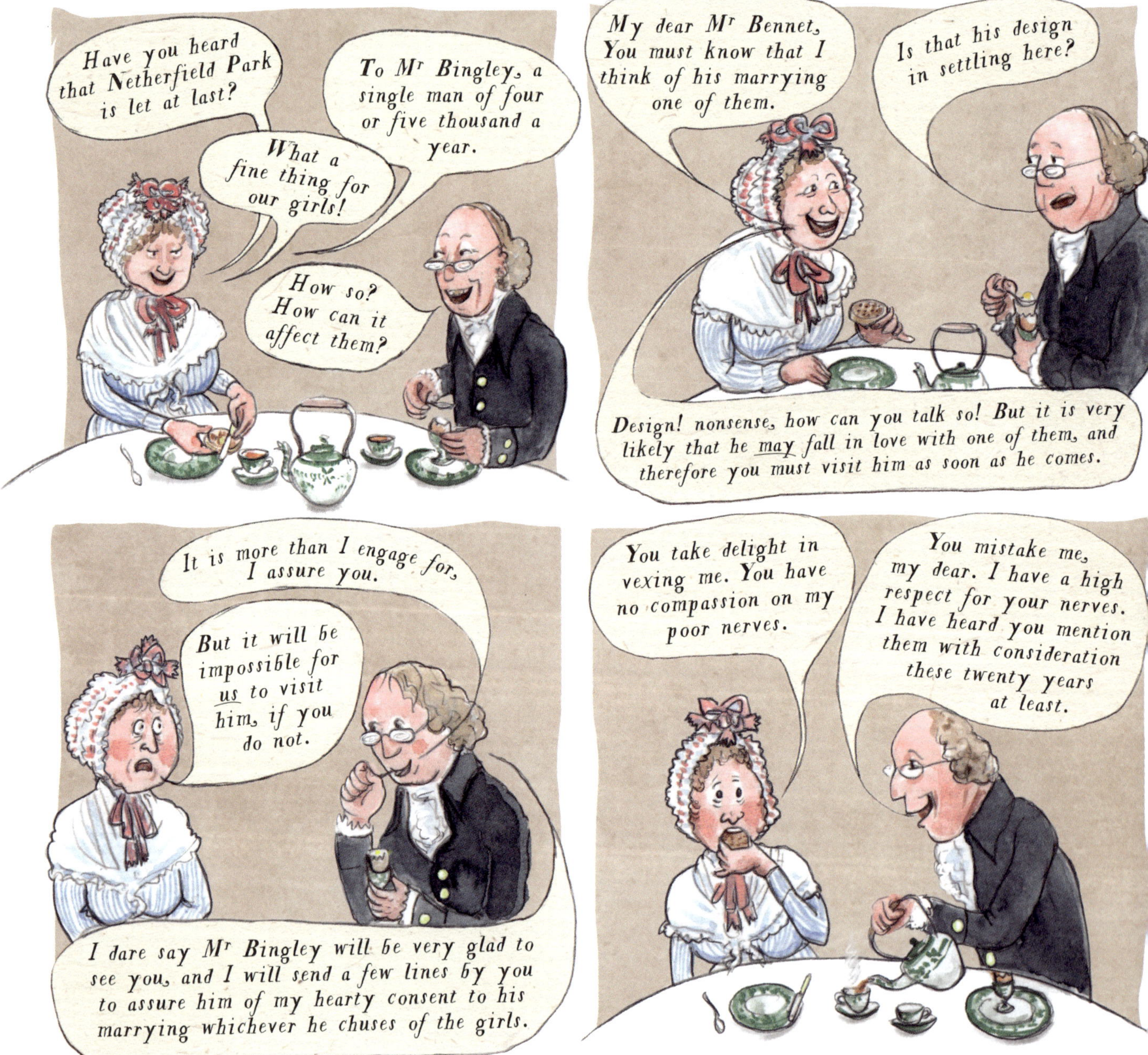

Have you heard that Netherfield Park is let at last?
To Mr Bingley, a single man of four or five thousand a year.
What a fine thing for our girls!
How so? How can it affect them?
My dear Mr Bennet, You must know that I think of his marrying one of them.
Is that his design in settling here?
Design! nonsense, how can you talk so! But it is very likely that he may fall in love with one of them, and therefore you must visit him as soon as he comes.
It is more than I engage for, I assure you.
But it will be impossible for us to visit him, if you do not.
I dare say Mr Bingley will be very glad to see you, and I will send a few lines by you to assure him of my hearty consent to his marrying whichever he chuses of the girls.
You take delight in vexing me. You have no compassion on my poor nerves.
You mistake me, my dear. I have a high respect for your nerves. I have heard you mention them with consideration these twenty years at least.

It is also a novel about the power of language. The heroine, Elizabeth Bennet, enchants the eligible but reserved Mr Darcy, not with beauty, modesty or riches, but with her sparkling eyes, confidence, and wit.

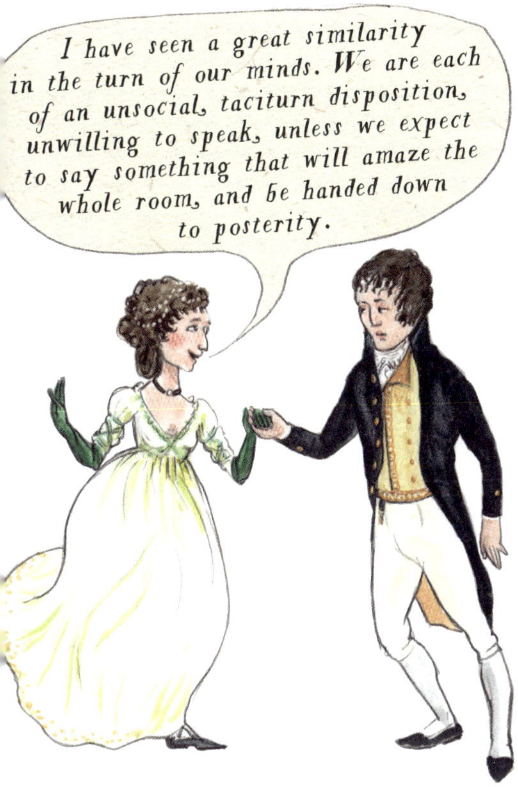
I have seen a great similarity in the turn of our minds. We are each of an unsocial, taciturn disposition, unwilling to speak, unless we expect to say something that will amaze the whole room, and be handed down to posterity.

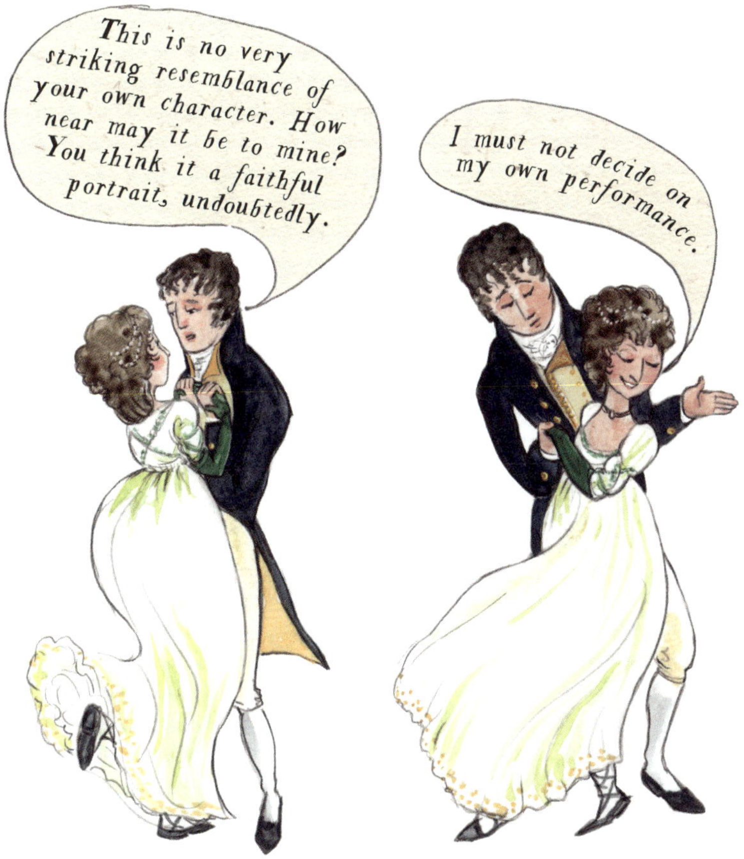
This is no very striking resemblance of your own character. How near may it be to mine? You think it a faithful portrait, undoubtedly.
I must not decide on my own performance.

In a carefully plotted, climactic central scene, Lizzy Bennet responds to Darcy's surprise proposal with an outright rejection:

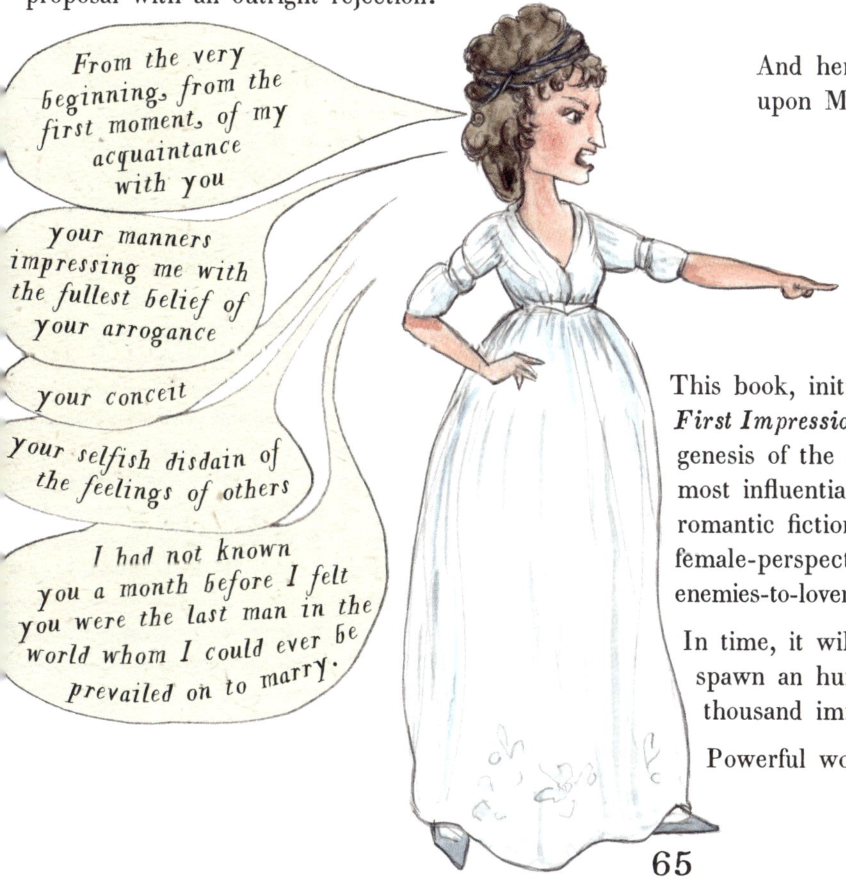
From the very beginning, from the first moment, of my acquaintance with you
your manners impressing me with the fullest belief of your arrogance
your conceit
your selfish disdain of the feelings of others
I had not known you a month before I felt you were the last man in the world whom I could ever be prevailed on to marry.

And her speech works its magic upon Mr Darcy.

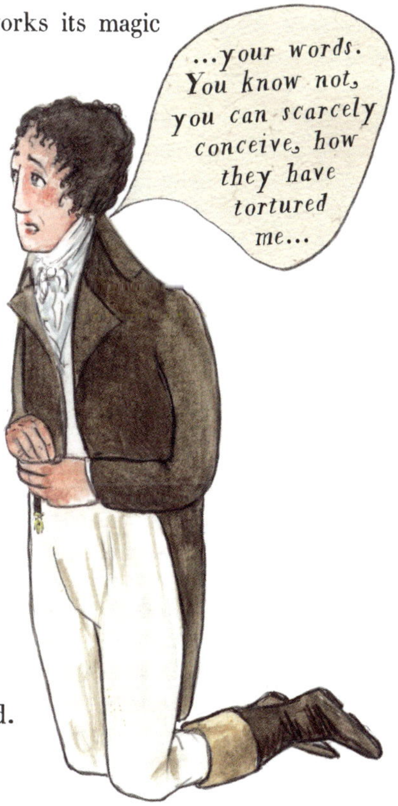
...your words. You know not, you can scarcely conceive, how they have tortured me...

This book, initially called *First Impressions*, is the genesis of the single most influential trope in romantic fiction: the female-perspective, enemies-to-lovers story.

In time, it will spawn an hundred thousand imitations.

Powerful words, indeed.

Jane sprinkles the narrative with fully fleshed comedic characters; the pompous cousin, the wittily bickering parents, the silly younger sisters. Her friends and family clamour for installments.

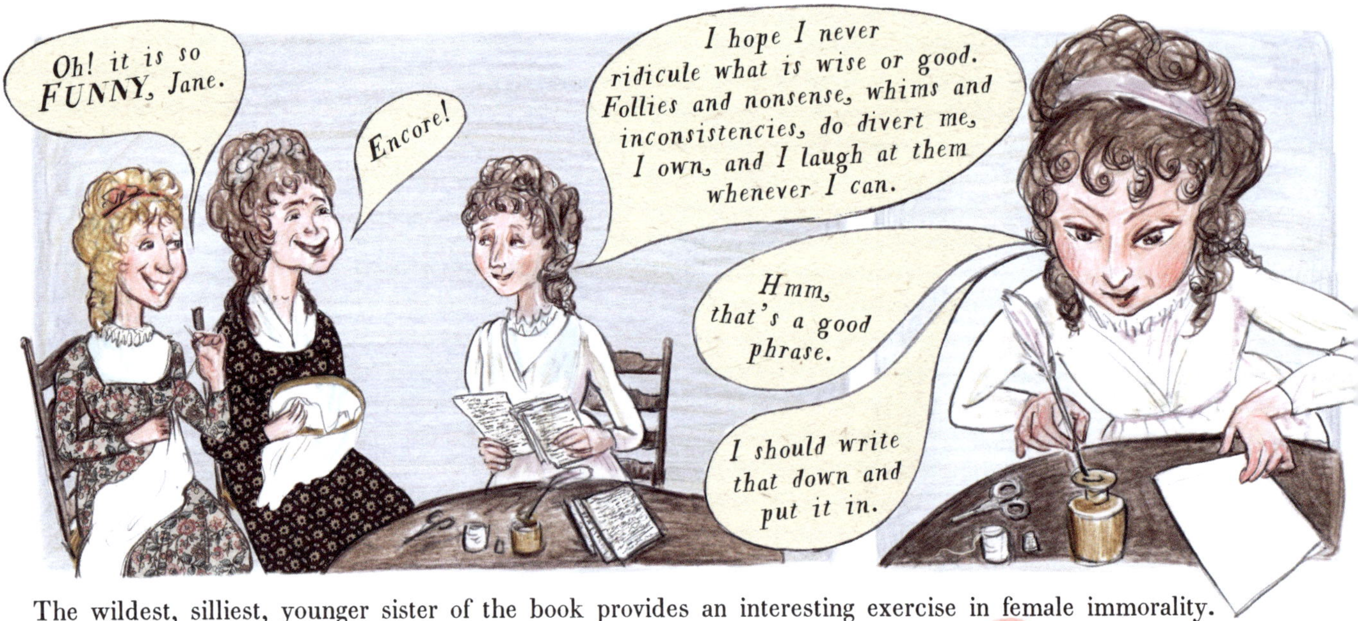

Oh! it is so FUNNY, Jane.
Encore!
I hope I never ridicule what is wise or good. Follies and nonsense, whims and inconsistencies, do divert me, I own, and I laugh at them whenever I can.
Hmm, that's a good phrase.
I should write that down and put it in.

The wildest, silliest, younger sister of the book provides an interesting exercise in female immorality. We watch Lydia's development from

...a stout, well-grown girl of fifteen, with high animal spirits and a sort of natural self-consequence...

under the influence of parental misguidance, and a surfeit of army officers, into

...the most determined flirt that ever made herself and her family ridiculous.

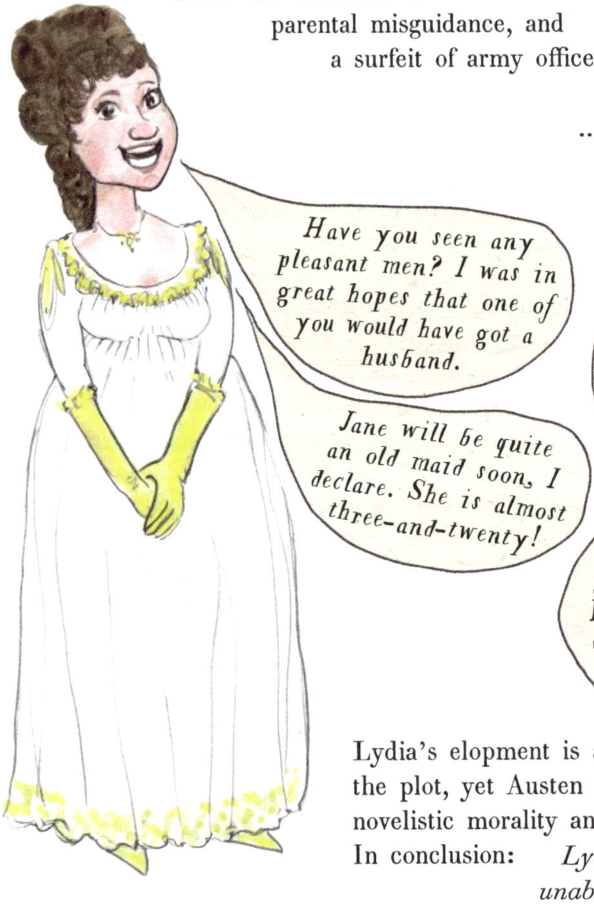

Have you seen any pleasant men? I was in great hopes that one of you would have got a husband.
Jane will be quite an old maid soon, I declare. She is almost three-and-twenty!

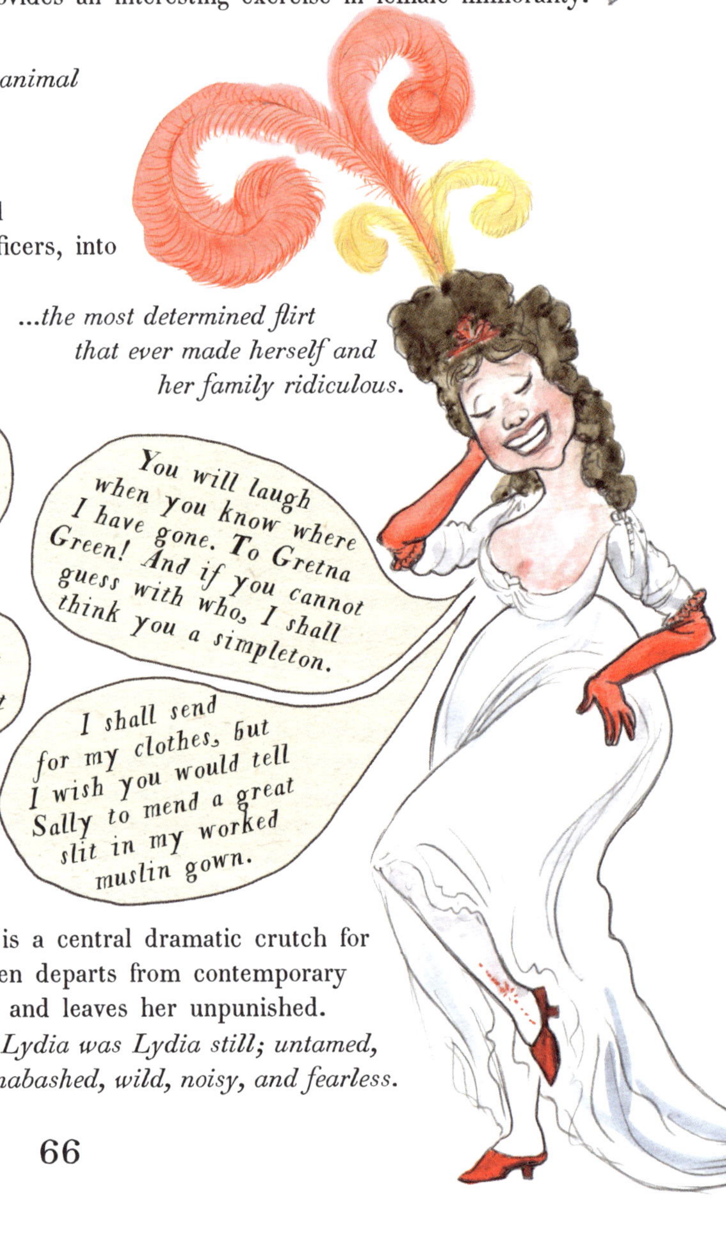

You will laugh when you know where I have gone. To Gretna Green! And if you cannot guess with who, I shall think you a simpleton.
I shall send for my clothes, but I wish you would tell Sally to mend a great slit in my worked muslin gown.

Lydia's elopment is a central dramatic crutch for the plot, yet Austen departs from contemporary novelistic morality and leaves her unpunished.

In conclusion: *Lydia was Lydia still; untamed, unabashed, wild, noisy, and fearless.*

And Elizabeth is Austen's most straightforwardly self-assured heroine. Towards the end of the book, she is confronted by lady Catherine de Bourgh, a person who demands deference to her wealth, her age, and her caste.

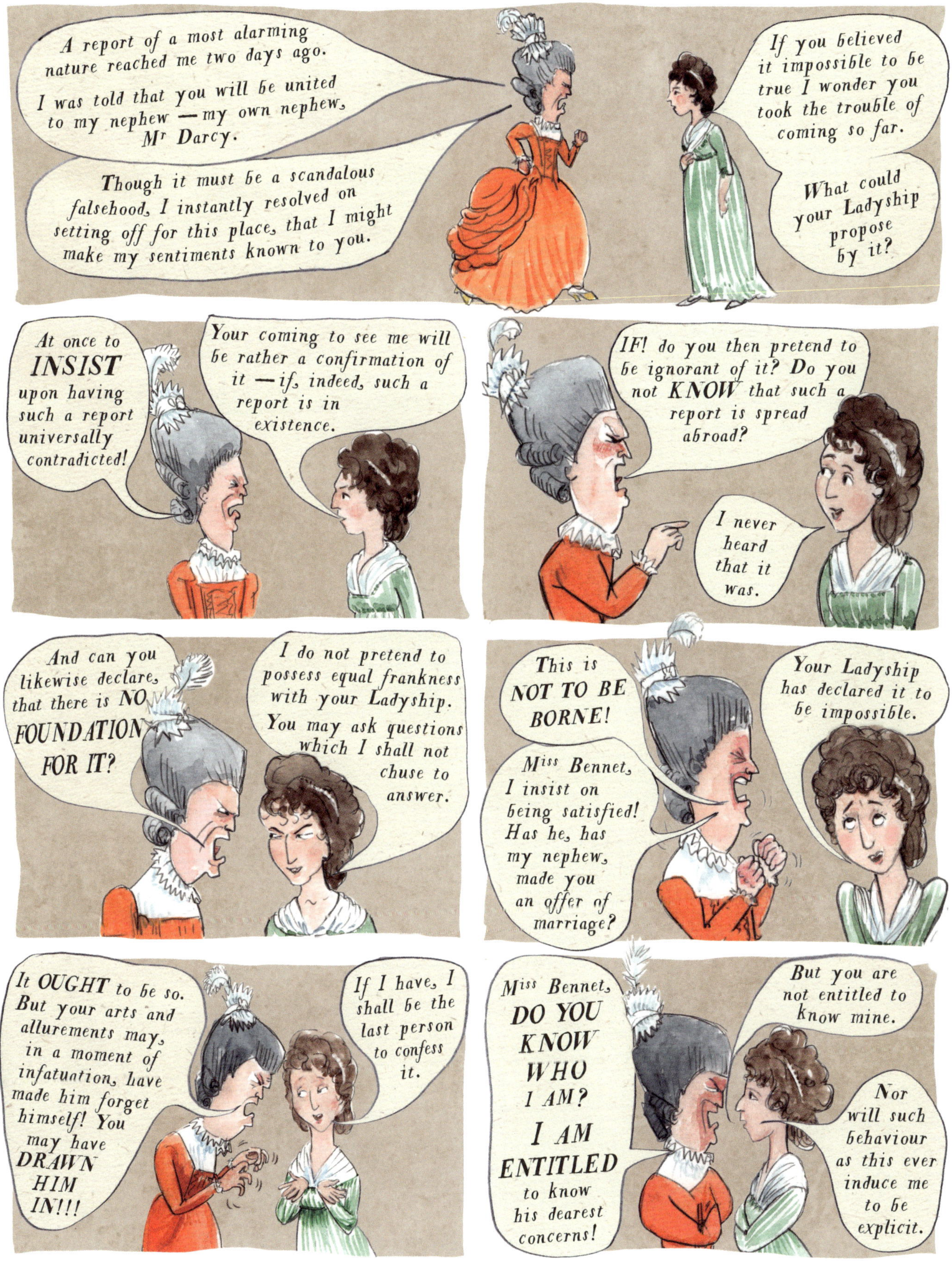
A report of a most alarming nature reached me two days ago.
I was told that you will be united to my nephew — my own nephew, Mr Darcy.
Though it must be a scandalous falsehood, I instantly resolved on setting off for this place, that I might make my sentiments known to you.
If you believed it impossible to be true I wonder you took the trouble of coming so far.
What could your Ladyship propose by it?
At once to INSIST upon having such a report universally contradicted!
Your coming to see me will be rather a confirmation of it — if, indeed, such a report is in existence.
IF! do you then pretend to be ignorant of it? Do you not KNOW that such a report is spread abroad?
I never heard that it was.
And can you likewise declare, that there is NO FOUNDATION FOR IT?
I do not pretend to possess equal frankness with your Ladyship. You may ask questions which I shall not chuse to answer.
This is NOT TO BE BORNE!
Miss Bennet, I insist on being satisfied! Has he, has my nephew, made you an offer of marriage?
Your Ladyship has declared it to be impossible.
It OUGHT to be so. But your arts and allurements may, in a moment of infatuation, have made him forget himself! You may have DRAWN HIM IN!!!
If I have, I shall be the last person to confess it.
Miss Bennet, DO YOU KNOW WHO I AM? I AM ENTITLED to know his dearest concerns!
But you are not entitled to know mine.
Nor will such behaviour as this ever induce me to be explicit.

August 1797. The work is finished! Reverend Austen enthusiastically writes to the London publisher Thomas Cadell, offering to pay for publication out of his own pocket...

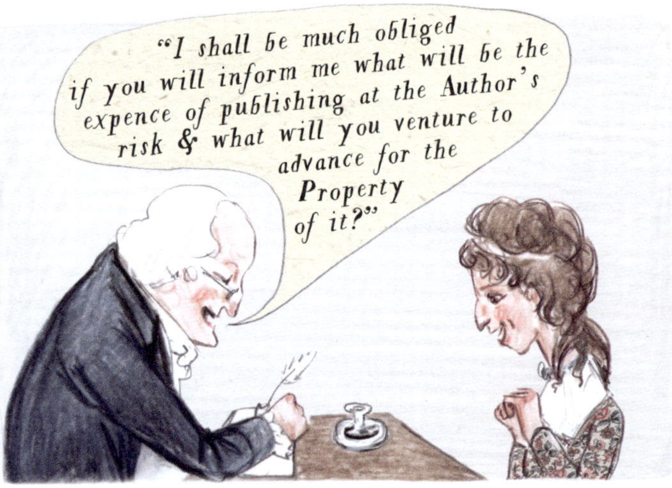

"I shall be much obliged if you will inform me what will be the expence of publishing at the Author's risk & what will you venture to advance for the Property of it?"

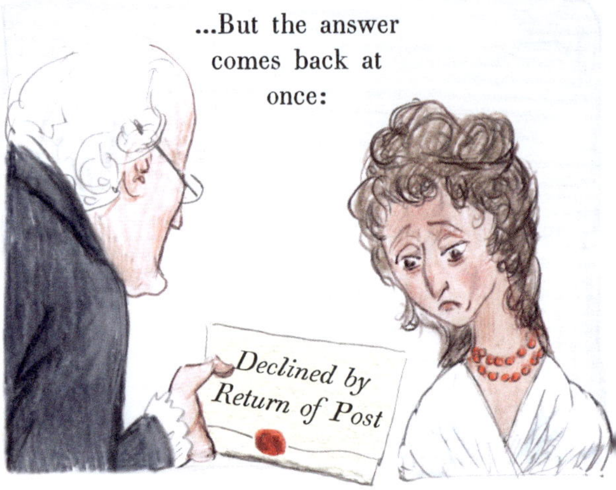

...But the answer comes back at once:
Declined by Return of Post

Jane has no perspective on her work, no resilience in the face of rejection. The verdict has been pronounced: "inadequate." *First Impressions* is set aside.

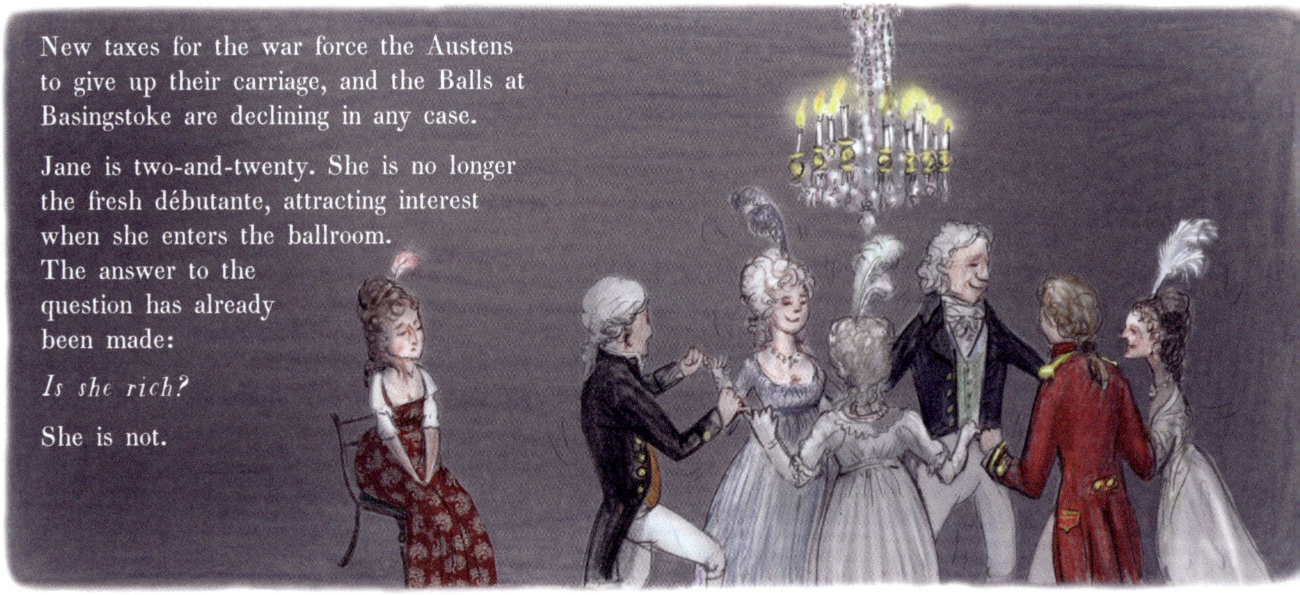

New taxes for the war force the Austens to give up their carriage, and the Balls at Basingstoke are declining in any case.
Jane is two-and-twenty. She is no longer the fresh débutante, attracting interest when she enters the ballroom. The answer to the question has already been made:
Is she rich?
She is not.

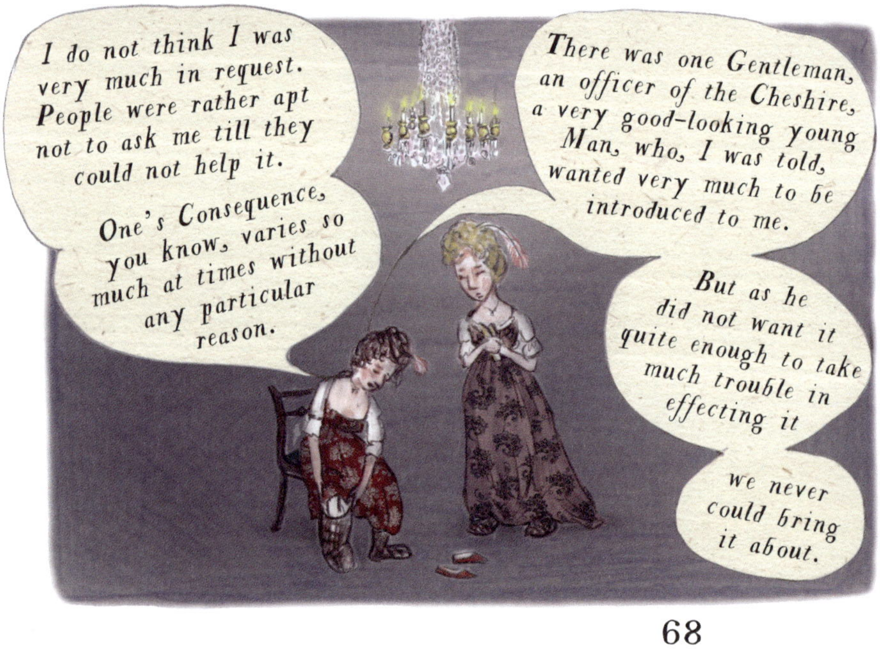

I do not think I was very much in request. People were rather apt not to ask me till they could not help it.
One's Consequence, you know, varies so much at times without any particular reason.
There was one Gentleman, an officer of the Cheshire, a very good-looking young Man, who, I was told, wanted very much to be introduced to me.
But as he did not want it quite enough to take much trouble in effecting it
we never could bring it about.

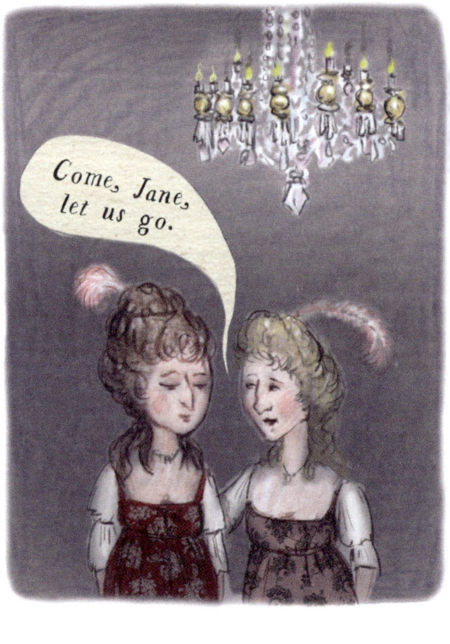

Come, Jane, let us go.

To Bath! A change of scene is required.

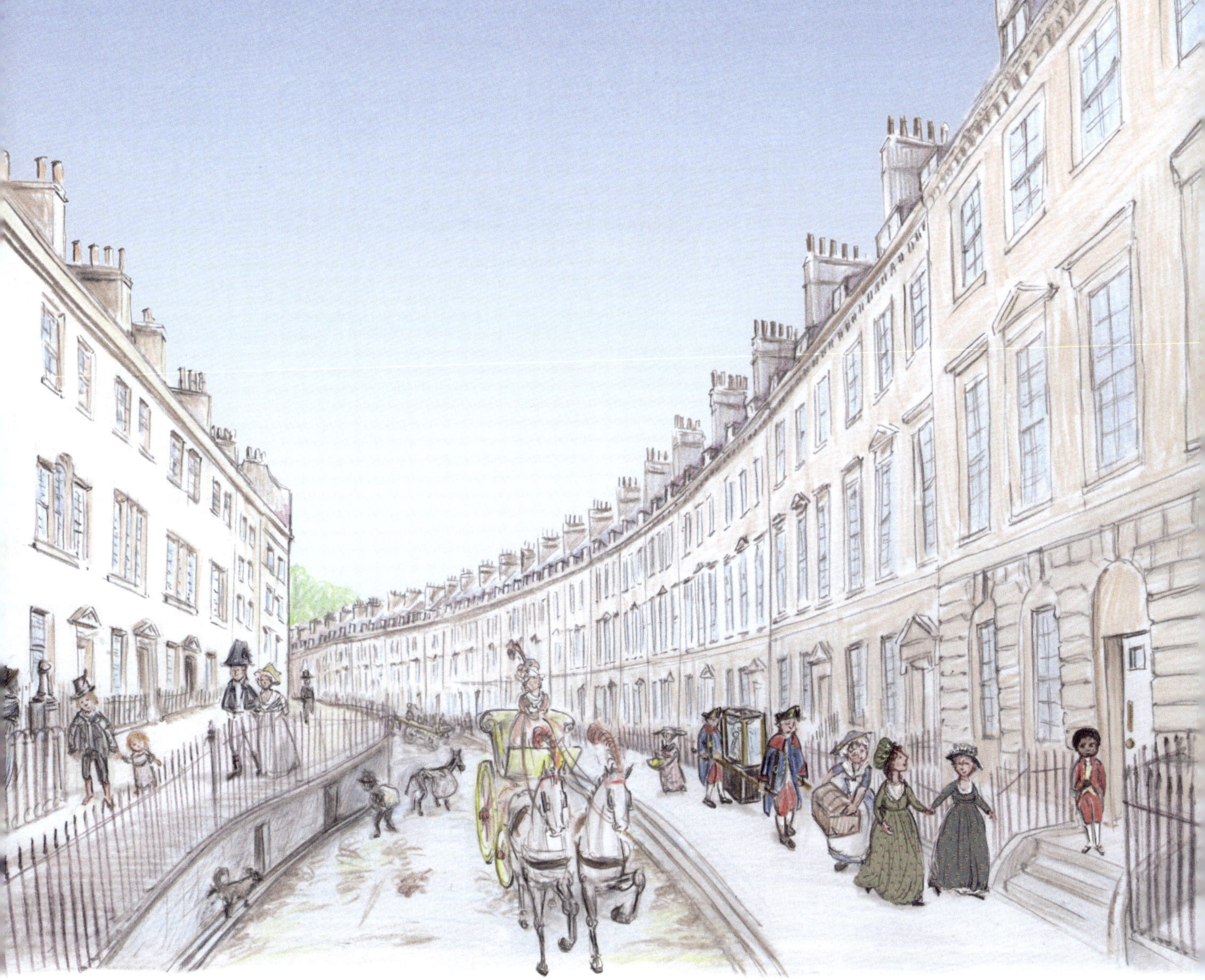

Meet the Leigh-Perrots.

Mrs Austen's brother James acquired the surname Perrot along with a fortune from their mother's sister. (Money that could have gone to Mrs Austen, but of course, it was settled upon the male.)

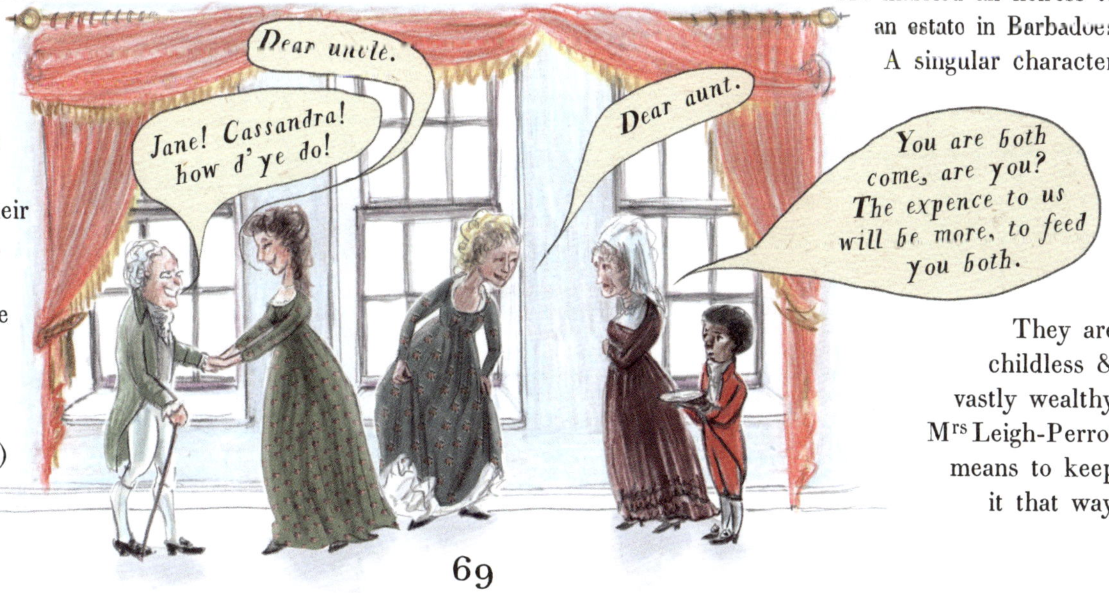

Dear uncle.
Jane! Cassandra! how d'ye do!
Dear aunt.
You are both come, are you? The expence to us will be more, to feed you both.

He married an heiress to an estate in Barbadoes. A singular character.

They are childless & vastly wealthy. Mrs Leigh-Perrot means to keep it that way.

NO PLACE IN ENGLAND affords so brilliant a circle of polite company as Bath. The young, the old, the grave, the gay, the infirm, and the healthy all resort to this place of amusement. Jane is come to be happy and feels happy already.

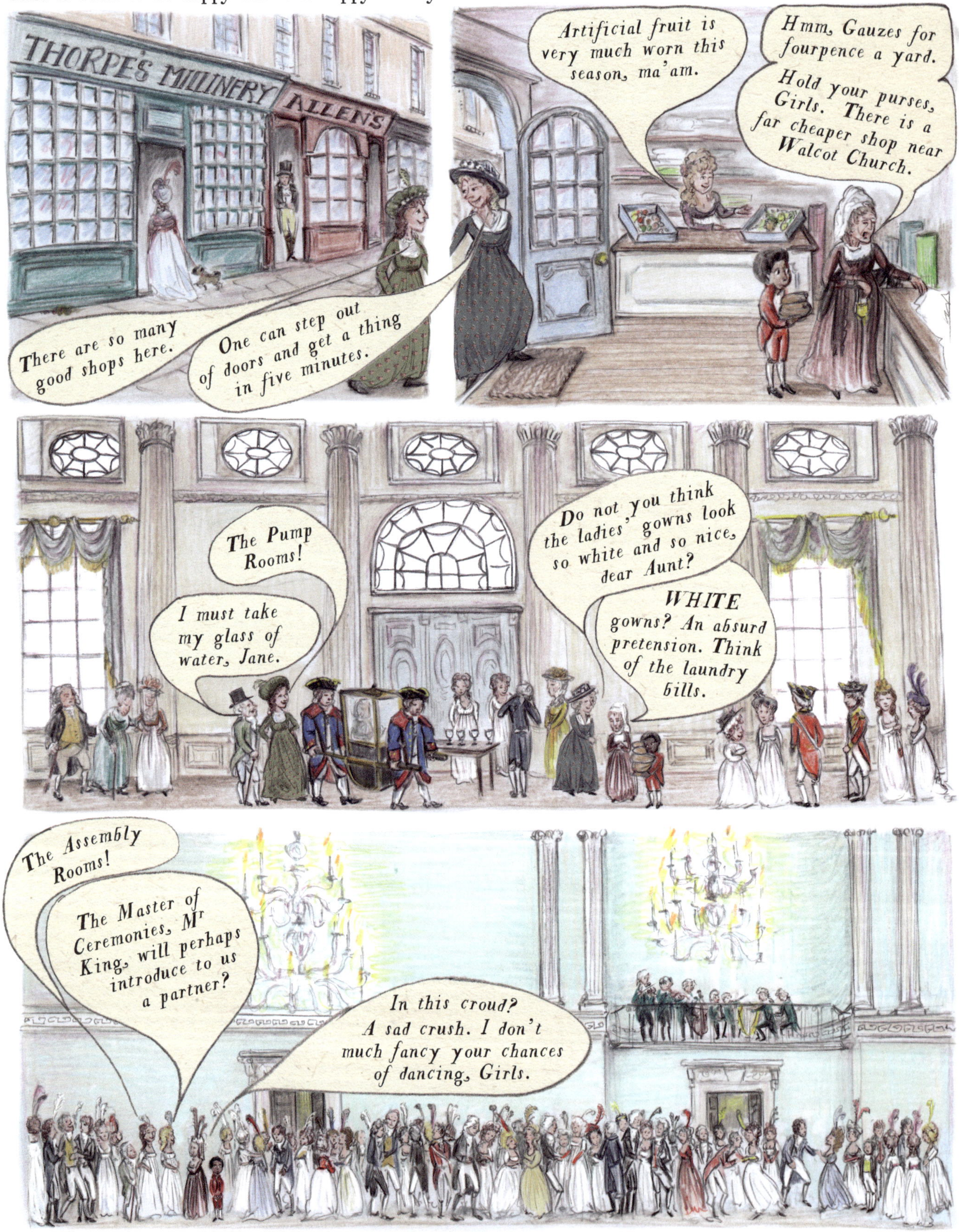
THORPE'S MILLINERY
ALLEN'S
There are so many good shops here.
One can step out of doors and get a thing in five minutes.
Artificial fruit is very much worn this season, ma'am.
Hmm, Gauzes for fourpence a yard.
Hold your purses, Girls. There is a far cheaper shop near Walcot Church.
The Pump Rooms!
I must take my glass of water, Jane.
Do not you think the ladies' gowns look so white and so nice, dear Aunt?
WHITE gowns? An absurd pretension. Think of the laundry bills.
The Assembly Rooms!
The Master of Ceremonies, Mr King, will perhaps introduce to us a partner?
In this croud? A sad crush. I don't much fancy your chances of dancing, Girls.

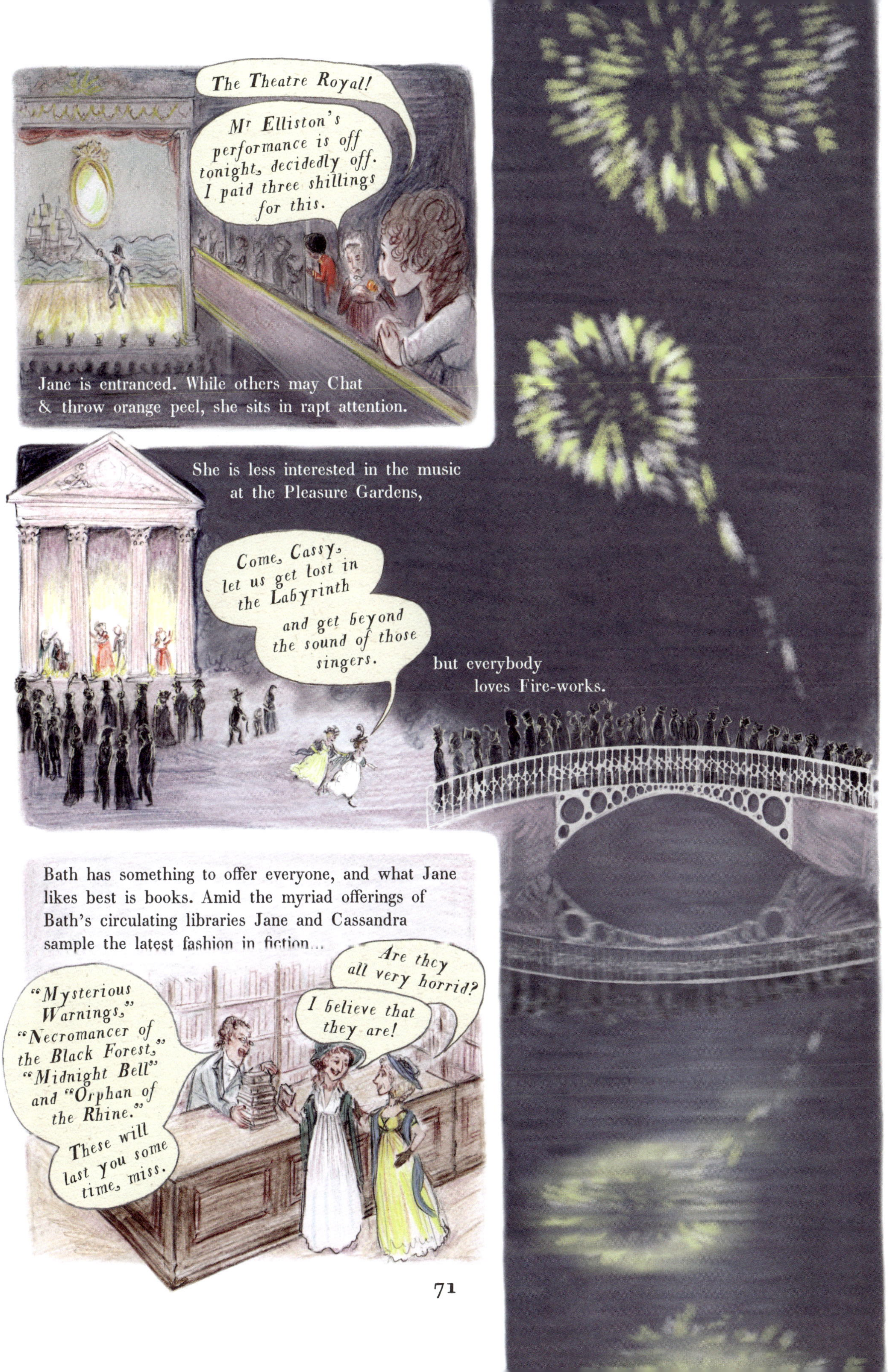
The Theatre Royal!
Mr Elliston's performance is off tonight, decidedly off. I paid three shillings for this.
Jane is entranced. While others may Chat & throw orange peel, she sits in rapt attention.
She is less interested in the music at the Pleasure Gardens,
Come, Cassy, let us get lost in the Labyrinth
and get beyond the sound of those singers.
but everybody loves Fire-works.
Bath has something to offer everyone, and what Jane likes best is books. Amid the myriad offerings of Bath's circulating libraries Jane and Cassandra sample the latest fashion in fiction...
"Mysterious Warnings," "Necromancer of the Black Forest," "Midnight Bell" and "Orphan of the Rhine."
These will last you some time, miss.
Are they all very horrid?
I believe that they are!

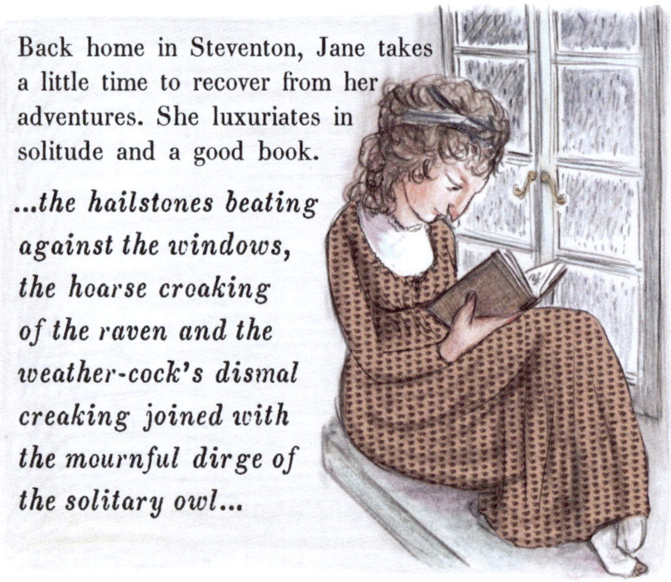
Back home in Steventon, Jane takes a little time to recover from her adventures. She luxuriates in solitude and a good book.
...the hailstones beating against the windows, the hoarse croaking of the raven and the weather-cock's dismal creaking joined with the mournful dirge of the solitary owl...

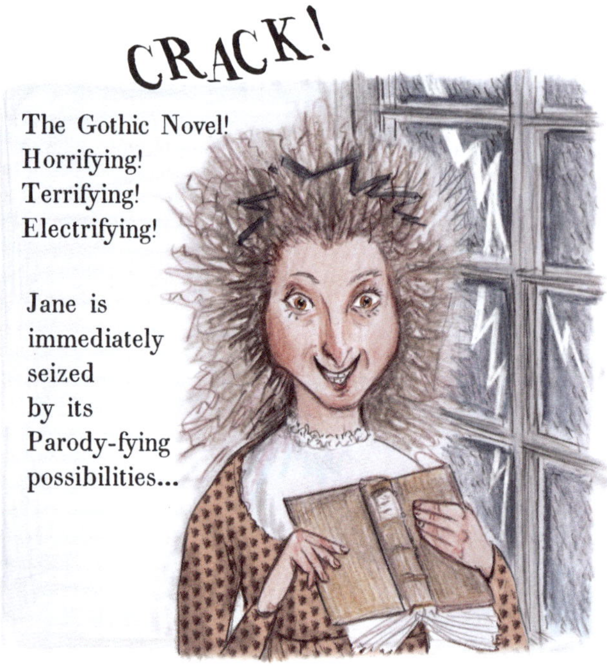
CRACK!
The Gothic Novel!
Horrifying!
Terrifying!
Electrifying!
Jane is immediately seized by its Parody-fying possibilities...

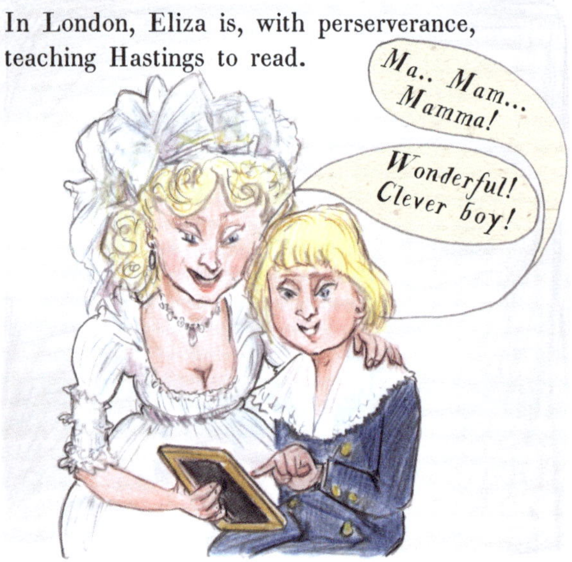
In London, Eliza is, with perserverance, teaching Hastings to read.
Ma.. Mam... Mamma!
Wonderful! Clever boy!

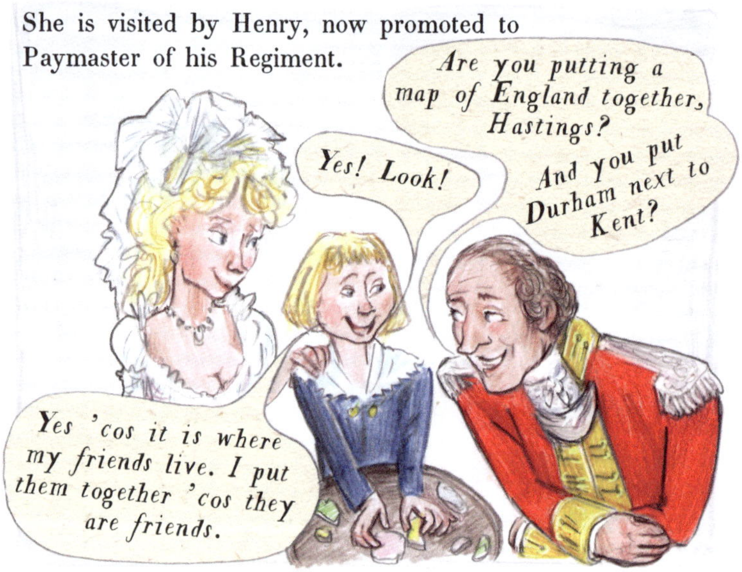
She is visited by Henry, now promoted to Paymaster of his Regiment.
Are you putting a map of England together, Hastings?
Yes! Look!
And you put Durham next to Kent?
Yes 'cos it is where my friends live. I put them together 'cos they are friends.

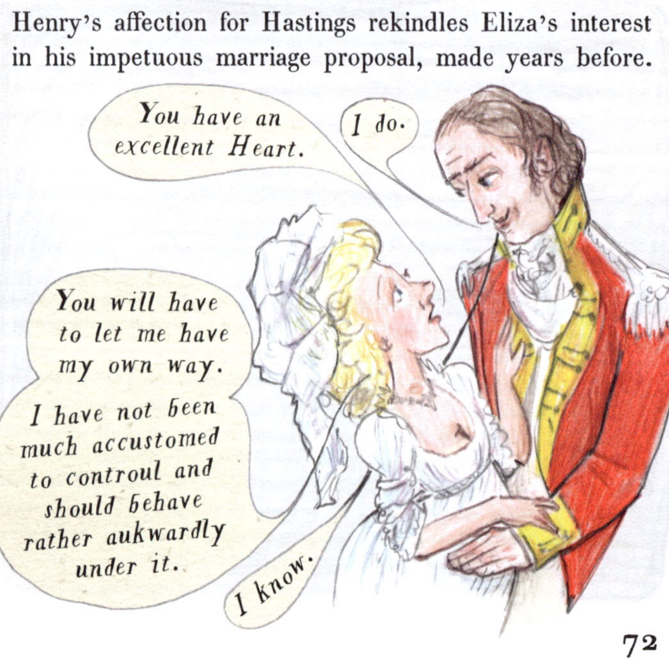
Henry's affection for Hastings rekindles Eliza's interest in his impetuous marriage proposal, made years before.
You have an excellent Heart.
I do.
You will have to let me have my own way.
I have not been much accustomed to controul and should behave rather aukwardly under it.
I know.

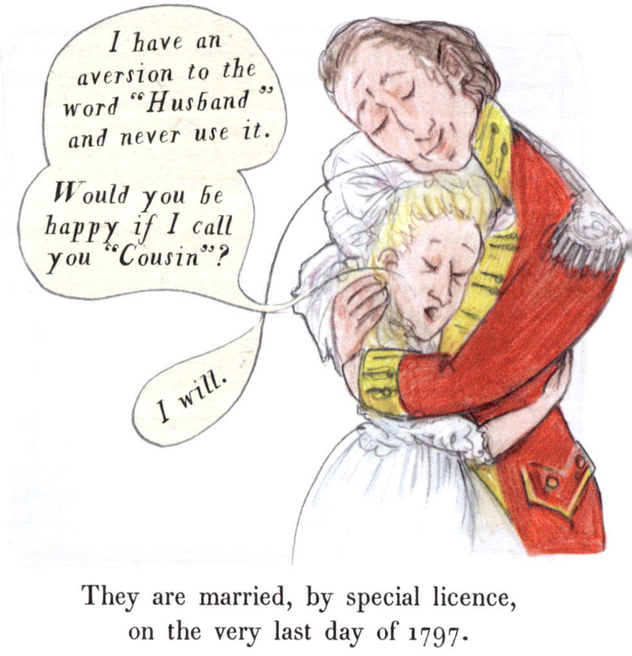
I have an aversion to the word "Husband" and never use it.
Would you be happy if I call you "Cousin"?
I will.
They are married, by special licence, on the very last day of 1797.

And so, Jane writes a love story about a Henry, and she sets it in Bath.

Perhaps uniquely in romantic fiction, she establishes her hero, Henry Tilney, firmly in the reader's favour by demonstrating his knowledge of dressmaking.

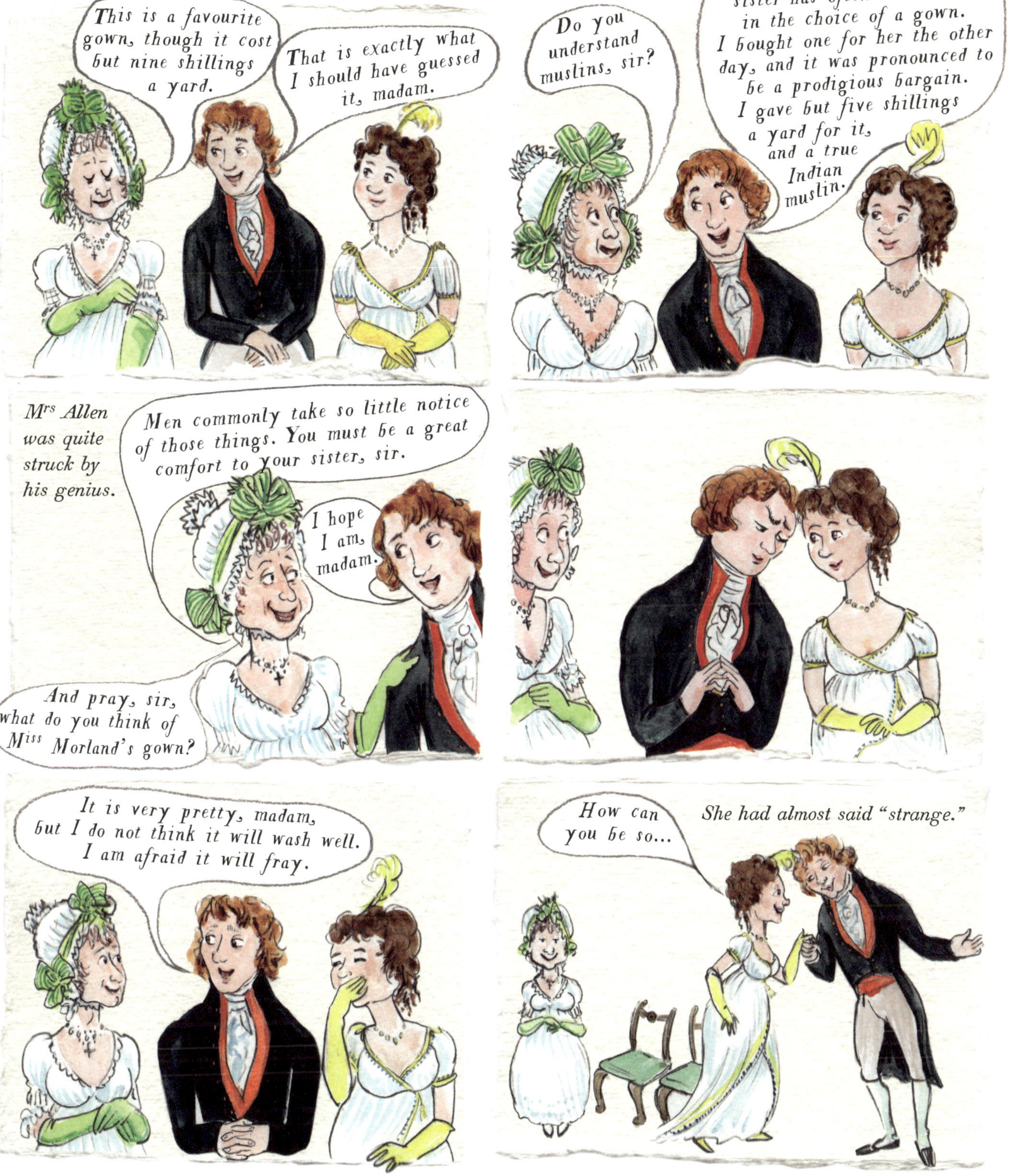

This is a favourite gown, though it cost but nine shillings a yard.
That is exactly what I should have guessed it, madam.
Do you understand muslins, sir?
Particularly well. I always buy my own cravats, and am allowed to be an excellent judge, and my sister has often trusted me in the choice of a gown. I bought one for her the other day, and it was pronounced to be a prodigious bargain. I gave but five shillings a yard for it, and a true Indian muslin.
Mrs Allen was quite struck by his genius.
Men commonly take so little notice of those things. You must be a great comfort to your sister, sir.
I hope I am, madam.
And pray, sir, what do you think of Miss Morland's gown?
It is very pretty, madam, but I do not think it will wash well. I am afraid it will fray.
How can you be so...
She had almost said "strange."

Ever the innovator, Austen simplifies the tortuous, star-crossed fortunes of the traditional heroine down to a simple story of boy meets girl. Because the real focus of the book is not Henry Tilney's love of Susan Morland, it's impressionable Susan Morland's love of spooky, scary, Gothic novels.

When admitted to Tilney's family home of Northanger Abbey, Susan's imagination takes full flight...

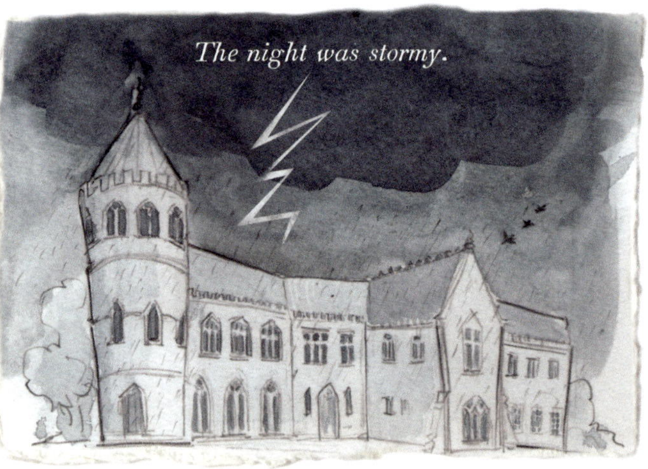
The night was stormy.

Susan listened to the tempest with sensations of awe; and felt for the first time that she was really in an abbey. The sounds brought to her recollection a countless variety of dreadful situations and horrid scenes, which such buildings had witnessed, and such storms ushered in.

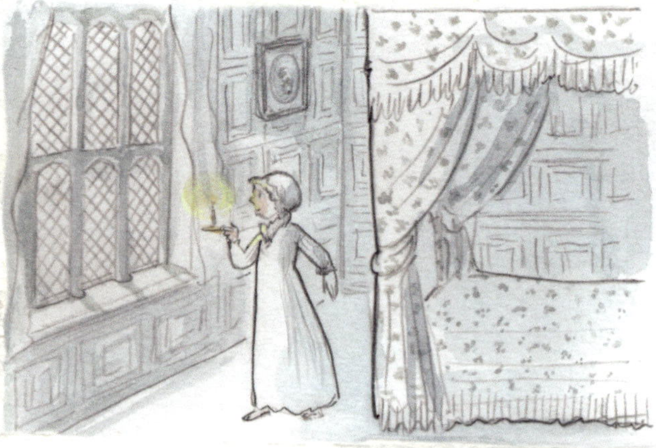

The fire died away, and Susan was beginning to think of stepping into bed, when, she was struck by the appearance of a high, old-fashioned black cabinet, which, though in a situation conspicuous enough, had never caught her notice before.

She took her candle and looked closely at the cabinet. She seized the key with a tremulous hand and tried to turn it; but it resisted her utmost strength.

Alarmed, but not discouraged, she tried it another way; a bolt flew, and she believed herself successful; but how strangely mysterious!

The door was still immovable!

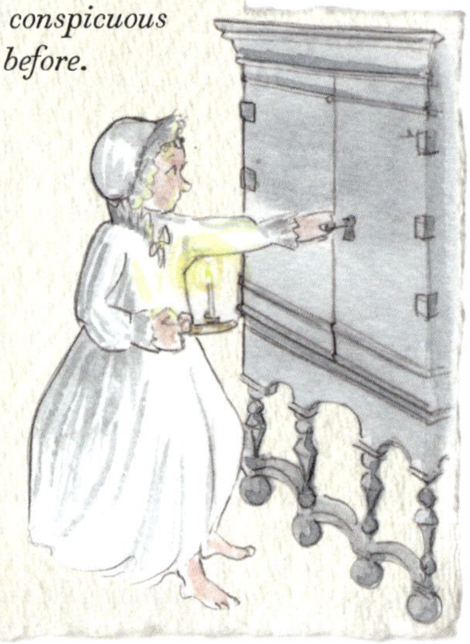

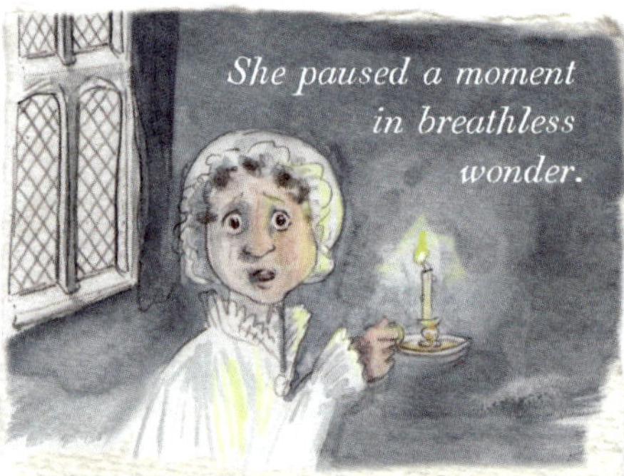
She paused a moment
in breathless
wonder.

The wind roared down the chimney, the rain beat in torrents against the windows, and everything seemed to speak the awfulness of her situation.

Again, she applied herself to the key, and after moving it in every possible way for some instants with the determined celerity of hope's last effort, the door suddenly yielded to her hand.

A double range of small drawers appeared in view, with some larger drawers above and below them; and in the centre, a small door, closed also with a lock and key, secured in all probability a cavity of importance.

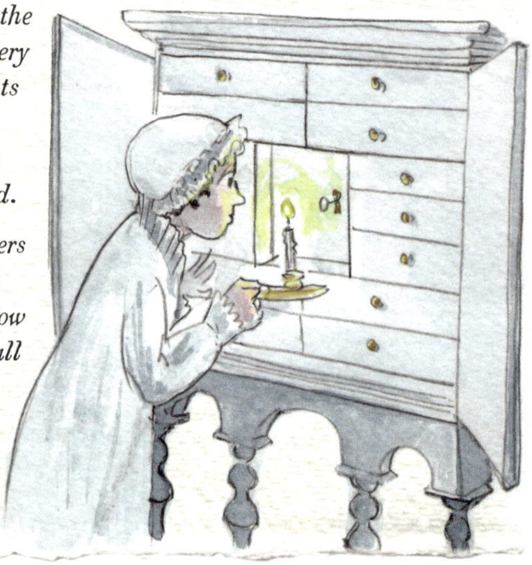

Susan's heart beat quick, but her courage did not fail her.

With a cheek flushed by hope, and an eye straining with curiosity, her fingers grasped the handle of a drawer and drew it forth.

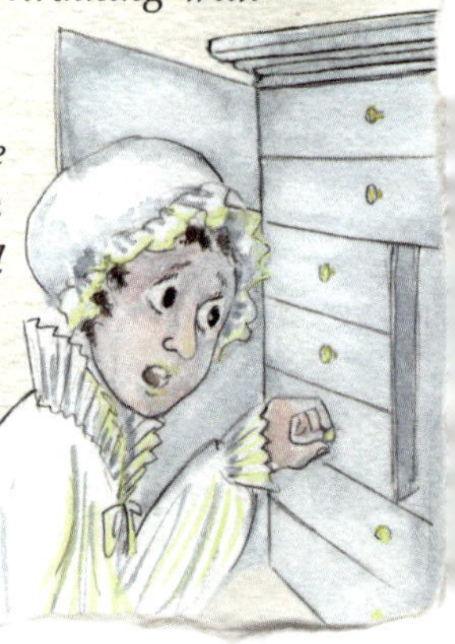

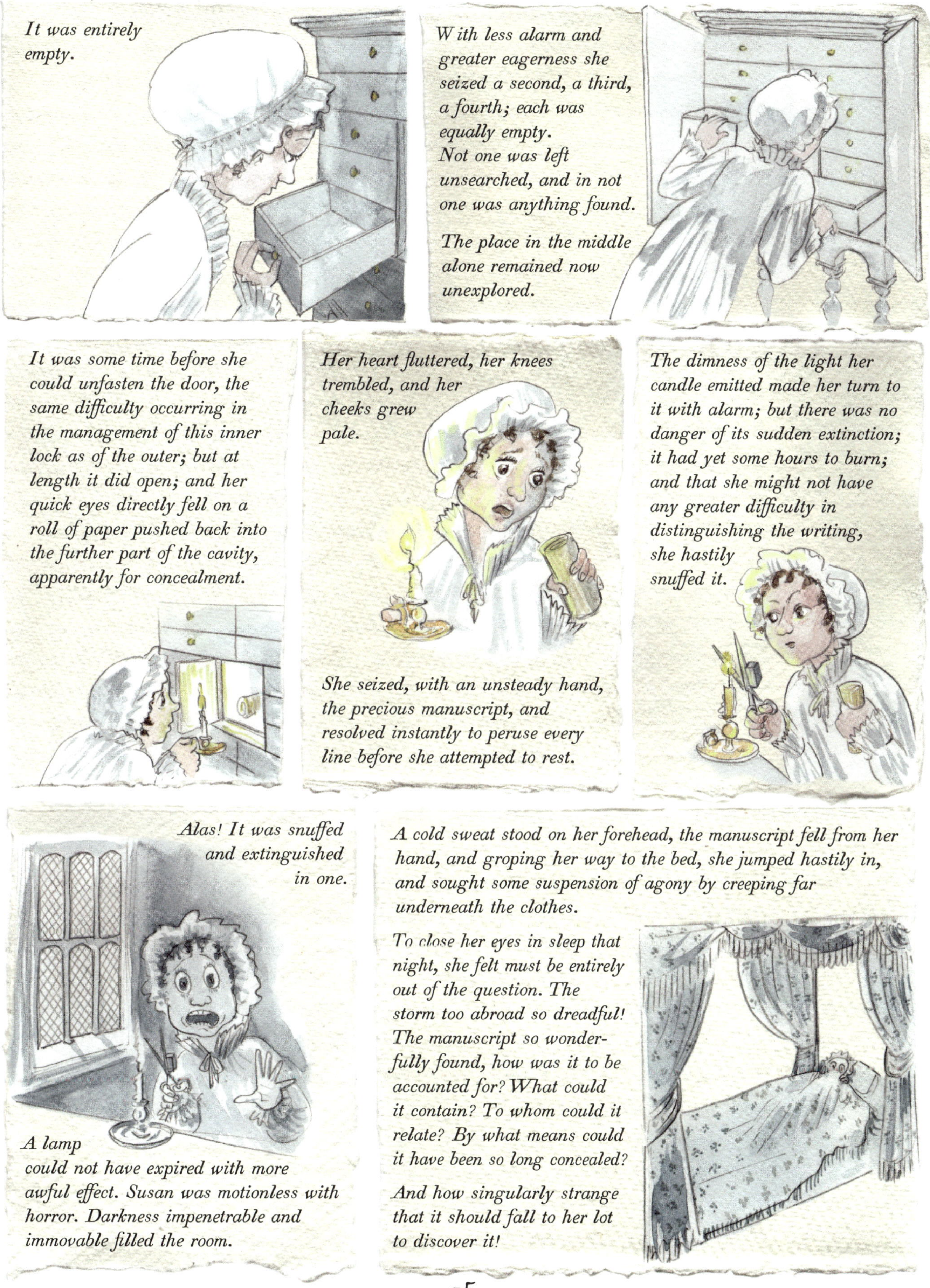
It was entirely empty.
With less alarm and greater eagerness she seized a second, a third, a fourth; each was equally empty. Not one was left unsearched, and in not one was anything found.
The place in the middle alone remained now unexplored.
It was some time before she could unfasten the door, the same difficulty occurring in the management of this inner lock as of the outer; but at length it did open; and her quick eyes directly fell on a roll of paper pushed back into the further part of the cavity, apparently for concealment.
Her heart fluttered, her knees trembled, and her cheeks grew pale.
She seized, with an unsteady hand, the precious manuscript, and resolved instantly to peruse every line before she attempted to rest.
The dimness of the light her candle emitted made her turn to it with alarm; but there was no danger of its sudden extinction; it had yet some hours to burn; and that she might not have any greater difficulty in distinguishing the writing, she hastily snuffed it.
Alas! It was snuffed and extinguished in one.
A lamp could not have expired with more awful effect. Susan was motionless with horror. Darkness impenetrable and immovable filled the room.
A cold sweat stood on her forehead, the manuscript fell from her hand, and groping her way to the bed, she jumped hastily in, and sought some suspension of agony by creeping far underneath the clothes.
To close her eyes in sleep that night, she felt must be entirely out of the question. The storm too abroad so dreadful! The manuscript so wonderfully found, how was it to be accounted for? What could it contain? To whom could it relate? By what means could it have been so long concealed?
And how singularly strange that it should fall to her lot to discover it!

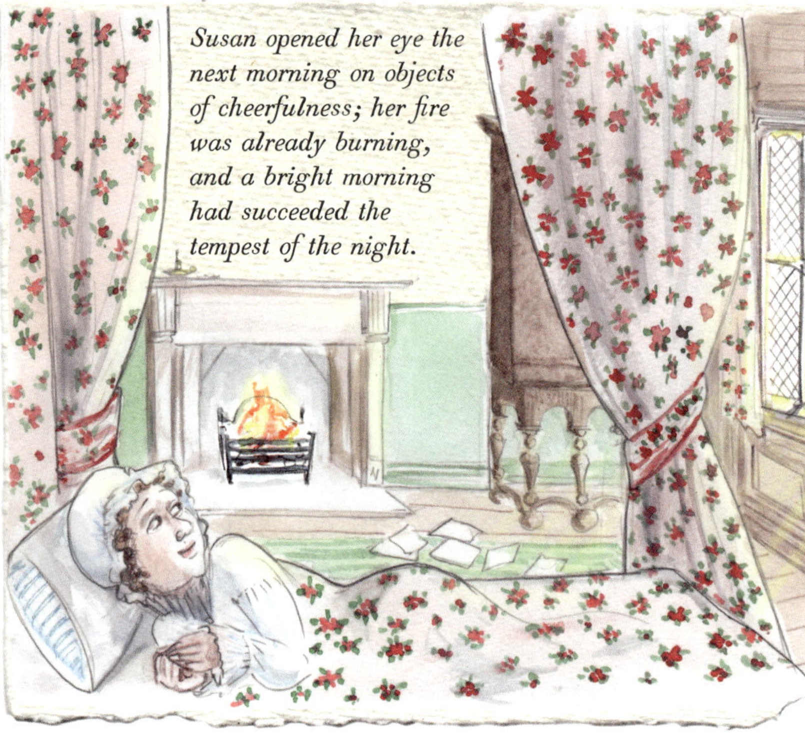

Susan opened her eye the next morning on objects of cheerfulness; her fire was already burning, and a bright morning had succeeded the tempest of the night.

Instantaneously, with the consciousness of existence, returned her recollection of the manuscript; and springing from the bed, she eagerly collected every scattered sheet and flew back to enjoy the luxury of their perusal on her pillow.

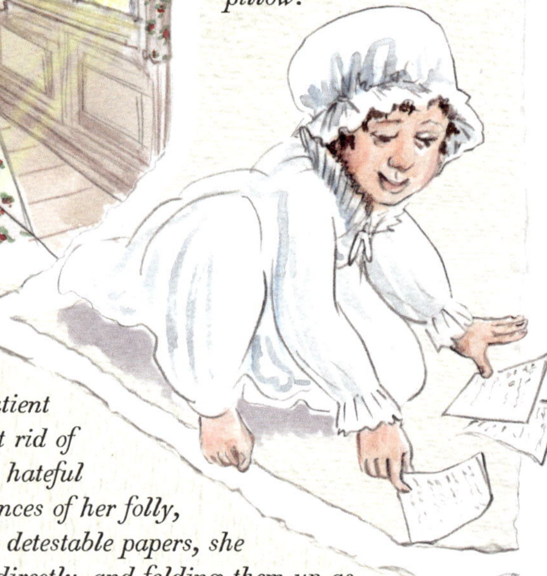

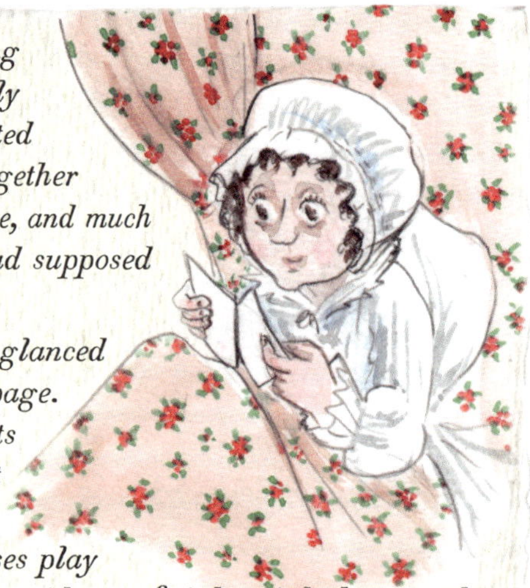

The roll, seeming to consist entirely of small disjointed sheets, was altogether but of trifling size, and much less than she had supposed it to be at first.

Her greedy eye glanced rapidly over a page. She started at its import. Could it be possible, or did not her senses play her false? If the evidence of sight might be trusted... she held a washing-bill in her hand.

She seized another sheet, and saw the same articles with little variation; a third, a fourth, and a fifth presented nothing new. Shirts, stockings, cravats, and waistcoats faced her in each. Two others, penned by the same hand, marked an expenditure scarcely more interesting, in letters, hair-powder, shoe-string, and breeches-ball. And the larger sheet, which had enclosed the rest, seemed by its first cramp line, "To poultice chestnut mare" – a farrier's bill! Such was the collection of papers which had filled her with expectation and alarm, and robbed her of half her night's rest!

She felt humbled to the dust.

Impatient to get rid of those hateful evidences of her folly, those detestable papers, she rose directly, and folding them up as nearly as possible in the same shape as before, returned them to the same spot within the cabinet.

Why the locks should have been so difficult to open, however, was still something remarkable, for she could now manage them with perfect ease.

In this there was surely something mysterious, and she indulged in the flattering suggestion for half a minute, till the possibility of the door's having been at first unlocked, and of being herself its fastener, darted into her head, and cost her another blush.

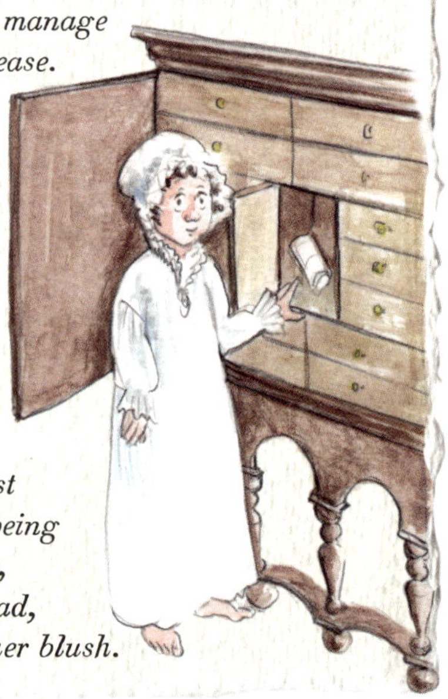

Objects of cheerfulness.

A stroll in the Elm Walk in the Rectory grounds.

Jane and Cassandra's snug sitting room.

A laptop open upon a table

and upon it, the completed manuscript of a third, exceptional, beautifully crafted novel.

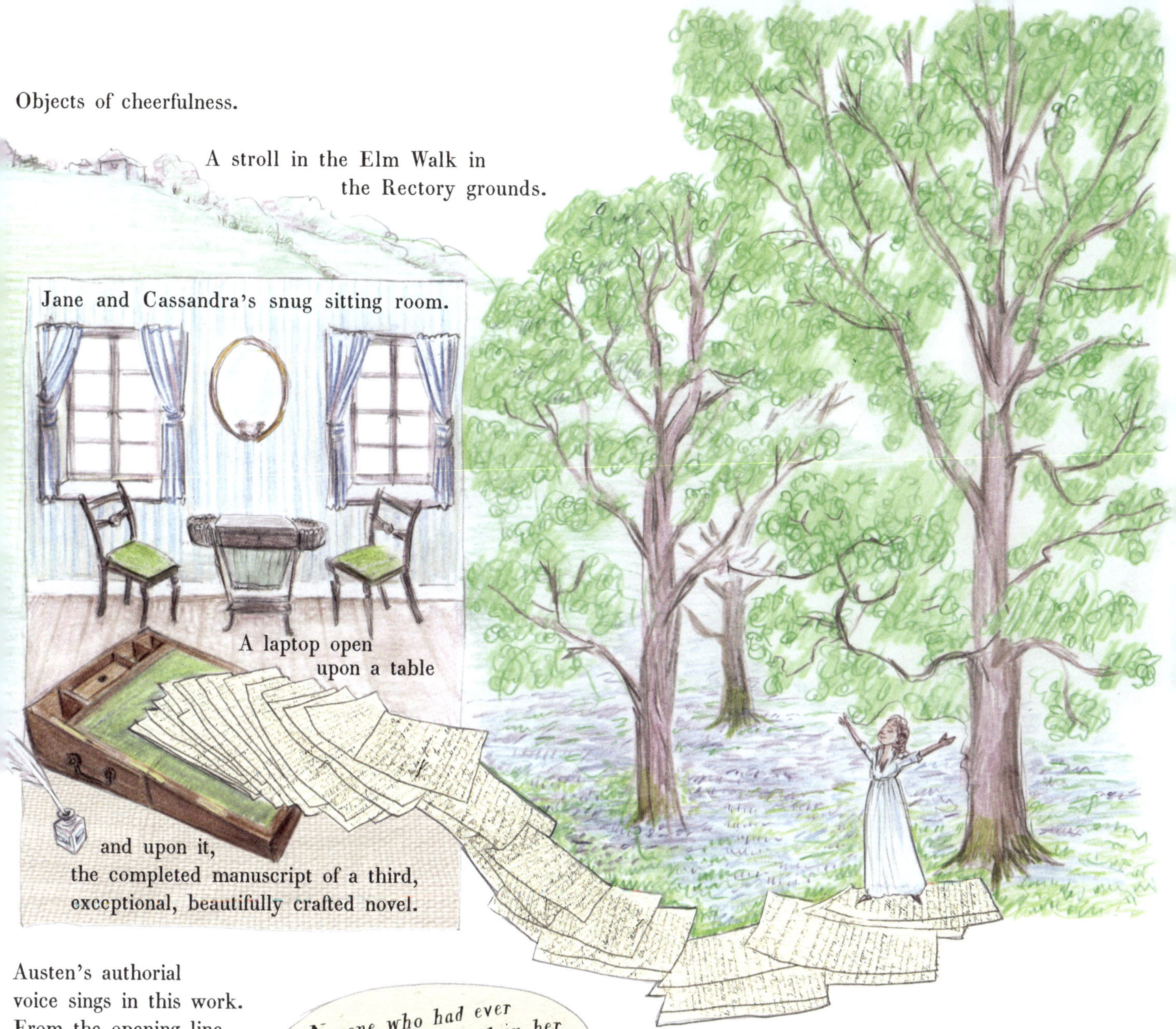

Austen's authorial voice sings in this work. From the opening line

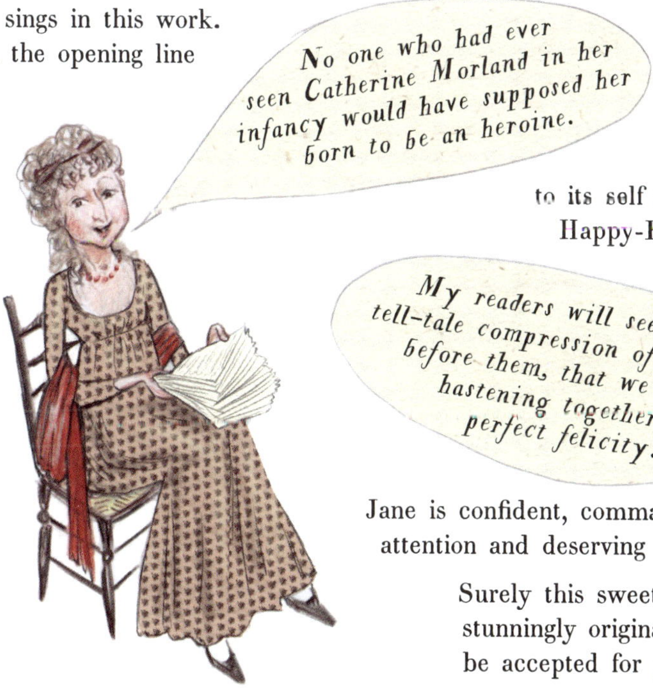
No one who had ever seen Catherine Morland in her infancy would have supposed her born to be an heroine.

to its self referential Happy-Ever-After

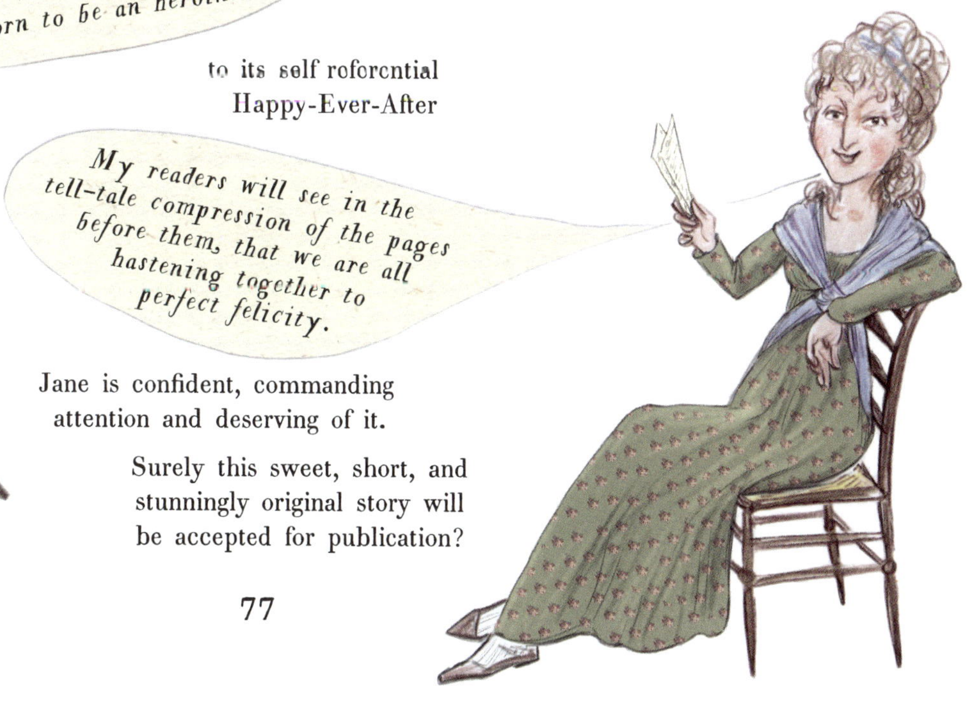
My readers will see in the tell-tale compression of the pages before them, that we are all hastening together to perfect felicity.

Jane is confident, commanding attention and deserving of it.

Surely this sweet, short, and stunningly original story will be accepted for publication?

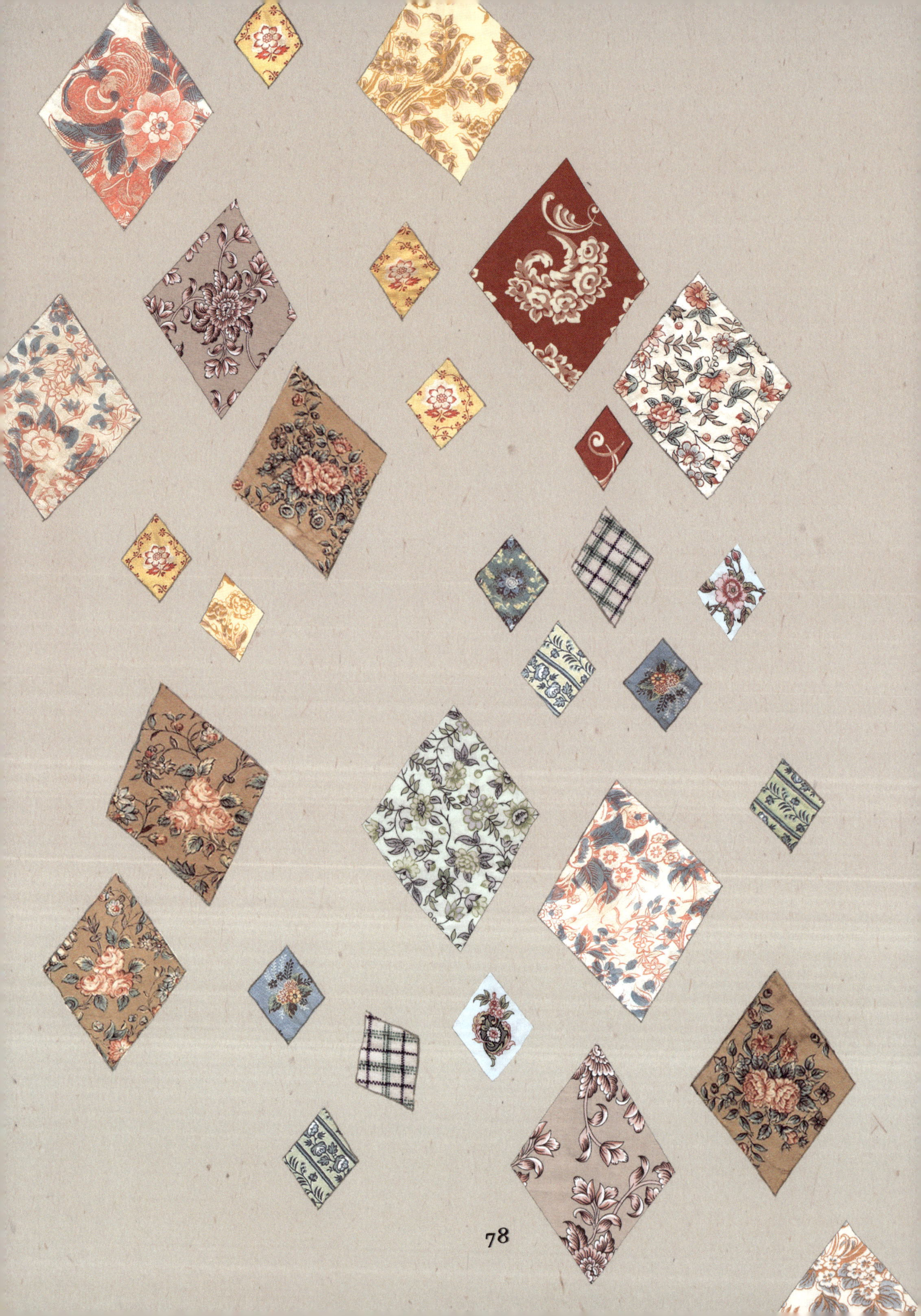

Mrs LEIGH-PERROT BUYS SOME LACE

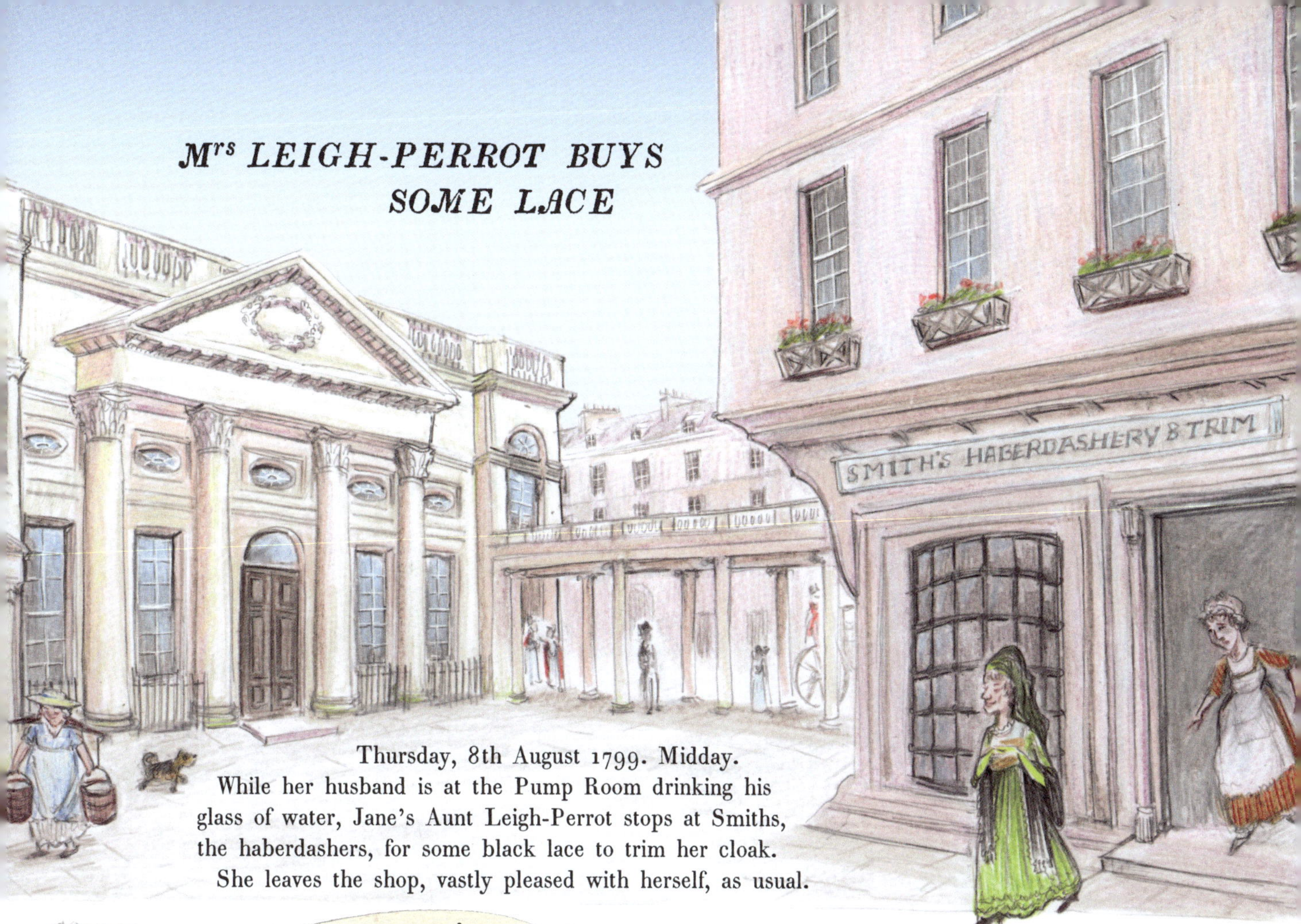
SMITH'S HABERDASHERY & TRIM

Thursday, 8th August 1799. Midday.
While her husband is at the Pump Room drinking his glass of water, Jane's Aunt Leigh-Perrot stops at Smiths, the haberdashers, for some black lace to trim her cloak. She leaves the shop, vastly pleased with herself, as usual.

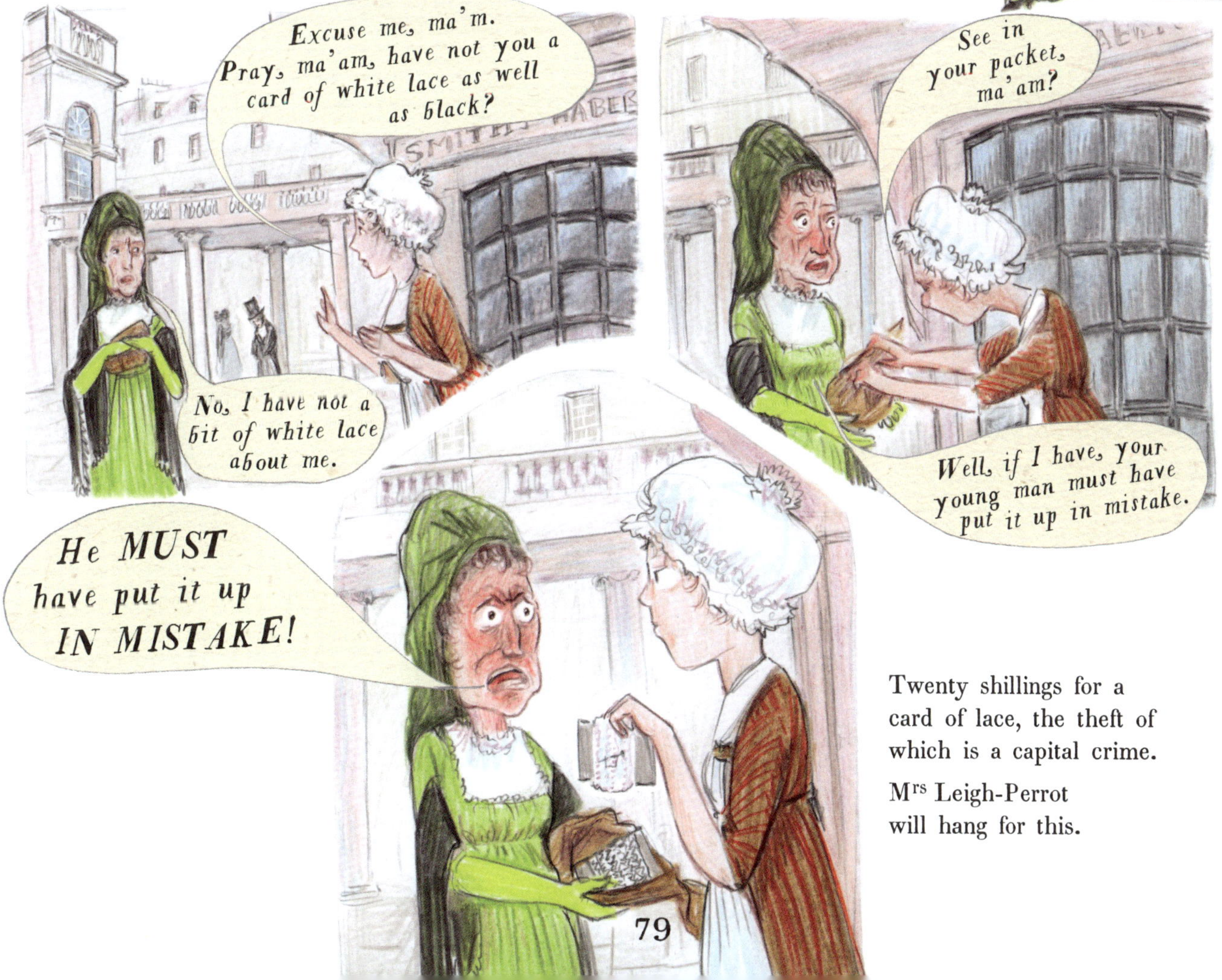
Excuse me, ma'm. Pray, ma'am, have not you a card of white lace as well as black?
No, I have not a bit of white lace about me.
See in your packet, ma'am?
Well, if I have, your young man must have put it up in mistake.
He MUST have put it up IN MISTAKE!

Twenty shillings for a card of lace, the theft of which is a capital crime.

Mrs Leigh-Perrot will hang for this.

Wednesday, 14th August 1799. Mrs Leigh-Perrot is committed to Ilchester gaol. Her husband voluntarily accompanies her. They are lodged in the Govenor's house, with his wife and five young children.

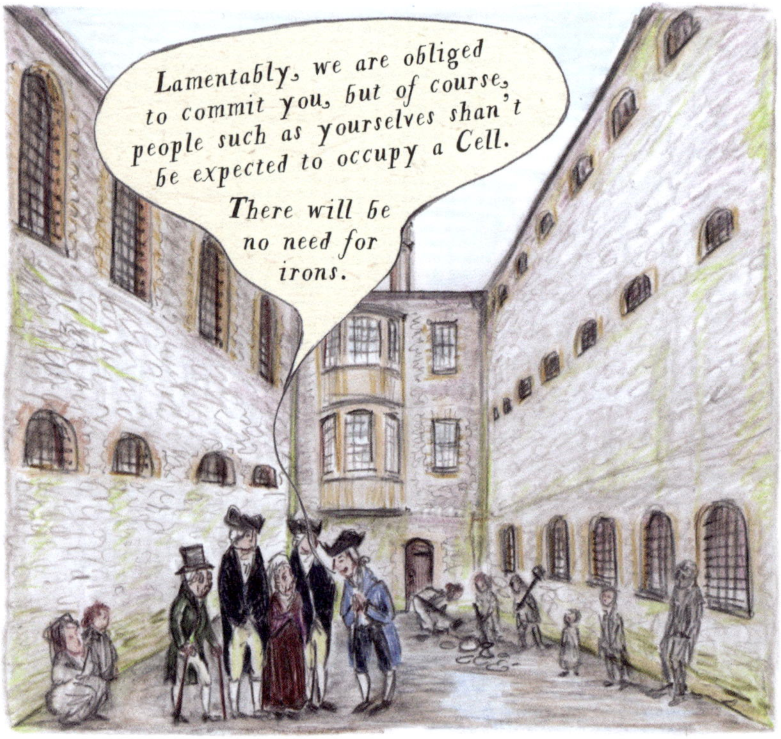

Lamentably, we are obliged to commit you, but of course, people such as yourselves shan't be expected to occupy a Cell.
There will be no need for irons.

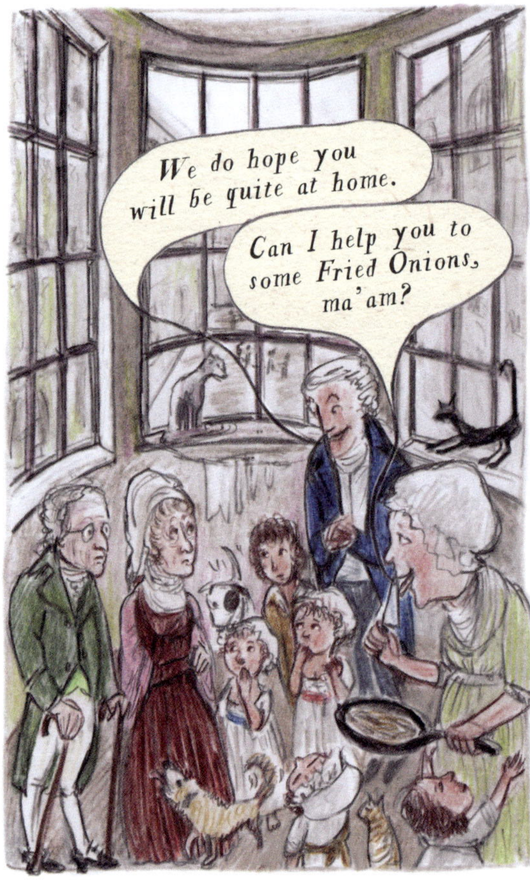

We do hope you will be quite at home.
Can I help you to some Fried Onions, ma'am?

Months pass. Mrs Austen offers to send Jane and Cassandra to share the Leigh-Perrot's confinement. Thankfully, they decline.

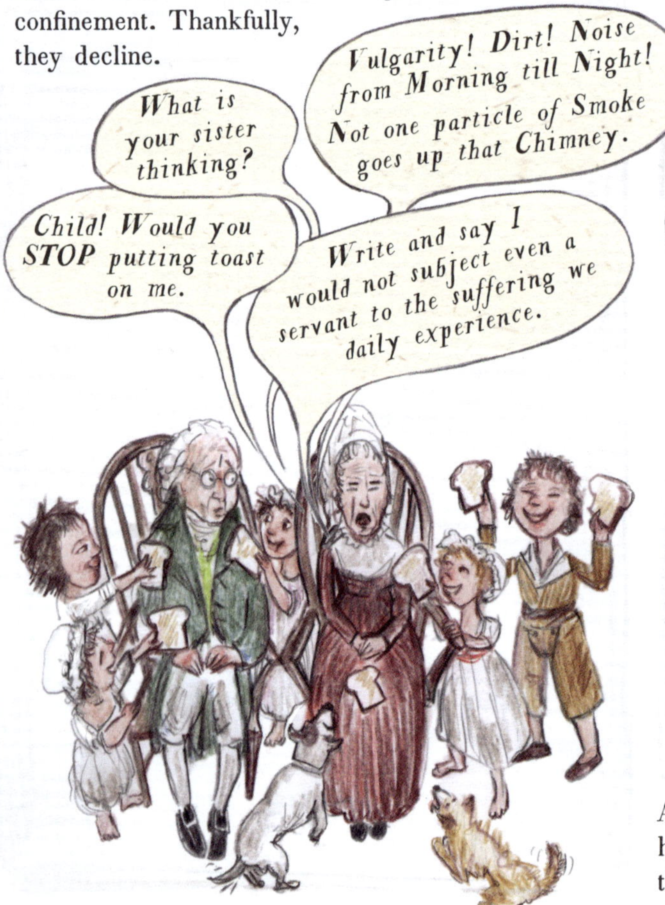

What is your sister thinking?
Vulgarity! Dirt! Noise from Morning till Night! Not one particle of Smoke goes up that Chimney.
Child! Would you STOP putting toast on me.
Write and say I would not subject even a servant to the suffering we daily experience.

Their lawyer, Mr Watts, offers cold comfort.

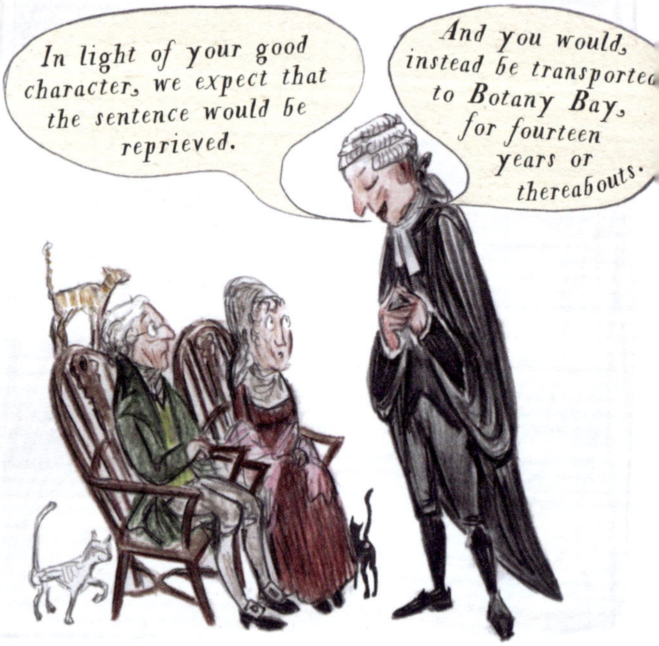

In light of your good character, we expect that the sentence would be reprieved.
And you would, instead be transporte to Botany Bay, for fourteen years or thereabouts.

Accordingly, and seemingly in not much doubt of her guilt, Mr Leigh-Perrot makes arrangments for the sale of their estate, to follow her to Australia.

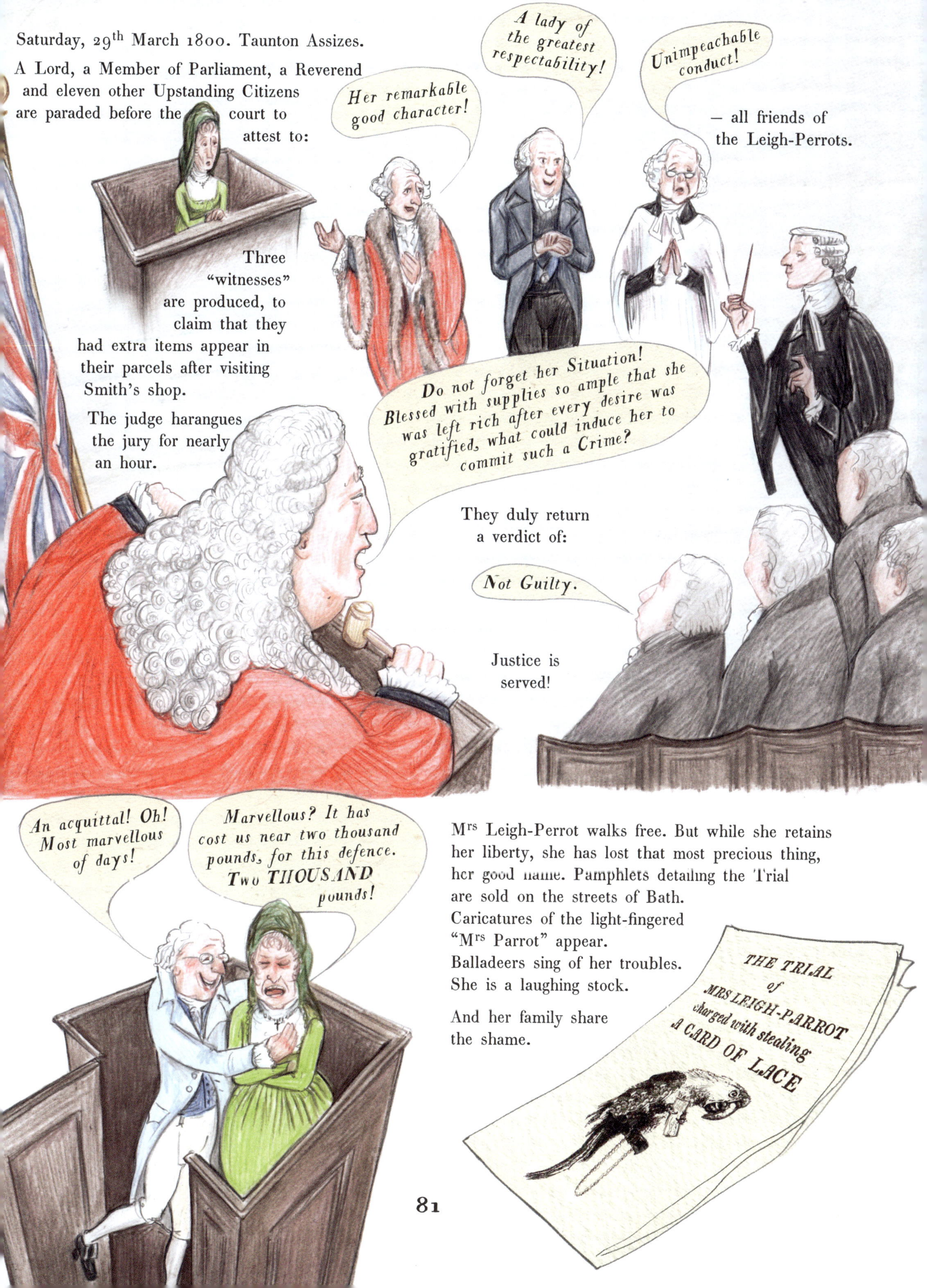
Saturday, 29th March 1800. Taunton Assizes.
A Lord, a Member of Parliament, a Reverend and eleven other Upstanding Citizens are paraded before the court to attest to:
Her remarkable good character!
A lady of the greatest respectability!
Unimpeachable conduct!
— all friends of the Leigh-Perrots.
Three "witnesses" are produced, to claim that they had extra items appear in their parcels after visiting Smith's shop.
The judge harangues the jury for nearly an hour.
Do not forget her Situation! Blessed with supplies so ample that she was left rich after every desire was gratified, what could induce her to commit such a Crime?
They duly return a verdict of:
Not Guilty.
Justice is served!
An acquittal! Oh! Most marvellous of days!
Marvellous? It has cost us near two thousand pounds, for this defence. Two THOUSAND pounds!
Mrs Leigh-Perrot walks free. But while she retains her liberty, she has lost that most precious thing, her good name. Pamphlets detailing the Trial are sold on the streets of Bath. Caricatures of the light-fingered "Mrs Parrot" appear. Balladeers sing of her troubles. She is a laughing stock.
And her family share the shame.
THE TRIAL
of
MRS LEIGH-PARROT
charged with stealing
A CARD OF LACE

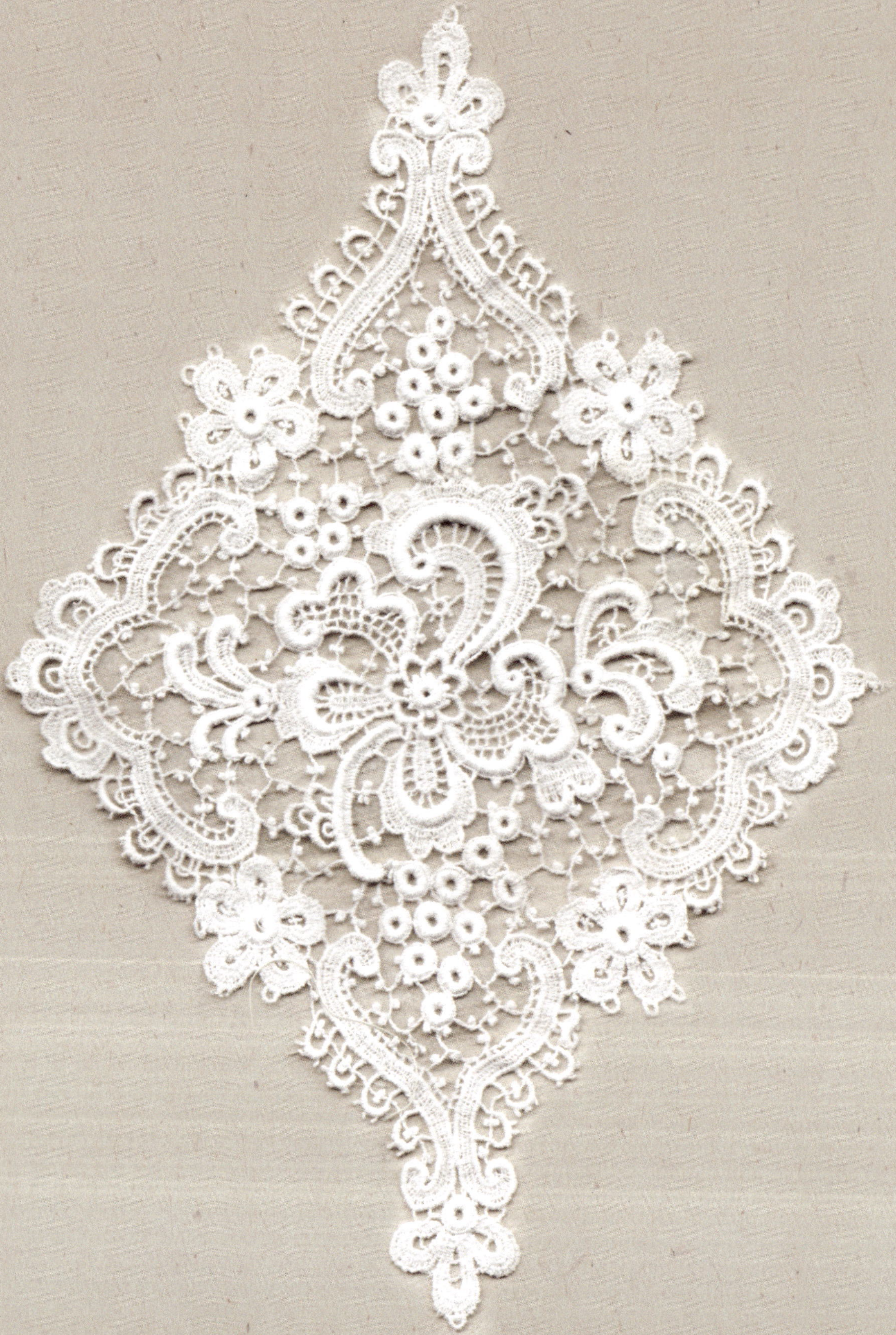

December 1800.

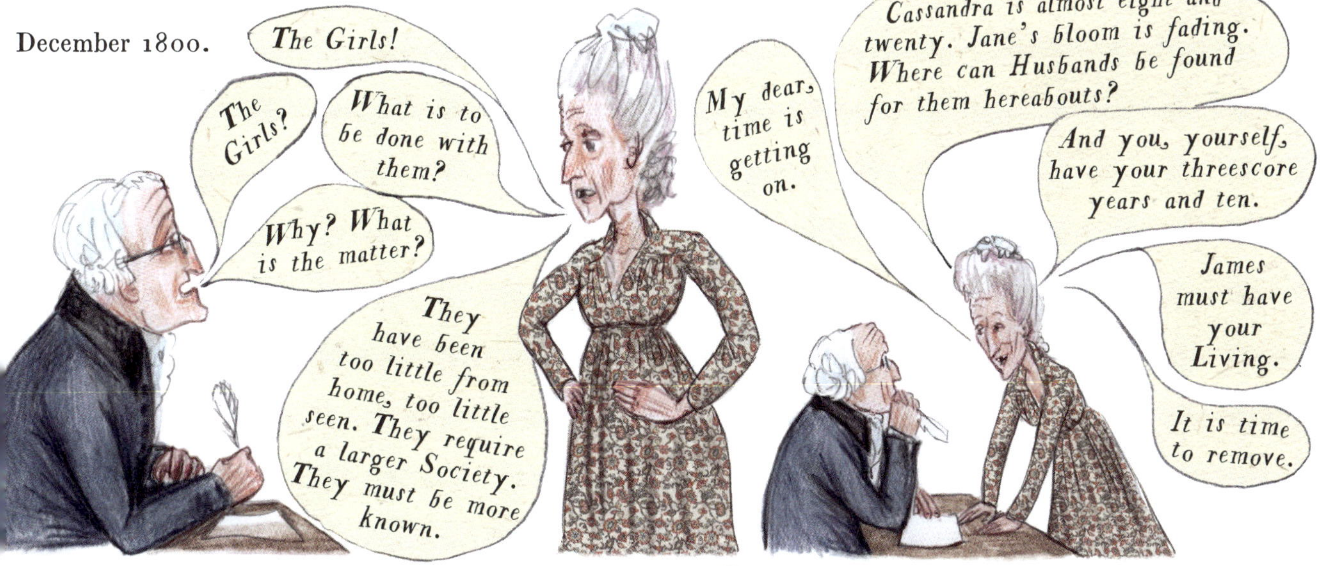
The Girls!
The Girls?
What is to be done with them?
Why? What is the matter?
They have been too little from home, too little seen. They require a larger Society. They must be more known.
My dear, time is getting on.
Cassandra is almost eight and twenty. Jane's bloom is fading. Where can Husbands be found for them hereabouts?
And you, yourself, have your threescore years and ten.
James must have your Living.
It is time to remove.

And so, it is decided. The family will move to Bath! Without consultation, of course. What interest could a daughter have in directing her own affairs?

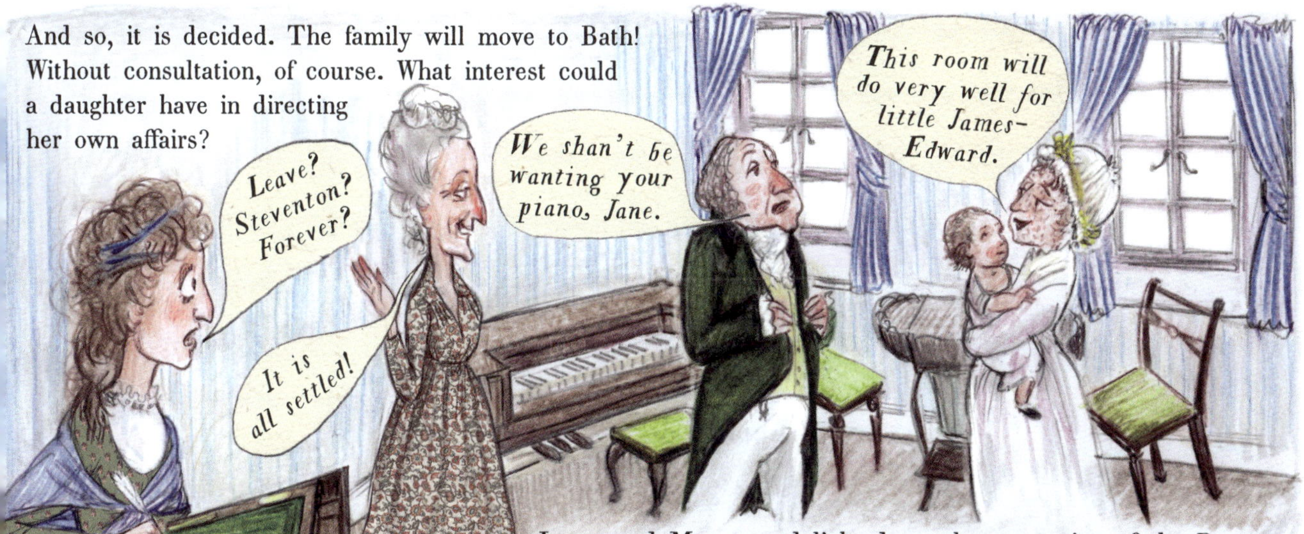
Leave? Steventon? Forever?
It is all settled!
We shan't be wanting your piano, Jane.
This room will do very well for little James-Edward.

James and Mary are delighted to take possession of the Rectory.

Ever-favoured James.

Jane is filled with inexpressible rage, as, with almost indecent haste, the contents of her life are packed up and auctioned off. Her bed. Her piano. The farm animals. The old theatre sets. The beloved books that have been her life-long companions.

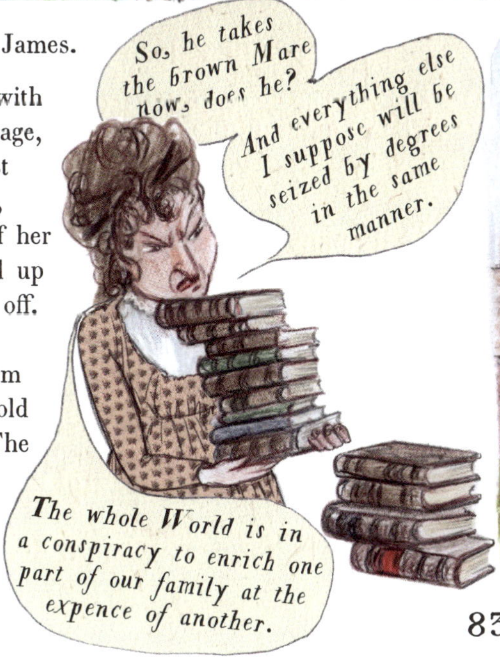
So, he takes the brown Mare now, does he?
And everything else I suppose will be seized by degrees in the same manner.
The whole World is in a conspiracy to enrich one part of our family at the expence of another.

Spring 1801.

Jane bids goodbye to the only home she can remember.

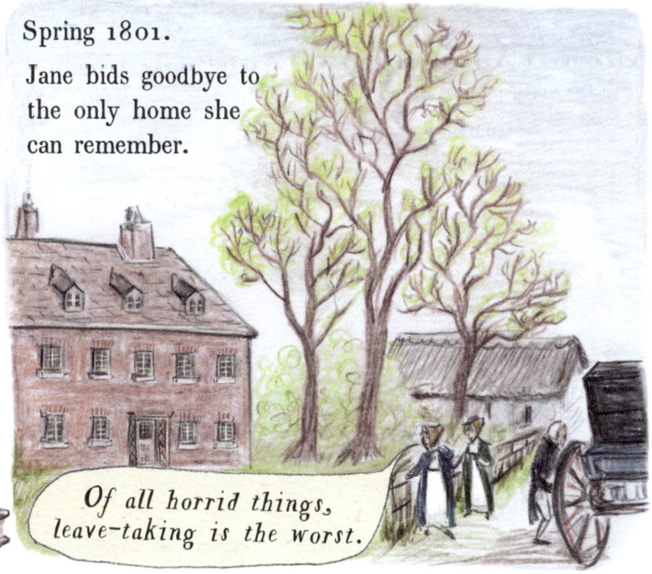
Of all horrid things, leave-taking is the worst.

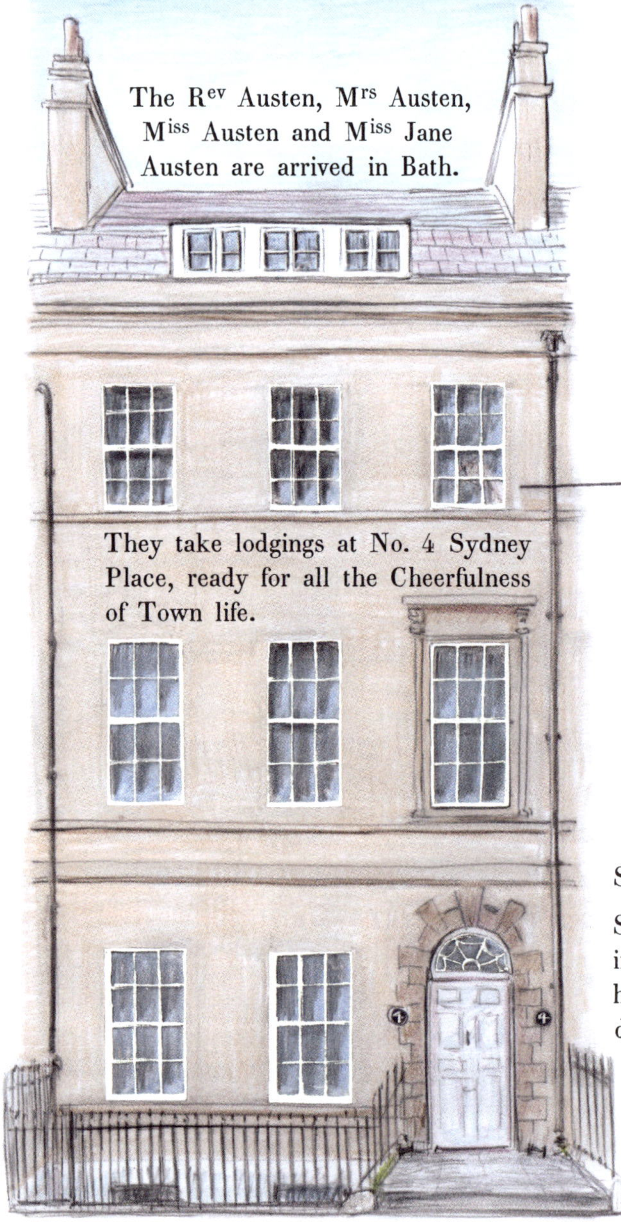

The Rev Austen, Mrs Austen, Miss Austen and Miss Jane Austen are arrived in Bath.

They take lodgings at No. 4 Sydney Place, ready for all the Cheerfulness of Town life.

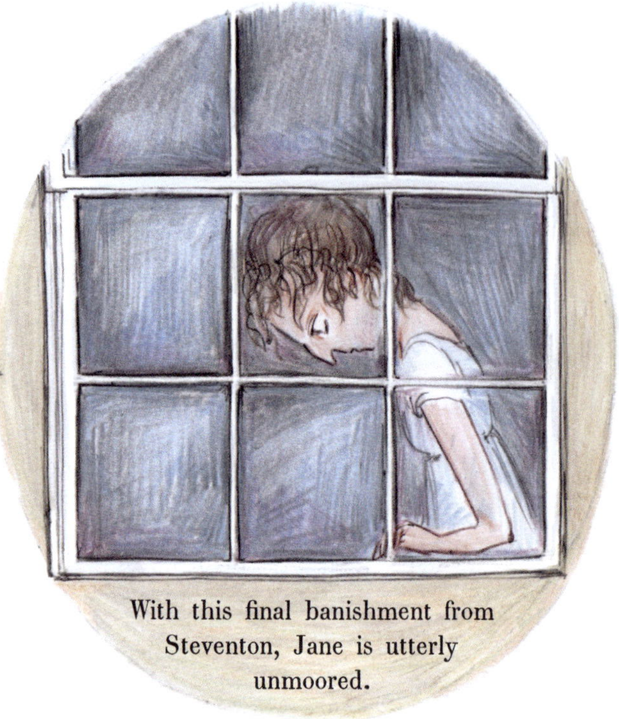

With this final banishment from Steventon, Jane is utterly unmoored.

She feels it at first as the loss of the pleasures of Spring.

She had not known before how much the unfurling flowers in the garden, the glory of the budding woods, had delighted her – what animation, both of body and mind she had derived from watching the advance of that Season. To be losing such pleasures is no trifle. To be losing them, because she is in the midst of closeness and noise, to have confinement, bad air, bad smells, substituted for liberty, freshness, fragrance, and verdure, is infinitely worse.

She sighs for the air, the liberty, the quiet of the country.

The sun's rays falling strongly into the parlour make her still more melancholy, for sunshine appears to her a totally different thing in a town and in the country.

Here, its power is only a glare, a stifling, sickly glare, dazzling on white pavements.

There is neither health nor gaiety in sunshine in a town.

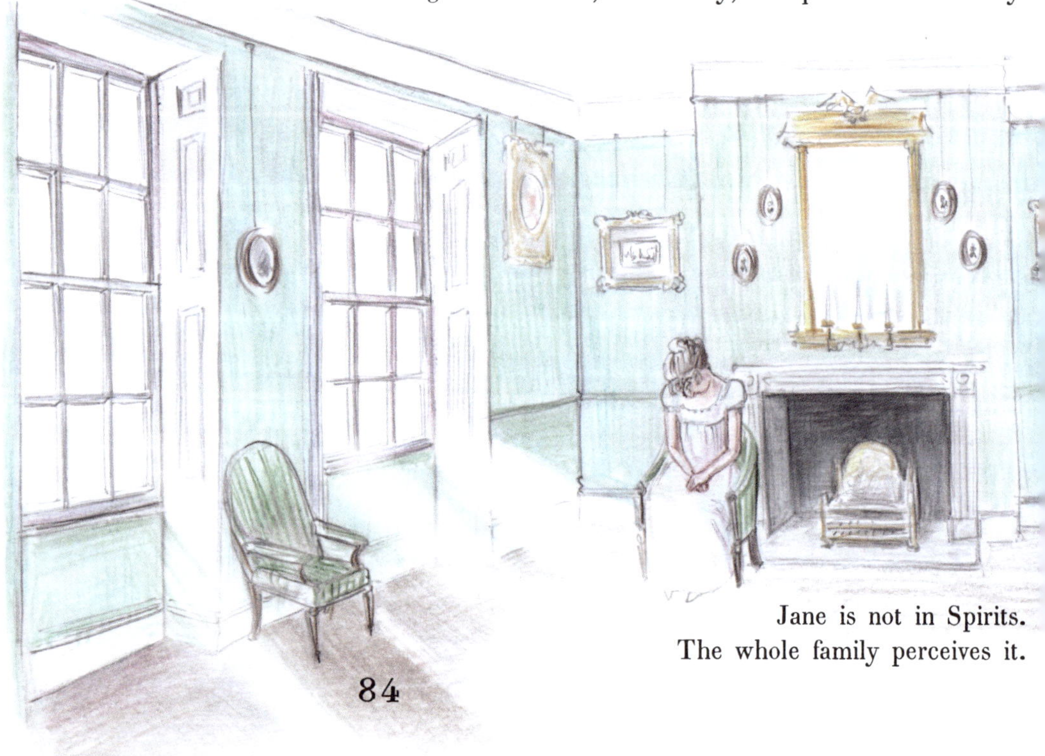

Jane is not in Spirits. The whole family perceives it.

She is propelled, like an automaton, through the whirl of social engagements.

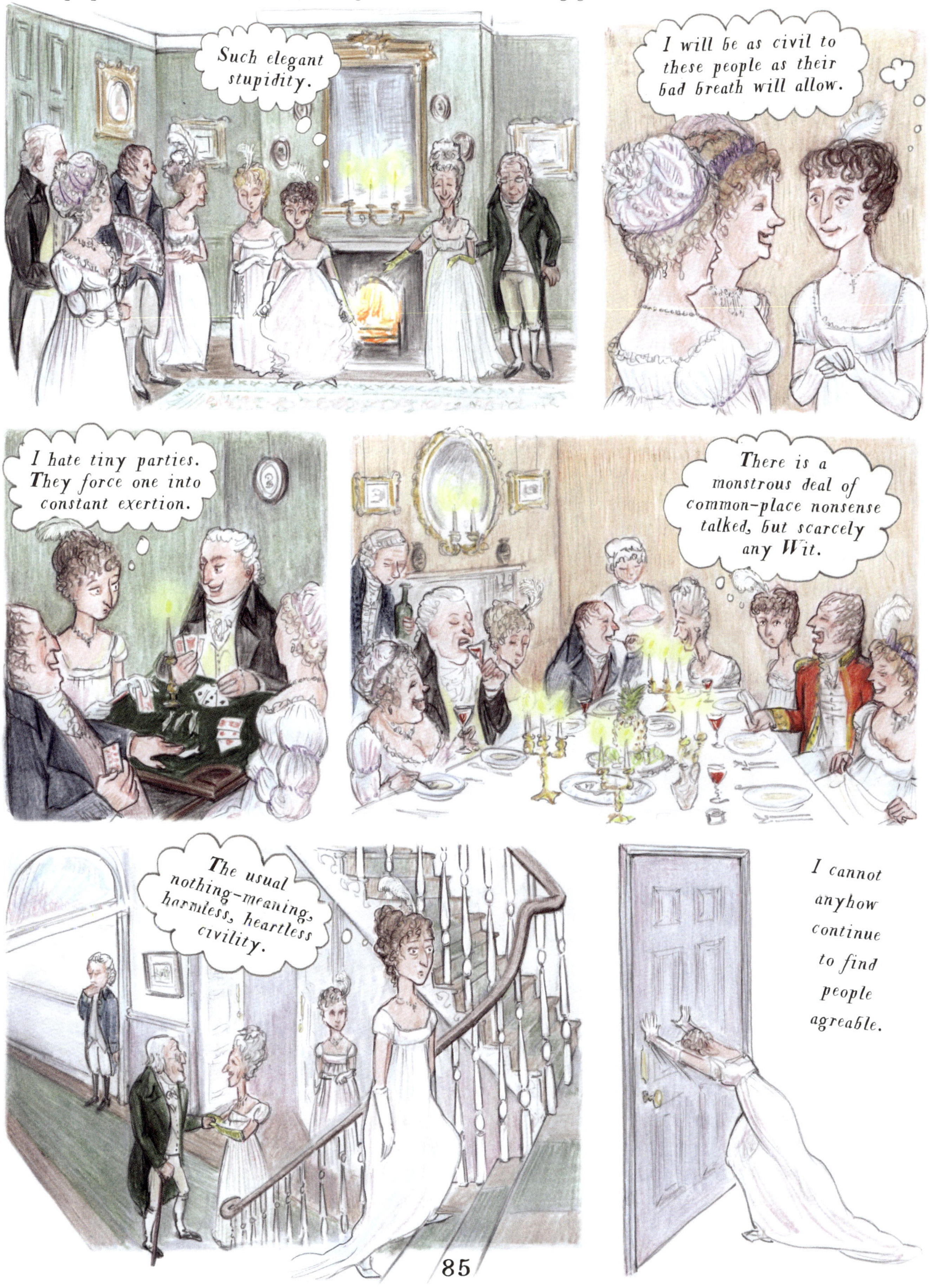
Such elegant stupidity.
I will be as civil to these people as their bad breath will allow.
I hate tiny parties. They force one into constant exertion.
There is a monstrous deal of common-place nonsense talked, but scarcely any Wit.
The usual nothing-meaning, harmless, heartless civility.
I cannot anyhow continue to find people agreable.

Cassandra and Jane are not stupid. They full know the reason for their removal. The object is to captivate some Man of much better fortune than their own.

But, by the same token, they know how desirable they aren't: the portionless, ageing daughters of a country parson.

Even Bath itself is past its best. These days, the truly fashionable frequent Brighthelmstone, or perhaps, the Isle of Wight.

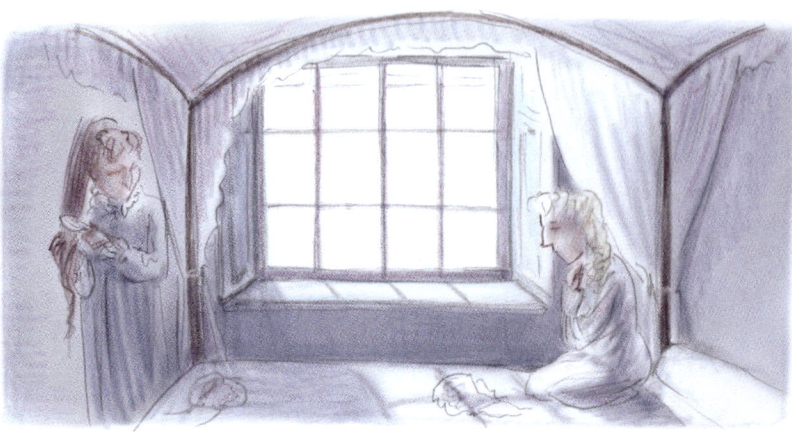

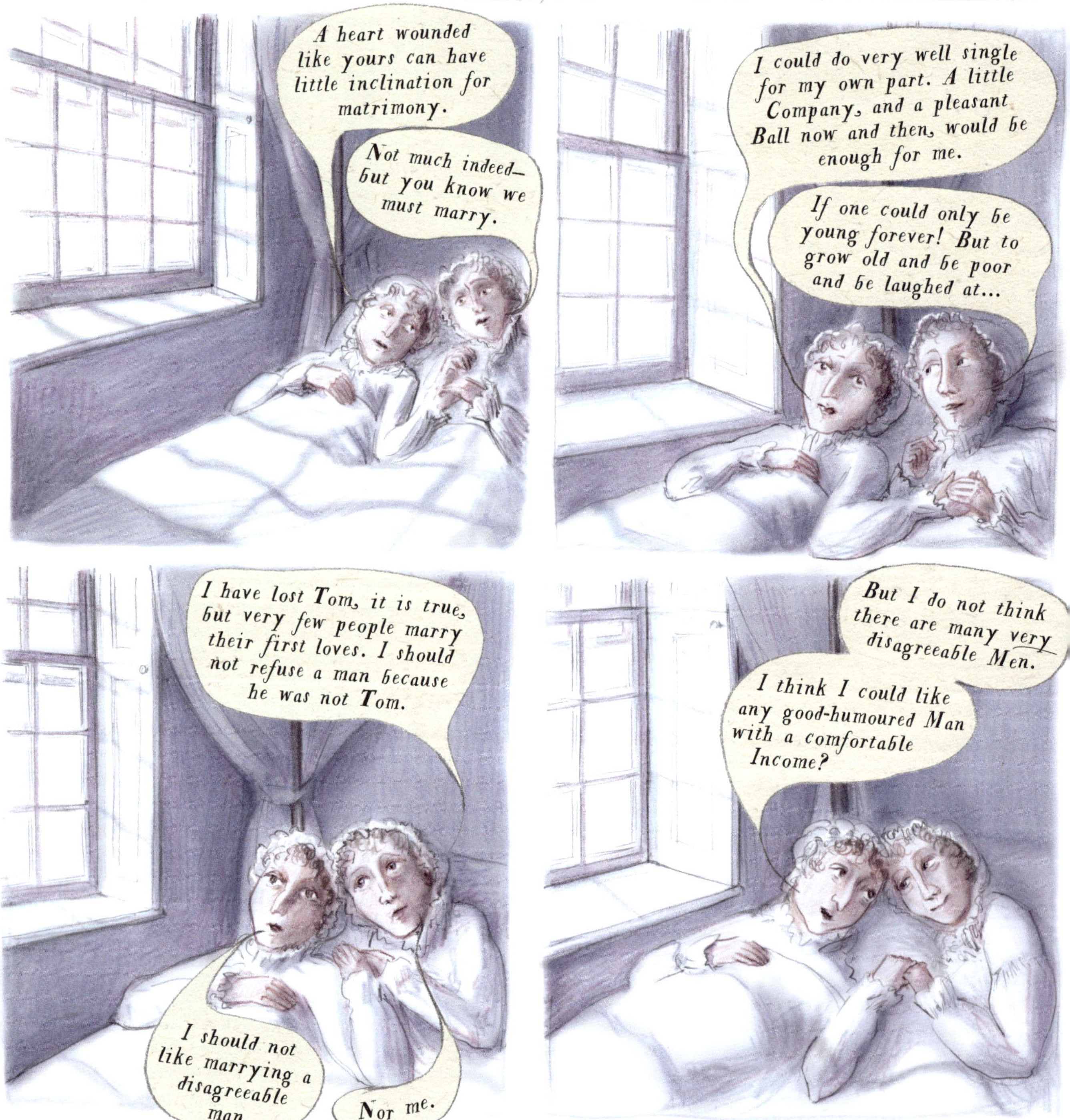
A heart wounded like yours can have little inclination for matrimony.
Not much indeed— but you know we must marry.
I could do very well single for my own part. A little Company, and a pleasant Ball now and then, would be enough for me.
If one could only be young forever! But to grow old and be poor and be laughed at...
I have lost Tom, it is true, but very few people marry their first loves. I should not refuse a man because he was not Tom.
I should not like marrying a disagreeable man.
Nor me.
But I do not think there are many very disagreeable Men.
I think I could like any good-humoured Man with a comfortable Income?

Before the year is out, little Hastings dies suddenly, of a seizure.

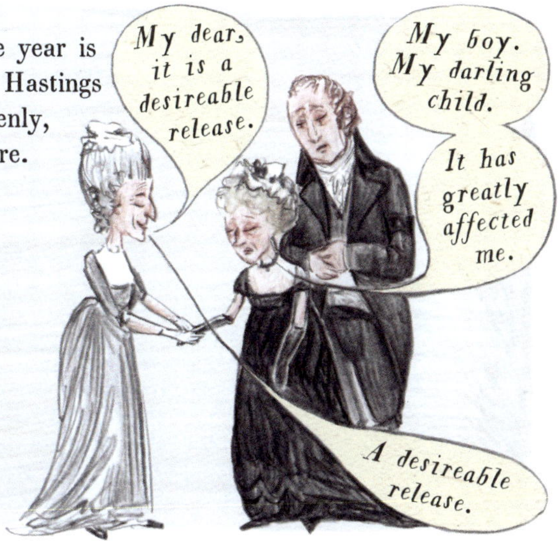

My dear, it is a desireable release.
My boy. My darling child.
It has greatly affected me.
A desireable release.

While Eliza loses her only child, Edward gains his seventh. Baby Marianne joins siblings Elizabeth, Edward J^nr^, William, Henry, George, and Fanny under the care of the indomitable Godmersham nursery-maid, Sackree.

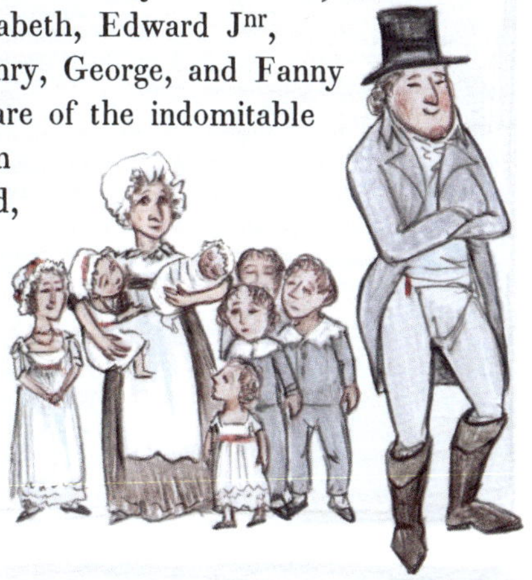

The colour has bled from Jane's life.

She dully copies out her novels, making fair copies in hope of publication, but no new words flow to her quill.

How can she write, without a room for composition?

How can she write, with no reprieve from social calls?

How can she write? Mother is complaining and must be attended to.

How can she write, with three completed novels sitting, mocking her, in manuscript form?

If Jane has thoughts, it is unacceptable to think them.

So she does not.

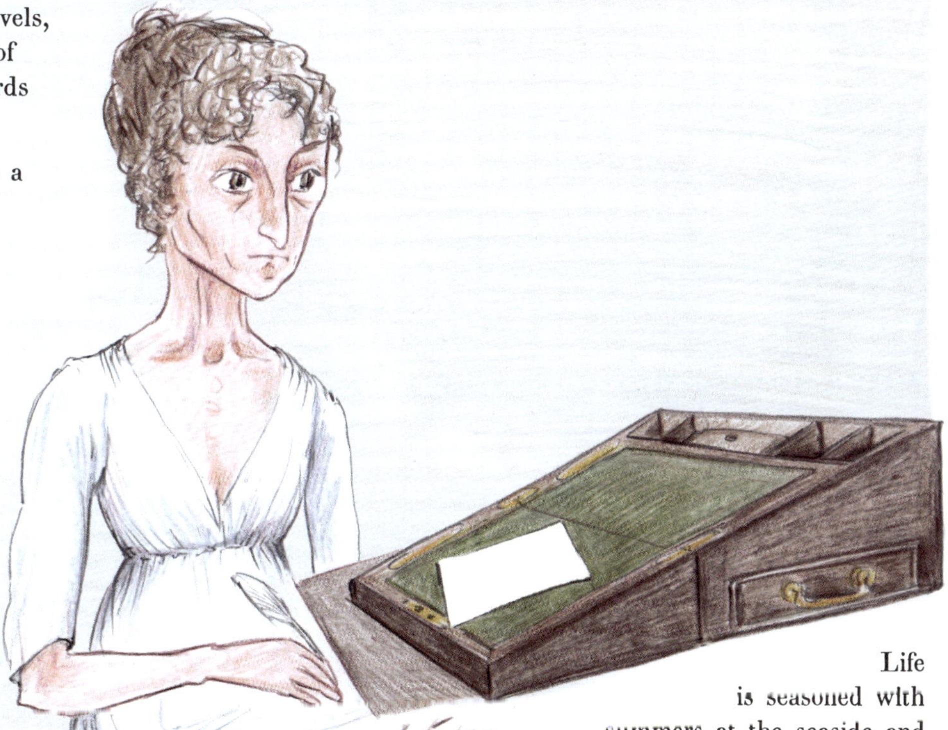

Life is seasoned with summers at the seaside and trips in the winters to visit friends. The Girls are taken, like parcels, from one place to another. Never unaccompanied. Never free.

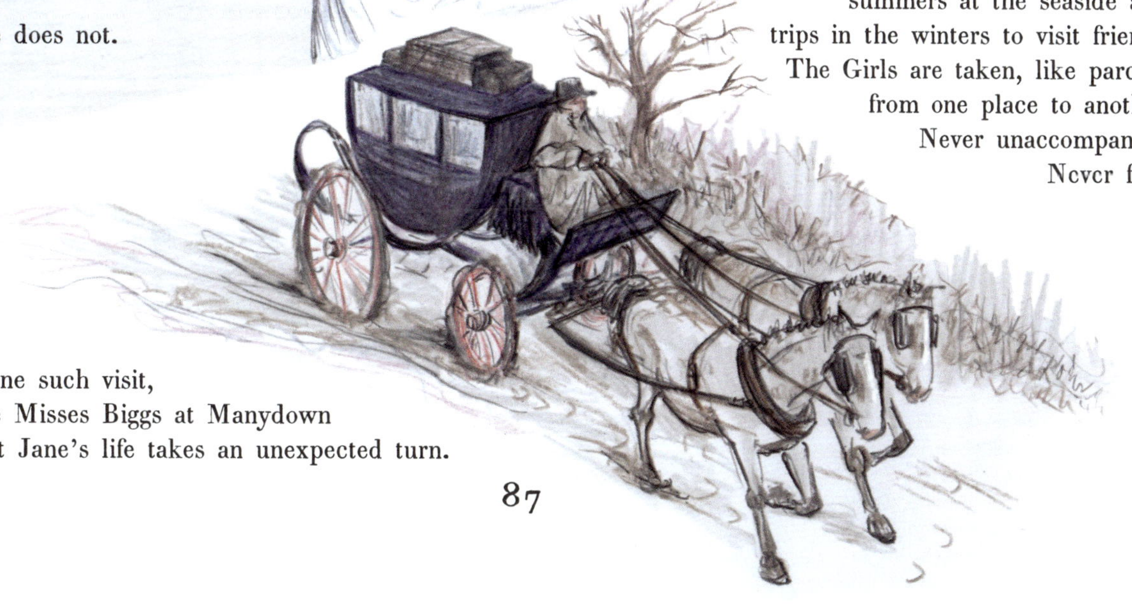

It is on one such visit, to see the Misses Biggs at Manydown Park, that Jane's life takes an unexpected turn.

2nd December 1802.

Catherine and Alethea have left the room, by evident prearrangement, leaving Jane alone with their shy, stumbling younger brother.

Harris Bigg-Wither.

Jane has never given him much notice before. He makes a short speech. Jane is unsure she has heard him correctly.

You want me? to be your Wife?

Me?

Jane is saved! Marriage is the only honourable provision for a well-educated young woman of small fortune, and, however uncertain of giving happiness, must be her pleasantest preservative from want.

The connexion offers nothing but good. Consideration, independence from her mother, a proper home — for herself, for her sister, for her friends Catherine & Alethea. At this moment, she feels that to be mistress of Manydown Park might be something!

Yes. *Yes, I will.*

Acceptance! Her friends are jubilant!

Immediately, Jane is seized by doubt.

to marry without Affection...
...to be bound without Love

She lies awake that whole night, possessed by the most wearing anxiety.

And in the morning, with burning embarrassment, she explains her mistake to Mr Bigg-Withers.

In many respects I think very highly of you.

But we should not suit.

I cannot marry you.

Jane must prevail upon James to accompany her home to Bath. More humiliation.

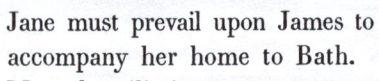

Most inconvenient! I cannot now be back for Sunday. I have Responsibilities, Jane.

And so she must confess the reason for the necessity of her immediate removal, and he, in turn, of course, informs...

...Mother, who is incandescent.

...and if you take it into your head to go on refusing every offer of marriage in this way, you will never get a husband at all and I am sure I do not know who is to maintain you when your father is dead, I shall not be able to keep you, and so I warn you...

Jane's birthday, a few weeks later, is a sombre occasion. She is haunted by her own words, written in jest many years before...

A woman of seven and twenty can never hope to feel or inspire affection again.

Spring 1803. A shard of sunshine pierces Jane's gloom.

Henry, who has, like every military man, a very large acquaintance, utilises it for his sister's benefit. He brings *Susan* to the attention of London publisher Benjamin Crosby & Son.

Acceptance! Jane is jubilant!

Crosby buys the copyright for Ten Pounds.

The money is trifling, but what it represents means more than gold to Jane. Her dream of being a novelist is solidifying into reality.

Jane is thrilled. She waits eagerly to see what happens next..

And she waits.
And waits.
And waits.

The unvarying themes of her life consist in:

Her mother's ailments, real or imagined...

"I have a Dreadful cold in my head. Dreadful."

"I am quite plagued by Rheumaticks."

"We must call Dr Bowen."

"Jane, you know not how it feels to grow Old."

"I have not much compassion for colds in the head without Fever or Sore throat."

...and the continual forging of new acquaintance on the shallow Bath social scene.

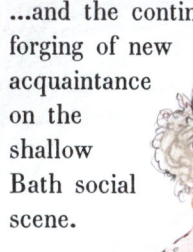

"This one is just like any other short girl with a broad nose and a fashionable dress and an exposed bosom."

Acquaintance which is necessarily truncated by the end of every visitor's six week stay.

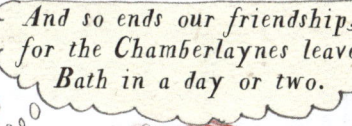

"And so ends our friendship, for the Chamberlaynes leave Bath in a day or two."

Waiting. Waiting. Eighteen months tick by... Twenty months...

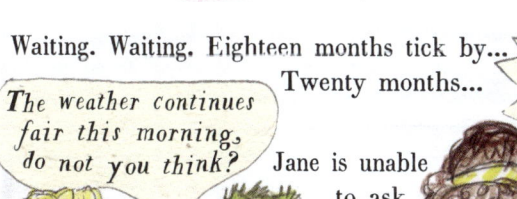

"The weather continues fair this morning, do not you think?"

Jane is unable to ask

"HOW-LONG-DO-NOVELS-TAKE-TO-APPEAR-IN-PRINT?"

SMASH

"I beg your pardon? Did you say something, Miss Austen?"

"Oh! I... I made a comment upon this fine muslin. Lovely print."

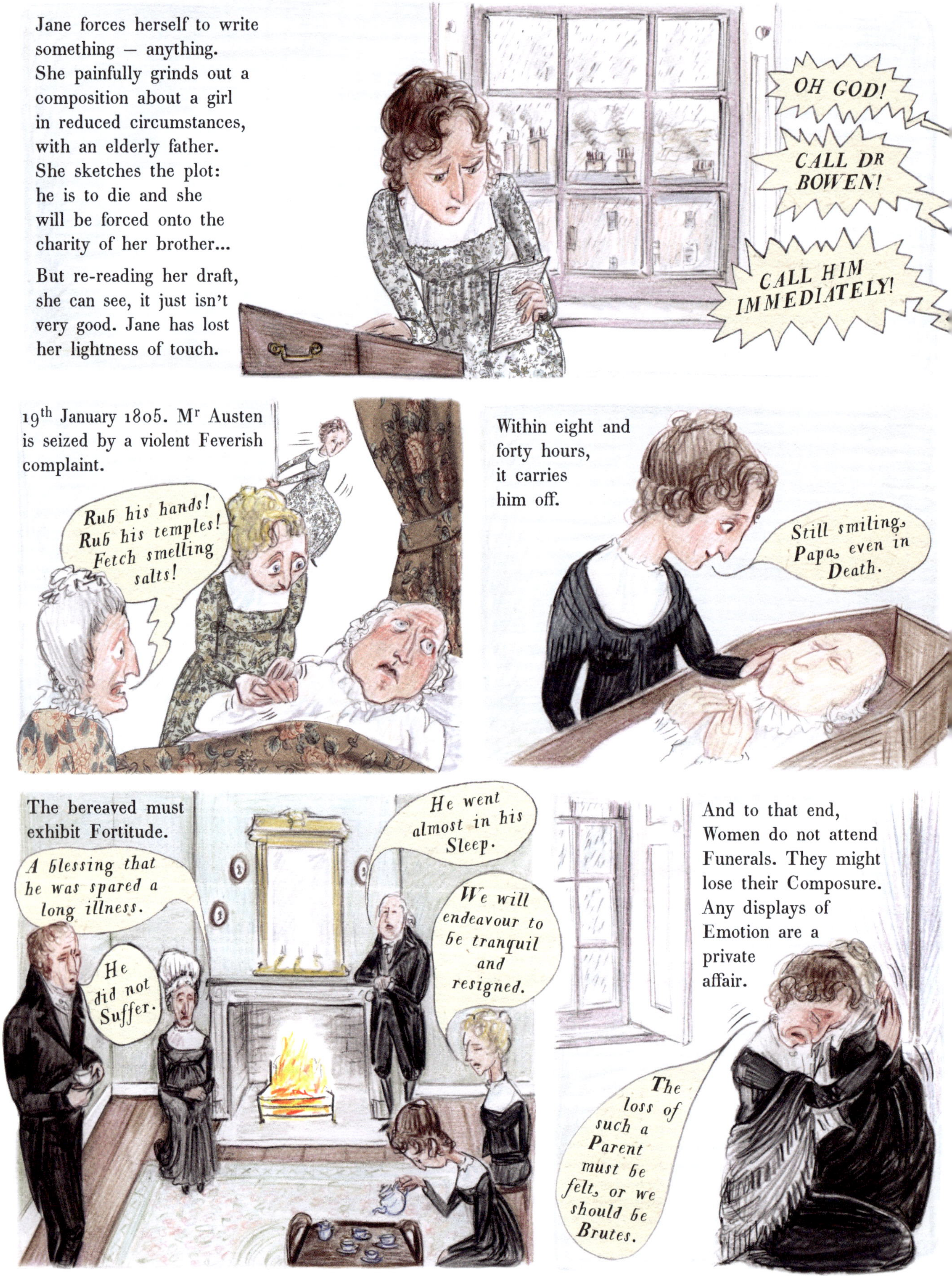
Jane forces herself to write something – anything. She painfully grinds out a composition about a girl in reduced circumstances, with an elderly father. She sketches the plot: he is to die and she will be forced onto the charity of her brother...
But re-reading her draft, she can see, it just isn't very good. Jane has lost her lightness of touch.
OH GOD!
CALL DR BOWEN!
CALL HIM IMMEDIATELY!
19th January 1805. Mr Austen is seized by a violent Feverish complaint.
Rub his hands! Rub his temples! Fetch smelling salts!
Within eight and forty hours, it carries him off.
Still smiling, Papa, even in Death.
The bereaved must exhibit Fortitude.
A blessing that he was spared a long illness.
He did not Suffer.
He went almost in his Sleep.
We will endeavour to be tranquil and resigned.
And to that end, Women do not attend Funerals. They might lose their Composure. Any displays of Emotion are a private affair.
The loss of such a Parent must be felt, or we should be Brutes.

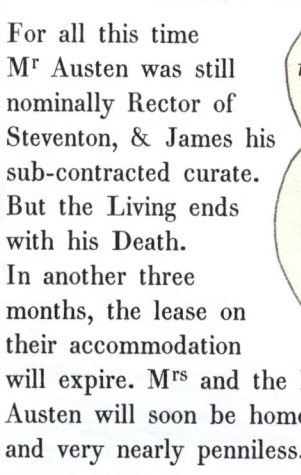

For all this time Mr Austen was still nominally Rector of Steventon, & James his sub-contracted curate. But the Living ends with his Death. In another three months, the lease on their accommodation will expire. Mrs and the Misses Austen will soon be homeless, and very nearly penniless.

The men decide between themselves how best to support them.

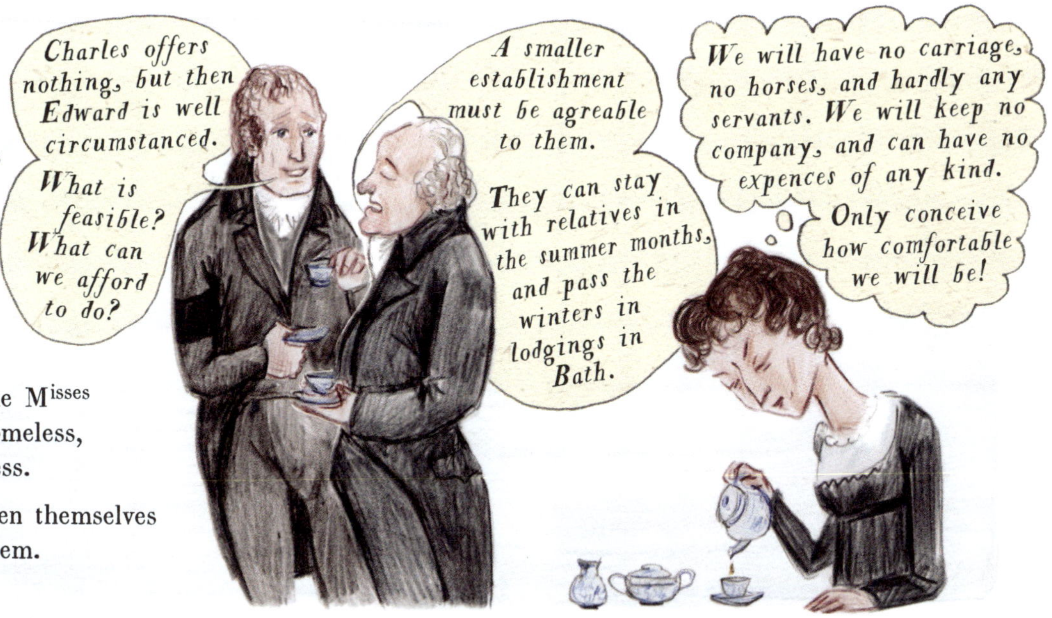
Charles offers nothing, but then Edward is well circumstanced.
A smaller establishment must be agreable to them.
What is feasible? What can we afford to do?
They can stay with relatives in the summer months, and pass the winters in lodgings in Bath.
We will have no carriage, no horses, and hardly any servants. We will keep no company, and can have no expences of any kind.
Only conceive how comfortable we will be!

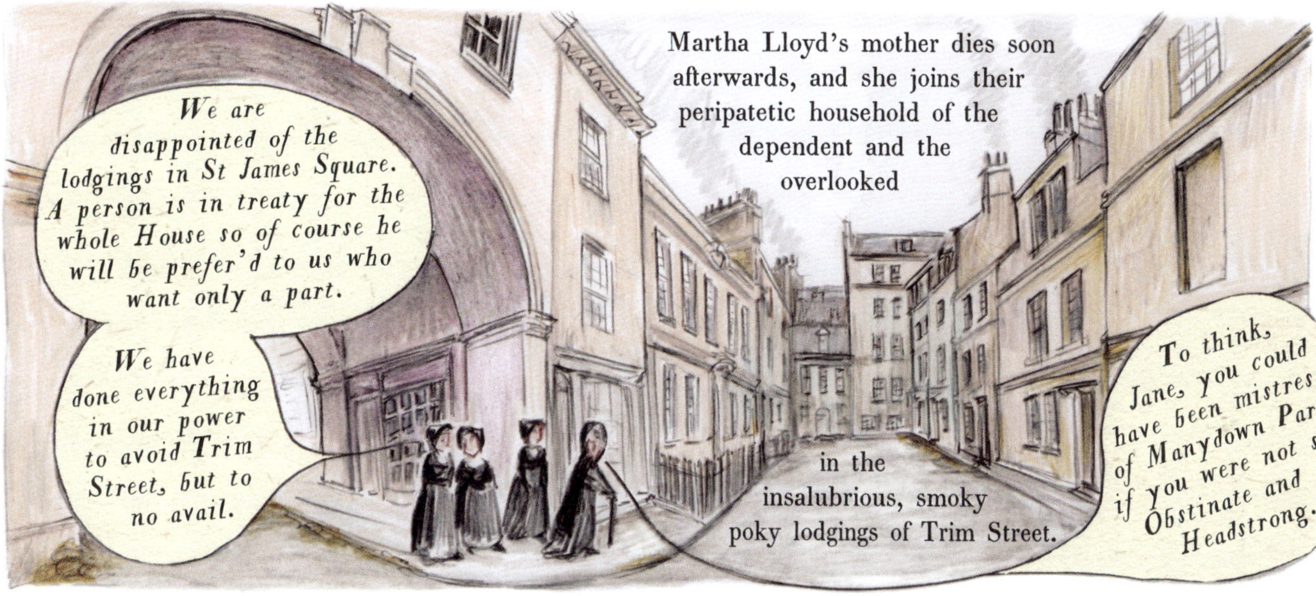
Martha Lloyd's mother dies soon afterwards, and she joins their peripatetic household of the dependent and the overlooked
We are disappointed of the lodgings in St James Square. A person is in treaty for the whole House so of course he will be prefer'd to us who want only a part.
We have done everything in our power to avoid Trim Street, but to no avail.
in the insalubrious, smoky poky lodgings of Trim Street.
To think, Jane, you could have been mistress of Manydown Park if you were not so Obstinate and Headstrong.

And *still* there is no sign of *Susan* appearing in print.

When, after *six years*, another publisher brings out a different novel of that same name, Jane is convinced that it never will.

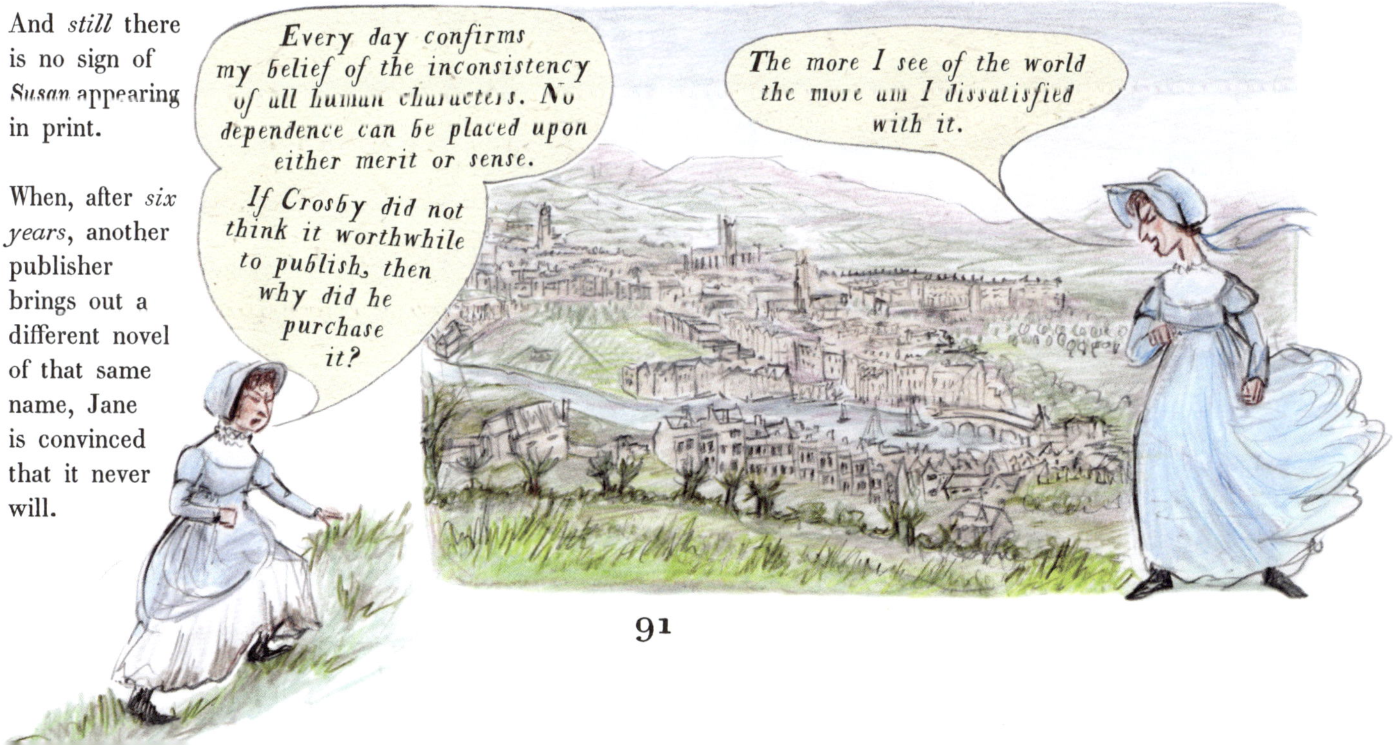
Every day confirms my belief of the inconsistency of all human characters. No dependence can be placed upon either merit or sense.
If Crosby did not think it worthwhile to publish, then why did he purchase it?
The more I see of the world the more am I dissatisfied with it.

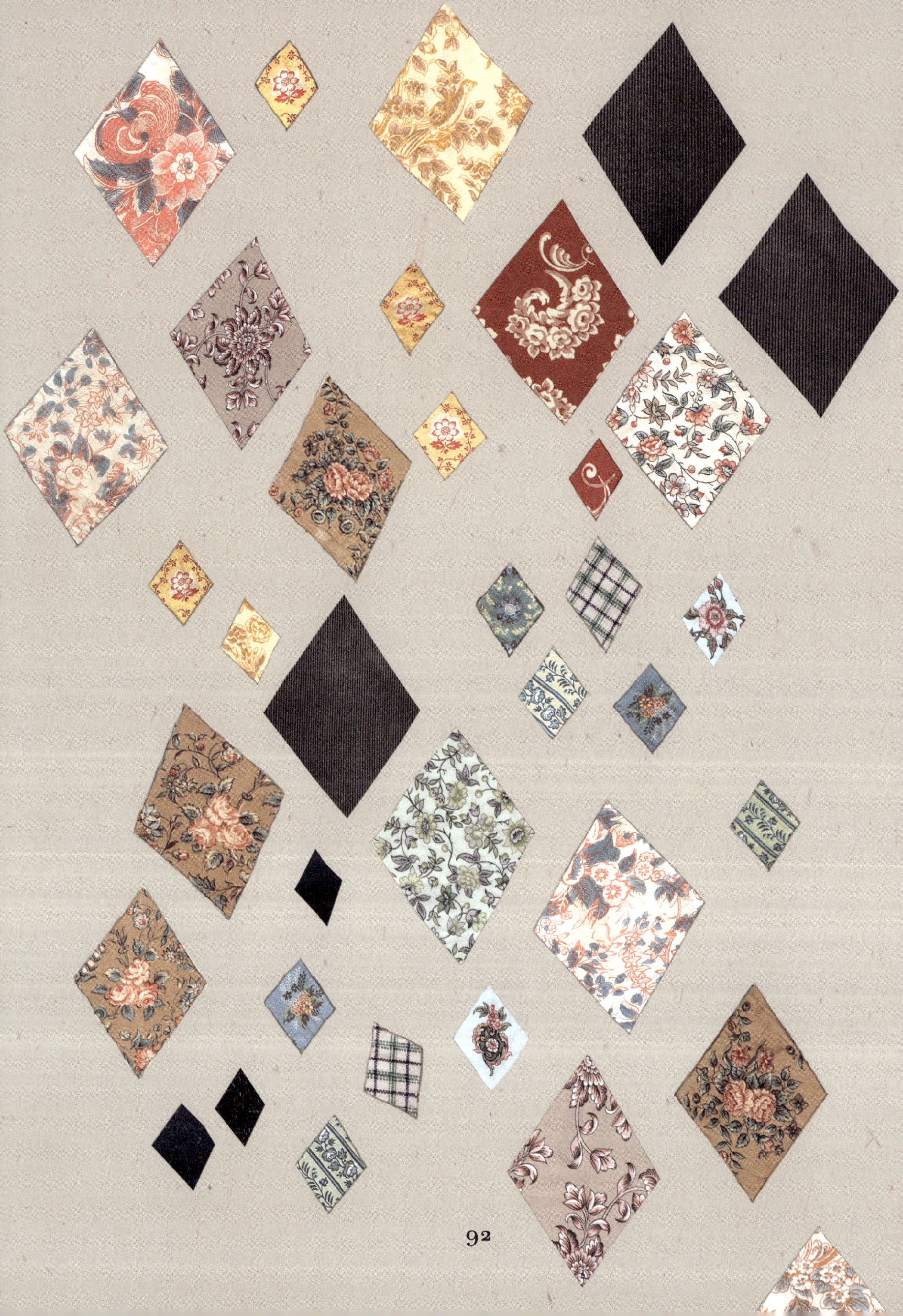

THE WAVES

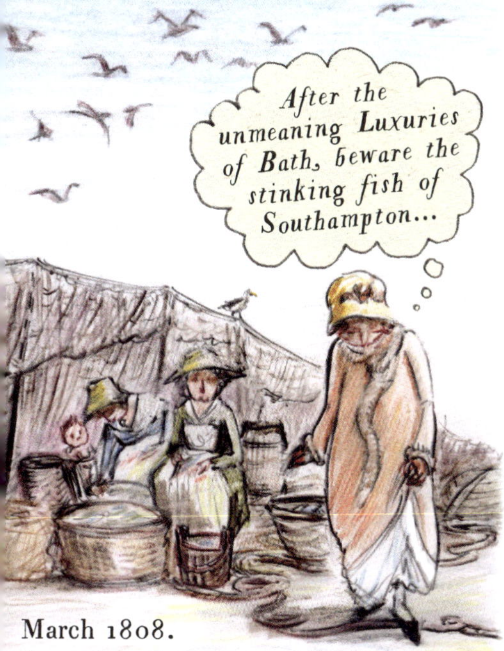
After the unmeaning Luxuries of Bath, beware the stinking fish of Southampton...

March 1808.
Jane picks her way through coils of rope in the dockyards.

The Austen women have washed up in Southampton. Frank has decided that they will be company for his new wife, Mary. It is more than a year since they left Bath, with what happy feelings of escape!

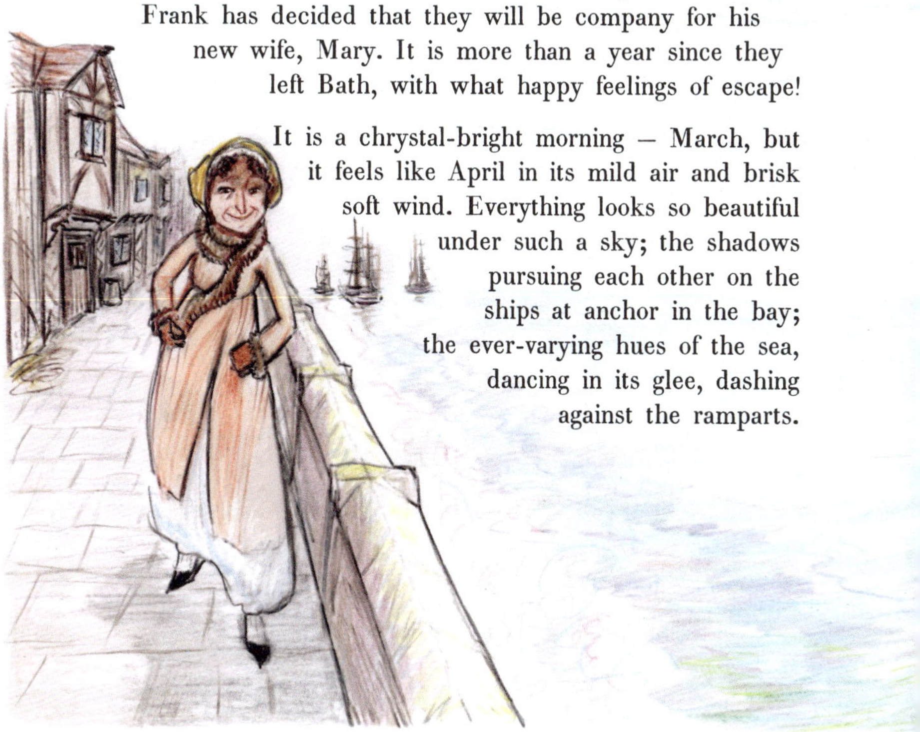

It is a chrystal-bright morning – March, but it feels like April in its mild air and brisk soft wind. Everything looks so beautiful under such a sky; the shadows pursuing each other on the ships at anchor in the bay; the ever-varying hues of the sea, dancing in its glee, dashing against the ramparts.

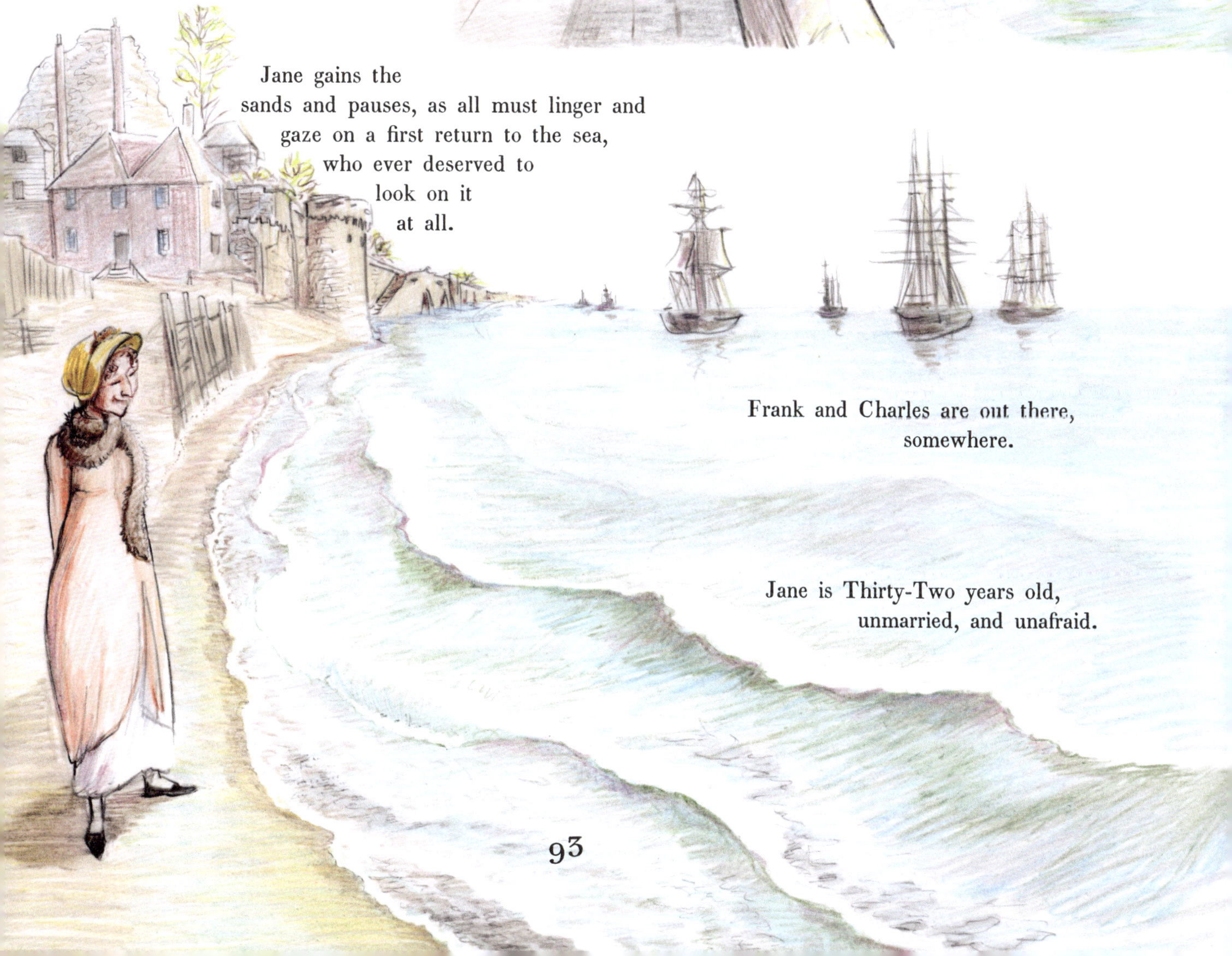

Jane gains the sands and pauses, as all must linger and gaze on a first return to the sea, who ever deserved to look on it at all.

Frank and Charles are out there, somewhere.

Jane is Thirty-Two years old, unmarried, and unafraid.

She is here by appointment.

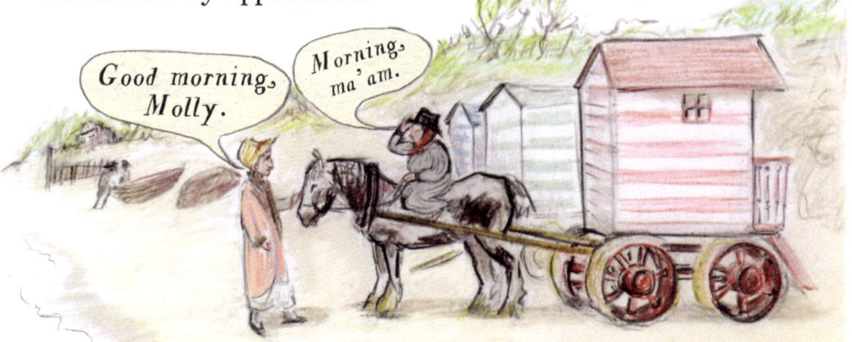
Good morning, Molly.
Morning, ma'am.

So she greets her Dipper, absent mindedly pats the whiskery muzzle of the stolid cob pony, and mounts the painted steps of the Bathing Machine.

It trundles into the waves and wheels around.

It halts.

Jane emerges.

She plunges in.

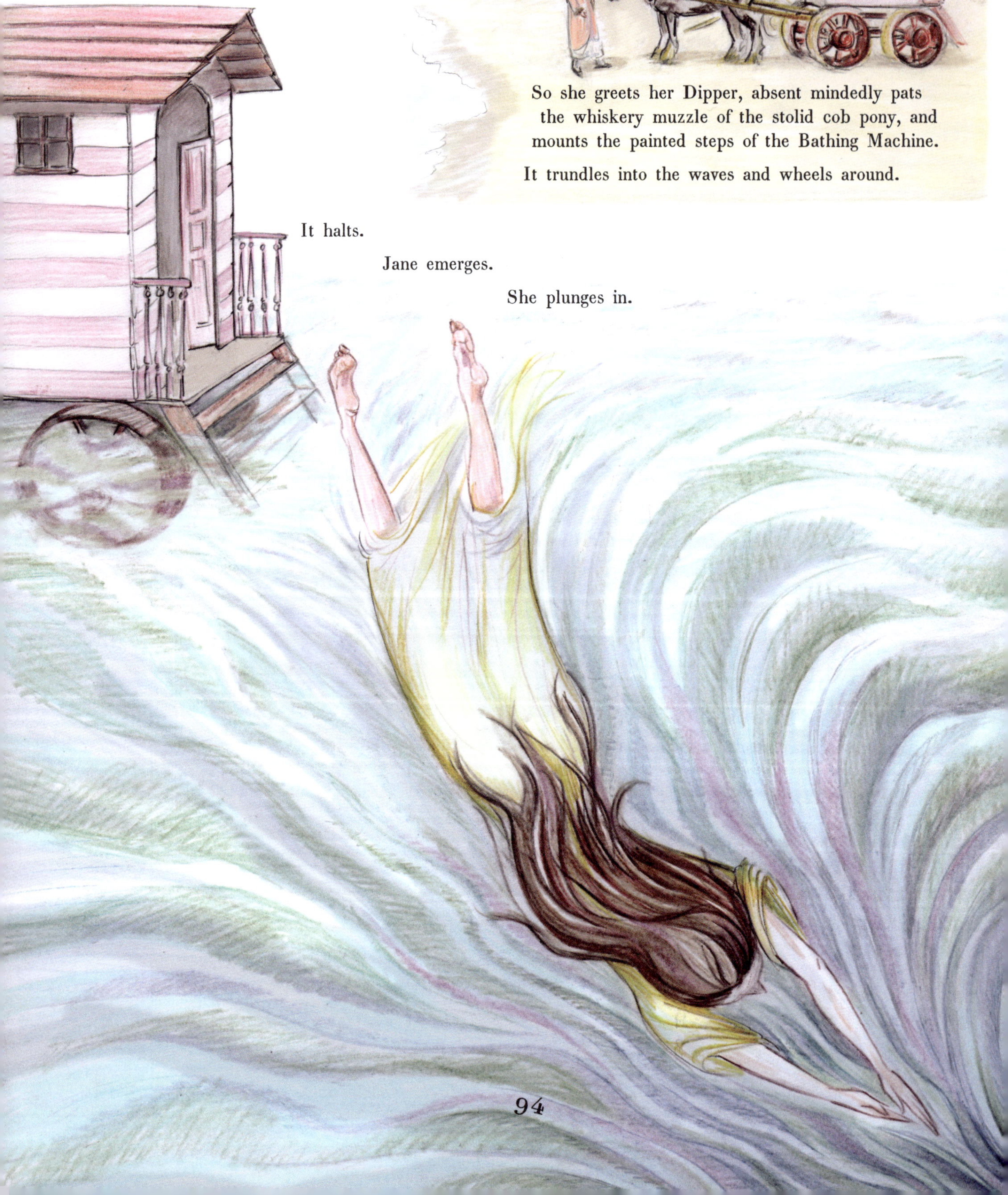

Her nerves are thrilled,

her senses sated,

her spirits soar.

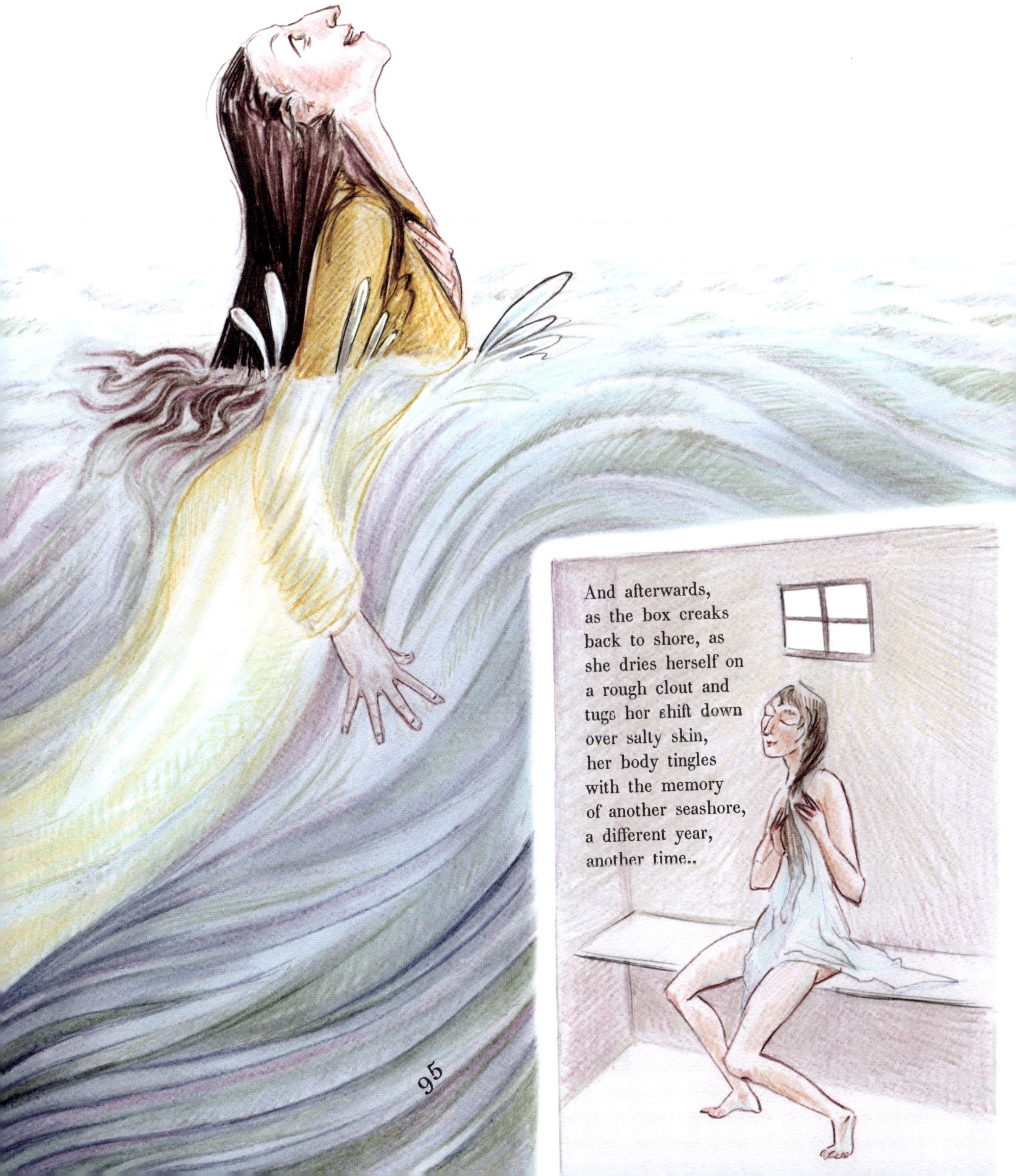

And afterwards,
as the box creaks
back to shore, as
she dries herself on
a rough clout and
tugs her shift down
over salty skin,
her body tingles
with the memory
of another seashore,
a different year,
another time..

They say every body is in love once in their lives.

Aunt Cassandra, in old age, tells a story:
Jane met a Gentleman, one summer, by the sea.

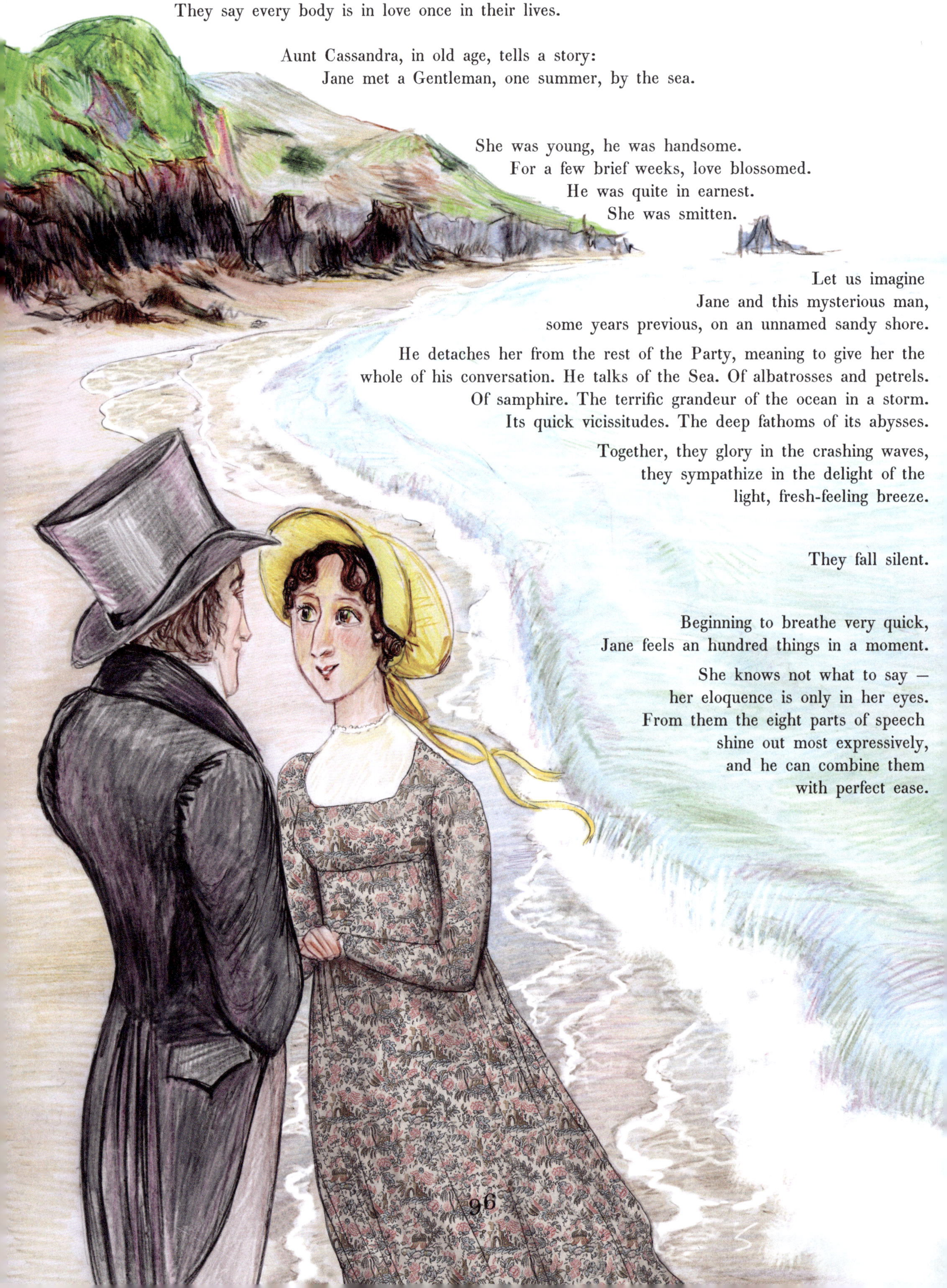

She was young, he was handsome.
For a few brief weeks, love blossomed.
He was quite in earnest.
She was smitten.

Let us imagine
Jane and this mysterious man,
some years previous, on an unnamed sandy shore.

He detaches her from the rest of the Party, meaning to give her the whole of his conversation. He talks of the Sea. Of albatrosses and petrels. Of samphire. The terrific grandeur of the ocean in a storm. Its quick vicissitudes. The deep fathoms of its abysses.

Together, they glory in the crashing waves,
they sympathize in the delight of the
light, fresh-feeling breeze.

They fall silent.

Beginning to breathe very quick,
Jane feels an hundred things in a moment.

She knows not what to say –
her eloquence is only in her eyes.
From them the eight parts of speech
shine out most expressively,
and he can combine them
with perfect ease.

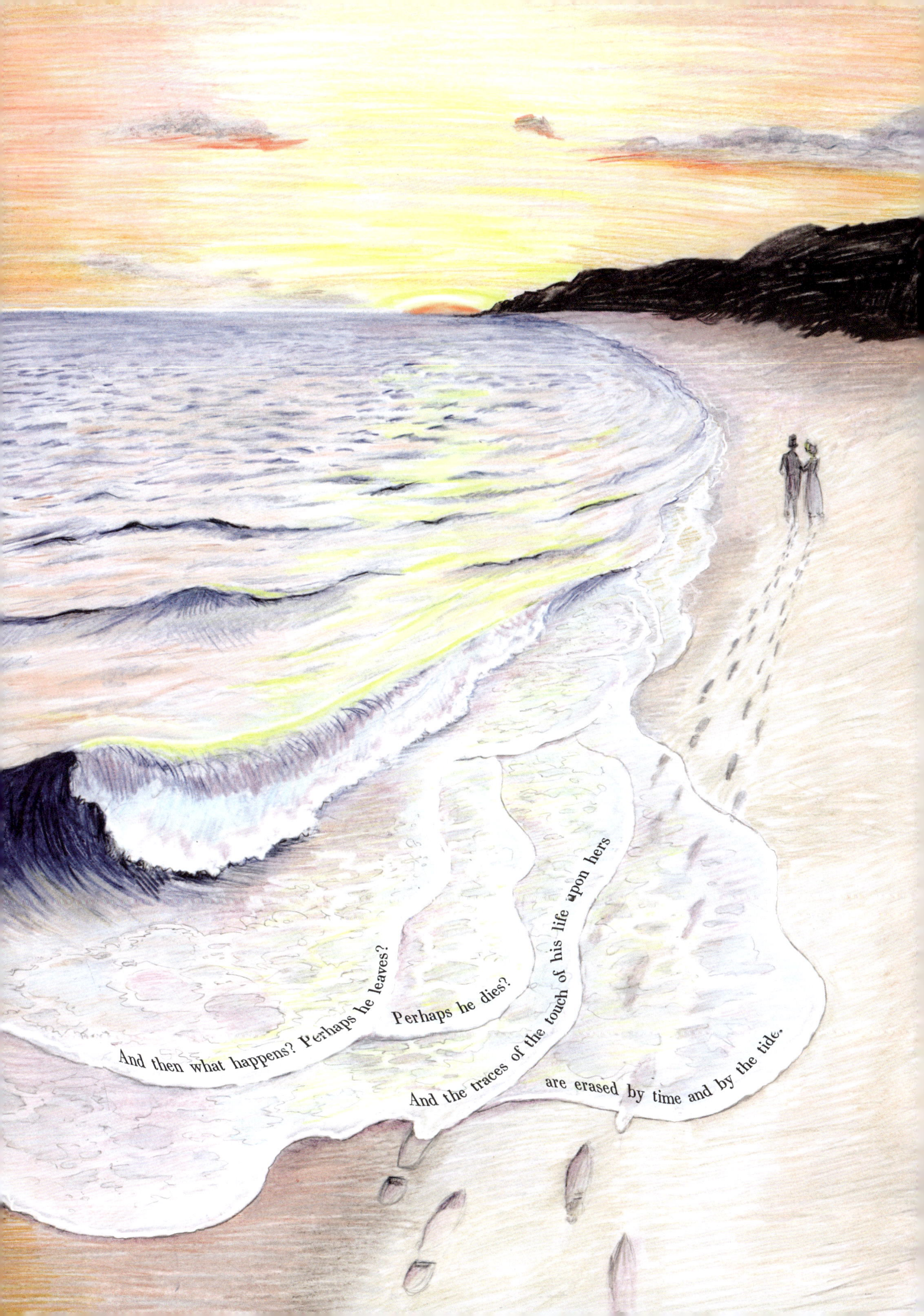
And then what happens? Perhaps he leaves?
Perhaps he dies?
And the traces of the touch of his life upon hers
are erased by time and by the tide.

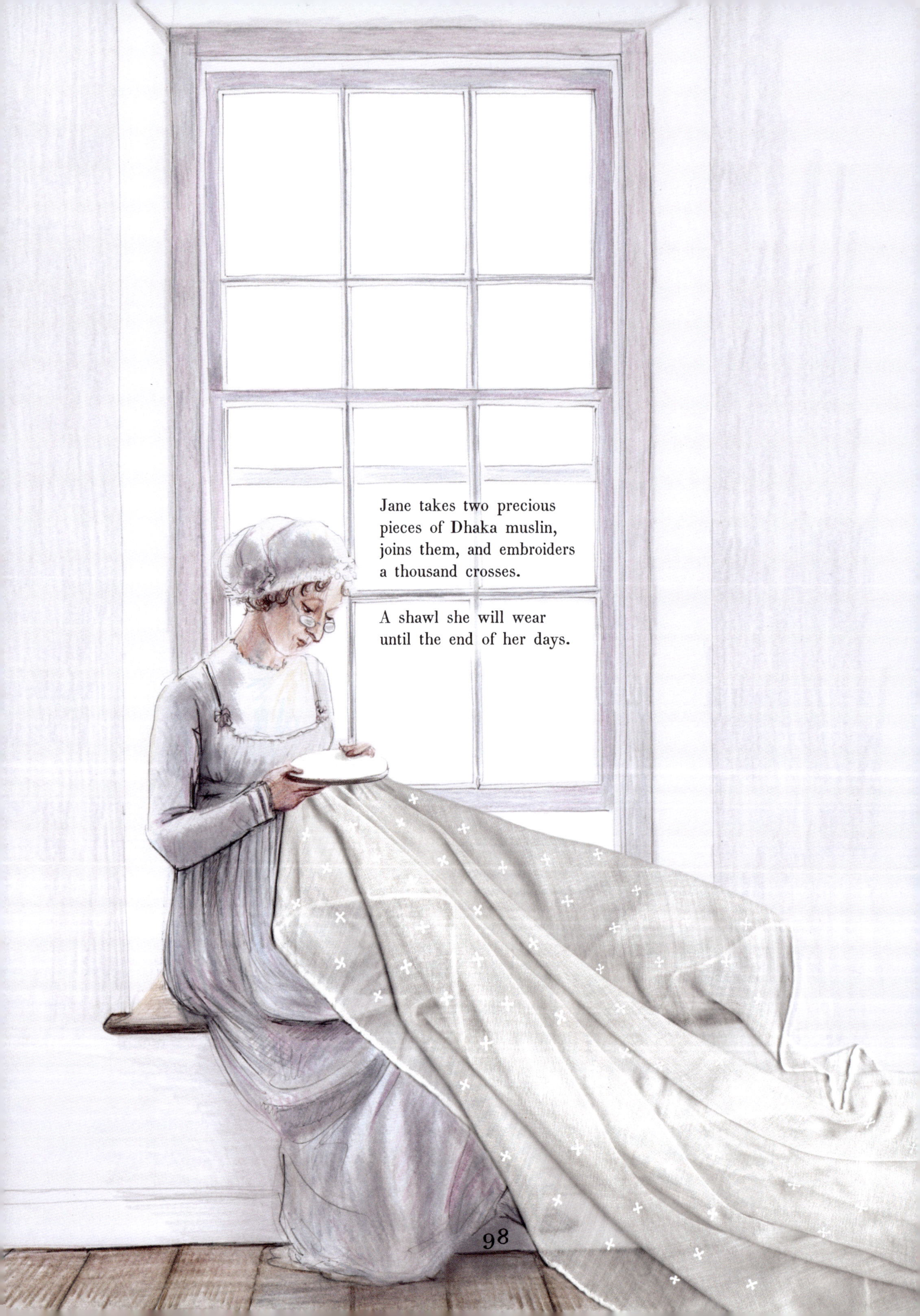

Jane takes two precious pieces of Dhaka muslin, joins them, and embroiders a thousand crosses.

A shawl she will wear until the end of her days.

INTERLUDE
We piece together Jane's words, like patchwork.
But there are other voices in these fabrics,
if we choose to hear them.

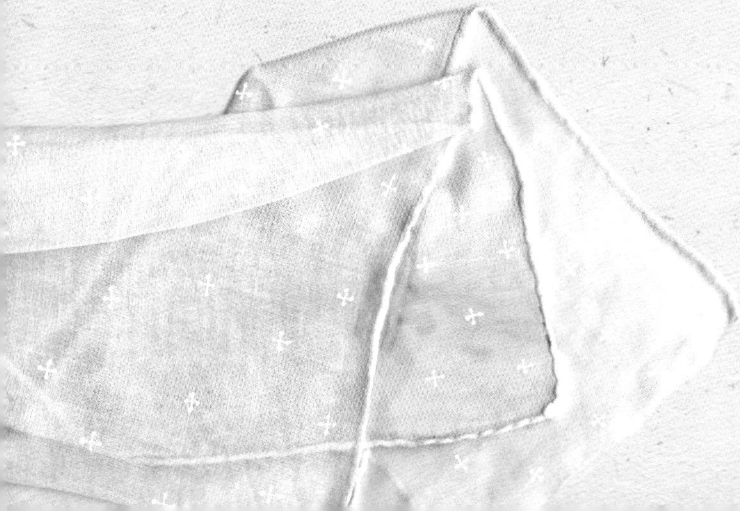

THE MUSLIN

The year is 1809.

A woman sits, at dawn,
in a boat on the river Meghna,
and spins, and as she spins,
she sings

ভররে পরে কাপড় তৈয়ের কইরল — *Cloth on the loom is made*
দীনবন্ধু কারকির — *By the craftsman, friend of the poor,*
মনপুির কামিনী মিলে — *Together with Manipuri woman.*
ওরে পাছ পাইড়তে দিচ্ছে জুইড়ে — *Along its borders, they are connecting*
প্রেমে রসরে মার লাগাইয়ে — *The colours of love...*

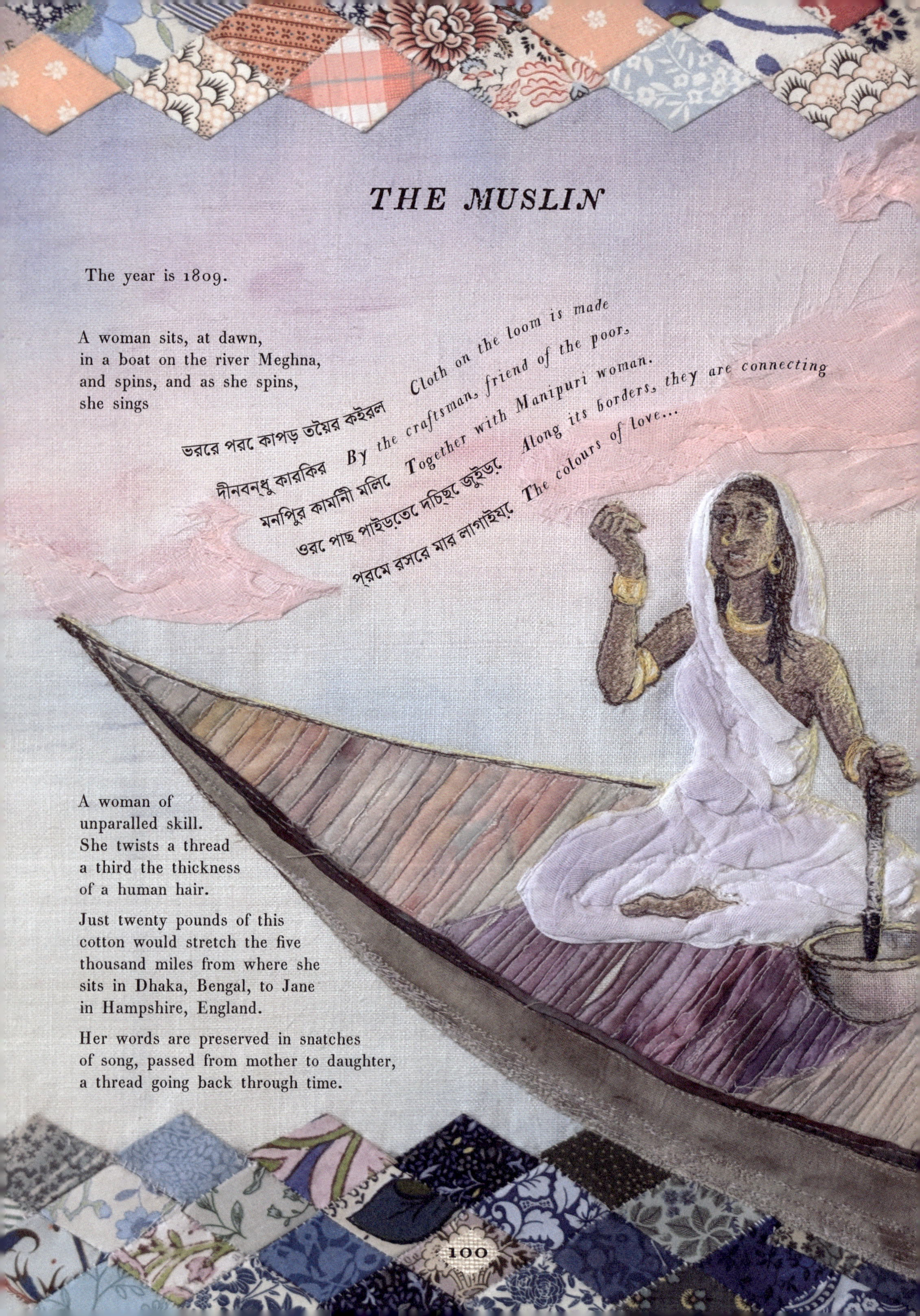

A woman of
unparalled skill.
She twists a thread
a third the thickness
of a human hair.

Just twenty pounds of this cotton would stretch the five thousand miles from where she sits in Dhaka, Bengal, to Jane in Hampshire, England.

Her words are preserved in snatches of song, passed from mother to daughter, a thread going back through time.

The phuti karpas
cotton plant grows only by
these waters.

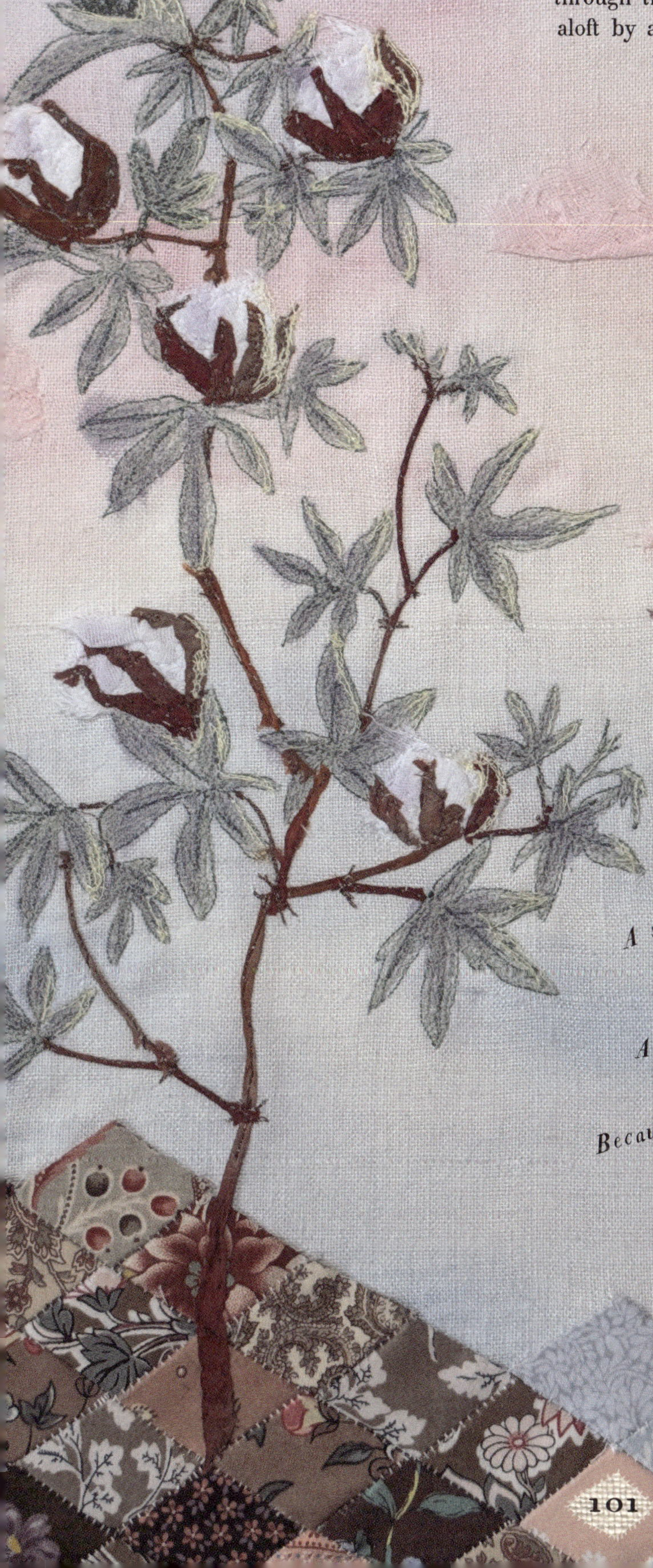

The soft cotton bolls are combed
through the jawbone of a catfish, fibres thrummed
aloft by a vibrating bow, collected on a lacquered
reed, stored in a supple eelskin,
spun in the mists of dawn.

The thread is boiled in
parched rice water. Strung on a loom
in a flooded pit. Deftly, delicately,
painstakingly woven.

The cloth is steamed
and bleached with lime juice
and dried and bleached and steamed
again and polished smooth with
conch shells.

So many hands.

So many
voices.

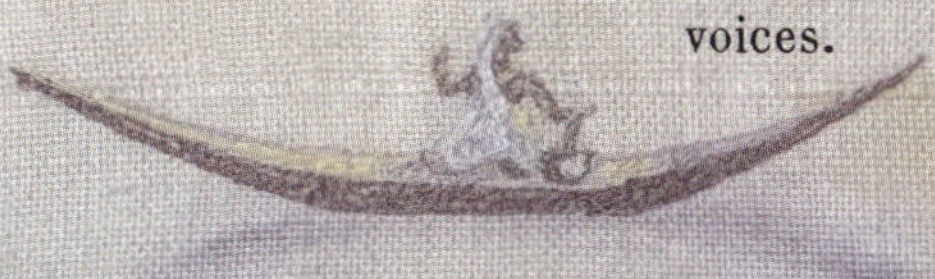

What is
this she is singing?

চরকা আমার ছেলে মেয়ে

A spinning wheel my son, my bridegroom,

চরকা নাতিপুতি

A spinning wheel my grandchild

চরকার দৌলতে আমার

Because of a wheel outside my room,

দরজায় বান্ধা হাতি লো সজনী

An elephant by my door, I find.

The British East India Company Agent stands by the door of the weaver's hut.
He inspects the cloth.

A cloth so fine that it may pass through his wedding ring.
Cloth that robed Mughal princes and Roman emperors.
That poets described as "the skin of the moon," as "the light vapours of dawn," as "webs of woven wind." That bewildered British clothmakers said "might be thought the work of faeries."

He is not here to appreciate its poetry.
He is here to assess its value.

He points out some imaginary imperfections in the muslin, and gives less than he said he would. He gives less than the debt that the weaver already owes, debt which grows larger year by year, no matter how diligently the weaver works his heddles and shuttles. Debt that will be passed on to the weaver's sons and his sons' sons.

The weaver has no choice. It is illegal to sell to anyone except the British East India Company.

"I gave but five shillings a yard for it, and a true Indian muslin."

And now the
weaver must pay
income tax,
special tax,
ceremonial tax
incidental tax,
land rent, loom
charge, loom tax,
arbitrary tax.

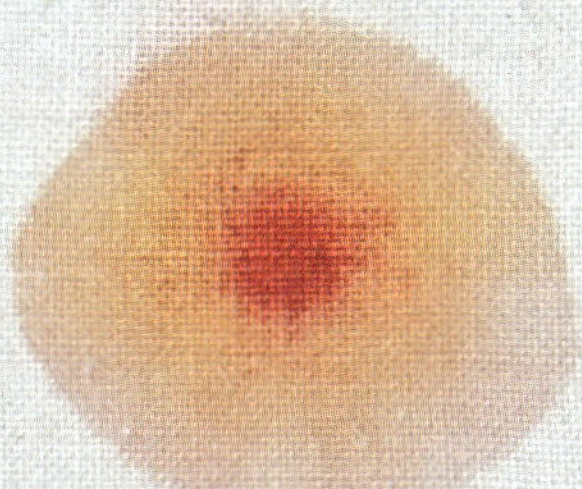

The rains fail.
The fields bleach dry.
Famine.

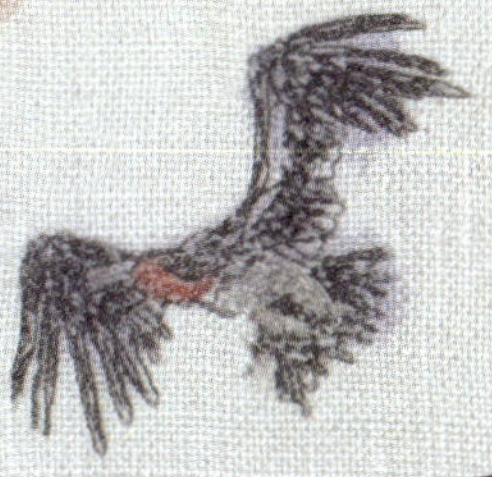

East India Company
Officials buy up the
rice and inflate
the price.

Children cannot
eat muslin.

The spindles are
stilled. Looms broken
up for firewood.

She sings

এখন কাপড় বোনায় লভ্য নাইক উল্টো দেনায় হয় সারা

Now there is no profit in weaving cloth. Instead, you are fully in debt.

কাপাস তুলো নেইক দেশে কেশেরে ফুলকোয় মাঠ ভরা

No karpas cotton in the country. Fields are filled with puffs of catkins.

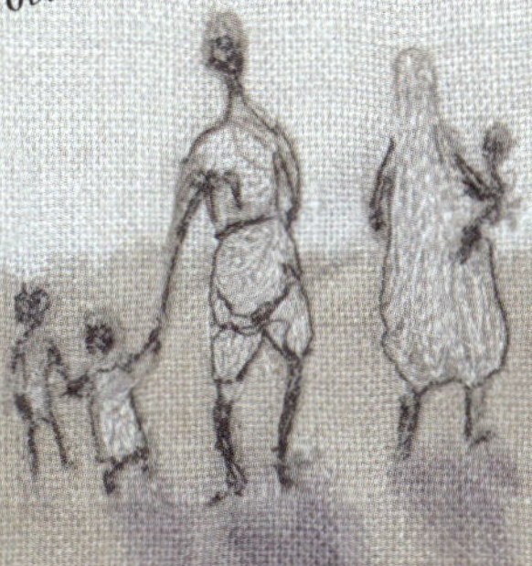

In another nine years,
the Company Commercial
Residency at Dhaka will close.

The phuti karpas plant will be lost to the wild.

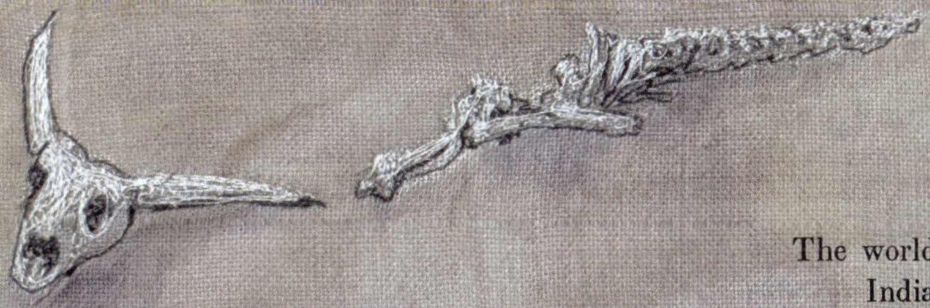

The world will never see true
Indian muslin again.

THE CHINTZ

The British East India Company.

A private corporation which has the power to raise an army, invade a country, tax the populace, mint a currency, and spend the funds thus raised upon more soldiers to consolidate its hold.

And its business? Cloth. Perfect, brilliant, and beautiful.

...Cotton calicoes, chintzes, seersuckers, dimities, muslins lighter than air, silks from Malda, Pullicat and Cossimbazar...

More than 75 per cent of its exports are textiles: tens of millions of yards per year.

As Company profits increase, and share-holders reap their dividends, the income of the Indian worker falls.

The weaver. The dyer. The carver of the intricate shesham wood blocks. The printer. The washerwoman.

Their income is less than a fifth of that of their grandparents.

These chintz printers, pinning out the cotton and carefully placing and tapping down the designs — they might as well be printing pound notes.

কৃষকরে ধনে পুরাণে, দহিলে নীল আগুনে
Our hearts and lives have been burnt with blue flame.

গুণরাশি কি কুদিনে, কল্লে হতো পদারপণ।
On what a bad day you have come here.

দাদনের সুকৌশলে, শ্বেতে সমাজের বলে,
With cunning loans, with the power of White society,

লুঠছে সকল তো হে
You have looted it all.

কি আর আছে এখন
What are the remains now?

"Indian Cotton Manufactures, from whence that astonishing Mass of Wealth has flowed which Bengal has poured into the Lap of Great Britain."

The year is 1809.

Jane's brother Frank is escorting a convoy of East India Company cargo.

The Company gifts him a thousand pounds for his service.

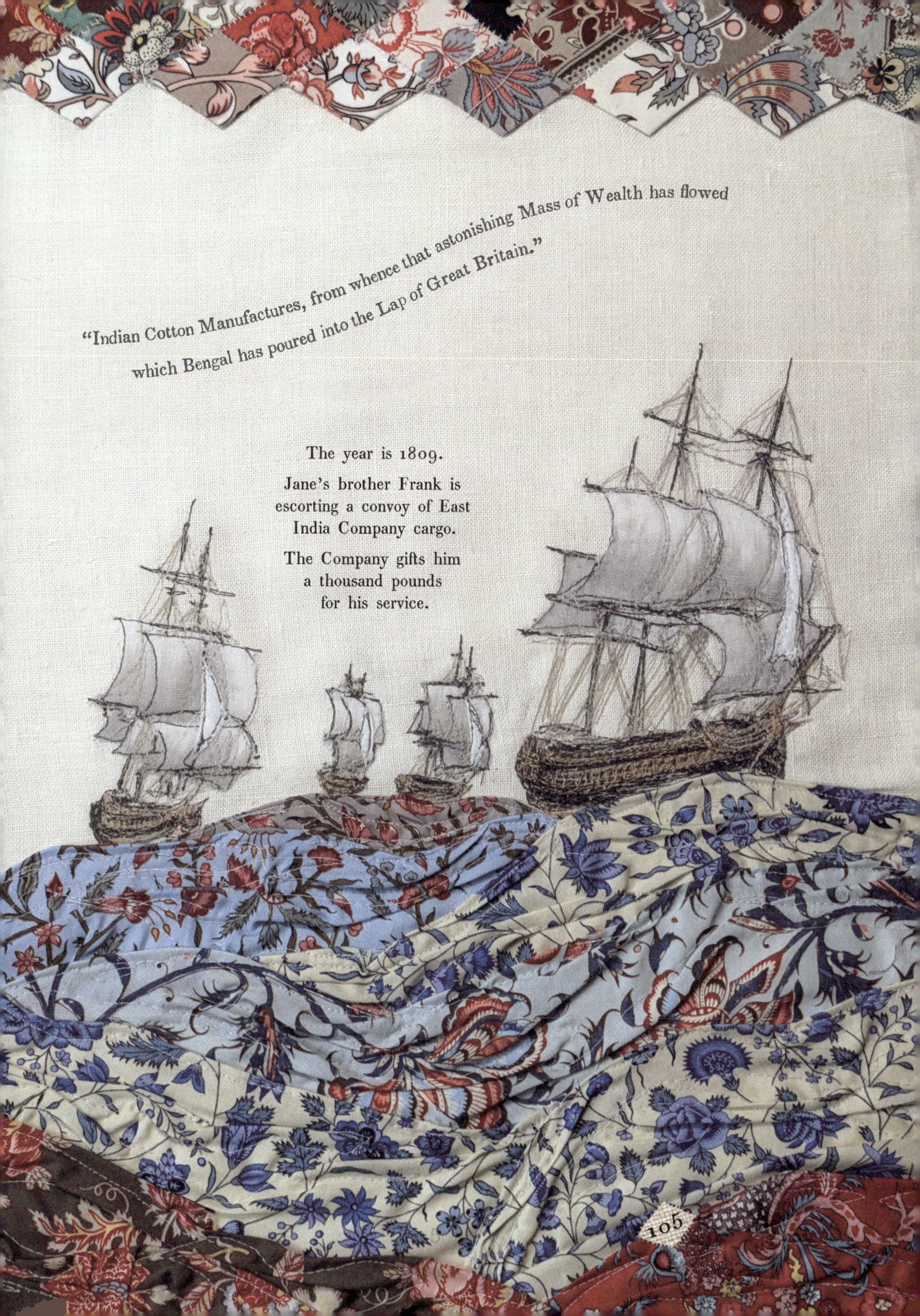

Here is the Great Warren Hastings, one-time Govenor-General of Bengal.

He relaxes by his fireside at his grand estate in Gloucestershire, bought with East India Company funds.
Indian maidens ornament the fire surround. The arms of his chair are carved into tiger heads. The ceiling cornices are gilded lotus leaves.
The furnishings, are, of course, all of the finest Indian chintz.

His words are proclaimed before Parliament. They are printed in books. We may read of his achievements.

"Mr Hastings has not only preserved and extended our dominions, he has increased the revenues of the Company above two million pounds annually. By those strong measures which he took he saved India, and by no other measure could India have been preserved."

Warren Hastings went off to India to seek his fortune.

"His" fortune.

And became so rich that he could casually gift ten thousand pounds to Eliza, a child who was *not even* his daughter.

Indian weavers' money, bequeathed to Eliza, that becomes Henry's upon marriage, and that Jane shall have the use of, to stand surety for her publication ventures.

Such are the threads that criss-cross the fabric of society.

1809. Mr Hastings breakfasts upon lychees and custard apples from his Hot House. He receives a letter, and a gift, from Eliza:

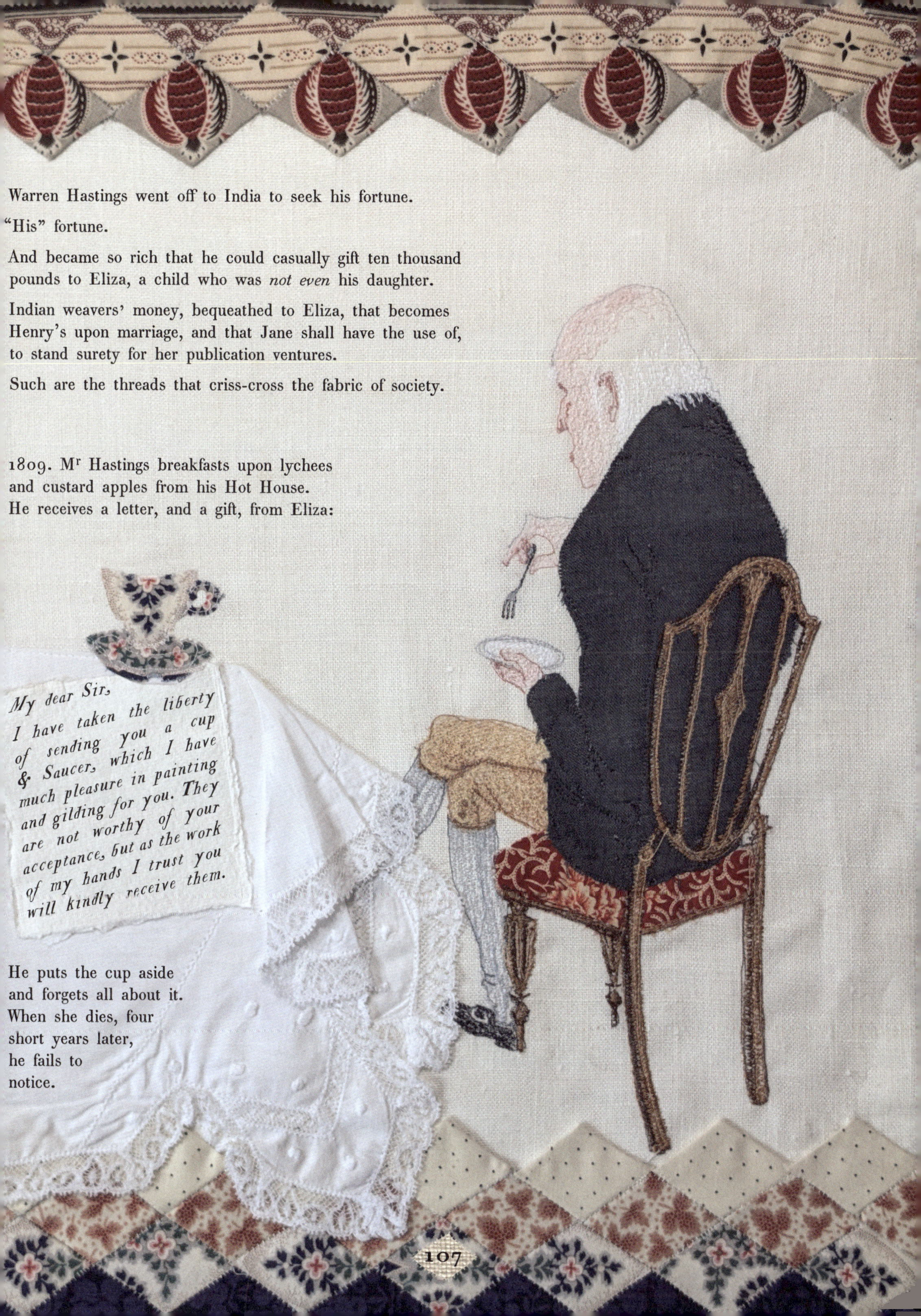
My dear Sir,
I have taken the liberty of sending you a cup & Saucer, which I have much pleasure in painting and gilding for you. They are not worthy of your acceptance, but as the work of my hands I trust you will kindly receive them.

He puts the cup aside and forgets all about it. When she dies, four short years later, he fails to notice.

THE LINEN

In fields all across Ireland, the wee blue blossom of the flax bobs merrily in the breeze.

The plants are pulled by Irish hands, retted in Irish bogs, weighted down with Irish stones.

The stems are scutched and heckled into masses of glossy golden fibres, all bound about with ribbon.

They are spun, by nimble Irish fingers, into supple linen thread.

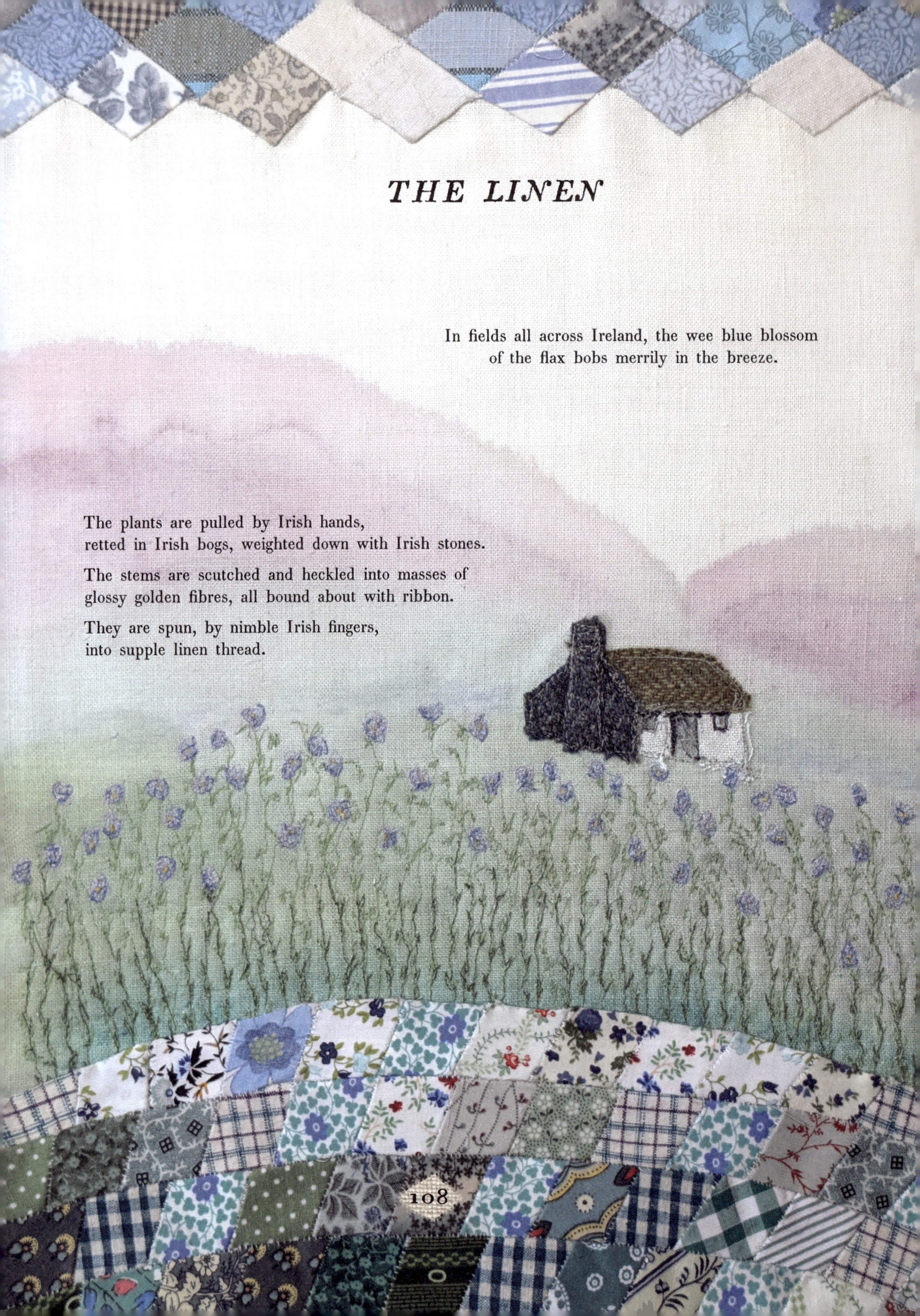

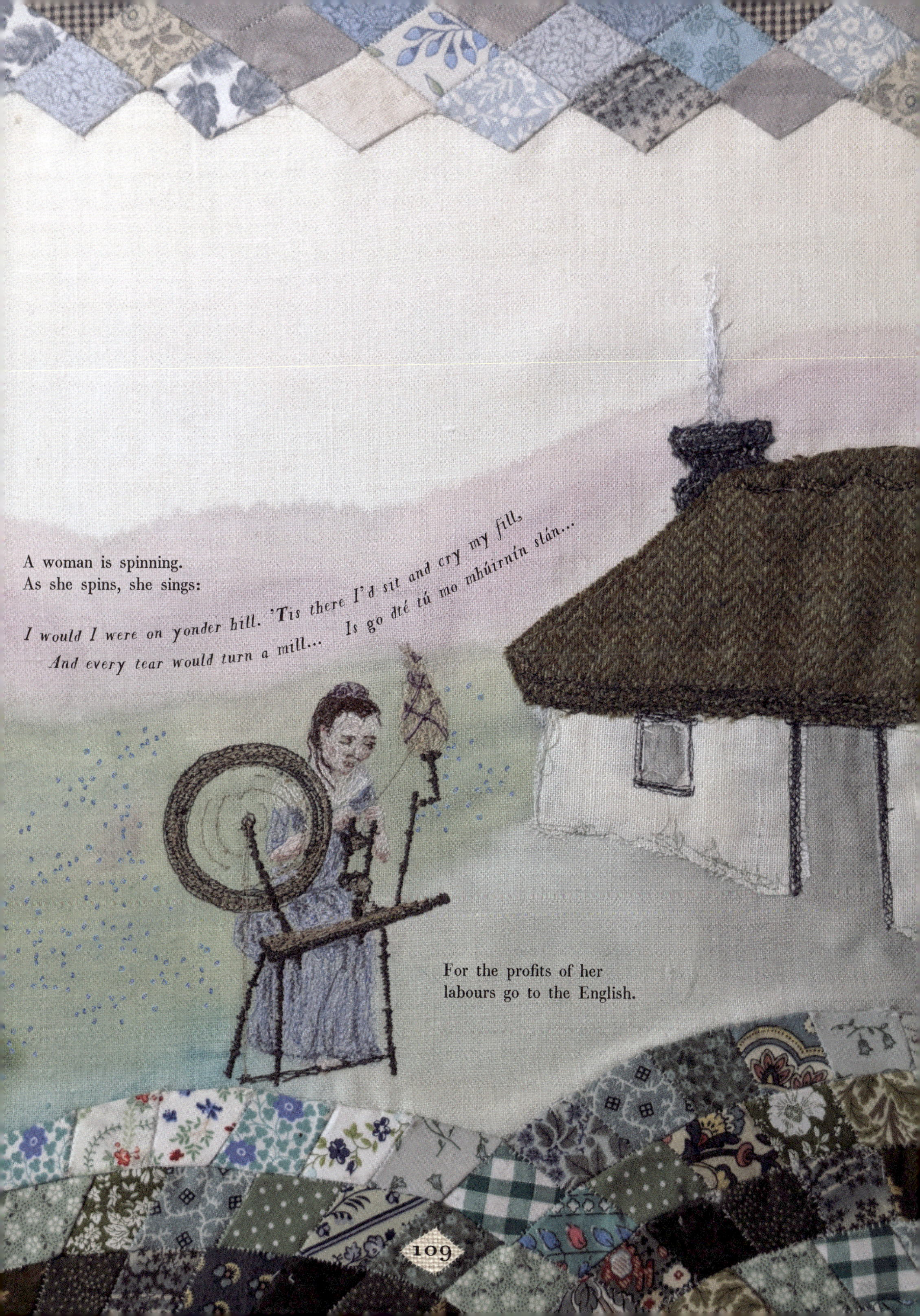

A woman is spinning.
As she spins, she sings:

I would I were on yonder hill. 'Tis there I'd sit and cry my fill,
And every tear would turn a mill... Is go dté tú mo mhúirnín slán...

For the profits of her
labours go to the English.

Jane buys yards of finest linen and works it into shirts, shifts & petticoats.

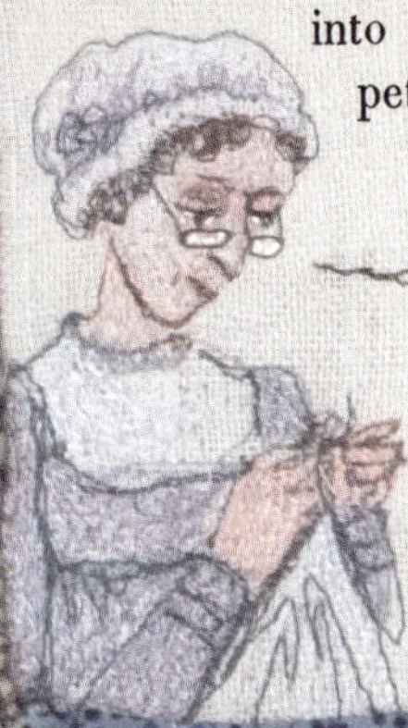

The Irish is not so fine as I should like it, but as I gave as much money for it as I intended, I have no reason to complain. It cost me 3 shillings per yard.

"Irish" in her letters is synonomous with linen.
The Irish can only make linen.
The British forbade them to export wool.

I'll sell my rock, I'll sell my reel, I'll sell my only spinning wheel
To buy for my love a sword of steel... Is go dté tú mo mhúirnín slán...

Dispossessed of the lands, their language, their forests, their futures: the Irish rise up.

OUR INDEPENDENCE MUST BE HAD AT ALL HAZARDS!

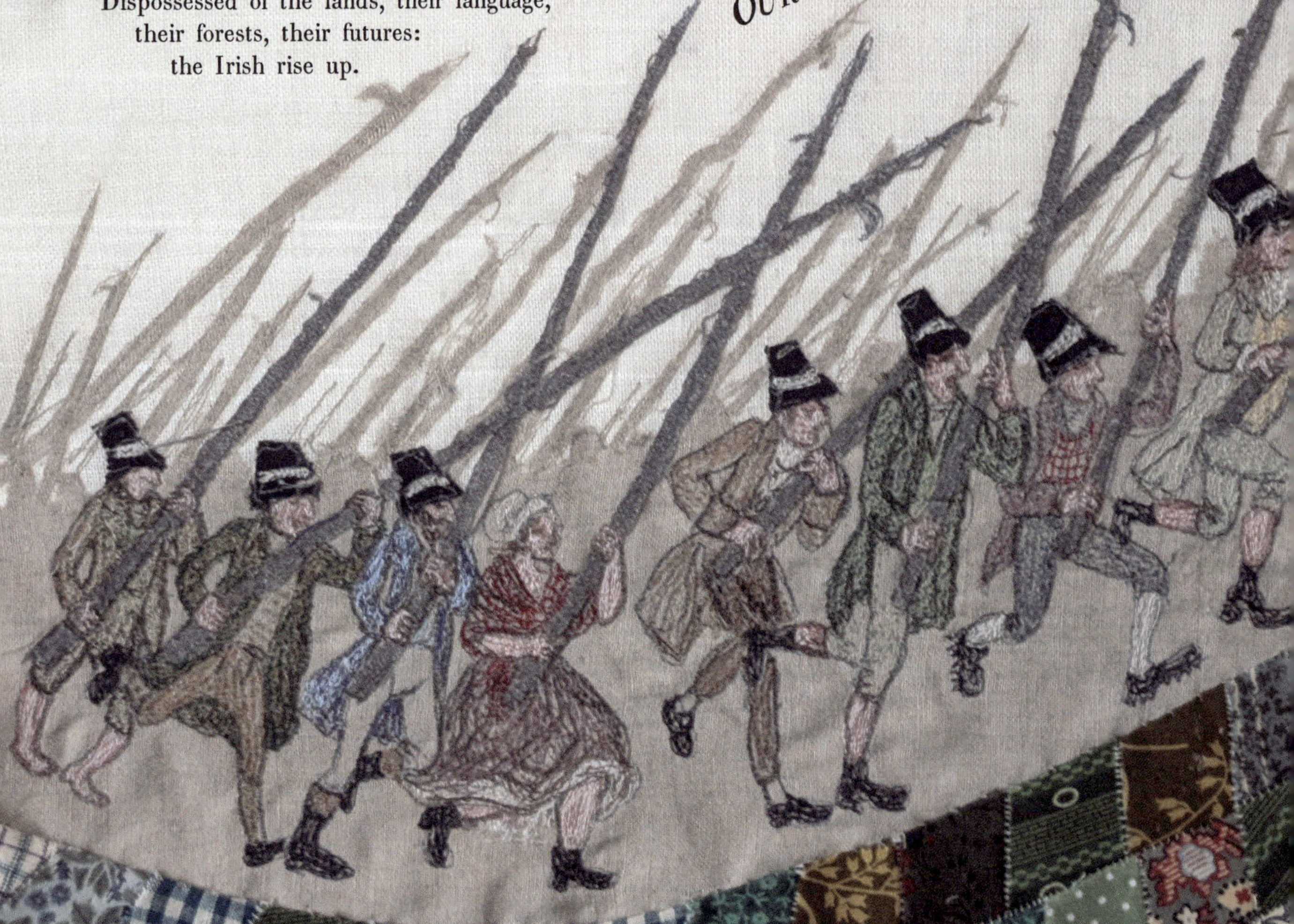

They are brutally repressed.

Henry Austen is sent to Ireland,
with the Oxfordshire Militia, to preserve the peace.
Arraigning, detaining, deporting and executing
the United Irishmen.

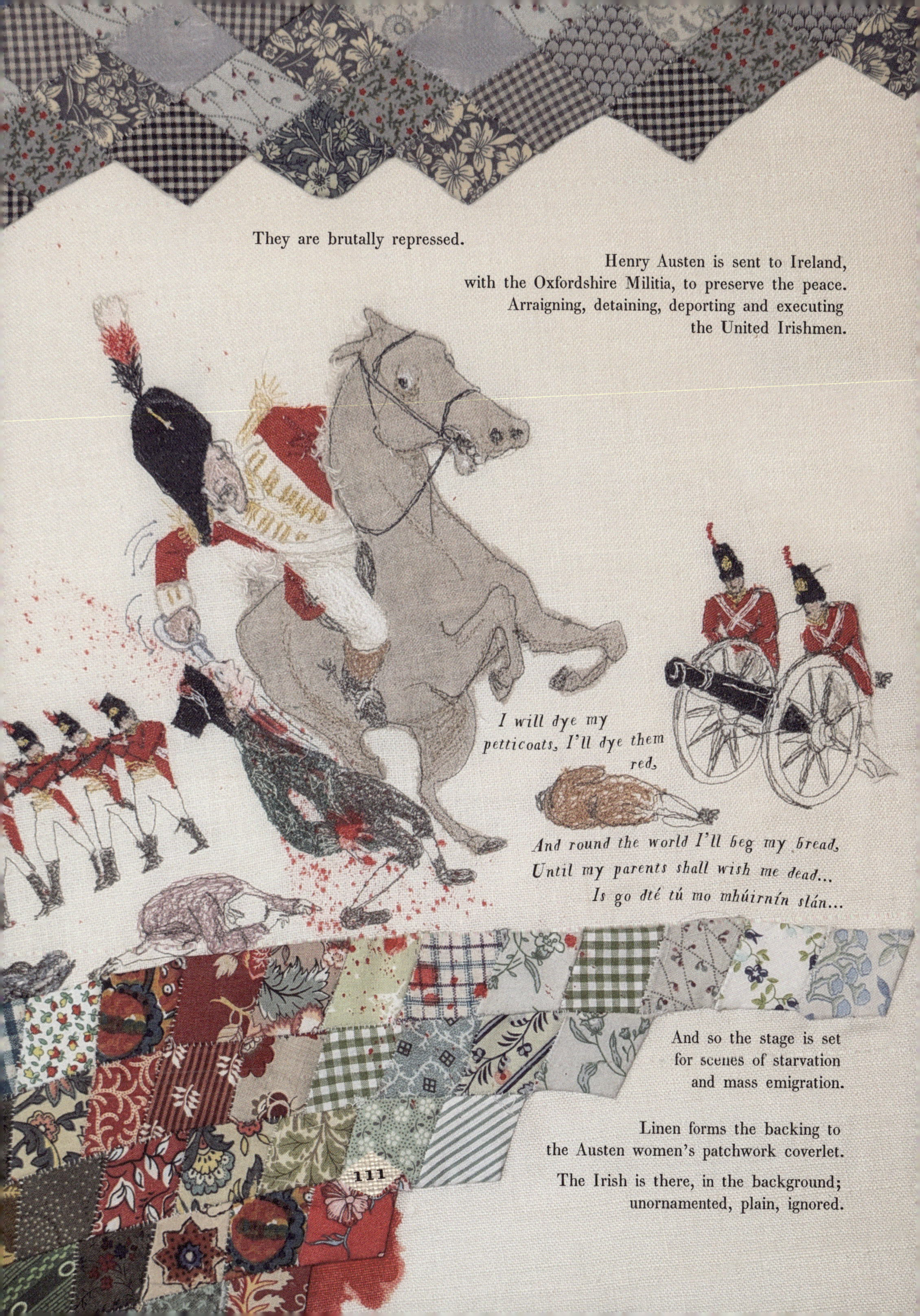

I will dye my
petticoats, I'll dye them
red,

And round the world I'll beg my bread,
Until my parents shall wish me dead...
Is go dté tú mo mhúirnín slán...

And so the stage is set
for scenes of starvation
and mass emigration.

Linen forms the backing to
the Austen women's patchwork coverlet.

The Irish is there, in the background;
unornamented, plain, ignored.

THE COTTON

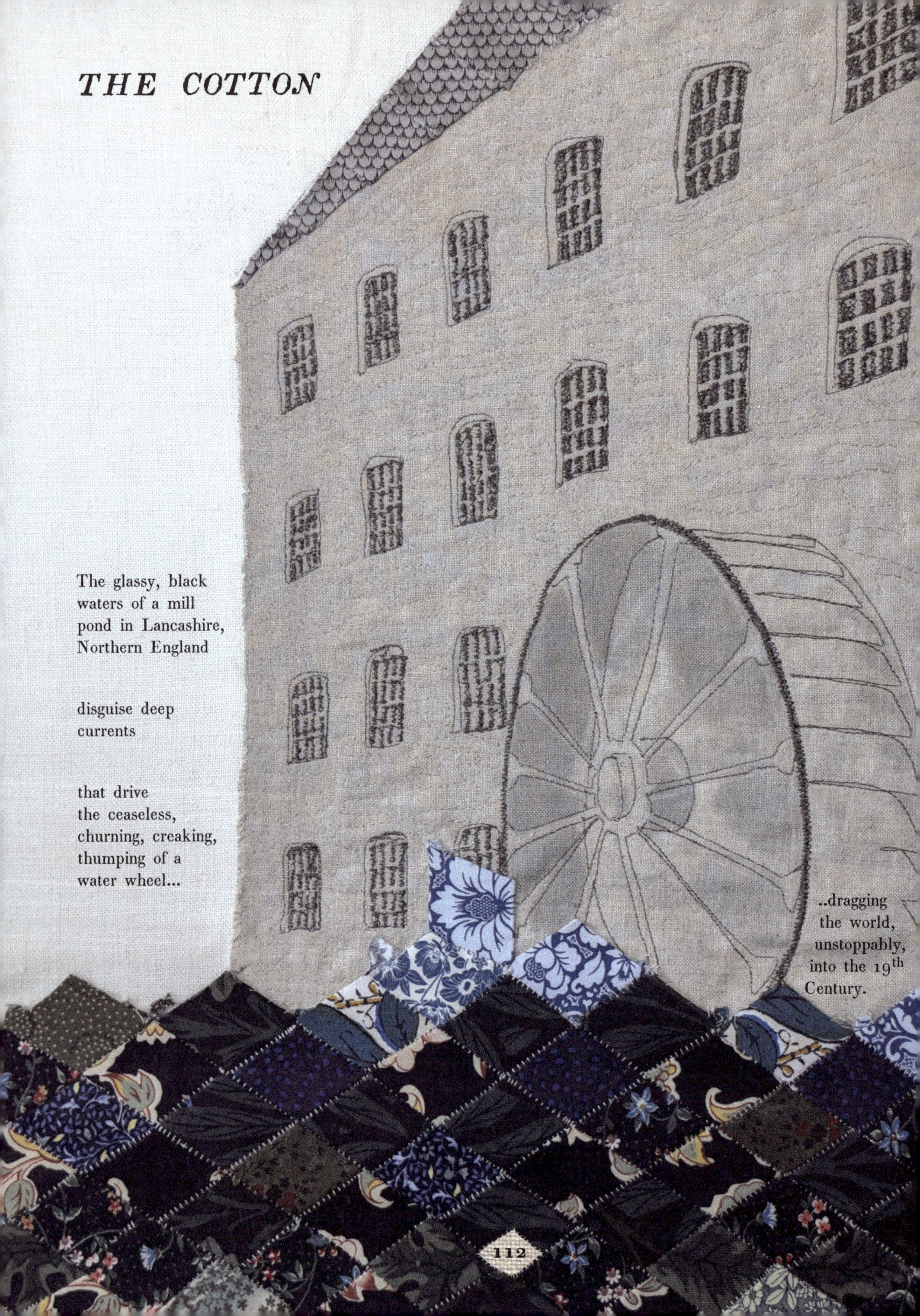

The glassy, black
waters of a mill
pond in Lancashire,
Northern England

disguise deep
currents

that drive
the ceaseless,
churning, creaking,
thumping of a
water wheel...

..dragging
the world,
unstoppably,
into the 19th
Century.

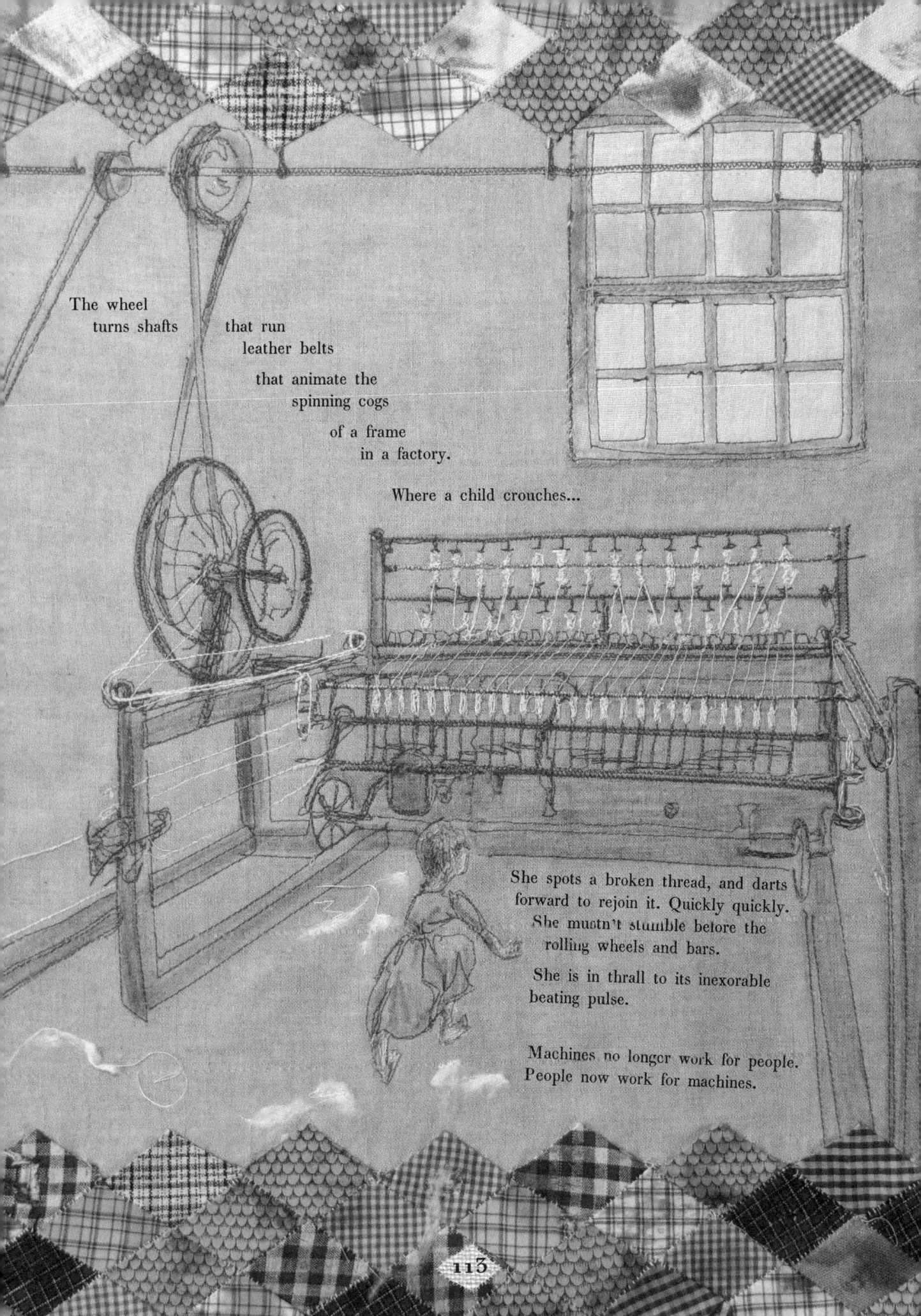

The wheel
turns shafts that run
leather belts
that animate the
spinning cogs
of a frame
in a factory.

Where a child crouches...

She spots a broken thread, and darts forward to rejoin it. Quickly quickly. She mustn't stumble before the rolling wheels and bars.

She is in thrall to its inexorable beating pulse.

Machines no longer work for people. People now work for machines.

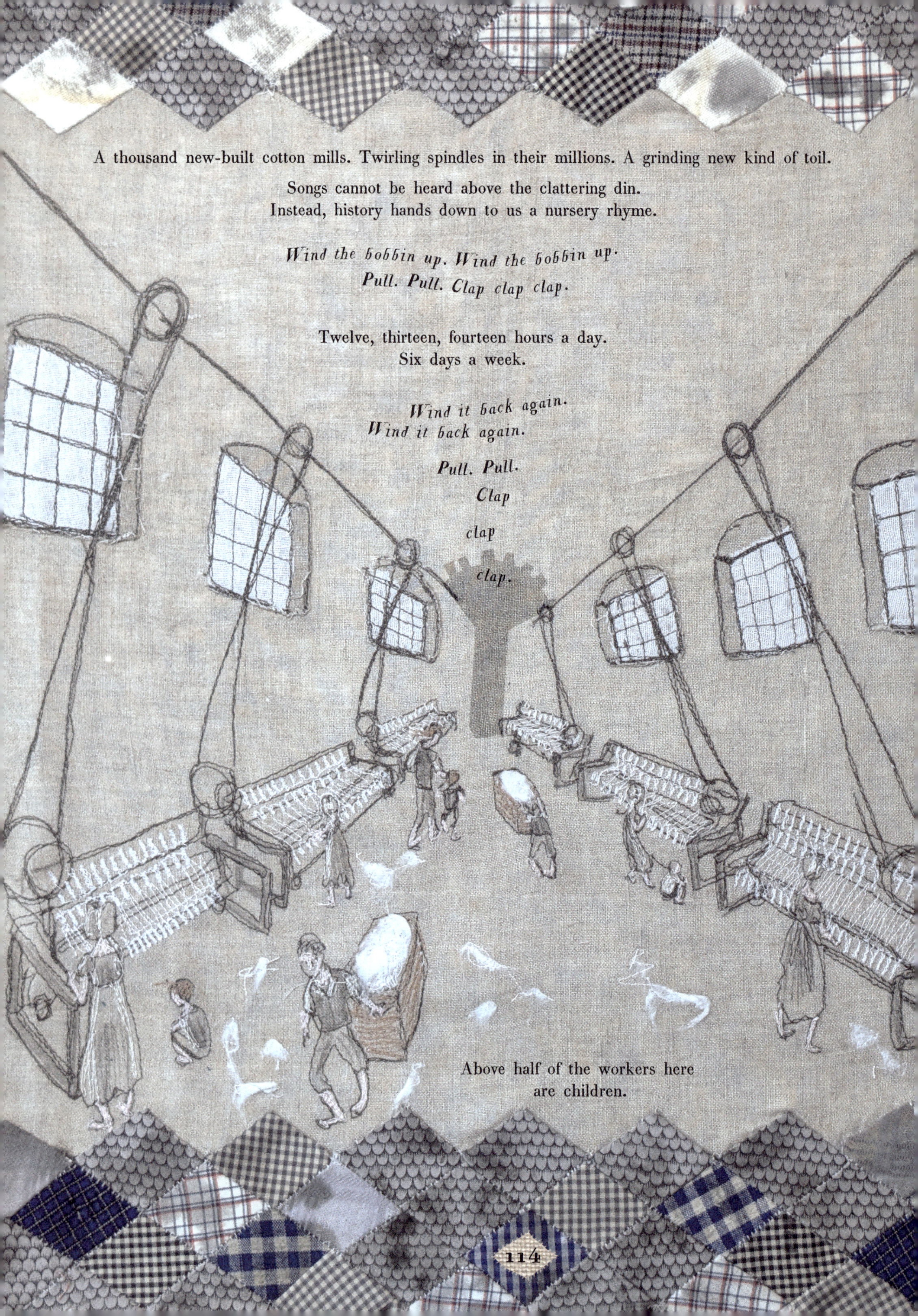

A thousand new-built cotton mills. Twirling spindles in their millions. A grinding new kind of toil.

Songs cannot be heard above the clattering din.
Instead, history hands down to us a nursery rhyme.

Wind the bobbin up. Wind the bobbin up.
Pull. Pull. Clap clap clap.

Twelve, thirteen, fourteen hours a day.
Six days a week.

Wind it back again.
Wind it back again.

Pull. Pull.
Clap

clap

clap.

Above half of the workers here
are children.

Point to the window. Point to the door. Point to the ceiling. Point to the floor.

The children's knee bones bend grotesquely. Their feet drop and splay.
They say it is the pressure of standing all day at the machine.
They do not know it is the consequence of never seeing daylight.

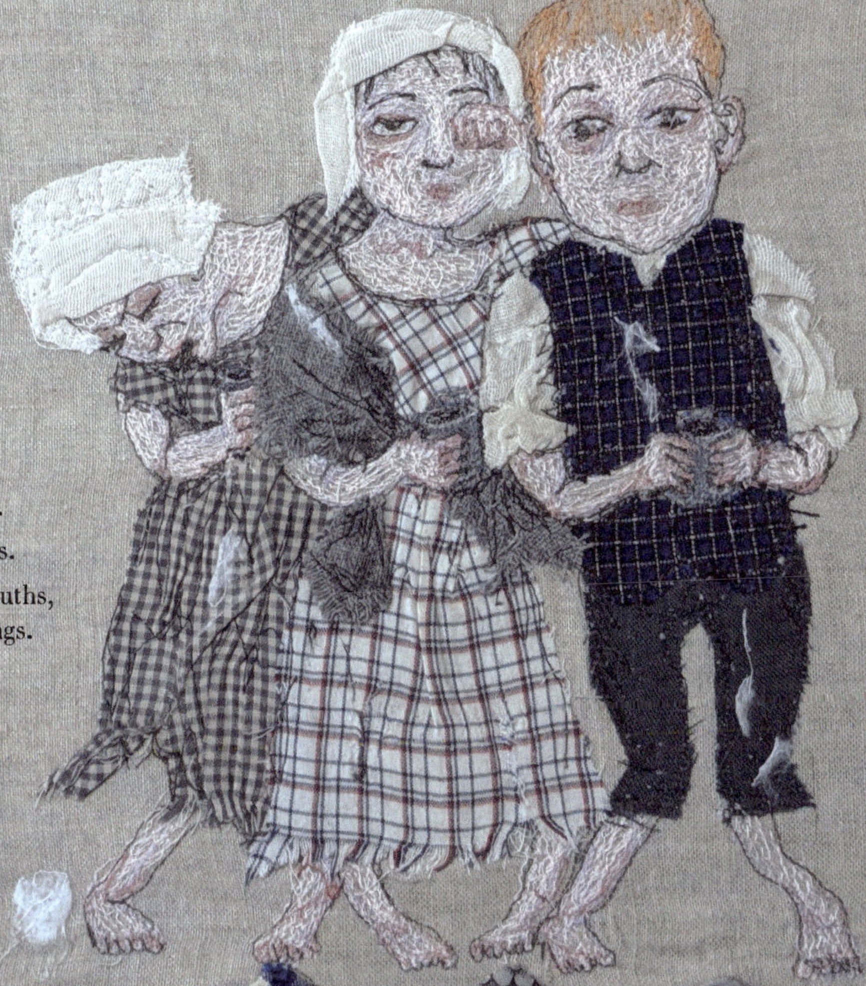

The working week is done.
They wait patiently for meagre
wages, in a little pewter cup.

They spit cotton flue from their
throats; rub their reddened eyes.

Grease and dust coats their mouths,
their noses, their hair, their lungs.

What is this cotton fluff?
Where does it come from?
It doesn't grow in
Lancashire.

It comes from the Land of the Free.

Cotton explodes out across the southern States of America,
unfurling just like the tight seed heads expand into massy clouds.

Everything is perfect for the new crop: American upland cotton.

The climate.

Vast fertile lands (freshly emptied of their original inhabitants).

The new Whitney cotton 'gin, which wrests the fibre from its recalcitrant seed heads.

And almost limitless free labour.

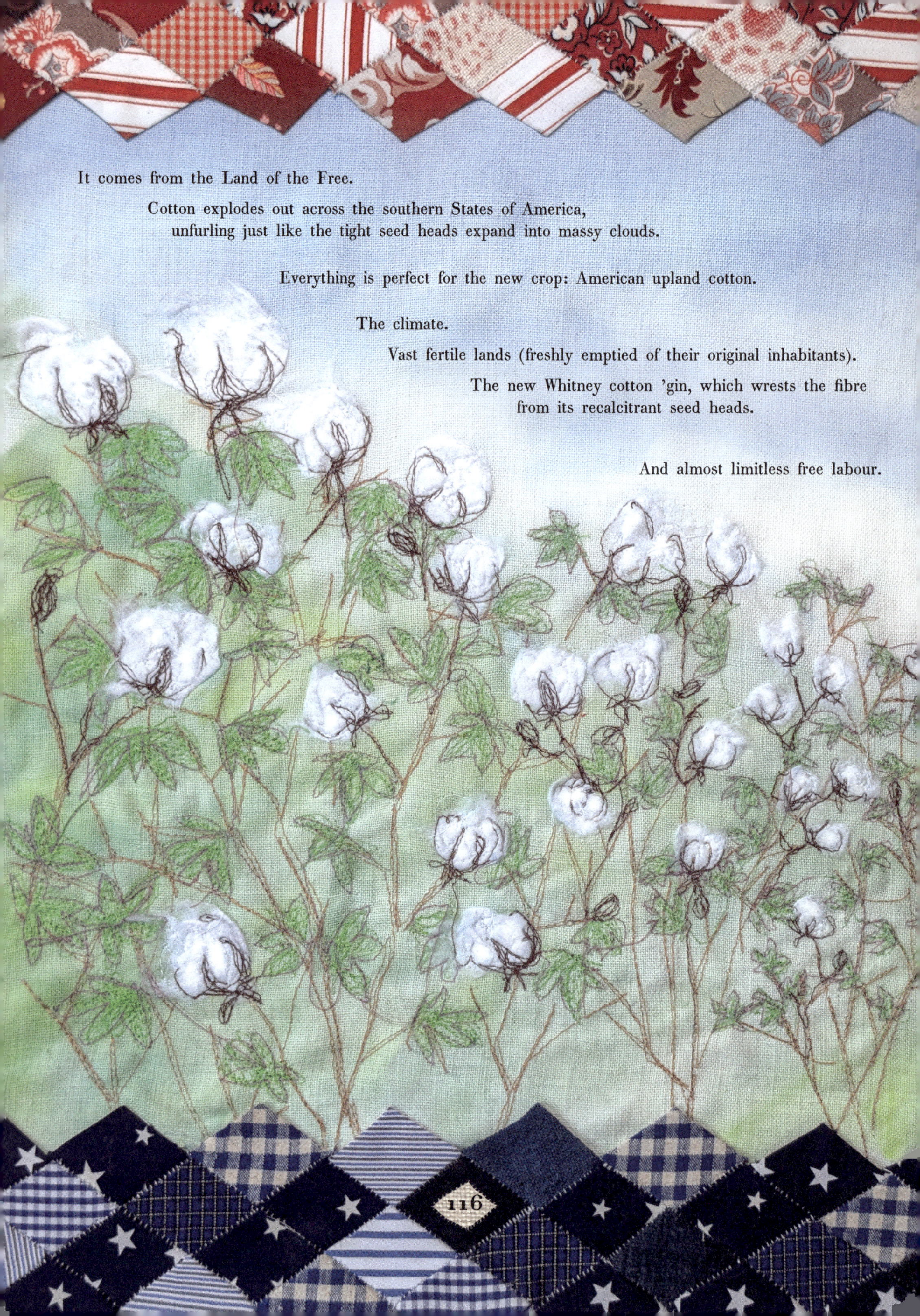

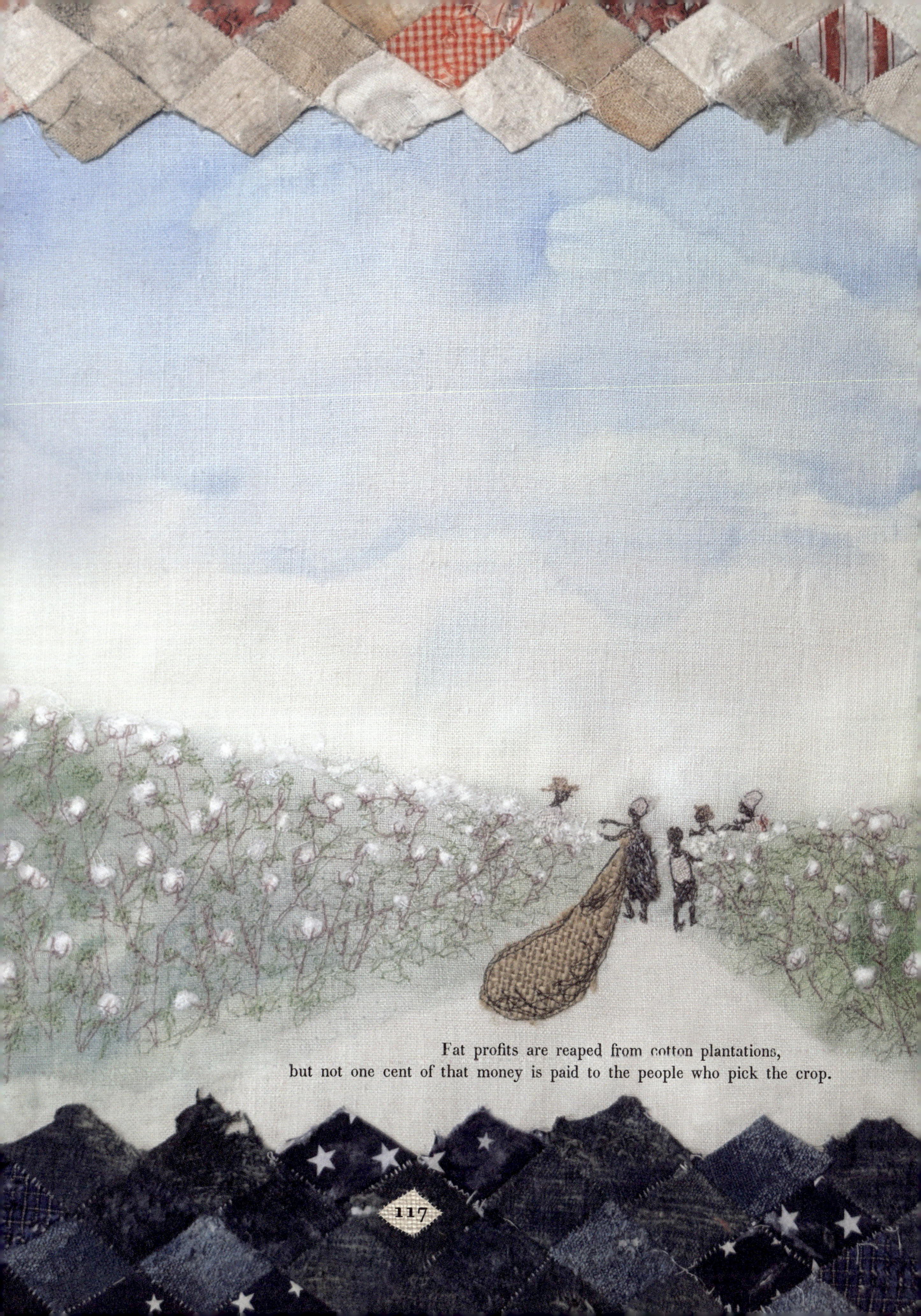

Fat profits are reaped from cotton plantations,
but not one cent of that money is paid to the people who pick the crop.

A woman picks cotton, picks cotton, picks cotton,
as the blistering sun inches towards the horizon.

Her true name has been lost.
She is "Mary" now, or "Sarah," or "Phyllis."

She has been bought and sold by the white men,
like livestock. Her children have been wrenched
from her, screaming, to the auction block.

Her back has known the lash of the whip.
Her body has known worse.

Incessant labour. Fourteen, fifteen,
sixteen hours a day.
Six days a week.

She raises her voice in a work song.
A song of sorrow. A song of redemption.
A song which promises freedom
in the life to come

How long? How long?

My father, how long?

My father, how long
Poor sinner suffer here?

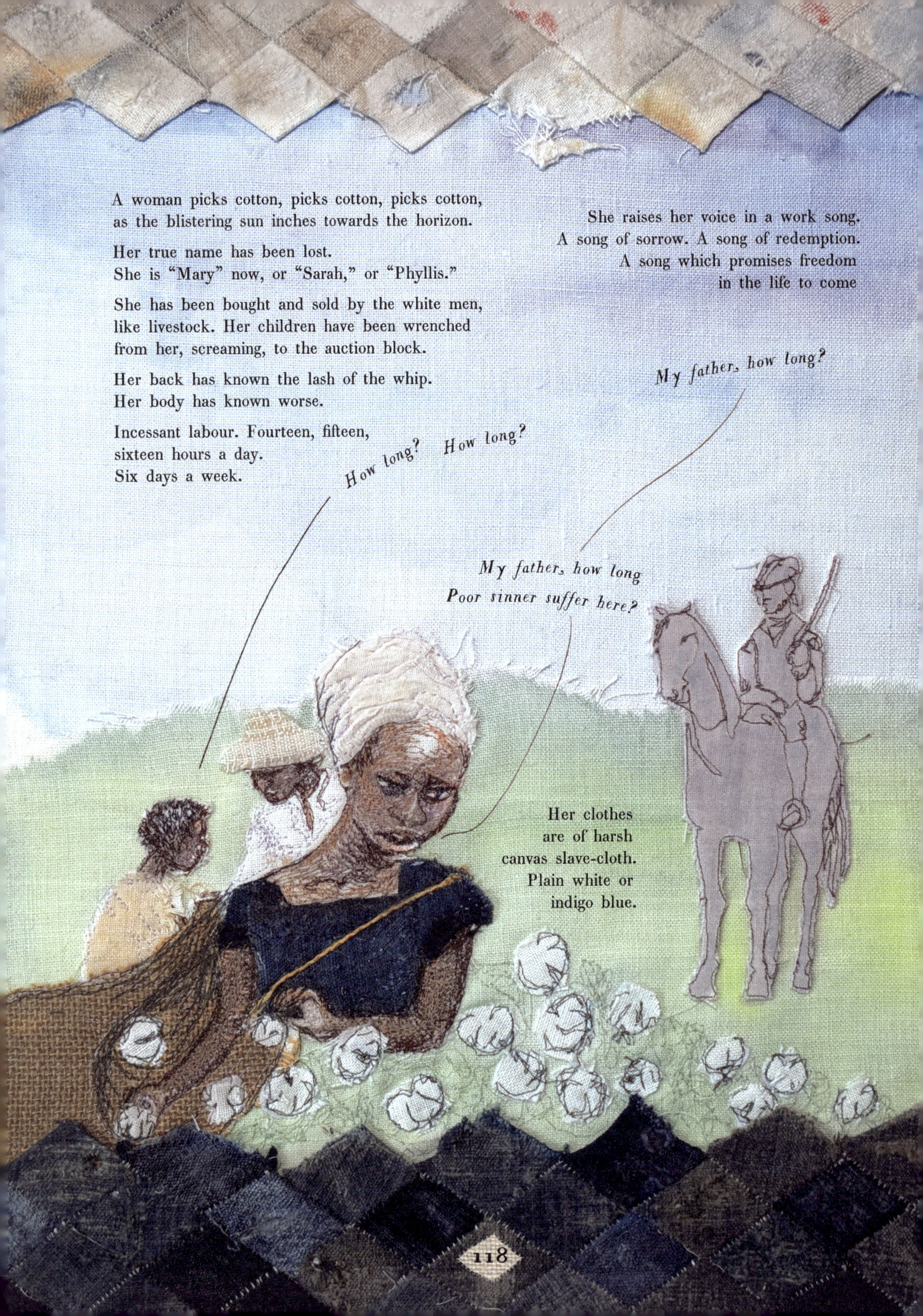

Her clothes
are of harsh
canvas slave-cloth.
Plain white or
indigo blue.

She knows other songs. Songs to be sung in secret. Songs which code the landscape of escape routes, the way North. Songs of resistance, shared softly in the dead of night.

When she loudly sings that same tune with different words before the buckra (white folk), her sistren and brethren know her true meaning

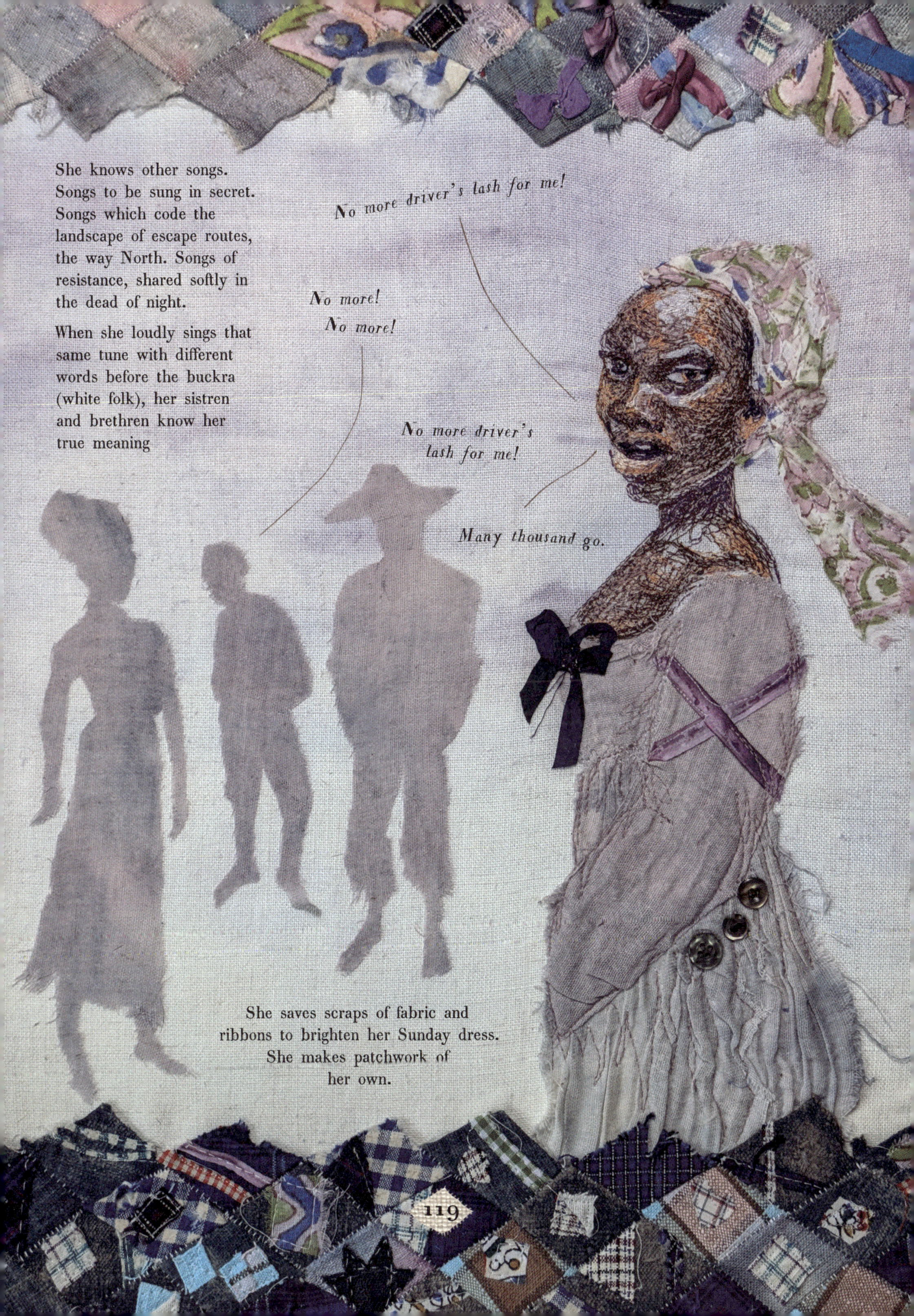

No more driver's lash for me!
No more!
No more!
No more driver's lash for me!
Many thousand go.

She saves scraps of fabric and ribbons to brighten her Sunday dress. She makes patchwork of her own.

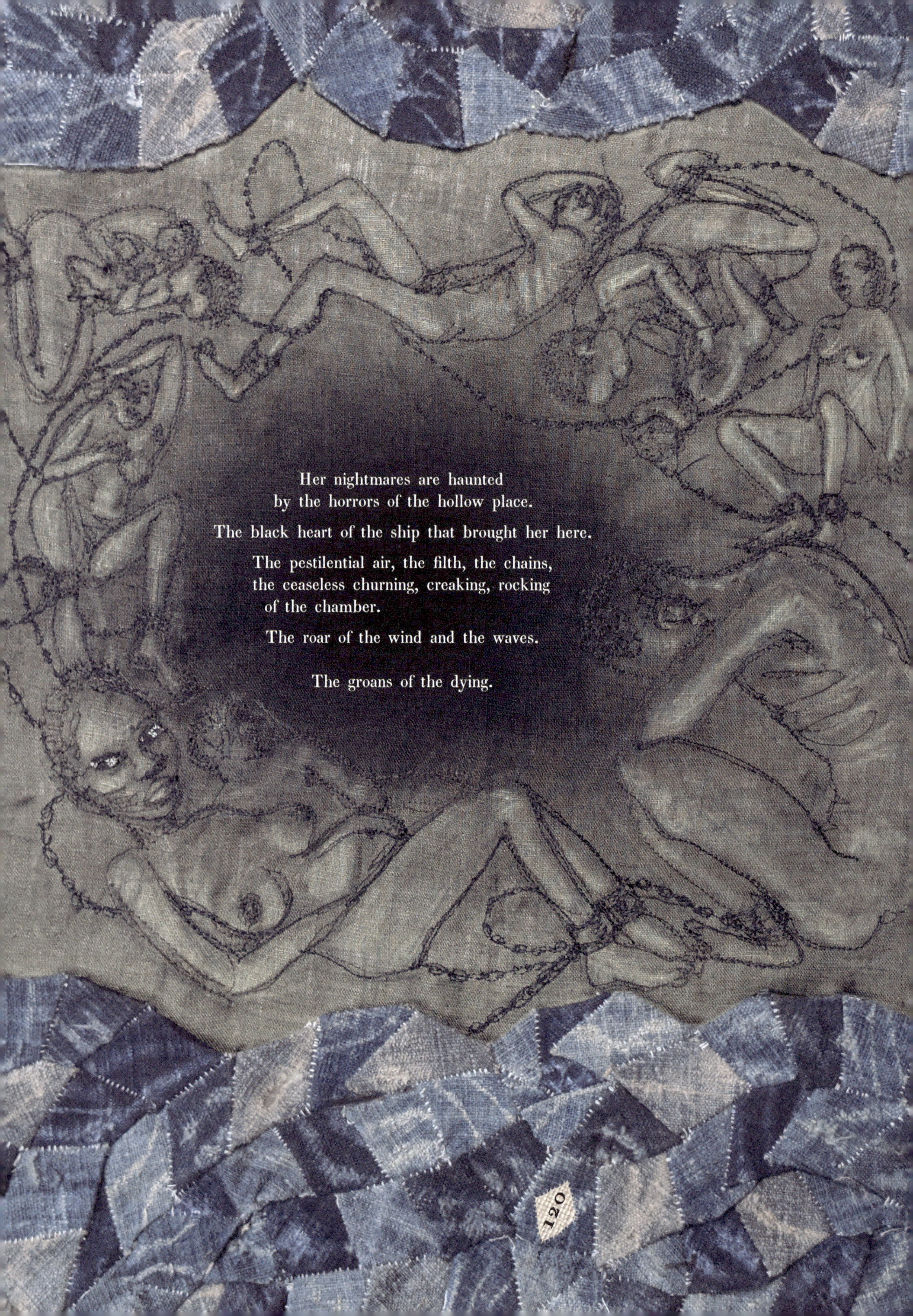

Her nightmares are haunted
by the horrors of the hollow place.

The black heart of the ship that brought her here.

The pestilential air, the filth, the chains,
the ceaseless churning, creaking, rocking
of the chamber.

The roar of the wind and the waves.

The groans of the dying.

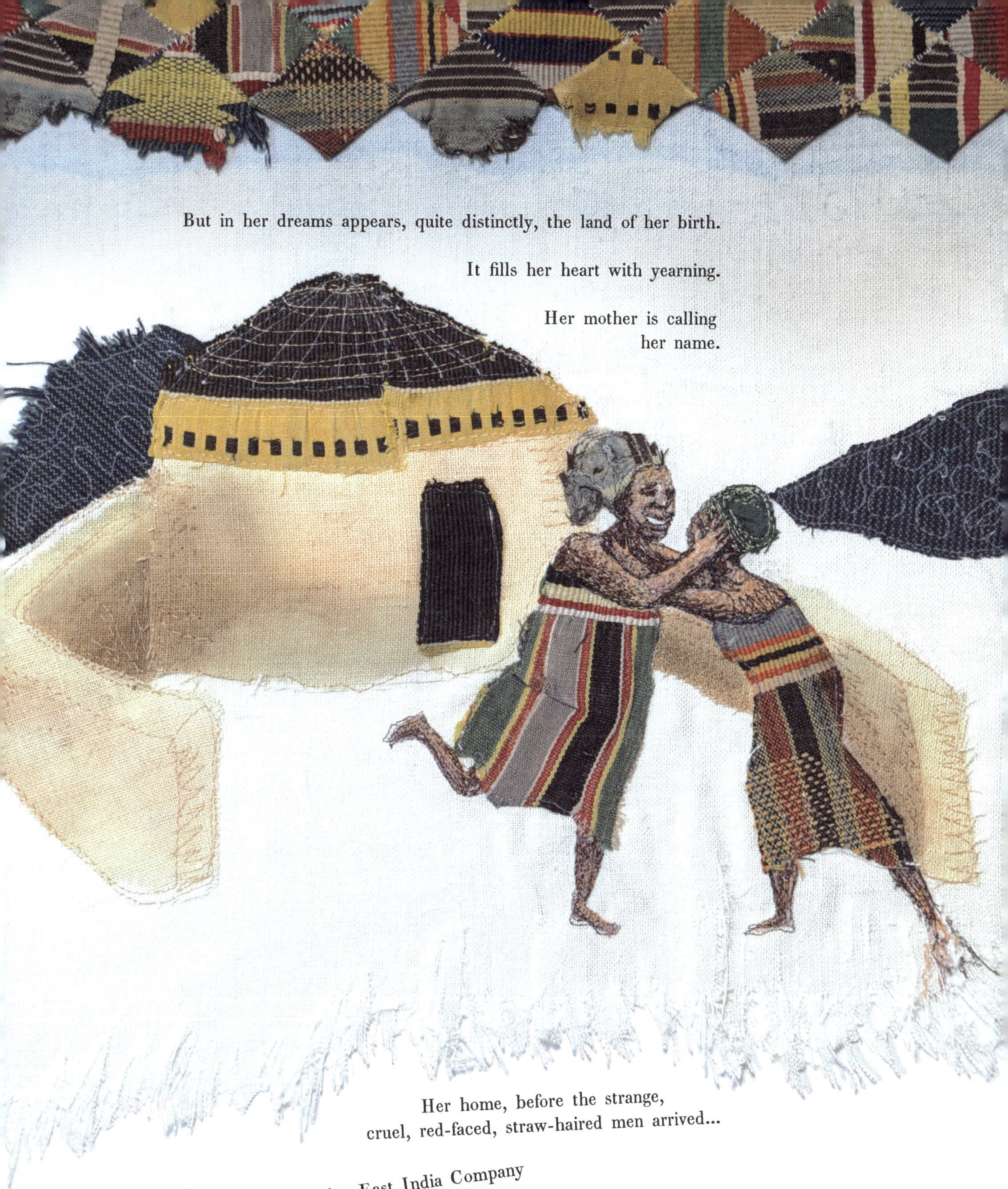

But in her dreams appears, quite distinctly, the land of her birth.

It fills her heart with yearning.

Her mother is calling
her name.

Her home, before the strange,
cruel, red-faced, straw-haired men arrived...

(They bring East India Company products, woven according to exacting market specifications, for West Africans are known to prefer a Cross-barred Indigo Check.)

...and she was seized...

...and traded, by her kidnappers...

...for cloth.

What has this to do with Jane? Jane reads the abolitionists. She abhors slavery, as all right-thinking people should.
But how can her fortunes be untangled from others?

Did Mr Darcy build Pemberley without income from West Indian investments? His friend Mr Bingley – his money was acquired in trade – did that happen without child labour? The £10,000 a year that her heroes boast: this money does not materialise from thin air.

Where is the line between imagination and reality, when a legal fiction can, with the stroke of a pen, condemn people to be properties? commodites? The very first slave codes are written by the British: laws which make humans into chattel. An act of creative writing that redefines inhumanity.

Then that peculiarly British invention, the Joint Stock corporation, outsources the unspeakable. Merchant adventurers roam the globe: country parsons and kind aged widows from the comfort of their drawing-rooms purchase the shares and provide the collateral.

They cannot see the bodies.
They see the neat round figures
of dividends on balance sheets.

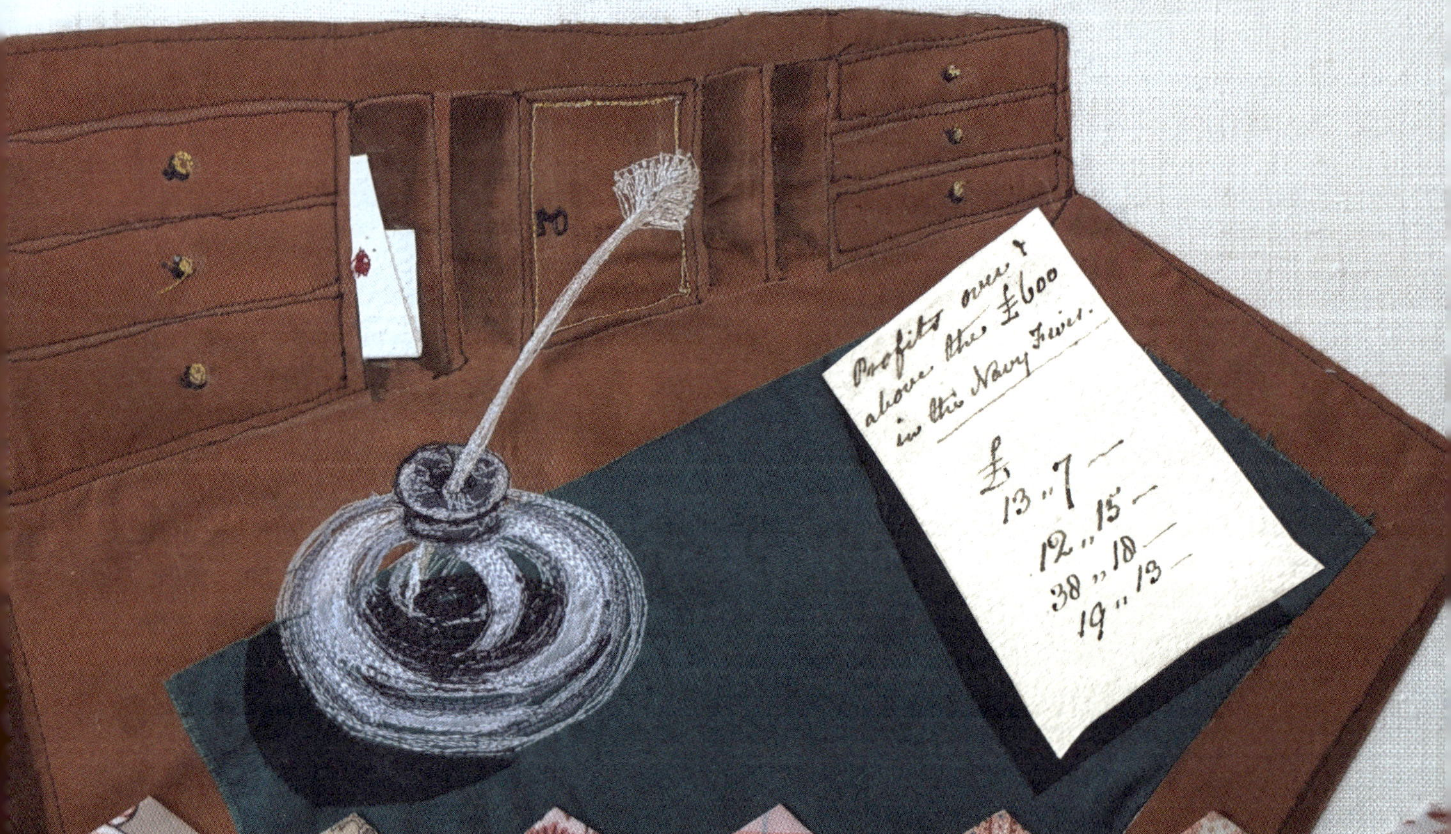

Profits over & above the £600 in the Navy Fives.
£
13 „ 7 –
12 „ 15 –
38 „ 10 –
19 „ 13 –

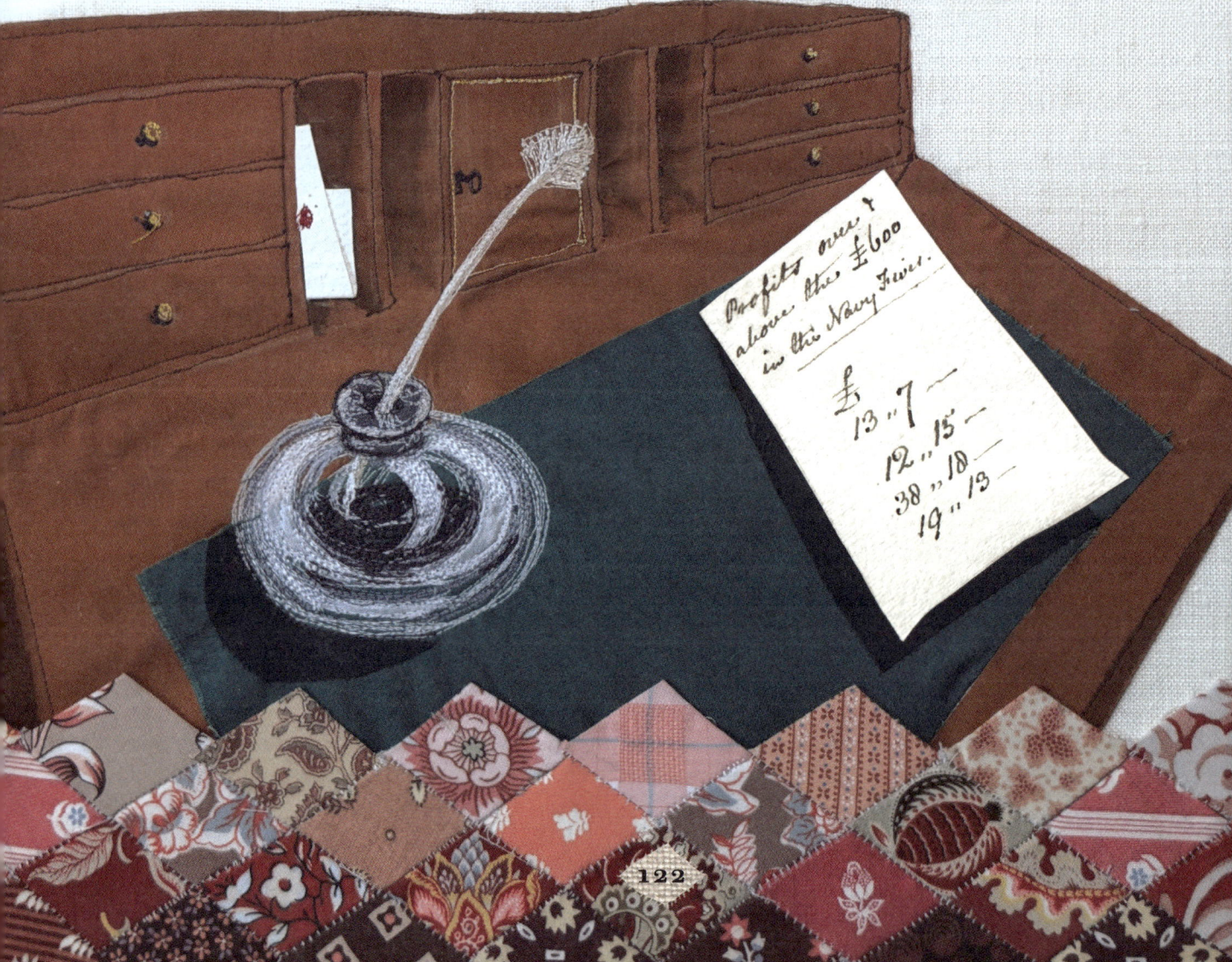

In 1809, slave ships no longer legally ply their trade. A new prohibition on the *transport* of people from Africa has come into effect.

Charles Austen is stationed at Bermuda, patrolling on his Royal Navy sloop. Should he encounter a slaver, his orders are to impound it.

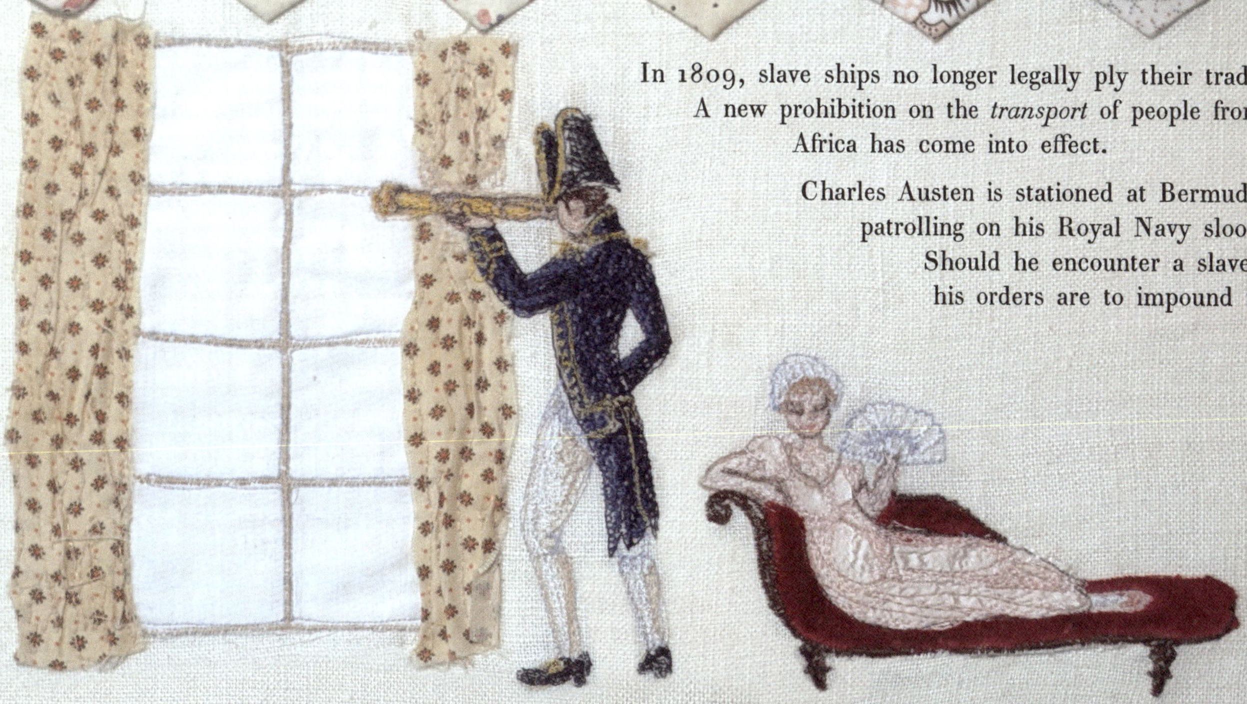

But there is no prohibition on *ownership*.

His beautiful wife procures a girl to watch their beloved new baby.

She is tender and attentive.

She is still too young to understand rightly her condition as a slave.

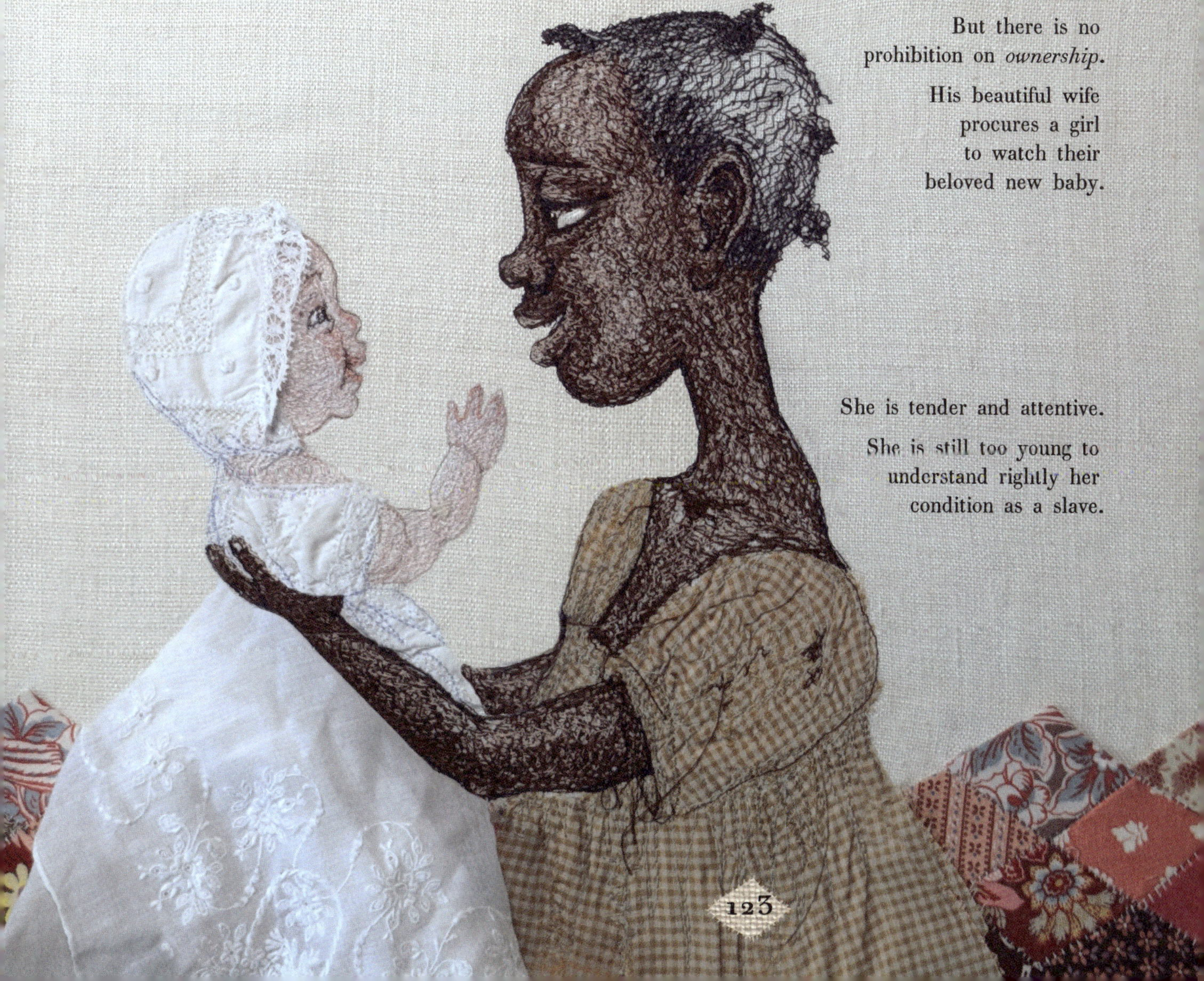

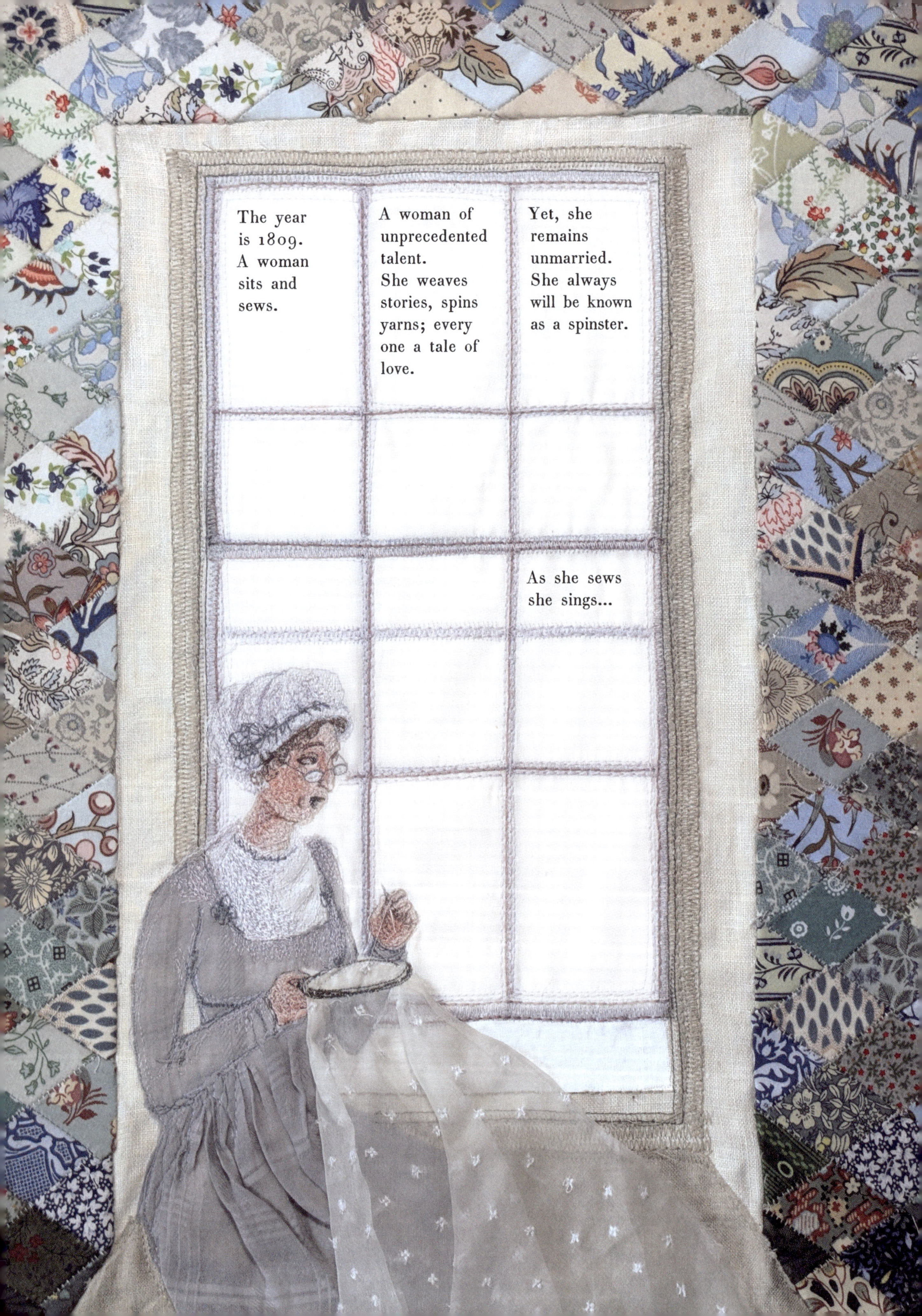
The year is 1809. A woman sits and sews.
A woman of unprecedented talent. She weaves stories, spins yarns; every one a tale of love.
Yet, she remains unmarried. She always will be known as a spinster.
As she sews she sings...

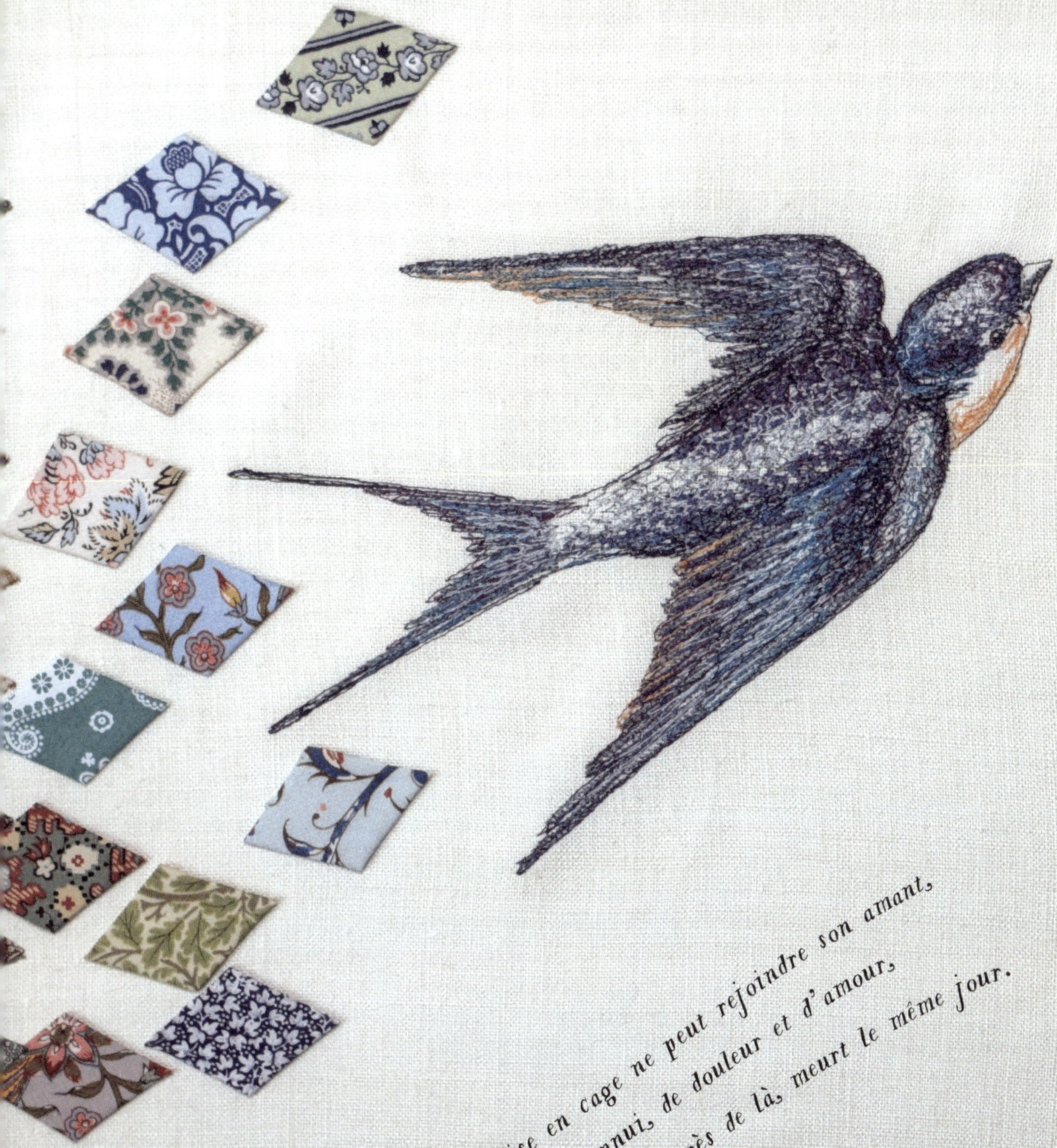

Si une hirondelle mise en cage ne peut rejoindre son amant,
Vous voyez mourir l'hirondelle, d'ennui, de douleur et d'amour,
Tandis que son amant fidèle, près de là, meurt le même jour.

If a swallow
trapped in a cage
cannot join her lover

You will see the swallow die
of world-weariness, pain and love

While her faithful lover, nearby, dies the same day.

THE

PAPERS

10th October 1808. Edward's wife, Elizabeth, after producing her eleventh child in seventeen years, unsurprisingly, expires. From this tragedy, the Austen women reap an unexpected reward. Edward is awakened to the value of having a grandmother and two maiden aunts to attend to his brood, and remembers that he has *two* vast country estates at his disposal, one in Chawton, Hampshire, one in Kent. And so, he offers them...

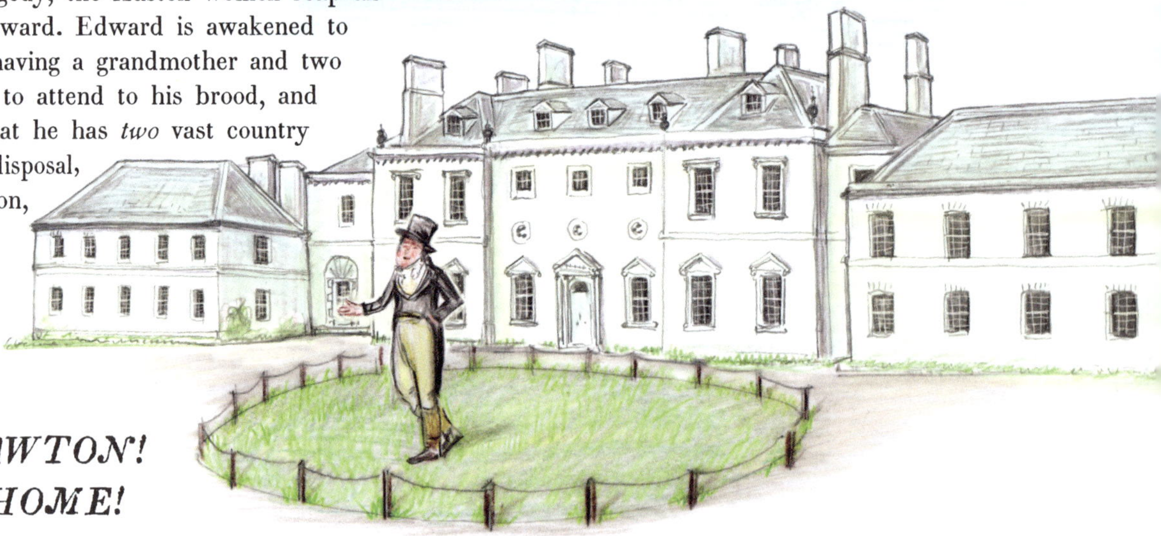

CHAWTON! A HOME!

...his old bailiff's cottage.

He does put in some nice wallpaper though, and revise the plumbing.

It has no advantage of situation. It stands full on the thoroughfare from London to Winchester, almost as close to the road as it can be. Stagecoaches make the windows rattle. The stairs are dark and narrow. The kitchen smokes.

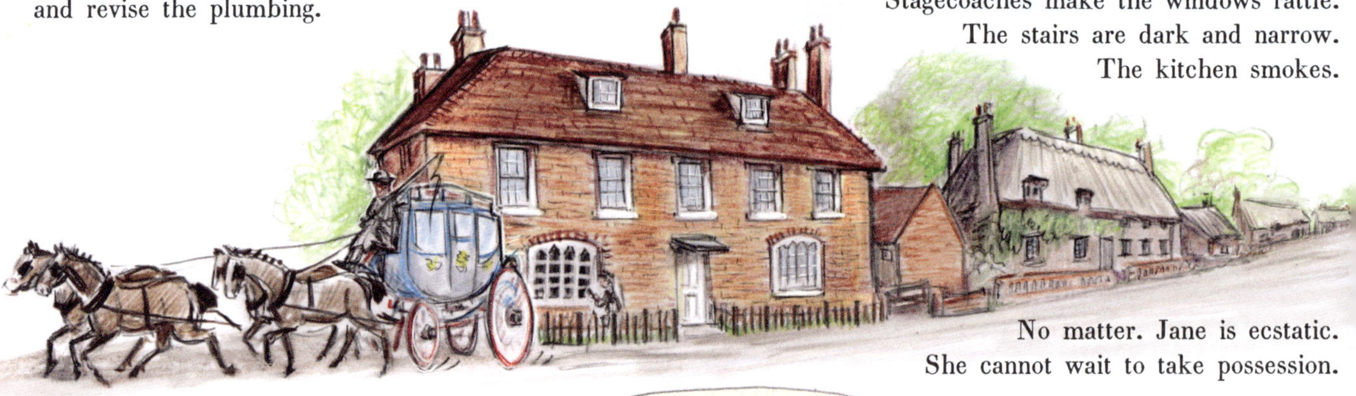

No matter. Jane is ecstatic. She cannot wait to take possession.

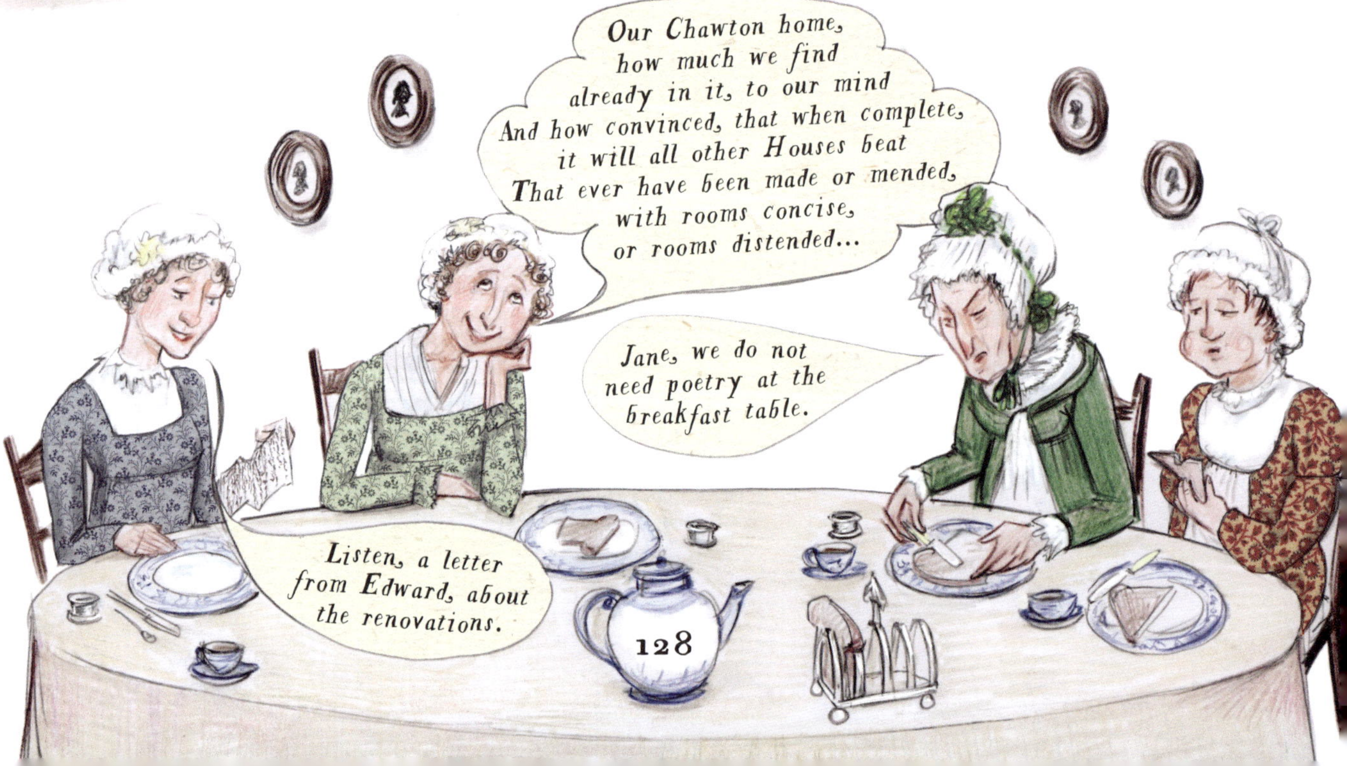

Listen, a letter from Edward, about the renovations.
Our Chawton home, how much we find already in it, to our mind And how convinced, that when complete, it will all other Houses beat That ever have been made or mended, with rooms concise, or rooms distended...
Jane, we do not need poetry at the breakfast table.

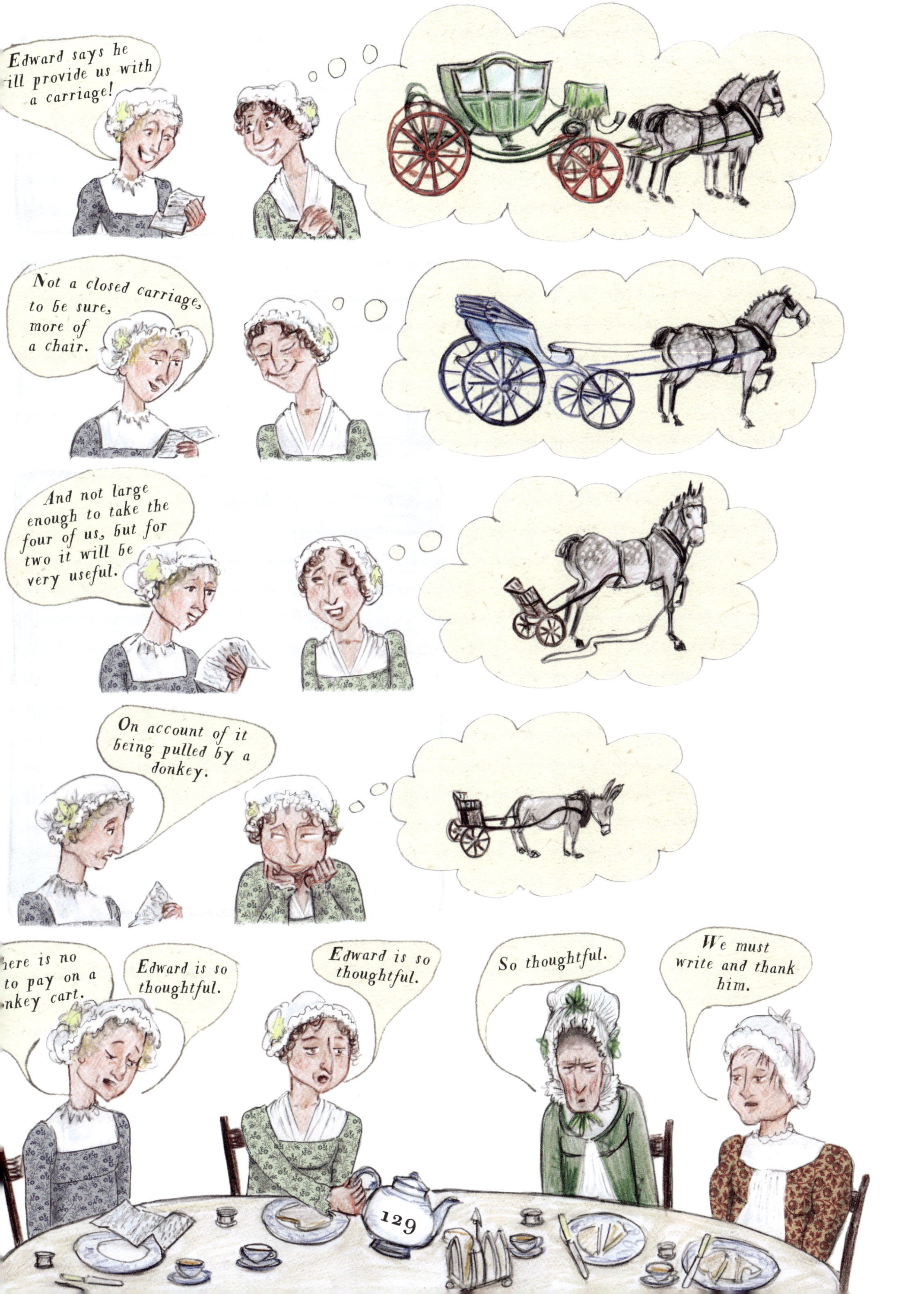

Edward says he
ill provide us with
a carriage!
Not a closed carriage,
to be sure,
more of
a chair.
And not large
enough to take the
four of us, but for
two it will be
very useful.
On account of it
being pulled by a
donkey.
here is no
to pay on a
nkey cart.
Edward is so
thoughtful.
Edward is so
thoughtful.
So thoughtful.
We must
write and thank
him.

7th July 1809. They are in! Jane and Cassandra and Martha and Mother. Each of them is busy in arranging their particular concerns; endeavouring to form themselves a home.

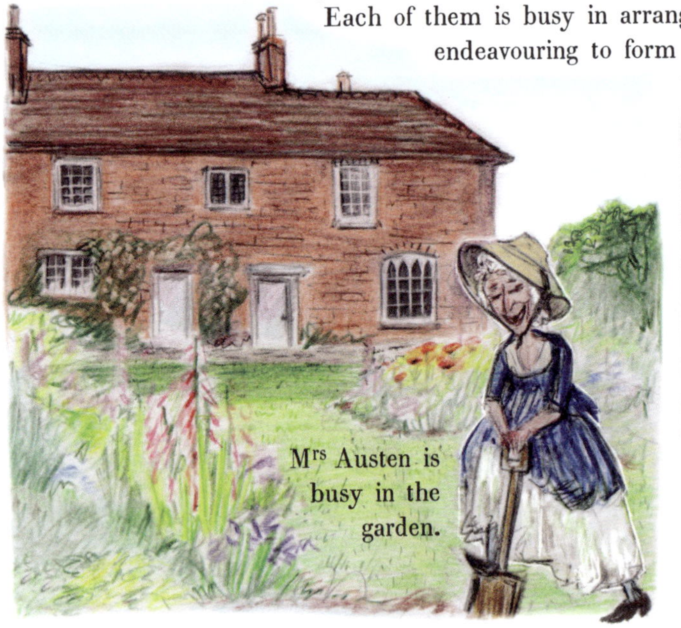
Mrs Austen is busy in the garden.

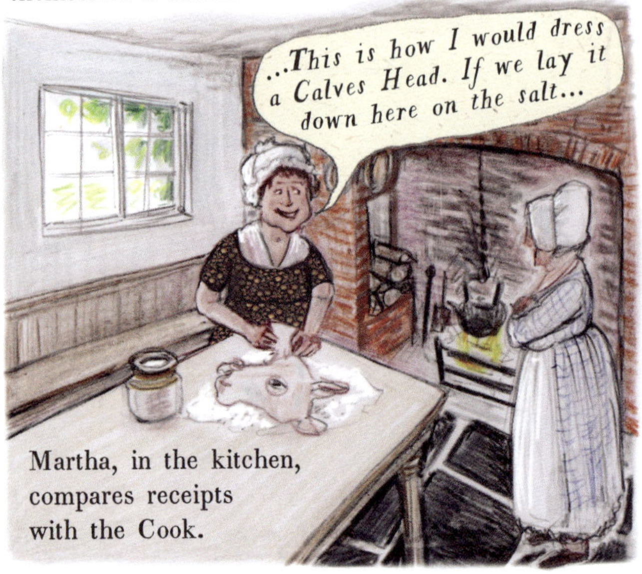
...This is how I would dress a Calves Head. If we lay it down here on the salt...
Martha, in the kitchen, compares receipts with the Cook.

Jane is responsible for getting Breakfast to the table. She has the keys for the tea and the sugar. After that, her day is her own, deliberately so.

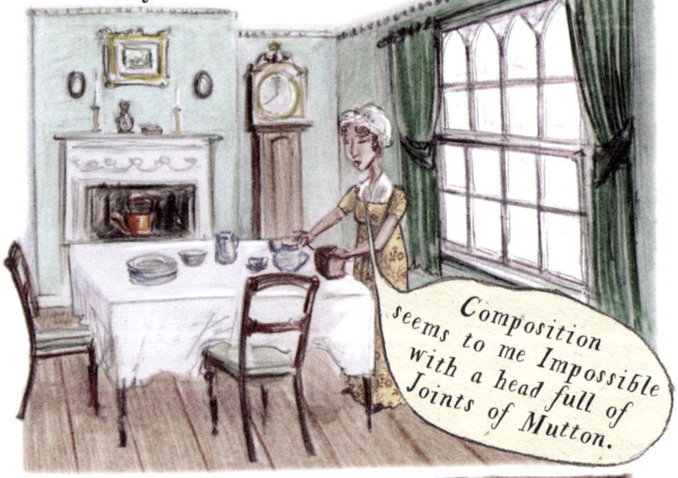
Composition seems to me Impossible with a head full of Joints of Mutton.

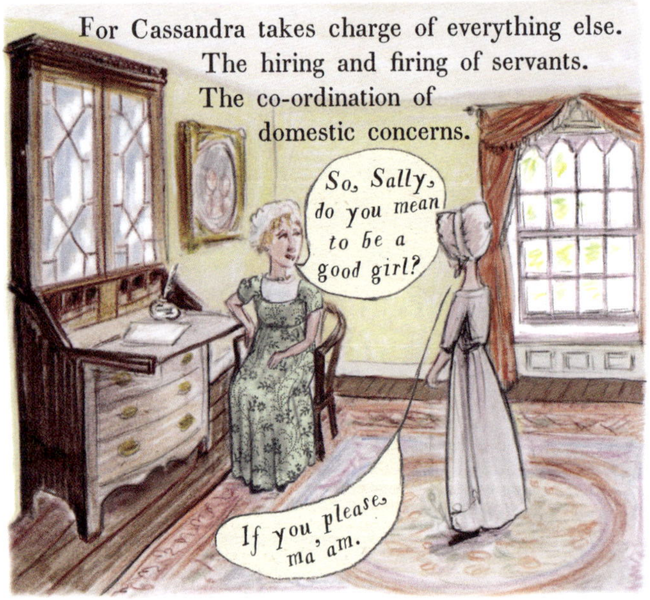
For Cassandra takes charge of everything else. The hiring and firing of servants. The co-ordination of domestic concerns.
So, Sally, do you mean to be a good girl?
If you please, ma'am.

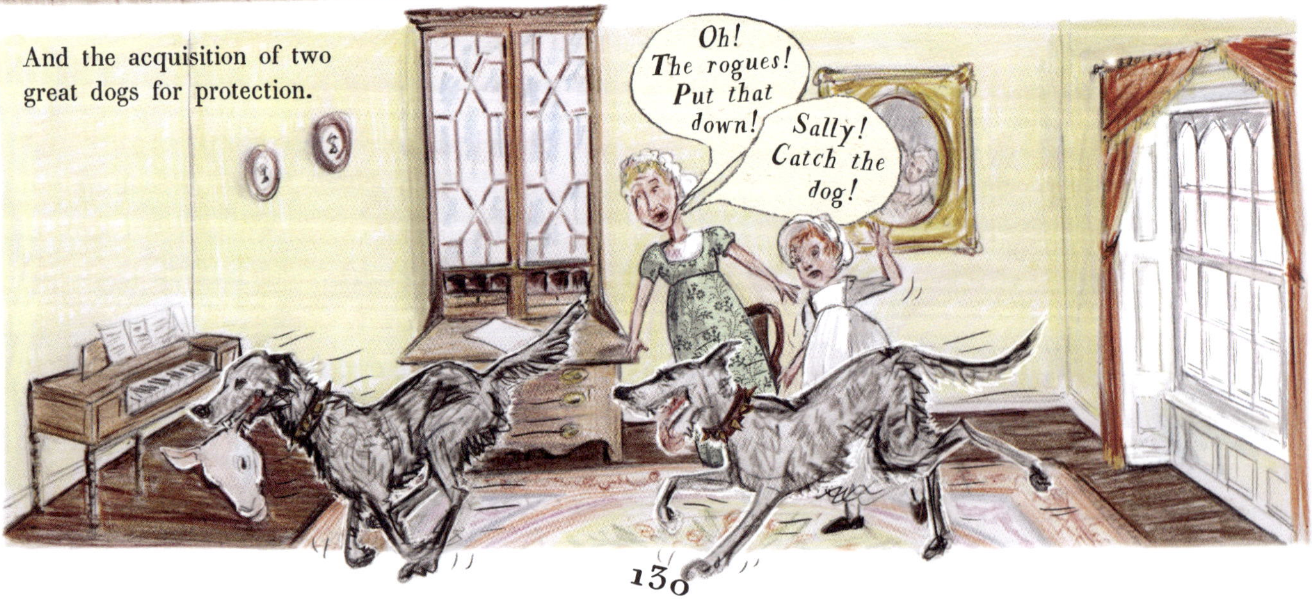
And the acquisition of two great dogs for protection.
Oh! The rogues! Put that down!
Sally! Catch the dog!

There are social calls, of course, but thankfully, not too many. The Austens live in a very small way.

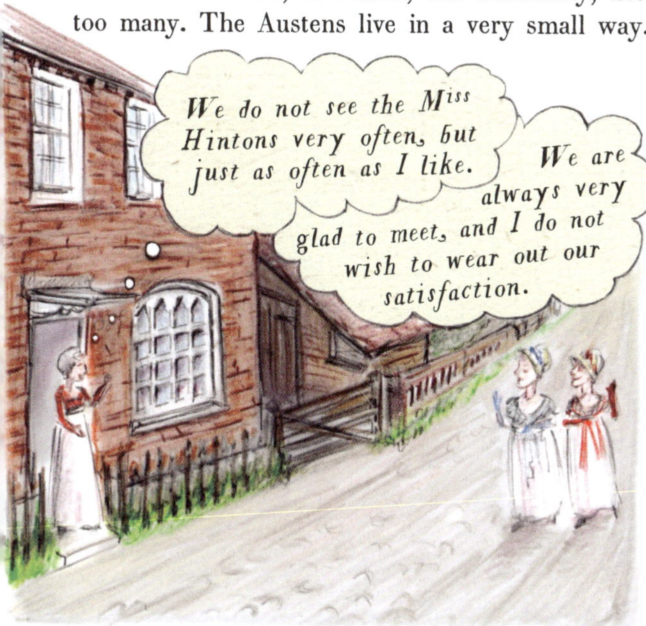
We do not see the Miss Hintons very often, but just as often as I like.
We are always very glad to meet, and I do not wish to wear out our satisfaction.

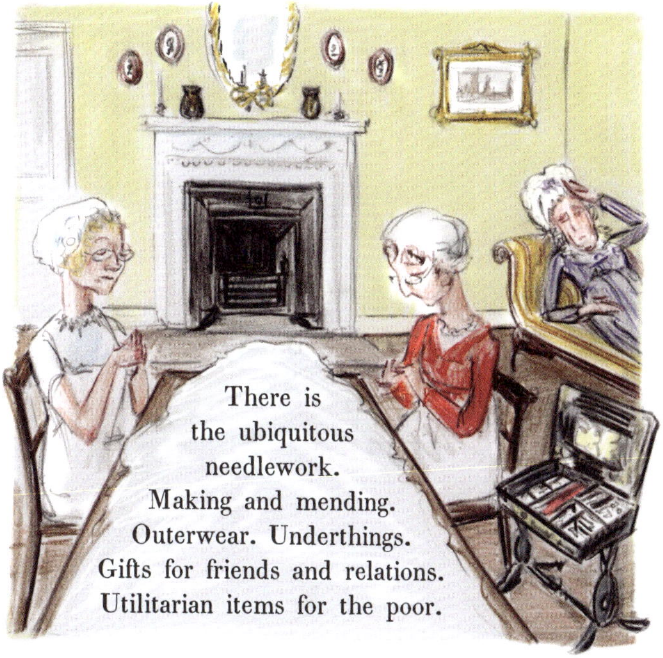
There is the ubiquitous needlework.
Making and mending.
Outerwear. Underthings.
Gifts for friends and relations.
Utilitarian items for the poor.

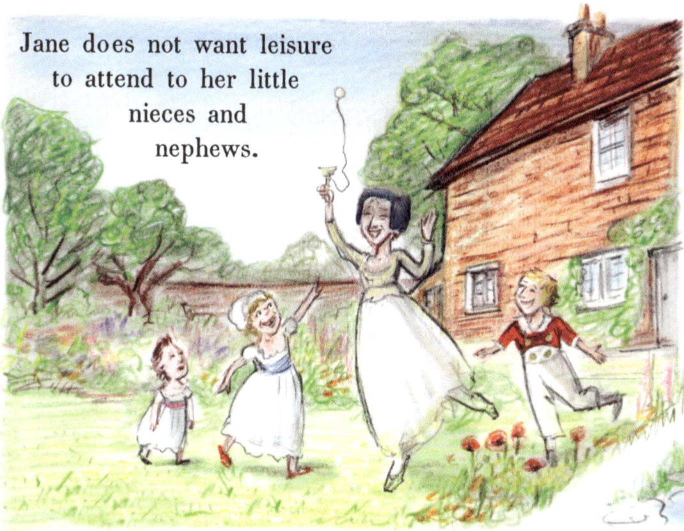
Jane does not want leisure to attend to her little nieces and nephews.

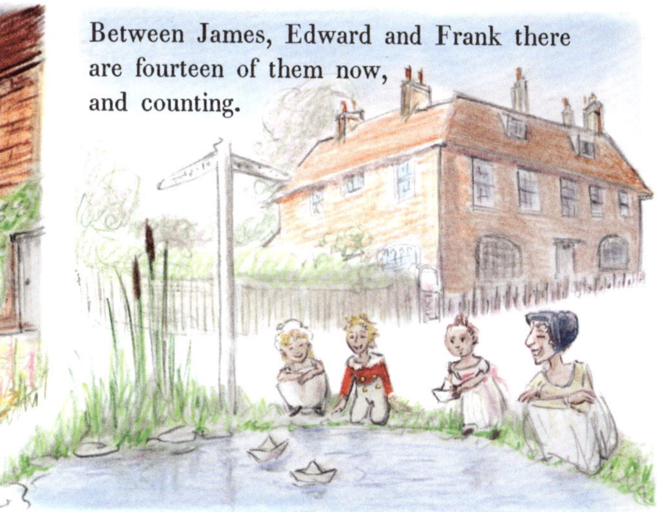
Between James, Edward and Frank there are fourteen of them now, and counting.

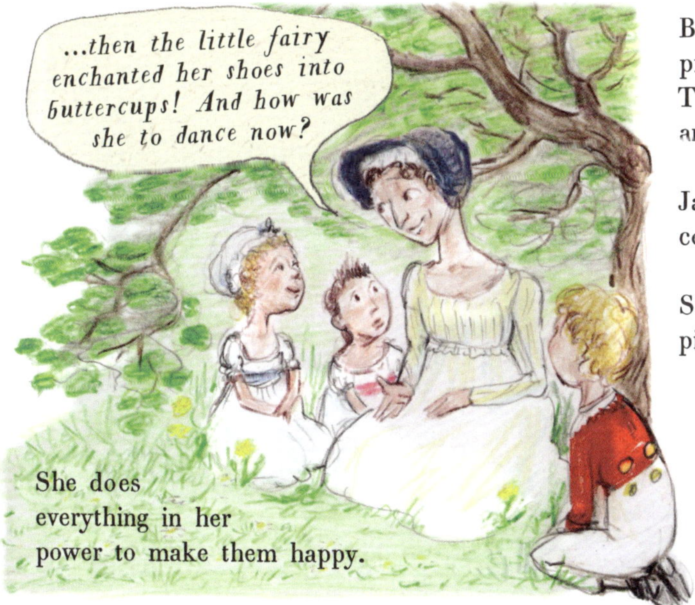
...then the little fairy enchanted her shoes into buttercups! And how was she to dance now?
She does everything in her power to make them happy.

But her chief delight is the Quiet. Chawton Cottage provides her with exemption from the Interruptions, Thoughts & Contrivances which any sort of Company gives.

Jane is able to concentrate once more.

She opens her laptop and picks up her pen.

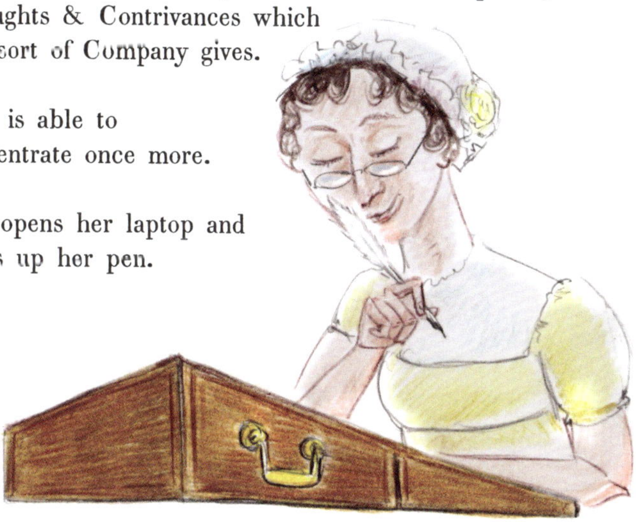

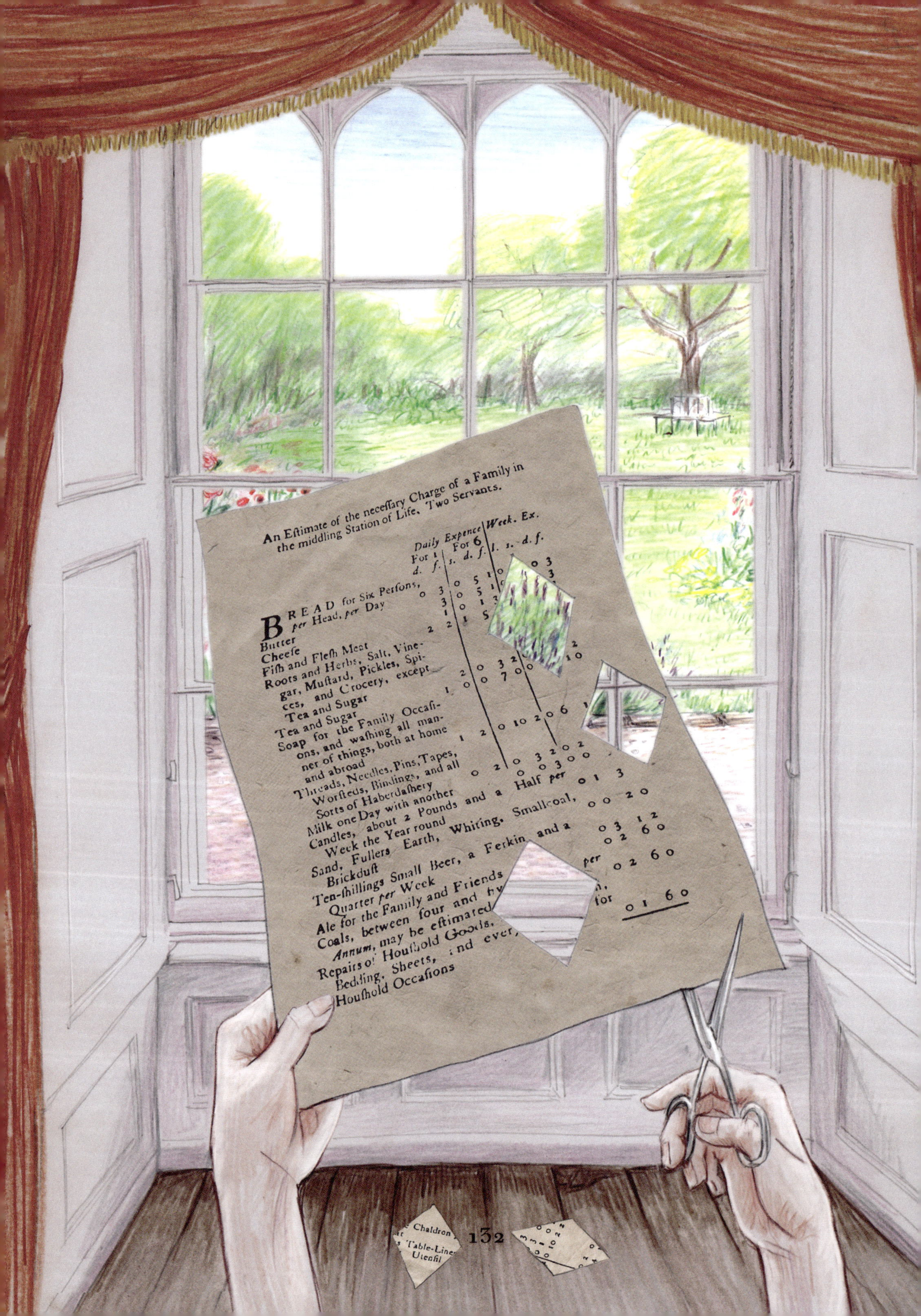
An Estimate of the necessary Charge of a Family in the middling Station of Life, Two Servants.
Daily Expence
For 1
For 6
Week. Ex.
BREAD for Six Persons, per Head, per Day
Butter
Cheese
Fish and Flesh Meat
Roots and Herbs, Salt, Vinegar, Mustard, Pickles, Spices, and Grocery, except Tea and Sugar
Tea and Sugar
Soap for the Family Occasions, and washing all manner of things, both at home and abroad
Threads, Needles, Pins, Tapes, Worsteds, Bindings, and all Sorts of Haberdashery
Milk one Day with another
Candles, about 2 Pounds and a Half per Week the Year round
Sand, Fullers Earth, Whiting, Smallcoal, Brickdust
Ten-shillings Small Beer, a Ferkin and a Quarter per Week
Ale for the Family and Friends
Coals, between four and five
Annum, may be estimated
Repairs of Houshold Goods,
Bedding, Sheets,
Houshold Occasions
Chaldron
Table-Line
Utensil

TO BUSINESS!

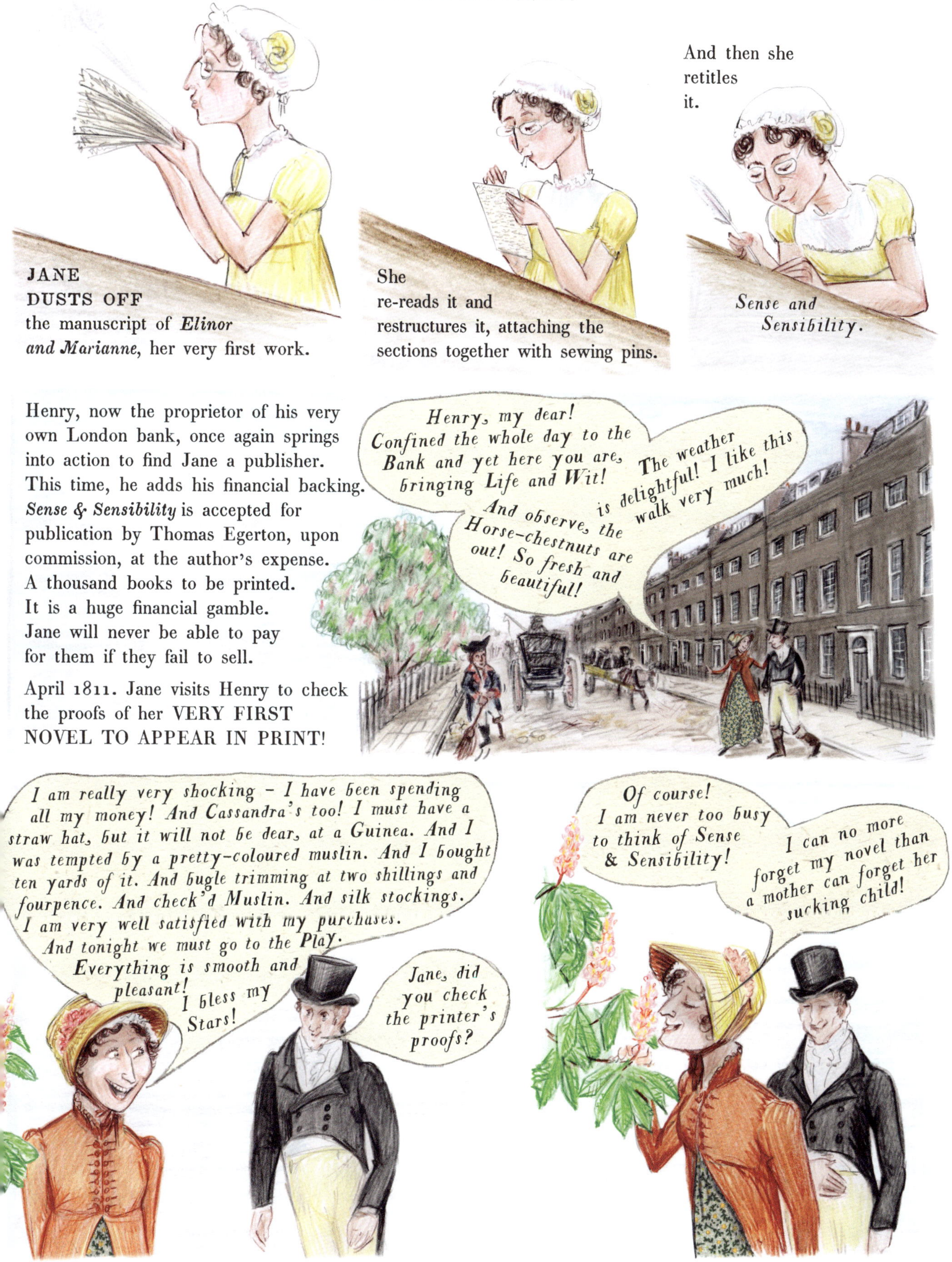
JANE DUSTS OFF the manuscript of *Elinor and Marianne*, her very first work.
She re-reads it and restructures it, attaching the sections together with sewing pins.
And then she retitles it.
Sense and Sensibility.
Henry, now the proprietor of his very own London bank, once again springs into action to find Jane a publisher. This time, he adds his financial backing. *Sense & Sensibility* is accepted for publication by Thomas Egerton, upon commission, at the author's expense. A thousand books to be printed. It is a huge financial gamble. Jane will never be able to pay for them if they fail to sell.
April 1811. Jane visits Henry to check the proofs of her VERY FIRST NOVEL TO APPEAR IN PRINT!
Henry, my dear! Confined the whole day to the Bank and yet here you are, bringing Life and Wit!
The weather is delightful! I like this walk very much!
And observe, the Horse-chestnuts are out! So fresh and beautiful!
I am really very shocking – I have been spending all my money! And Cassandra's too! I must have a straw hat, but it will not be dear, at a Guinea. And I was tempted by a pretty-coloured muslin. And I bought ten yards of it. And bugle trimming at two shillings and fourpence. And check'd Muslin. And silk stockings. I am very well satisfied with my purchases. And tonight we must go to the Play. Everything is smooth and pleasant! I bless my Stars!
Jane, did you check the printer's proofs?
Of course! I am never too busy to think of Sense & Sensibility!
I can no more forget my novel than a mother can forget her sucking child!

IT IS REALLY HAPPENING!

An editor is imposing paragraph-breaks and Standard Capitalization into Jane's free-flowing prose.

A type-setter is selecting each letter, and assembling them into pages; upside-down and back-to-front.

A printer is blacking the plate and introducing a sheet of paper to the press.

A bookbinder is folding the printed sheets and sewing up the spine.

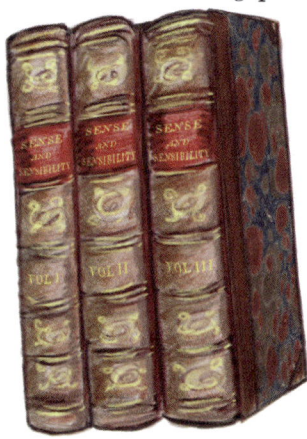

The discerning reader will commission a hand-tooled calfskin binding, in addition to the fifteen shilling price.

But Jane's copy arrives in plain boards.

October. After many months more frustrating delay, Jane finally holds her very own book in her hands.

Sense & Sensibility: A Novel. In Three Volumes. By a Lady. Printed for The Author. & Published by T. Egerton, Whitehall, London, 1811.

At last!

There are Advertisements. There are Reviews. Word of the book spreads...

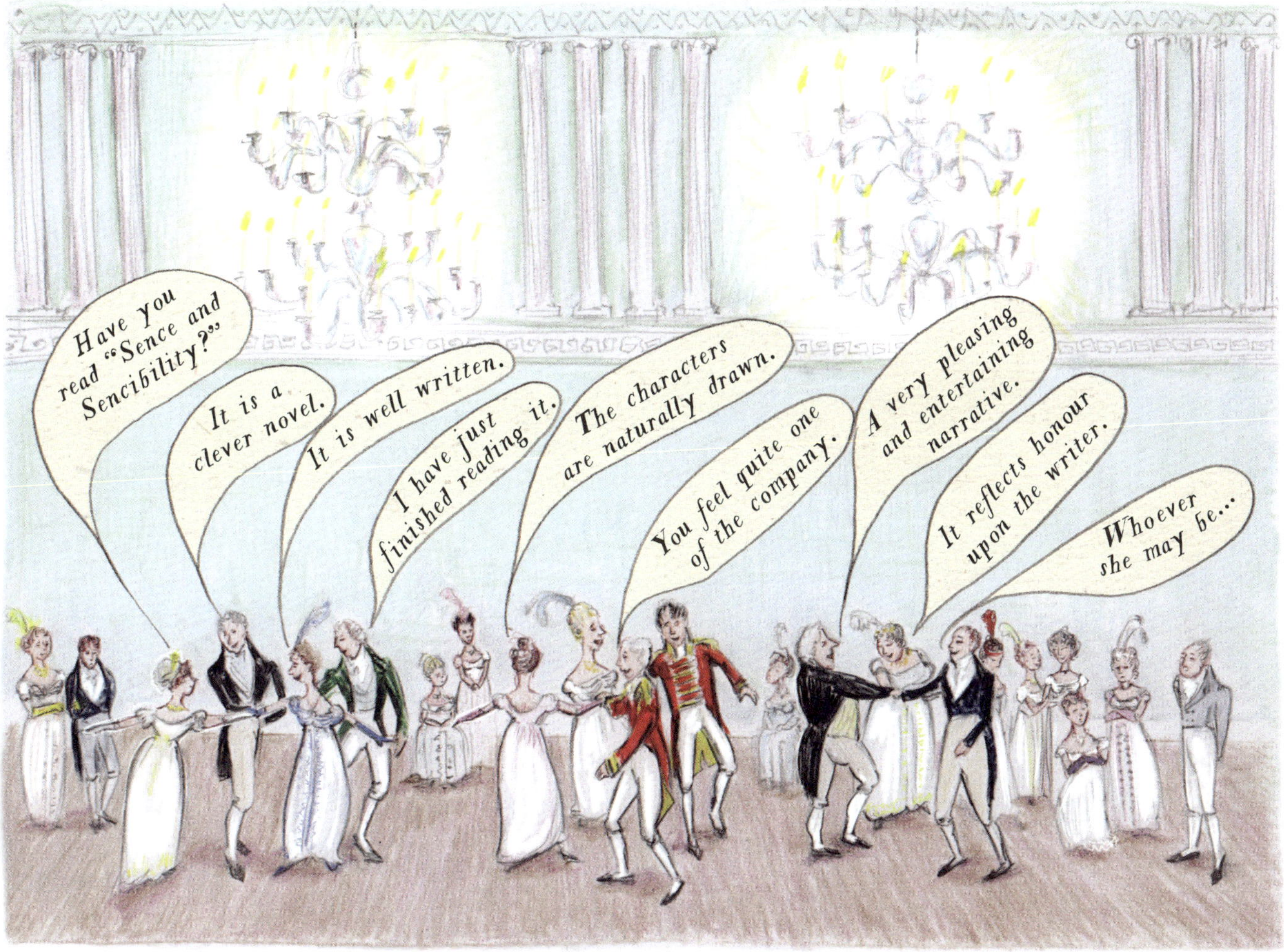

Have you read "Sence and Sencibility?"
It is a clever novel.
It is well written.
I have just finished reading it.
The characters are naturally drawn.
You feel quite one of the company.
A very pleasing and entertaining narrative.
It reflects honour upon the writer.
Whoever she may be...

Jane is anonymous. Her name never appears on her work in her lifetime. Secluded in Chawton, she knows nothing of the "buzz" about her book, but she does spot a copy in Alton circulating library...

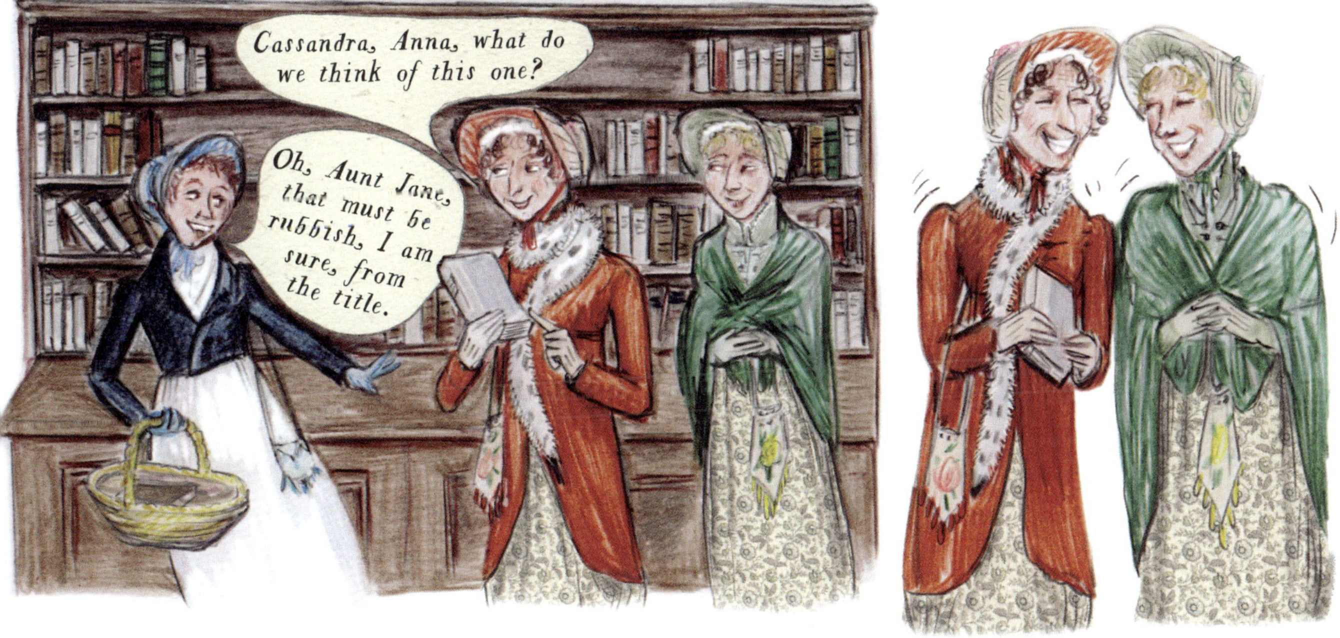

Cassandra, Anna, what do we think of this one?
Oh, Aunt Jane, that must be rubbish, I am sure, from the title.

A success! Every single copy sells in seven short months! Jane clears a handsome profit of £140. Henry's opinion of his sister's financial motives differs somewhat from her own.

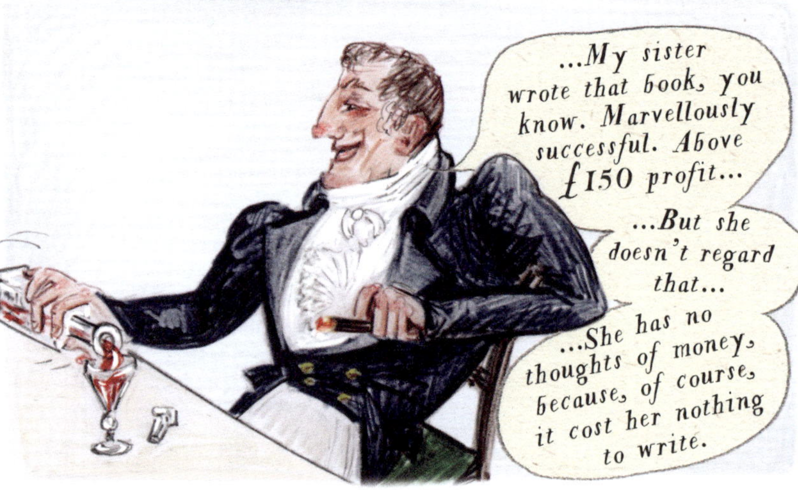
...My sister wrote that book, you know. Marvellously successful. Above £150 profit...
...But she doesn't regard that...
...She has no thoughts of money, because, of course, it cost her nothing to write.

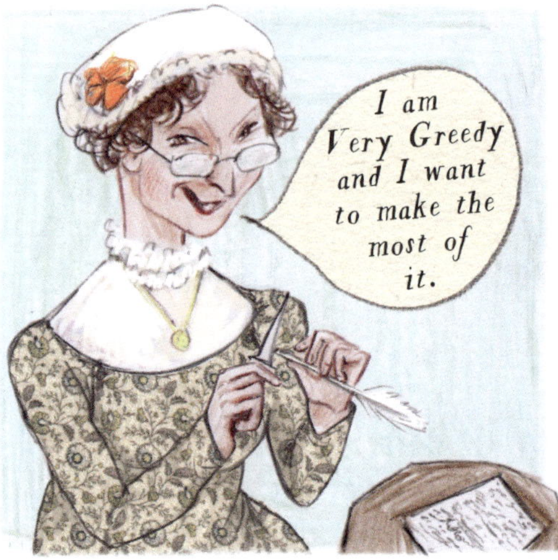
I am Very Greedy and I want to make the most of it.

Spurred on, Jane eagerly sets to work on her other extant manuscript. She lops and crops and whips *First Impressions* into shape. Again, she selects a new name:

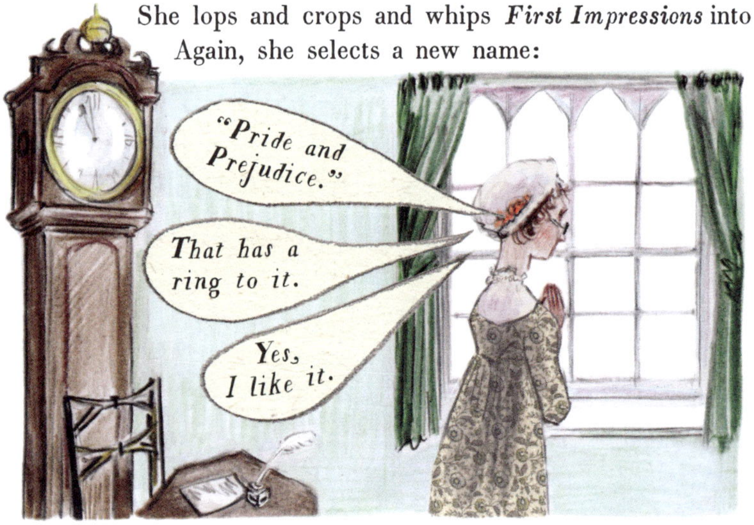
"Pride and Prejudice."
That has a ring to it.
Yes, I like it.

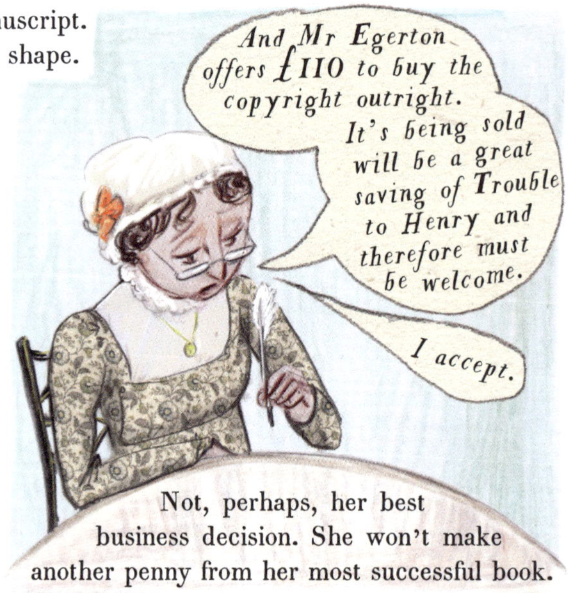
And Mr Egerton offers £110 to buy the copyright outright. It's being sold will be a great saving of Trouble to Henry and therefore must be welcome.
I accept.

Not, perhaps, her best business decision. She won't make another penny from her most successful book.

Egerton prints faster when he stands to keep the profits. January 1813, Jane receives her copy. She eagerly slices the pages apart.

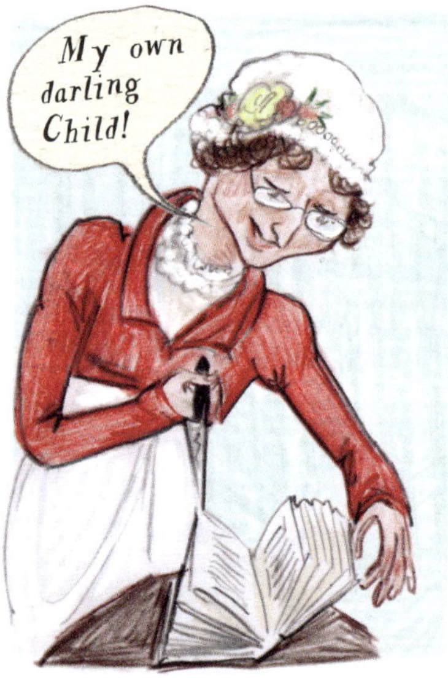
My own darling Child!

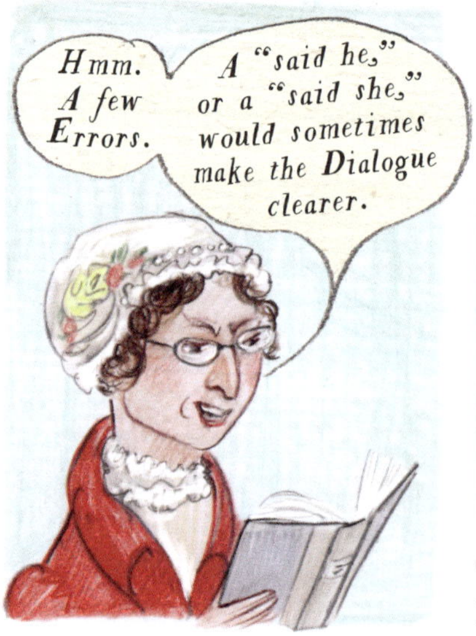
Hmm. A few Errors.
A "said he," or a "said she," would sometimes make the Dialogue clearer.

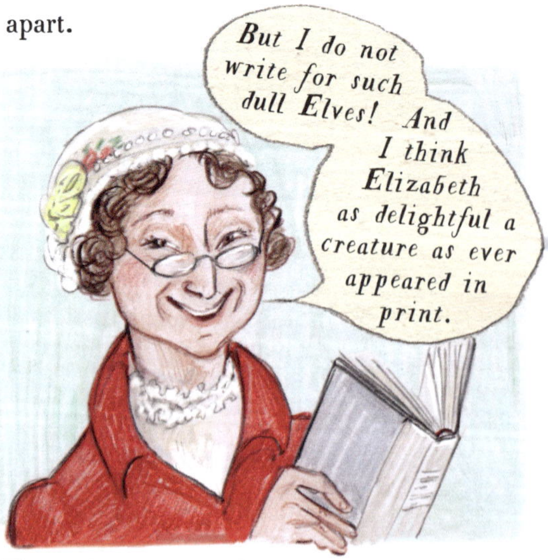
But I do not write for such dull Elves! And I think Elizabeth as delightful a creature as ever appeared in print.

The Public agrees. It is a runaway success. Egerton will reprint within the year.

Curiosity grows about Jane's identity...

"I wish very much to know who is the author." "It is much too clever to have been written by a woman."

but for now, her secret is safe.

She celebrates her new book by reading it to her neighbour, Miss Benn, who is unaware that she is in the presence of the authoress herself.

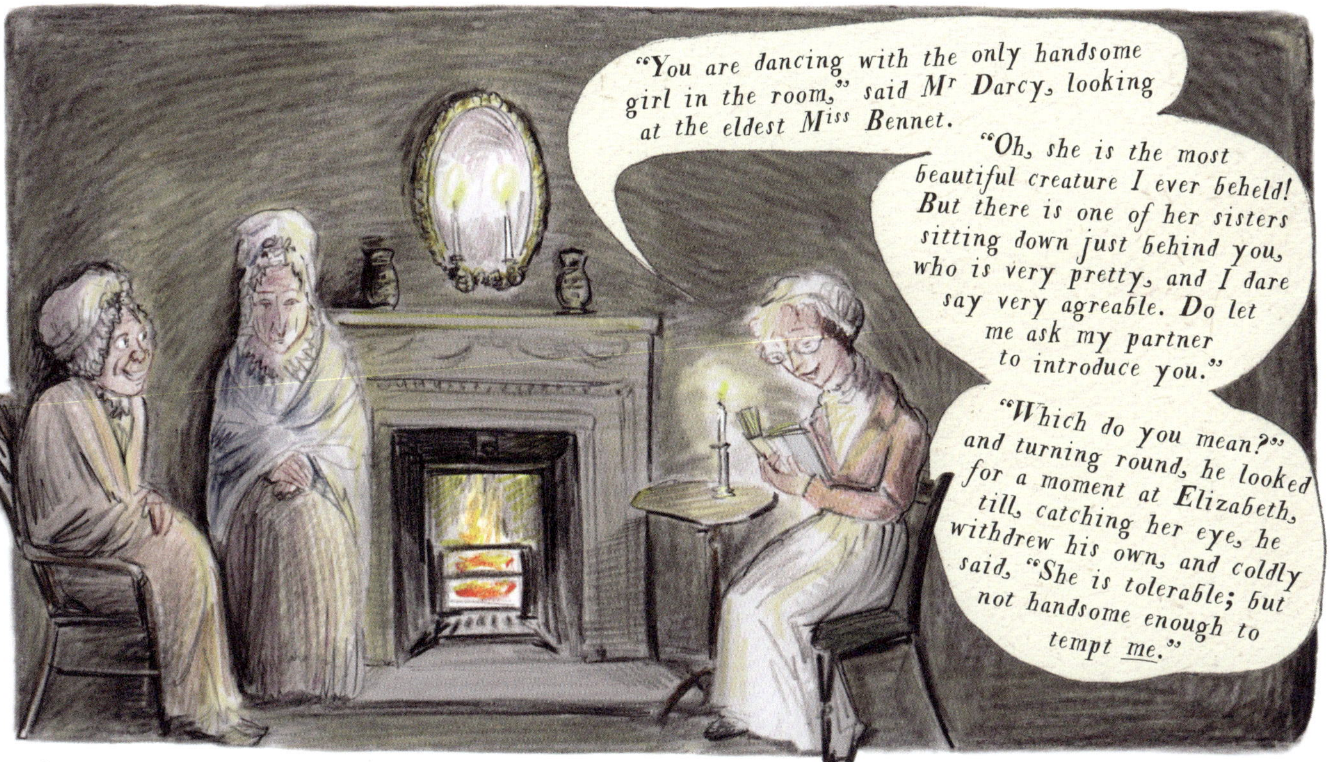
"You are dancing with the only handsome girl in the room," said Mr Darcy, looking at the eldest Miss Bennet.
"Oh, she is the most beautiful creature I ever beheld! But there is one of her sisters sitting down just behind you, who is very pretty, and I dare say very agreable. Do let me ask my partner to introduce you."
"Which do you mean?" and turning round, he looked for a moment at Elizabeth, till, catching her eye, he withdrew his own, and coldly said, "She is tolerable; but not handsome enough to tempt me."

Miss Benn returns the next evening, but Mrs Austen takes over the reading of the book and gabbles through the narrative. Jane cannot, of course, protest.

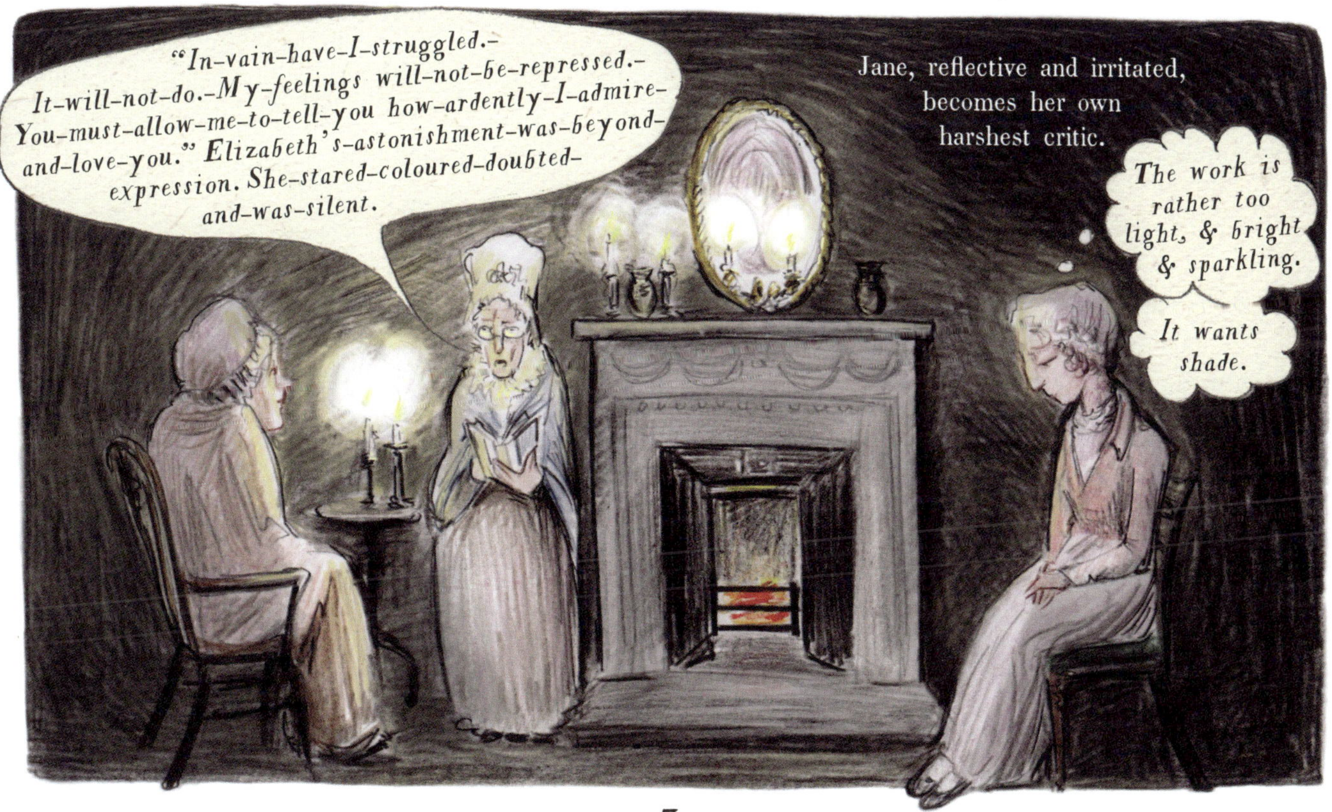
"In-vain-have-I-struggled.-It-will-not-do.-My-feelings will-not-be-repressed.-You-must-allow-me-to-tell-you how-ardently-I-admire-and-love-you." Elizabeth's-astonishment-was-beyond-expression. She-stared-coloured-doubted-and-was-silent.
Jane, reflective and irritated, becomes her own harshest critic.
The work is rather too light, & bright & sparkling.
It wants shade.

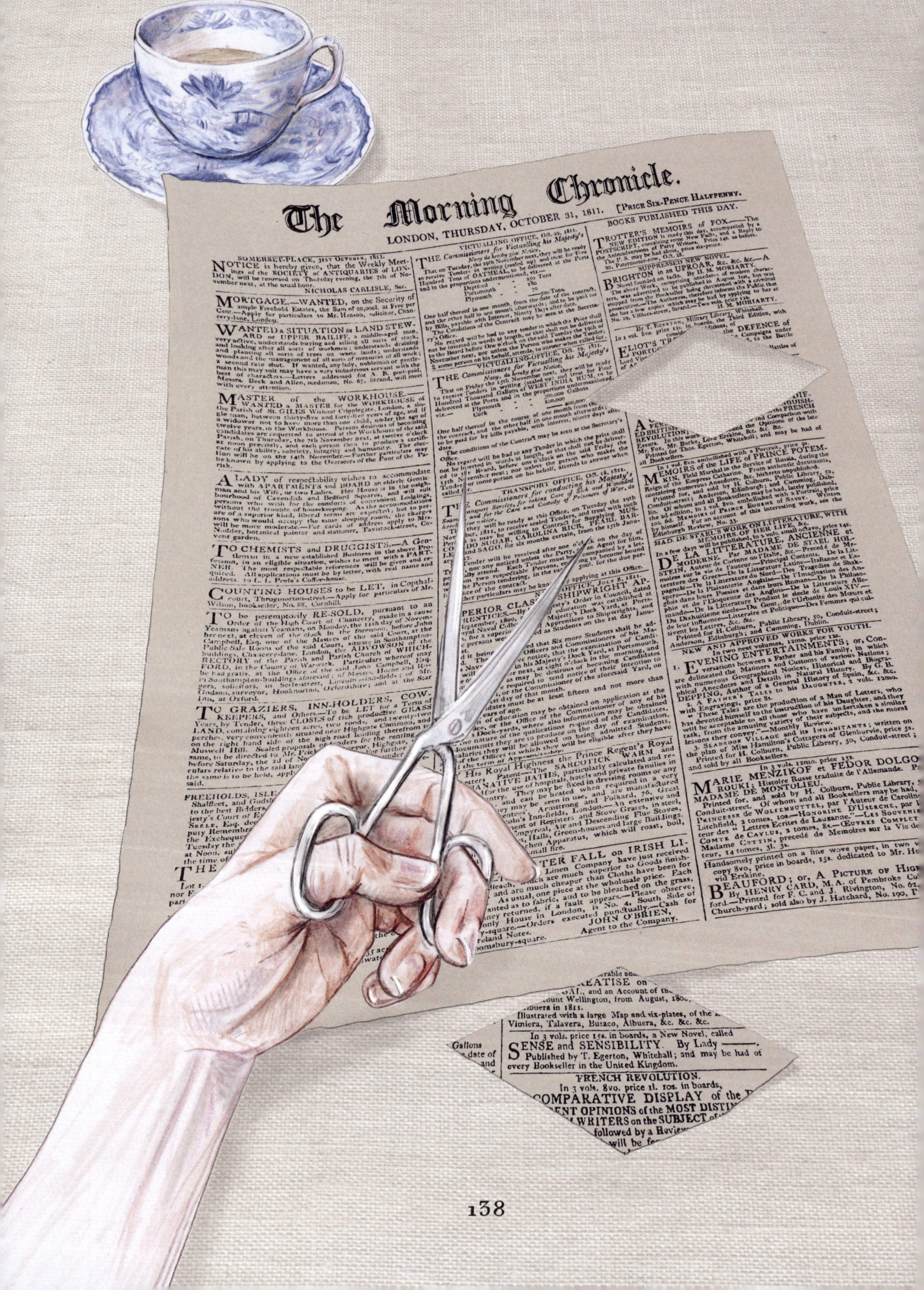
The Morning Chronicle.
LONDON, THURSDAY, OCTOBER 31, 1811.
[PRICE SIX-PENCE HALFPENNY.
BOOKS PUBLISHED THIS DAY.
In 3 vols. price 15s. in boards, a New Novel, called
SENSE and SENSIBILITY. By Lady ——.
Published by T. Egerton, Whitehall; and may be had of every Bookseller in the United Kingdom.
FRENCH REVOLUTION.
In 3 vols. 8vo. price 1l. 10s. in boards,
COMPARATIVE DISPLAY of the

February 1811. Simultaneously with arranging the publication of ***Sense and Sensibility*** and revising the manuscript of ***Pride and Prejudice***, Jane starts work on an entirely new composition.

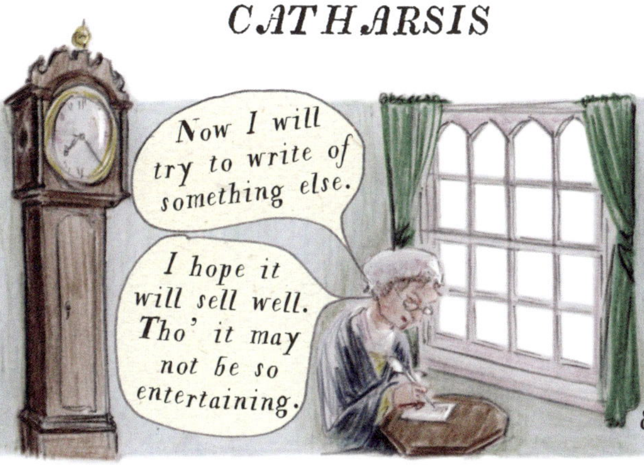
Now I will try to write of something else.
I hope it will sell well. Tho' it may not be so entertaining.

Jane's new novel is certainly something else. Nobody could accuse it of being too light and sparkling. She is writing explicitly for publication, and on the surface, ***Mansfield Park*** celebrates modesty and virtue. But from Jane's unconscious, & her pen, darker themes emerge.

Jane paints a portrait of a child, a girl, a poor relation, Fanny Price, plucked from her home to live with her wealthy Uncle's family.

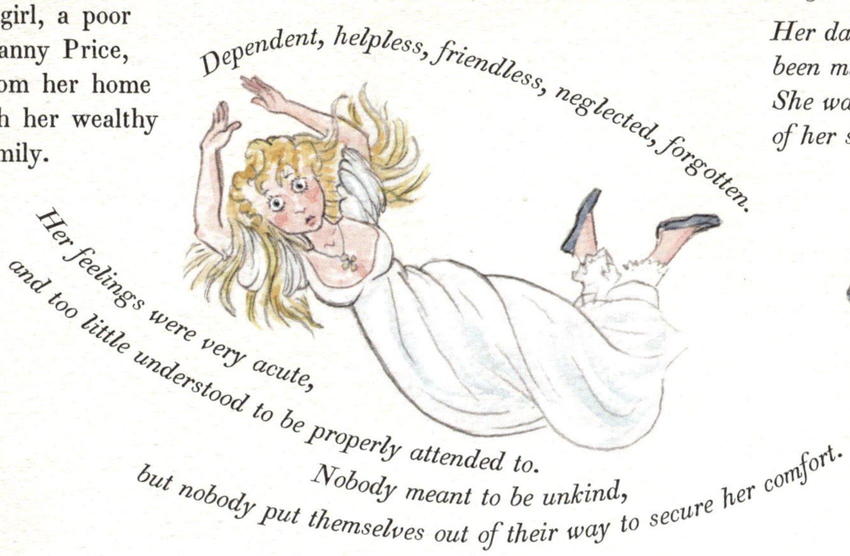
Dependent, helpless, friendless, neglected, forgotten.
Her feelings were very acute, and too little understood to be properly attended to.
Nobody meant to be unkind, but nobody put themselves out of their way to secure her comfort.

Neglected by her Mother...

Her daughters never had been much to her. She was fond of her sons.

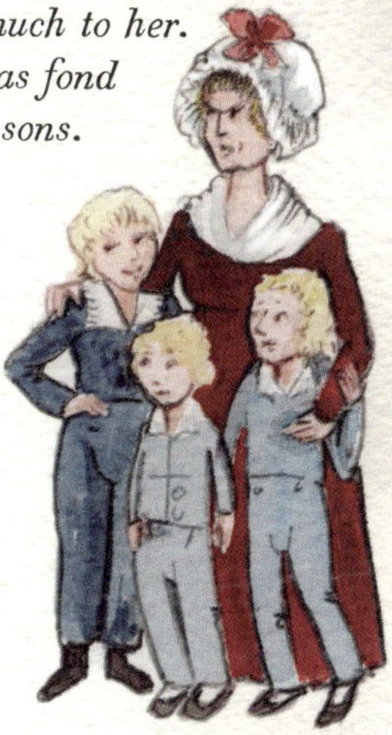

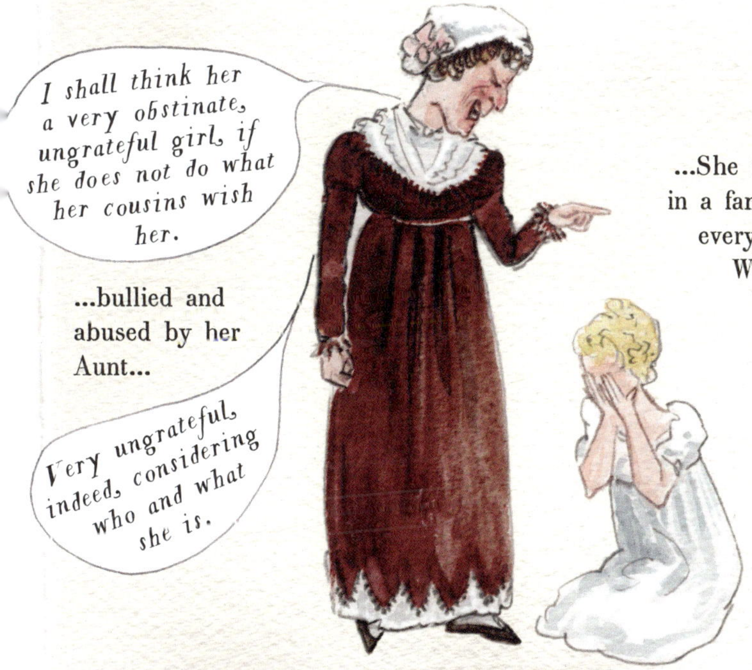
I shall think her a very obstinate, ungrateful girl, if she does not do what her cousins wish her.
...bullied and abused by her Aunt...
Very ungrateful, indeed, considering who and what she is.

...She is trapped in a family where everything is Wrong.

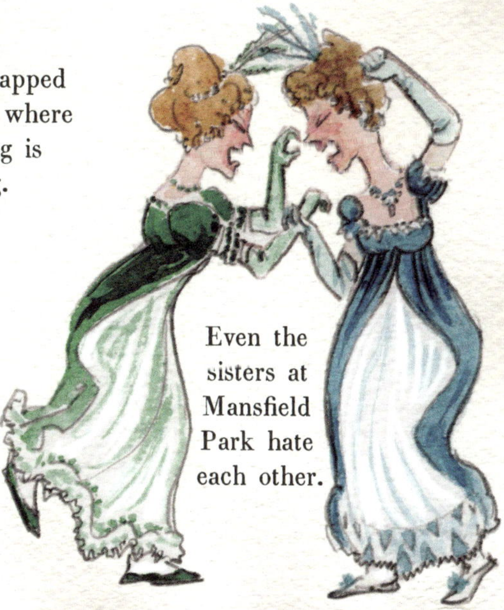
Even the sisters at Mansfield Park hate each other.

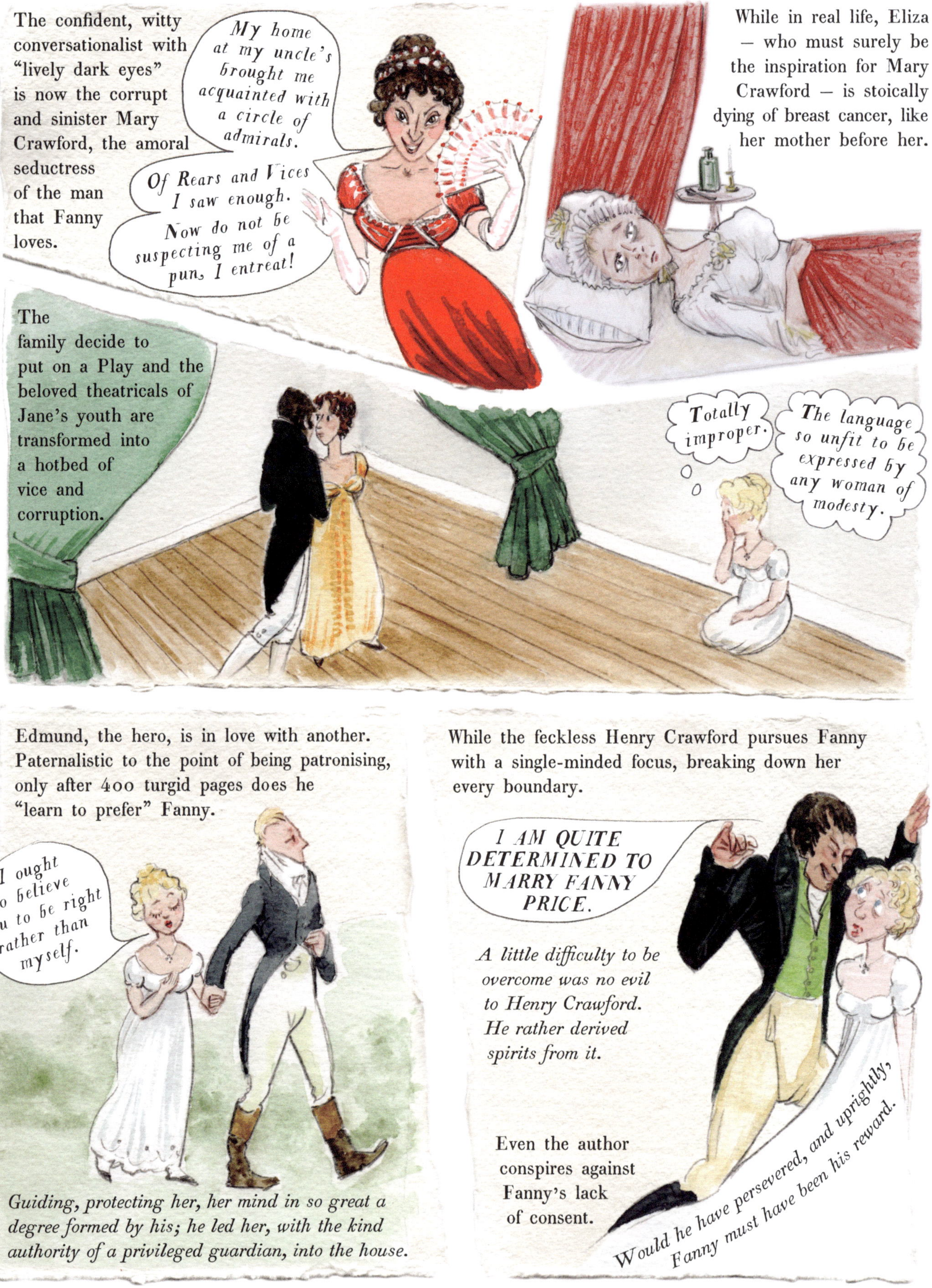

The confident, witty conversationalist with "lively dark eyes" is now the corrupt and sinister Mary Crawford, the amoral seductress of the man that Fanny loves.
My home at my uncle's brought me acquainted with a circle of admirals.
Of Rears and Vices I saw enough. Now do not be suspecting me of a pun, I entreat!
While in real life, Eliza – who must surely be the inspiration for Mary Crawford – is stoically dying of breast cancer, like her mother before her.
The family decide to put on a Play and the beloved theatricals of Jane's youth are transformed into a hotbed of vice and corruption.
Totally improper.
The language so unfit to be expressed by any woman of modesty.
Edmund, the hero, is in love with another. Paternalistic to the point of being patronising, only after 400 turgid pages does he "learn to prefer" Fanny.
I ought to believe you to be right rather than myself.
Guiding, protecting her, her mind in so great a degree formed by his; he led her, with the kind authority of a privileged guardian, into the house.
While the feckless Henry Crawford pursues Fanny with a single-minded focus, breaking down her every boundary.
I AM QUITE DETERMINED TO MARRY FANNY PRICE.
A little difficulty to be overcome was no evil to Henry Crawford. He rather derived spirits from it.
Even the author conspires against Fanny's lack of consent.
Would he have persevered, and uprightly, Fanny must have been his reward.

Something is rotten in the house of Mansfield.

Slavery.

(Austen's audience would have understood the significance of the name: Judge Mansfield famously ruled that slavery had never been legal in England.

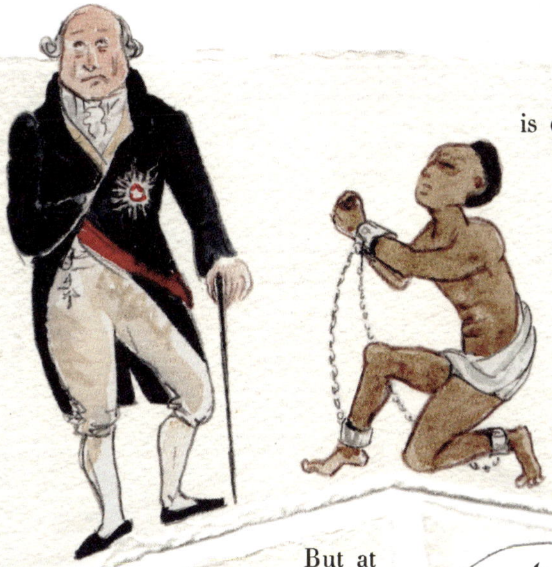

S^ir^ Thomas Bertram, the patriarch, is called away to visit his West Indian plantations, and in his absence his daughters' morals are corrupted. Jane's tepid exploration of the evils of enslavement is couched entirely in terms of the damage it inflicts upon rich white men.

And to make that argument, she must emphasise S^ir^ Thomas's *honour*, his *morality*, his *kind parental solicitude* – hardly the attributes of an enslaver.

But at the point where Jane touches most directly upon the issue, her representation holds real resonance...

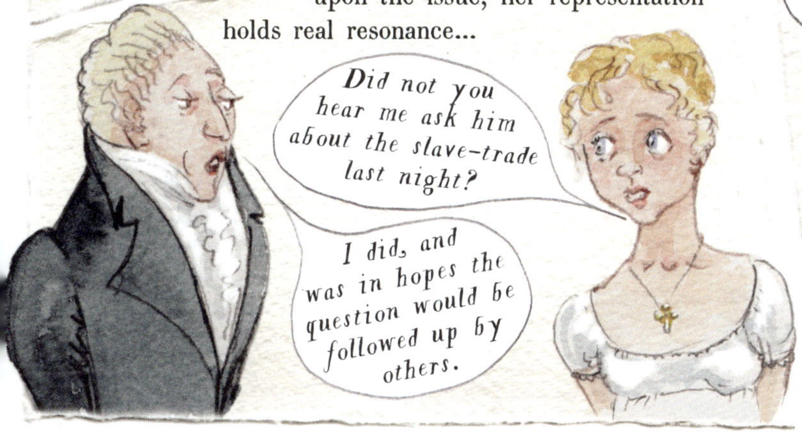
Did not you hear me ask him about the slave-trade last night?
I did, and was in hopes the question would be followed up by others.

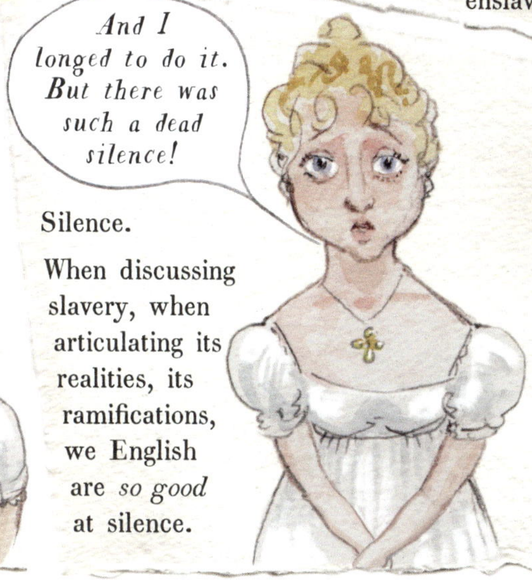
And I longed to do it. But there was such a dead silence!

Silence.

When discussing slavery, when articulating its realities, its ramifications, we English are *so good* at silence.

And there is something else within this "something else."

Fanny's passivity, her muteness, her incapability, the way that she is spoken about in the third person, how her life is dictated by others...

Fanny could not speak, but he did not want her to speak.

Timid, anxious, doubting.

She alone was sad and insignificant: she had no share in anything.

...Fanny echoes the horror at the heart of the Austen family.

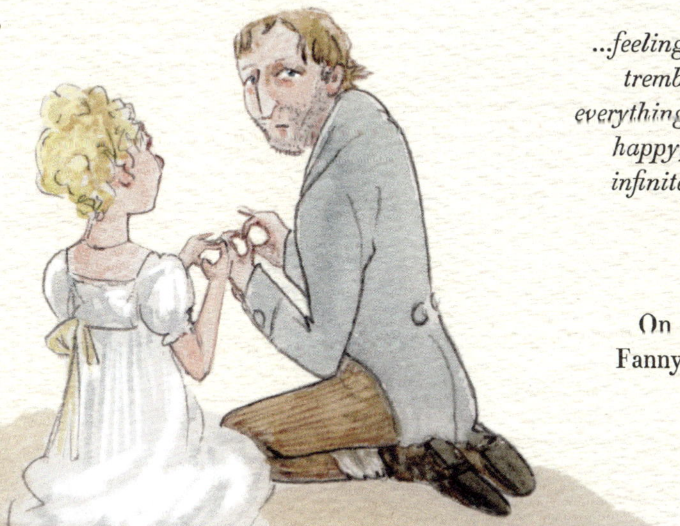

That truly dependent, helpless, friendless, neglected, forgotten person.

...feeling, thinking, trembling about everything; agitated, happy, miserable, infinitely obliged, absolutely angry...

On some level, Fanny is George.

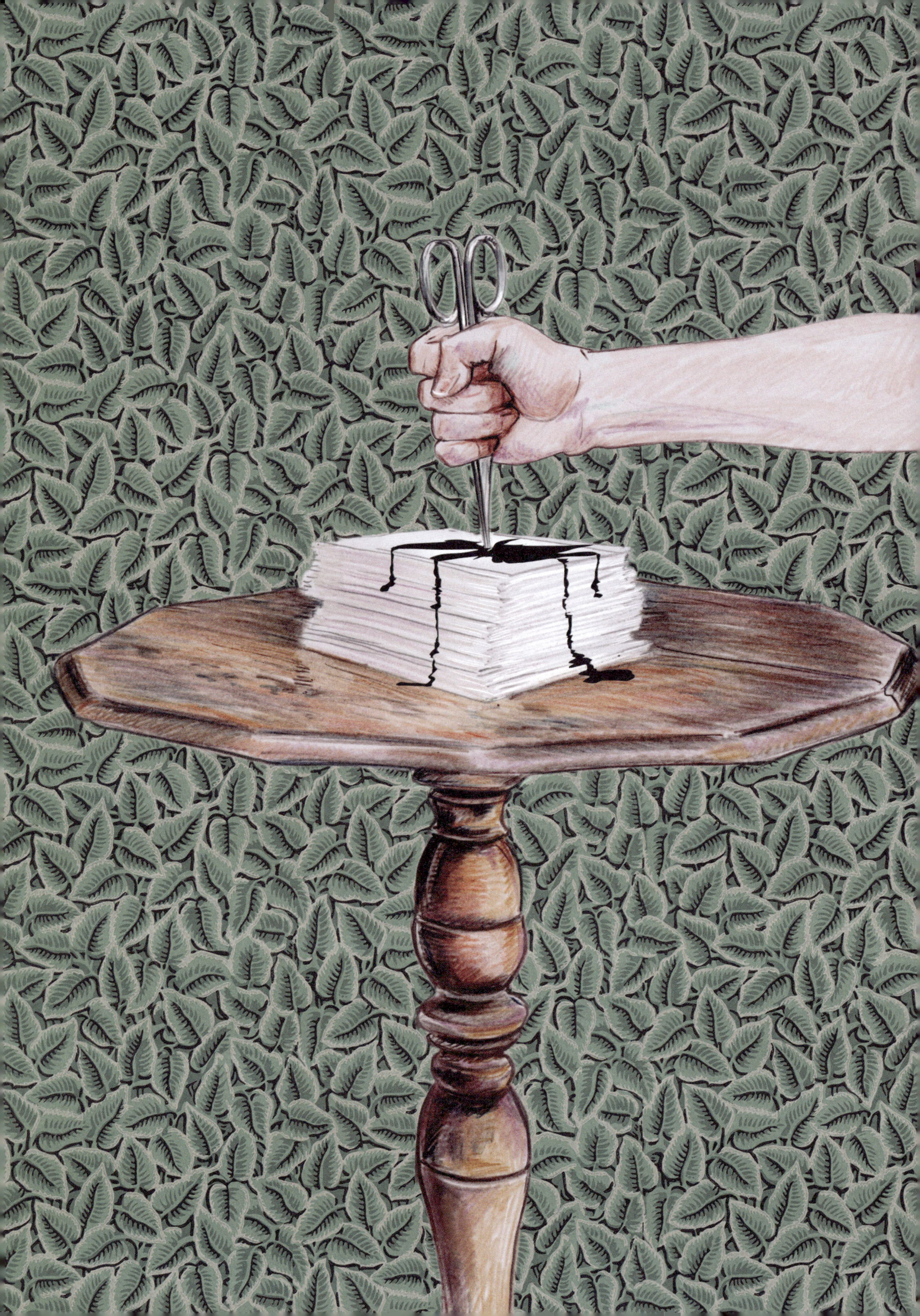

YOUNG LADIES OF AN INTERESTING AGE

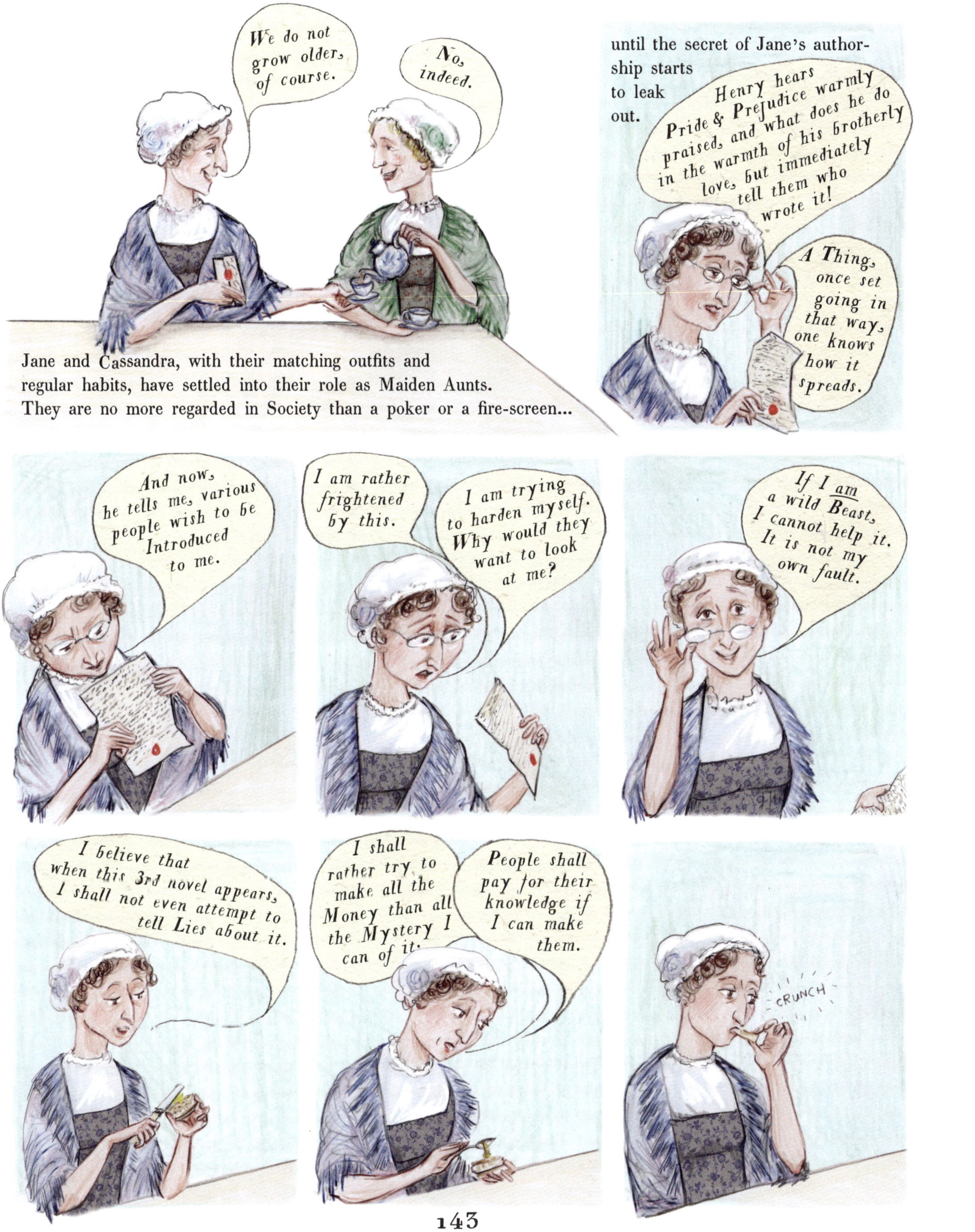
We do not grow older, of course.
No, indeed.
Jane and Cassandra, with their matching outfits and regular habits, have settled into their role as Maiden Aunts. They are no more regarded in Society than a poker or a fire-screen...
until the secret of Jane's authorship starts to leak out.
Henry hears Pride & Prejudice warmly praised, and what does he do in the warmth of his brotherly love, but immediately tell them who wrote it!
A Thing, once set going in that way, one knows how it spreads.
And now, he tells me, various people wish to be Introduced to me.
I am rather frightened by this.
I am trying to harden myself. Why would they want to look at me?
If I am a wild Beast, I cannot help it. It is not my own fault.
I believe that when this 3rd novel appears, I shall not even attempt to tell Lies about it.
I shall rather try to make all the Money than all the Mystery I can of it.
People shall pay for their knowledge if I can make them.
CRUNCH

Of all the nieces and nephews that enliven the Aunt Austens' lives, the two first remain the most special. Anna, James' eldest and Fanny, Edward's firstborn, have now reached an *interesting* age. Who can keep pace with the fluctuations of their Fancies, the Capprizios of their Tastes, and the Contradictions of their Feelings?

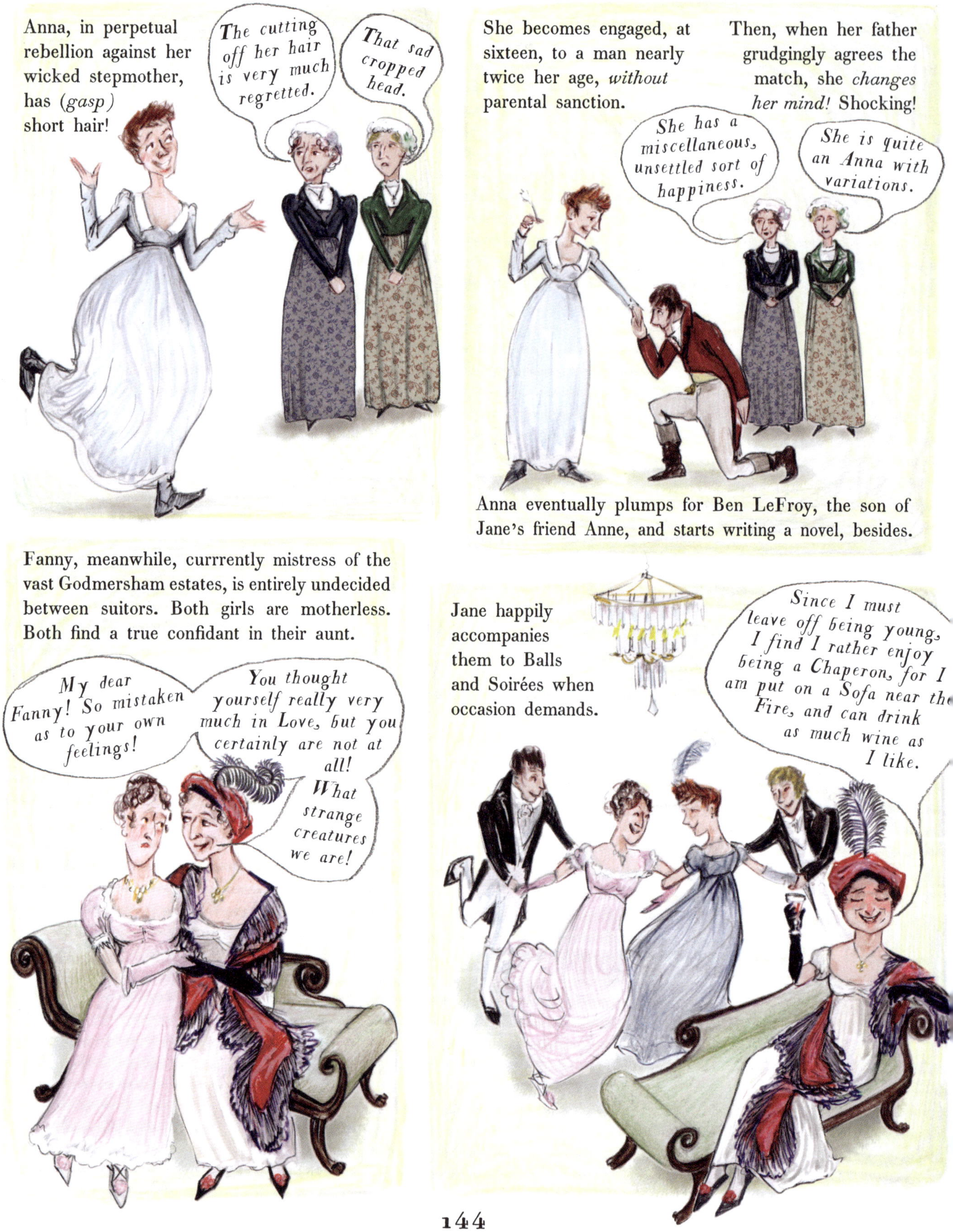
Anna, in perpetual rebellion against her wicked stepmother, has (gasp) short hair!
The cutting off her hair is very much regretted.
That sad cropped head.
She becomes engaged, at sixteen, to a man nearly twice her age, without parental sanction.
Then, when her father grudgingly agrees the match, she changes her mind! Shocking!
She has a miscellaneous, unsettled sort of happiness.
She is quite an Anna with variations.
Anna eventually plumps for Ben LeFroy, the son of Jane's friend Anne, and starts writing a novel, besides.
Fanny, meanwhile, currrently mistress of the vast Godmersham estates, is entirely undecided between suitors. Both girls are motherless. Both find a true confidant in their aunt.
My dear Fanny! So mistaken as to your own feelings!
You thought yourself really very much in Love, but you certainly are not at all! What strange creatures we are!
Jane happily accompanies them to Balls and Soirées when occasion demands.
Since I must leave off being young, I find I rather enjoy being a Chaperon, for I am put on a Sofa near the Fire, and can drink as much wine as I like.

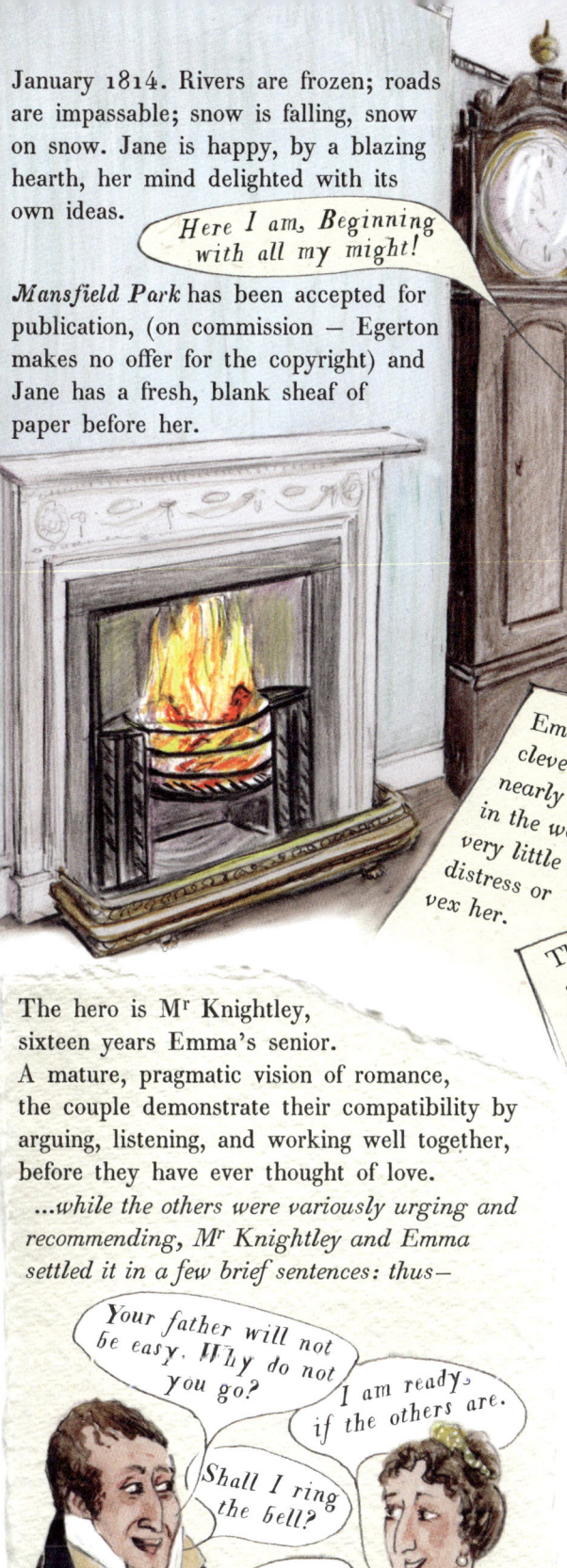

January 1814. Rivers are frozen; roads are impassable; snow is falling, snow on snow. Jane is happy, by a blazing hearth, her mind delighted with its own ideas.

Mansfield Park has been accepted for publication, (on commission – Egerton makes no offer for the copyright) and Jane has a fresh, blank sheaf of paper before her.

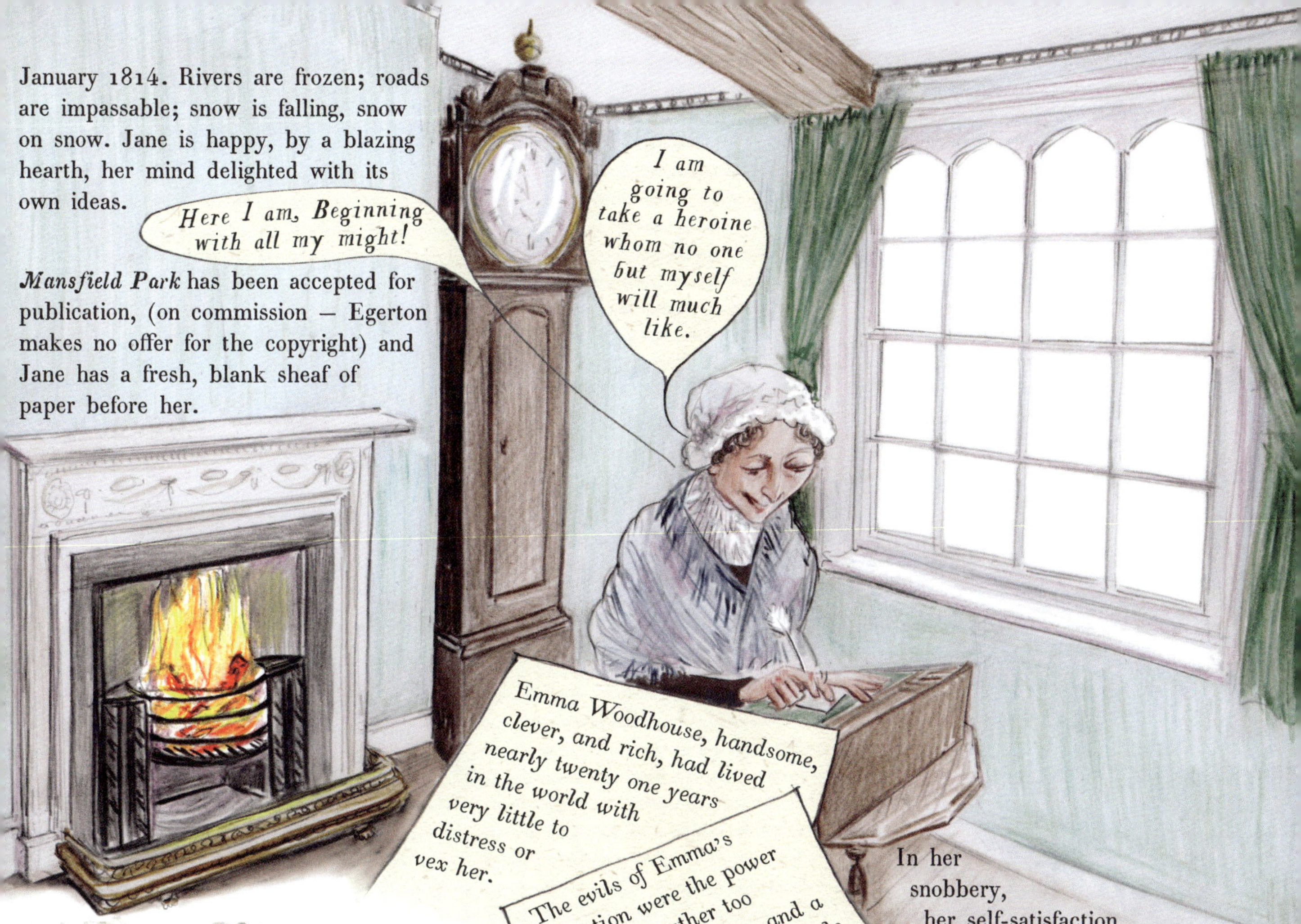
Here I am, Beginning with all my might!
I am going to take a heroine whom no one but myself will much like.
Emma Woodhouse, handsome, clever, and rich, had lived nearly twenty one years in the world with very little to distress or vex her.
The evils of Emma's situation were the power of having rather too much her own way, and a disposition to think a little too well of herself.

In her snobbery, her self-satisfaction, and also the loss of her mother, her character and situation exactly match Fanny Knight's.

The hero is Mr Knightley, sixteen years Emma's senior. A mature, pragmatic vision of romance, the couple demonstrate their compatibility by arguing, listening, and working well together, before they have ever thought of love.

...while the others were variously urging and recommending, Mr Knightley and Emma settled it in a few brief sentences: thus–

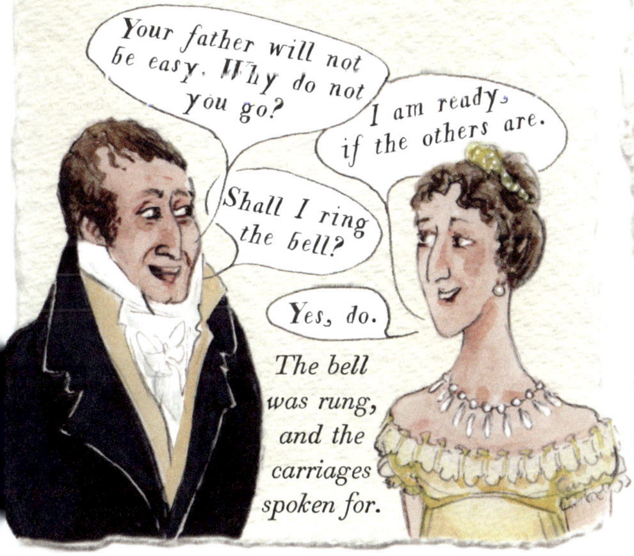
Your father will not be easy. Why do not you go?
I am ready, if the others are.
Shall I ring the bell?
Yes, do.

The bell was rung, and the carriages spoken for.

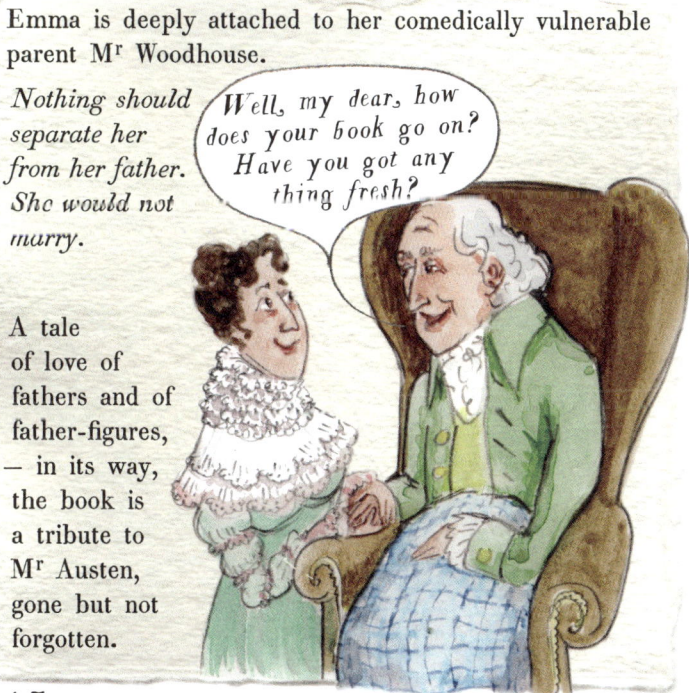

Emma is deeply attached to her comedically vulnerable parent Mr Woodhouse.

Nothing should separate her from her father. She would not marry.

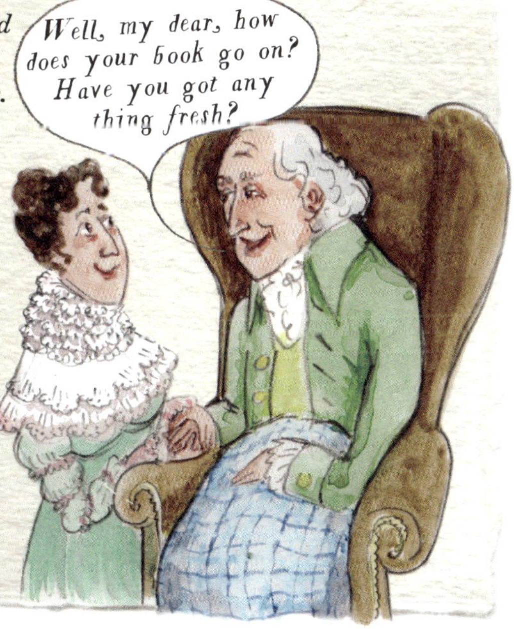
Well, my dear, how does your book go on? Have you got any thing fresh?

A tale of love of fathers and of father-figures, – in its way, the book is a tribute to Mr Austen, gone but not forgotten.

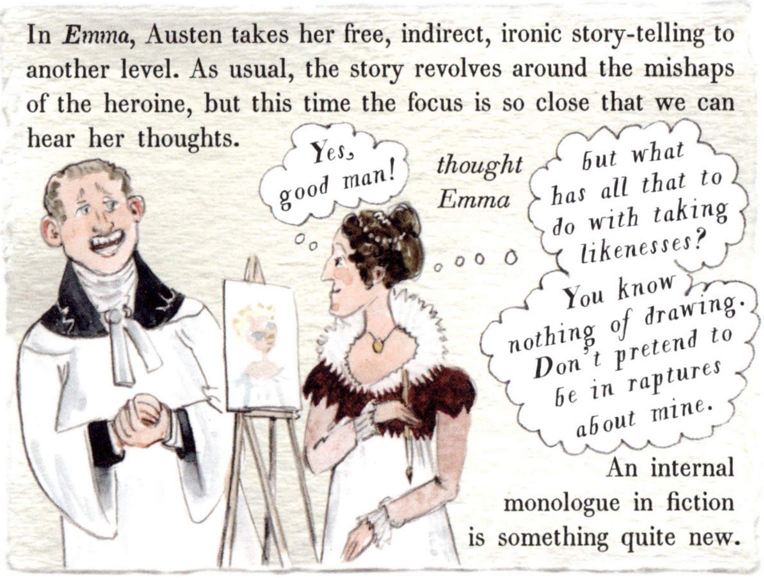
In *Emma*, Austen takes her free, indirect, ironic story-telling to another level. As usual, the story revolves around the mishaps of the heroine, but this time the focus is so close that we can hear her thoughts.
Yes, good man!
thought Emma
but what has all that to do with taking likenesses?
You know nothing of drawing. Don't pretend to be in raptures about mine.
An internal monologue in fiction is something quite new.

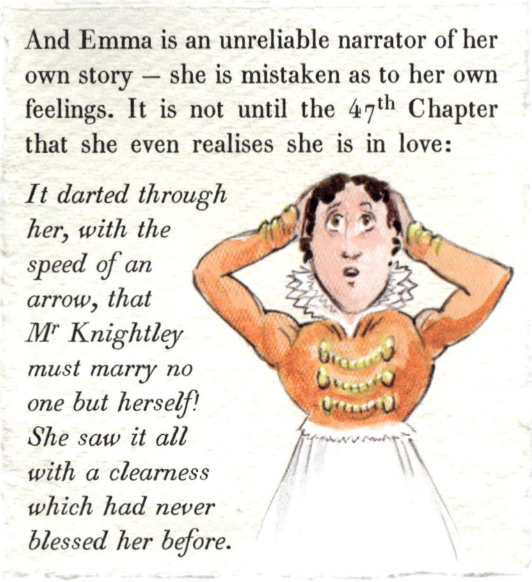
And Emma is an unreliable narrator of her own story – she is mistaken as to her own feelings. It is not until the 47th Chapter that she even realises she is in love:
It darted through her, with the speed of an arrow, that Mr Knightley must marry no one but herself! She saw it all with a clearness which had never blessed her before.

On the surface, the book is a gentle comedy of manners. Deeper currents swirl beneath.

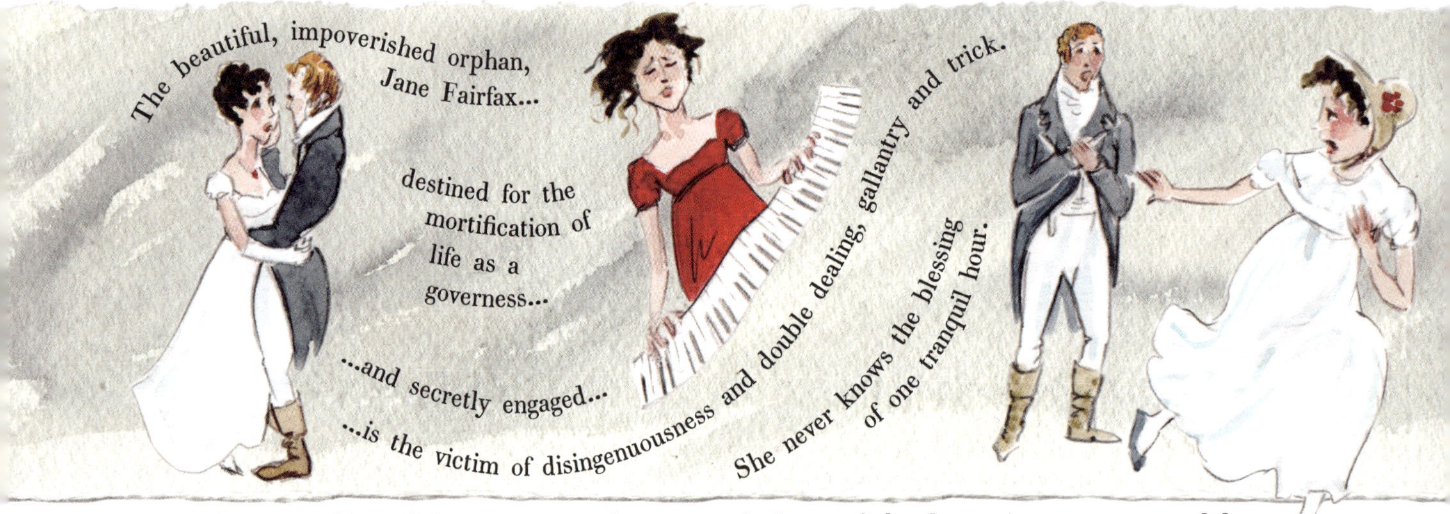
The beautiful, impoverished orphan, Jane Fairfax...
destined for the mortification of life as a governess...
...and secretly engaged...
...is the victim of disingenuousness and double dealing, gallantry and trick.
She never knows the blessing of one tranquil hour.

Emma knows nothing of these events, and so, we only learn of the drama in retrospect, and by one remove. And thus, a second reading of the novel produces an entirely new story. It is deftly done.

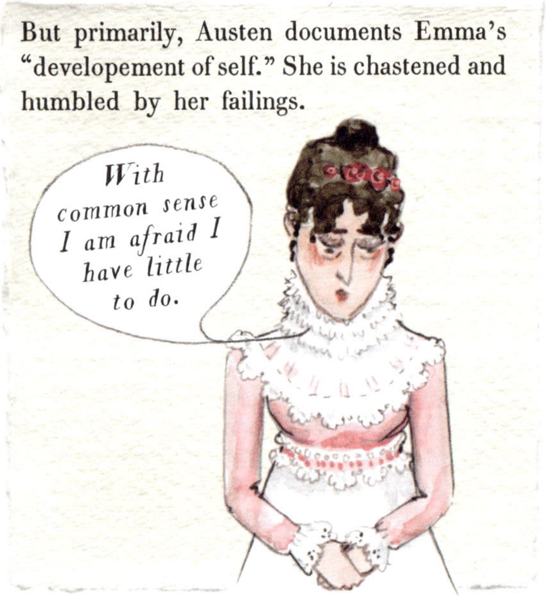
But primarily, Austen documents Emma's "developement of self." She is chastened and humbled by her failings.
With common sense I am afraid I have little to do.

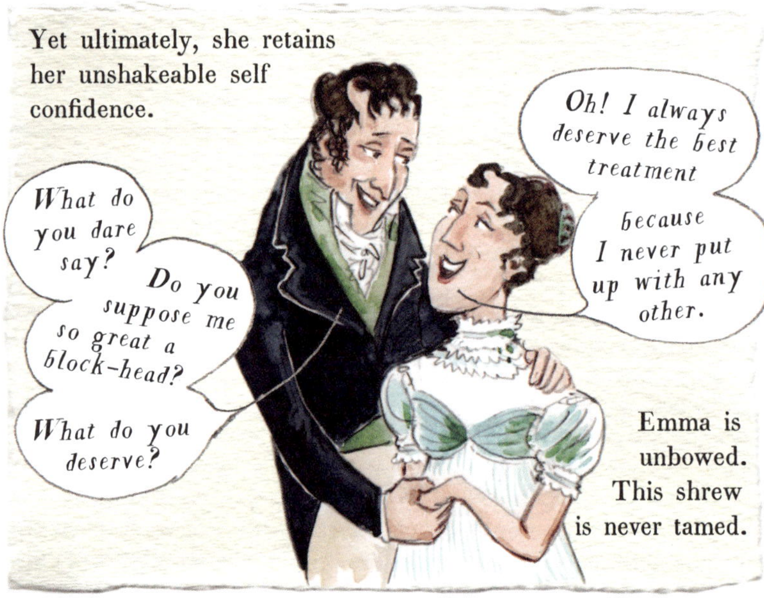
Yet ultimately, she retains her unshakeable self confidence.
What do you dare say?
Do you suppose me so great a block-head?
What do you deserve?
Oh! I always deserve the best treatment
because I never put up with any other.
Emma is unbowed. This shrew is never tamed.

And then, there is Miss Bates, Austen's finest comic character. Jane makes the unmarried spinster the butt of the joke, with the most extraordinary, unbroken walls of speech:

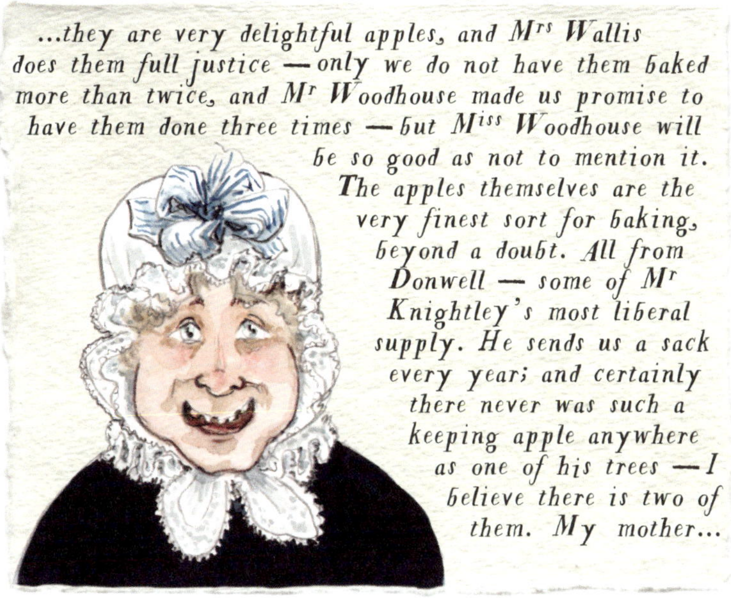
...they are very delightful apples, and Mrs Wallis does them full justice — only we do not have them baked more than twice, and Mr Woodhouse made us promise to have them done three times — but Miss Woodhouse will be so good as not to mention it. The apples themselves are the very finest sort for baking, beyond a doubt. All from Donwell — some of Mr Knightley's most liberal supply. He sends us a sack every year; and certainly there never was such a keeping apple anywhere as one of his trees — I believe there is two of them. My mother...

Yet simultaneously, she makes it clear that Miss Bates is a force for good in the world. Emma's most regretted error is to publically ridicule the sweet woman.

And surprisingly for a romance (and to the delight of generations of unmarried readers) *Emma* lays out a case *against* marriage.

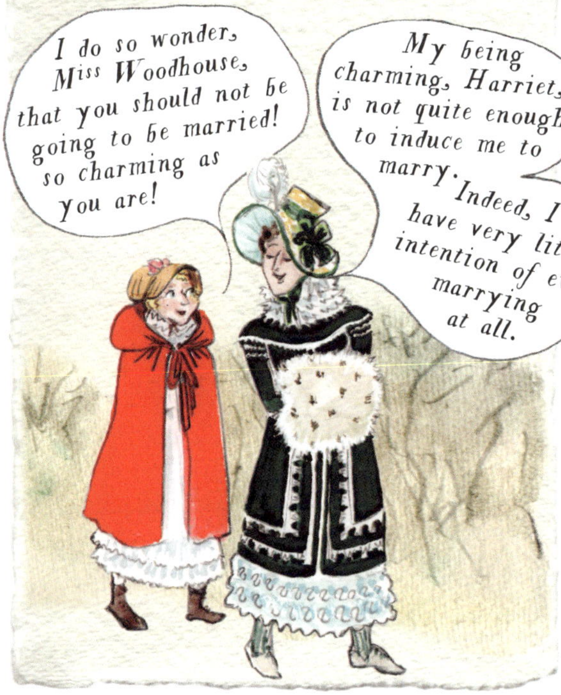
I do so wonder, Miss Woodhouse, that you should not be going to be married! so charming as you are!
My being charming, Harriet, is not quite enough to induce me to marry.
Indeed, I have very little intention of ever marrying at all.

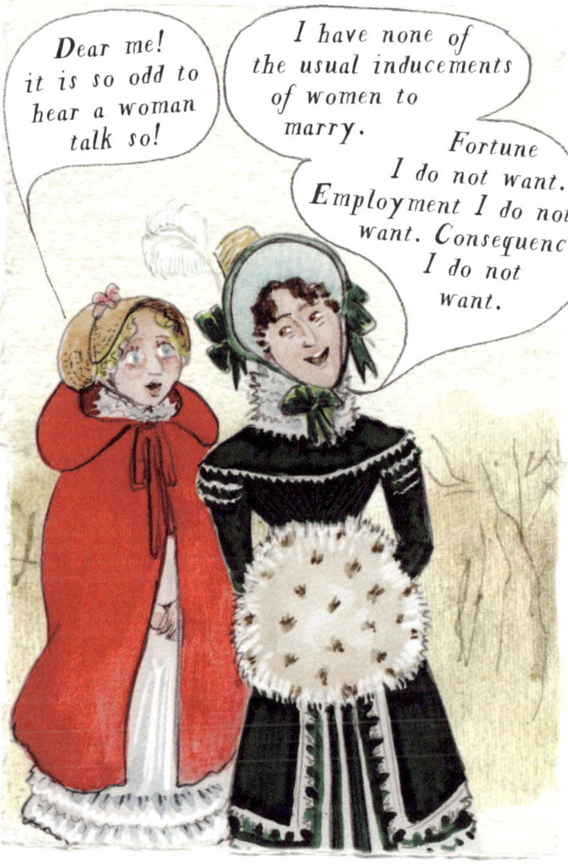
Dear me! it is so odd to hear a woman talk so!
I have none of the usual inducements of women to marry.
Fortune I do not want. Employment I do not want. Consequence I do not want.

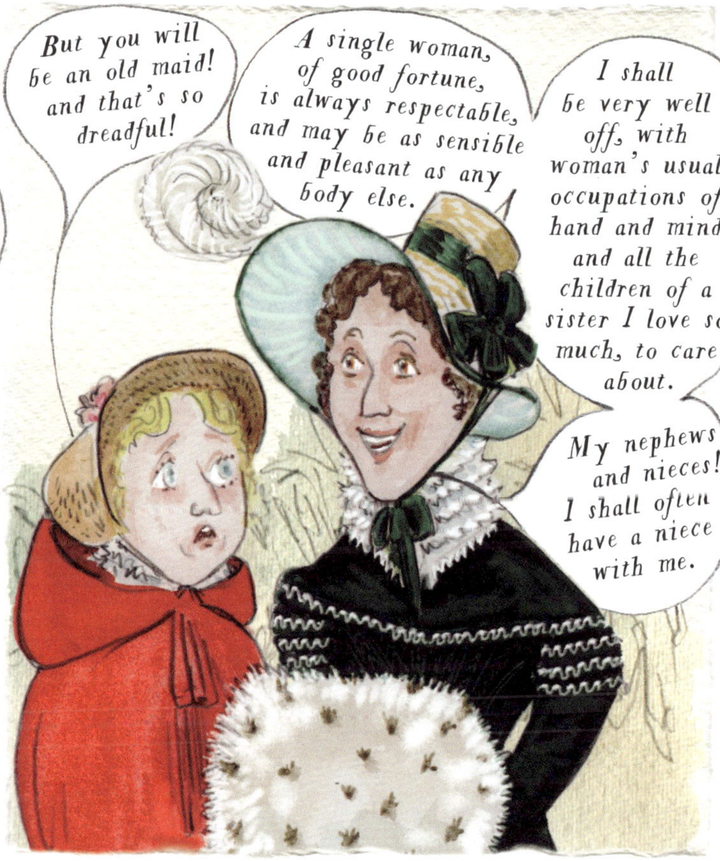
But you will be an old maid! and that's so dreadful!
A single woman, of good fortune, is always respectable, and may be as sensible and pleasant as any body else.
I shall be very well off, with woman's usual occupations of hand and mind, and all the children of a sister I love so much, to care about.
My nephews and nieces! I shall often have a niece with me.

The book is a vehicle for Austen's ambivalence about marriage. Perpetually pregnant Elizabeth Knight expired at the age of thirty-five. During the writing of *Emma*, Charles's wife, Fanny Palmer, dies horrifically, of childbirth, on board ship. And when beloved niece Anna marries, in Autumn 1814, her novel-writing is, of course, abandoned.

So much lives in Jane's imagination, so many little particulars. In *Emma*, she writes very beautifully of the small, ordinary moments of life.

Emma went to the door of the haberdasher's shop and looked out. Much could not be hoped from the traffic of even the busiest part of Highbury.

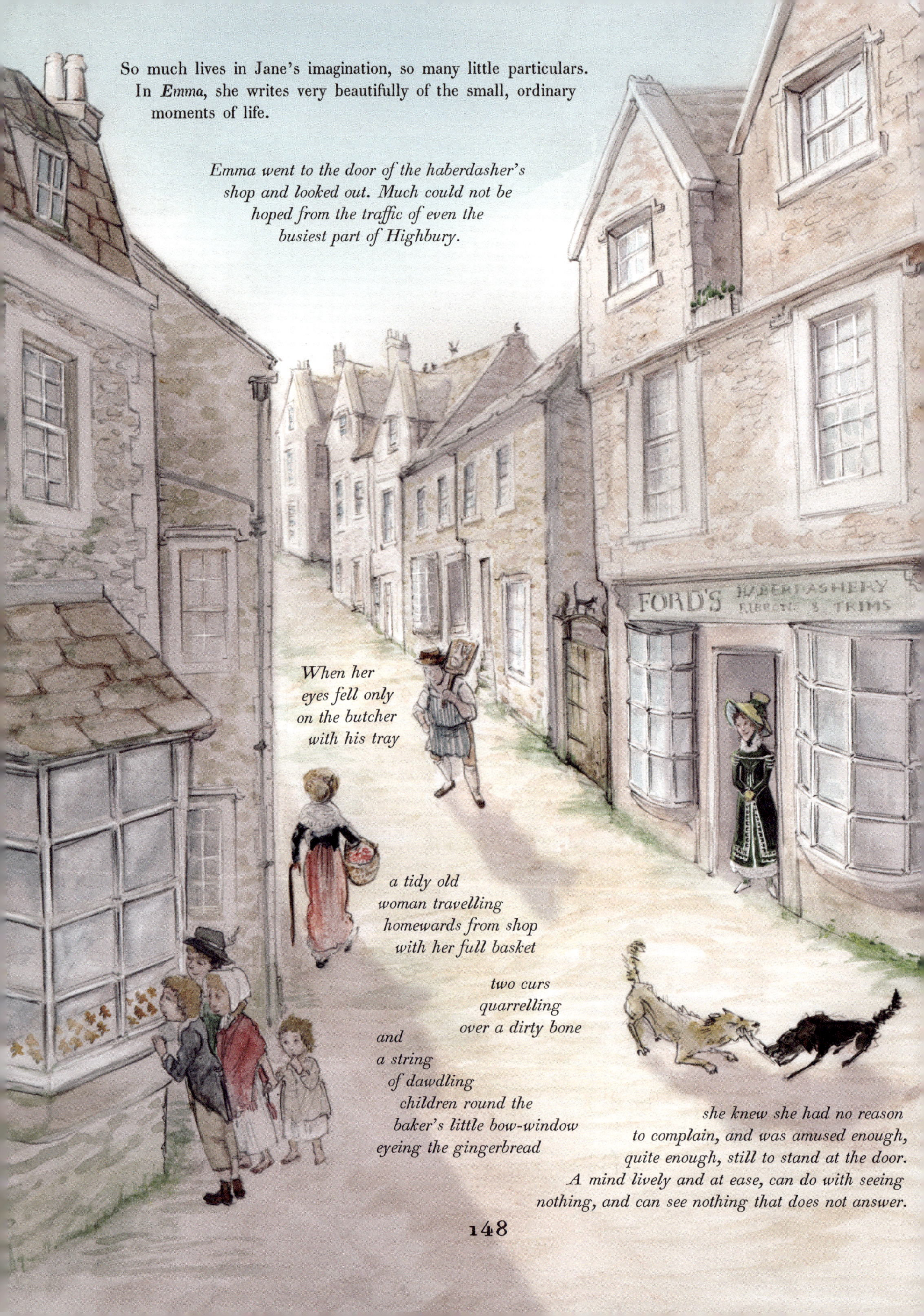
FORD'S HABERDASHERY
RIBBONS & TRIMS

When her eyes fell only on the butcher with his tray

a tidy old woman travelling homewards from shop with her full basket

two curs quarrelling over a dirty bone

and a string of dawdling children round the baker's little bow-window eyeing the gingerbread

she knew she had no reason to complain, and was amused enough, quite enough, still to stand at the door. A mind lively and at ease, can do with seeing nothing, and can see nothing that does not answer.

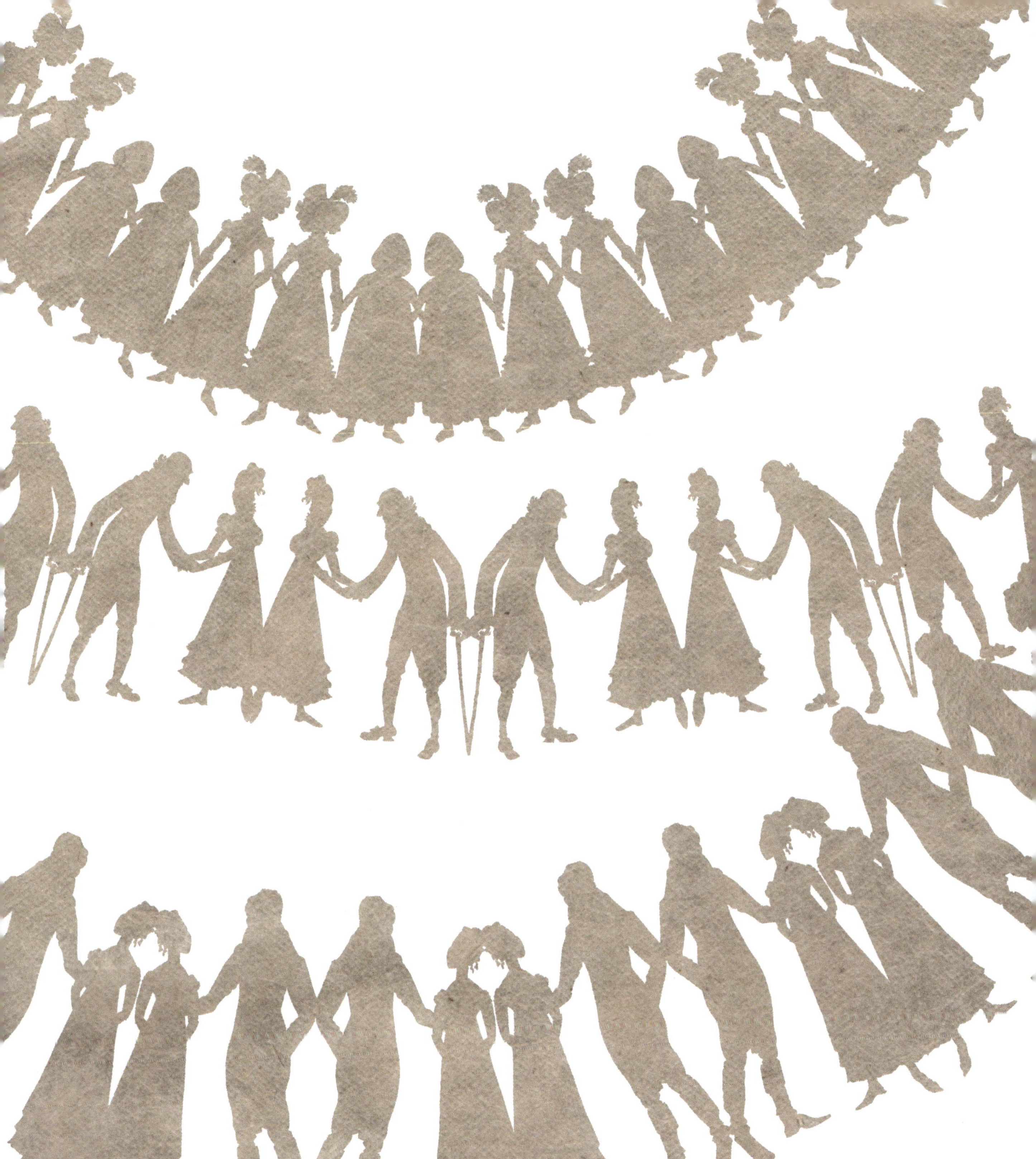

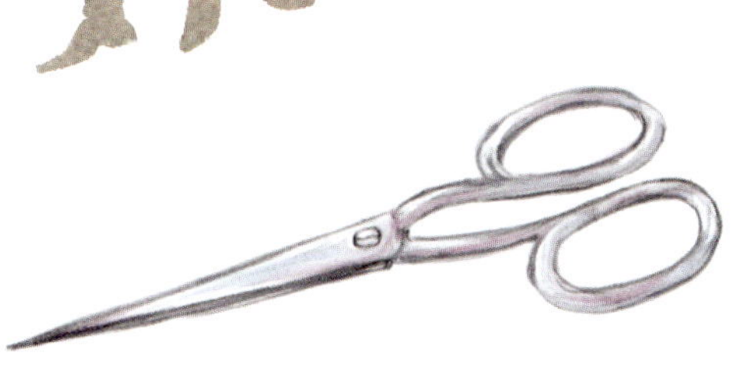

A mind lively, and at ease.

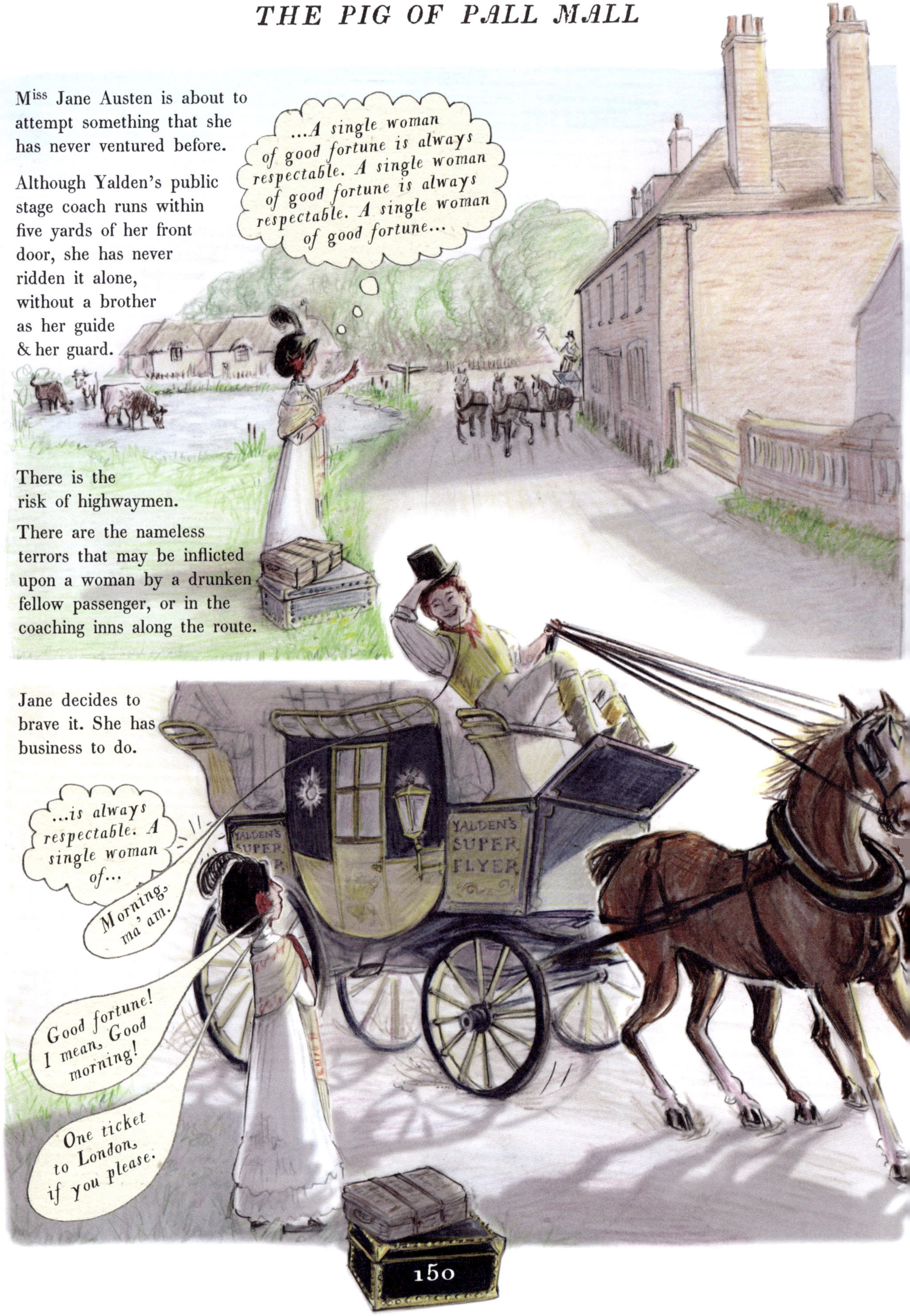
Miss Jane Austen is about to attempt something that she has never ventured before.
Although Yalden's public stage coach runs within five yards of her front door, she has never ridden it alone, without a brother as her guide & her guard.
...A single woman of good fortune is always respectable. A single woman of good fortune is always respectable. A single woman of good fortune...
There is the risk of highwaymen.
There are the nameless terrors that may be inflicted upon a woman by a drunken fellow passenger, or in the coaching inns along the route.
Jane decides to brave it. She has business to do.
...is always respectable. A single woman of...
Morning, ma'am.
YALDEN'S SUPER FLYER
Good fortune! I mean, Good morning!
One ticket to London, if you please.

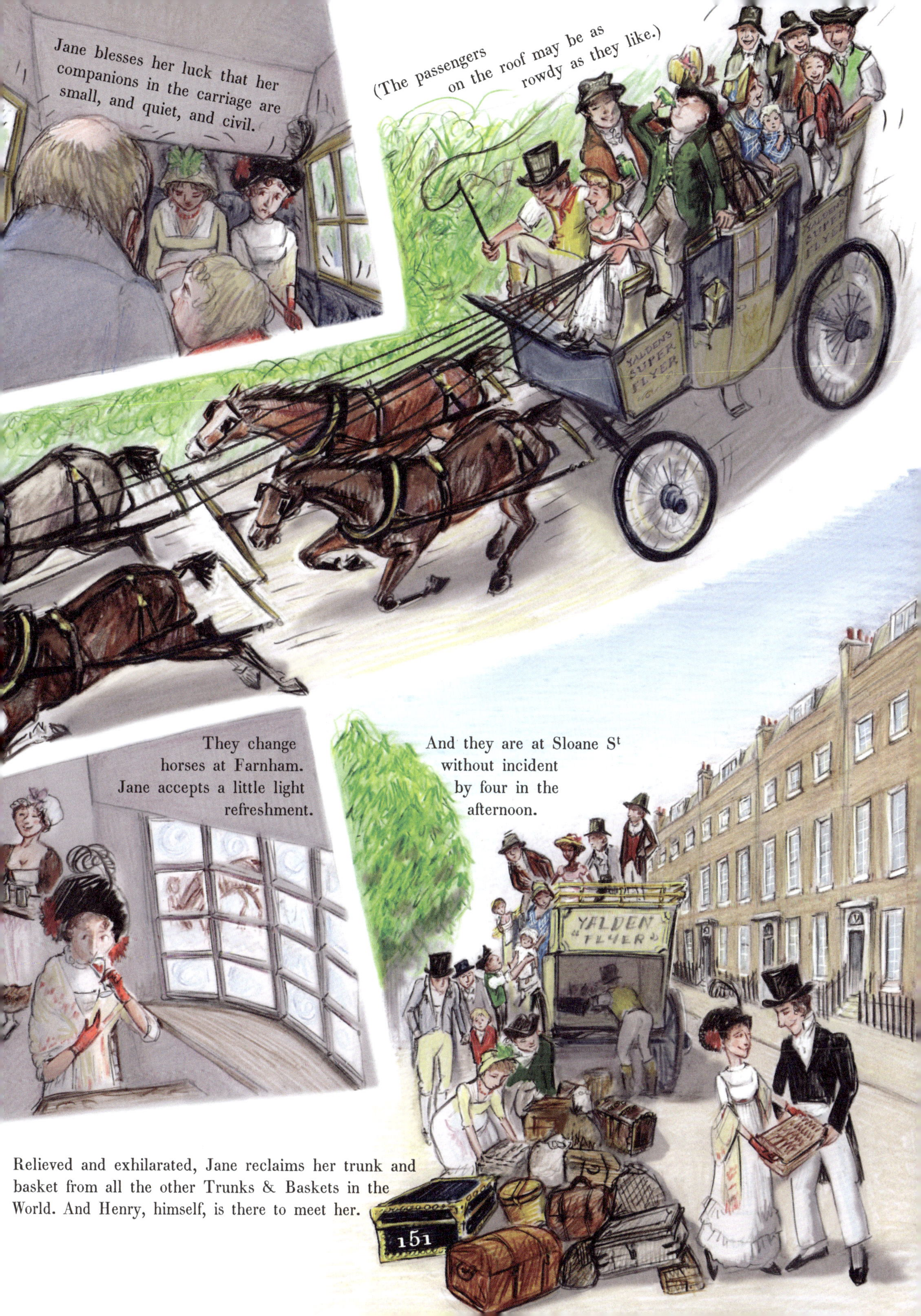
Jane blesses her luck that her companions in the carriage are small, and quiet, and civil.
(The passengers on the roof may be as rowdy as they like.)
YALDEN'S SUPER FLYER
They change horses at Farnham. Jane accepts a little light refreshment.
And they are at Sloane St without incident by four in the afternoon.
YALDEN "FLYER"
Relieved and exhilarated, Jane reclaims her trunk and basket from all the other Trunks & Baskets in the World. And Henry, himself, is there to meet her.
151

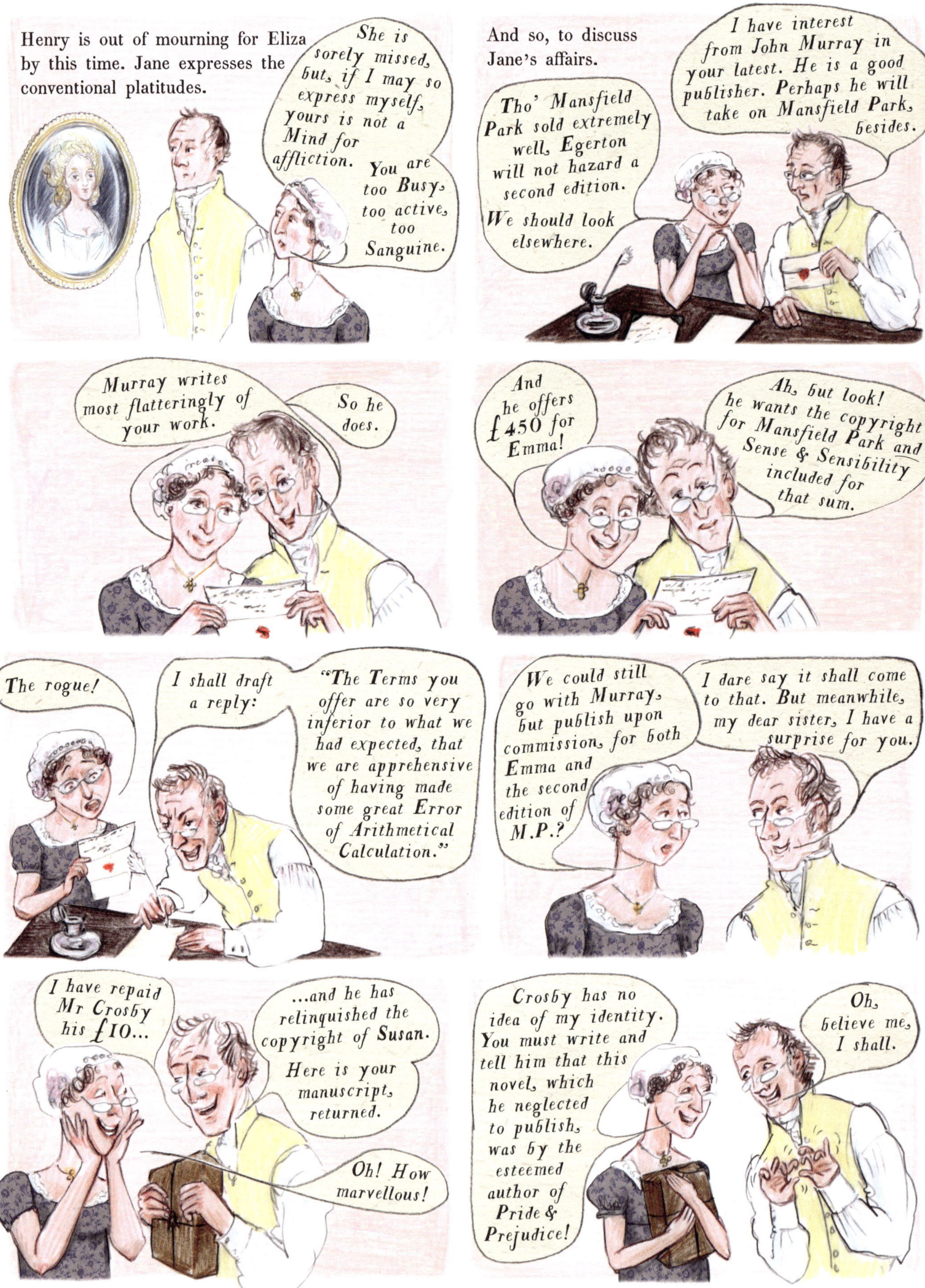
Henry is out of mourning for Eliza by this time. Jane expresses the conventional platitudes.
She is sorely missed, but, if I may so express myself, yours is not a Mind for affliction.
You are too Busy, too active, too Sanguine.
And so, to discuss Jane's affairs.
Tho' Mansfield Park sold extremely well, Egerton will not hazard a second edition.
We should look elsewhere.
I have interest from John Murray in your latest. He is a good publisher. Perhaps he will take on Mansfield Park, besides.
Murray writes most flatteringly of your work.
So he does.
And he offers £450 for Emma!
Ah, but look! he wants the copyright for Mansfield Park and Sense & Sensibility included for that sum.
The rogue!
I shall draft a reply:
"The Terms you offer are so very inferior to what we had expected, that we are apprehensive of having made some great Error of Arithmetical Calculation."
We could still go with Murray, but publish upon commission, for both Emma and the second edition of M.P.?
I dare say it shall come to that. But meanwhile, my dear sister, I have a surprise for you.
I have repaid Mr Crosby his £10...
...and he has relinquished the copyright of Susan.
Here is your manuscript, returned.
Oh! How marvellous!
Crosby has no idea of my identity. You must write and tell him that this novel, which he neglected to publish, was by the esteemed author of Pride & Prejudice!
Oh, believe me, I shall.

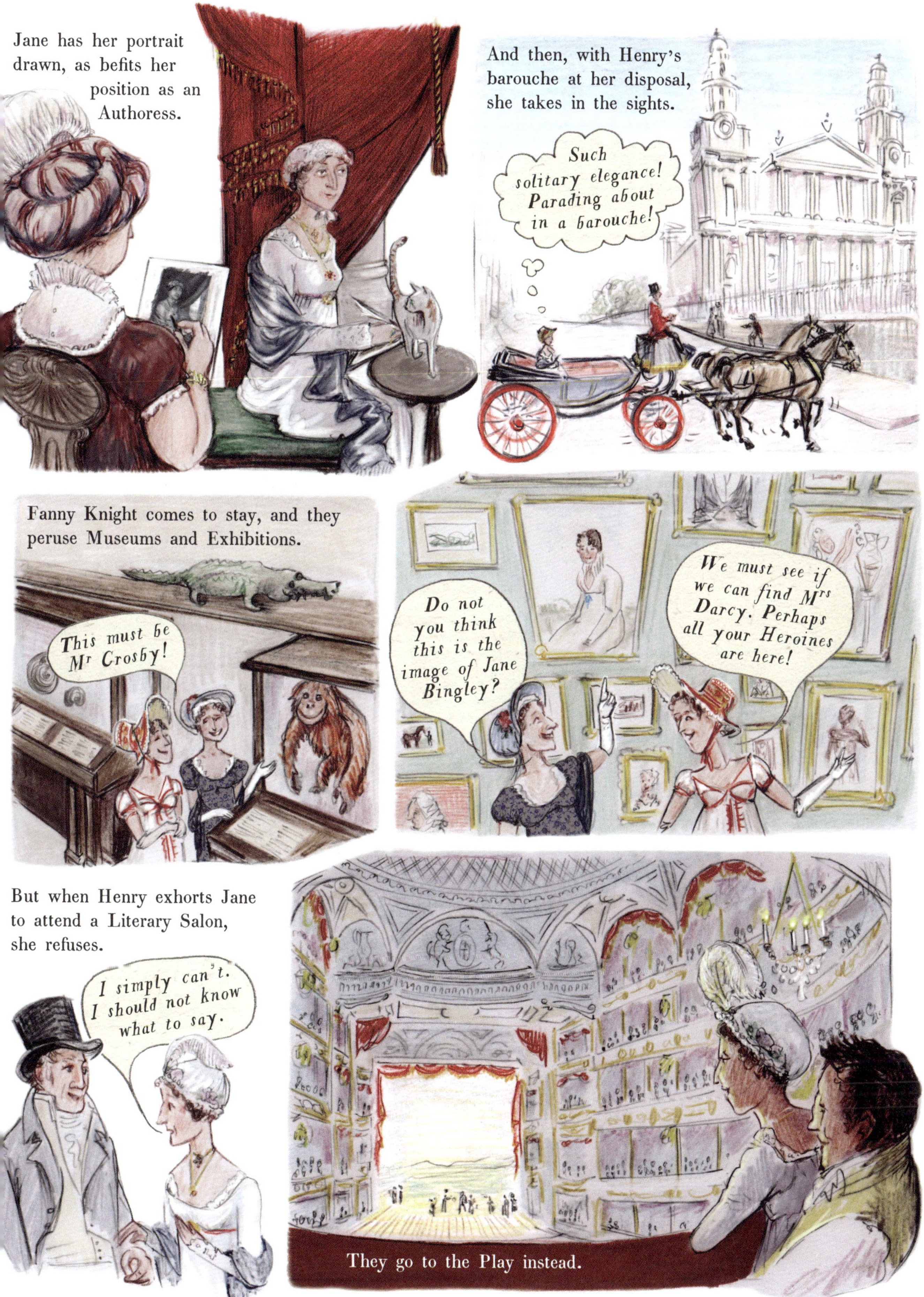
Jane has her portrait drawn, as befits her position as an Authoress.
And then, with Henry's barouche at her disposal, she takes in the sights.
Such solitary elegance! Parading about in a barouche!
Fanny Knight comes to stay, and they peruse Museums and Exhibitions.
This must be Mr Crosby!
Do not you think this is the image of Jane Bingley?
We must see if we can find Mrs Darcy. Perhaps all your Heroines are here!
But when Henry exhorts Jane to attend a Literary Salon, she refuses.
I simply can't. I should not know what to say.
They go to the Play instead.

October 4th, 1815. Henry has a touch of bilious fever.
Jane, my dear, bring me some calomel.
Just the thing! Mercury Salts to purge the body of sickness.
The latest medical advice is that one should take a "heroic dose."
A larger amount is said to be gentler upon the body.
Here goes!
The next morning, Henry is worse!
How could this be?
The mercury must not have been effective.
I had better take some more.
Henry deteriorates alarmingly.
Call Mr Haden!
Mr Haden is so worried that he summons the great Dr Baillie, physician to the Prince Regent himself.
22nd October, Jane dispatches express letters to her siblings, Henry is not expected to survive.
But he rallies!
The Pulse is much improved. As is the Stool.
And soon he is quite himself again.
Did you know that my sister wrote Pride & Prejudice?
I did not! The Mystery Authoress! His Royal Highness a great admirer her novels.

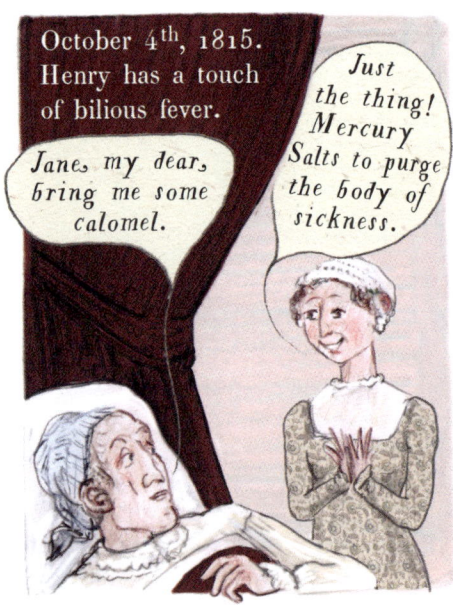

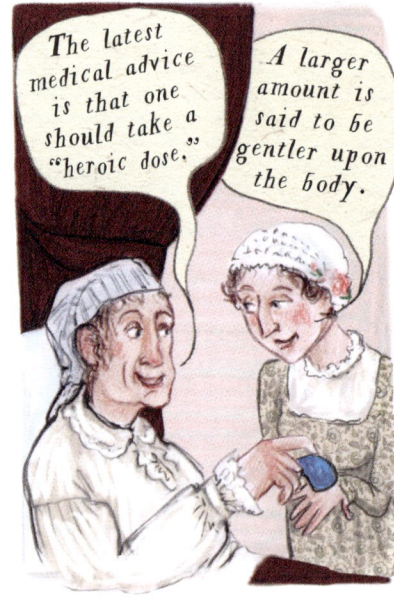

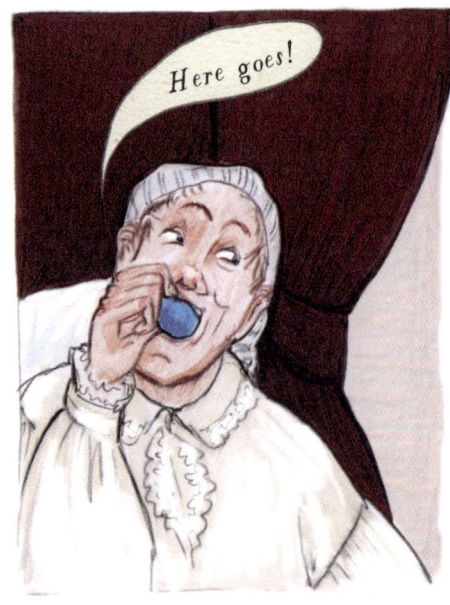

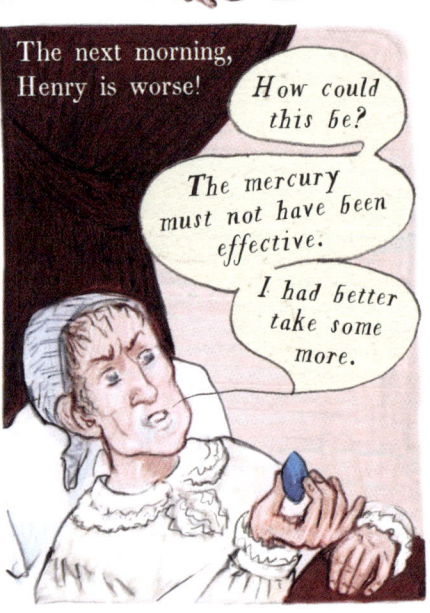

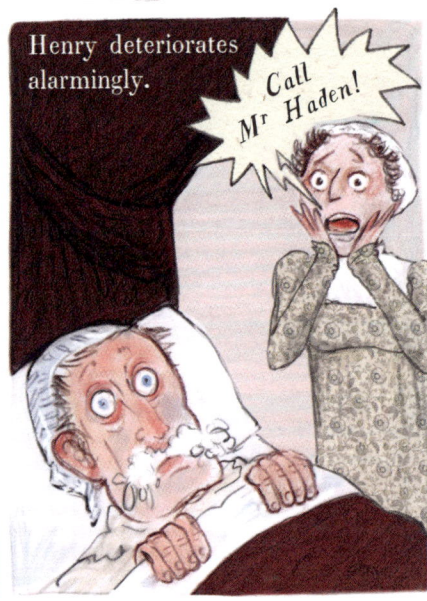

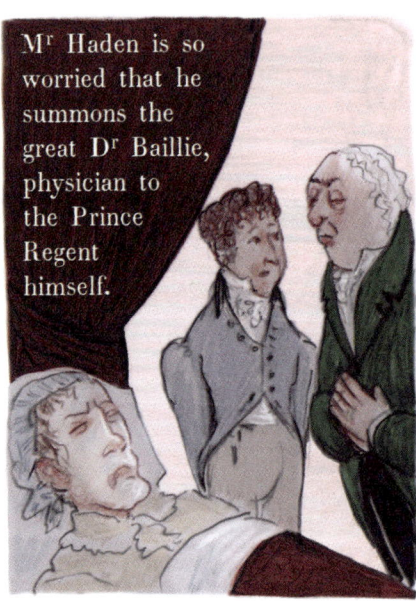

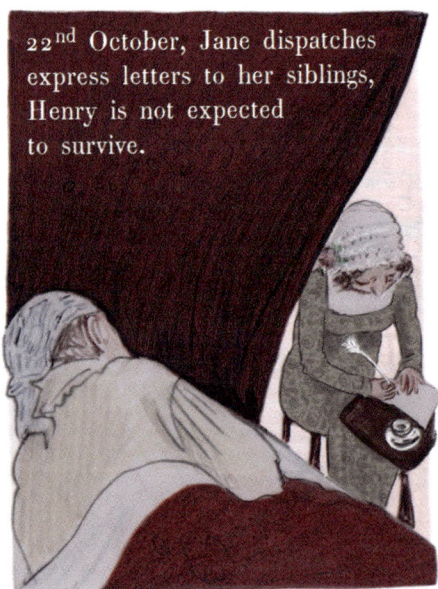

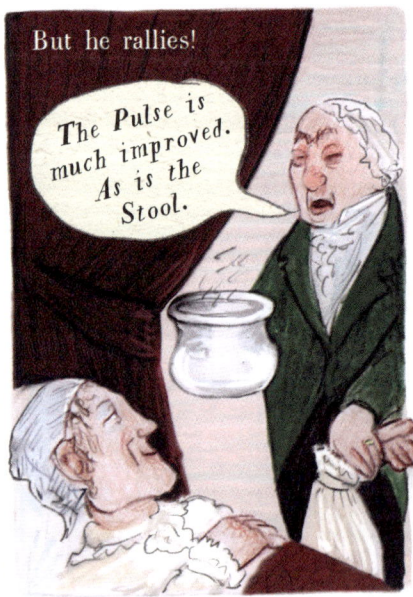

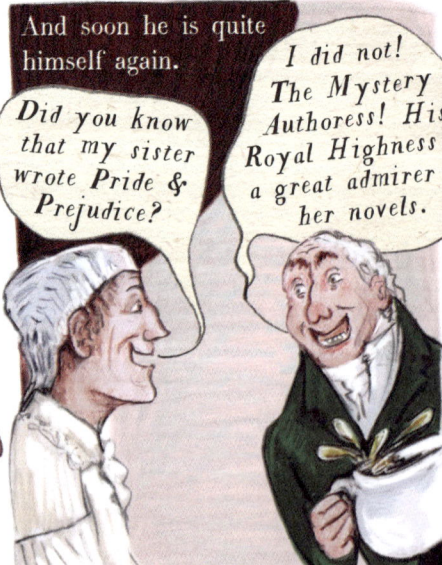

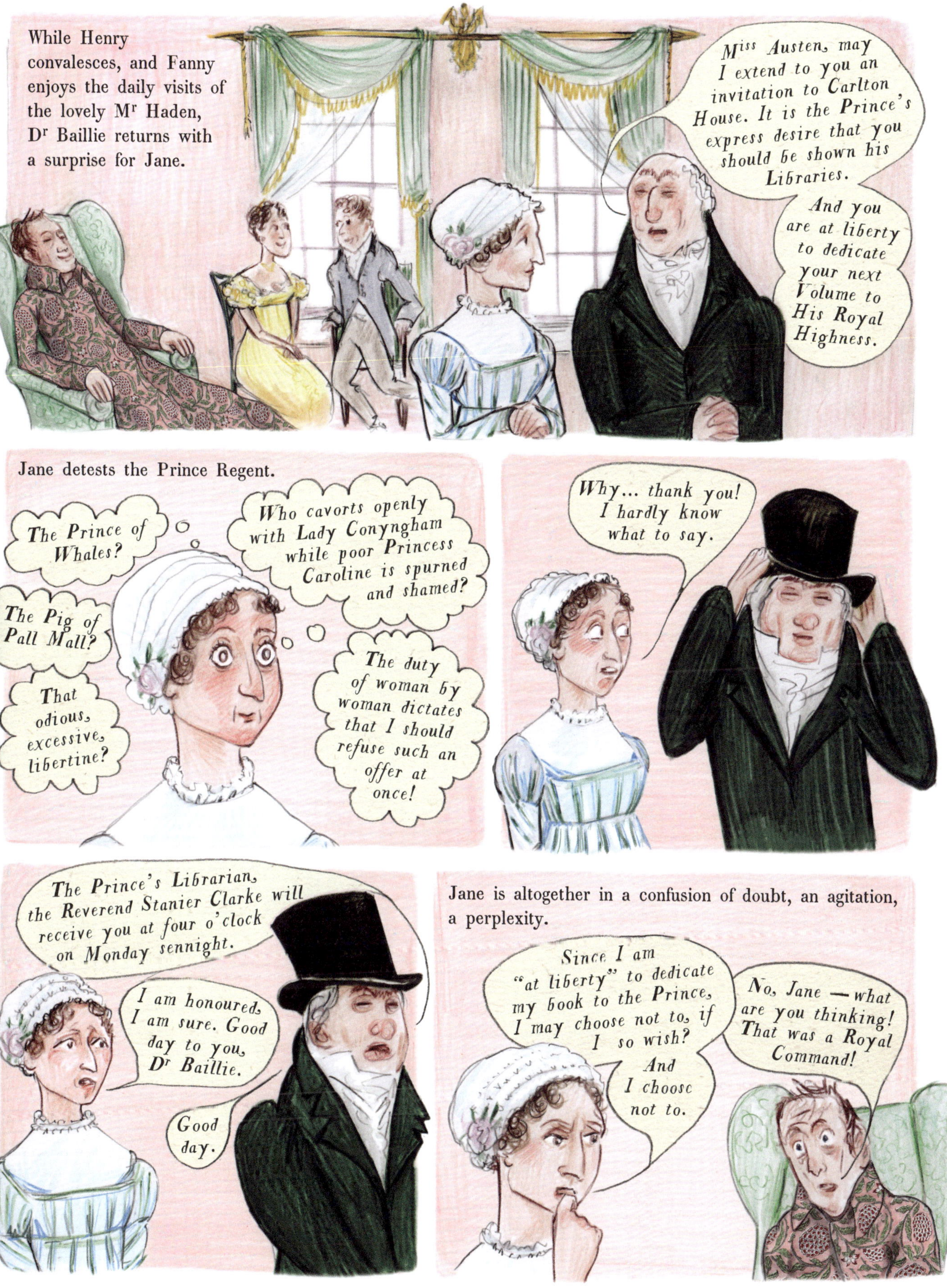
While Henry convalesces, and Fanny enjoys the daily visits of the lovely Mr Haden, Dr Baillie returns with a surprise for Jane.
Miss Austen, may I extend to you an invitation to Carlton House. It is the Prince's express desire that you should be shown his Libraries.
And you are at liberty to dedicate your next Volume to His Royal Highness.
Jane detests the Prince Regent.
The Prince of Whales?
The Pig of Pall Mall?
That odious, excessive, libertine?
Who cavorts openly with Lady Conyngham while poor Princess Caroline is spurned and shamed?
The duty of woman by woman dictates that I should refuse such an offer at once!
Why... thank you! I hardly know what to say.
The Prince's Librarian, the Reverend Stanier Clarke will receive you at four o'clock on Monday sennight.
I am honoured, I am sure. Good day to you, Dr Baillie.
Good day.
Jane is altogether in a confusion of doubt, an agitation, a perplexity.
Since I am "at liberty" to dedicate my book to the Prince, I may choose not to, if I so wish?
And I choose not to.
No, Jane — what are you thinking! That was a Royal Command!

Accordingly, on 13th November 1815 Miss Austen is admitted to that monument to the Prince Regent's profligacy, Carlton House.

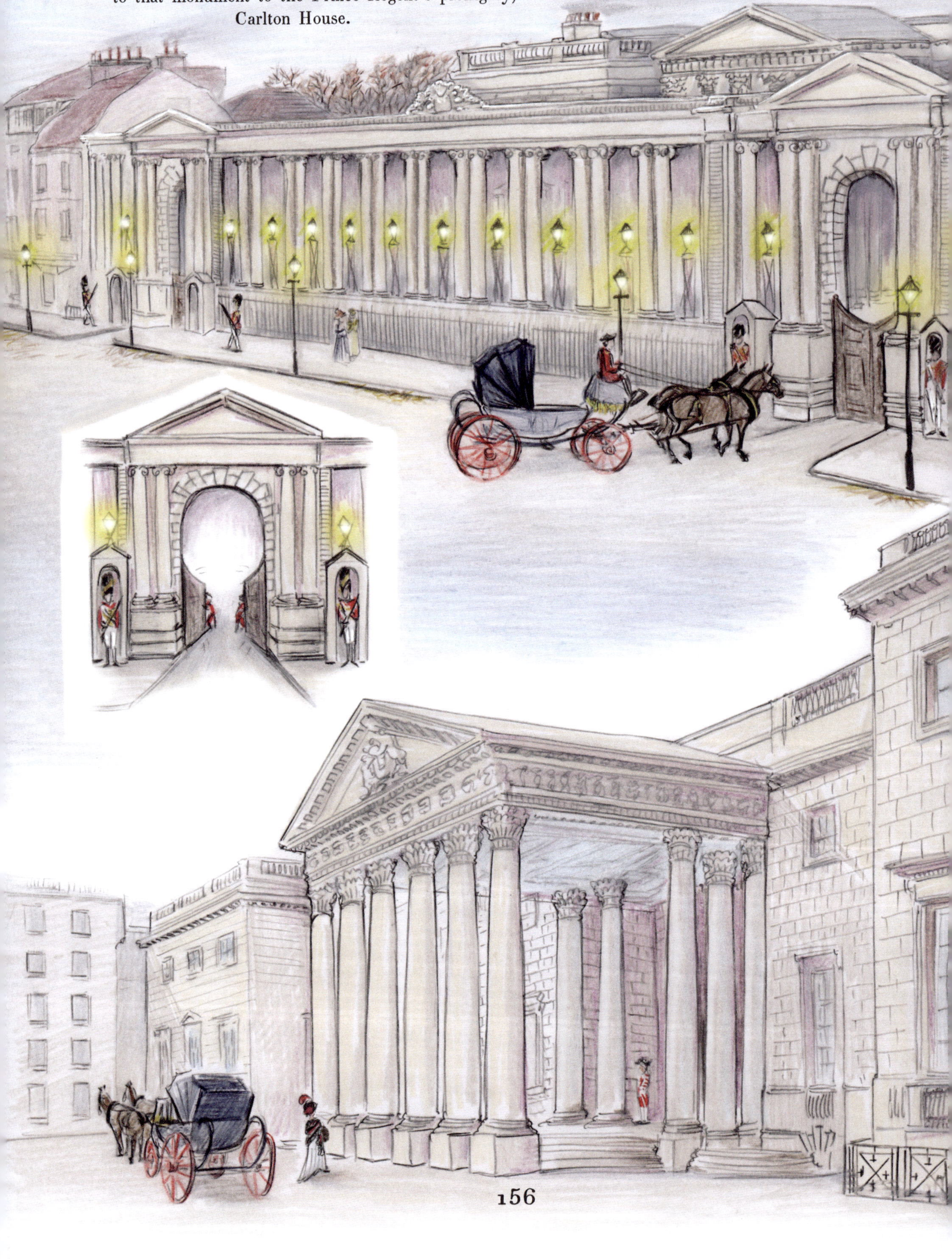

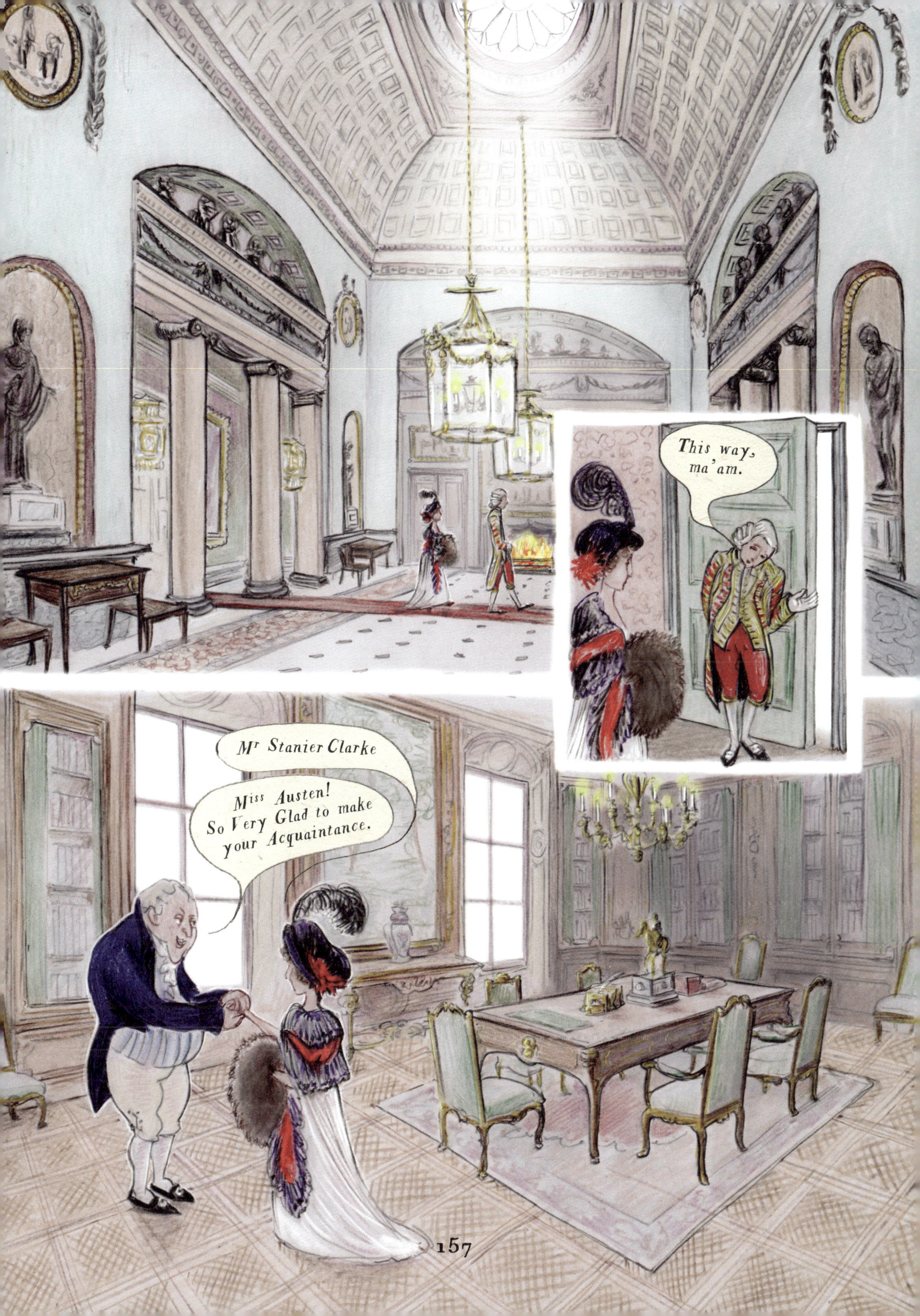
This way, ma'am.
Mr Stanier Clarke
Miss Austen! So Very Glad to make your Acquaintance.

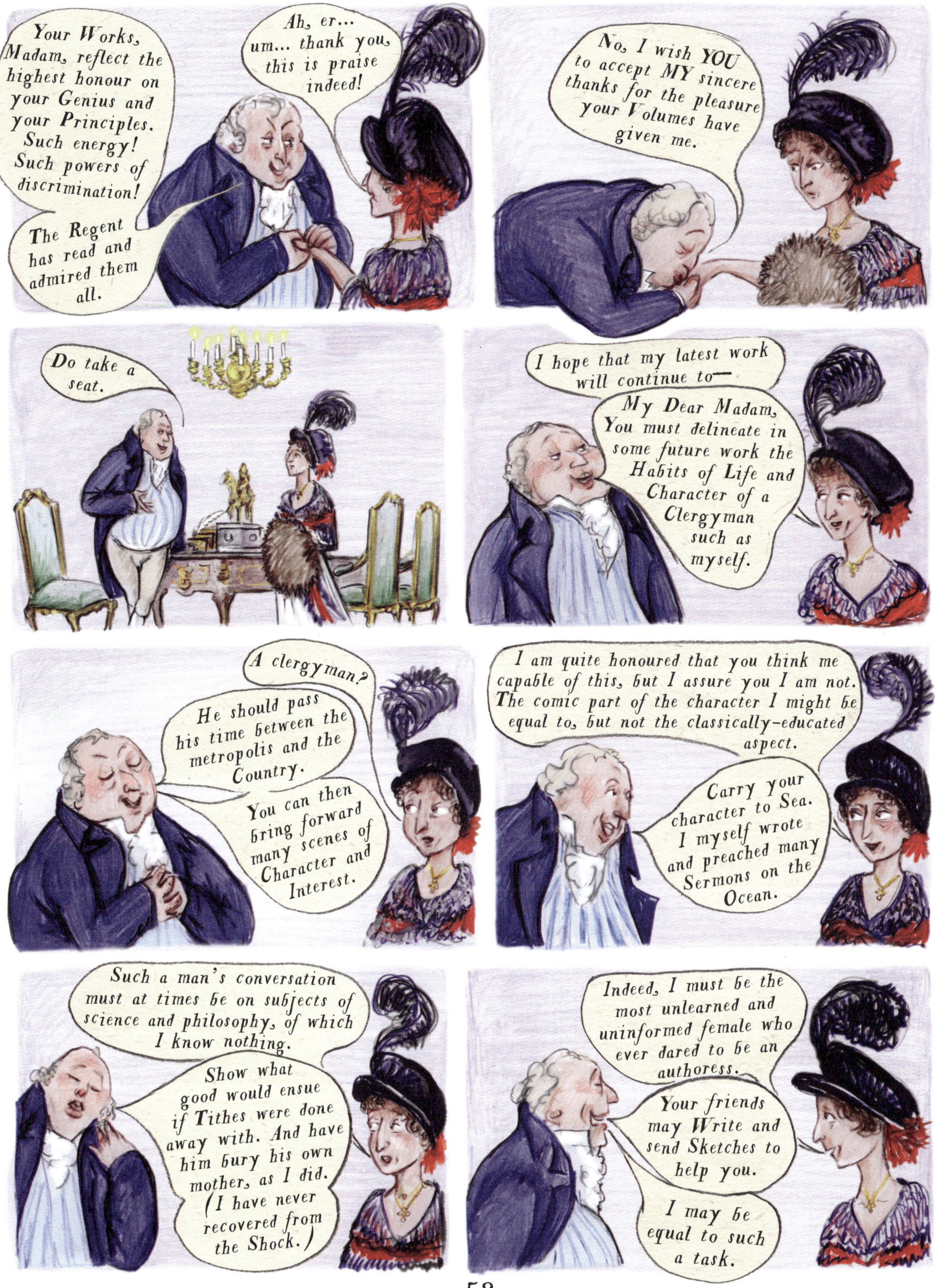
Your Works, Madam, reflect the highest honour on your Genius and your Principles. Such energy! Such powers of discrimination!
The Regent has read and admired them all.
Ah, er... um... thank you, this is praise indeed!
No, I wish YOU to accept MY sincere thanks for the pleasure your Volumes have given me.
Do take a seat.
I hope that my latest work will continue to—
My Dear Madam, You must delineate in some future work the Habits of Life and Character of a Clergyman such as myself.
A clergyman?
He should pass his time between the metropolis and the Country.
You can then bring forward many scenes of Character and Interest.
I am quite honoured that you think me capable of this, but I assure you I am not. The comic part of the character I might be equal to, but not the classically-educated aspect.
Carry your character to Sea. I myself wrote and preached many Sermons on the Ocean.
Such a man's conversation must at times be on subjects of science and philosophy, of which I know nothing.
Show what good would ensue if Tithes were done away with. And have him bury his own mother, as I did. (I have never recovered from the Shock.)
Indeed, I must be the most unlearned and uninformed female who ever dared to be an authoress.
Your friends may Write and send Sketches to help you.
I may be equal to such a task.

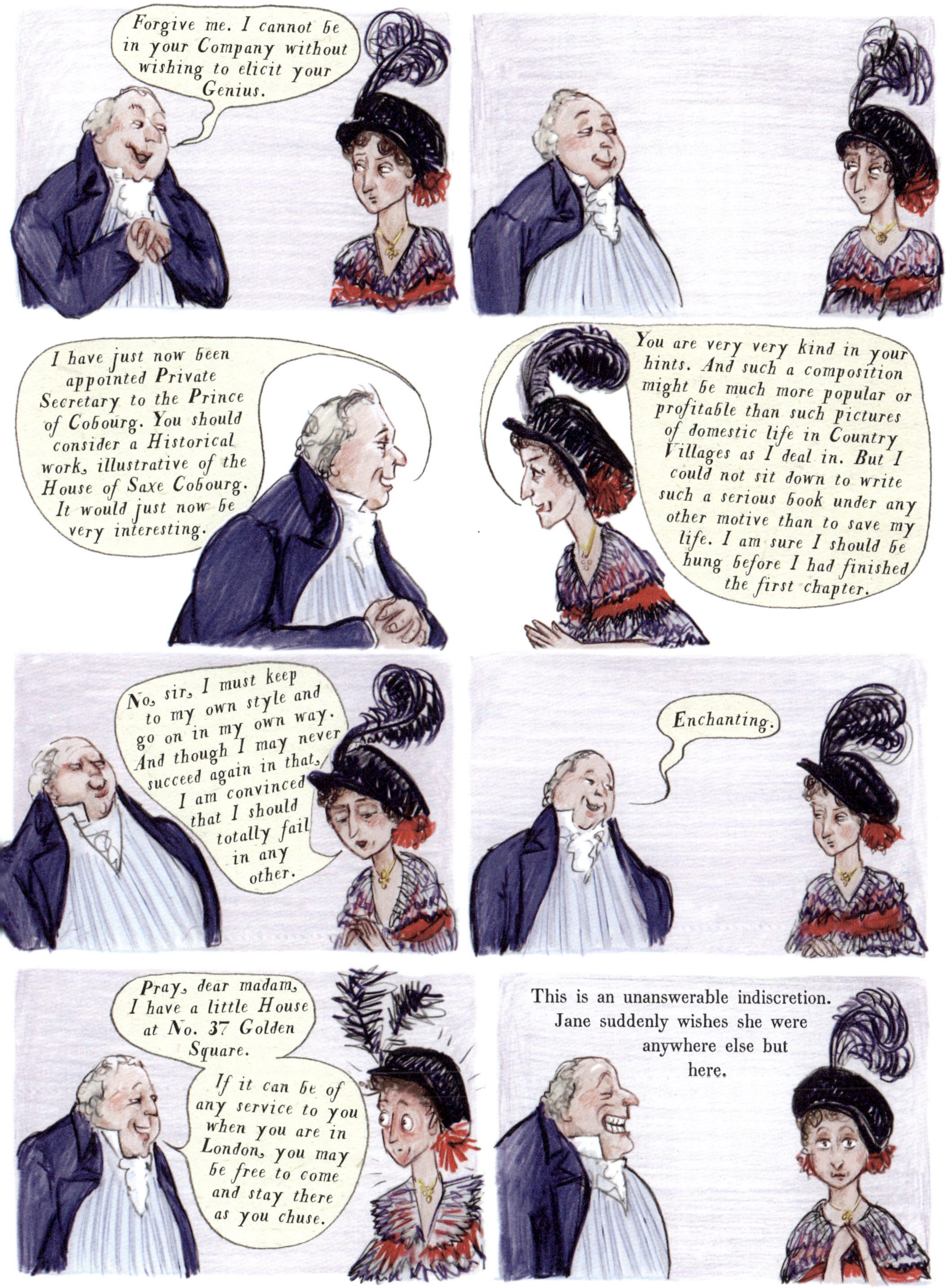
Forgive me. I cannot be in your Company without wishing to elicit your Genius.
I have just now been appointed Private Secretary to the Prince of Cobourg. You should consider a Historical work, illustrative of the House of Saxe Cobourg. It would just now be very interesting.
You are very very kind in your hints. And such a composition might be much more popular or profitable than such pictures of domestic life in Country Villages as I deal in. But I could not sit down to write such a serious book under any other motive than to save my life. I am sure I should be hung before I had finished the first chapter.
No, sir, I must keep to my own style and go on in my own way. And though I may never succeed again in that, I am convinced that I should totally fail in any other.
Enchanting.
Pray, dear madam, I have a little House at No. 37 Golden Square.
If it can be of any service to you when you are in London, you may be free to come and stay there as you chuse.
This is an unanswerable indiscretion. Jane suddenly wishes she were anywhere else but here.

PLAN OF A NOVEL
ACCORDING TO HINTS FROM VARIOUS QUARTERS

Jane is not cast down by this encounter. Alive, as ever, to the reception of her work by others, and mindful of the guidance that *many* people have *so kindly* provided as to how she should proceed with subsequent compositions, she sits down to draft a summary of all the Hints to date.

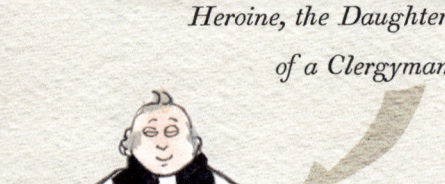

Heroine, the Daughter of a Clergyman.

He, the most excellent Man that can be imagined, perfect in Character, Temper, Manners, without the smallest drawback or peculiarity to prevent his being the most delightful companion to his Daughter from one year's end to the other.

Heroine a faultless Character herself, perfectly good, with much tenderness and sentiment, and not the least Wit. Her Person quite beautiful — dark eyes and plump cheeks.

Father and Daughter are to converse in long speeches, elegant Language and a tone of high serious sentiment. The Father to be induced, at his Daughter's earnest request, to relate to her the past events of his Life. This Narrative will reach through the greatest part of the first volume as it will comprehend...

...his going to sea as Chaplain to a distinguished naval character...

...his going afterwards to Court, which introduced him to a great variety of Characters and involved him in many interesting situations...

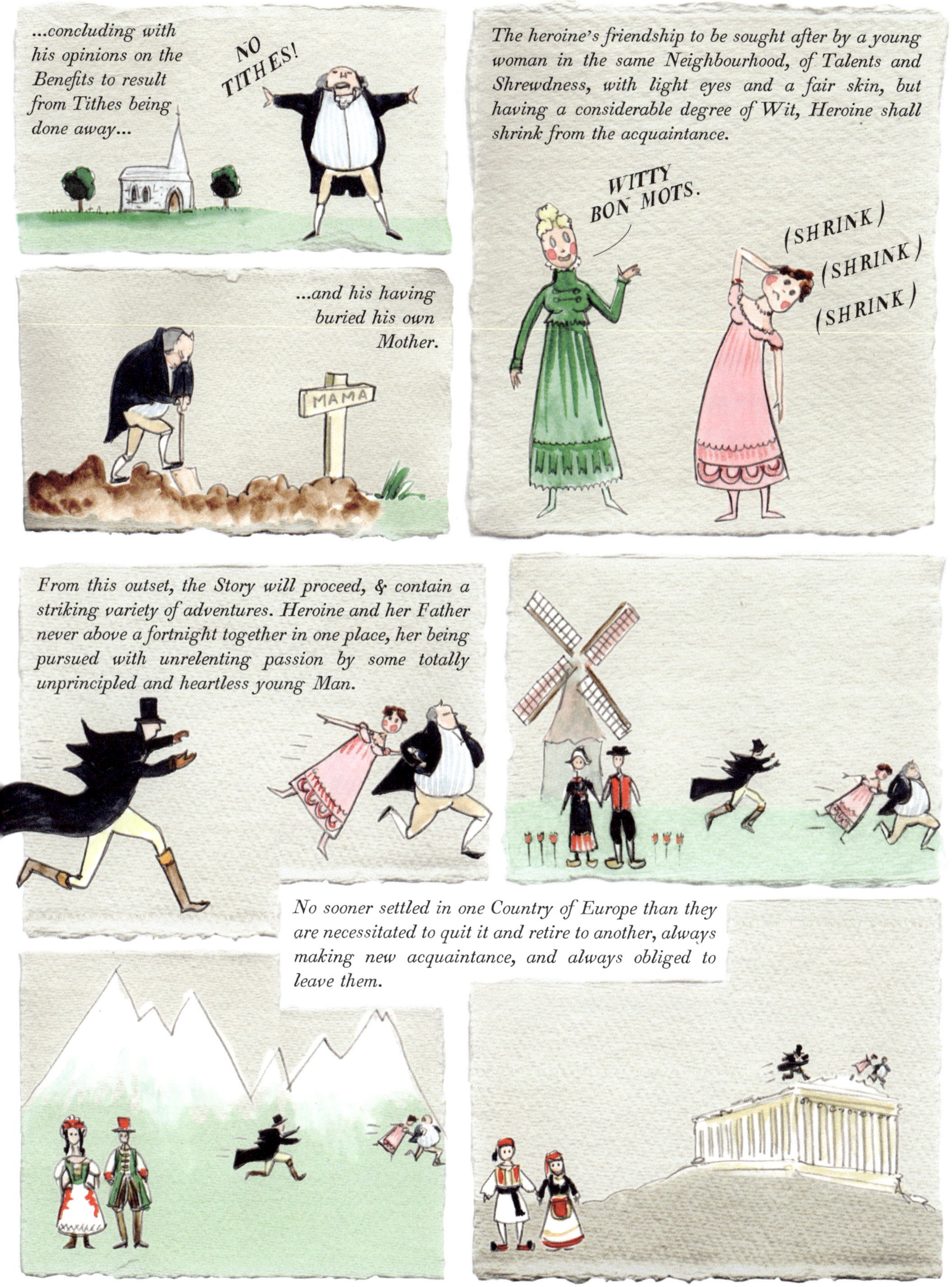
...concluding with his opinions on the Benefits to result from Tithes being done away...
NO TITHES!
...and his having buried his own Mother.
MAMA
The heroine's friendship to be sought after by a young woman in the same Neighbourhood, of Talents and Shrewdness, with light eyes and a fair skin, but having a considerable degree of Wit, Heroine shall shrink from the acquaintance.
WITTY BON MOTS.
(SHRINK)
(SHRINK)
(SHRINK)
From this outset, the Story will proceed, & contain a striking variety of adventures. Heroine and her Father never above a fortnight together in one place, her being pursued with unrelenting passion by some totally unprincipled and heartless young Man.
No sooner settled in one Country of Europe than they are necessitated to quit it and retire to another, always making new acquaintance, and always obliged to leave them.

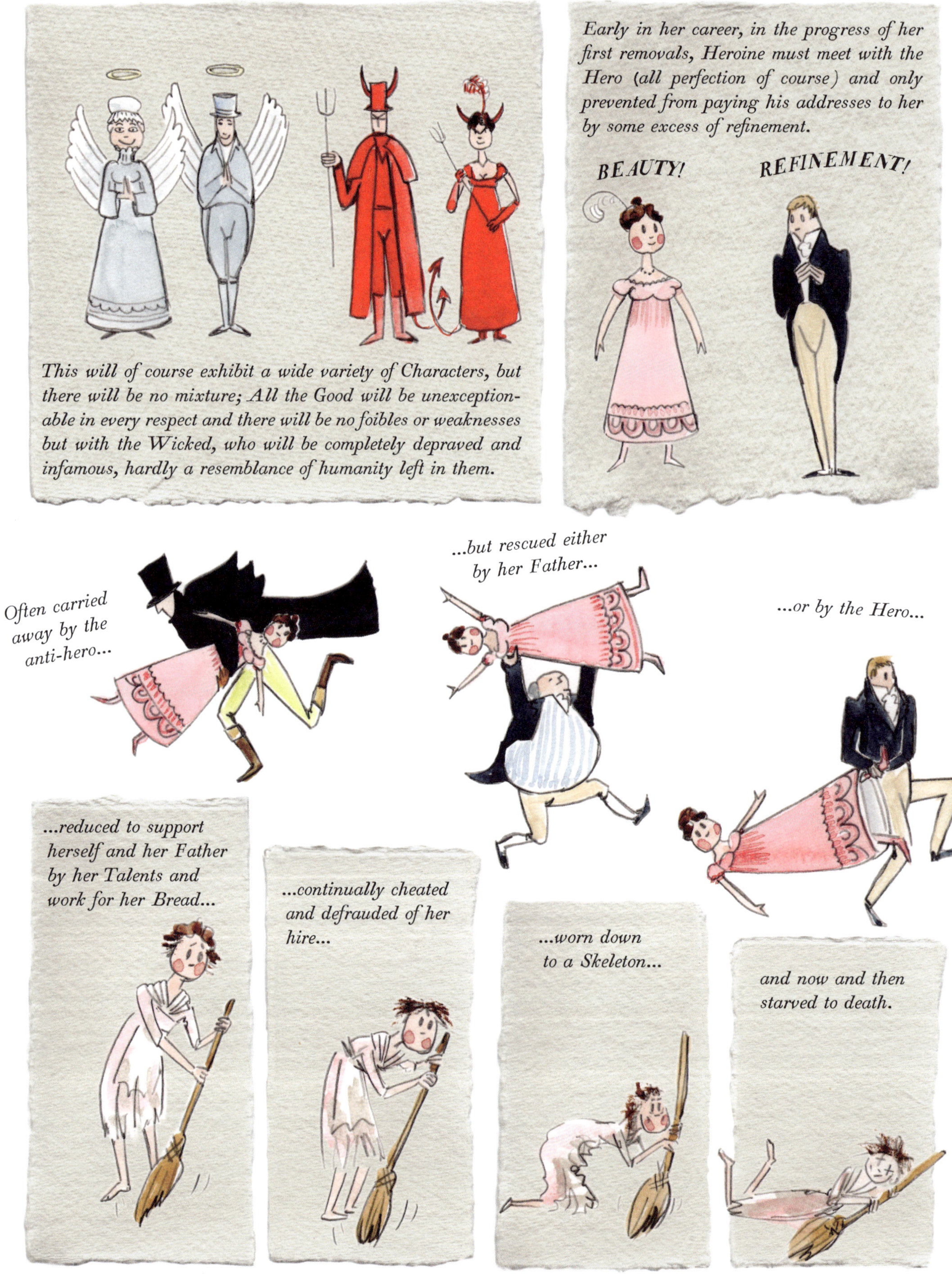
This will of course exhibit a wide variety of Characters, but there will be no mixture; All the Good will be unexceptionable in every respect and there will be no foibles or weaknesses but with the Wicked, who will be completely depraved and infamous, hardly a resemblance of humanity left in them.
Early in her career, in the progress of her first removals, Heroine must meet with the Hero (all perfection of course) and only prevented from paying his addresses to her by some excess of refinement.
BEAUTY!
REFINEMENT!
Often carried away by the anti-hero...
...but rescued either by her Father...
...or by the Hero...
...reduced to support herself and her Father by her Talents and work for her Bread...
...continually cheated and defrauded of her hire...
...worn down to a Skeleton...
and now and then starved to death.

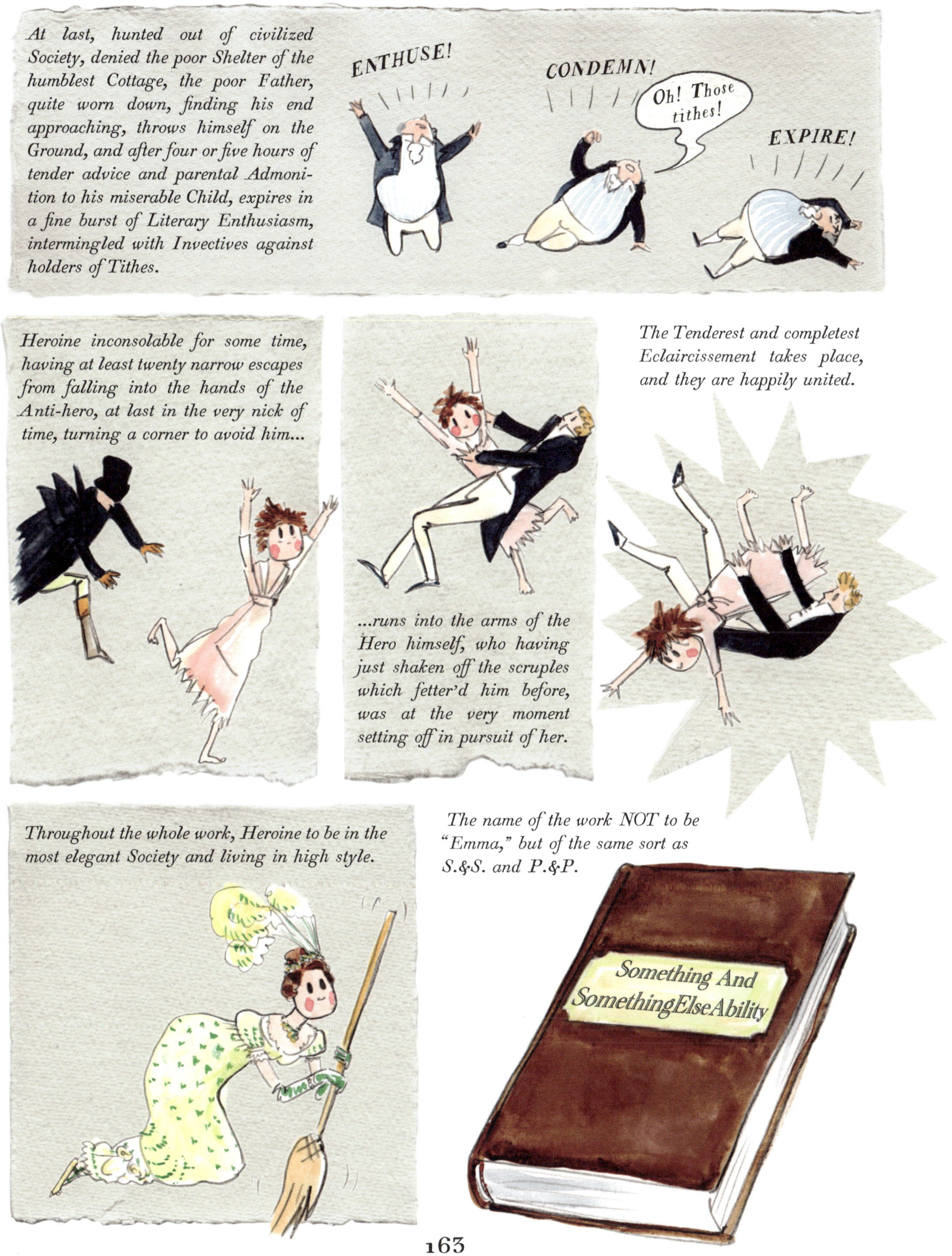
At last, hunted out of civilized Society, denied the poor Shelter of the humblest Cottage, the poor Father, quite worn down, finding his end approaching, throws himself on the Ground, and after four or five hours of tender advice and parental Admonition to his miserable Child, expires in a fine burst of Literary Enthusiasm, intermingled with Invectives against holders of Tithes.
ENTHUSE!
CONDEMN!
Oh! Those tithes!
EXPIRE!
Heroine inconsolable for some time, having at least twenty narrow escapes from falling into the hands of the Anti-hero, at last in the very nick of time, turning a corner to avoid him...
...runs into the arms of the Hero himself, who having just shaken off the scruples which fetter'd him before, was at the very moment setting off in pursuit of her.
The Tenderest and completest Eclaircissement takes place, and they are happily united.
Throughout the whole work, Heroine to be in the most elegant Society and living in high style.
The name of the work NOT to be "Emma," but of the same sort as S.&S. and P.&P.
Something And SomethingElseAbility

Cassandra has been appraised of the burgeoning Romance between Fanny and Mr Haden. She writes to Jane with concern at the potential alliance with a lowly Apothecary. Jane is giddy in her reply:

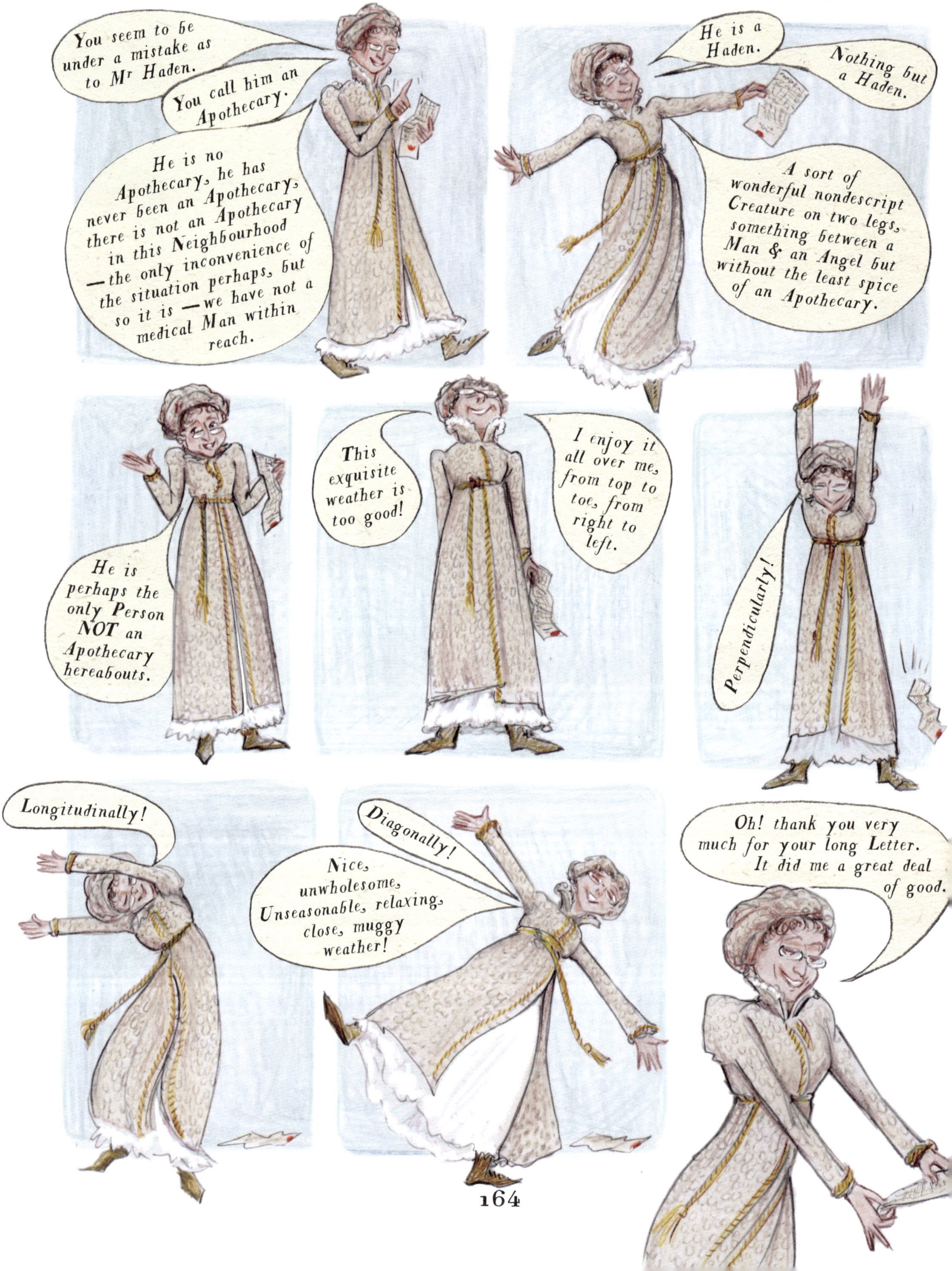
You seem to be under a mistake as to Mr Haden.
You call him an Apothecary.
He is no Apothecary, he has never been an Apothecary, there is not an Apothecary in this Neighbourhood —the only inconvenience of the situation perhaps, but so it is —we have not a medical Man within reach.
He is a Haden.
Nothing but a Haden.
A sort of wonderful nondescript Creature on two legs, something between a Man & an Angel but without the least spice of an Apothecary.
He is perhaps the only Person NOT an Apothecary hereabouts.
This exquisite weather is too good!
I enjoy it all over me, from top to toe, from right to left.
Perpendicularly!
Longitudinally!
Diagonally!
Nice, unwholesome, Unseasonable, relaxing, close, muggy weather!
Oh! thank you very much for your long Letter. It did me a great deal of good.

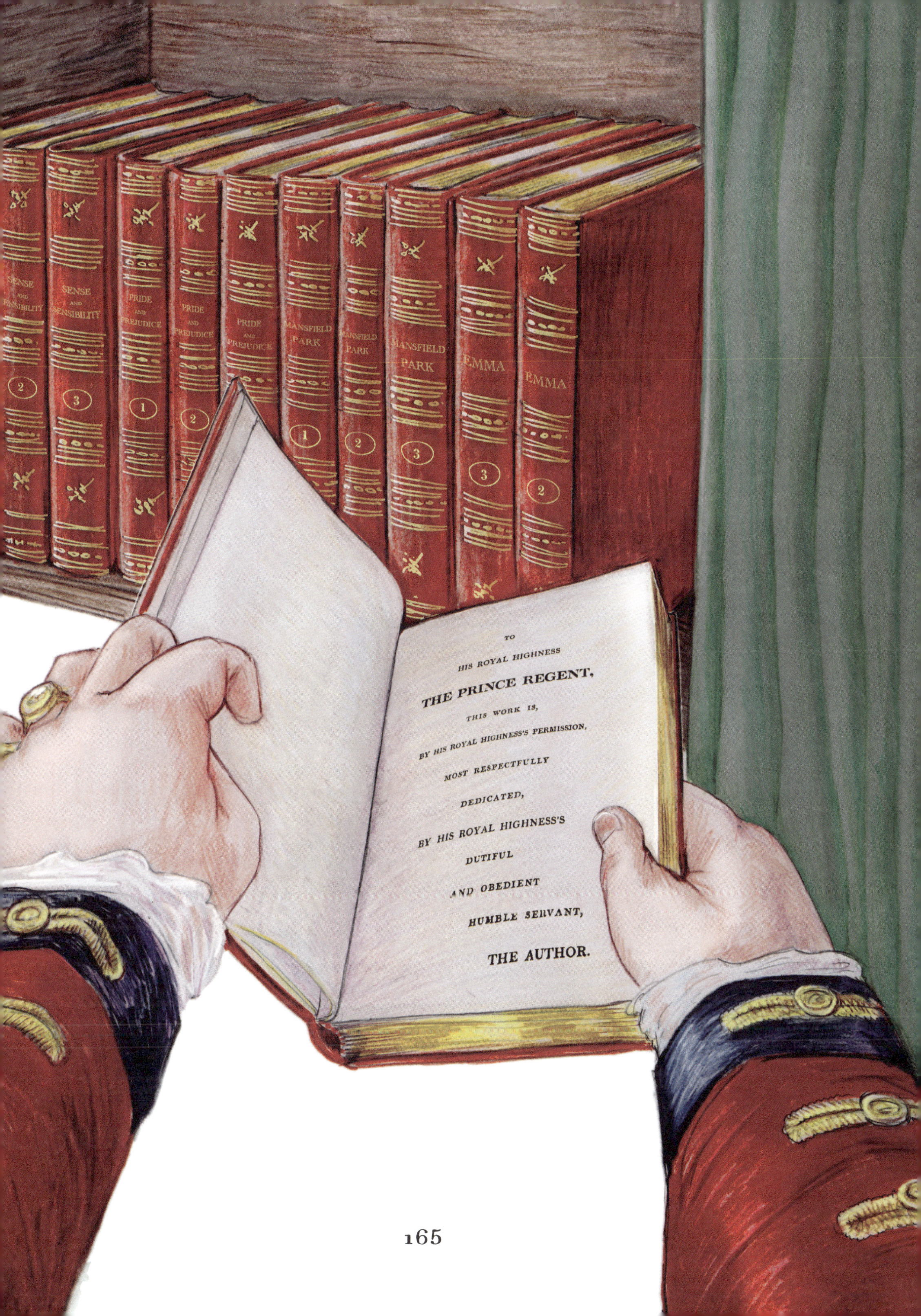
SENSE AND SENSIBILITY
SENSE AND SENSIBILITY
PRIDE AND PREJUDICE
PRIDE AND PREJUDICE
PRIDE AND PREJUDICE
MANSFIELD PARK
MANSFIELD PARK
MANSFIELD PARK
EMMA
EMMA
TO
HIS ROYAL HIGHNESS
THE PRINCE REGENT,
THIS WORK IS,
BY HIS ROYAL HIGHNESS'S PERMISSION,
MOST RESPECTFULLY
DEDICATED,
BY HIS ROYAL HIGHNESS'S
DUTIFUL
AND OBEDIENT
HUMBLE SERVANT,
THE AUTHOR.

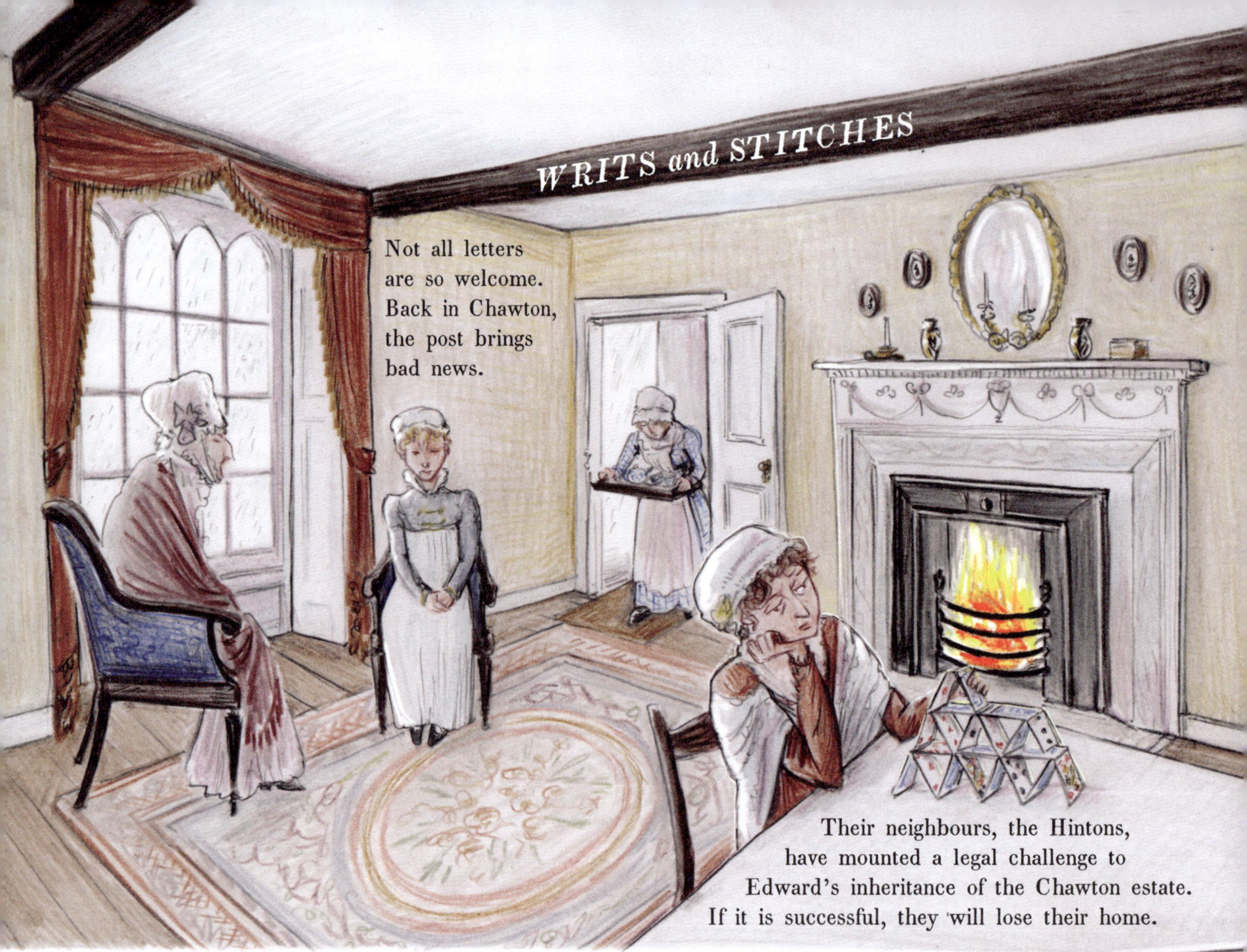
WRITS and STITCHES
Not all letters are so welcome. Back in Chawton, the post brings bad news.
Their neighbours, the Hintons, have mounted a legal challenge to Edward's inheritance of the Chawton estate. If it is successful, they will lose their home.

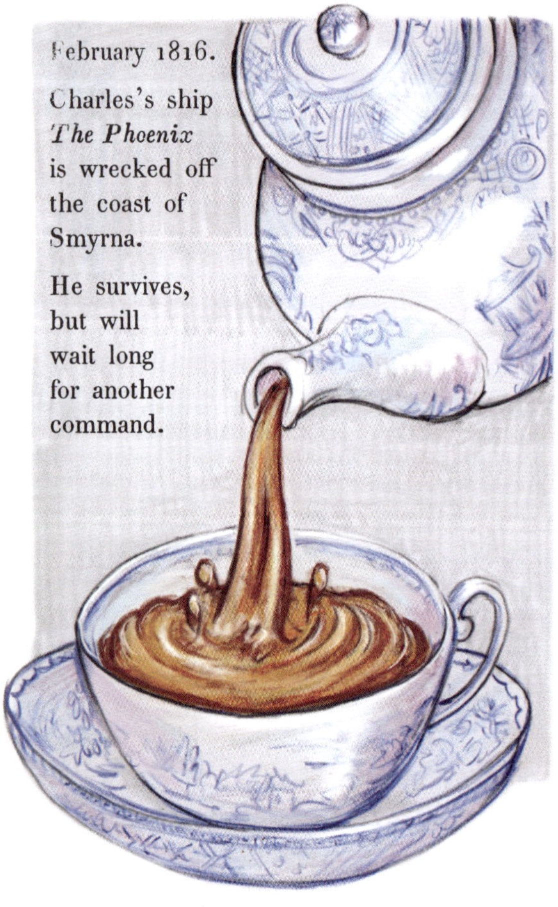
February 1816.
Charles's ship *The Phoenix* is wrecked off the coast of Smyrna.
He survives, but will wait long for another command.

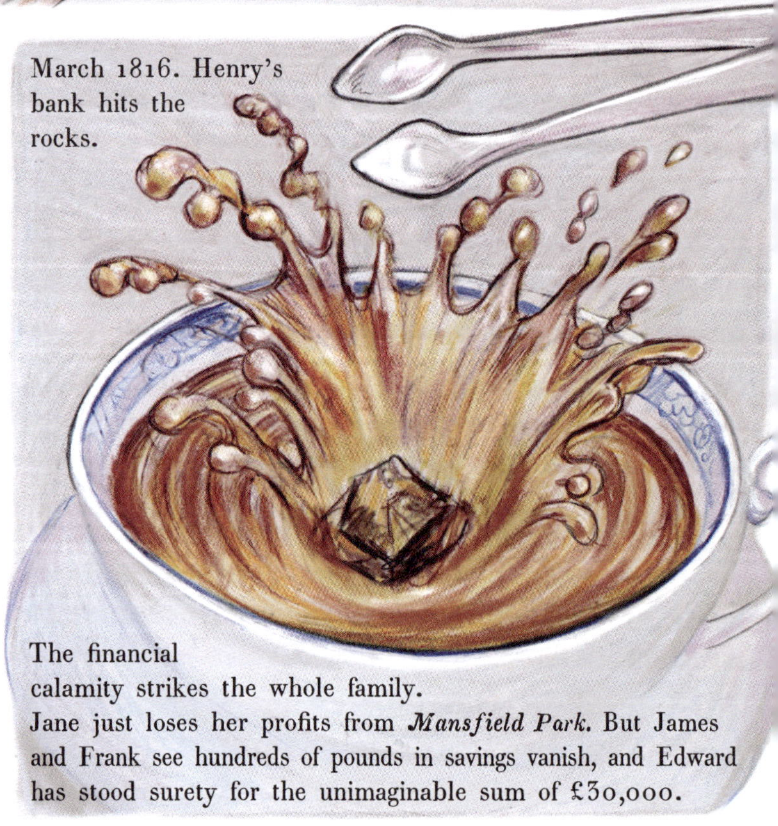
March 1816. Henry's bank hits the rocks.
The financial calamity strikes the whole family.
Jane just loses her profits from *Mansfield Park.* But James and Frank see hundreds of pounds in savings vanish, and Edward has stood surety for the unimaginable sum of £30,000.

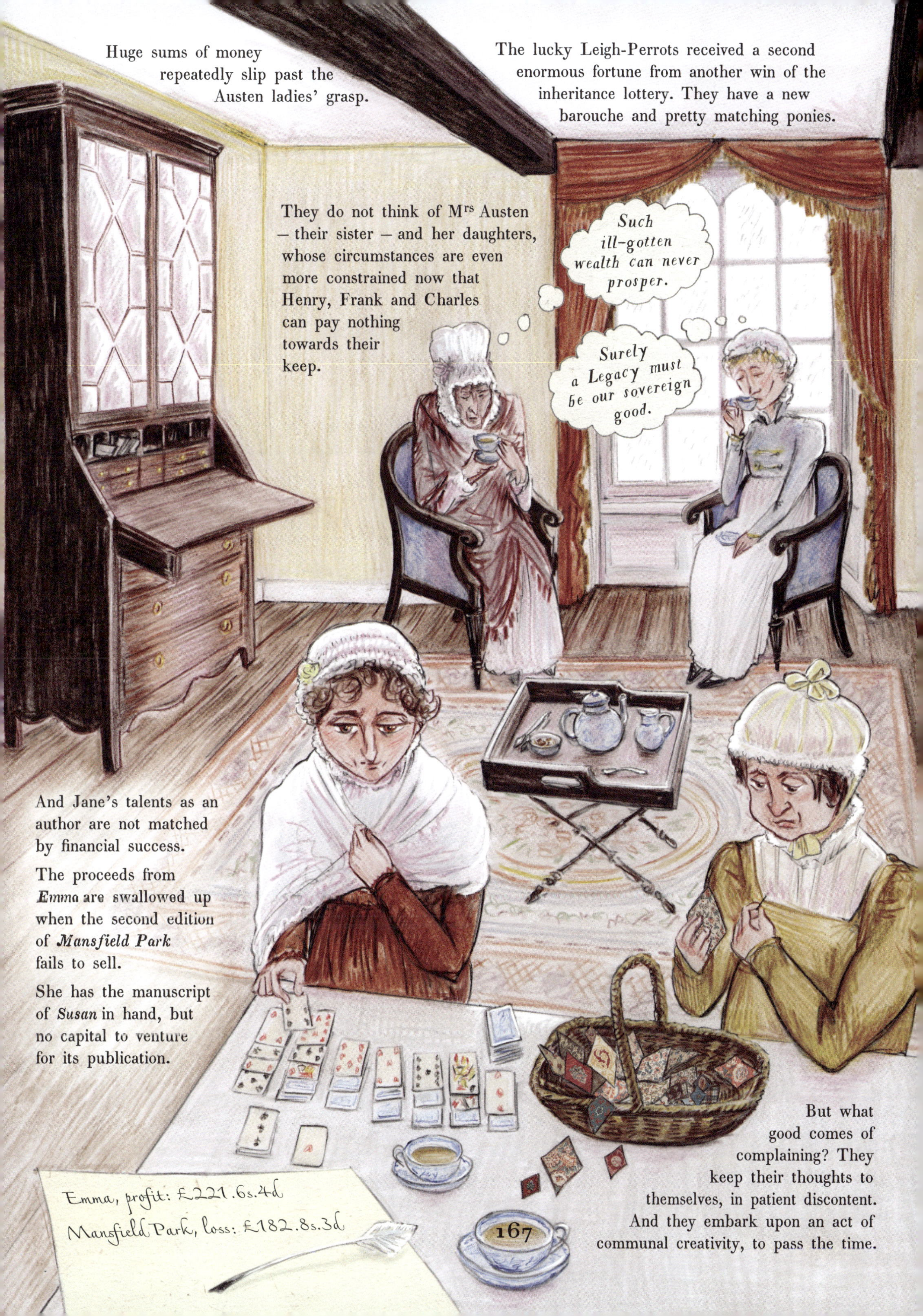
Huge sums of money repeatedly slip past the Austen ladies' grasp.
The lucky Leigh-Perrots received a second enormous fortune from another win of the inheritance lottery. They have a new barouche and pretty matching ponies.
They do not think of Mrs Austen – their sister – and her daughters, whose circumstances are even more constrained now that Henry, Frank and Charles can pay nothing towards their keep.
Such ill-gotten wealth can never prosper.
Surely a Legacy must be our sovereign good.
And Jane's talents as an author are not matched by financial success.
The proceeds from *Emma* are swallowed up when the second edition of *Mansfield Park* fails to sell.
She has the manuscript of *Susan* in hand, but no capital to venture for its publication.
But what good comes of complaining? They keep their thoughts to themselves, in patient discontent. And they embark upon an act of communal creativity, to pass the time.
Emma, profit: £221.6s.4d
Mansfield Park, loss: £182.8s.3d

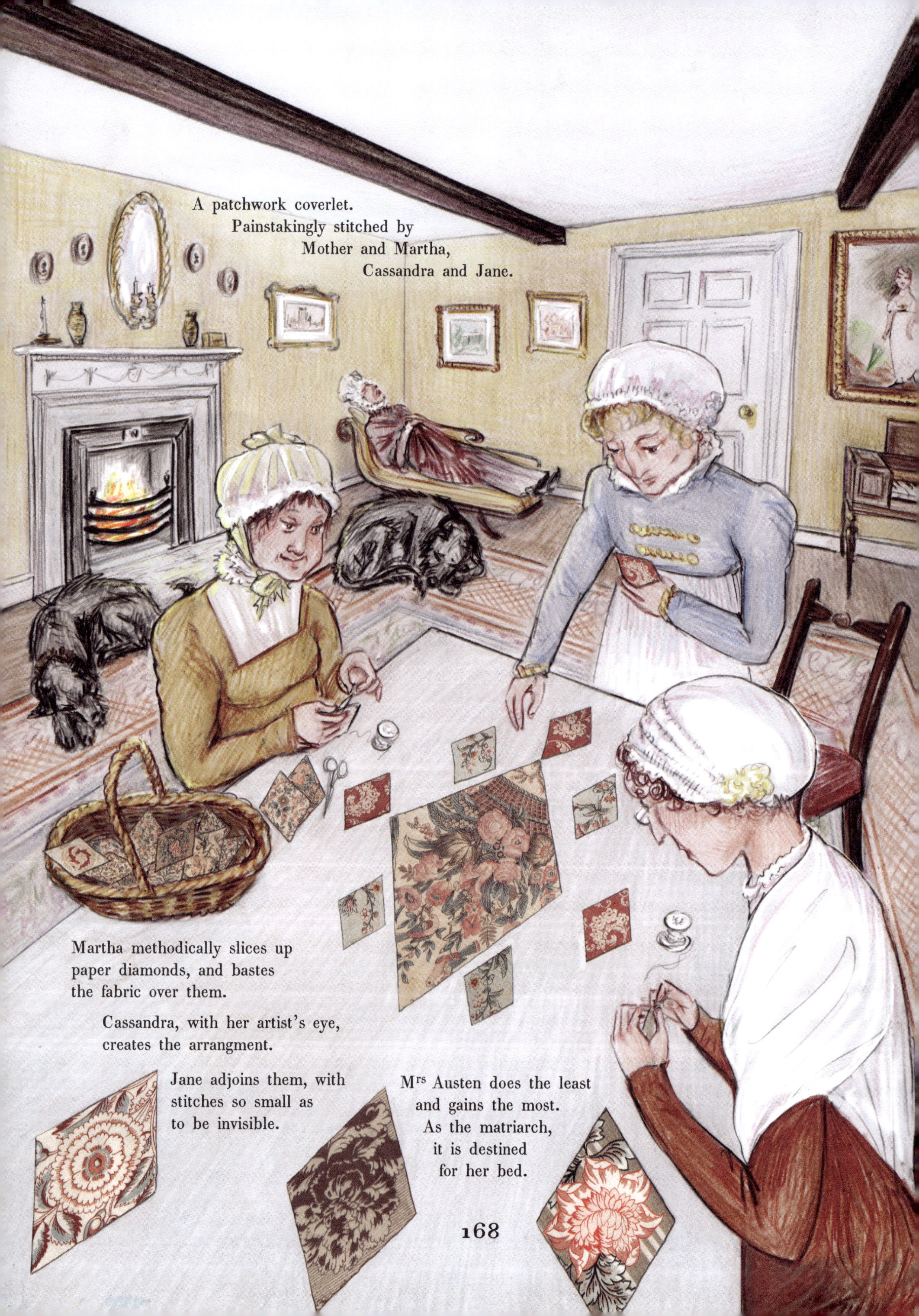

A patchwork coverlet.
Painstakingly stitched by
Mother and Martha,
Cassandra and Jane.

Martha methodically slices up paper diamonds, and bastes the fabric over them.

Cassandra, with her artist's eye, creates the arrangment.

Jane adjoins them, with stitches so small as to be invisible.

Mrs Austen does the least and gains the most. As the matriarch, it is destined for her bed.

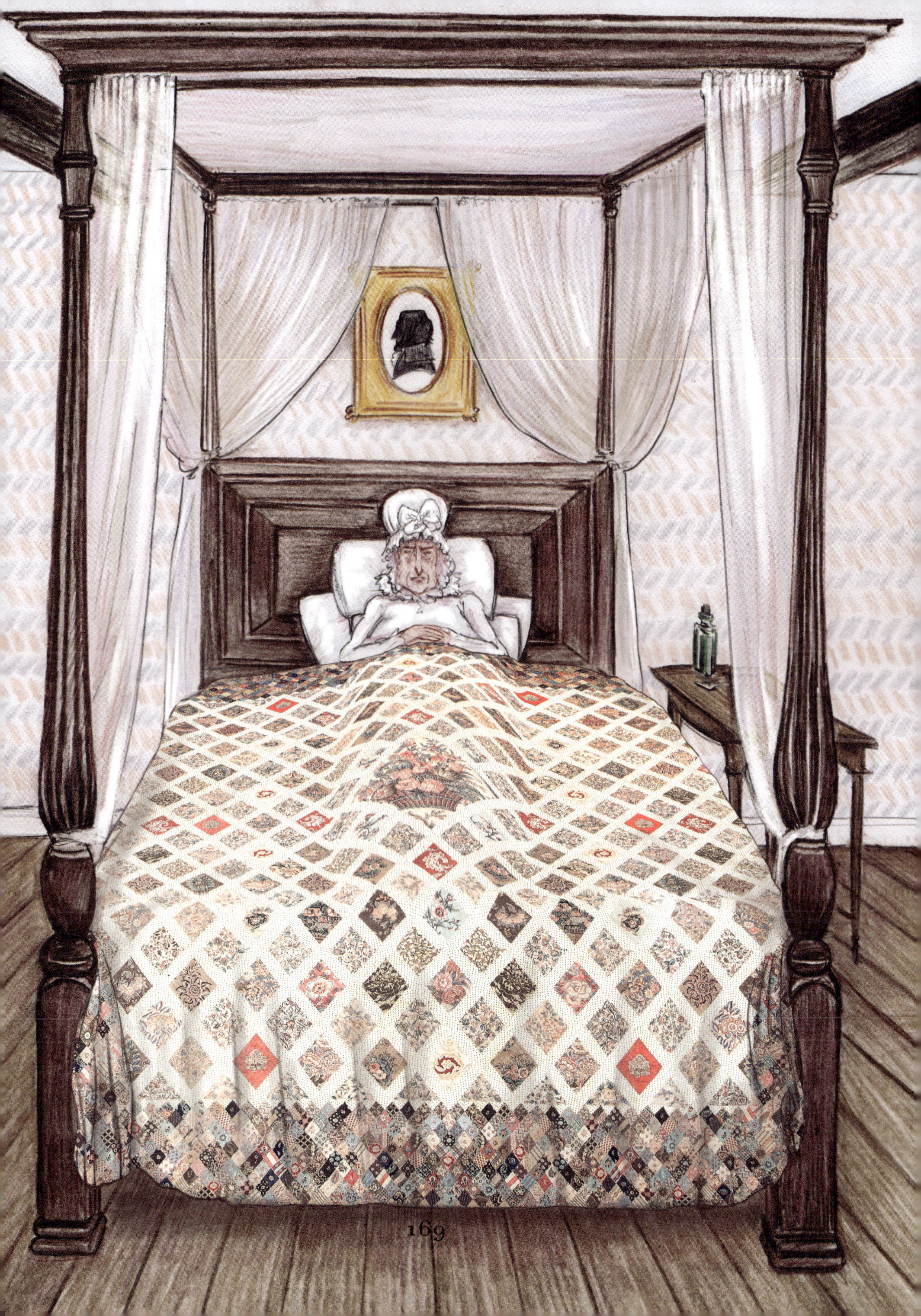

PASSION

Of course, Jane has another novel underway. Of course she does. Her creative passions, once ignited, are not easily quenched. She sets pen to paper on August 8th, 1815, and completes it on August 6th, 1816. Almost exactly one year for her most perfect, august work.

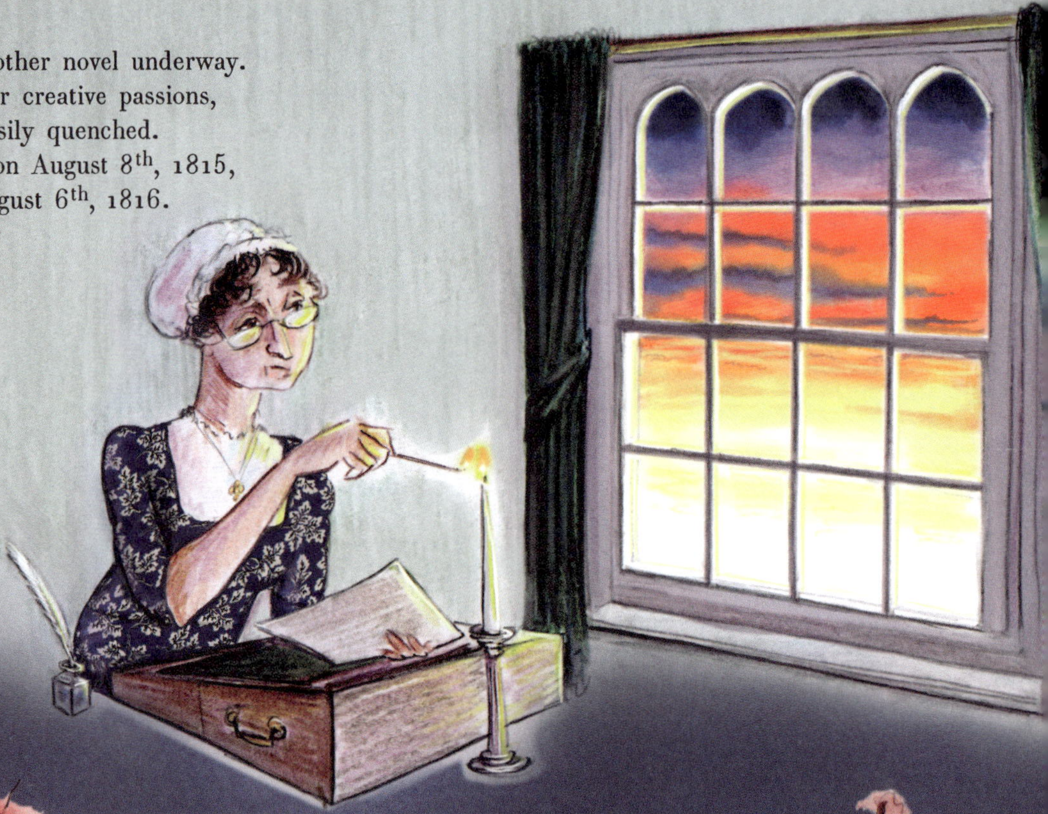

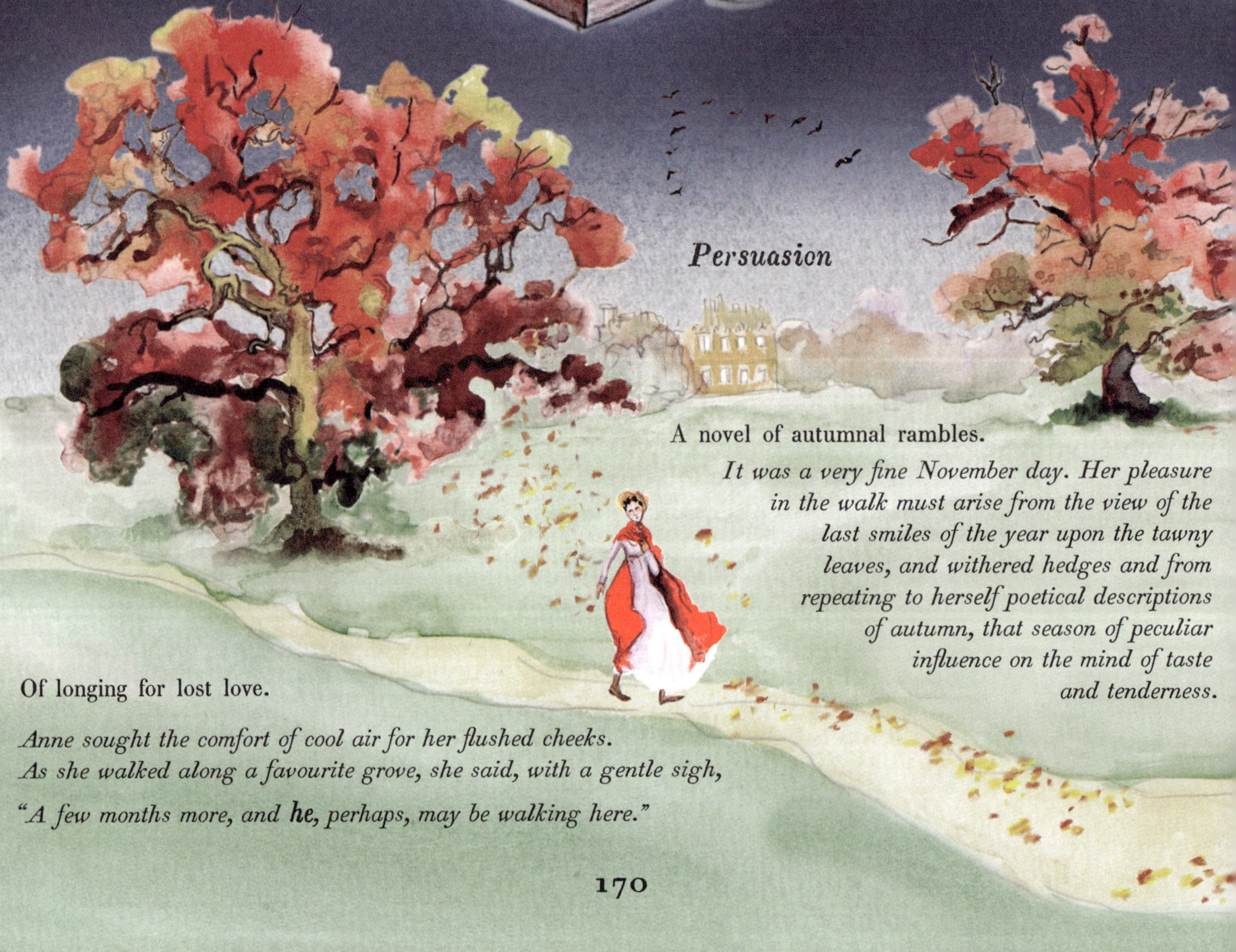

Persuasion

A novel of autumnal rambles.

It was a very fine November day. Her pleasure in the walk must arise from the view of the last smiles of the year upon the tawny leaves, and withered hedges and from repeating to herself poetical descriptions of autumn, that season of peculiar influence on the mind of taste and tenderness.

Of longing for lost love.

Anne sought the comfort of cool air for her flushed cheeks. As she walked along a favourite grove, she said, with a gentle sigh, "A few months more, and **he***, perhaps, may be walking here."*

Of sensuous physicality.

A thousand feelings rushed on Anne... Her eye half met Captain Wentworth's, a bow, a curtsey passed; she heard his voice; he said all that was right... the room seemed full, full of persons and voices, but a few minutes ended it... Their visitor had bowed and was gone... the room was cleared.

All the overpowering, blinding, bewildering, first effects of strong surprise were over with her. Still, however, she had enough to feel! It was agitation, pain, pleasure, a something between delight and misery.

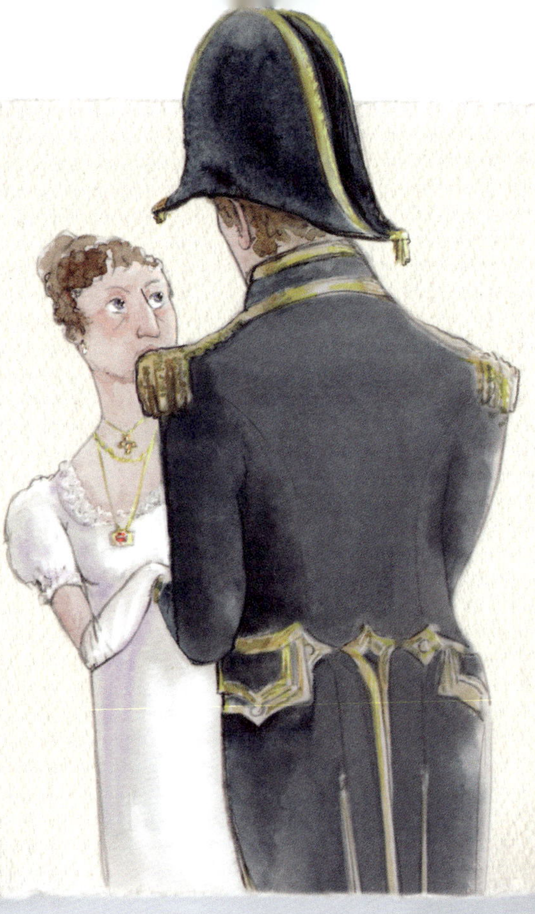

Of patient waiting for just rewards.

She began to reason with herself, and try to be feeling less. Eight years, almost eight years had passed, since all had been given up. How absurd to be resuming the agitation which such an interval had banished into distance and indistinctness!

Alas! with all her reasoning, she found, that to retentive feelings eight years may be little more than nothing.

And of the sea: the place where passions are rekindled.

She was looking remarkably well; her very regular, very pretty features, having the bloom and freshness of youth restored by the fine wind which had been blowing on her complexion, and by the animation of eye which it had also produced.

Captain Wentworth looked round at her instantly in a way which shewed his noticing of it. He gave her a momentary glance, a glance of brightness, which seemed to say, "I, at this moment, see something like Anne Elliot again."

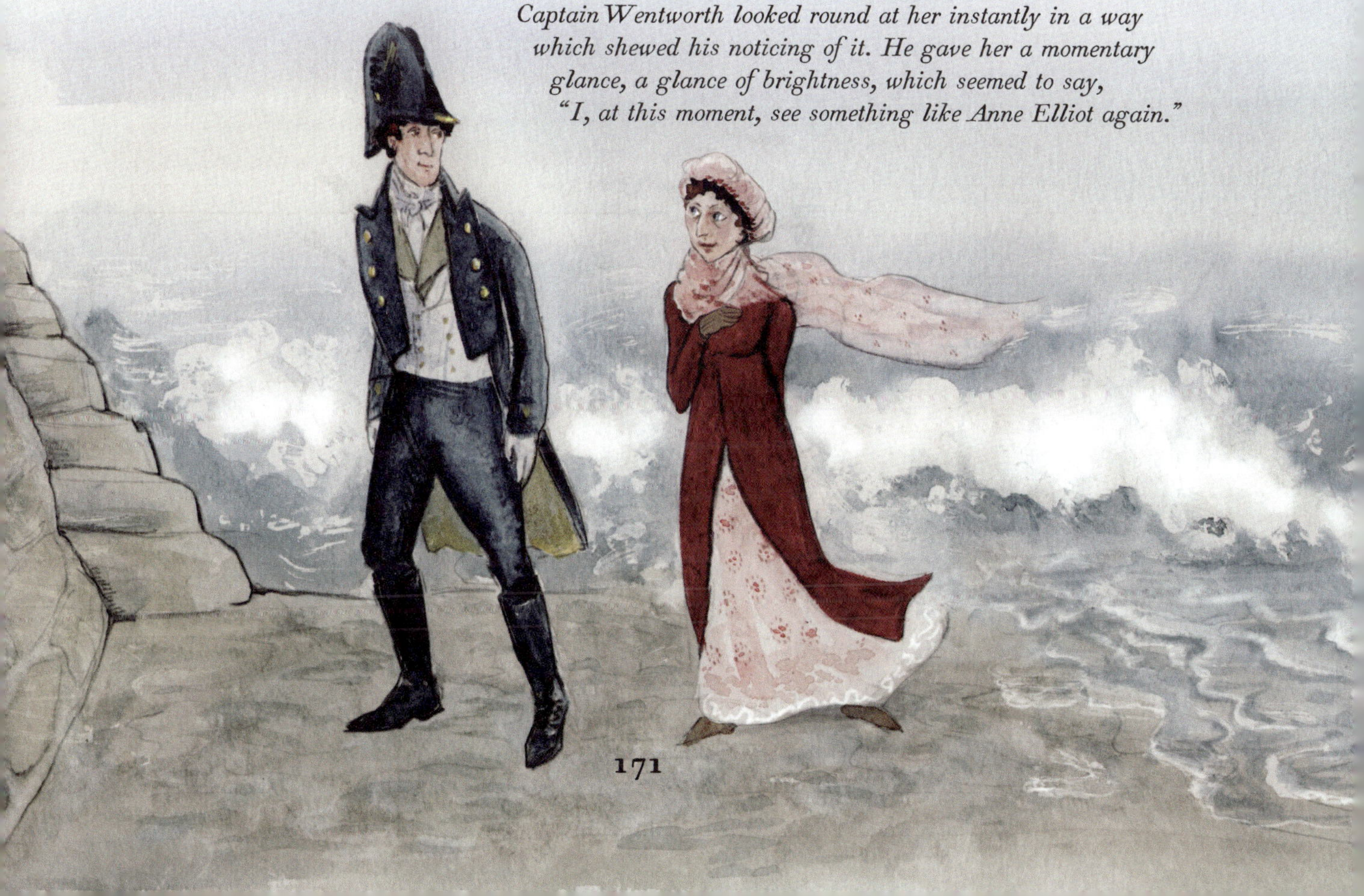

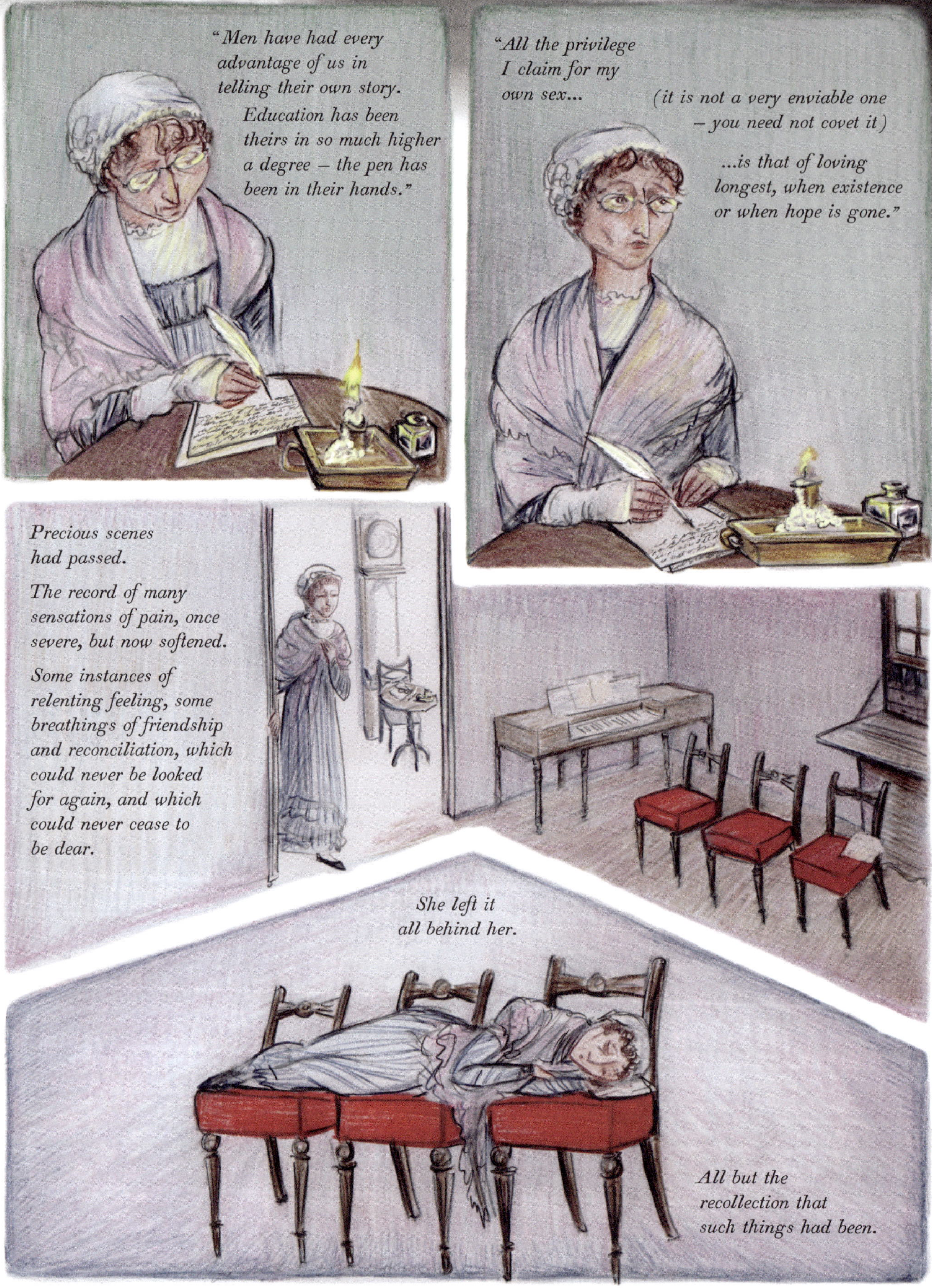
"Men have had every advantage of us in telling their own story. Education has been theirs in so much higher a degree – the pen has been in their hands."
"All the privilege I claim for my own sex...
(it is not a very enviable one – you need not covet it)
...is that of loving longest, when existence or when hope is gone."
Precious scenes had passed.
The record of many sensations of pain, once severe, but now softened.
Some instances of relenting feeling, some breathings of friendship and reconciliation, which could never be looked for again, and which could never cease to be dear.
She left it all behind her.
All but the recollection that such things had been.

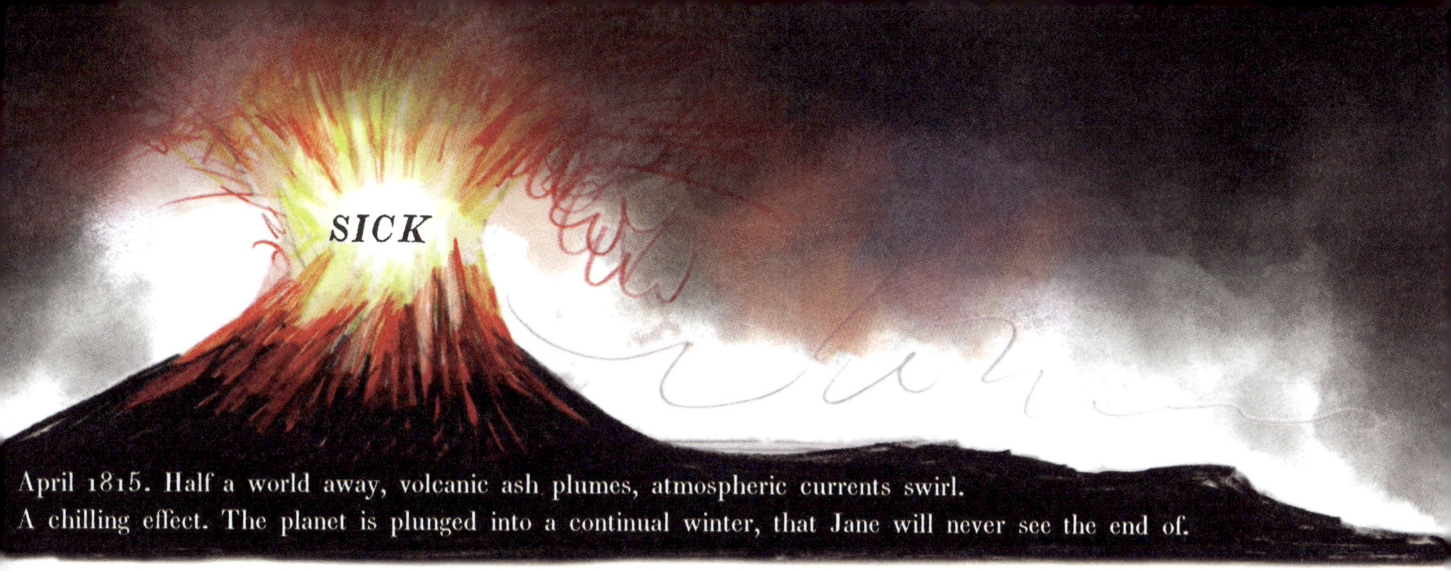
SICK
April 1815. Half a world away, volcanic ash plumes, atmospheric currents swirl.
A chilling effect. The planet is plunged into a continual winter, that Jane will never see the end of.

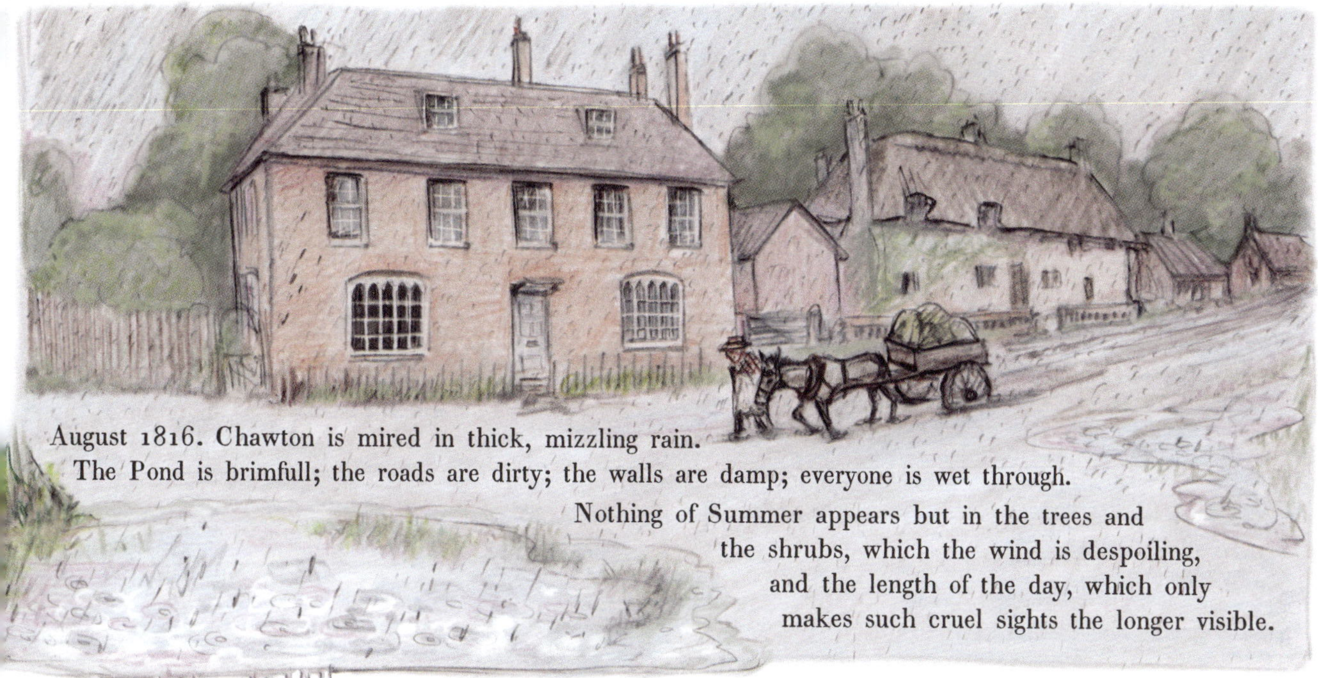
August 1816. Chawton is mired in thick, mizzling rain.
The Pond is brimfull; the roads are dirty; the walls are damp; everyone is wet through.
Nothing of Summer appears but in the trees and the shrubs, which the wind is despoiling, and the length of the day, which only makes such cruel sights the longer visible.

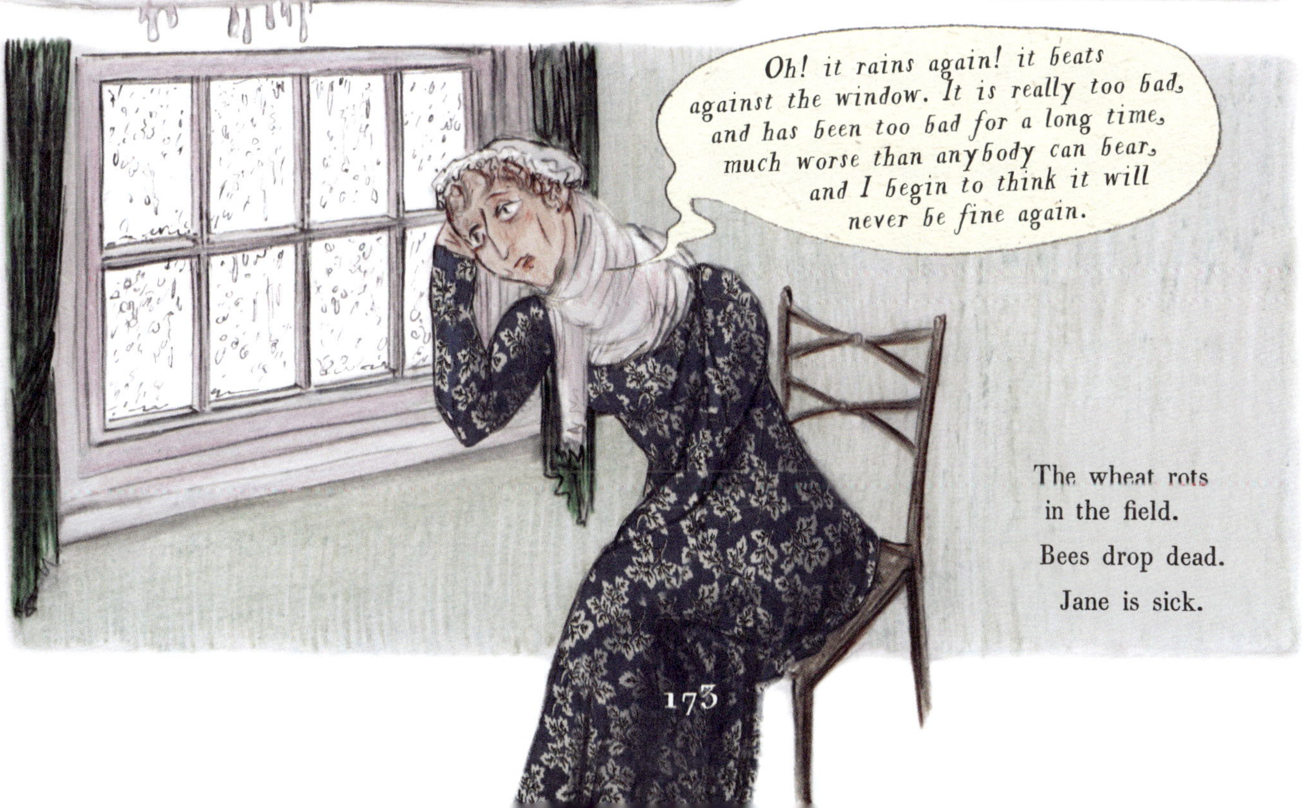
Oh! it rains again! it beats against the window. It is really too bad, and has been too bad for a long time, much worse than anybody can bear, and I begin to think it will never be fine again.
The wheat rots in the field.
Bees drop dead.
Jane is sick.

The symptoms are vague, and troubling, and long standing; a pain in the face; an ache in the back; an overwhelming fatigue. It comes and goes, but she cannot doubt, when she looks back, that she is now in a weaker state of health than she was half a year ago. Her appearance has exactly that of a confirmed Decline.

But she will be the last to own it.

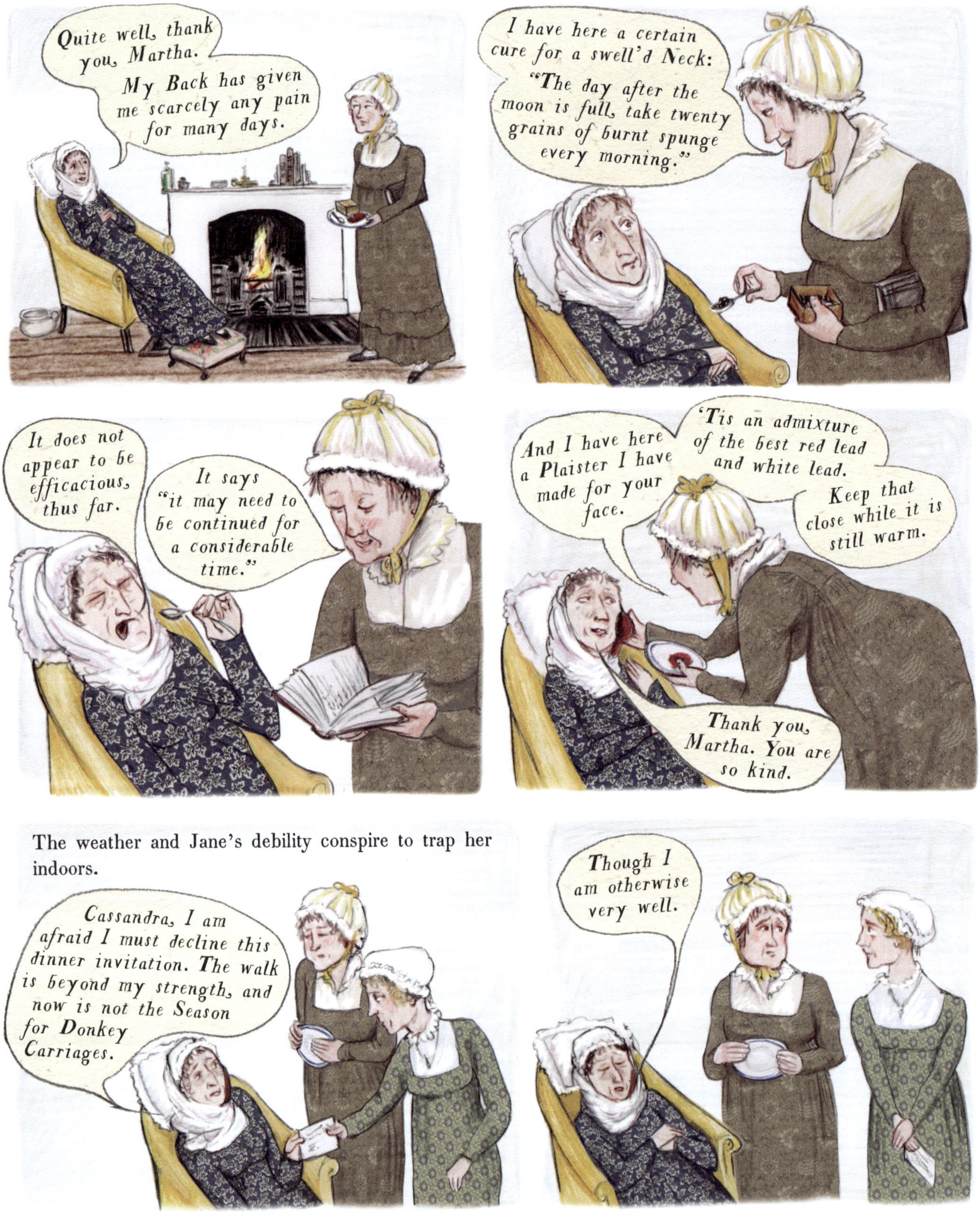

Quite well, thank you, Martha.
My Back has given me scarcely any pain for many days.
I have here a certain cure for a swell'd Neck:
"The day after the moon is full, take twenty grains of burnt spunge every morning."
It does not appear to be efficacious, thus far.
It says "it may need to be continued for a considerable time."
And I have here a Plaister I have made for your face.
'Tis an admixture of the best red lead and white lead.
Keep that close while it is still warm.
Thank you, Martha. You are so kind.
The weather and Jane's debility conspire to trap her indoors.
Cassandra, I am afraid I must decline this dinner invitation. The walk is beyond my strength, and now is not the Season for Donkey Carriages.
Though I am otherwise very well.

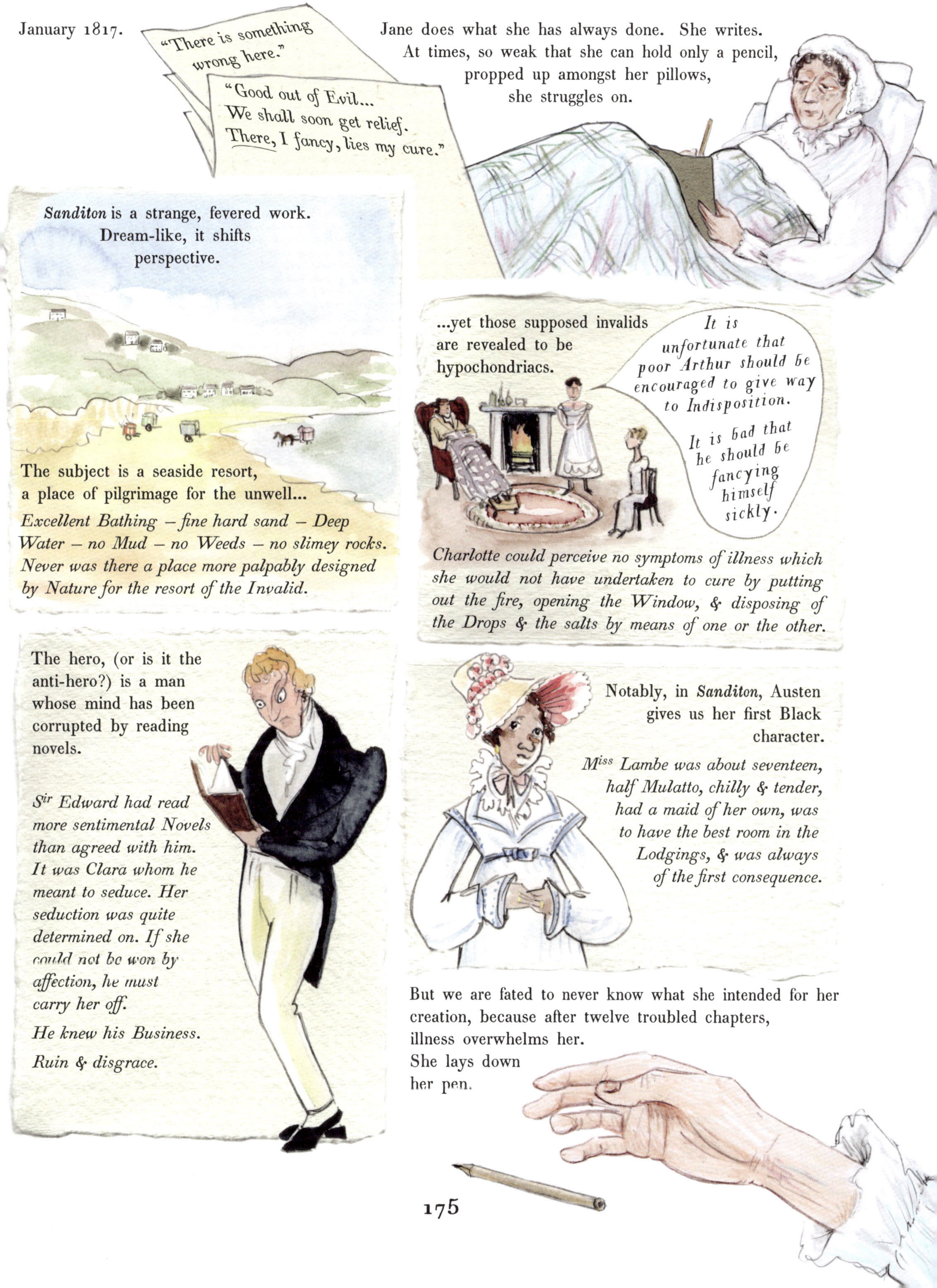
January 1817.
"There is something wrong here."
"Good out of Evil... We shall soon get relief. There, I fancy, lies my cure."
Jane does what she has always done. She writes. At times, so weak that she can hold only a pencil, propped up amongst her pillows, she struggles on.
Sanditon is a strange, fevered work. Dream-like, it shifts perspective.
The subject is a seaside resort, a place of pilgrimage for the unwell...
Excellent Bathing – fine hard sand – Deep Water – no Mud – no Weeds – no slimey rocks. Never was there a place more palpably designed by Nature for the resort of the Invalid.
...yet those supposed invalids are revealed to be hypochondriacs.
It is unfortunate that poor Arthur should be encouraged to give way to Indisposition.
It is bad that he should be fancying himself sickly.
Charlotte could perceive no symptoms of illness which she would not have undertaken to cure by putting out the fire, opening the Window, & disposing of the Drops & the salts by means of one or the other.
The hero, (or is it the anti-hero?) is a man whose mind has been corrupted by reading novels.
Sir Edward had read more sentimental Novels than agreed with him. It was Clara whom he meant to seduce. Her seduction was quite determined on. If she could not be won by affection, he must carry her off.
He knew his Business.
Ruin & disgrace.
Notably, in *Sanditon*, Austen gives us her first Black character.
Miss Lambe was about seventeen, half Mulatto, chilly & tender, had a maid of her own, was to have the best room in the Lodgings, & was always of the first consequence.
But we are fated to never know what she intended for her creation, because after twelve troubled chapters, illness overwhelms her.
She lays down her pen.

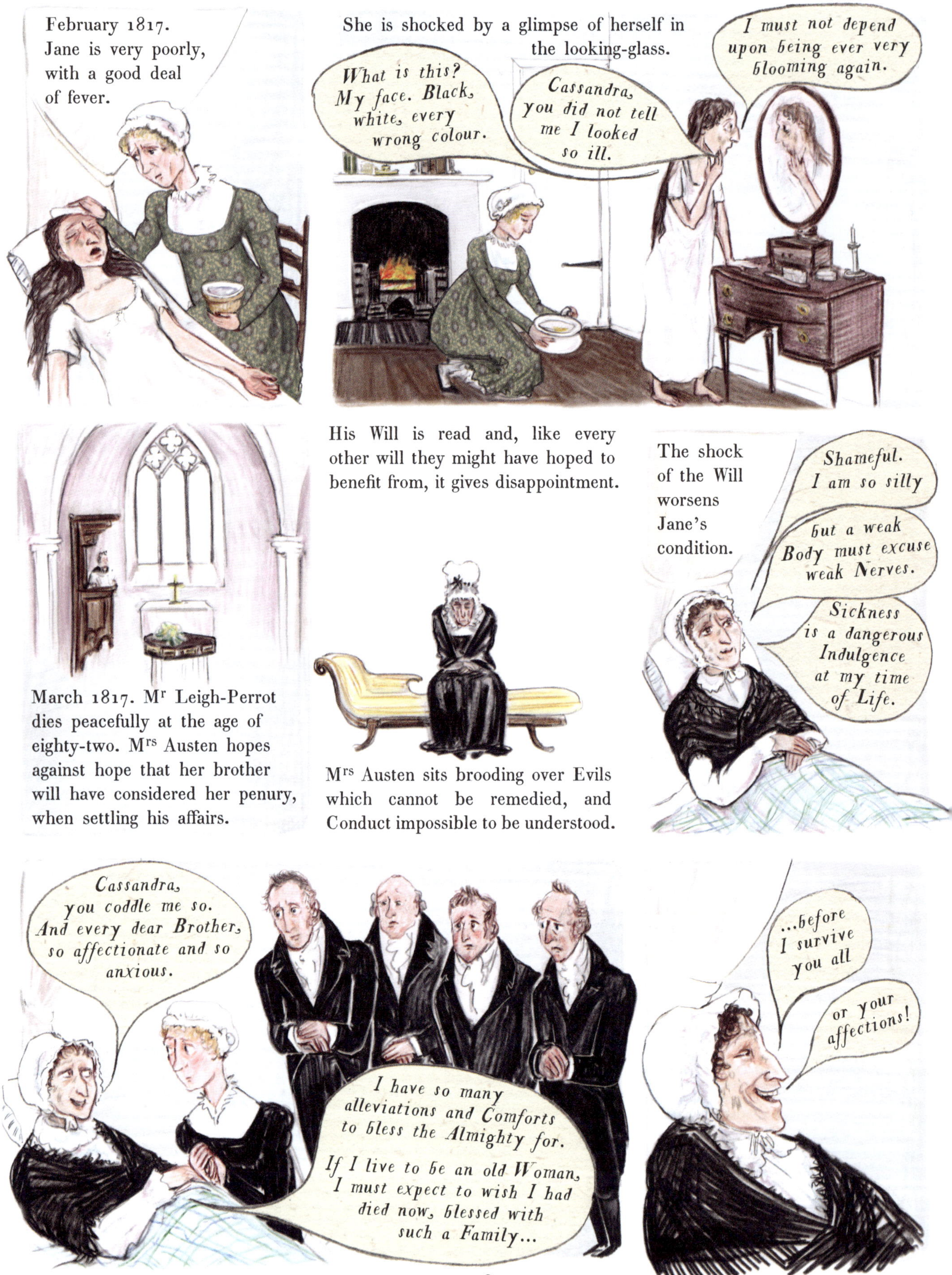

February 1817.
Jane is very poorly, with a good deal of fever.
She is shocked by a glimpse of herself in the looking-glass.
What is this? My face. Black, white, every wrong colour.
Cassandra, you did not tell me I looked so ill.
I must not depend upon being ever very blooming again.
March 1817. Mr Leigh-Perrot dies peacefully at the age of eighty-two. Mrs Austen hopes against hope that her brother will have considered her penury, when settling his affairs.
His Will is read and, like every other will they might have hoped to benefit from, it gives disappointment.
Mrs Austen sits brooding over Evils which cannot be remedied, and Conduct impossible to be understood.
The shock of the Will worsens Jane's condition.
Shameful. I am so silly
but a weak Body must excuse weak Nerves.
Sickness is a dangerous Indulgence at my time of Life.
Cassandra, you coddle me so. And every dear Brother, so affectionate and so anxious.
I have so many alleviations and Comforts to bless the Almighty for.
If I live to be an old Woman, I must expect to wish I had died now, blessed with such a Family...
...before I survive you all
or your affections!

St SWITHIN'S DAY

24th May 1817.

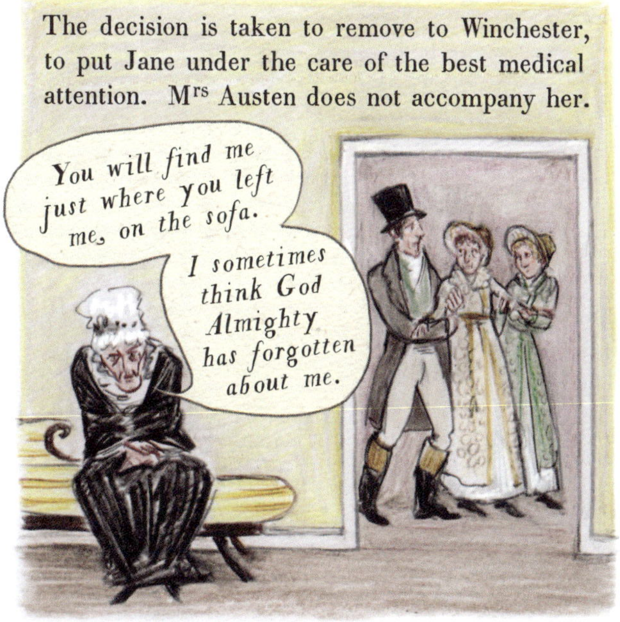
The decision is taken to remove to Winchester, to put Jane under the care of the best medical attention. Mrs Austen does not accompany her.
You will find me just where you left me, on the sofa.
I sometimes think God Almighty has forgotten about me.

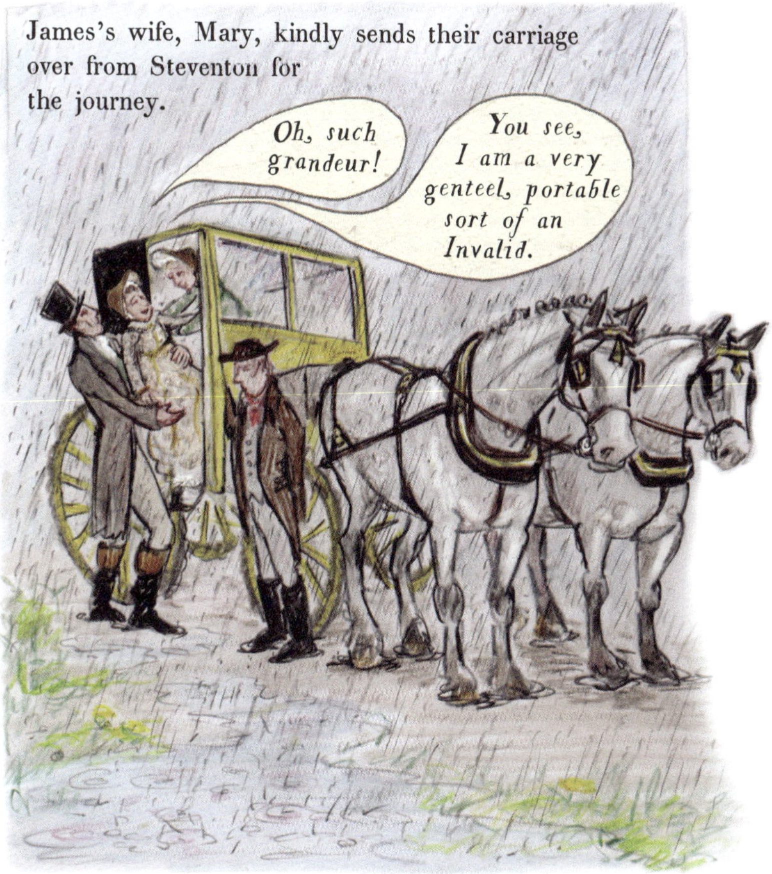
James's wife, Mary, kindly sends their carriage over from Steventon for the journey.
Oh, such grandeur!
You see, I am a very genteel, portable sort of an Invalid.

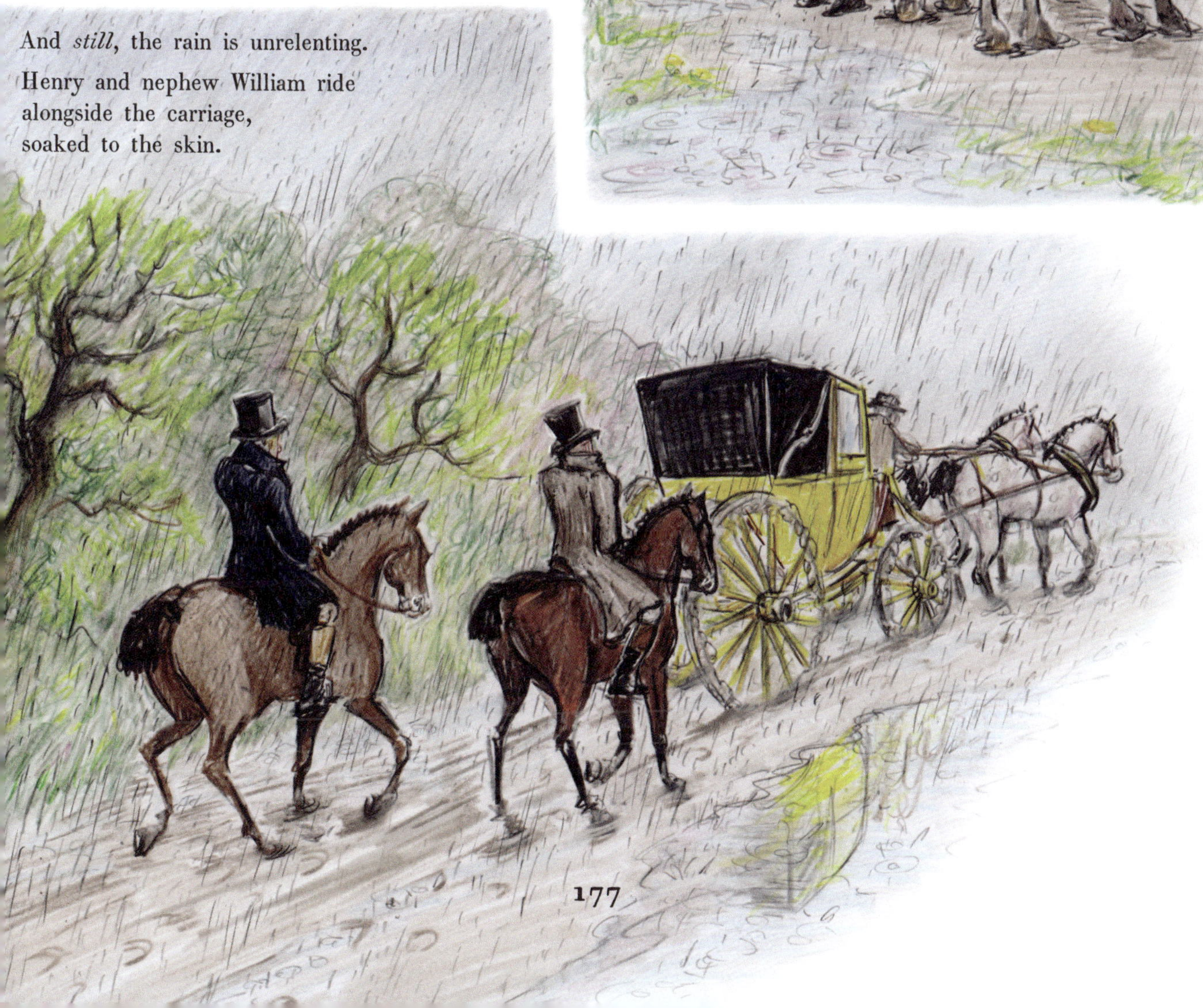
And *still*, the rain is unrelenting.
Henry and nephew William ride alongside the carriage, soaked to the skin.

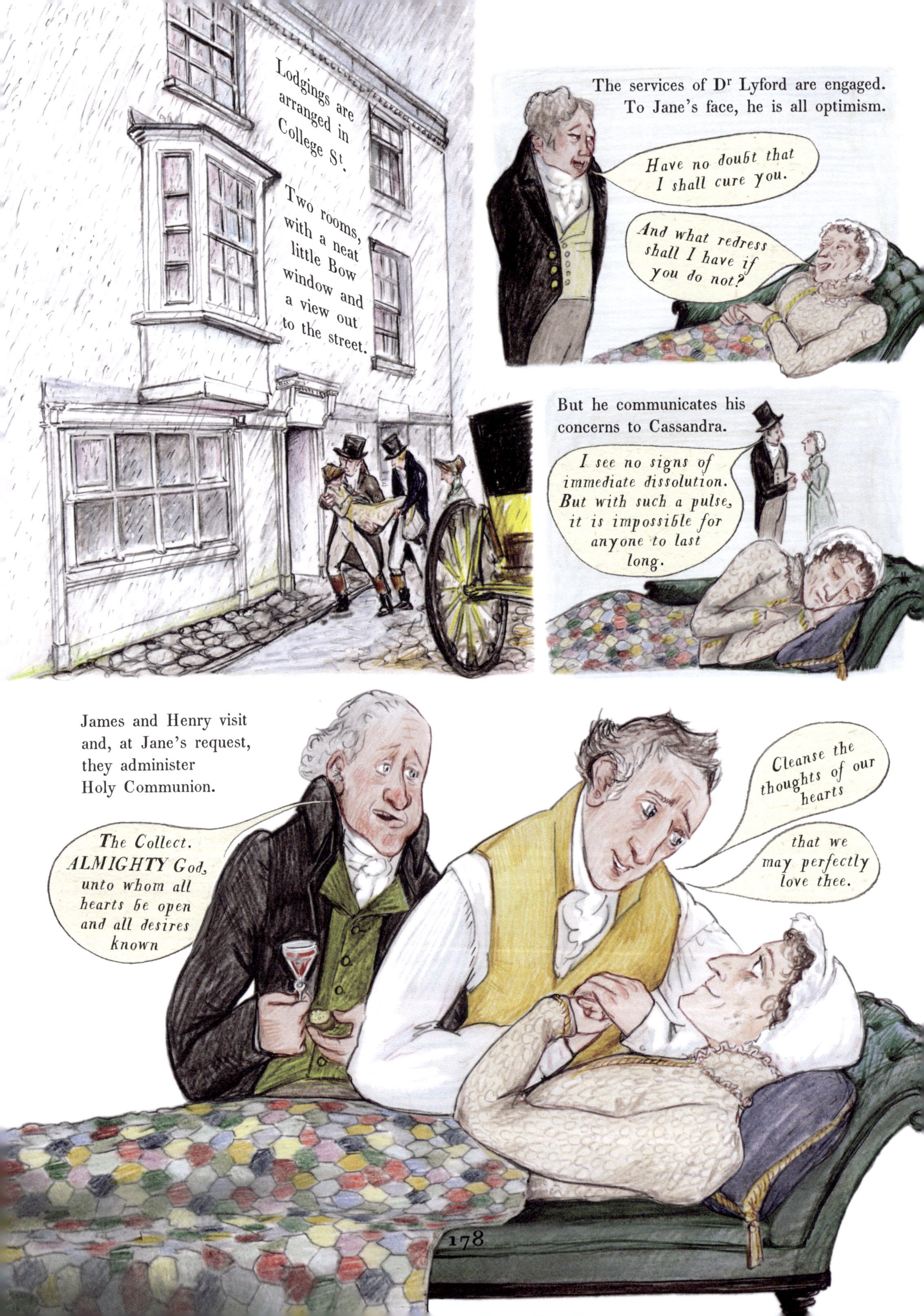
Lodgings are arranged in College S^t.
Two rooms, with a neat little Bow window and a view out to the street.
The services of Dr Lyford are engaged. To Jane's face, he is all optimism.
Have no doubt that I shall cure you.
And what redress shall I have if you do not?
But he communicates his concerns to Cassandra.
I see no signs of immediate dissolution. But with such a pulse, it is impossible for anyone to last long.
James and Henry visit and, at Jane's request, they administer Holy Communion.
The Collect. ALMIGHTY God, unto whom all hearts be open and all desires known
Cleanse the thoughts of our hearts
that we may perfectly love thee.

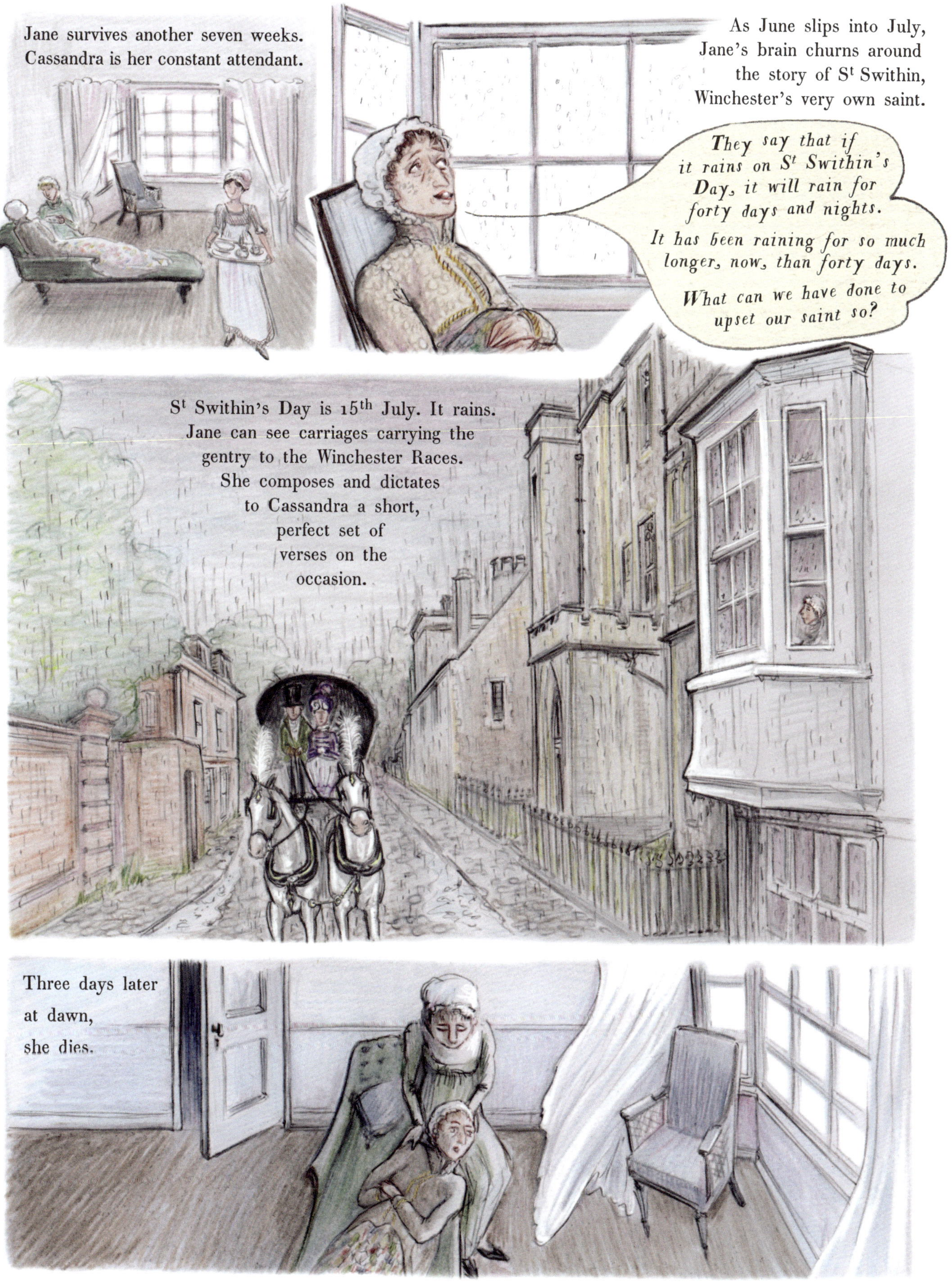
Jane survives another seven weeks. Cassandra is her constant attendant.
As June slips into July, Jane's brain churns around the story of St Swithin, Winchester's very own saint.
They say that if it rains on St Swithin's Day, it will rain for forty days and nights. It has been raining for so much longer, now, than forty days. What can we have done to upset our saint so?
St Swithin's Day is 15th July. It rains. Jane can see carriages carrying the gentry to the Winchester Races. She composes and dictates to Cassandra a short, perfect set of verses on the occasion.
Three days later at dawn, she dies.

THE WINCHESTER RACES *were fix'd and determin'd*
The company met & the Weather was charming
The Lords and the Ladies were sattin'd and ermined
And nobody saw any future alarming.

But when the old Saint was
inform'd of these doings
He made but one Spring
from his Shrine to the Roof
Of the Palace which now
lies so sadly in ruins
And thus he address'd them all
standing aloof:

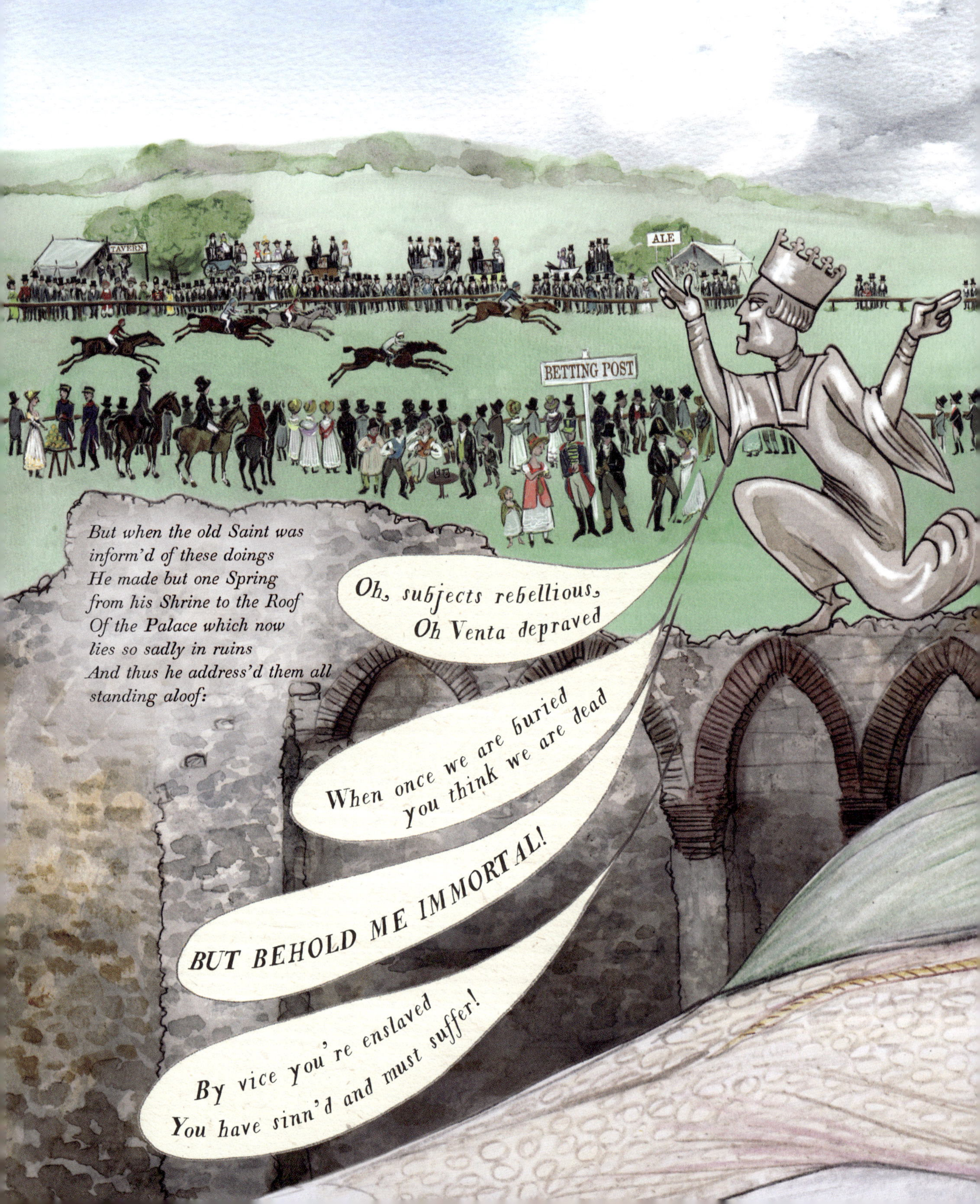
TAVERN
ALE
BETTING POST
Oh, subjects rebellious, Oh Venta depraved
When once we are buried you think we are dead
BUT BEHOLD ME IMMORTAL!
By vice you're enslaved You have sinn'd and must suffer!

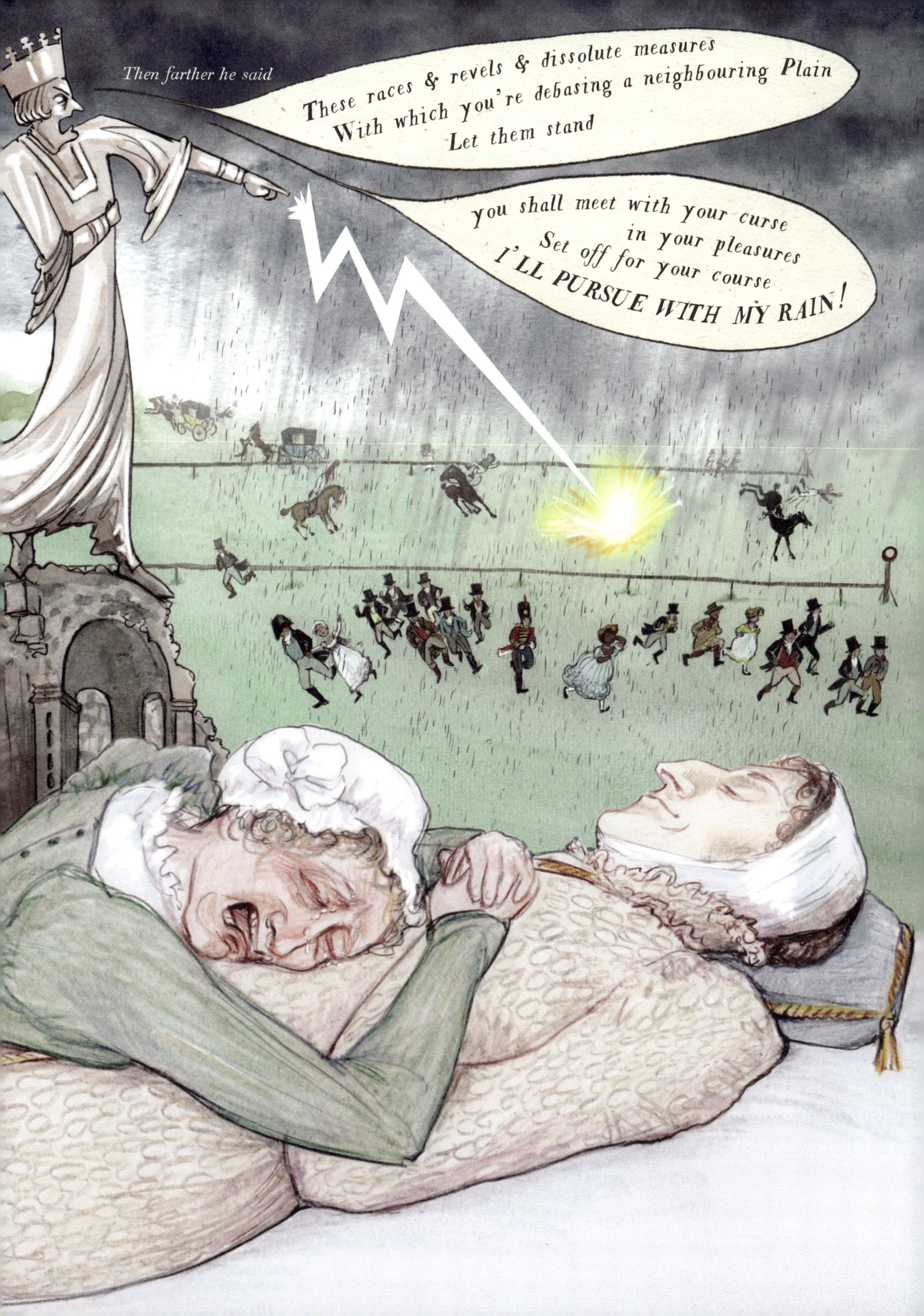
Then farther he said
These races & revels & dissolute measures
With which you're debasing a neighbouring Plain
Let them stand
you shall meet with your curse
in your pleasures
Set off for your course
I'LL PURSUE WITH MY RAIN!

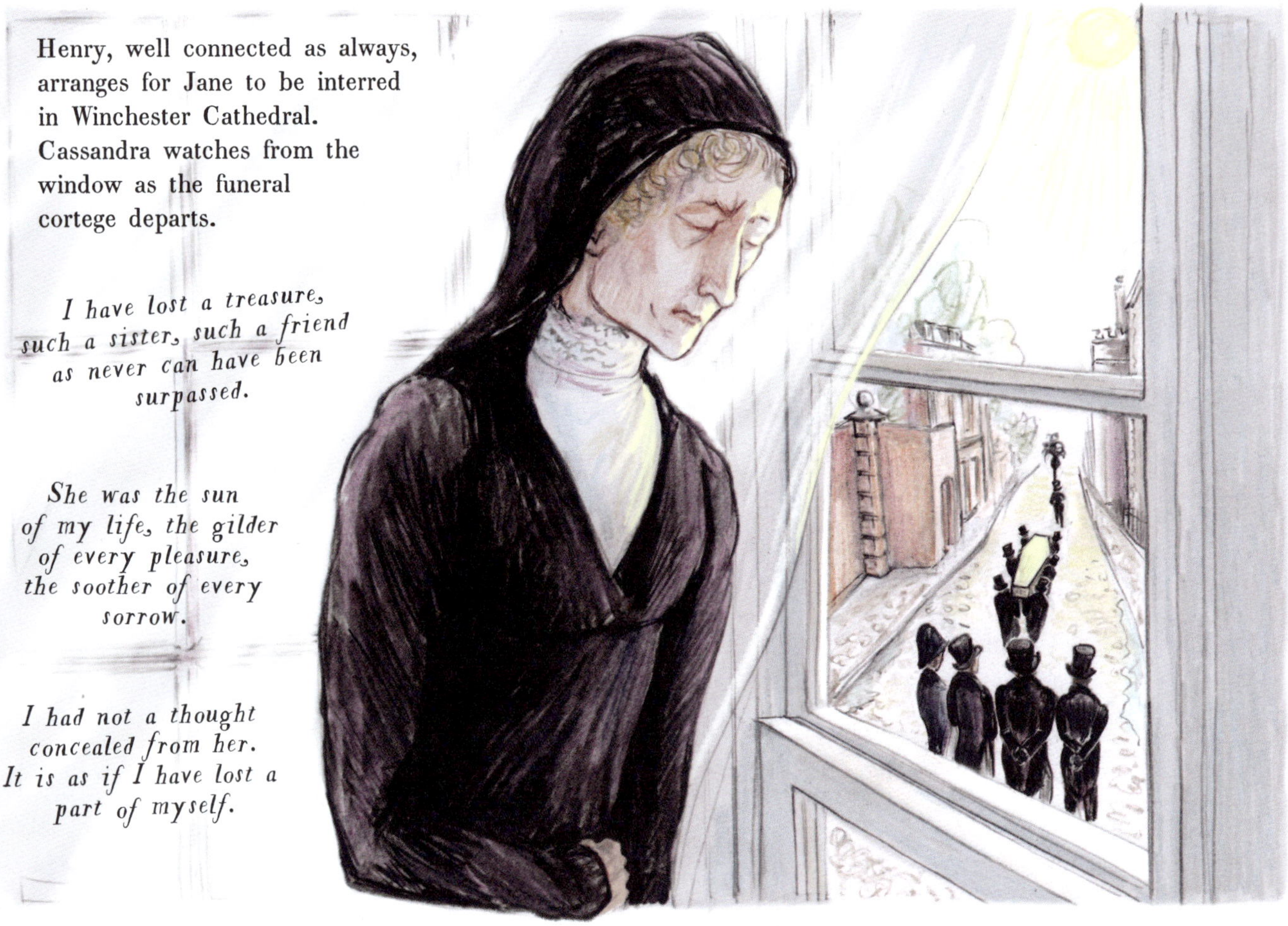
Henry, well connected as always, arranges for Jane to be interred in Winchester Cathedral. Cassandra watches from the window as the funeral cortege departs.
I have lost a treasure, such a sister, such a friend as never can have been surpassed.
She was the sun of my life, the gilder of every pleasure, the soother of every sorrow.
I had not a thought concealed from her. It is as if I have lost a part of myself.

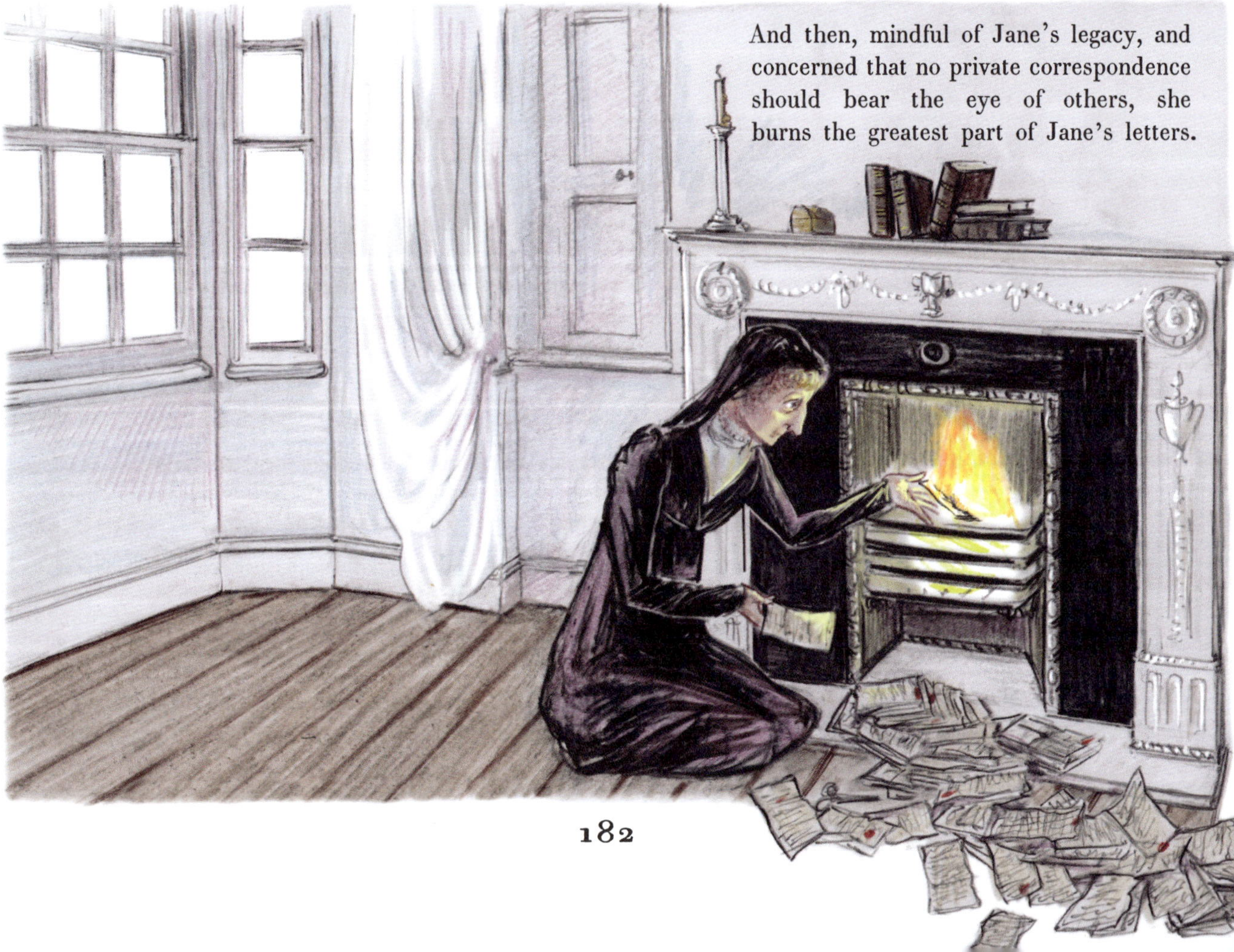
And then, mindful of Jane's legacy, and concerned that no private correspondence should bear the eye of others, she burns the greatest part of Jane's letters.

Persuasion and *Northanger Abbey* (the retitled novel *Susan*) were published posthumously as a four-volume set in December 1817. Just a single print run, of which the last few hundred copies were remaindered.

In 1832, the publisher Richard Bentley bought the copyright for all six of Austen's obscure, out-of-print, and slightly old-fashioned novels for £250.

He printed them in cheap, one-volume editions.

They have remained in print ever since.

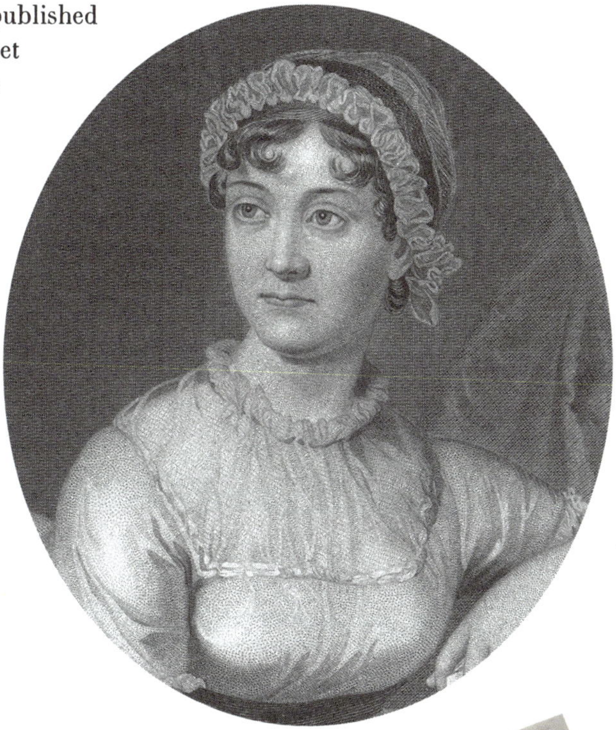

Dear Jane's life was not a life of event.

She had no hopes of fame or of profit.

She possessed perfect placidity of temper.

Never uttered a hasty, a silly, or a severe expression.

Faultless herself, as nearly as human nature could be.

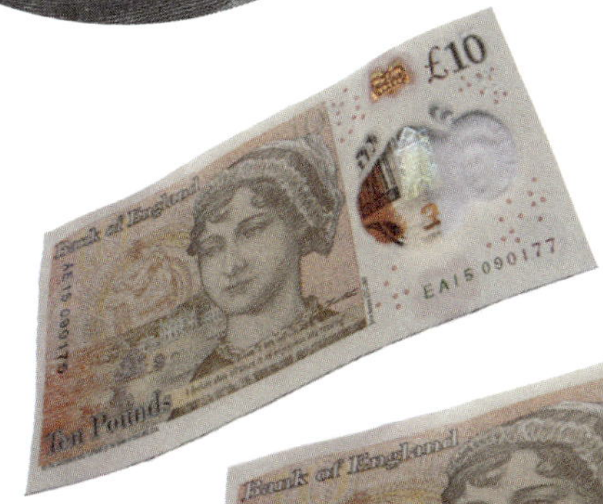
£10
Bank of England
Ten Pounds
EA15 090177

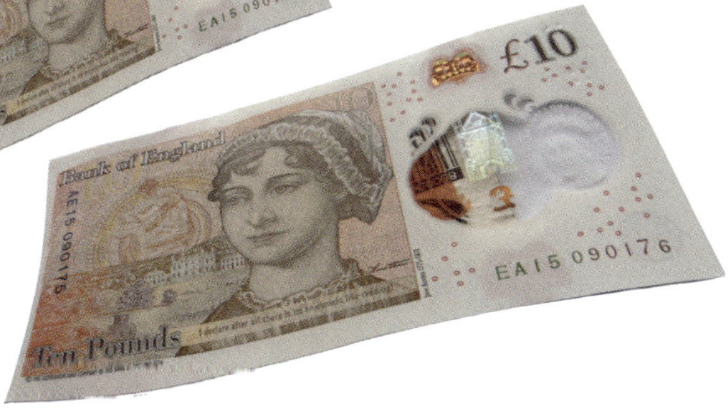
£10
Bank of England
Ten Pounds
EA15 090176

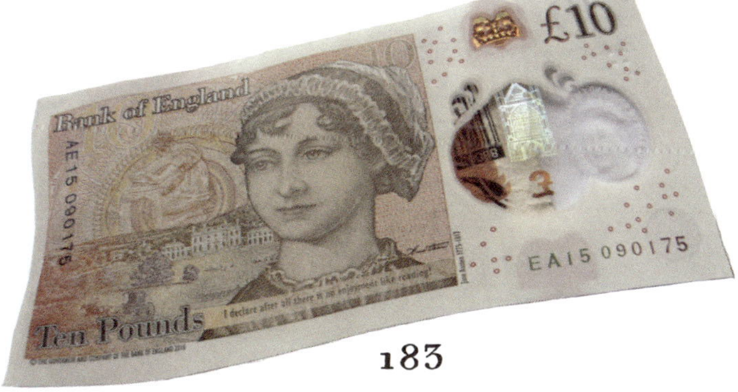
£10
Bank of England
Ten Pounds
EA15 090175

The portrait is a very pleasing, sweet face. It is not much like hers, but that, the public will not be able to detect.

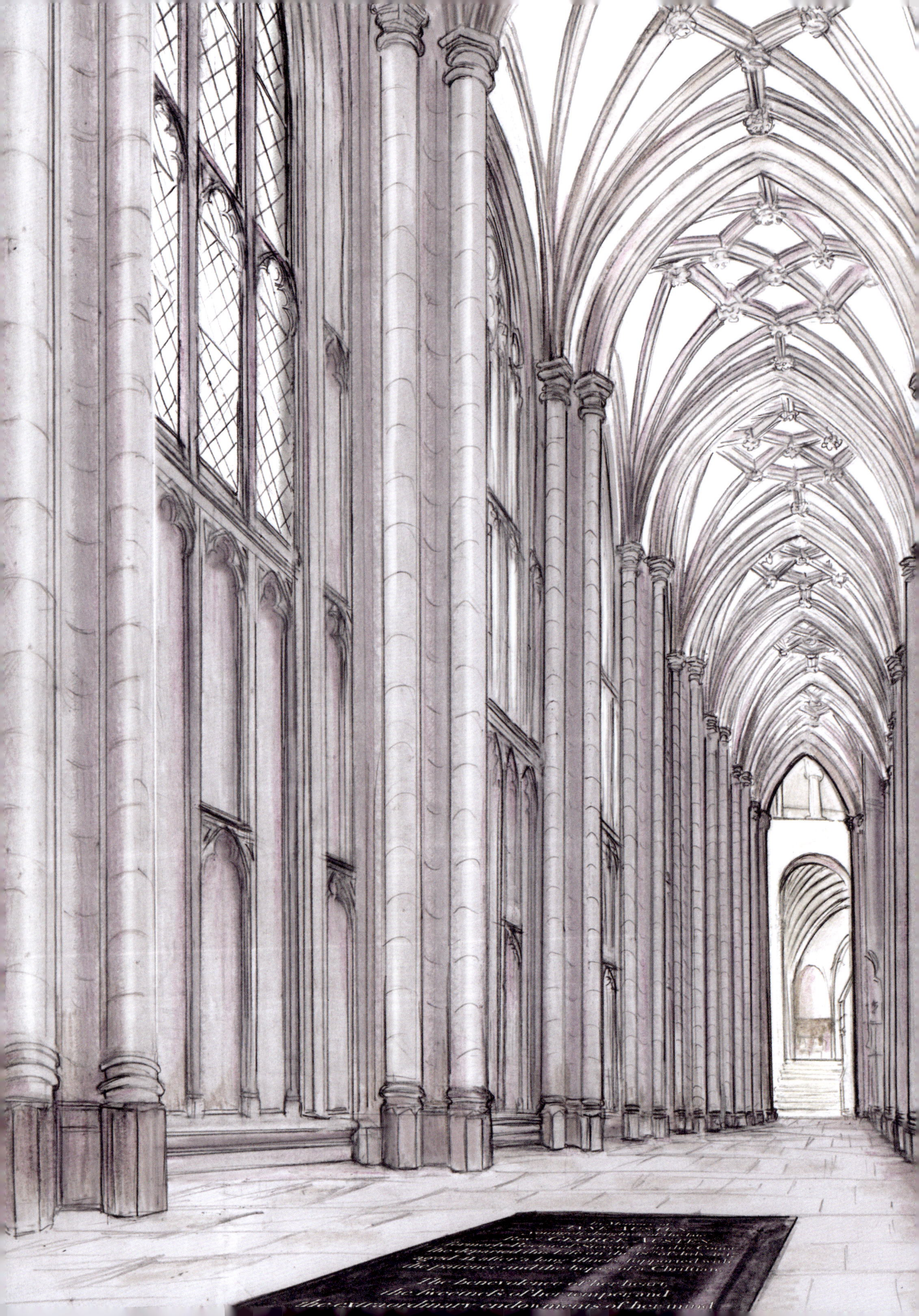
the patience and the hopes of a Chriſtian
The benevolence of her heart,
the ſweetneſs of her temper, and
the extraordinary endowments of her mind

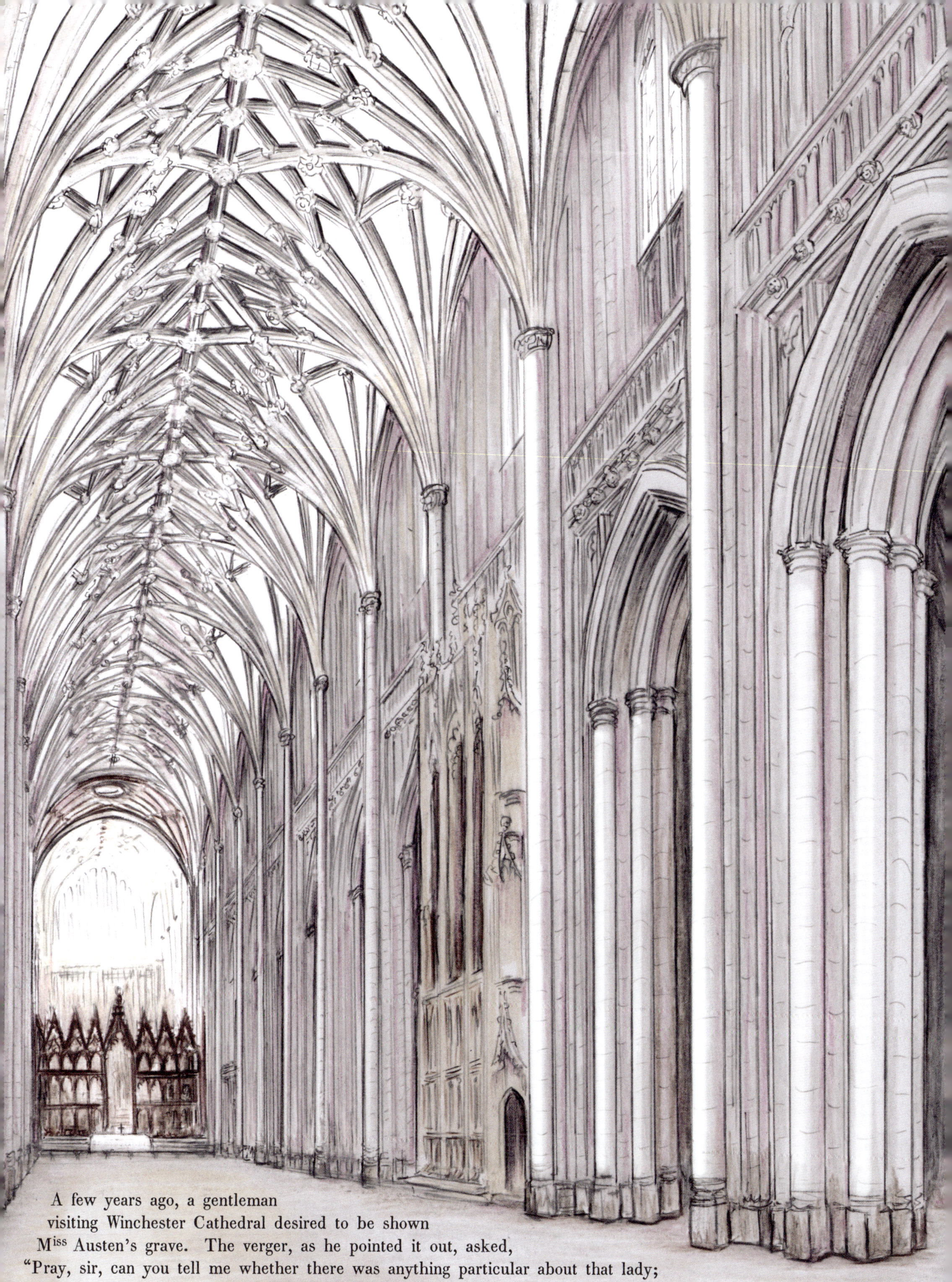

A few years ago, a gentleman visiting Winchester Cathedral desired to be shown Miss Austen's grave. The verger, as he pointed it out, asked, "Pray, sir, can you tell me whether there was anything particular about that lady; so many people want to know where she was buried?"

NOTES

The Austen patchwork coverlet still exists and is on display at Jane Austen's House, a museum and centre of Austen scholarship at Chawton Cottage, Hampshire. It is a coverlet, rather than a quilt, because it only contains two layers of fabric, the patchwork top and a linen backing – there is no layer of wadding in the middle. It was historically referred to as Mrs Austen's because that's who it belonged to, but we know that Jane worked on it and was instrumental in its creation from a reference she makes in a letter to Cassandra:

> Have you remembered to collect peices for the Patchwork? — We are now at a stand still.
> Letter No.74, May 1811, p. 190.

The materials of the coverlet are spread throughout this graphic novel as an artistic metaphor. In reality, many of the red and blue fabrics would only just have become available in 1811, as they utilised the latest lapis printing techniques for combining mordants and dyes.

If you want to recreate Jane Austen's quilt yourself, then Riley Blake Designs produce an authentic reproduction quilt kit. It includes preprinted panels which spare the maker the labour of stitching together the thousands of tiny diamonds which make up the borders. Some of the fabrics used in the collage sections of this book are reproductions of the actual cloth from the Austen coverlet, also available from Riley Blake Designs.

BIRTH

page 1

Anna LeFroy drew three sketches of Steventon rectory which show contradictory indications of the size, number and style of windows. An archaeological excavation of the Steventon site in 2012 confirmed that the larger version of the house is the more accurate one. Comparison of this with LeFroy's sketch of the back of the house confirms that it had a mansard roof. One of Anne's sketches shows the house with casement windows, and the other shows sash panes. She must have been drawing from memory to be so inconsistent. But maybe the house had both? In *Emma*, Frank Churchill describes the house where Jane Fairfax lives as:

> a brick house, sashed windows below, and casements above *Emma*, Chapter 50, p. 409.

Could this be a description of Steventon Rectory?

The house was demolished in 1824. If you visit Steventon nowadays, all that remains is part of the old water pump in a field. The farmer keeps bulls there to stop us Austen maniacs from trampling all over it.

page 2

Mr Austen writes to his sister:

> Cassy certainly expected to have been brought to bed a month ago; however, last night the time came, and without a great deal of warning, everything was soon happily over. We have now another girl, a present plaything for her sister Cassy, and a future companion. She is to be Jenny ... Your sister, thank God, is pure well after it.
> *Life and Letters*, p. 23.

page 3

Chintz bed robes and bed furnishings were extremely fashionable in the eighteenth century. The Calico Acts had made import of Indian printed cottons illegal between 1700 and 1774 — this did not make them less desirable, but meant that they were primarily used in the bed chamber, a private sphere.

CONGREGATION

page 5

Steventon church is open to the public. There is a wall safe for donations to its upkeep next to the font. The box pews were mostly removed in the nineteenth century, but the largest "Squire's pew" reserved for Steventon's first family, the Digweeds, has been saved and relocated to the back of the church where it is used as a vestry.

The opening Collect and the christening service are taken from the *1662 Book of Common Prayer*.

> Mary behaved very well, and was not at all fidgetty. Letter No.18, Jan 1799, p. 38.

page 7

> such a superfluity of children, and such a want of almost everything else *Mansfield Park*, Chapter 1, p. 6.

page 8

> the joyful surprise that lighted up their faces, and displayed itself over their whole bodies, in a variety of capers and frisks, was the first pleasing earnest of their welcome.
> *Pride & Prejudice*, Chapter 47, p. 271.

Fellow Austen nerds will be delighted to see my depiction of willow pattern china, evidence of which was found at the Steventon rectory archeological dig. Specialists in Staffordshire pottery might be annoyed, however, given that that Spode only started mass producing the design in 1784, and the events here are from 1776. Oh well. They look pretty. This is what the footnotes are for.

LITTLE WORTH

page 11

Mrs Austen, writing about Cassandra:
> I suckled my little Girl thro' the first quarter; she has been wean'd and settled at a good Woman's at Dean just Eight weeks
> *Family Record*, p. 26.

Lizzy Littleworth was older than my representation of her suggests, but I wanted to show her as vibrant and attractive as an embodiment of the attachment that she would have engendered in the Austen babies. Littleworth represents the fundamental disruption visited upon generations of upper-class children who were primarily maternally attached to women of a different class (and in many cases, race), and who were subsequently taught to despise the object of that maternal bond.

Austen makes no reference to Dame Littleworth in her letters, but she does in her fiction:
> Some of the objects of [Frank Churchill's] curiosity spoke very amiable feelings ... on recollecting that an old woman who had nursed him was still living, [he] walked in quest of her cottage from one end of the street to the other
> *Emma*, Chapter 24, p. 185.

I read the entire *Glossary of Hampshire Words and Phrases*, compiled in 1883 by the Reverend Sir William Cope, searching for terms of endearment. The nearest I could find was "chuffy", meaning "broad faced, healthy". There were, however, multiple words for "hit". So either rural Hampshire was a very violent and unloving place, or Victorian men should not be allowed to compile dictionaries.

page 12

Austen would originally have spoken in Hampshire dialect. In a poem about her brother Frank as a small child she describes him in the nursery saying, "Bet, my be not come to bide" ("Bet, maybe come and stay here," asking his nurse to stay with him). Letter No. 69, p. 177.

Jane's nephew James Edward claimed that:
> the infant was daily visited by one or both of its parents, and frequently brought to them at the house, but the cottage was its home, and must have remained so till it was old enough to run about and talk. *Memoir*, p. 30.

But this account is directly contradicted by the fact that both Mr and Mrs Austen were in London visiting Philadelphia Hancock in the summer of 1776 when she learned of Saul Tysoe Hancock's death (*Family Record*, p. 36). Whatever the frequency or intensity of the visits, Mrs Austen's parenting practices resulted in a lack of attachment between her and her children. Mr Austen comments that the little ones "bear their mother's absence with great philosophy" (*Austen Papers*, p. 24). They don't seem to care whether their mother is present.

SCHOOL HOUSE

page 17

In a private joke to her family, Jane has the odious General Tilney perfectly describe Steventon Parsonage:
> I believe there are few country parsonages in England half so good. It may admit of improvement, however. Far be it from me to say otherwise; and anything in reason — a bow thrown out, perhaps — though, between ourselves, if there is one thing more than another

my aversion, it is a patched-on bow.
Northanger Abbey, Chapter 26, p. 199.

It's fun spotting private jokes in Austen's works. Given that Mr Austen, James, and Edward have undershot jaws, here is another one:

> Sir Walter ... did justice to his very gentlemanlike appearance, his air of elegance and fashion, his good shaped face, his sensible eye; but, at the same time, "must lament his being very much under-hung," *Persuasion*, Chapter 15, p. 131.

Tithes were a tax on produce payable by everyone (whether you were an Anglican Christian or not) to the local parish. Originally paid in physical goods, such as wool, grain, or timber, and stored in a tithe barn — see page 22 — monetary payments were gradually being substituted. The phrase "ten percent tithes" is an oxymoron: "tithe" means ten percent.

> "The manners I speak of might rather be called conduct, perhaps, the result of good principles; the effect, in short, of those doctrines which it is their duty to teach and recommend"
> *Mansfield Park*, Chapter 9, p. 88.

Not much evidence exists of George Austen's views on meritocracy, but he

does write to Frank, when his son goes off to sea:

> With your inferiors perhaps you will have but little intercourse, but when it does occur there is a sort of kindness they have a claim on you for, and which, you may believe me, will not be thrown away on them   *Sailor Brothers*, p. 18.

which suggests a kindly paternalism towards "the lower orders" and not much awareness that Frank is about to be sharing a 137-foot sailing ship with at least 250 common sailors.

> we took a quiet walk round the farm, with George and Henry to animate us by their races and merriment. Letter No.45, Aug 1805, p. 107.

> the magistrates, and overseers, and churchwardens, are always wanting his opinion.
> *Emma*, Chapter 52, p. 426.

page 18

Country estates and grand houses were self-sufficient farming enterprises, an aspect of Regency life that doesn't often make it into modern period dramas, but is well-reflected in Austen's novels. Grand General Tilney reports with satisfaction on the number of pineapples he grows, and the happy ending of *Sense & Sensibility* is delineated with the words:

> Elinor and her husband ... one of the happiest couples in the world ... had in fact nothing to wish for, but ... rather better pasturage for their cows.
> *Sense & Sensibility*, Chapter 50, p. 348.

Mrs Austen wrote "My flesh is much warmer, my blood freer flows/ When I work in the garden with rakes & with hoes" as part of her "Poem to rhyme with Rose," Selwyn, p. 21.

James was accepted into St John's College, Oxford at the precocious age of fourteen. This wasn't such a remarkable academic achievment since he qualified automatically for his place through Mrs Austen being a direct descendant of the original Founder of the College.

Fowle's speech should, of course, read "dolorem ipsum, quia dolor sit amet consectetur adipiscing velit, sed quia non numquam do eius modi tempora incididunt." Fowle is slurring his words. It's almost like the words are just there to fill up space on the page.

page 19

the sons, who, at seventeen and sixteen, and tall

of their age, had all the grandeur of men in the eyes of their little cousin.
Mansfield Park, Chapter 2, p. 13.

she had nothing worse to endure on the part of Tom than that sort of merriment which a young man of seventeen will always think fair with a child of ten. He was just entering into life, full of spirits, and with all the liberal dispositions of an eldest son, who feels born only for expense and enjoyment. *Mansfield Park*, Chapter 2, p. 18.

There is an authenticity and naturalness to Austen's recreation of male discourse which must have come from growing up in a predominantly male household.

"only see how he moves; that horse cannot go less than ten miles an hour: tie his legs and he will get on. What do you think of my gig, Miss Morland? ... Curricle-hung, you see; seat, trunk, sword-case, splashing-board, lamps, silver moulding, all you see complete"
Northanger Abbey, Chapter 7, pp. 45–6.

As the proud owner of a copy of *A Treatise on Carriages* by William Felton, I can confirm that this is an accurate representation of a curricle-hung, chair-back gig with a sword case. It takes a bit of research to learn the differences between Regency carriages, phaetons, landaus, chaises and gigs, but it is fun re-reading the books with that knowledge, because it enables you to visualise what Austen is writing rather than mentally skipping those parts. They are as significant to the Regency readership as cars are in the modern day.

Her ... daughters were inevitably left to shift for themselves *Northanger Abbey*, Chapter 1, p. 17.

page 20

Frank's little hunting outfit survives and is on display at Chawton House. Frank really was nicknamed Fly, his pony was called Squirrel, and the older boys did tease him by calling it Scug. He sold it at a profit when he outgrew it (*Life and Letters*, p. 23). There is no record of the name of Edward's pony.

There are references to needlework, or "work," throughout Austen's writings. Once you recognise them, you will spot them everywhere. Yet I have never seen any dramatic realisation on the screen of the fact that the characters in Austen's novels are continuously creating clothing, carpets and accessories.

She sat intently at work, striving to be composed, and without daring to lift up her eyes
Pride & Prejudice, Chapter 56, p. 316.

The netting-box, just leisurely drawn forth, was closed with joyful haste, and she was ready to attend him in a moment.
Northanger Abbey, Chapter 22, p. 167.

[Lady Bertram's] time had been irreproachably spent during his absence: she had done a great deal of carpet-work, and made many yards of fringe. *Mansfield Park*, Chapter 19, p. 167.

"Good God!" she cried. – "Well!" – Then having recourse to her workbasket, in excuse for leaning down her face, and concealing all the exquisite feelings of delight *Emma*, Chapter 54, p. 441.

"My dear Catherine ... I do not know when poor Richard's cravats would be done, if he had no friend but you."
Northanger Abbey, Chapter 30, p. 224.

Jane did not stitch the phrase "I wish I had done" onto her sampler, but she did doodle it on the inside cover of her French dictionary, together with the poignant phrase "Mothers angry Fathers gone out" (Worsley, p. 58).

She was fond of all boy's plays ... it was not very wonderful that Catherine ... should prefer cricket, base ball ... and running about the country *Northanger Abbey*, Chapter 1, pp. 15–17.

While Austen indicates, in *Northanger Abbey*, that girls could be inattentive and disengaged from the work that was expected of them, it's also important to note that needlework was both economically important, and women's central creative outlet. Austen created beautiful whitework embroidery, and had special glasses, in her later life, to better see the tiny stitches.

page 21

she was ... noisy and wild, hated confinement and cleanliness, and loved nothing so well in the world as rolling down the green slope at the back of the house.
Northanger Abbey, Chapter 1, p. 16.

pages 22–5

Dame Bushell washes for us only one week more Letter No.10, Oct 1798, p. 17.

Wash day was a big event. The Austens would hire extra servants for the day. Laundry was done only about once

every six weeks (though let's hope that people washed some things by hand in between times).

> Cassandra ... described to me her return to Steventon one fine summer evening ... my Grandfather had to go, I think as far as Andover to meet her — He might have conveyed himself by Coach, but he brought his Daughter home in a Hack chaise ... they met Jane & Charles, the two little ones of the family, who had got as far as New down to meet the chaise.
> Recollection of Anna LeFroy, *Memoir*, p. 160.

page 26

> the girls were ranging over the town and making what acquaintance they chose
> *Sense & Sensibility*, Chapter 31, p. 197.

> "You want to tell me, and I have no objection to hearing it." *Pride & Prejudice*, Chapter 1, p. 5.

> "my youngest is not sixteen. Perhaps she is full young to be much in company."
> *Pride & Prejudice*, Chapter 29, p. 162.

> when the elder was sent to [school] the younger went with her, not because she was thought old enough to profit much by the instruction there imparted, but because she would have been miserable without her sister; her mother observing that "if Cassandra were going to have her head cut off, Jane would insist on sharing her fate." *Memoir*, p. 12.

There is no direct evidence of corporal punishment at Mrs Cawley's school, a contemporary source describes her as "stiff-mannered" rather than cruel (Boardman, p. 201). However, English people in the eighteenth century were astonishingly casual about physical violence by modern standards, so it is more likely that pupils at the school were beaten than not. Jane writes jovially:

> Little Edward was breeched yesterday for good and all [transitioned into trousers from skirts] and was whipped into the bargain.
> Letter No.5, Sep 1796, p. 8.

page 27

Typhus, also known at the time as "Camp fever," is spread via the human body louse when people live in close quarters. There was little understanding of the vectors of disease transmission, which were generally thought to be caused by miasmas — bad smells — in the air.

Were she well enough to travel, Mrs Austen would certainly have viewed her sister's body. Regency people were not squeamish about death in this regard. Jane asks Cassandra, after the sudden death of their sister-in-law:

> "I suppose you see the Corpse? How does it appear?" Letter No.59, Oct 1808, p. 147.

page 28

> Mrs. Goddard was the mistress of a School ... a real, honest, old-fashioned Boarding-school, where a reasonable quantity of accomplishments were sold at a reasonable price, and where girls might be sent to be out of the way, and scramble themselves into a little education, without any danger of coming back prodigies. Mrs. Goddard's school was in high repute — and very deservedly; for Highbury was reckoned a particularly healthy spot: she ... gave the children plenty of wholesome food, let them run about a great deal in the summer, and in winter dressed their chilblains with her own hands. *Emma*, Chapter 3, pp. 22–3.

> Anne had gone unhappy to school, grieving for the loss of a mother whom she had dearly loved, feeling her separation from home, and suffering as a girl of fourteen, of strong sensibility and not high spirits, must suffer at such a time;
> *Persuasion*, Chapter 17, p. 143.

What is become of all the Shyness in the World? ... Our little visitor ... is a nice, natural, open-hearted, affectionate girl ... so unlike anything that I was myself at her age
Letter No.50, Feb 1807, p. 120.

"I never wish to offend, but I am so foolishly shy" *Sense & Sensibility*, Chapter 17, p. 93.

so great was her agitation in finding herself as one of the family, and so fearful was she of not doing exactly what was right
Northanger Abbey, Chapter 20, p. 147.

The living in incessant noise was, to a frame and temper delicate and nervous like Fanny's, an evil. *Mansfield Park*, Chapter 39, p. 363.

London was not the place for her. She could not endure its noise. Her nerves were under continual irritation and suffering
Emma, Chapter 37, p. 297.

an agitation of mind
Northanger Abbey, Chapter 30, p. 231.

She treated her therefore, with all the indulgent fondness of a parent towards a favourite child on the last day of its holidays. Marianne was to have the best place by the fire, was to be tempted to eat by every delicacy in the house
Sense & Sensibility, Chapter 30, p. 183.

The eggcup in the picture was excavated in the Steventon Rectory archaeological dig.

page 30

The quotes from Mrs and Mr Austen are from *Family Record*, pp. 23–4.

There are no portraits of George Austen Jr. This is a fictionalised representation of him as having Fragile X syndrome, because it is the commonest heritable cause of epilepsy and intellectual disability. His face and ears are not "too long" and "too large" — the ableist language here is reflective of Mrs Austen's discriminatory attitudes. George's facial features are perfect and right for him.

Whatever George's disability, he was left on a farm in Monk Sherborne with Mrs Austen's brother, who was similiarly incapacitated. He died in 1838 at the age of seventy-two and his death certificate lists him as "a gentleman." Nobody attended his funeral except his caregiver. Mrs Austen even forgot to include him in her will.

Austen's intriguing reference to her command of sign language is contained in a letter of 1808:

> Mr. Fitzhugh ... poor Man! is so totally deaf that they say he c^d not hear a Cannon, were it fired close to him; having no cannon at hand to make the experiment, I took it for granted, & talked to him a little with my fingers, which was funny enough. I recommended him to read Corinna.
> Letter No.63, Dec 1808, pp. 160–1.

EFFUSIONS OF FANCY BY A VERY YOUNG LADY IN A STYLE ENTIRELY NEW

page 31

Rev. George Austen pencilled the words "Effusions of Fancy by a very Young Lady consisting of Tales in a Style entirely new" inside the front cover of Jane Austen's third notebook volume of *Juvenilia*, 6th May 1792.

The books represent Austen's literary foremothers and contemporaries. They would not have been single volume editions; this is an artistic representation.

pages 32–3

"Without a governess, you must have been neglected."
"Compared with some families, I believe we were; but such of us as wished to learn never wanted the means. We were always encouraged to read, and had all the masters that were necessary. Those who chose to be idle certainly might."
Pride & Prejudice, Chapter 29, p. 161.

"Give him a book, and he will read all day long."
"He will sit poring over his book, and not know when a person speaks to him"
Persuasion, Chapter 14, p. 124.

They found Mr. Bennet still up. With a book, he was regardless of time;

Pride & Prejudice, Chapter 3, p. 14.

she ... mentioned such works of our best moralists, such collections of the finest letters, such memoirs of characters of worth and suffering, as occurred to her at the moment as calculated to rouse and fortify the mind by the highest precepts, and the strongest examples of moral and religious endurances.

Persuasion, Chapter 11, p. 94.

Let us leave it to the reviewers to abuse ... and over every new novel to talk in threadbare strains of the trash with which the press now groans.

Northanger Abbey, Chapter 5, p. 38.

"Miss Morland has been talking of nothing more dreadful than a new publication which is shortly to come out, in three duodecimo volumes, two hundred and seventy-six pages in each, with a frontispiece to the first, of two tombstones and a lantern – do you understand?"

Northanger Abbey, Chapter 14, p. 108.

a book was produced; but on beholding it (for everything announced it to be from a circulating library) he started back, and, begging pardon, protested that he never read novels.

Pride & Prejudice, Chapter 14, p. 67.

The eighteenth century moral panic about novel-reading seem hilarious today, when children are actively encouraged to read novels rather than spend time on screens. Quotes are edited from Vogorinčić, pp. 104 and 113.

Caroline Austen remembers her aunt reading aloud:

I knew her take up a volume of *Evelina* and read a few pages of Mr. Smith and the Brangtons and I thought it was like a play. She had a very good speaking voice.

Memoir, p. 174.

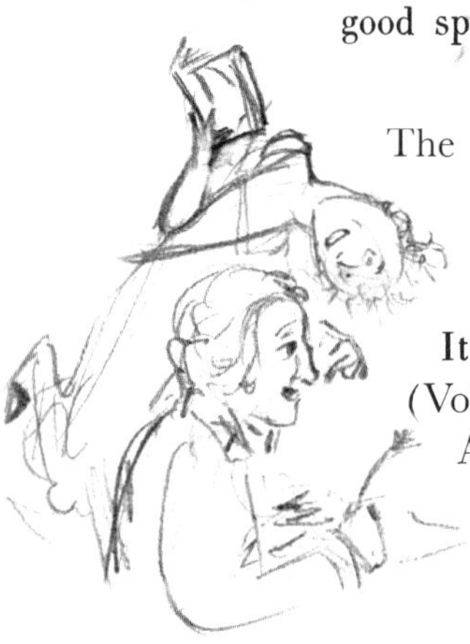

The quotes from *Evelina*, by Fanny Burney, are: **a country parson's daughter** (Vol I, Letter XII, p. 37). **It seems time to declare it** (Vol I, Letter XXXI, p. 132.) **A sister who is most warmly** (Vol III, Letter XVI, p. 363). **Motherless, fatherless** (edited) (Vol II, Letter XIX, p. 219). **Such haughtiness** (Vol II, Letter XV, p. 200). **The height to which thou** (edited) (Vol III, Letter XXII, p. 405). **Wretched adventurer** (edited) (Vol III, Letter XVI, p. 363). **Live upon learning** (paraphrased) (Vol II, Letter XI p. 177). **His person is all elegance** (edited) (Vol I, Letter XII, p. 37). **You don't know no more of the world than if you was a baby** (Vol II, Letter XIII, p. 245).

[Mrs Austen] was amusingly particular about people's noses, having a very aristocratic one herself. Anne LeFroy, *Homes & Friends*, p. 120.

the bride's "going away" dress seems to have been a scarlet riding habit. *Life and Letters*, p. 10.

"I have formed my plan, and am determined to enter on a course of serious study."

Sense & Sensibility, Chapter 46, p. 320.

page 34

Jane explores her Aunt Phila's situation in her Juvenilia:

"do you call it lucky, for a Girl of Genius and Feeling to be sent in quest of a Husband to Bengal, to be married there to a Man of whose Disposition she has not opportunity of judging till her Judgement is of no use to her, who may be a Tyrant, or a Fool or both."

"Catherine, or the Bower," *Love and Freindship*, p. 225.

We know for certain that Warren Hastings was Eliza's godfather, and that he bequeathed her £10,000 (more than a million pounds in 2020's money). Robert Clive, Governor-General of Bengal wrote to his wife in 1765:

In no circumstances whatever keep company with Mrs. Hancock for it is beyond a doubt that she abandoned herself to Mr. Hastings, indeed, I would rather you had no acquaintance with the ladies who have been in India, they stand in such little esteem in England that their company cannot be of credit to Lady Clive

Outlandish Cousin, pp. 19–20.

Whether this claim is true, whether it is slander, and whether Clive (a deeply unpleasant man) is endeavouring here to limit and control his wife's acquaintance by fair means or foul, is all a subject of conjecture. In later life, Eliza was keen to emphasise her close connections with Warren Hastings, and in Joshua Reynolds' two portraits of the Hancock family and Warren Hastings, young Eliza looks more like Hastings than Hancock. But, on the other hand, Eliza's legal father, Saul Tysoe Hancock was a devoted, active father figure, Hasting's continued friend and business partner, and Hasting's recorded generosity does make it possible that he could have gifted money to his god-daughter whether or not she was his biological child.

It seems unlikely, if Eliza was illegitimate, that Jane would have been made aware of the fact.

"Hancock constantly sent home to Philadelphia supplies of the Indian foods she had grown to like during her sojourn there — a bag of leaves for curries, pickled mangoes, pickled limes, chillies, balychongspice and cassoondy sauce — together with as much of her favourite scent as he could acquire, the precious attar of roses from Patna or Echharabad. He also maintained a supply of fine Indian fabric — soosy quilts and palampores for bed-linen, and seersuckers, sannow, doreas, muslin, dimity, atlas, Maida silks, chintz and flowered shawl ... He procured silks from Cossimbazar and silk handkerchiefs from Pullicat ... [He] reminded Philadelphia to see that Betsy had the best masters available to teach her writing, arithmetic, music and dancing, that she should have a Kirkman harpsichord to play and a pony to ride, and that she should also learn French" (*Family Record*, pp. 34–5).

page 35

The following quotes are all from Eliza's letters:

> We were a few days ago at Versailles ... The Queen is a very fine woman, she has a most beautiful complexion, & is indeed exceedingly handsome Ibid. p. 37.

> Every Body now goes to Longchamps not to say their Prayers but to shew their fine Cloaths & fine Equipages Ibid. p. 39.

> I gave you some account of the Globes or Ballons in my last ... M. Blanchard had ... the courage ... to set out alone for the aerial regions; he ascended to the height of 1500 fathoms & returned from thence in perfect health & safety to the astonishment of most of the spectators.
> Ibid. p. 39.

> I have without doubt already mentioned to You a Donation made by the King to Mons. de Feuillide & his heirs for ever, of 5000 Acres of Land little distant from his Paternal Estate
> Ibid. p. 40.

> It is too little to say he loves me, since he literally adores me; entirely devoted to me, & making my inclinations the guide of all his actions, the whole study of his life seems to be to contribute to the happiness of mine. Ibid. p. 38.

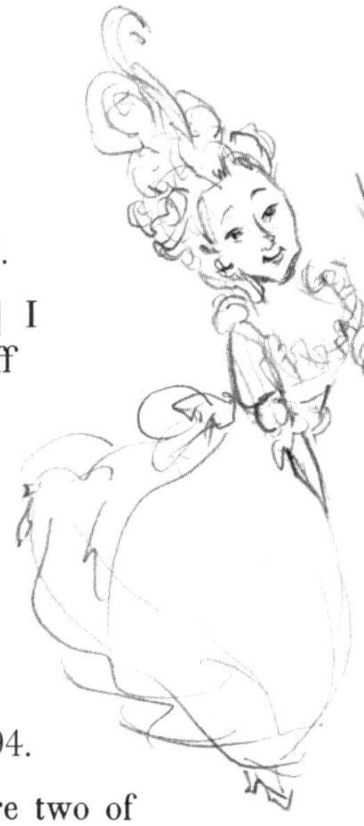

> [writing when newly-married] I have of course entirely left off *trade* but I can however discover that Captn Tilson is remarkably handsome.
> *Outlandish Cousin*, p. 154.

> I [shall] tell You all the wonderful endowments of my wonderful Brat. Ibid. p. 94.

> I hear her Sister & herself are two of the prettiest girls in England. Ibid. p. 108.

> Henry is now rather more than Six Foot high I believe, He is also much improved, and is certainly endowed with uncommon Abilities
> Ibid. p. 116.

page 36

> a love of the theatre is so general, an itch for acting so strong among young people
> *Mansfield Park*, Chapter 13, p. 113.

> "We must have a curtain," said Tom Bertram; "a few yards of green baize for a curtain, and perhaps that may be enough."
> *Mansfield Park*, Chapter 13, pp. 115–6.

Eliza's cousin Phylla Walters writes in September 1787:

> They go at Xmas to Steventon and mean to act a play *Which is the Man?* and *Bon Ton*. My uncle's barn is fitting up quite like a theatre and all the young folks take their part. The Countess [Eliza] is Lady Bob Lardoon in the former and Miss Tittup in the latter.
> *Outlandish Cousin*, pp. 80–81.

Bon Ton, or High Life Below Stairs, is a play by David Garrick, from which Miss Tittup's quote is verbatim. *Which is the Man?* is by Hannah Cowley.

page 37

Quotes from Suzanne Centlivre's *The Wonder: a Woman Keeps a Secret*. It's terrible. I read it so you don't have to.

> Everybody around her was gay and busy, prosperous and important; each had their object of interest, their part, their dress, their favourite scene *Mansfield Park*, Chapter 17, p. 147.

James's speech is paraphrased from the epilogue to The Sultan, which the Steventon party performed the following year. I changed the third person narration to direct speech (*poetrynook.com/poem/epilogue-sultan*).

Mrs Austen on James:
> Classical Knowledge, Literary Taste, and the power of Elegant Composition he possessd in the highest degree. *Family Record*, p. 53.

page 38

Edited from "Henry and Eliza: A Novel," *Minor Works*, pp. 36–7. The chronology of Jane's juvenilia is rearranged in this chapter for artistic effect.

> every raw girl while she reads, is tempted to fancy that she can also write. More, p. 170.

page 39

> The evening conversation, when they were all assembled, had lost much of its animation, and almost all its sense, by the absence of Jane and Elizabeth. *Pride & Prejudice*, Chapter 12, p. 59.

> The subject of reading aloud was farther discussed ... giving instances of blunders, and failures ... the want of management of the voice, of proper modulation and emphasis, of foresight and judgment ...
> "how little the art of reading has been studied! how little a clear manner, and good delivery, have been attended to!"
> *Mansfield Park*, Chapter 34, p. 314.

The quotes about Miss Dickins and Charles Adams are from "Jack and Alice," *Minor Works*, pages 17 and 22–3.

page 40

> "Nonsensical girl!" was his reply, but not at all in anger. *Emma*, Chapter 26, p. 200.

The Henry Austen bank demand is from the dedication to "Lesley Castle." Henry probably jokingly drafted it to Jane rather than the other way around (*Minor Works*, p. 110).

> The History of England from the reign of Henry the 4th to the death of Charles the 1st By a partial, prejudiced, and ignorant Historian.
> N.B There will be very few Dates in this History.
> *Love and Freindship*, p. 151.

Cassandra was an accomplished watercolourist and drew various members of the Austen family into Jane's History of England. Queen Mary is almost certainly Cassandra 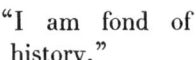 — it has the "what do I look like?" expression common in self portraits. Mrs Austen is Queen Elizabeth and Jane is Mary Queen of Scots. Charles and Henry also make an appearance (*Love and Freindship*, pp. 159–60.)

> "I am fond of history."
> "I wish I were too. I read it a little as a duty, but it tells me nothing that does not either vex or weary me. The quarrels of popes and kings, with wars or pestilences, in every page; the men all so good for nothing, and hardly any women at all — it is very tiresome: and yet I often think it odd that it should be so dull, for a great deal of it must be invention ... and invention is what delights me in other books."
> *Northanger Abbey*, Chapter 14, p. 104.

page 41

The quote about "insipid Vanities" is from "Love and Freindship: a novel in a series of letters," *Minor Works*, pp. 78–9. I changed "idle Dissipations" to "idle Debaucheries" because we have a scene of "Dissipation & vice" further down the page.

The trip to Sevenoaks was in July 1788. Mr Francis Motley Austen's house is the Red House.

Cousin Phylla Walters writes:
> The younger is ... not at all pretty & very prim, unlike a girl of twelve. *Family Record*, p. 64.

> she had heard that Miss Darcy was exceedingly proud; but the observation of a very few minutes convinced her that she was only exceedingly shy. She found it difficult to obtain even a word from her beyond a monosyllable.
> *Pride & Prejudice*, Chapter 44, p. 249.

> Here I am once more in this scene of Dissipation & vice, and I begin already to find my Morals corrupted. Letter No.3, Aug 1796, p. 5.

The speech "Madam, you are a Phoenix" is the dedication at the beginning of "The Beautifull Cassandra" (*Minor Works*, p. 44).

pages 42–3

This is very nearly the entire text of "The Beautifull Cassandra," Austen's most anarchic, subversive and succinct work (*Minor Works*, pp. 44–7).

page 44

Jane is reading from the *Lady's Magazine*, May 1789, p. 274. My dad bought the 1789 bound edition years ago because he knew the Austens took it and he was curious about the reportage of the French Revolution that Jane would have read. It's in there.

Eliza writes:
> my spouse, who is a strong Aristocrate or Royalist in his heart, has joined this latter party ... now at Turin where the French Princes of the Blood are assembled and watching some favourable opportunity to reinstate themselves in the country they have quitted. I am no politician, but think they will not easily accomplish their purpose; time alone can decide this matter, and in the interim you will easily imagine I cannot be wholly unconcerned about events.
> *Life and Letters*, p. 42.

> my son and Heir who promises to be as great a pickle as any who ever deserved that appellation
> *Outlandish Cousin*, p. 102.

> he has not the least of the greediness and Love of Dainties which children usually shew, and will absolutely offer his half muncht apples or cakes to the whole company altho' I have remonstrated on the impropriety of the proceeding.   Ibid. p. 95.

This confrontation between Mrs Austen and Eliza is invented. I extrapolated it from the circumstances.

Eliza writes:
> this said Son of mine is ... most exceedingly good tempered and I do not think he will ever be either Alderman or Lord Mayor as he has not the least of the greediness.   Ibid. pp. 94–5.

> To crown all his accomplishments I have taught him to say Cousin – Philly is rather too difficult but I trust it will be attempted in Time.   Ibid. p. 95.

> The Sea has strengthened him wonderfully & I think has likewise been of great service to myself.   Ibid. p. 99.

pages 45–6

This is the complete text of Austen's play *The Mystery*, a surrealist piece, with a very modern feel. It would have been composed to be played at Steventon as part of the family theatricals. Edward is unlikely to have been part of the production, but the chance to cast him as Sir Edward Spangle was too good to miss (*Love and Freindship*, pp. 62–4).

page 48

It was a tradition of the time amongst the super-rich to commission a new carriage for one's wedding day. Fans of the snobbish Mrs Elton will be delighted to know that this is a barouche-landau.

Because I save all the best bits for the Notes for you all, here is Eliza, wrtiting about her mother's illness:
> considerable portions of the swelling are now continually detaching themselves, whether this change is for the better or the worse I am too ignorant to determine, but yet I cannot help but hope the whole of the Tumour will thus be removed in time ... My Mothers spirits are surprisingly good ... She is able to leave off the Laudanum   *Outlandish Cousin*, p. 107.

Eliza writes of Henry:
> You know that his Family design him for the Church.   Ibid. p. 116.

Edmund's situation in *Sense & Sensibility* is the inverse of Henry's:
> I always preferred the church, as I still do. But that was not smart enough for my family. They recommended the army. That was a great deal too smart for me.
> *Sense & Sensibility*, Chapter 19, p. 100.

> "what is to be done in the church? Men love to distinguish themselves, and in either of the other lines distinction may be gained, but not in the church. A clergyman is nothing." ... said she, with an arch smile; "I am just as much surprised now as I was at first that you should intend to take orders. You really are fit for something better. Come, do change your mind. It is not too late. Go into the law."
> *Mansfield Park*, Chapter 9, pp. 86–88.

page 49

Jane comments on the superiority of Cassandra's handwriting:
> why is my alphabet so much more sprawly than yours?   Letter No.10, Oct 1798, p. 17.

Jane's doodled names were discovered at the front of the

Steventon marriage register. They have been preserved in the Hampshire Archives.

> They were of a respectable family in the north of England; a circumstance more deeply impressed on their memories than that their brother's fortune and their own had been acquired by trade. *Pride & Prejudice*, Chapter 4, p. 17.

COMING OUT

page 51

> Miss Crawford [was] supposing Fanny was now preparing for her appearance, as of course she would come out when her cousin was married.
> *Mansfield Park*, Chapter 15, p. 137.

> "A girl not out has always the same sort of dress: a close bonnet, for instance; looks very demure, and never says a word."
> *Mansfield Park*, Chapter 5, p. 46.

> she lay awake ten minutes on Wednesday night debating between her spotted and her tamboured muslin. *Northanger Abbey*, Chapter 10, p. 71.

> I cannot determine what to do about my new gown; I wish such things were to be bought ready-made ... I want to have something suggested which will give me no trouble of thought or direction. Letter No.15, Dec 1798, p. 29.

Did Jane and Cassandra make their own clothes? Given that the words "gown" and "shift" were used interchangeably to refer both to the unmade cloth and the finished garment, the historical record is murky. There are details in Jane's letters of them making their own garments:

> I beleive I shall make my new gown like my robe, but the back of the latter is all in a piece with the tail, and will 7 yards enable me to copy it in that respect? Letter No.14, Dec 1798, p. 27.

> [Martha] is pleased with my Gown, & particularly bids me say that if you could see me in it for five minutes, she is sure you would be eager to make up your own. Letter No.28, Nov 1800, p. 65.

> I believe I put five breadths of linsey also into my flounce; Letter No.51, Feb 1807, p. 123.

And also of their employing others:

> I have got over the dreadful epocha of Mantuamaking much better than I expected. My Gown is made very much like my blue one, which you always told me sat very well
> Letter No.17, Jan 1799, p. 33.

> Miss Summers has made my gown very well indeed, & I grow more and more pleased with it.
> Letter No.27, Nov 1800, p. 61.

> Mrs. Mussell has got my gown, and I will endeavour to explain what her intentions are
> Letter No. 35, May 1801, p. 83.

They definitely make shirts for their brothers:

> When you come home you will have some shirts to make up for Charles. Mrs. Davies frightened him into buying a piece of Irish when we were in Basingstoke. Letter No.18, Jan 1799, p. 38.

> I have heard from Charles, & am to send his shirts by half-dozens as they are finished; — one sett will go next week. Letter No.24, Nov 1800, p. 53.

Jane suggests that she doesn't sew enough:

> I wish I *could* help you in your Needle-work. I have two hands and a new Thimble that lead a very easy life. Letter No.63, Dec 1808, p. 159.

And, occasionally, the men sew too:

> William will be quite recovered, I trust, by the time you receive this. What a comfort his cross-stitch must have been! Pray tell him that I should like to see his work very much.
> Letter No.64, Jan 1809, p. 163.

> Frank has got a very bad cough for an Austen, but it does not disable him from making very nice fringe for the drawing-room curtains.
> Letter No.51, Feb 1807, p. 123.

> I make no apologies for my Heroine's vanity. — If there are young Ladies in the World at her time of Life, more dull of Fancy & more careless of pleasing, I know them not, & never wish to know them. *Sanditon*, p. 395.

page 52

Jane's debut was made at a private ball at Enham House (*Family Record*, p. 78). She subsequently attended regular balls at Basingstoke Assembly Rooms.

> in a very few minutes, the party were transported from the quiet and warmth of a snug parlour to the bustle, noise, & draughts of air of the broad Entrance-passage of an inn. — Mrs Edwards, carefully guarding her own dress, while she

attended with yet greater Solicitude to the proper security of her young Charges' Shoulders and Throats, led the way up the wide staircase
The Watsons, p. 327.

The party passed on. Mrs E's sattin gown swept along the clean floor of the Ball-room to the fireplace at the upper end *The Watsons*, p. 327.

They ... heard their names announced from one landing-place to another in an audible voice, and entered a room splendidly lit up, quite full of company *Sense & Sensibility*, Chapter 28, p. 166.

continual accessions of portly Chaperons & strings of smartly-dressed girls were received, with now & then a fresh gentleman straggler
The Watsons, p. 327.

Anne LeFroy, who was a talented writer herself, seems to have been a second mother to Jane. She died from a fall from a runaway horse on Jane's twenty-ninth birthday. Four years later, Jane was still so grief-stricken as to compose a long set of verses in her memory.

Mrs. Gardiner ... was an amiable, intelligent, elegant woman, and a great favourite with her Longbourn nieces. Between the two eldest and herself especially, there subsisted a very particular regard.
Pride & Prejudice, Chapter 25, p. 137.

page 53

Jane Austen loved dancing:
In cold weather & with few couples I fancy I could just as well dance for a week together as for half an hour. Letter No.15, Dec 1798, pp. 29–30.

she bounded higher than ever, flew farther down the middle, and was in a continual course of smiles. *Emma*, Chapter 38, p. 307.

a general spirit of ease and enjoyment seemed diffused, and they all stood about and talked and laughed, and every moment had its pleasure and its hope.
Mansfield Park, Chapter 28, p. 252.

I am very glad You liked my lace, & so are You, & so is Martha, — & we are all glad together.
Letter No.21, Jun 1799, p. 45.

pursued by the ceaseless country-dance, feverish with hopes and fears, soup and negus, sore-footed and fatigued, restless and agitated, yet feeling, in spite of everything, that a ball was indeed delightful. *Mansfield Park*, Chapter 28, p. 259.

page 54

That the Miss Lucases and the Miss Bennets should meet to talk over a ball was absolutely necessary; and the morning after the assembly brought the former to Longbourn to hear and to communicate. *Pride & Prejudice*, Chapter 5, p. 19.

the morning afforded her an opportunity of talking over Thursday night ... with all the heightenings of imagination, and all the laughs of playfulness which are so essential to the shade of a departed ball *Mansfield Park*, Chapter 29, pp. 261–2.

There were twenty Dances, & I danced them all, and without any fatigue.
Letter No.15, Dec 1798, pp. 29–30.

Instances of people sending their Best Love and their Best Regards abound in Austen's letters. Servants also send their Best Duty.

"The profession, either navy or army, is its own justification. It has everything in its favour: heroism, danger, bustle, fashion."
Mansfield Park, Chapter 11, p. 101.

It was next to impossible that their cousin should come in a scarlet coat, and it was now some weeks since they had received pleasure from the society of a man in any other colour.
Pride & Prejudice, Chapter 13, p. 63.

Annoyingly, Cassandra's picture of Henry in "A History of England" shows him in a blue coat, not a red one, but I was not prepared to let the truth get in the way of a *Pride & Prejudice* reference.

Now that you are become an Aunt, you are a person of some consequence & must excite great Interest whatever you do. I have always maintained the importance of Aunts as much as possible, & I am sure of your doing the same now. Letter No.123, Oct 1815, p. 294.

Notes to pages 55–6

Austen's useful advice to her nieces is from her "Letter from a Young Lady" (*Love and Freindship*, p. 194). She is parodying the sensational, true-life, *Confessions of the Countess of Strathmore* published earlier in the year.

page 55

> Sir Thomas had the pleasure of receiving, in his protégé, certainly a very different person ... a young man   *Mansfield Park*, Chapter 24, p. 216.

> William ... complete in his lieutenant's uniform, looking and moving all the taller, firmer, and more graceful for it
> *Mansfield Park*, Chapter 38, p. 356.

> Young as he was, William had already seen a great deal ... and in the course of seven years had known every variety of danger which sea and war together could offer. With such means in his power he had a right to be listened to;
> *Mansfield Park*, Chapter 24, p. 218.

> We had not been six hours in the Sound, when a gale came on, which lasted four days and night   *Persuasion*, Chapter 8, p. 61.

Eliza writes:
> The last day of my Liberty, mind I do not say Widowhood, I spent at Mr Hampson's, when Mrs Stevenson & myself did our best to entertain eleven beaux   *Outlandish Cousin*. p. 132.

Eliza, writing about herself in the third person:
> you may preach to herself and rehearse all the wise things ... concerning the dangers of flirtation ... but She will have her own way, and I am more & more convinced that she is not at all calculated for sober Matrimony.   Ibid. p. 142.

"Several suitors" is speculation, but we know that she refused Henry and her letters suggest that she refused James. She has ten thousand pounds. There will have been other offers.

> she was the happiest creature in the world. "'Tis too much!" she added, "by far too much. I do not deserve it. Oh, why is not everybody as happy?" ... [He] claimed the good wishes and affection of a sister.
> *Pride & Prejudice*, Chapter 55, pp. 327–8.

> "He has only two thousand pounds of his own; it would be madness to marry upon that ... We must wait, it may be for many years"
> *Sense & Sensibility*, Chapter 24, p. 141.

> [I] have had A Weakness in my Eyes [and] I could not now make petticoats, Pockets & dressing Gowns for any Bride expectant
> Letter No.103, July 1814, p. 266.

page 56

There has been a lot of hype over Austen's romance with Tom LeFroy: a largely fictionalised romantic movie has been constructed from just a few lighthearted references in Jane's letters. LeFroy, who went on to become Lord Chief Justice of Ireland, confessed in old age to having felt a "boyish love" for Jane, but he married "an Irish lady who ... had the convenience of money" soon after their brief dalliance (*Family Record*, p. 278). For Jane's part, if there had been anything particularly serious about her feelings for Tom, Cassandra would have burned those letters.

> [the] celebration of that festival which requires a more than ordinary share of private balls and large dinners to proclaim its importance.
> *Sense & Sensibility*, Chapter 25, p. 145.

> He ... if not quite handsome, was very near it ... Catherine felt herself in high luck.
> *Northanger Abbey*, Chapter 3, p. 24.

> With what sparkling eyes and ready motion she granted his request
> *Northanger Abbey*, Chapter 10, pp. 72–3.

> I am almost afraid to tell you how my Irish friend and I behaved. Imagine to yourself everything most profligate and shocking in the way of dancing and sitting down together ... he has but one fault, which time will, I trust, entirely remove – it is that his morning coat is a great deal too light.
> Letter No.1, Jan 1796, pp. 1–2.

listening with sparkling eyes to everything he said; and, in finding him irresistible, becoming so herself. *Northanger Abbey*, Chapter 16, p. 125.

A handsome young fellow like him, will go smirking & smiling about & paying girls compliments, but he knows he must marry for Money.
Sanditon, p. 400.

"I would have you be on your guard. Do not involve yourself, or endeavour to involve him, in an affection which the want of fortune would make so very imprudent ... if he had the fortune he ought to have, I should think you could not do better. But as it is — you must not let your fancy run away with you."
Pride & Prejudice, Chapter 26, p. 142.

"It had better have happened to you, Lizzy; you would have laughed yourself out of it sooner"
Pride & Prejudice, Chapter 25, pp. 138–9.

I mean to confine myself in future to Mr. Tom Lefroy, for whom I don't care sixpence.
Letter No.2, Jan 1796, p. 4.

page 57

At length the day is come on which I am to flirt my last with Tom Lefroy, & when you receive this it will be over. My tears flow as I write at the melancholy idea. Letter No.2, Jan 1796, p. 4.

"handsome young men must have something to live on as well as the plain."
Pride & Prejudice, Chpt 26, p. 148.

Her heart had been but slightly touched, and her vanity was satisfied with believing that she would have been his only choice, had fortune permitted it. The sudden acquisition of ten thousand pounds was the most remarkable charm of the young lady to whom he was now rendering himself agreeable; but Elizabeth ... did not quarrel with him for his wish of independence.
Pride & Prejudice, Chapter 26, p. 147.

"a girl likes to be crossed in love a little now and then. It ... gives her a sort of distinction among her companions." *Pride & Prejudice*, Chapter 24, p. 135.

"I am quite enough in love. I should be sorry to be more." *Emma*, Chapter 31, p. 245.

It was an English Christmas tradition to save an ember of the yule log to light the following year's fire.

Mrs Austen writes to Mary Lloyd:
I look forwards to you as a real comfort to me in my old age, when Cassandra is gone to Shropshire & Jane — the Lord knows where.
Family Record, p. 99.

Jane writes to Cassandra:
By this time therefore they are at Barbadoes I suppose. *Family Record*, p. 91.

Tom Fowle is private chaplain to Lord Craven, Colonel of the 3rd Foot. They are travelling to the West Indies to suppress uprisings by enslaved people (*Family Record*, p. 91). He died in February 1797. The Austens learned of his death in May of that year.

I WRITE ONLY FOR FAME

page 59

I am very much flattered by your commendation of my last Letter, for I write only for Fame, and without any view to pecuniary Emolument.
Letter No.2, Jan 1796, p. 3.

The Georgian version of Ugg boots were list shoes, made from the offcut selvedges from woven woollen cloth and lined with thick baize. Austen refers to them in Letter 66, Jan 1809, p. 170.

The laptop writing desk was a nineteenth birthday present from her loving and supportive father. There is a record of his having bought "a Small Mahogany Writing Desk with 1 Long Drawer and Glass Ink Stand Compleat" on 5th December 1794 (*Family Record*, p. 89). It is now in the British Library.

"Oh! It is only a novel!" replies the young lady, while she lays down her book with affected indifference, or momentary shame. "It is only Cecilia, or Camilla, or Belinda"; or, in short, only some work in which the greatest powers of the mind are displayed, in which the most thorough knowledge of human nature, the happiest delineation of its varieties, the liveliest effusions of wit and humour, are conveyed to the world in the best-chosen language.
Northanger Abbey, Chapter 5, pp. 36–7.

Lady Susan isn't particularly good, and is a useful example of how extremely talented people require time and opportunity to practice their craft before their full potential can emerge. Interestingly, Austen creates a powerfully evil female central character who never once departs

Notes to pages 60–3

from the conventional dictates of propriety, critiquing the ideal of the virtuous heroine.

Quotes are from Letter 25, *Love and Freindship*, p. 317 and Letter 16, *Love and Freindship*, p. 289. The conclusion was composed in 1803 when Austen made a fair copy of the story.

pages 60–1

> "I did not know before," continued Bingley, immediately, "that you were a studier of character. It must be an amusing study."
> "Yes; but intricate characters are the most amusing. They have at least that advantage."
> "The country," said Darcy, "can in general supply but few subjects for such a study. In a country neighbourhood you move in a very confined and unvarying society."
> "But people themselves alter so much, that there is something new to be observed in them for ever." *Pride & Prejudice*, Chapter 9, p. 42.

Jane gives advice to her niece Anna on novel-writing:
> —You are now collecting your People delightfully, getting them exactly into such a spot as is the delight of my life; — 3 or 4 Families in a Country Village is the very thing to work on — & I hope you will write a great deal more, & make full use of them while they are so very favourably arranged.
> Letter No.107, Sept 1814, p. 275.

Professor Kathryn Sutherland has done some fascinating textual analysis of Austen's extant manuscripts. "When she reaches a point where her characters are in conversation, her hand runs smoothly, often without a pause, a mistake, a slip or correction" (*British Library film: Jane Austen's manuscripts*).

> This brief account of the family is intended to supersede the necessity of a long and minute detail from Mrs. Thorpe herself, of her past adventures and sufferings, which might otherwise be expected to occupy the three or four following chapters; in which the worthlessness of lords and attorneys might be set forth, and conversations, which had passed twenty years before, be minutely repeated.
> *Northanger Abbey*, Chapter 3, p. 33.

The chronology around Austen's rewrite is more complicated. She wrote *Elinor and Marianne* in epistolary form in 1795, then wrote *First Impressions* (*Pride & Prejudice*), and

after that, in November 1797, went back and reworked it into a third person narrative.

The quote about John Dashwood being ill-disposed is from Chapter 1, p. 7. The references to Elinor's self-governance are gleaned from Chapter 1, p. 8 and Chapter 19, p. 101. The dialogue between John and his wife is edited from Chapter 2, pp. 11–14; the dramatic opening chapter. The accomplished nature of the prose suggests that it was rewritten when Austen later revised the work for publication, while living at Chawton Cottage. Reading this, and the various pointed references to shoddy cottage accomodation, as Jane's commentary on the actions of Edward and Elizabeth Austen-Knight gives the work extra bite.

page 63

Edward doesn't actually know that Mrs Knight is about to make over the estate to him the following year. But he does shortly inherit it.

> for every body must now "move in a Circle", — to the prevalence of which rototory Motion, is perhaps to be attributed the Giddiness & false steps of many. *Sanditon*, p. 422.

Mrs Knight would have met Jane before, but this is the probable start date of her patronage of Austen's writing.

Eliza writes:
> both Mrs James & Mrs Edward Austen are in the encreasing way. *Outlandish Cousin*, p. 118.

> I have taken little George once in my arms since I have been here, which I thought very kind.
> Letter No.4, Sep 1796, p. 6.

Austen's attitude to childcare changes over time. Her representation of the terrors of small children in *Sense & Sensibility* mellows into much more personal and engaged relations with the young nieces and nephews in *Emma*.

Susannah Sackree was a valued member of the Austen-Knight household. Her portrait was painted, wearing a valuable lace cap and collar, and now hangs at Chawton House. She is presumably the inspiration for Sarah, the Musgrove's nursery-maid, in *Persuasion*.

pages 64–5

The opening quote and Bennets's speech are edited from *Pride & Prejudice*, Chapter 1 pp. 5–7. Lizzy Bennet's words to Mr Darcy are edited from Chapter 18, p. 90 and Chapter 34, p. 188. His reply is from Chapter 58, pp. 347–8.

pages 66–7

Jane lends the manuscript of *First Impressions* to friends and family for repeated re-reading. She writes to Cassandra, with heavy sarcasm:

> I do not wonder at your wanting to read *First Impressions* again, so seldom as you have gone through it, and that so long ago.
> Letter No.17, Jan 1799, p. 35.

> I would not let Martha read *First Impressions* again upon any account, & am very glad that I did not leave it in your power. — She is very cunning, but I saw through her design; — she means to publish it from Memory, & one more perusal must enable her to do it.
> Letter No.21, Jun 1799, p. 44.

The quote "I hope I never ridicule what is wise or good" is from Chapter 11, p. 56, and the Lydia references are from Chapter 9, p. 45, Chapter 39, pp. 212–3, Chapter 41, p. 223, Chapter 47, pp. 276–7 and Chapter 51, p. 298.

Lydia's fictional flirting: "she saw herself ... tenderly flirting with at least six officers at once" (*Pride & Prejudice*, Chapter 41, p. 22) tallies very closely with Cousin Eliza's real-life adventures: "Mrs Stevenson & myself did our best to entertain eleven beaux " (*Outlandish Cousin*. p. 132).

Elizabeth is Austen's most straightforwardly self-assured heroine: Emma Woodhouse has more self-confidence, but it is misplaced. Elizabeth Bennet's confrontation with lady Catherine is edited from Chapter 56, pp. 334–5 with added capitalisation for dramatic emphasis.

page 68

Mr Austen's letter is reproduced in *Family Record*, p. 104.

> There is to be a ball at Basingstoke next Thursday. Our assemblies have very kindly declined ever since we laid down the carriage, so that dis-convenience and dis-inclination to go have kept pace together.   Letter No.1, Jan 1796, p. 20.

Jane's speech about not being very much in request is from Letter No.17, Jan 1799, p. 35.

page 69

Jane made several trips to Bath with various family members, which are conflated in this representation. Cassandra would have been in mourning for Tom for the second half of 1797, which I have not included here because it looks incongruous at Assembly Room balls and Sydney Gardens galas.

Jane is mindful of the the Leigh-Perrots' parsimony and the expense of feeding her and her sister:

> I do not know how to give up the idea of our both going to Paragon in May [The Bath address of the Leigh-Perrots]. Your going I consider as indispensably necessary, and I shall not like being left behind ... and though, to be sure, the keep of two will be more than of one, I will endeavour to make the difference less by disordering my stomach with Bath buns.
> Letter No.29, Jan 1801, p. 67.

> Frank whose black head was in waiting at the hall window, received us very kindly.
> Letter No.35, May 1801, p. 81.

Some commentators have taken this reference to mean that Frank had black hair, rather than that he was Black. Firstly, there is no other reference to any aspect of the physical appearance of a servant in all Jane's letters, so Frank's "black"ness was remarkable. And secondly, c'mon, Mrs Leigh-Perrot, or Jane Cholmley to give her her maiden name, is a West Indian enslaver. We can surmise that when she came over to England to be married she would brought the enslaved child Frank with her as her page boy, and he would have been her adult manservant by this time. I drew him younger to highlight the fact that Black children were once a fashion accessory and that child labour was ubiquitous.

page 70

> No place in England ... affords so brilliant a circle of polite company as Bath. The young, the old, the grave, the gay, the infirm, and the healthy all resort to this place of amusement.
> *New Bath Guide*, Worsley p. 177.

> They arrived at Bath. Catherine was all eager delight ... She was come to be happy, and she felt happy already. *Northanger Abbey*, Chapter 2, p. 20.

> "Bath is a charming place, sir; there are so many

good shops here ... one can step out of doors and get a thing in five minutes."
Northanger Abbey, Chapter 3, p. 28.

I saw some gauzes in a shop in Bath Street yesterday at only 4d. a yard ... My aunt has told me of a very cheap [shop], near Walcot Church,
Letter No.20, Jun 1799, p. 42.

There is a reference to Aunt Leigh-Perrot's love of money in Jane's letters:

> My Aunt is in a great hurry to pay me for my Cap, but cannot find in her heart to give me good money.   Letter No.44, April 1805, p. 103.

> their gowns look so white and so nice (which, by the bye, my aunt thinks an absurd pretension in this place)   Letter No.37, May 1801, p. 88.

> When my uncle went to take his second glass of water I walked with him
> Letter No. 35, May 1801, p. 83.

The ball would have been at the Lower Rooms, because Mr King was Master of Ceremonies there until 1805. My illustration shows the Upper Rooms, because the Lower Rooms were destroyed by fire in 1820 and so there are no reference photos. Sue me.

> The season was full, the room crowded, and the two ladies squeezed in as well as they could ... With more care for the safety of her new gown than for the comfort of her protégée, Mrs. Allen made her way through the throng of men by the door, as swiftly as the necessary caution would allow; Catherine, however, kept close at her side, and linked her arm too firmly within her friend's to be torn asunder by any common effort of a struggling assembly. But to her utter amazement she found that to proceed along the room was by no means the way to disengage themselves from the crowd; it seemed rather to increase as they went on, whereas she had imagined that when once fairly within the door, they should easily find seats and be able to watch the dances with perfect convenience. But this was far from being the case, and though by unwearied diligence they gained even the top of the room, their situation was just the same; they saw nothing of the dancers but the high feathers of some of the ladies.   *Northanger Abbey*, Chapter 2, p. 21.

page 71

It would be very pleasant to be near Sidney Gardens! — we might go into the Labyrinth every day.   Letter No.32, Jan 1801, p. 76.

There is to be a grand gala on Tuesday evening in Sidney Gardens ... the concert will have more than its usual charm for me, as the gardens are large enough for me to get pretty well beyond the reach of its sound.   Letter No.20, Jun 1799, p. 43.

Last night we were in Sidney Gardens again ... in very good time for the Fire-works, which were really beautiful   Letter No.22, Jun 1799, p. 47.

> "...Castle of Wolfenbach, Clermont, Mysterious Warnings, Necromancer of the Black Forest, Midnight Bell, Orphan of the Rhine, and Horrid Mysteries. Those will last us some time."
> "Yes, pretty well; but are they all horrid, are you sure they are all horrid?"
> *Northanger Abbey*, Chapter 6, p. 39.

page 72

"The hurricane was howling" is the opening line to *The Necromancer of the Black Forest* by Karl Friedrich Kahlert, translated by Peter Teuthold, 1794.

Austen makes multiple references to solitude and the need for breaks from social interaction:

> an agitation of mind which many solitary hours were required to compose
> *Northanger Abbey*, Chapter 30, p. 231.

> "I am worn out with civility," said he. "I have been talking incessantly all night, and with nothing to say. But with you, Fanny, there may be peace. You will not want to be talked to. Let us have the luxury of silence."
> *Mansfield Park*, Chapter 28, p. 257.

Some more quotes from Eliza's letters:

> Hastings ... is putting the Map of England together and sticks Kent close to Durham, because he says that his two best friends live in those Countries — Have I told you that I have begun teaching him to write and that he regularly comes to school to me every day, for that & French & English reading
> *Outlandish Cousin*, p. 135.

> I have consented to an Union with my Cousin, Captain Austen ... He has been for some time in Possession of a comfortable income, and the excellence of his Heart, Temper and Understanding, together with steady attachment to me, his Affection for my little Boy ... have at

length induced me to an acquiescence which I have withheld for more than two years.
Outlandish Cousin, p. 151.

all the Comfort which can result from the tender Affection & Society of a Being who is possessed of an excellent Heart, Understanding, & Temper I have at least ensured — to say nothing of the pleasure of having my own way in every thing, for Henry well knows that I have not been much accustomed to controul and should probably behave rather awkwardly under it
Outlandish Cousin, p. 152.

I have an aversion to the word Husband & never make use of it   *Outlandish Cousin*, p. 155.

pages 73–7

Henry Tilney's appreciation of muslin comes from *Northanger Abbey*, Chapter 3, p. 28. The spooky adventures on the following three pages are from Chapter 21, pp. 158–162, and Chapter 22, pp. 163–4; the original name of the heroine "Susan" has been reinstated in place of Austen's later substitution "Catherine" and the words "the next morning" added. The quotes illustrating Austen's authorial voice are edited from Chapter 1, p. 16 and Chapter 31, p. 233.

Mrs LEIGH-PERROT BUYS SOME LACE

page 79

> Witness [Gregory] went across to them and addressing herself to Mrs. Leigh-Perrot, said "Pray ma'am have not you a card of white lace as well as black?" — Mrs. Leigh Perrot answered, "No, I have not a bit of white lace about me." — Witness then said to her, "See in your pocket ma'am." Mrs. Leigh Perrot then took out her arm from under her cloak and gave a paper parcel to Witness, saying "If I have your young man must have put it up in mistake."   *Gye*, p. 2.

Mrs Leigh-Perrot left the shop and then visited the Post Office before returning and passing Smiths where she was confronted by Gregory. The shop was on Stall Street, not, as my picture shows, in the Abbey churchyard.

page 80

Mrs Leigh-Perrot writes:
> The Mayor and magistrates, to whom we were well known, lamented their being obliged to commit me [but] to prison I was sent. *Honan*, p. 150.

> Vulgarity, Dirt, Noise from Morning till Night. The People, not conscious that this can be Objectionable to anybody, fancy we are very happy, and to do them justice they mean to make us quite so ... this Room joins to a Room where the Children all lie, and not Bedlam itself can be half so noisy, besides which, as not one particle of Smoke goes up the Chimney, except you leave the door or window open, I leave you to judge of the Comfort I can enjoy in such a Room ... No! my Good Cousin, I cannot subject even a Servant to the suffering we daily experience ... My dearest Perrot, Cleanliness has ever been his greatest delight and yet he sees the greasy toast laid by the dirty Children on his Knees, and feels the small Beer trickle down his sleeves on its way across the table unmoved ... Mrs. Scadding's knife well licked to clean it from fried onions helps me now and then — you may believe how the Mess I am helped to is disposed of — here are two dogs and three Cats always full as hungry as myself.   *Family Record*, p. 121.

page 81

> She made an affecting address to the Judge and Jury: "Placed in a situation the most eligible that any woman could desire, with supplies so ample that I was left rich after every wish was gratified, blessed in the affection of the most generous man as a husband, what could induce me to commit such a crime?"
> *Reading Mercury*, 19th March 1892.

These are Mrs Leigh-Perrot's words, not the judge's.

The case has been made that Leigh-Perrot was the innocent victim of a plot by the shopkeepers to blackmail her. This is a prominent shop on the main thoroughfare in Bath, and for the shopkeepers to be in the habit of planting items into people's parcels makes dubious

Notes to pages 83–5

financial sense. Her own barrister, Joseph Jekyll, thought she was guilty. He subsequently wrote:

> Mrs. L.P [and other ladies] frequent bazaars and mistake other people's property for their own. It was the blunder of my client, Mrs Leigh Perrot.
> *Honan*, p. 150.

Pamphlets about the trial were published by J. W. Myers, and William Gye. There is no evidence of balladeers singing about Mrs Leigh-Perrot, I invented that, but songs and printed ballad sheets were a common form of working-class commentary on contemporary events.

EXILE

page 83

> Anne had been too little from home, too little seen. Her spirits were not high. A larger society would improve them. She wanted her to be more known. *Persuasion*, Chapter 2, p. 15.

> Anne Elliot had been a very pretty girl, but her bloom had vanished early *Persuasion*, Chapter 1, p. 7.

Mrs Austen planned the move in consultation with Mary, James's wife, and announced it to Jane when she returned from a visit with the words: "Well, girls, it is all settled, we have decided to leave Steventon in such a week and go to Bath" (*Family Record*, p. 128).

> The brown Mare, which, as well as the black, was to devolve on James at our removal, has not had patience to wait for that, and has settled herself even now at Deane ... & everything else I suppose will be seized by degrees in the same manner. Letter No.30, Jan 1801, pp. 71–2.

> The whole world is in a conspiracy to enrich one part of our family at the expense of another.
> Letter No.37, May 1801, p. 88.

> "Of all horrid things, leave-taking is the worst."
> *Emma*, Chapter 30, p. 241.

page 84

The Austens lodged at first with the Leigh-Perrots and took the lease of 4 Sydney Place at the end of the summer of 1801. They moved to 27 Green Park Buildings in January 1805.

> [Mr and Mrs Austen] seemed to enjoy the cheerfulness of their Town life, and especially perhaps the rest which their advancing years entitled them to. *Family Record*, p. 136.

> It was sad to Fanny to lose all the pleasures of spring. She had not known before what pleasures she had to lose in passing March and April in a town. She had not known before how much the beginnings and progress of vegetation had delighted her. What animation, both of body and mind, she had derived from watching the advance of that season which cannot, in spite of its capriciousness, be unlovely, and seeing its increasing beauties from the earliest flowers in the warmest divisions of her aunt's garden, to the opening of leaves of her uncle's plantations, and the glory of his woods. To be losing such pleasures was no trifle; to be losing them, because she was in the midst of closeness and noise, to have confinement, bad air, bad smells, substituted for liberty, freshness, fragrance, and verdure, was infinitely worse.
> *Mansfield Park*, Chapter 45, pp. 400–1.

> She sighed for the air, the liberty, the quiet of the country; *Sense & Sensibility*, Chapter 39, p. 261.

> the sun's rays falling strongly into the parlour, instead of cheering, made her still more melancholy, for sunshine appeared to her a totally different thing in a town and in the country. Here, its power was only a glare: a stifling, sickly glare, serving but to bring forward stains and dirt that might otherwise have slept. There was neither health nor gaiety in sunshine in a town. *Mansfield Park*, Chapter 46, p. 408.

> When first we came, all the umbrellas were up, but now the pavements are getting very white again Letter No.19, May 1799, p. 41.

> he was not in spirits. The whole family perceived it. *Sense & Sensibility*, Chapter 17, p. 89.

page 85

> the elegant stupidity of private parties
> *Persuasion*, Chapter 19, p. 169.

> I was as civil to them as their bad breath would allow me Letter No.27, Nov 1800, p. 61.

> We are to have a tiny party here to-night. I hate tiny parties — they force one into constant exertion. Letter No.37, May 1801, p. 88.

> There was a monstrous deal of stupid quizzing, & common-place nonsense talked, but scarcely any Wit; Letter No.44, April 1805, p. 104.

> his usual nothing-meaning, harmless, heartless civility. Letter No.70, April 1811, p. 179.

> Another stupid party last night; perhaps if larger they might be less intolerable, but here there were only just enough to make one card-table, with six people to look on & talk nonsense to each other ... I cannot anyhow continue to find people agreable
>
> Letter No.36, May 1801, pp. 85–6.

page 86

> the object of all, was to captivate some Man of much better fortune than their own. *Sanditon*, p. 421.

> He had, by that time, realised an easy competence ... enough to marry a woman as portionless even as Miss Taylor *Emma*, Chapter 2 p. 17.

There is a popular conception of Cassandra as some kind of nun, who remained unmarried because she foreswore any other romantic interest after the death of Tom Fowle. But this is a post hoc rationalisation. These passages about openness to subsequent romantic encounters in *The Watsons*, written during the Austen sisters' time in Bath, speak directly to Cassandra's situation. We don't know that they reflect Cassandra's views, but they certainly contain Jane's analysis of Cassandra's options:

> "A heart wounded like yours can have little inclination for matrimony."
> "Not much indeed — but you know we must marry. — I could do very well single for my own part — A little Company, & a pleasant Ball now & then, would be enough for me, if one could be young forever; but my Father cannot provide for us, & it is very bad to grow old & be poor & laughed at. I have lost Purvis, it is true; but very few people marry their first loves. I should not refuse a man because he was not Purvis."
>
> *The Watsons*, p. 317

> I should not like marrying a disagreeable man any more than yourself; — but I do not think there are many very disagreeable men; — I think I could like any good-humoured Man with a comfortable Income." *The Watsons*, p. 318.

page 87

I am libelling Mrs Austen again. The phrase "desirable release" was written to Eliza by her cousin Phila, and alluded to in Eliza's reply:

> an event which though, as You justly consider it, a desirable release has greatly affected my spirits. So awful a dissolution of a near & tender tie must ever be a severe shock *Outlandish Cousin* p. 159.

Regarding unaccompanied travel, public stagecoaches would trap a woman in a confined space for many hours with men she had never met before, in a period with no police force, when rape was endemic. The inns and coachouses where journeys were broken up facilitated drunkenness and sex work. There was the additional risk of highway robbery. Catherine Morland's being forced to leave *Northanger Abbey* unaccompanied is a genuinely perilous moment of novelistic drama.

The prohibition on women travelling alone did not extend to servants. There are references in Austen's letters and her novels of maids being sent by public transport:

> "It will only be sending Betty by the coach, and I hope I can afford *that*. We three shall be able to go very well in my chaise."
>
> *Sense & Sensibility*, Chapter 26, p. 146.

page 88

I followed the tradition of Austen novels and skipped the words used in Bigg Wither's proposal. Austen's reluctance to include details in her novels which she doesn't have direct experience of extends to her avoiding, wherever possible, writing the words of imaginary successful proposals and acceptances. This is a remarkable shortcoming in a writer of romances.

> marriage ... was the only honourable provision for well-educated young women of small fortune, and, however uncertain of giving happiness, must be their pleasantest preservative from want.
>
> *Pride & Prejudice*, Chapter 22, p. 120.

> "This is a connexion which offers nothing but good. It will give you every thing that you want — consideration, independence, a proper home"
>
> *Emma*, Chapter 9, p. 72.

> at that moment she felt that to be mistress of Pemberley might be something!
>
> *Pride & Prejudice*, Chapter 43, p. 235.

Jane, advising Fanny Knight about love:

> Anything is be preferred or endured rather than

marrying without Affection *Family Record*, p. 219.

nothing can be compared to the misery of being bound without Love
  Letter No.114, Nov 1814, pp. 285–6.

She was awake the whole night, and she wept the greatest part of it
  Sense & Sensibility, Chapter 16, p. 83.

many hours of the most wearing anxiety
  Sense & Sensibility, Chapter 45, p. 312.

"Mr Elliot is an exceedingly agreeable man, and in many respects I think highly of him," said Anne; "but we should not suit."
  Persuasion, Chapter 17, p. 150.

Mrs Austen's tirade is lifted, with the punctuation altered, from *Pride & Prejudice*, Chapter 20, p. 111.

"A woman of seven and twenty," said Marianne, after pausing a moment, "can never hope to feel or inspire affection again"
  Sense & Sensibility, Chapter 8, pp. 39–40.

page 89

his father, like every military man, had a very large acquaintance. *Northanger Abbey*, Chapter 12, p. 91.

Jane makes frequent sardonic references to the state of her mother's health in her letters:

> She is tolerably well — better upon the whole than she was some weeks ago. She would tell you herself that she has a very dreadful cold in her head at present; but I have not much compassion for colds in the head without fever or sore throat. Letter No.18, Jan 1799, p. 38.

> I left my Mother very well when I came away, & left her with strict orders to continue so.
> Letter No.28, Nov 1800, p. 64.

How can Mrs J. Austen be so provokingly ill-judging? — I should have expected better from her professed if not her real regard for my Mother. Now my Mother will be unwell again.
  Letter No.89, Sept 1813, p. 225.

Mr. Lyford ... recommended her to take twelve drops of Laudanum when she went to bed as a Composer, which she accordingly did.
  Letter No.10, Oct 1798, p. 16.

Miss Langley is like any other short girl, with a broad nose and wide mouth, fashionable dress and exposed bosom.
  Letter No.36, May 1801, pp. 85–6.

And so ends our friendship, for the Chamberlaynes leave Bath in a day or two.
  Letter No.38, May 1801, pp. 89–90.

page 90

The abandoned novel fragment is called *The Watsons*.

"Rub her hands, rub her temples; here are salts; take them, take them."
  Persuasion, Chapter 12, p. 102.

An illness of only eight & forty hours carried him off yesterday morning between ten & eleven ... he did not suffer ... The Serenity of the Corpse is most delightful! — It preserves the sweet, benevolent smile which always distinguished him.
  Letter No.41, Jan 1805, pp. 97–8.

Jane writes about her bereaved niece Fanny, upon the death of her mother: "we may hope that ... she will try to be tranquil and resigned" (Letter No.59, Oct 1808, p. 147). The prohibition on displaying emotion was so extreme that, on the same occasion, Jane writes to Cassandra: "We are anxious to be assured that E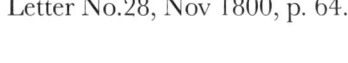dwd will not attend the funeral; but when it comes to the point I think he must feel it impossible" (Letter No.59, Oct 1808, p. 147). She is afraid that he will cry at his own wife's funeral.

My Mother ... feels all the blessing of his being spared a long Illness ... The loss of such a Parent must be felt, or we should be Brutes.
  Letter No.40, Jan 1805, pp. 95–6.

page 91

Edward pays £100 a year towards the Austen women's keep, Charles nothing and Henry, James and Frank £50 each. Edward sends his adoptive mother, Mrs Knight, an

annual allowance of £2,000 and he is happy supporting his mother and both sisters on a twentieth part of that between them. Given that James had previously been Mr Austen's curate, there is exactly the same amount of money in the Austen family after the death, but James keeps a far larger proportion of it.

Henry writes:
> She will be very comfortable, & as a smaller establishment will be as agreeable to them, as it cannot but be feasible, I really think that my Mother & Sisters will be to the full as rich as ever *Family Record*, p. 147.

James writes:
> I believe her summers will be spent in the country amongst her Relations & chiefly I trust among her children — the winters she will pass in comfortable lodgings in Bath.
>
> *Family Record*, p. 147.

> We are disappointed of the lodgings in St James' Square. A person is in treaty for the whole House so of course he will be prefer'd to us who want only a part.
>
> Letter from Mrs Austen, *Family Record*, p. 153.

> she will do everything in her power to avoid Trim Street Letter No.29, Jan 1801, pp. 66–7.

> "Obstinate, headstrong girl! I am ashamed of you!" *Pride & Prejudice*, Chapter 56, p. 336.

> That any bookseller should think it worthwhile to purchase what he did not think it worthwhile to publish seems extraordinary.
>
> "Advertisement by the Authoress"
> *Northanger Abbey*, p. 13.

> The more I see of the world the more am I dissatisfied with it; and every day confirms my belief of the inconsistency of all human characters, and of the little dependence that can be placed on the appearance of either merit or sense.
>
> *Pride & Prejudice*, Chapter 24, p. 133.

page 93

> It will be two years to-morrow since we left Bath for Clifton, with what happy feelings of escape! Letter No.55, June 1808, p. 138.

> the clouds cleared away, and we had a very bright *chrystal* afternoon. Letter No.9, Oct 1798, p. 15.

> The day was uncommonly lovely. It was really March; but it was April in its mild air, brisk soft wind, and bright sun, occasionally clouded for a minute; and everything looked so beautiful under the influence of such a sky, the effects of the shadows pursuing each other on the ships at Spithead and the island beyond, with the ever-varying hues of the sea, now at high water, dancing in its glee and dashing against the ramparts *Mansfield Park*, Chapter 42, p. 380.

> The party ... soon found themselves on the sea-shore; and lingering only, as all must linger and gaze on a first return to the sea, who ever deserved to look on it at all
>
> *Persuasion*, Chapter 11, pp. 89–90.

page 94

A Bathing machine was an enclosed chamber on wheels which was driven into the sea, providing a secure, private changing room for sea bathing and the supervision of a personal lifeguard (in this case, Molly, the Dipper). Jane describes sea bathing in her letter of September 1804: "The Bathing was so delightful this morning & Molly so pressing with me to enjoy myself that I believe I staid in rather too long" (Letter No.39, p. 95). Georgians were fans of the medicinal effects of all-weather sea bathing: in *Persuasion* Mary Musgrave is depicted bathing at Lyme in December, and Eliza writes: "I still continue bathing notwithstanding the severity of the Weather & Frost & Snow which is I think somewhat courageous" (*Outlandish Cousin* p. 99). I took some artistic licence with the bathing machines which were not yet painted like this.

page 97

> "they say every body is in love once in their lives"
> *Emma*, Chapter 31, p. 246.

> Stationing himself close by her, he seemed to mean to detach her as much as possible from the rest of the Party & to give her the whole of his Conversation. He began ... to talk of the Sea & the Sea shore ... The terrific Grandeur of the Ocean in a Storm, its glassy surface in a calm, it's Gulls & its Samphire, & the deep fathoms of it's Abysses, it's quick vicissitudes
>
> *Sanditon* p. 396.

> They praised the morning; gloried in the sea; sympathized in the delight of the fresh-feeling breeze — and were silent
>
> *Persuasion*, Chapter 12, p. 95.

Notes to pages 98–108

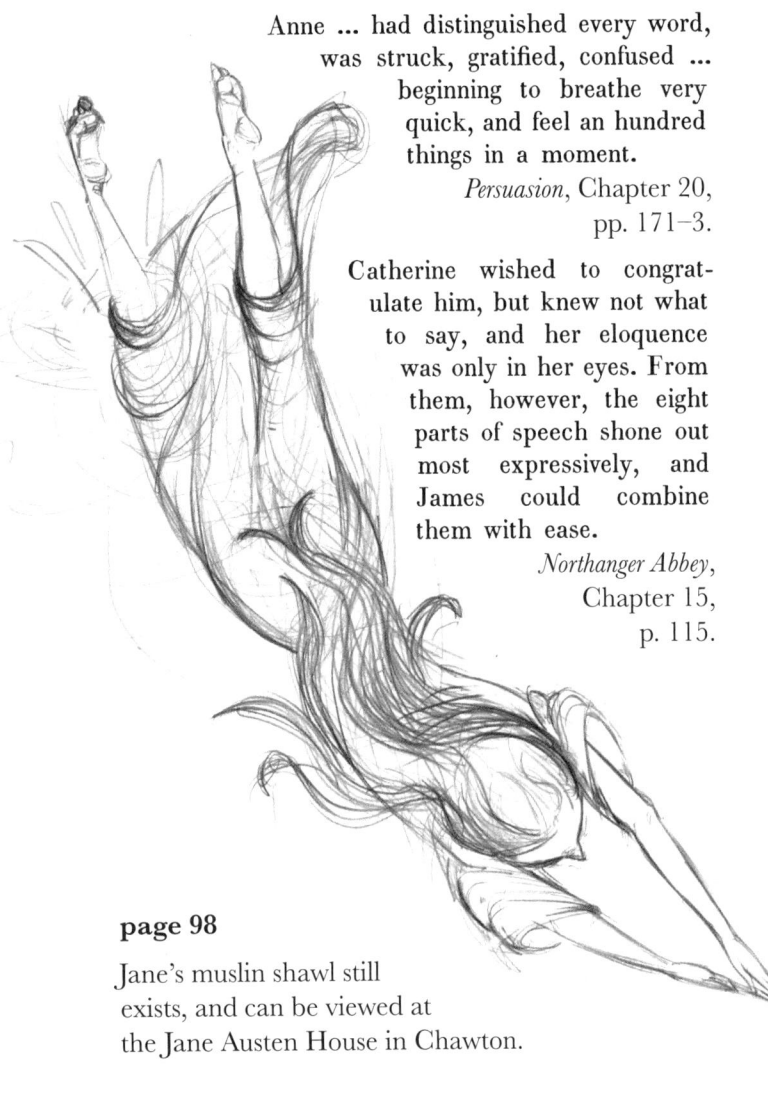

> Anne ... had distinguished every word, was struck, gratified, confused ... beginning to breathe very quick, and feel an hundred things in a moment.
>
> *Persuasion*, Chapter 20, pp. 171–3.

> Catherine wished to congratulate him, but knew not what to say, and her eloquence was only in her eyes. From them, however, the eight parts of speech shone out most expressively, and James could combine them with ease.
>
> *Northanger Abbey*, Chapter 15, p. 115.

page 98

Jane's muslin shawl still exists, and can be viewed at the Jane Austen House in Chawton.

MUSLIN

page 100

The songs in this section are sourced from Islam, p. 191.

A thread a third the thickness of a human hair would be the fabled 1200 count cotton thread, a pound of which stretched 250 miles. This was impractial to weave and most superfine muslins were in the 400 to 600 count range. Modern muslin cloth is forty to eighty count. Recent attempts to recreate Dhaka muslin with artisanal weavers has resulted in a 300 count piece.

page 101

The soft cotton bolls are combed ... collected ... stored... (Islam, p. 72) woven ... bleached ... (ibid. p. 82).

page 102

This is an artistic interpretation of an interaction between a Bengali artisan and an East India Company (EIC) agent. In reality, the Agent would have been an Indian intermediary, not a white British man: there were remarkably few British people in India co-ordinating company business. Military historians have informed me that my soldier can't have both the ammunition straps of an artillery man and the epaulettes of an officer, but I'm not about to unpick it.

Descriptions of Dhaka muslin: **like the light vapours of dawn** — Yuan Chwang, (629–45 CE) Chinese traveller visiting India, (ibid. p. 17). **The skin of the moon** — Abdul Hasan Yaminuddin Khusrow (1253–1325) (ibid. p. 21). **Webs of woven wind** — Roman author Petronius, (Beckert, p. 8). **Thought the work of fairies** (ibid. p. 8).

The pricing for the muslin was set two years in advance (Islam, p. 164). Nine regulatory acts restricting its sale, from 1775 to 1789, are listed in Islam, p. 157.

page 103

In addition to the taxes listed, the weavers were paid in a variety of currencies and then subject to punitive exchange rates. Some of these taxes were paid to the local zamindar or landowner, not directly to the EIC, but the Company had increased the duties payable by those zamindars who then passed them on to the weavers (ibid. p. 156).

At a conservative estimate, one in five Bengali people died in the famine of 1770: 1.2 million people. The area had always been vulnerable to intermittent crop failure, but previous Mughal administrators created grain stores and engaged in public relief works to alleviate the effects of famine. The East India Company did not. As well as diverting food supplies to the military, the EIC continued to collect taxes from the starving populace, in some cases increased them, and hanged people for non-payment. A report to Company directors in 1771 was able to boast:

> notwithstanding the great severity of the late famine, and the great reduction of people thereby, some increase [in revenue] has been made.
>
> Dalrymple, pp. 215–220.

According to a contemporary account in Gentleman's Magazine:

> As soon as the dryness of the season foretold the

approaching dearness of rice, our gentlemen in the Company's service, particularly those whose stations gave them the best opportunities, were as early as possible in buying up all they could lay hold of. *Ibid.* p. 220.

"Now there is no profit in weaving cloth" is from the song "Manikganj" by Saidur Rahman Boyati (b. 1931). It would not have been sung in 1809 but it is about events from that time.

Despite efforts to locate it in the wild, the plant *Gossypium arboreum var. Neglecta* now only exists as dried specimens in the collections of Victorian botanists. Some high-quality muslin continued to be woven until the 1870s. As can be seen from the time frame, the extinction of Dhaka muslin was not a direct result of the 1770 famine, but resulted from a combination of a heavy burden of direct taxation with unfair trade practices which made India into a captive market for exports of British mechanised cotton spinning and weaving.

CHINTZ

page 104

Seventy five per cent of East India Company exports were textiles in 1766 (Beckert, p. 33). Eighty million yards a year is the combined European export figure for Indian textiles in the 1790s (Beckert, p. 46).

The statement that weavers' incomes fell to less than a fifth of that of their grandparents, is an extrapolation from their proportion of the sale price of the cloth which decreased from one-third in the late seventeenth century to less than 6 percent 100 years later. Variations in the final price of the cloth and changed economics of production have would altered the amount received (Beckert, p. 45).

The song "the hearts and lives of the peasants have been burnt with blue flame" is "Hey Nirdoy Nilkorgon / O Merciless Indigo Planters" (Biswas, p. 497).

page 105

> Branches of Induſtry and Wealth, which that Country is, from a Variety of Cauſes, ſo peculiarly adapted to encourage, which have been the great Sources of its Proſperity for Ages paſt, and from whence that aſtoniſhing Maſs of Wealth has flowed, which Bengal has in the laſt 30 years poured into the lap of Great Britain

> "Report of the Select Committee of the Court of Directors of the East India Company," p. 10.

When the British East India Company first arrived in 1700, India's share of global GDP was 27 per cent, centred around the technological skill of its cloth producers. When the British left in 1947, its share was just over 3 per cent (Tharoor pp. 32–3).

"[Captain Austen] afforded protection, to and from the East, to several large convoys of Indiamen. For his gallant exertions, in the autumn of 1809, in bringing to a successful issue a dispute with the Chinese, he was ... presented by the East India Company with the sum of 1000 guineas" (O'Byrne, p. 28). The resolution of the "dispute with the Chinese" was Capt Austen skillfully failing to prosecute British sailors for the murder of a Chinese man (Steer, 18th July 2020). The cargo would almost certainly have been opium.

page 106

The details of Hasting's Daylesford estate are from Ginger, pp. 80–102.

> By those strong measures which he took he saved India   Debrett, J, p. 318.

page 107

Eliza's letter is from *Outlandish Cousin*, pp. 164–5.

Eliza died in April 1813, and Warren Hastings did not mention the fact in his diary. When Henry visited him in August, Hastings made none of the conventional remarks upon his bereavement, causing Jane to write:

> Mr Hastings never *hinted* at Eliza in the smallest degree.   *Outlandish Cousin*, p. 173.

LINEN

page 108

The song is "Siúil a Rún." The Irish chorus exhorts her lover to take up arms with the French against the English.

page 110

Austen refers to Irish linen in Letter No. 12, Nov 1798, p. 22.

Wool exports were banned under the Irish Woollen Export Prohibition Act of 1699. By the end of the eighteenth century, Ireland was the world's largest producer of linen. Exports grew from 1.3 million yards of linen cloth in 1712, to 46 million yards by 1796 (Gill, p. 375).

For information on the dispossession from Irish lands and language see "The Statute of Kilkenny" "The Ulster Plantations" and "The Administration of Justice (Language) Act." The almost complete deforestation was the result of timber extraction by absentee landlords.

Events here are specifically referencing the 1798 Irish Rebellion. There were others. There were armed uprisings across the British empire, including India. See Gott and Gopal in the bibliography.

> Our independence must be had at all hazards.
> Tone, p. 270.

page 111

Henry was stationed between Drogheda and Dundalk from April 26th to November 3rd 1799. This is the year after the active fighting of the 1798 Rebellion, represented on this page (Caplan, pp. 138–141). According to the online records of the County Louth Archeological and Historical society, the Oxfordshires were a cavalry regiment.

A million Irish people died and another million emigrated during the Great Hunger, or the Potato Famine, from 1847 to 1852. This resulted from absentee landlords, overwhelmingly British, continuing to export every other form of food from Ireland after the potato crop had been afflicted by blight.

COTTON

page 112

In the absence of precise figures for 1809, "a thousand mills and spindles in their millions" is estimated from the existence of 900 factories in 1797, and 50,000 mule spindles in 1788 rising to 7 million in 1821 (Beckert, p. 67).

"[Cotton] became the driving commodity behind the Industrial Revolution. From tufted white bolls emerged a new global system: industrial capitalism. There was of course inventiveness and innovation in other industries, but cotton was the only one with a global scope, a strong connection to coercive labor, and a unique level of the state's imperial attention to capture the necessary markets across the world" (Beckert, p. 81).

In a survey in 1788, children made up two-thirds of the workforce on powered equipment in 143 water mills in England and Scotland. The share of cotton mill workers under eighteen in surveys in Manchester, Stockport, and Preston in 1816–1819 were 47 per cent, 58 per cent, and 65 per cent respectively (Galbi, p. 358). The Sadler Report into child labour, 1833, found that managers were forthcoming in stating their preference for child workers: "Children are most expert, active, and complete when taken young" (ibid. p. 359).

page 115

> The position in which the piecer stands to his work is with his right foot forward ... the chief weight of his body rests upon his right knee, which is almost always the first joint to give way ... The continual pressure of the body upon [the arch of the foot] causes it to give way: the bones fall gradually down, the foot then becomes broad and flat, and the owner drags it after him.
> Dodd, p. 10.

The skeletal deformities were rickets, caused by Vitamin D deficiency as a result of inadequate diet and no exposure to sunlight (Gowland, pp. 15–17).

Child workers in factories were frequently unpaid. Children sent from the workhouse were indentured from the ages of seven to 21 (Blincoe, p. 26).

> The fat of horses, dogs, pigs [is] kept for the purpose of greasing the heavy machinery. It may be imagined what sort of effluvia will arise from the application of this fat to shafts almost on fire. I have ... had to apply it to a shaft very much heated, and as one piece melted away, another was laid on ... and all the time the smoke was arising almost sufficient to suffocate me. Dodd, p. 15.

Quarry Bank Mill in Manchester is open to the public as an industrial museum, and includes tours of the Apprentice House detailing the lives of the indentured children. Unusually for the time, a doctor was employed, and medical records include the application of leeches to around children's eyes to reduce inflammation. The pewter cups are from here.

page 116

"In 1790, three years before Whitney's invention, the United States had produced 1.5 million pounds of cotton; in 1800 that number grew to 36.5 million pounds, and in 1820, to 167.5 million pounds ... By 1802 the United States was already the single most important supplier of cotton to the British market" (Beckert, p. 104).

page 117

The "fat profits" specifically references large plantations, which were the most profitable: "85 percent of all cotton picked in the South in 1860 was grown on units larger than a hundred acres; the planters who owned these farms owned 91.2 percent of all slaves" (Beckert, p. 110).

I am paraphrasing the speech of Sarah Remond to British textile workers, circa 1858:

> When I walk through the streets of Manchester and meet load after load of cotton, I think of those 80,000 cotton plantations on which was grown the $125 million worth of cotton which supply your market, and I remember that not one cent of that money ever reached the hands of the labourers. Brown, 30th March 2023.

page 118

> Slaves are generally expected to sing as well as to work. A silent slave is not liked by masters or overseers. "Make a noise"... are the words usually addressed to the slaves when there is silence amongst them. This may account for the almost constant singing heard in the southern states. Douglass, *My Bondage*, p. 97.

> I have often been utterly astonished, since I came to the north, to find persons who could speak of the singing, among slaves, as evidence of their contentment and happiness. It is impossible to conceive of a greater mistake. Slaves sing most when they are most unhappy. The songs of the slave represent the sorrows of his heart; and he is relieved by them, only as an aching heart is relieved by its tears. Douglass, *Narrative*, pp. 14–15.

"My Father How Long?" is recorded in Allen p. 112.

> The allowance of clothes made yearly to each slave ... is a certain number of yards of ... what they call plains — an extremely stout, thick, heavy woollen cloth, of a dark grey or blue colour, which resembles the species of carpet we call drugget.
> Kemble, pp. 52–3.

page 119

Escape routes were coded into songs such as "Follow the Drinking Gourd," which directed people to follow the Big Dipper constellation to the North (Songs of the Underground Railroad).

> [Many Thousand Go] was composed by nobody knows whom ... and had been sung in secret to avoid detection. It is certainly plaintive enough.
> Allen, p. 48.

A heavily edited passage from Fanny Kemble's deeply problematic *Journal of a Residence on a Georgian Plantation* describes the Sabbath dress of enslaved Gullah Geechee people:

> frills, flounces, ribbands, combs ... finery, every colour in the rainbow, and the deepest possible shades blended in fierce companionship ... beads, bugles, flaring sashes, and ... aprons, which finish ... with a sort of airy grace. Kemble, p. 58.

My representation of patchwork here is informed by the album quilts of Harriet Powers and the nineteenth and twentieth century quilters of Gees Bend. Patchwork has always existed as a proletarian art form, accessible to the poor and the oppressed.

page 120

> I could not help expressing my fears and apprehensions to some of my countrymen: I asked them if these people had no country, but lived in this hollow place (the ship): they told me they did not, but came from a distant one.
> Equiano, p. 34.

> The stench of the hold while we were on the coast was so intolerably loathsome, that it was dangerous to remain there for any time, and some of us had been permitted to stay on deck for fresh air; but now that the whole ship's cargo was confined together, it became absolutely pestilential. Ibid. p. 35.

page 121

> I asked them if we were not to be eaten by those white men with their horrible looks, red faces, and long hair Ibid. p. 33.

East India Company imports were central to the British slave trade. British legislation banned domestic consumption of Indian textiles between 1700 and 1774, but actively encouraged their being brought to Britain for re-export to Africa and the colonies. Accounts from Slave ship log books list large quantities and varieties of Indian textiles (Inkori, pp. 343–79).

The indigo checked cloth was known as "Guinea cloth."

page 122

Austens's comment "I am as much in love with the author as ever I was with Clarkson" (Letter No.78, Jan 1813, p. 198) is generally taken to be a reference to the abolitionist Thomas Clarkson, author of *An Essay on the Slave Trade*. Austen's novels contain contradictory references to slavery. In *Mansfield Park* she constructs her most overt condemnation of it. But in *Persuasion*, the virtuous, poverty-stricken widow Mrs Smith is unable to access "some property of her husband in the West Indies" and at the happy ending of the novel the hero Captain Wentworth restores it to her. The reality of property (both land and people) in a plantation colony is obscured by the income that it represents.

The Barbados Slave Code of 1661 established the principle that black people can be owned as property. Subsequent slave codes in other British colonies, including in North America, were based upon this legisation.

The first joint stock company was the Company of Merchant Adventurers to New Lands, founded in England in 1551.

The Centre for the Study of the Legacies of British Slavery has a searchable database of known enslavers, including widows and clergymen. Jane's Aunt Leigh Perrot is listed (ucl.ac.uk/lbs).

Jane Austen did not directly invest in companies or enterprises that enslaved people; she put the profits of her novels into Government bonds, known as Navy Fives (Avery Jones).

page 123

The transatlantic slave trade was officially proscribed by the British in 1807 and the Americans in 1808.

That Fanny Palmer would utilise enslaved domestic help is an extrapolation from probable circumstances. Charles's teenage wife, Fanny, was the daughter of the Attorney General of Bermuda, John Palmer. Palmer's family owned household slaves (Kindred, p. 12) and his attitude to racial equality may be inferred from the fact that he imprisoned a white Methodist preacher, John Stephenson, for preaching to black audiences. Given Fanny's upbringing and social circle, it is vanishingly unlikely that she didn't.

The History of Mary Prince, the testimony of an enslaved domestic maid in Bermuda makes fascinating parallel reading against the life of Fanny Palmer. She says of her childhood:

> This was the happpiest period of my life; for I was too young to understand rightly my condition as a slave. Prince, p. 7.

page 124

> the song I heard her sing oftenest, was a little French ditty ... The 2 first lines were "Que j'aime à voir les Hirondelles" ... As a child, this was my favourite.

Recollection of Caroline Austen, *Memoir*, p. 193.

CHAWTON! A HOME!

pages 128–9

Austen fans are in for a treat, visiting Chawton. Not only is her original cottage, the Jane Austen House, open to the public as an incredible living museum of her life and work, but you can also visit Edward's country home Chawton House which is now a dedicated study centre for eighteenth century women's literature. All the portraits are of women, like a parallel historical reality where the Matriarchy ran the show. Ask to see the library. It's amazing. Tell them I sent you.

> an old and not very good house, almost as close to the road as it could be. It had no advantage of situation; but had been very much smartened up by the present proprietor.
> *Emma*, Chapter 11, p. 81.

> "were I rich enough I would instantly pull Combe down, and build it up again in the exact plan of this cottage."
> "With dark narrow stairs and a kitchen that smokes, I suppose," said Elinor.
> *Sense & Sensibility*, Chapter 14, p. 73.

The cottage was remodelled when the Austens moved in, and the window closest to the road bricked up. I have shown a false window painted onto the space, as would have been common at the time of the window tax.

Jane's poem is from Letter No.68, July 1809, p. 176.

The donkey cart has been preserved and is on display at Chawton Cottage.

page 130

> each of them was busy in arranging their particular concerns, and endeavoring, by placing around them books and other possessions, to form themselves a home.
> *Sense & Sensibility*, Chapter 6, p. 31.

Martha Lloyd references dressing "a Calves head" on page 80 of her *Household Book*.

> Composition seems to me Impossible, with a head full of Joints of Mutton & doses of rhubarb.
> Letter No.145, Sept 1816, p. 321.

> Sally knows your kind intentions & has received your message, & in return for it all, she & I have between us made out that she sends her Duty & thanks you for your goodness & means to be a good girl if I please.
> Letter No.77, Nov 1812, p. 196.

Jane writing to Cassandra with a message for Martha about the dogs:

> Tell her that I hunt away the rogues every night from under her bed, they feel the difference of her being gone. Letter No.78, Jan 1813, p. 200.

page 131

> She lived with her single daughter in a very small way *Emma*, Chapter 3, p. 22.

> "I should like to know ... why I am to be supposed in danger of wanting leisure to attend to the little boys" [her nephews]
> *Emma*, Chapter 36, p. 291.

Notes to pages 133–5

[about her nephews] "I shall do all in my power to make them happy"   *Emma*, Chapter 36, p. 289.

> Her performances with cup and ball were marvellous. The one used at Chawton was an easy one, and she has been known to catch it on the point above an hundred times in succession, till her hand was weary.   *Memoir*, p. 77.

> We do not want amusement: bilbocatch, at which George is indefatigable, spillikins, paper ships, riddles, conundrums, and cards
> Letter No.60, Oct 1808, p. 160.

This story is invented; as were Jane's:
> She would tell us the most delightful stories chiefly of Fairyland, and her Fairies had characters all of their own – The tale was invented, I am sure, at the moment, and was sometimes continued for 2 or 3 days.
> *Family Record*, p. 177.

> fanny & I have the Library to ourselves in delightful quiet.   Letter No.92, Oct 1813, p. 239.

> I was not sorry when friday came. It had been a busy week, & I wanted a few days quiet, & exemption from the Thought & contrivances which any sort of company gives.
> Letter No.145, Sept 1816, p. 321.

TO BUSINESS!

page 133

Estimates of the first print run of *Sense & Sensibility* vary from 750 to 1000 copies.

Jane's letters from London are a torrent of excitement:
> Henry, who had been confined the whole day to the Bank, took me in his way home, and, after putting Life and Wit into the party for a quarter of an hour, put himself & his Sister into a hackney coach. I bless my stars that I have done with tuesday – But, alas! – Wednesday was likewise a day of great doings ... I am sorry to tell you that I am getting very extravagant, and spending all my Money, and, what is worse for you, I have been spending yours too ... I was tempted by a pretty-coloured muslin, and bought 10 yds of it on the chance of your liking it ... I liked my walk very much; it was shorter than I had expected, & the weather was delightful ... I was very well satisfied with my purchases – my bugle trimming at 2s. 4d. and

> three pair silk stockings for a little less than 12s. a pair ... I am really very shocking ... I find all these little parties very pleasant ... To-night I might have been at the Play ... everything is smooth and pleasant;
> Letter No.70, April 1811, pp. 179–81.

The fact that Jane now finds tiny parties "very pleasant" indicates that her mood has changed considerably since Bath.

> The Horse-chestnuts are quite out, & the Elms almost. I had a pleasant walk in Kensington Gns on Sunday ... everything was fresh and beautiful.
> Letter No.71, April 1811, p. 184.

Presumably, Cassandra replies to all this crazy talk, asking if Jane is even actually working on her book, and Jane then writes back with:

> No, indeed, I am never too busy to think of S&S. I can no more forget it than a mother can forget her sucking child.
> Letter No.71, April 1811, p. 181.

page 135

The reactions to "Sence and Sensibility" are given in *Family Record*, pp. 188–9.

Why is Jane anoymous? Partly this is because there is an absolute prohibition on upper-class women having paid employment. None of the women in Austen novels work. Even when Mrs Smith is reduced to near destitution in *Persuasion*, she knits and sews items to sell for the charitable relief of poor families, not to pay her own rent. But also, the plot of *Sense & Sensibility* hinges on the selfishness of an older brother who leaves his sisters in penury – perhaps that's too close to the bone for her to publically put her name to it?

It was in searching this Library that my mother [Anna] came across a copy of *Sense & Sensibility* which she threw aside with careless contempt, little imagining who had written it, exclaiming to the great amusement of her Aunts who stood by "Oh that must be rubbish I am sure from the title."   Recollection of Fanny-Catherine LeFroy, *Family Record*, p. 191.

pages 136–7

She could scarcely believe what she termed her great good fortune when *Sense & Sensibility* produced a clear profit of about £150. Few so gifted were so truly unpretending. She regarded the above sum as a prodigious recompense for for that which had cost her nothing.
    Henry's Biographical Notice of the Author, *Northanger Abbey*, p. 6.

You will be glad to hear that the first Edit: of M. P. is all sold ... I am very greedy & want to make the most of it;
    Letter No.109, Nov 1814, p. 281.

The new title was lifted from *Cecilia* by Fanny Burney: "The whole of this unfortunate business," said Dr Lyster, "has been the result of pride and prejudice."

P. & P. is sold. — Egerton gives £110 for it. — I would rather have had £150, but we could not both be pleased ... It's being sold will I hope be a great saving of Trouble to Henry, & therefore must be welcome to me.
    Letter No.77, Nov 1812, p. 197.

I want to tell you that I have got my own darling child from London; on Wednesday I received one copy ... Miss Benn dined with us on the very day of the books coming & in the even^g we set fairly at it, and read half the 1st vol. to her ... She was amused, poor soul! That she could not help, you know, with two such people to lead the way, but she really does seem to admire Elizabeth. I must confess that I think her as delightful a creature as ever appeared in print, and how I shall be able to tolerate those who do not like her at least I do not know. There are a few typical errors; and a "said he," or a "said she," would sometimes make the Dialogue more immediately clear; but I do not write for such dull Elves.   Letter No.79. Jan 1813, pp. 201–2.

Reactions to the novel, are from *Family Record* p. 196. The excerpts are from Chapter 3, pp. 13–4 and Chapter 34, p. 185.

—our 2^d evening's reading to Miss Benn had not pleased me so well, but I believe something must be attributed to my Mother's too rapid way of getting on ... The work is rather too light, & bright, & sparkling; it wants shade; it wants to be stretched out here and there with a long Chapter — of sense, if it could be had; if not, of solemn specious nonsense, about something unconnected with the story; an Essay on Writing, a critique on Walter Scott, or the history of Buonaparte   *Letter No.80*, Feb 1813, p. 203.

Clearly, Jane is being ironic when she says that the work is too bright and sparkling. I removed the playful wit in order to use her words as foreshadowing.

CATHARSIS

pages 139–40

Now I will try to write of something else, & it shall be a complete change of subject
    Letter No.79. Jan 1813, pp. 201–2.

I have something in hand — which I hope on the credit of P. & P. will sell well, tho' not half so entertaining.   Letter No.86, July 1813, p. 217.

The quoted passages from *Mansfield Park* are:
Dependent, helpless (Chapter 30, p. 274). Her feelings were very acute (Chapter 2, p. 15). Her daughters never had been much to her (Chapter 39, p. 361). "a very obstinate, ungrateful girl" (Chapter 15, p. 137). her lively dark eye (Chapter 5, p. 42). "Of Rears and Vices I saw enough" (Chapter 6, p. 57). so totally improper [edited] (Chapter 14, p. 128). Loving, guiding, protecting her (Chapter 48, pp. 436–7). "I am quite determined" (Chapter 30, p. 268). A little difficulty to be overcome (Chapter 33, p. 302). Fanny must have been his reward (Chapter 48, pp. 433–4).

page 141

The image of the kneeling enslaved man was a wildly popular contemporary visual from the anti-slavery movement, accompanied by the text "Am I not a man and a brother?" The image is problematic: it fetishises Black bodies as muscled and animalistic, placed in the subordinate position of begging for emancipation rather than claiming it. I used it because Austen's anti-slavery argument is also problematic and crude.

Quoted passages from *Mansfield Park*, continued:
> Sir Thomas's parental solicitude and high sense of honour and decorum (Chapter 45, p. 410). "Did not you hear me ask him about the slave-trade last night?" (Chapter 21, pp. 183–4). Fanny could not speak (Chapter 31, p. 275). **Timid, anxious, doubting** (Chapter 48, p. 437). She alone was sad and insignificant (Chapter 17, p. 147). Agitated, happy, miserable, infinitely obliged, absolutely angry (Chapter 31, p. 279).

YOUNG LADIES OF AN INTERESTING AGE
page 143

> [Newphew James-]Edward's visit has been a great pleasure to us. He has not lost one good quality or good Look, & is only altered in being improved by being some months older than when we saw him last. He is getting very near our own age, for *we* do not grow older of course.
> Letter No.143, Jul 1816, p. 318.

> she has stiffened into the most perpendicular, precise, taciturn piece of "single blessedness" that ever existed, and that, till *Pride & Prejudice* showed what a precious gem was hidden in that unbending case, she was no more regarded in society than a poker or a fire-screen.
Recollection of Nancy Mitford, *Family Record*, p. 221.

> the truth is that the Secret has spread so far as to be scarcely the Shadow of a secret now — & that I beleive whenever the 3ᵈ appears, I shall not even attempt to tell Lies about it. — I shall rather try to make all the Money than all the Mystery I can of it. — People shall pay for their knowledge if I can make them. — Henry heard P. & P. warmly praised ... & what does he do in the warmth of his Brotherly vanity & Love, but immediately tell them who wrote it! A Thing once set going in that way — one knows how it spreads!   Letter No.90, Sept 1813, p. 231.

> I should like to see Miss Burdett very well, but that I am rather frightened by hearing that she wishes to be introduced to me. If I *am* a wild Beast, I cannot help it. It is not my own fault.
> Letter No.85, May 1813, pp. 212–3.

page 144

> Who can keep pace with the fluctuations of your Fancy, the Capprizios of your Taste, the Contradictions of your Feelings?
> Letter No.151, Feb 1817, pp. 328–9.

> Anna will not be surprised that the cutting off her hair is very much regretted by several of the party in this house
> Letter No.52, June 1808, p. 128.

> that sad cropped head
> Letter No.66, Jan 1809, p. 170.

> Anna ... has had plenty of the miscellaneous, unsettled sort of happiness which seems to suit her best.   Letter No.75, June 1811, p. 193.

> She is quite an Anna with variations
> Letter No.71, April 1811, p. 184.

From Fanny Knight's diary:
> "Aunt Jane and I had a very interesting conversation"; "Aunt Jane and I had a delicious morning together"; "Aunt Jane and I very snug"
> *Life and Letters*, p. 341.

> My dear Fanny ... so mistaken as to your own feelings ... I thought you really very much in Love — But you certainly are not at all ... What strange creatures we are!
> Letter No.109, Nov 1814, p. 279.

> By the bye, as I must leave off being young, I find many Douceurs in being a sort of Chaperon for I am put on the Sofa near the Fire & can drink as much wine as I like.
> Letter No.96, Nov 1813, p. 251.

page 145

> Here I am, my dearest Cassandra, seated in the Breakfast, Dining, sitting-room, beginning with all my might. Letter No.87, Sept 1813, p. 217.

> with the real good-will of a mind delighted with its own ideas *Emma*, Chapter 3, p. 25.

> She was very fond of Emma, but did not reckon on her being a general favourite; for, when commencing that work, she said, "I am going to take a heroine whom no one but myself will much like." *Memoir*, p. 119.

Fanny is so similar to Emma Woodhouse that she even shares her "true hazle eye" colour. How snobby is Fanny? Well, here are her recollections of beloved Aunt Jane:

> not so refined as she ought to have been ... They were not rich & the people around with whom they chiefly mixed, were not at all high bred ... very much below par as to good Society & its ways *Family Record*, pp. 279–9.

Austen noted that Fanny "could not bear Emma herself" (*Minor Works*, p. 436). I wonder why?

The quoted passages from *Emma* are:

> while the others were variously urging and recommending (Chapter 15, p. 122). Nothing should separate her from her father (Chapter 48, p. 390). "Well, my dears, how does your book go on?" (NB slight misquotation) (Chapter 9, p. 76).

pages 146–9

Regarding the originality of Austen's prose, Lawrence Sterne and Daniel Defoe had previously narrated inner thoughts, but recounted in the first person, not inserted into a third person narrative. See Provenzano Oberman pp. 7–9 and pp. 18–46.

The situation of the real heroine of *Emma*, Jane Fairfax, is inspired by Austen's good friendship with Anne Sharp, governess to the Knight family. So Austen's descriptions of the life of a governess as "penance and mortification for ever" (Chapter 20. p. 155) and her tone-deaf comparisons of the governess trade with the slave trade (Chapter 35, p. 280) are... interesting.

Quoted passages, continued:

> "Yes, good man!" (Chapter 6, p. 42). It darted through her, with the speed of an arrow (edited) (Chapter 47, p. 382). Disingenuousness and double dealing seemed to meet him at every turn. These letters were but the vehicle for gallantry and trick. (Chapter 41, pp. 326–7). "I have never known the blessing of one tranquil hour" (Chapter 48, p. 392). developement of self (Chapter 47, p. 383) (spelling from the Chapman 1954 edition) "But, with common sense," she added, "I am afraid I have had little to do." (Chapter 47, p. 377). "Do you dare to suppose me so great a blockhead" (edited) (Chapter 54, p. 443). "they are very delightful apples" (Chapter 27, pp. 221–2). "I do so wonder, Miss Woodhouse, that you should not be married" (edited) (Chapter 10, pp. 82–3). Emma went to the door (edited) (Chapter 27, p. 217).

> Much that lived in Harriet's memory, many little particulars... *Emma*, Chapter 47, p. 384.

THE PIG OF PALL MALL

I took liberties in this chapter to aid the narrative flow:

* Jane first writes of taking Yalden's coach in August 1814, a year earlier than my representation. She does travel up to London in August 1815, but accompanied by Henry, so presumably in his carriage. She is visiting London in October 1815 when Henry becomes ill, but there is no record of how she travelled.

* The expeditions to art galleries are from 1813.

* Henry made the reply to Murray's offer for the copyright of *Emma* after he became ill.

* Fanny Knight does visit and flirt with Mr Hayden, but this does not coincide with Jane's trips to exhibitions and museums; she writes to tell Fanny about them.

* Jane instructed Henry to retrieve the copyright to *Susan* in 1816, after the publication of *Emma*; it wasn't a surprise.

pages 150 1

I had a very good Journey, not crouded, two of the three taken up at Bentley being Children, the others of a reasonable size; & they were all very quiet & civil. — We were late in London, from

Notes to pages 152-3

being a great Load & from changing Coaches at Farnham, it was nearly 4 I beleive when we reached Sloane S^t; Henry himself met me, & as soon as my Trunk & Basket could be routed out from all the other Trunks & Baskets in the World ... There were 4 in the Kitchen part of Yalden — & I was told 15 at top.

Letter 105, Aug 1814, p. 270.

There were 15 people on the roof of that stage coach. Even including infants, I could only fit 11 into my drawing.

page 152

If I may so express myself, his Mind is not a Mind for affliction. He is too Busy, too active, too sanguine. Letter No.86, July 1813, pp. 215–6.

Mr Murray's letter is come. He is a rogue of course, but a civil one. He offers £450 but wants to have the copyright of M. P. & S. & S. included. It will end in my publishing for myself I daresay. He sends more praise however than I expected.

Letter No.121, Oct 1815, p. 291.

Henry writes:

> The Terms you offer are so very inferior to what we had expected, that I am apprehensive of having made some great Error in my Arithmetical Calculation *Family Record*, p. 224.

> [S]he wished to recover the copyright of this early work. One of her brothers undertook the negotiation. He found the purchaser very willing to receive back his money, and to resign all claim to the copyright. When the bargain was concluded and the money paid, but not till then, the negotiator had the satisfaction of informing him that the work which had been so lightly esteemed was by the author of *Pride & Prejudice*. *Memoir*, p. 106.

page 153

This is the Byrne portrait, a recently discovered graphite sketch on vellum with "Miss Austin" written on the back.

"One of Jane's sightseeing destinations was William Bullock's collection of natural history specimens in Piccadilly, which included a stuffed boa snake and more than sixty different kinds of monkeys." (Worsely, p. 351). The dialogue "This must be Mr Crosby" is invented, but Austen did have a caustic wit. Although Cassandra expunged most of the venom from her letters, such gems remain as:

> Mrs Hall, of Sherborne, was brought to bed yesterday of a dead child, some weeks before she expected, owing to a fright. I suppose she happened unawares to look at her husband.
> Letter No.10, Oct 1798, p. 17.

Henry & I went to the Exhibition in Spring Gardens ... I was very well pleased, — particularly ... with a small portrait of Mrs Bingley, excessively like her. I went in hopes of seeing one of her Sister, but there was no Mrs Darcy.

Letter No.85, May 1813, p. 212.

the Driving about, the Carriage being open, was very pleasant. — I liked my solitary elegance very much, & was ready to laugh all the time, at my being where I was. — I could not but feel that I had naturally small right to be parading about London in a Barouche.

Letter No.85, May 1813, pp. 213–4.

Miss Austen was on a visit in London soon after the publication of *Mansfield Park*: a nobleman, personally unknown to her, but who had good reasons for considering her to be the authoress of that work, was desirous of her joining a literary

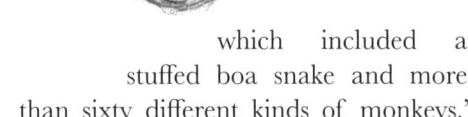

circle at his house ... Miss Austen immediately declined the invitation.
> Recollection of Henry Austen, *Memoir*, pp. 149–50.

page 154

Henry is not quite well – a bilious attack with fever ... He is calomeling & therefore in a way to be better & I hope may be well to-morrow.
> Letter No.121, Oct 1815, p. 291.

Specific recommendations to take "heroic doses" of calomel were not published until 1824, so this is fictionalised for dramatic effect. But toxic mercury salts were freely prescribed in uncontrolled doses, and Henry did suddenly deteriorate immediately after this documented case of ingesting calomel. See Haller, pages 29 and 32.

page 155

Jane's views on Princess Caroline:
> Poor Woman, I shall support her as long as I can, because she is a Woman, & because I hate her Husband.
> Worsley p. 361.

> She doubted whether she had not transgressed the duty of woman by woman
> *Emma*, Chapter 28, p. 215.

> It was altogether a confusion of images and doubts – a perplexity, an agitation which she could not see the end of.
> *Persuasion*, (alternative ending) quoted in *Memoir*, p. 177.

> Mr Clarke, speaking again of the Regent's admiration of her writing, declared himself charged to say, that if Miss Austen had any other Novel forthcoming, she was quite at liberty to dedicate it to the Prince. My Aunt made all proper acknowledgments at the moment, but had no intention of accepting the honor offered – until she was avised by some of her friends that she must consider the permission as a command.
> Recollection of Caroline Austen, *Memoir*, p. 176.

page 156

The Prince Regent was so insanely profligate that once he was crowned George IV he had Carlton House, his personal palace, demolished.

pages 158–9

We have no record of the conversation that passed between Miss Austen and Mr Stanier Clarke; she could well have been chaperoned when she visited Carlton House. The conversation here is a dramatisation of their subsequent exchanges of letters. Bear in mind that there is a social prohibition against a woman writing to a man to whom she is not related or married, and you can see that Mr Stanier Clarke takes advantage of Austen's professional overtures with repeated indiscretions, informing her of his whereabouts and ultimately, scandalously, offering that she, an unmarried woman, should stay at his Town house. Stanier Clarke was a sleaze bag. He is the subject of a satirical cartoon *Petworth Frolics, or the Divine and the Donkey*, which shows him being drunkenly bundled into bed with a donkey dressed in a petticoat, as punishment for an "assignation" with a servant girl. It was based on real events at the Earl of Egremont's residence, Petworth House (Hughes, pp. 24–5).

Jane's outfit is based on a watercolour sketch by Stanier Clarke which is thought to be of her.

From Stanier Clarke:
> Your late Works, Madam, and in particular *Mansfield Park* reflect the highest honour on your Genius & your Principles; in every new work your mind seems to increase its energy and powers of discrimination. The Regent has read & admired all your publications.
>
> Accept my sincere thanks for the pleasure your Volumes have given me: in the perusal of them I felt a great inclination to write & say so. And I also dear Madam wished to be allowed to ask you, to delineate in some future Work the Habits of Life and Character and enthusiasm of a Clergyman – who should pass his time between the metropolis & the Country
> Letter No.125(A), Nov 1815, p. 296.

Austen's reply:
> I am quite honoured by your thinking me capable of drawing such a Clergyman as you gave the sketch of in your note of N^{ov} 16. But I assure you I am not. The comic part of the Character I might be equal to, but not the Good, the Enthusiastic, the Literary. Such a Man's Conversation must at times be on subjects of Science & Philosophy, of which I know nothing ... A Classical Education, or at any rate a very extensive acquaintance with English Literature, Ancient & Modern, appears to me quite Indispensable for the person who w^d do any justice to your Clergyman – And I think I may boast myself to be, with all possible Vanity,

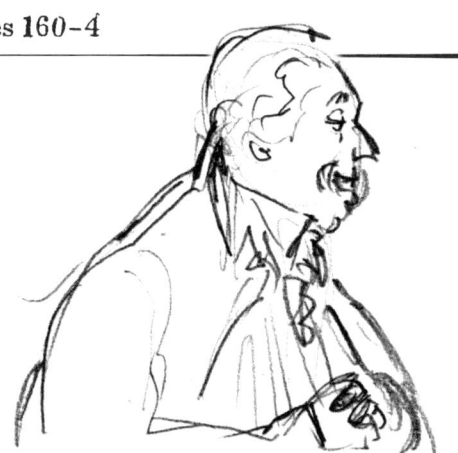

the most unlearned & uninformed Female who ever dared to be an Authoress.
   Letter No.132 (D), Dec 1815, pp. 305–6.

Stanier Clarke is undeterred:
> Pray continue to write, & make all your friends send Sketches to help you ... Do let us have an English Clergyman after *your* fancy – much novelty may be introduced – shew dear Madam what good would be done if Tythes were taken away entirely, and describe him burying his own mother – as I did – because the High Priest of the Parish in which she died – did not pay her remains the respect he ought to do. I have never recovered the Shock. Carry your Clergyman to Sea as the Friend of some distinguished Naval Character about a Court – you can then bring forward like Le Sage many interesting Scenes of Character & Interest.
>
> But forgive me, I cannot write to you without wishing to elicit your Genius; – & I fear I cannot do that, without trespassing on your Patience and Good Nature ... besides My Cell at Carlton House, I have another which Dr Barne procured for me at N° 37. Golden Square – where I often hide myself. There is a small Library there much at your Service – and if you can make the Cell render you any service as a sort of Half-way House, when you come to Town – I shall be most happy. There is a Maid Servant of mine always there
>
>   Letter 132 (A), Dec 1815, pp. 306–7.

Austen ghosts him on receipt of this letter, with its spelled-out indiscretion. But the correspondance is resumed when Stanier Clarke acknowledges receipt of the presentation copy of *Emma*:
> I have to return you the thanks of His Royal Highness, the Prince Regent, for the handsome copy you sent him of your last excellent novel ... any historical romance, illustrative of the history of the august House of Cobourg, would just now be very interesting.
>   Letter No. 138 (A), Mar 1816, p. 311.

Austen writes back, as she knows she must, and apologises politely and insincerely for not replying previously:
> I am honoured by the Prince's thanks, & very much obliged to yourself for the kind manner in which You mention the Work. I have also to acknowledge a former letter forwarded to me from Hans Place. I assure You I felt very grateful for the friendly Tenor of it, and hope my silence will have been considered, as it was truely meant, to proceed only from an unwillingness to tax your Time with idle Thanks ... You are very very kind in your hints as to the sort of Composition which might recommend me at present, and I am fully sensible that an Historical Romance, founded on the House of Saxe Cobourg, might be much more to the purpose of Profit or Popularity than such pictures of domestic Life in Country Villages as I deal in. But I could no more write a Romance than an Epic Poem. I could not sit seriously down to write a serious Romance under any other motive than to save my Life, & if it were indispensable for me to keep it up & never relax into laughing at myself, I am sure I should be hung before I had finished the first Chapter. – No – I must keep to my own style and go on in my own Way; And though I may never succeed again in that, I am convinced that I should totally fail in any other. Letter No 138 (D), April 1816, p. 312.

pages 160–3

Edited from "Plan of a Novel, according to hints from various quarters" *Minor Works*, Vol IV, pp. 428–30.

page 164

Edited from Letter No.129, Dec 1815, pp. 302–3.

WRITS & STITCHES

pages 166–9

The Hinton-Baverstock lawsuit was first lodged in 1814. It was setttled in April 1818 when Edward felled £15,000 worth of timber in Chawton Park to buy off his opponents.

The Leigh-Perrot inheritance from the Stoneleigh estate had happened back in July 1806. They got £24,000 and an annuity of £2,000. Jane was provoked into writing:

> Such ill-gotten wealth can never prosper.
> Letter No.51, Feb 1807, p. 122.

> a Legacy is our sovereign good.
> Letter No.54, June 1808, p. 134.

Jane, who has to ride in a donkey cart, makes this acidic reference to Aunt Leigh-Perrot in 1811:

> her Barouche ... gives her a headache — a comfortable proof, I suppose, of the uselessness of the new Carriage when they have got it.
> Letter No.73, May 1811, p. 187.

By 1816, the Austen women appear to be living (rent free and with free firewood) on £250 p.a. not counting income from Jane's novels and any other investments. The Leigh-Perrots did, however, also lose large sums of money when Henry's bank collapsed.

> Such were her thoughts, but she kept them to herself, and put on her bonnet in patient discontent.
> *Northanger Abbey*, Chapter 22, p. 168.

Austen's letter dates the construction of the patchwork coverlet as 1811, not 1816 as per my representation, but since I structured the whole graphic novel around this quilt, I had to put it in more towards the end.

> We are very busy making Edward's shirts, and I am proud to say that I am the neatest worker of the party.
> Letter No.4, Sep 1796, p. 6.

The Austen coverlet is sewn at 12 stitches to the inch. It is a show piece, not intended for warmth (it has no wadding) but for display. Many of the diamonds are fussy cut – a practice which is wasteful of cloth – and, unusually for the time period, none of the elements are pieced together from smaller scraps of fabric. It would have required a large quantity of paper to make, and could well have been pieced using the manuscript of *Sense & Sensibility*. The larger pieces of chintz are a useful indication of the probable fabric of curtains and chair coverings in Chawton Cottage.

PASSION

pages 170–1

Quotes from *Persuasion* are as follows:

> It was a very fine November day (edited) (Chapter 10, p. 78). Anne ... left the room, to seek the comfort of cool air for her flushed cheeks (edited) (Chapter 3, p. 25). a thousand feelings rushed on Anne ... to retentive feelings eight years may be little more than nothing (edited) (Chapter 7, p. 56). All the overpowering, blinding, bewildering, first effects of strong surprise (Chapter 19, p. 165). She was looking remarkably well (Chapter 12, p. 97). "Men have had every advantage of us in telling their own story" (Chapter 23, p. 220). "All the privilege I claim" (Chapter 23, p. 221).

> Scenes had passed in Uppercross which made it precious. It stood the record of many sensations of pain, once severe, but now softened; and of some instances of relenting feeling, some breathings of friendship and reconciliation, which could never be looked for again, and which could never cease to be dear.
> *Persuasion*, Chapter 13, p. 115.

Why is Jane lying on three chairs?

> The sitting-room contained only one sofa, which was frequently occupied by [Mrs Austen]. Jane would never use it, even in her mother's absence; but she contrived a sort of couch for herself with two or three chairs, and was pleased to say that this arrangement was more comfortable to her than a real sofa.
> *Memoir*, pp. 165–6.

Jane told her niece that if she lay on the real sofa, Mother wouldn't use it any more, like they were all stuck in some hell of mutual politeness and self-denial. And either that was true, or she was disguising her assumption that her mother would resent her lying on the good sofa, even though she was seriously ill.

SICK

page 173

The eruption of Mount Tambora on the island of Sumbawa (present-day Indonesia) is the largest volcanic event in recorded history. It directly killed 71,000 people and led to a volcanic winter which starved many more. 1816 is known as "the year without a summer," and it seems likely that the unrelentingly cold, wet weather precipitated Austen's decline. It also caused spectacular sunsets in England in 1815.

a thick mizzling rain...
Northanger Abbey, Chapter 20, pp. 152–3.

> Our Pond is brimfull & our roads are dirty & our walls are damp, & we sit wishing every bad day may be the last.
> Letter No.137, Mar 1816, pp. 310–1.

> A cold stormy rain set in, and nothing of July appeared but in the trees and shrubs, which the wind was despoiling, and the length of the day, which only made such cruel sights the longer visible. *Emma*, Chapter 48, p. 395.

> It is really too bad, & has been too bad for a long time, much worse than anybody can bear, & I begin to think it will never be fine again ... Oh! it rains again; it beats against the window. – Mary Jane & I have been wet through once already today, we set off in the Donkey Carriage for Farringdon ... but we were obliged to turn back before we got there, but not soon enough to avoid a Pelter all the way home. We met Mr. Woolls – I talked of it's being bad weather for the Hay – & he returned me the comfort of it's being much worse for the Wheat.
> Letter No.142, Jul 1816, pp. 315–6.

We hear now that there is to be no Honey this year. Letter No.145, Sept 1816, p. 322.

page 174

References to fatigue and pain in Jane's letters date back as far as 1813:

> We were in a private box –Mr. Spencer's ... One is infinitely less fatigued than in the common way ... I have had no pain in my face since I left you. Letter No.87, Sept 1813, pp. 219–20.

> he could not doubt, when he looked back, that she was in a weaker state of health than she had been half a year ago. *Emma*, Chapter 37, p. 296.

> [writing from Bath, about an acquaintance] his appearance has exactly that of a confirmed Decline. *Letter No.43*, April 1805, p. 100.

> Thank you, my Back has given me scarcely any pain for many days. – I have an idea that agitation does it as much harm as fatigue, & that I was ill at the time of your going, from the very circumstance of your going.
> Letter No.145, Sept 1816, p. 320.

Martha's "certain cure for a swell'd Neck" can be found in her *Household Book* (Gehrer, p. 133). Her recipe for a Plaister is on page 145. Lead is toxic, but it is toxic to bacteria as well as humans, so perhaps it's unsurprising that the Georgians used it to dress wounds.

> Ben was here on Saturday, to ask Uncle Charles & me to dine with them [a distance of less that two miles] ... I was forced to decline it, the walk is beyond my strength (though I am otherwise very well) & this is not a Season for Donkey Carriages Letter No.146, Dec 1816, p. 323.

page 175

Sanditon quote page references are:
"There is something wrong here... There, I fancy lies my cure." (*Minor Works*, p. 364). "Excellent Bathing..." (*Minor Works*, p. 369). "it is unfortunate for poor Arthur" (edited) (*Minor Works*, pp. 388–9). Charlotte could perceive no symptoms of illness (edited) (*Minor Works*, p. 413) . Sir E^{dw} ... had read more sentimental Novels than agreed with him ... It was Clara whom he meant to seduce ... ruin & disgrace... (*Minor Works*, pp. 404–6). Miss Lambe was beyond comparison the most important & precious, as she paid in proportion to her fortune. – She was about 17 (*Minor Works*, p. 421).

page 176

What was Jane Austen's last illness? We don't know. Tentative posthumous diagnoses have been made of Addison's disease, Hodgkin's lymphoma (Upfal, pp. 3–11) or lupus (Sanders pp. 1–5). She could even have contracted arsenic poisoning from the green wallpaper in the room where she worked and ate. Austen herself said:

> I think I understand my own case now so much better than I did, as to be able by care to keep off any serious return of illness. I am more & more convinced that bile is at the bottom of all I have suffered, which makes it easy to know how to treat myself.   Letter No. 150, Jan 1817, p. 327.

I hope that clears that up.

> I certainly have not been well for many weeks, and about a week ago I was very poorly, I have had a good deal of fever at times & indifferent nights, but am considerably better now, & recovering my Looks a little, which have been bad enough, black & white & every wrong colour. I must not depend upon being ever very blooming again. Sickness is a dangerous Indulgence at my time of Life.
> Letter No. 155, Mar 1817, pp. 335–6.

> The old gentleman died: his will was read, and like almost every other will, gave as much disappointment as pleasure.
> *Sense & Sensibility*, Chapter 1, p. 6.

> the expectation of [Mr Leigh-Perrot's death] keeps us in a worry, your Grandmama especially; she sits brooding over Evils which cannot be remedied & Conduct impossible to be understood.
> Letter No. 155, Mar 1817, p. 336.

> I am ashamed to say that the shock of my Uncle's Will brought on a relapse ... I live upstairs however for the present & am coddled. I am the only one of the Legatees who has been so silly, but a weak Body must excuse weak Nerves.   Letter No. 157, April 1817, p. 338.

> Every dear Brother so affectionate & so anxious! – and as for my Sister! – Words must fail me in any attempt to describe what a Nurse she has been to me ... I have so many alleviations & comforts to bless the Almighty for! ... if I live to be an old Woman, I must expect to wish I had died now; blessed in the tenderness of such a Family, & before I had survived either them or their affection.
> Letter No. 159, May 1817, pp. 340–1.

St SWITHIN'S DAY

page 177

> [Mrs Austen] once said to me, "Ah, my dear, you find me just where you left me – on the sofa. I sometimes think that God Almighty must have forgotten me; but I dare say He will come for me in His own good time."
> Recollection of James-Edward, *Memoir*, p. 15.

> I am going to Winchester ... to see what Mr Lyford can do farther towards re-establishing me in tolerable health. – On Sat^y next, I am actually going thither – my dearest Cassandra with me I need hardly say – and as this is only two days off you will be convinced that I am now really a very genteel, portable sort of an Invalid. – The Journey is only 16 miles, we ... are to have the accomodation of my elder Brother's Carriage which will be sent over from Steventon on purpose. Now, that's a sort of thing which Mrs J. Austen does in the kindest manner!   Letter 159, May 1817, pp. 340–1.

> my Journey hither on Saturday was performed with very little fatigue, & had it been a fine day I think I should have felt none, but it distressed me to see uncle Henry & W^m K – who kindly attended us on horseback, riding in rain almost all the way.   Letter No. 160, May 1817, p. 342.

I drew a demi-landau carriage. It has to be a two-seater because there's no room for Henry and William Knight.

page 178

Jane jokingly discusses her doctor's optimistic promises:
> Mr Lyford says he will cure me, & if he fails I shall draw up a Memorial & lay it before the Dean & Chapter, & have no doubt of redress from that Pious, Learned & Disinterested Body.
> *Family Record*, p. 249.

Cassandra writes:
> Lyford said he saw no signs of immediate dissolution, but added that with such a pulse it was impossible for any person to last long, and indeed no one can wish it – an easy departure from this to a better world is all that we can pray for.   *Family Record*, p. 251.

After his bank failed, Henry became an evangelical clergyman: I tried, but I couldn't shoehorn that fact into the narrative. The prayer is the "Collect for Purity" from the *Book of Common Prayer* (Baskerville p. 288).

page 179

Cassandra:

> I sat close to her with a pillow in my lap to assist in supporting her head, which was almost off the bed, for six hours; fatigue made me then resign my place to Mrs J. A. for two hours and a-half, when I took it again, and in about an hour more she breathed her last.
>
> Letter No. CEA.1. July 1817, p. 343.

pages 180–1

This is an edited extract from Austen's poem "Venta" (*Minor Works*, pp. 451–2) with altered punctuation. As Cassandra transcribed the poem, she presumably sanitised the phrase "When once we are buried you think we are dead" to the more palatable "you think we are gone." I changed it back.

Cassandra:

> ...even now, in her coffin, there is such a sweet, serene air over her countenance as is quite pleasant to contemplate
>
> Letter No. CEA.1. July 1817, p. 343.

page 182

Cassandra:

> I have lost a treasure, such a sister, such a friend as never can have been surpassed. She was the sun of my life, the gilder of every pleasure, the soother of every sorrow; I had not a thought concealed from her, and it is as if I had lost a part of myself.
>
> Letter No CEA.1. July 1817, p. 343.

Cassandra burns Jane's letters years later, in 1843, not on the day of the funeral (I messed with the chronology again one last time). There has been much speculation from anguished Austen scholars as to why Cassandra did this. I think this reference to the sanctity of private correspondence in *Persuasion* is a complete explanation as to her motives:

> her seeing the letter was a violation of the laws of honour ... no one ought to be judged or to be known by such testimonies ... no private correspondence could bear the eye of others
>
> *Persuasion*, Chapter 21, pp. 191–2.

BEHOLD ME IMMORTAL

page 183

Henry's "Biographical Notice of the Author" at the front of the posthumous joint edition of *Northanger Abbey* and *Persuasion* contains the following gems:

> Short and easy will be the task of the mere biographer. A life of usefulness, literature, and religion, was not by any means a life of event ... She became an authoress entirely from taste and inclination. Neither the hope of fame nor profit mixed with her early motives. Most of her works, as before observed, were composed many years previous to their publication. It was with extreme difficulty that her friends, whose partiality she suspected whilst she honoured their judgement, could prevail on her to publish her first work. ... that perfect placidity of temper ... She never uttered either a hasty, a silly, or a severe expression ... Faultless herself, as nearly as human nature could be...
>
> *Northanger Abbey*, pp. 3–6.

This iconic engraving of Austen is from 1873. The artist is unknown, but it is based on William Home Lizars' 1870 interpretation of James Andrew's 1869 rendition of Cassandra's original sketch, so the "likeness" is made at third remove. Charles's daughter Cassy-Esten gave this appraisal of the James Andrew watercolour:

> I think the portrait ... is a very pleasing, sweet face, – tho', I confess, to not thinking it much like the original; – but *that*, the public will not be able to detect.
>
> *Family Record*, p. 280.

page 185

The quote is from James Austen-Leigh's *Memoir*, p. 91.

BIBLIOGRAPHY

Semi-bold italics indicate the titles of major works as referred to in the Notes.

AUSTEN'S WRITINGS:

If you have not yet read the novels, start with *Northanger Abbey* and *Pride and Prejudice*. If you like those, read *Persuasion* and *Emma*. *Sense and Sensibility* and *Mansfield Park* contain some lovely writing, but the plots are less satisfying. The first two volumes of *Juvenilia* are hilarious.

Editions cited:
Sense & Sensibility, **Pride & Prejudice**, **Northanger Abbey**, **Mansfield Park**, **Emma**, **Persuasion**, **Love & Freindship**, all *Jane Austen: the Complete Works*, Penguin clothbound boxed set, 2009.
The Watsons, **Sanditon** and selected **Juvenilia**, from *The Works of Jane Austen, Volume VI, Minor Works*, (ed.) R.W. Chapman, 1954.
Jane Austen's **Letters**, collected and edited by Deirdre Le Fay, 1995. Cassandra cut the juicy parts out of Jane's letters, which makes reading them a rather dry experience, although leavened with some silly asides. The ones from the end of her life have survived unexpurgated, and are very moving.

EARLY AUSTEN BIOGRAPHIES:

The abundance of books with similar titles and content by Austen's relatives is somewhat confusing.
In 1869, James's children, James Edward Austen-Leigh, Caroline Austen-Leigh and Anna LeFroy collaborated to produce a volume of reminiscences of their aunt: *A* **Memoir** *of Jane Austen, and other Family Recollections*, (edition cited: ed. Kathryn Sutherland, 2002).
In 1884, Fanny Knight's son Lord Brabourne followed with a bowdlerised collection of her letters, which was extended and republished by James Edward's sons William Austen-Leigh and Richard Arthur Austen-Leigh as *Jane Austen — Her* **Life and Letters** *a Family Record*, 1913.
Frank's grandson and great-granddaughter John and Edith Hubback then produced **Jane Austen's Sailor Brothers,** 1906.
The refreshingly unrelated Constance Hill went on a "pilgrimage in Austen's footsteps" with her illustrator sister Ellen in 1901 to create the enlightening *Jane Austen: Her Homes & Her Friends* (**Homes & Friends**), 1902.
And Richard Arthur Austen-Leigh then pulled together a wider assortment of family letters, which he privately published in 1942 as **Austen Papers** *1704–1856*.

CONTEMPORARY BIOGRAPHIES:

Deirdre Le Faye, *Jane Austen: a* **Family Record**, 2004. Le Faye, the greatest Austen historian of all time, wrote a meticulously researched and incredibly comprehensive, original biography in 1989, which she then, incomprehensibly, titled *Jane Austen: a Family Record*, which is very nearly the same as William Austen-Leigh's 1913 book. Just, why?
She also published a very entertaining compilation of Eliza's letters: *Jane Austen's* **Outlandish Cousin**: *The Life and Letters of Eliza de Feuillide*, Deirdre Le Faye, 2002.

Of the slew of biographical works listed below, honorable mentions go to Lucy Worsley's *Jane Austen at Home*, Paula Byrne's *The Real Jane Austen, a Life in Small Things* and Hilary Davidson's *Jane Austen's Wardrobe*, which are outstanding.

ADDITIONAL RESEARCH:

Adkins, Roy and Lesley, *Eavesdropping on Jane Austen's England*, 2014.
Allen, W. F et al. *Slave songs of the United States*, 1867.
Avery Jones, John, "Jane Austen's income: insights from the Bank of England archives," bankunderground.co.uk, 2019.
Baskerville, John, (pub.) *The Book Of Common Prayer*, 1762.
Beckert, Sven, *Empire of Cotton: A New History of Global Capitalism*, 2014.
Bielenberg, Andrew, *Industrial Growth in Ireland, 1790–1910*, 1994.
Biswas, Probin, "Protest in Bengali Folk Songs" *International Journal of Creative Research Thoughts* Vol 11, Issue 2, February 2023, pp. 497–500.
Blincoe, Robert, *A Memoir of Robert Blincoe, An Orphan Boy*, 1832.
Boardman, Elizabeth, "Mrs Cawley and Brasenose College" *Jane Austen Society Collected Reports 2001–2005*, pp. 201–8.
Brooks–Davies, Douglas, *Jane Austen: Poems and Favourite Poems*, 1998.
Brown, Deneen L, "The Gullah Geecheefight for a legacy after Slavery," Guardian, 30th March 2023.
Brownlow, Graham, et. al, "Puzzles in the economic institutions of capitalism: production coordination, contracting and work organisation in the Irish linen trade, 1750–1850," *Cambridge Journal of Economics*, Vol 29, Issue 4, 2005, pp. 559–76.
Burney, Frances, *Evelina*, Oxford World Classics, 2002.
Byrne, Paula, *The Genius of Jane Austen: Her Love of Theatre*

Bibliography

and *Why she is a Hit in Hollywood*, 2002.

Byrne, Paula, *The Real Jane Austen: A Life in Small Things*, 2013.

Caplan, Clive, "Jane Austen's Soldier Brother: The Military Career of Captain Henry Thomas Austen of the Oxfordshire Regiment of Militia, 1793–7801" *Persuasions*, Vol.18, 1996, pp. 122–43.

Clayton, Tim, *James Gillray: a Revolution in Satire*, 2022.

Cohen, Marilyn, *The Warp of Ulster's Past: Interdisciplinary Perspectives in the Irish Linen Industry 1700–1920*, 1997.

Cope, Rev. Sir William, *A Glossary of Hampshire Words and Phrases*, 1883.

Corfield, Penelope, *The Georgians: The Deeds & Misdeeds of 18th Century Britain*, 2022.

Cotton Capital: *How Slavery shaped the Guardian, Britain & the World*, Guardian newspaper special edition, 2023.

Cunnington, Phillis, *The History of Underclothes*, 1951.

Cunnington, Phillis, *A Dictionary of English Costume*, 1960.

Dadzie, Stella, *A Kick in the Belly: Women, Slavery and Resistance*, 2021.

Dalrymple, William, *The Anarchy: The Relentless Rise of the East India Company*, 2019.

Davidson, Hillary, *Dress in the Age of Jane Austen*, 2019.

Davidson, Hillary, *Jane Austen's Wardrobe*, 2023.

Davies, C. Collin (ed.) *The Benares Diary of Warren Hastings*, 1948.

Debrett, J pub. *The History of the Trial of Warren Hastings Esq, Late Governor-General of Bengal*, 1796.

Dodd, William, *A Narrative of the Experiences and Sufferings of William Dodd, a Factory Cripple*, 1841.

Donald, Diana, *The Age of Caricature: Satirical Prints in the Reign of George III*, 1996.

Douglass, Frederick, *My Bondage and My Freedom*, 1855.

Douglass, Frederick, *Narrative of the Life of Frederick Douglass, an American Slave*, 1846.

Durkin, Hannah, *Survivors: the Lost Stories of the Last Captives of the Atlantic Slave Trade*, 2024.

Equiano, Olaudah, *The Interesting Narrative of the life of Olaudah Equiano*, 2021.

Fawcett, Trevor, *Georgian Imprints: Printing and Publishing at Bath, 1729–1815*, 2008.

Fee, Sarah, (ed.) *Cloth that Changed the World: The Art and Fashion of Indian Chintz*, 2019.

Felton, William, *A Treatise on Carriages*, Vol. 2, 1796.

Finlay, Victoria, *Fabric: The Hidden History of the Material World*, 2021.

Galbi, Douglas A, "Child Labor and the Division of Labor in the early English Cotton Mills," *Journal of Population Economics*, Vol. 10, Issue 4, 1997, pp. 357–75.

Gehrer, Julienne, *Martha Lloyd's Household Book, The original manuscript from Jane Austen's kitchen*, 2021.

George, M. Dorothy, *Hogarth to Cruikshank: Social Change in Graphic Satire*, 1967.

Gerzina, Getchen, *Black England: A Forgotten Georgian History*, 2022.

Gill, Conrad, *The Rise of the Irish Linen Industry*, 1925.

Ginger, Andrew, "Daylesford House and Warren Hastings," *The Georgian Group Report & Journal*, 1989, pp. 80–102

Gott, Richard, *Britain's Empire, Resistance, Repression and Revolt*, 2011.

Gowland, Rebecca L. et al, "The expendables: Bioarchaeological evidence for pauper apprentices in 19th century England and the health consequences of child labour," *Plos One*, 2023, pp. 1–29.

Grier, Sydney (ed.) *Letters of Warren Hastings to his Wife* 1905.

Gye, W pub. *The Trial of Jane Leigh Perrot, Wife of James Leigh Perrot, Esq., Charged with Stealing a Card of Lace*, 1800.

Hadlow, Janice, *The Strangest Family: the Private Lives of George III, Queen Charlotte and the Hanoverians*, 2014.

Haller, John S. "Samson of the Materia Medica: Medical Theory and the Use and Abuse of Calomel," *Pharmacy in History*, Vol. 13, 1971, pp. 27–34.

Hennelly, Des, "Colonialism, Landlordism and the Rift of Ireland," *Rupture: Eco Socialist Quarterly*, 2021.

Holland, William, *Paupers & Pig Killers: The Diary of William Holland, A Somerset Parson, 1799–1818*, 2003.

Honan, Park, *Jane Austen: Her Life*, 1988.

Howard, Tamara, "Black Cotton: 3 part series," *Curated Quilts* Issue 20, pp. 38–44, Issue 21, pp. 38–43, Issue 22, pp. 70–75.

Hughes, Annabelle, "The Old Rectory, Tillington," *The Petworth Society Magazine*, No.171, March 2018, pp. 22–5.

Hurston, Zora Neale, *Barracoon; The Story of the Last Slave* 2019.

Inikori, Joseph E. "Slavery and the Revolution in Cotton Textile Production in England," *Social Science History*, Vol. 13, No. 4, pp. 343–79.

Islam, Saiful, *Muslin: Our Story*, 2016.

Jenkins, Elizabeth, *Jane Austen*, 1973.

Kemble, Frances Anne, *Journal of a Residence on a Georgian Plantation*, 1863.

Kindred, Sheila, *Jane Austen's Transatlantic Sister*, 2017.

Lane, Maggie, *Jane Austen and Lyme Regis*, 2003.

Le Faye, Deirdre, *Jane Austen's Steventon*, 2007.

Le Faye, Deirdre, "'The Business of Mothering': Two Austenian Dialogues," *The Book Collector*, 1983, pp. 296–314.

Manjapra, Kris, *Black Ghost of Empire: The Long Death of Slavery and the Failure of Emancipation*, 2022.
Moore, Wendy, *Wedlock: How Georgian Britain's Worst Husband Met His Match*, 2009.
More, Hannah, *Modern System of Female Education*, 1799.
Mortimer, Ian, *The Time Traveller's Guide to Regency Britain*, 2020.
Murray, John pub. *The Answer of Warren Hastings Esq. to the Articles*, 1788.
Nicolson, Nigel, *Godmersham Park, Kent*, 2003.
Northrup, Solomon, *Twelve Years a Slave*, 1853.
O'Byrne, William R, *A Naval Biographical Dictionary*, 1849.
Parker, Rozsika, *The Subversive Stitch: Embroidery and the Making of the Feminine*, 2010.
Peal, Robert, *Meet the Georgians: Epic Tales from Britain's Wildest Century* 2021.
Prichard, Sue (ed.) *Quilts 1700–2010: Hidden Histories, Untold Stories*, 2010.
Prince, Mary, *The History of Mary Prince, A West Indian Slave*, 1831.
Provenzano Oberman, Rachel, *Inner voices: Narrated monologue and narrative voice in Jane Austen, George Eliot, and Virginia Woolf*, 2007.
Ramaswamy, Vijaya, "The Genesis and Historical Role of the Master Weavers in South Indian Textile Production," *Journal of the Economic and Social History of the Orient*, Vol. 28, No. 3, 1985, pp. 294–325.
Ramaswamy, Vijaya, *The Song of the Loom: Weaver Folk Traditions in South India*, 2013.
Renton, Alex, *Blood Legacy: Reckoning with a Family's Story of Slavery*, 2022.
"Report from the Select Committee Appointed to Examine the Reports of the Directors of the East India Company, 1794," accessed via ProQuest UK Parliamentary Papers, 14th April 2024.
"Report of the Select Committee of the Court of Directors of the East India Company on the Subject of the Cotton Manufacture of this Country: with Appendixes, 1793," accessed via ProQuest UK Parliamentary Papers, 14th April 2024.
Reynolds, Sophie, *Jane Austen's House Souvenir Guidebook*, 2022.
Richardson, Samuel, *Pamela; or, Virtue Rewarded*, 1740.
Sanders, Michael D and Graham, Elizabeth M, "Black and white and every wrong colour: The medical history of Jane Austen and the possibility of systemic lupus erythematosus" *Lupus*, 2021, pp. 1–5.
Sanghera, Sathnam, *Empireland: How Imperialism has Shaped Modern Britain*, 2021.

Selwyn, David (ed.) *The Poetry of Jane Austen and the Austen Family*, 1997.
Sir John Soane's Museum: a Complete Description, 2018.
Songs of the Underground Railroad, harriet-tubman.org
Spence, Jon, *Becoming Jane Austen*, 2003.
Spence, Jon, (ed.) *Jane Austen's Brother Abroad: The Grand Tour Journals of Edward Austen*, 2005.
Sperling, Diana, *Mrs Hurst Dancing & Other Scenes from Regency Life*, 1981.
St Clair, Kassia, *The Golden Thread: How fabric changed history*, 2019.
Steer, Julie with Pappalardo, Bruno, "The Royal Naval inspiration behind Jane Austen's work," blog.nationalarchives.gov.uk, accessed 18th July 2020.
Stowell, Lauren with Abby Cox, *The American Duchess Guide to 18th Dressmaking*, 2017.
Stowell, Lauren with Abby Cox, *The American Duchess Guide to 18th Century Beauty*, 2019.
Swain, Margaret, *Embroidered Georgian Pictures*, 1994.
Takei, Ahiro, "The First Irish Linen Mills, 1800–1824," *Irish Social and Economic History*, Vol 21, 1994, pp. 28–38.
Tharoor, Shashi, *Inglorious Empire: What the British did to India*, 2016.
The Lady's Magazine, Bound edition Vol XX, 1789.
Tomalin, Claire, *Jane Austen: A Life*, 1997.
Tone, T. Wolfe, *Memoirs of Theobald Wolfe Tone*, 1837.
Trollope, Frances, *The Life and Adventures of Michael Armstrong, the Factory Boy*, 1840.
Truth, Sojourner, *Ain't I a Woman?* 2020.
Upfal, A. "'Austen's lifelong health problems and final illness: New evidence points to a fatal Hodgkin's disease and excludes the widely accepted Addison's," *Medical Humanities*, Vol. 31, 2005. pp. 3–11.
Vick, Robin, "The Sale at Steventon Parsonage," *Annual Report of the Jane Austen Society: 1993, Jane Austen Collected Reports 1986–1995*, pp. 295–8.
Vogorinčić, Ana, "The Novel-Reading Panic in 18th Century England: An Outline of an Early Moral Media Panic," *Media Research: Croatian journal for Journalism and the Media*, Vol. 14, No. 2, 2008, pp. 103–24.
White, Diana, *Jane Austen: The Life and Times of the Woman Behind the Books*, 2017.
Wilkins, Charles, *The Bhagvat–Geeta, or Dialogues of Kreeshna and Arjoon introduction by Warren Hastings*, 1785.
Wong, Teresa Duryea, "Old Newspapers & Everyday Paper are the Magic Behind the Quilt," *Curated Quilts*, pp. 10–17.
Worsley, Lucy, *Jane Austen at Home*, 2018, also the 2017 BBC documentary *Jane Austen: Behind Closed Doors*.

WHAT DID JANE AUSTEN LOOK LIKE?

The starting point for the graphic biographer. We think we know what Jane Austen looks like from the familiar image on the ten pound note, and we don't.

The only authenticated portrait that shows Austen's face is this tiny, unfinished, watercolour sketch by Cassandra.

And Cassandra's sketch of Mary Queen of Scots in *A History of England* could also plausibly be Jane.

"There is my sister; and really quite her own little elegant figure! – and the face not unlike."
Emma, Chapter 6, p. 44.

Then there are two non-authenticated portraits: the Rice portrait which Austen family tradition says is Jane, and the Byrne portrait, a recently discovered pencil sketch marked as "Miss Austin" on the reverse. Some people have for various reasons decided that these aren't Jane Austen, but comparison of them with Cassandra's sketches show that they could easily be the same person.

"Such an eye!
– the true hazle eye – and so brilliant!"
Emma, Chapter 5, p. 38

I arrived at my take on Jane using all of these pictures, together with portraits and photographs of her parents and siblings. I was particularly inspired by this contemporary account of Jane, the 1838 recollection by Fulwar William Fowle:

> "She was pretty – certainly pretty – bright & a good deal of colour in her face – like a doll – no that wd. not give at all the idea for she had so much expression – she was like a child – quite a child very lively & full of humour – most amiable – most beloved."
> *Family Record*, p. 165.

"Doll like" suggests that she shared her brother Edward's small mouth and round, pink cheeks. Her fine eyes, which rendered her face "uncommonly intelligent" (*Pride & Prejudice*, Chapter 6, p. 24) are similar to her brother Henry's.

Edward's mouth.   *Henry's fine eyes.*

Frank's nose and chin.

Her nose was hooked like her brother Frank – though carefully minimised in some of the portraits of her – and she shared his oval face shape.